Steps in Analyzing a Transaction

STEP 1. What accounts are involved?

STEP 2. What are the classifications of the accounting involved (asset, liability, capital, drawing, revenue, expenses)?

STEP 3. Are the accounts increased or decreased?

STEP 4. Write the transaction as a debit to one account (or accounts) and a credit to another account (or accounts).

STEP 5. Is the equation in balance after the transaction has been recorded?

Journalizing and Posting

① Date of transaction
② Amount of transaction
③ Page number of the journal
④ Ledger account number

The Work Sheet

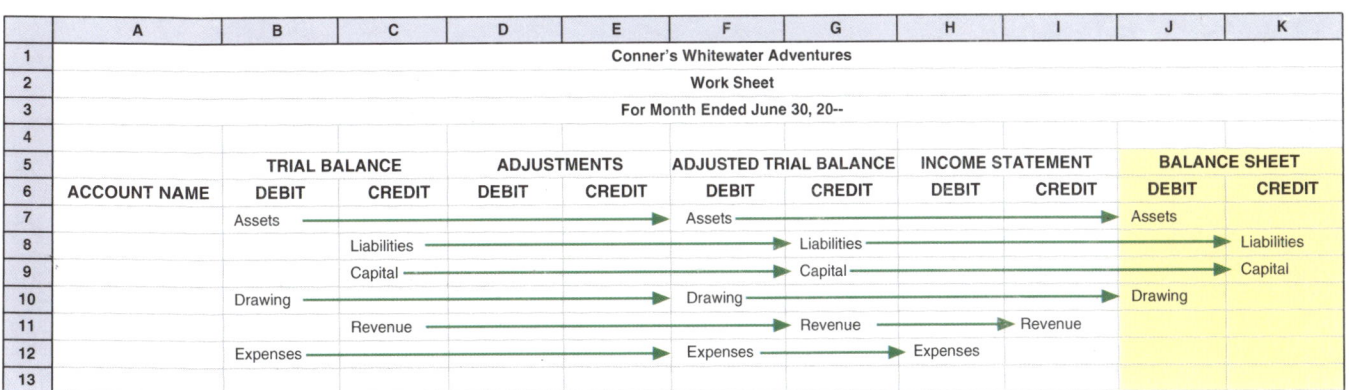

	A	B	C	D	E	F	G	H	I	J	K
1					Conner's Whitewater Adventures						
2					Work Sheet						
3					For Month Ended June 30, 20--						
4											
5		TRIAL BALANCE		ADJUSTMENTS		ADJUSTED TRIAL BALANCE		INCOME STATEMENT		BALANCE SHEET	
6	ACCOUNT NAME	DEBIT	CREDIT	DEBIT	CREDIT	DEBIT	CREDIT	DEBIT	CREDIT	DEBIT	CREDIT
7		Assets				Assets				Assets	
8			Liabilities				Liabilities				Liabilities
9			Capital				Capital				Capital
10		Drawing				Drawing				Drawing	
11			Revenue				Revenue		Revenue		
12		Expenses				Expenses		Expenses			
13											

College Accounting

A Career Approach

13e

Cathy J. Scott

Navarro College

CENGAGE

Australia • Brazil • Mexico • Singapore • United Kingdom • United States

College Accounting: A Career Approach,
Thirteenth Edition
Cathy J. Scott

Vice President, General Manager,
Social Science & Qualitative Business: Erin Joyner

Executive Product Director: Mike Schenk

Product Director: Jason Fremder

Associate Content Developer: Brian Pierce

Product Assistant: Aiyana Moore

Executive Marketing Manager: Robin LeFevre

Marketing Coordinator: Hillary Johns

Senior Digital Production Project Manager: Sally Nieman

Senior Digital Content Specialist: Tim Ross

Senior Content Project Manager: Tim Bailey

Manufacturing Planner: Doug Wilke

Production Service: Lumina Datamatics, Inc.

Senior Art Director: Michelle Kunkler

Cover and Internal Designer: Lou Ann Thesing

Cover Image: iStockPhoto.com/guvendemir

Design Images:

   Accounting in Your Future: J. Helgason/Shutterstock.com

   Small Business Success: VaskaSM/Shutterstock.com

   You Make the Call: Img Raj/Shutterstock.com

   All About You Spa: alekleks/Shutterstock.com

Intellectual Property

   Analyst: Brittani Morgan

   Project Manager: Carly Belcher

For product information and technology assistance, contact us at
**Cengage Customer & Sales Support, 1-800-354-9706
or support.cengage.com.**

For permission to use material from this text or product, submit all requests online at **www.cengage.com/permissions.**

Unless otherwise noted, all items are © Cengage Learning.

Microsoft Excel® is a registered trademark of Microsoft Corporation. © 2016 Microsoft.

All screen shots in this text are taken from QuickBooks software, created by Intuit. Reprinted with permission © Intuit Inc. All rights reserved.

Library of Congress Control Number: 2016962112

Student Edition with Access Card ISBN: 978-1-337-28056-3
Student Edition ISBN: 978-1-337-28057-0

Cengage
20 Channel Street
Boston, MA 02210
USA

Cengage is a leading provider of customized learning solutions with employees residing in nearly 40 different countries and sales in more than 125 countries around the world. Find your local representative at: **www.cengage.com.**

Cengage products are represented in Canada by Nelson Education, Ltd.

To learn more about Cengage platforms and services, register or access your online learning solution, or purchase materials for your course, visit **www.cengage.com.**

Printed in the United States of America
Print Number: 09   Print Year: 2023

About the Author

Cathy J. Scott, Ph.D.

Cathy J. Scott is a Professor of Accounting and the Accounting Program Department Chair at Navarro College. She is a proud recipient of the American Accounting Association's Two Year Outstanding Educator of the Year Award, Navarro College's Teaching of Excellence Award, and the Texas Society of Certified Public Accountants Outstanding Educator Award. Professor Scott received her bachelor's degree from Nazareth College, an MBA from Amberton University, a post-graduate Accounting degree from Keller Graduate School of Management, and a Ph.D. from Capella University. Professor Scott made a career shift into academics after a 25-year accounting and consulting career within the automotive industry. Professor Scott is currently the Two Year Section Vice President and Council Representative for the American Accounting Association. She also serves as a board member for the Teachers of Accounting at Two Year Colleges, and is a member of the Texas 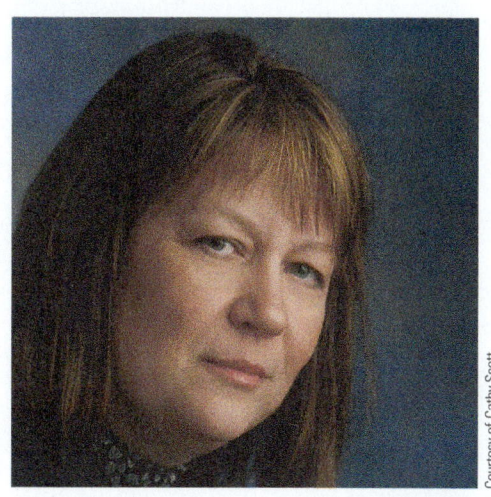 Society of Certified Public Accountants Educational Institutions committee. Professor Scott is also a member of the Academy of Management, Institute of Management Accountants, National Business Education Association, and Texas Community College Teachers Association. Professor Scott has a passion for improving accounting education and has spoken on numerous occasions about effectively using technology in the classroom, improving online education, and engaging students with active learning. Professor Scott is also the co-founder of the TeachingAndLearningToolbox.com, a teaching and learning website and blog that links technology to pedagogy as well as provides tips to successfully incorporate technology into courses. In her free time, Professor Scott enjoys spending time with her family on her farm in North Texas, in addition to raising and showing her Arabian horses.

Close the Gap

Between Homework and Exam Performance
with CengageNOWv2.

We've talked with hundreds of accounting instructors across the country and we are learning that online homework systems have created a new challenge in the accounting course.

We are hearing that students perform well on the homework but poorly on the exam, which leads instructors to believe that students are not truly learning the content, rather memorizing their way through the system.

CengageNOWv2 better prepares students for the exam by providing an online homework experience that is similar to what students will experience on the exam and in the real-world.

Read on to see how CengageNOWv2 helps close this gap.

Closing the gap, one step at a time.

Multi-Panel View

One of the biggest complaints students have about online homework is the scrolling, which prevents students from seeing the big picture and understanding the accounting system. This new Multi-Panel View in CengageNOWv2 enables students to see all the elements of a problem on one screen.

- Students make connections and see the tasks as connected components in the accounting process.

- Dramatically reduced scrolling eliminates student frustration.

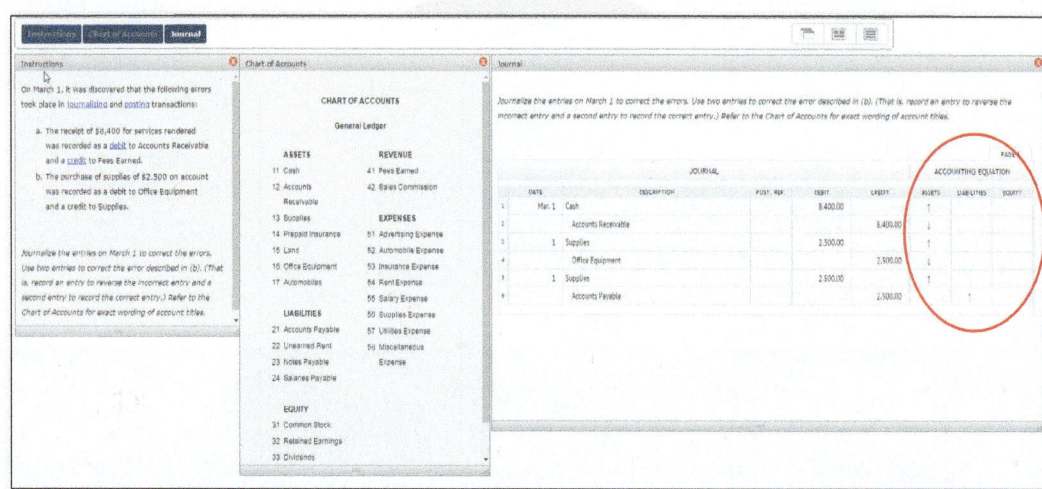

Adaptive Feedback

Adaptive Feedback responds to students based upon their unique answers and alerts them to the type of error they have made without giving away the answer.

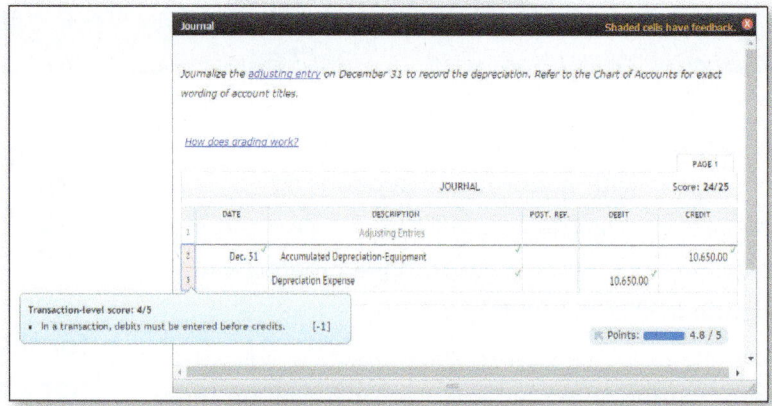

From Motivation to Mastery

MOTIVATION:
Engage students and better prepare them for class.

Adaptive Study Plan
The Adaptive Study Plan is an assignable/gradable study center that adapts to each student's unique needs and provides a remediation pathway to keep students progressing.

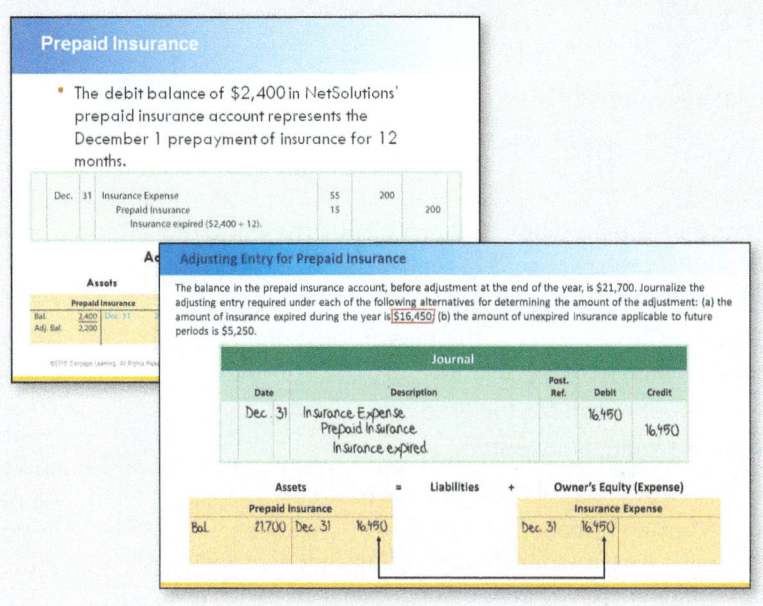

APPLICATION:
Help students apply accounting concepts.

Video: Show Me How
Linked to end-of-chapter problems in CengageNOWv2, Show Me How problem demonstration videos provide a step-by-step model of a similar problem.

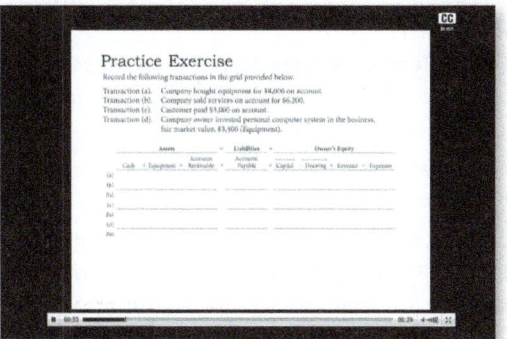

MASTERY:
Teach students to go beyond memorization to true understanding.

Comprehensive Review Problems for *College Accounting: A Career Approach*
These problems allow students to master fundamental accounting concepts and objectives for each chapter.

And that's not all...

You might also want to learn about the MindTap eReader, our LMS integration options, and more.

MindTap eReader

The MindTap eReader is the most robust digital reading experience available.

- Fully optimized for the iPad.
- Note-taking, highlighting, and more.
- Embedded digital media.

The MindTap eReader also features ReadSpeaker®, an online text-to-speech application that vocalizes, or "speechenables," online educational content.

LMS Integration

CengageNOWv2 can be seamlessly integrated with most Learning Management Systems. Adopters will enjoy:

- **A Seamless User Experience** — Access your Cengage resources seamlessly using only your LMS login credentials.
- **Simplified Registration Process** — Get students up and running faster!
- **Content Customization and Deep Linking** — Use our Content Selector to create a unique learning path for students that blends your content with Cengage Learning activities, eText and more within your LMS course.
- **Automatic Grade Synchronization*** — Need to have your course grades recorded in your LMS gradebook? No problem. Simply select the activities you want synched and grades will automatically be recorded in your LMS gradebook.

* Grade synchronization is currently available with Blackboard, Brightspace (powered by D2L), Angel 8 and Canvas.

ADA Accessibility

Cengage Learning is committed to making its educational materials accessible to users of all abilities. We are steadily working to increase accessibility and create a full spectrum of usable tools, features and choices that are accessible for users of all abilities. All new Cengage Learning products and services are designed with accessibility in mind.

- With the latest release of CengageNOWv2:
  - Images and graphics have been converted to HTML tables so that they can be read by screen readers.
  - The assignment experience now offers proper heading structure to support easy navigation with assistive technology.
- CengageNOWv2 solutions offer high contrast and well-structured HTML, which helps support screen reader interactivity.
- All videos are created with closed captioning and transcripts available for download.
- The MindTap eReader is HTML-based and compatible with most screen reading assistive software. The eReader supports browser settings for high-contrast narrative text, variable font sizes, and multiple foreground and background color options.

For more information on accessibility, please visit www.cengage.com/accessibility.

IPAD Tablet Compatibility

CengageNOWv2 is fully compatible with the IPAD and other tablet devices, with the exception of General Ledger (CLGL), which is flash based.

New to This Edition

- LEARN IT – Proven Pedagogy section
- Connecting the Classroom to the Real World
  - Accounting in Your Future
  - You Make the Call
  - Small Business Success
  - In the Real World
- Blueprint Problems
- Chapter Review and Self-Study
- Show Me How Videos (Author narrated)
  - Note these were in the last edition for the Practice Exercises. In this edition, these videos are noted with an icon for both the EOC Practice Exercises and related Exercises.
- This edition's revisions primarily focused on incorporating QuickBooks Online with the book. Additionally, this edition did revise some EOC problems, separated the display of FICA Social Security and Medicare taxes and revised the AAYS continuing problem. For the most part, this edition's updates were global across the text, rather than changed chapter-by-chapter.
- QuickBooks Online, a cloud-based accounting application.
  - Benefits Include:
    - Completely online. No CD drive required
    - QuickBooks Online Access Code included with each book
    - Works on both PCs and Macs
    - No data files to restore or back up
    - Instructor is the accountant. Providing the instructor online access to student work, including a date and time stamped audit trail

Introduction

- No new features

Chapter 1

- NEW! QuickBooks Online Tip margin notes provide useful tips related to accounting that can be applied with QuickBooks Online, a cloud-based accounting application.
- NEW! Accounting with QuickBooks Online
  - QuickBooks Online is a new feature for each chapter that is available as an Appendix on the Cengage Learning companion site at Cengage.com. This edition explains how to apply fundamentals of accounting processes using QuickBooks Online, a cloud-based accounting application. Complete with learning objectives, clear

step-by-step directions, and screen captures, this feature is a must for instructors who value the importance of teaching real-world technology skills in the classroom. This integrated approach of teaching the fundamentals of accounting with QuickBooks Online will help students understand how to utilize a real-world cloud-based accounting application, while developing marketable skills they can immediately apply in the workplace.

- NEW! QuickBooks Online Demonstration Videos on the Cengage Learning companion site at Cengage.com.

- A real-world, single company approach to learning QuickBooks Online. Students will apply accounting concepts in QuickBooks Online for Magnolia Spa.

Chapter 2

- NEW! QuickBooks Online Tip margin notes provide useful tips related to accounting that can be applied with QuickBooks Online, a cloud-based accounting application.

- NEW! Accounting with QuickBooks Online

  - QuickBooks Online is a new feature for each chapter that is available as an Appendix on the Cengage Learning companion site at Cengage.com. This edition explains how to apply fundamentals of accounting processes using QuickBooks Online, a cloud-based accounting application. Complete with learning objectives, clear step-by-step directions, and screen captures, this feature is a must for instructors who value the importance of teaching real-world technology skills in the classroom. This integrated approach of teaching the fundamentals of accounting with QuickBooks Online will help students understand how to utilize a real-world cloud-based accounting application, while developing marketable skills they can immediately apply in the workplace.

- NEW! QuickBooks Online Demonstration Videos on the Cengage Learning companion site at Cengage.com.

- NEW! A real-world, single company approach to learning QuickBooks Online. Students will apply accounting concepts in QuickBooks Online for Magnolia Spa.

Chapter 3

- NEW! QuickBooks Online Tip margin notes provide useful tips related to accounting that can be applied with QuickBooks Online, a cloud-based accounting application.

- NEW! Accounting with QuickBooks Online

  - QuickBooks Online is a new feature for each chapter that is available as an Appendix on the Cengage Learning companion site at Cengage.com. This edition explains how to apply fundamentals of accounting processes using QuickBooks Online, a cloud-based accounting application. Complete with learning objectives, clear step-by-step directions, and screen captures, this feature is a must for instructors who value the importance of teaching real-world technology skills in the classroom. This integrated approach of teaching the fundamentals of accounting with QuickBooks Online will help students understand how to utilize a real-world cloud-based accounting application, while developing marketable skills they can immediately apply in the workplace.

- NEW! QuickBooks Online Demonstration Videos on the Cengage Learning companion site at Cengage.com.

- REVISED! The All About You Spa continuous general ledger problem for a sole proprietorship business has been revised. This problem can still be solved manually, using CengageNow, or using Cengage Learning's Online General Ledger software (CLGL).

- NEW! A real-world, single company approach to learning QuickBooks Online. Students will apply accounting concepts in QuickBooks Online for Magnolia Spa.

Chapter 4

- NEW! QuickBooks Online Tip margin notes provide useful tips related to accounting that can be applied with QuickBooks Online, a cloud-based accounting application.

- NEW! Accounting with QuickBooks Online

  - QuickBooks Online is a new feature for each chapter that is available as an Appendix on the Cengage Learning companion site at Cengage.com. This edition explains how to apply fundamentals of accounting processes using QuickBooks Online, a cloud-based accounting application. Complete with learning objectives, clear step-by-step directions, and screen captures, this feature is a must for instructors who value the importance of teaching real-world technology skills in the classroom. This integrated approach of teaching the fundamentals of accounting with QuickBooks Online will help students understand how to utilize a real-world cloud-based accounting application, while developing marketable skills they can immediately apply in the workplace.

- NEW! QuickBooks Online Demonstration Videos on the Cengage Learning companion site at Cengage.com.

- REVISED! The All About You Spa continuous general ledger problem for a sole proprietorship business has been revised. This problem can still be solved manually, using CengageNow, or using Cengage Learning's Online General Ledger software (CLGL).

- NEW! A real-world, single company approach to learning QuickBooks Online. Students will apply accounting concepts in QuickBooks Online for Magnolia Spa.

Chapter 5

- NEW! QuickBooks Online Tip margin notes provide useful tips related to accounting that can be applied with QuickBooks Online, a cloud-based accounting application.

- NEW! Accounting with QuickBooks Online

  - QuickBooks Online is a new feature for each chapter that is available as an Appendix on the Cengage Learning companion site at Cengage.com. This edition explains how to apply fundamentals of accounting processes using QuickBooks Online, a cloud-based accounting application. Complete with learning objectives, clear step-by-step directions, and screen captures, this feature is a must for instructors who value the importance of teaching real-world technology skills in the classroom. This integrated approach of teaching the fundamentals of accounting with QuickBooks Online will help students understand how to utilize a real-world cloud-based accounting application, while developing marketable skills they can immediately apply in the workplace.

- NEW! QuickBooks Online Demonstration Videos on the Cengage Learning companion site at Cengage.com.

- REVISED! The All About You Spa continuous general ledger problem for a sole proprietorship business has been revised. This problem can still be solved manually, using CengageNow, or using Cengage Learning's Online General Ledger software (CLGL).

- NEW! A real-world, single company approach to learning QuickBooks Online. Students will apply accounting concepts in QuickBooks Online for Magnolia Spa.

Chapter 6

- NEW! QuickBooks Online Tip margin notes provide useful tips related to accounting that can be applied with QuickBooks Online, a cloud-based accounting application.

- NEW! Accounting with QuickBooks Online

  - QuickBooks Online is a new feature for each chapter that is available as an Appendix on the Cengage Learning companion site at Cengage.com. This edition explains how to apply fundamentals of accounting processes using QuickBooks Online, a cloud-based accounting application. Complete with learning objectives, clear step-by-step directions, and screen captures, this feature is a must for instructors who value the importance of teaching real-world technology skills in the classroom. This integrated approach of teaching the fundamentals of accounting with QuickBooks Online will help students understand how to utilize a real-world cloud-based accounting application, while developing marketable skills they can immediately apply in the workplace.

- NEW! QuickBooks Online Demonstration Videos on the Cengage Learning companion site at Cengage.com.

- NEW! A real-world, single company approach to learning QuickBooks Online. Students will apply accounting concepts in QuickBooks Online for Magnolia Spa.

Chapter 7

- NEW! QuickBooks Online Tip margin notes provide useful tips related to accounting that can be applied with QuickBooks Online, a cloud-based accounting application.

- NEW! Accounting with QuickBooks Online

  - QuickBooks Online is a new feature for each chapter that is available as an Appendix on the Cengage Learning companion site at Cengage.com. This edition explains how to apply fundamentals of accounting processes using QuickBooks Online, a cloud-based accounting application. Complete with learning objectives, clear step-by-step directions, and screen captures, this feature is a must for instructors who value the importance of teaching real-world technology skills in the classroom. This integrated approach of teaching the fundamentals of accounting with QuickBooks Online will help students understand how to utilize a real-world cloud-based accounting application, while developing marketable skills they can immediately apply in the workplace.

- NEW! QuickBooks Online Demonstration Videos on the Cengage Learning companion site at Cengage.com.

- NEW! A real-world, single company approach to learning QuickBooks Online. Students will apply accounting concepts in QuickBooks Online for Magnolia Spa.

Chapter 8

- NEW! QuickBooks Online Tip margin notes provide useful tips related to accounting that can be applied with QuickBooks Online, a cloud-based accounting application.

- NEW! Accounting with QuickBooks Online

  - QuickBooks Online is a new feature for each chapter that is available as an Appendix on the Cengage Learning companion site at Cengage.com. This edition explains how to apply fundamentals of accounting processes using QuickBooks Online, a cloud-based accounting application. Complete with learning objectives, clear step-by-step directions, and screen captures, this feature is a must for instructors who value the importance of teaching real-world technology skills in the classroom. This integrated approach of teaching the fundamentals of accounting with QuickBooks Online will help students understand how to utilize a real-world cloud-based accounting application, while developing marketable skills they can immediately apply in the workplace.

- NEW! QuickBooks Online Demonstration Videos on the Cengage Learning companion site at Cengage.com.

- NEW! A real-world, single company approach to learning QuickBooks Online. Students will apply accounting concepts in QuickBooks Online for Magnolia Spa.

Chapter 9

- NEW! QuickBooks Online Tip margin notes provide useful tips related to accounting that can be applied with QuickBooks Online, a cloud-based accounting application.

- NEW! Accounting with QuickBooks Online

  - QuickBooks Online is a new feature for each chapter that is available as an Appendix on the Cengage Learning companion site at Cengage.com. This edition explains how to apply fundamentals of accounting processes using QuickBooks Online, a cloud-based accounting application. Complete with learning objectives, clear step-by-step directions, and screen captures, this feature is a must for instructors who value the importance of teaching real-world technology skills in the classroom. This integrated approach of teaching the fundamentals of accounting with QuickBooks Online will help students understand how to utilize a real-world cloud-based accounting application, while developing marketable skills they can immediately apply in the workplace.

- NEW! QuickBooks Online Demonstration Videos on the Cengage Learning companion site at Cengage.com.

- REVISED! The All About You Spa continuous general ledger problem for a sole proprietorship business has been revised. This problem can still be solved manually, using CengageNow, or using Cengage Learning's Online General Ledger software (CLGL).

- NEW! A real-world, single company approach to learning QuickBooks Online. Students will apply accounting concepts in QuickBooks Online for Magnolia Spa.

Chapter 10

- NEW! QuickBooks Online Tip margin notes provide useful tips related to accounting that can be applied with QuickBooks Online, a cloud-based accounting application.

- NEW! Accounting with QuickBooks Online

  - QuickBooks Online is a new feature for each chapter that is available as an Appendix on the Cengage Learning companion site at Cengage.com. This edition explains how to apply fundamentals of accounting processes using QuickBooks Online, a cloud-based accounting application. Complete with learning objectives, clear step-by-step directions, and screen captures, this feature is a must for instructors who value the importance of teaching real-world technology skills in the classroom. This integrated approach of teaching the fundamentals of accounting with QuickBooks Online will help students understand how to utilize a real-world cloud-based accounting application, while developing marketable skills they can immediately apply in the workplace.

- NEW! QuickBooks Online Demonstration Videos on the Cengage Learning companion site at Cengage.com.

- REVISED! The All About You Spa continuous general ledger problem for a sole proprietorship business has been revised. This problem can still be solved manually, using CengageNow, or using Cengage Learning's Online General Ledger software (CLGL).

- NEW! A real-world, single company approach to learning QuickBooks Online. Students will apply accounting concepts in QuickBooks Online for Magnolia Spa.

Chapter 11

- NEW! QuickBooks Online Tip margin notes provide useful tips related to accounting that can be applied with QuickBooks Online, a cloud-based accounting application.

- NEW! Accounting with QuickBooks Online

  - QuickBooks Online is a new feature for each chapter that is available as an Appendix on the Cengage Learning companion site at Cengage.com. This edition explains how to apply fundamentals of accounting processes using QuickBooks Online, a cloud-based accounting application. Complete with learning objectives, clear step-by-step directions, and screen captures, this feature is a must for instructors who value the importance of teaching real-world technology skills in the classroom. This integrated approach of teaching the fundamentals of accounting with QuickBooks Online will help students understand how to utilize a real-world cloud-based accounting application, while developing marketable skills they can immediately apply in the workplace.

- NEW! QuickBooks Online Demonstration Videos on the Cengage Learning companion site at Cengage.com.

- REVISED! The All About You Spa continuous general ledger problem for a sole proprietorship business has been revised. This problem can still be solved manually, using CengageNow, or using Cengage Learning's Online General Ledger software (CLGL).

- NEW! A real-world, single company approach to learning QuickBooks Online. Students will apply accounting concepts in QuickBooks Online for Magnolia Spa.

Chapter 12

- NEW! QuickBooks Online Tip margin notes provide useful tips related to accounting that can be applied with QuickBooks Online, a cloud-based accounting application.

- NEW! Accounting with QuickBooks Online

  - QuickBooks Online is a new feature for each chapter that is available as an Appendix on the Cengage Learning companion site at Cengage.com. This edition explains how to apply fundamentals of accounting processes using QuickBooks Online, a cloud-based accounting application. Complete with learning objectives, clear step-by-step directions, and screen captures, this feature is a must for instructors who value the importance of teaching real-world technology skills in the classroom. This integrated approach of teaching the fundamentals of accounting with QuickBooks Online will help students understand how to utilize a real-world cloud-based accounting application, while developing marketable skills they can immediately apply in the workplace.

- NEW! QuickBooks Online Demonstration Videos on the Cengage Learning companion site at Cengage.com.

- REVISED! The All About You Spa continuous general ledger problem for a sole proprietorship business has been revised. This problem can still be solved manually, using CengageNow, or using Cengage Learning's Online General Ledger software (CLGL).

- NEW! A real-world, single company approach to learning QuickBooks Online. Students will apply accounting concepts in QuickBooks Online for Magnolia Spa.

- NEW! *Try It with QuickBooks Online* Comprehensive Problem

  - *Try It with QuickBooks Online* provides students with a comprehensive problem they can complete using QuickBooks Online. The *Try It with QuickBooks* feature is available on the Cengage Learning companion site at Cengage.com.

- NEW! End of Chapter - Statement of Cash Flows Appendix

Appendix A – E

- No new features

Acknowledgments

During the revision of the thirteenth edition, many instructors were consulted to review the text for thoughtful suggestions that helped guide the revision of *College Accounting: A Career Approach, 13e*. Those reviewers are as follows:

Kristy McAuliffe
San Jacinto College South

William Vermie
Bellevue College

Kristine Duke
Arizona Western College

Valerie Goodwin
SUNY-Jamestown Community College

Randy Schmitz
City College at Montana State University - Billings

Maria Bright
San Jacinto College North

Mellissa Youngman
Rochester Institute of Technology

Linda Snider
Grossmont College

Debra M. Johnson
Montana State University – Billings

Sherilyn Reynolds
San Jacinto College

Renee Richard
Pima Community College

Remy Orffeo
Erie Community College

Vaun Day
Central Arizona College

Michele Wehrle
Community College of Allegheny County

Chris Demaline
Central Arizona College

Rosemary Hall
Bellevue College

Anna Boulware
St. Charles Community College

Brenda Rudolph
Flathead Valley Community College

Ramona Braun
Miami University

Sam Wikamulia
City College of San Francisco

Lisa Taylor Weaver
Las Positas College

Mary L. McClelland
Wharton County Junior College

Marc Lafond
Arizona Western College

Cindy Hinz
Jamestown Community College

Celesta Bates
Martin University

Michele Adams
Erie Community College - South Campus

Jean Rodgers
Wenatchee Valley College at Omak

Leonor M Cabrera
Cañada College

Joel Glassman
Palomar College

Richard Bailey
Oregon Tech

Steven L Ernest
Baton Rouge Community College

Karen Scott
Malcolm X College

Ray Mathieu
LA Trade Technical College

Tory Vornholt
Agnes Scott College

Amery Klappert
Pima Community College

Kathy Boeger
Barton Community College

Doris Donovan
Dodge City Community College

Richard W. Stec JD, CPA, CGMA
CCAC-North Campus

Kim Hansen
Riverland Community College

Sherilyn Reynolds
San Jacinto College

Lorraine Rochon
Pima Community College

Barbara Newsham
St. Charles Community College

We would like to thank **Glen Owen** for his contributions and review of the Quickbooks Online content that is a part of this text. In addition, we would like to extend a thank you to **Erin Dischler, Toni Hartley**, and **Ken Martin** for their time and effort on the review and verification of the text and end of chapter content. Without their contributions, this book would not be possible.

Cathy Scott would like to thank her family, especially, Gale Tassell and her children, Erica Miller and Ryan Scott, for their never-ending patience, love and support. She would also like to thank her friends and colleagues for their continuous encouragement and professional collaboration as well as the many students who have inspired her as an educator over the years. A special thank you goes out to *"Team College Accounting"* at Cengage Learning for their enthusiastic support of this career approach to College Accounting. It has been a pleasure working with each of you. Cathy would also like to remember her late husband Forrest, who saw her passion as an educator and encouraged her to follow her dreams.

Brief Contents

*Appendix E is available for download on the text website at Cengage.com

Contents

PART 3 THE ACCOUNTING CYCLE FOR A MERCHANDISING BUSINESS

APPENDIX A
Methods of Depreciation   A-1

APPENDIX B
Bad Debts   B-1

APPENDIX C
Inventory Methods   C-1

APPENDIX D
Notes Payable and Notes Receivable   D-1

APPENDIX E
Departmental Accounting*   E-1

INDEX   I-1

*Appendix E is available for download on the text website at Cengage.com

College Accounting

A Career Approach

13e

Introduction to Accounting

Learning Objectives

After you have completed this introduction to accounting, you will be able to do the following:

1. Define accounting.
2. Explain the importance of accounting information.
3. Describe the various career opportunities in accounting.
4. Define ethics.

To: College Accounting Students
Subject: Welcome to the World of Accounting

College Accounting Students,

Welcome to the *World of Accounting*. This book holds one of the keys to your future—knowledge of accounting and business! Throughout the pages of this text, you'll be introduced to individuals, just like yourself, who dreamed about working in, operating, or even owning a business. You will read about many real world companies and learn about the important role accounting plays in each.

I understand this may be a new experience for many of you, and thus, this book is designed to help you navigate the material and ultimately succeed. As you go through this book, you will find numerous tools and activities to help you understand accounting and how accounting impacts business success. I look forward to being your guide into the world of accounting. So let's get started on this great adventure!

Dr. Cathy Scott

© iStockPhoto.com/AVAVA

Accounting is often called the *language of business* because when confronted with events of a business nature, all people in society—owners, managers, creditors, employees, attorneys, engineers, and so on—must use accounting terms and concepts to describe these events. Examples of accounting terms are *net, gross, yield, valuation, accrued, deferred*—the list goes on and on. So it is logical that anyone entering the business world should know enough of its *language* to communicate with others and to understand their communications.

As you acquire knowledge of accounting, you will gain an understanding of the way businesses operate and the reasoning involved in making business decisions. Even if you are not involved directly in accounting activities, you will certainly need to be sufficiently acquainted with the *language* in order to understand the meaning of accounting information and how it is compiled, how it can be used, and what its limitations are.

You may be surprised to find that you are already familiar with many accounting terms. Recalling your personal business activities and relating them to your study of accounting will be very helpful to you. For example, when you purchased this textbook, you exchanged cash or a promise to pay cash for the book. As you will see, this exchange is an accounting event. You are going to recognize many activities and terms as you begin your study of accounting.

I-1 WHAT IS ACCOUNTING?

A traditional definition of **accounting** is the process of analyzing, classifying, recording, summarizing, and interpreting business transactions in financial or monetary terms. A business **transaction** is an event that has a direct effect on the operation of an economic unit, is expressed in terms of money, and is recorded. Examples of business transactions are buying or selling goods, renting a building, paying employees, and buying insurance. However, in reality, Accounting is so much more. Accounting involves a wide range of activities required to make good decisions that lead to a prosperous society. The Pathways Commission, comprised of various leaders in the field of accounting, created

1 Define accounting.

Learning Objective

3

Figure 1
Pathways vision model

What is Accounting?

the *Pathways Vision Model* (Figure 1) in order to change *the perception* of accounting, which is often thought of as mundane and boring, into *the reality* of accounting today. The process of accounting starts with an economic activity. Accountants analyze these economic activities, using critical thinking skills and accounting judgments, in order to identify the information needed to make good decisions.

The primary purpose of accounting is to provide the financial information needed for the efficient operation of an economic unit. The term **economic unit** includes not only business enterprises but also not-for-profit entities such as government bodies, churches and synagogues, clubs, and public charities. Business enterprises or organizations may be called *firms* or *companies*.

Another important purpose of accounting is to provide useful information for decision making in the business enterprise. Similar to decisions you must make in your daily life, accounting helps businesses make decisions. For example, knowing whether there is enough cash to purchase new equipment or whether the business is making a profit requires knowledge of accounting.

All business entities require some type of accounting records. Basically, an **accountant** is a person who keeps the financial history of the transaction of an economic unit in written or computerized form.

I-1a Accounting Standards

Because it is important that everyone who receives accounting reports be able to interpret them, a set of rules or guidelines for the accounting process has been developed. These guidelines or rules are known as **generally accepted accounting principles (GAAP)** and are developed by the **Financial Accounting Standards Board (FASB)**.

The FASB was created by the **Securities and Exchange Commission (SEC)** in 1973. The SEC is the agency responsible for regulating public companies that are traded on a U.S. stock exchange. The SEC relies on the FASB to create accounting standards. However, the ultimate responsibility for setting and enforcing accounting standards for public companies lies with the SEC.

With the globalization of the world economy, an international standard-setting board, the **International Accounting Standards Board (IASB)**, has been created to provide guidelines or rules on international accounting standards known as **International Financial Reporting Standards (IFRS)**. The IASB and FASB are currently working to combine GAAP and IFRS into one set of standards.

I-1b Bookkeeping and Accounting

While bookkeeping and accounting are closely related, there are differences between the two processes. Generally, bookkeeping involves the systematic recording of business transactions in financial terms. Accounting functions at a higher level. An accountant sets up the system that a bookkeeper uses to record business transactions. An accountant may supervise the work of the bookkeeper and prepare financial statements and tax reports. Although the bookkeeper's work is more routine, it is hard to draw a line where the bookkeeper's work ends and the accountant's begins.

I-2 IMPORTANCE OF ACCOUNTING INFORMATION

Anyone who aspires to a position of leadership in business or government needs knowledge of accounting. A study of accounting gives a person the necessary background and gives him or her an understanding of the scope, functions, and policies of an organization. A person may not be doing the accounting work, but he or she will be dealing with accounting forms, language, and reports.

2 Explain the importance of accounting information.

Learning Objective

I-2a Users of Accounting Information

There are many users of accounting information, as outlined below.

OWNERS

Owners have invested their money or goods in a business organization. They want information regarding the company's earnings, its prospects for future earnings, and its ability to pay its debts.

MANAGERS

Managers and supervisors have to prepare financial reports, understand accounting data contained in reports and budgets, and express future plans in financial terms. People who have management jobs must know how accounting information is developed in order to evaluate performance in meeting goals.

CREDITORS

Creditors lend money or extend credit to the company for the purchase of goods and services. The company's creditors include suppliers, banks, and other lending institutions, such as loan companies. Creditors are interested in the firm's ability to pay its debts.

GOVERNMENT AGENCIES

Taxing authorities verify information submitted by companies concerning a variety of taxes, such as income taxes, sales taxes, and employment taxes. Public utilities, such as electric and gas companies, must provide financial information to regulatory agencies.

I-2b Accounting and Technology

Before the invention of computers, all business transactions were recorded by hand. Now computers perform routine recordkeeping operations and prepare financial reports. Computers are used today in all types of businesses, both large and small. All accounting positions now require workers to use computers, have knowledge of word processing and spreadsheet software, and possess an understanding of accounting software, such as QuickBooks®.

Even though virtually all businesses now use computers to do their accounting, the nature of accounting is the same. The computer is a powerful tool of the accountant. However, as a tool, the computer is only as useful as the operator's ability and understanding of accounting. The operator must be skilled to key the correct information into the computer program; otherwise, as the saying goes, "garbage in, garbage out."

I-3 CAREER OPPORTUNITIES IN ACCOUNTING

Learning Objective

3 Describe the various career opportunities in accounting.

There are a number of career opportunities in accounting in every industry. To find job opportunities in accounting, browse Internet job sites or read the newspapers' classified advertisements. Although the jobs listed in these ads require varying amounts of education and experience, many of them are for positions as accounting and auditing clerks, general bookkeepers, and accountants. The Bureau of Labor Statistics *Occupational Outlook Handbook* estimates that employment for accountants, auditors, and paraprofessionals is expected to grow faster than average. The number of accounting-related jobs is expected to grow by 11 percent between 2014 and 2024. The requirements and duties of these positions are discussed next. Figure 2, on page 7, provides a listing of the average salaries for some of these positions.

I-3a Accounting Clerk/Technician

An accounting clerk/technician performs routine recording of financial information. The duties of accounting clerks vary with the size of the company. In small businesses, accounting clerks handle most of the recordkeeping functions. In large companies, clerks specialize in one part of the accounting system, such as payroll, accounts receivable, accounts payable, cash, inventory, or purchases. The minimum requirement for most accounting clerk positions is usually one term or semester of accounting courses. Having experience in a related job and working in an office environment is also recommended. In addition, knowledge of word processing and spreadsheet software is helpful. Accounting clerks/technicians should be detail-oriented and have good communication skills.

I-3b Auditing Clerk

Auditing clerks are an organization's financial recordkeepers. An auditing clerk's primary responsibility involves verifying transactions and records posted by other employees. Additional responsibilities include maintaining and updating individual or groups of accounting records, checking documents to ensure that they are mathematically correct, and correcting or noting errors for accountants or other workers to adjust. Most auditing clerks are required to have a high school degree at a minimum, while an associate degree in business or accounting is often preferred for some positions. Knowledge of word processing and spreadsheet software in addition to experience in a related job are also recommended.

TITLE	SALARY RANGE
ACCOUNTING CLERK	$33,250–$43,500
– Accounts receivable/Accounts payable clerk	$36,250–$49,250[a]
	$36,250–$46,000[b]
	$33,000–$43,000[c]
– Inventory clerk	$35,250–$44,000[a]
	$33,000–$43,250[b]
– Payroll clerk	$37,250–$48,750[a]
	$35,500–$48,250[b]
	$33,000–$42,750[c]
BOOKKEEPER/PARAPROFESSIONAL ACCOUNTANT	$34,000–$45,500
ACCOUNTANT	
– Chief financial officer	$109,750–$484,500
– Controller	$83,250–$217, 250
– Financial analyst (entry level)	$50,000–$136,500[a]
	$48,250–$118,000[b]
	$45,250–$99,250[c]
– Forensic accountant	$74,750–$116,750
– General accountant (entry level)	$47,500–$123,500[a]
	$44,750–$102,250[b]
	$42,500–$93,500[c]
– Internal auditor (entry level)	$55,000–$151,250[a]
	$52,250–$127,000[b]

[a]Large companies
[b]Midsize companies
[c]Small companies

Source: Robert Half International, 2016 *Salary Guide—Accounting & Finance*, © 2016 Robert Half International.

Figure 2
Salary ranges for various accounting positions

I-3c General Bookkeeper

Many small- and medium-sized companies employ one person to oversee their bookkeeping operations. This person is called a general or full-charge bookkeeper. The general bookkeeper supervises the work of accounting clerks. Requirements for this job vary with the size of the company and the complexity of the accounting system. The minimum requirement for most general bookkeeper jobs is one or two years of accounting education as well as experience as an accounting clerk. Many companies

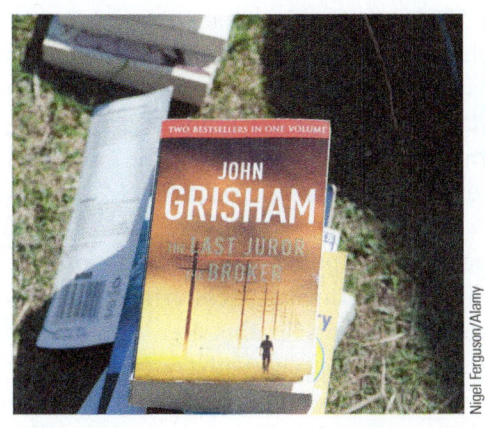

Nigel Ferguson/Alamy

In the Real World

Many famous people began their careers in accounting. For instance, author John Grisham received his undergraduate degree in accounting from Mississippi State University.

require a certificate in business or accounting and experience working with computers and accounting software.

I-3d Paraprofessional Accountant

To bridge a gap between the general bookkeeper and the professional accountant, many firms are hiring **paraprofessional accountants**. They manage the duties of the general bookkeeper as well as many of the duties of a professional accountant. Paraprofessional accountants work under the direct supervision of a professional accountant. Qualifications generally include a two-year degree in accounting, knowledge of accounting software, and prior experience.

I-3e Certifications Available

Several organizations offer certification for accounting and auditing clerks, bookkeepers, and paraprofessional accountants. The Certified Bookkeeper (CB) designation is awarded by the American Institute of Professional Bookkeepers (www.aipb.org) and certifies that an individual has the knowledge needed to carry out bookkeeping functions. For certification, candidates must have at least two years of bookkeeping experience, pass an examination, and adhere to a code of ethics. The Accreditation Council for Accountancy and Taxation (www.acatcredentials.org) offers an Accredited Business Accountant® (ABA) certification designed for individuals who work with small- to medium-sized businesses in the areas of financial accounting, tax, and ethics. For accreditation, candidates must pass a one-day, seven-hour exam.

I-3f Accountant

The term *accountant* describes a fairly broad range of jobs. The accountant may design and manage the entire accounting system for a business. The accountant may also prepare financial statements and tax returns and perform audits. Many accountants enter the field with a four-year college degree in accounting. However, it is not unusual for accountants to start at entry-level positions and work their way up to management positions. Although accountants are employed in every kind of economic unit, they are classified into one of four categories: public accounting, managerial or private accounting, government and not-for-profit accounting, and internal auditing. We'll briefly look at these categories.

PUBLIC ACCOUNTING

Most public accountants are certified public accountants (CPAs). To become a CPA, a person must have a bachelor's degree, complete 150 hours of college course work (in most states), pass a rigorous examination, and complete a work experience requirement. CPAs design accounting systems, prepare tax returns, provide financial advice about business operations, and audit financial statements. Many CPAs work for a public accounting firm such as Deloitte LLP or own their own small business. CPAs can also be employed by corporations in the private sector in finance positions such as chief financial officers (CFOs), controllers, and financial analysts.

A relatively new and upcoming career opportunity in public accounting is forensic accounting. Forensic accountants specialize in investigating business crimes such as fraud, embezzlement, and money laundering. Accountants in this area of specialty require knowledge of accounting, law, and finance and work closely with law enforcement personnel. Individuals wanting to specialize in forensic accounting can apply for a Certified Fraud Examiner (CFE) certificate (www.acfe.com). Requirements for CFE certification include a minimum of a bachelor's degree and two years of professional experience in a field directly or indirectly related to the detection or deterrence of fraud.

If you are interested in learning more about becoming a CPA or other public accounting jobs, the American Institute of Certified Public Accountants (www.aicpa.org) has an excellent website called This Way to CPA (www.thiswaytocpa.com) that describes accounting degrees and job opportunities. This site includes study information, simulation games, scholarship and internship listings, profiles of successful CPAs, and career opportunities.

MANAGERIAL OR PRIVATE ACCOUNTING

Most people who are accountants are employed by private business organizations. These accountants (not necessarily CPAs) manage the accounting system, prepare budgets, determine costs of products, and provide financial information for managers and owners. Accountants have many opportunities to advance into top management positions. The Certified Management Accountant (CMA) has a solid understanding of financial planning and analysis, internal controls, decision making, and professional ethics. Requirements for CMA certification include having a bachelor's degree (in any area), passing the CMA exam, and having two years' experience in management accounting and/or financial management. You can find more information about the CMA exam at http://imanet.org.

GOVERNMENT AND NOT-FOR-PROFIT ACCOUNTING

Not-for-profit accounting is used for government agencies, hospitals, churches and synagogues, and schools. Accountants for these organizations prepare budgets and maintain records of revenues and expenses. Local, state, and federal government bodies employ vast numbers of people in accounting positions. For example, a top federal government employer in the area of accounting is the Internal Revenue Service (IRS).

INTERNAL AUDITING

Due to recent accounting regulations, the demand for internal auditors has increased. Internal auditors verify the effectiveness of an organization's accounting system and controls. They examine and ensure that the company's financial information is accurate and protected. Internal auditors also ensure that organizations are following government regulations and corporate policies. The Institute of Internal Auditors (http://theiia.org) sets international standards for internal auditors and offers a certification opportunity called the Certified Internal Auditor (CIA). Requirements for certification include having a bachelor's degree (in any area), having two years' experience in internal auditing, and passing the Certified Internal Auditor exam.

I-4 ETHICS

Ethics is a philosophy or code or system of morality—that is, how we conduct ourselves from day to day in a variety of situations requiring a decision, usually of a right or wrong nature. Ethics, as it relates to accounting, is the way accountants and other keepers of financial information conduct the business of accounting according to laws of the state and their own personal code or system of morality.

 4 Define ethics.

Learning Objective

Many books, as well as classes, are available on the subject of ethics. All organizations provide a code of ethical conduct for their members. Your school may even have a Student Code of Conduct that discusses the ethical expectations and conduct of students.

With mounting evidence of questionable business ethics reported in print and portrayed through visual media, understanding and learning about ethics is very important in the world of accounting.

Related to ethics, a recent change to the accounting profession is the **Sarbanes-Oxley Act**, commonly referred to as SOX. SOX was created as a response to various large-scale corporate accounting frauds, such as Enron and WorldCom. The Sarbanes-Oxley Act established a wide range of new rules related to the audit environment and internal controls.

Chapter Review

Study and Practice

Learning Objective   Define accounting.

Accounting is the process of analyzing, classifying, recording, summarizing, and interpreting business **transactions** in financial or monetary terms. It is also an information system and the language of business.

Learning Objective   Explain the importance of accounting information.

A study of accounting gives a person the necessary background to understand the scope, functions, and policies of an organization.

Learning Objective   Describe the various career opportunities in accounting.

Accounting and auditing clerks, bookkeepers, **paraprofessional accountants**, and **accountants** will find employment opportunities in several areas—in the public sector, the private sector, and not-for-profit organizations.

Learning Objective   Define ethics.

Ethics is a code of morality—that is, how we respond to a variety of situations on a daily basis that require a decision, usually of a right or wrong nature. Ethics, as it relates to accounting, is the way accountants and other keepers of financial information conduct themselves according to laws of the state and their own personal code or system of morality.

Glossary

Accountant A person who keeps the financial history of the transactions of an economic unit in written form. (*p. 4*)

Accounting The process of analyzing, classifying, recording, summarizing, and interpreting business transactions in financial or monetary terms. (*p. 3*)

Economic unit Includes both business enterprises and not-for-profit entities. (*p. 4*)

Ethics A philosophy or code or system of morality—that is, how we conduct ourselves from day to day in a variety of situations requiring a decision, usually of a right or wrong nature. (*p. 9*)

Financial Accounting Standards Board (FASB) The organization, created in 1973 by the SEC, that creates GAAP. (*p. 4*)

Generally accepted accounting principles (GAAP) The rules or guidelines used for carrying out the accounting process. (*p. 4*)

International Accounting Standards Board (IASB) The international organization that provides standards or rules for international financial reporting. (*p. 5*)

International Financial Reporting Standards (IFRS) The rules or guidelines that guide international financial reporting. (*p. 5*)

Paraprofessional accountants People who are qualified in accounting to assume the duties of a general bookkeeper as well as some of the duties of a professional accountant under that accountant's supervision. (*p. 8*)

Sarbanes-Oxley Act A U.S. federal law enacted as a response to a number of major corporate and accounting scandals that establishes a wide range of rules related to the audit environment and internal controls. (*p. 10*)

Securities and Exchange Commission (SEC) The agency responsible for regulating public companies traded on a U.S. stock exchange. (*p. 4*)

Transaction An event directly affecting an economic entity that can be expressed in terms of money and that must be recorded in the accounting records. (*p. 3*)

Activities

Why Does It Matter?

In this book, you hold one of the keys to your future—knowledge of accounting and business! Throughout the pages of this text, you'll be introduced to individuals just like yourself, who dreamed about working in, operating, and even owning a business. You will read about businesses, such as a small cupcake business that has grown to international fame, an exotic catering business that brings food to far-reaching destinations, and an indoor rock-climbing business that caters to all ages. In all of these companies, one important skill stands out—knowing and understanding accounting!

So where do you see accounting in your future? Why is studying accounting so important?

Asset, Liability, Owner's Equity, Revenue, and Expense Accounts

Learning Objectives

After you have completed this chapter, you will be able to do the following:

1 Define and identify *asset, liability,* and *owner's equity* accounts.

2 Record, in column form, a group of business transactions involving changes in assets, liabilities, and owner's equity.

3 Define and identify *revenue* and *expense* accounts.

4 Record, in column form, a group of business transactions involving all five elements of the fundamental accounting equation.

To: **Amy Roberts, CPA**
Subject: **Starting My New Business**

_____

Hi Amy,

Well, I've given it a lot of thought and have decided to take the "plunge"! I'm going to start my own business. I've been working for many years as a whitewater rafting guide and helping in the business office. I think I'm ready to go out on my own. I know a lot about rafting and operating tours, but I don't know much about accounting. Do you think you could help? Would you recommend I purchase accounting software?

Thanks,

Janie

_____

To: **Janie Conner**
Subject: **RE: Starting My New Business**

_____

Hi Janie,

Great! I'm so glad you've finally taken my advice and decided to open your own business. I will definitely help you learn accounting, and I would strongly recommend that you purchase a cloud-based accounting software package like QuickBooks Online! There's a lot to learn—so let's take it step by step. I've made a list of some items for you to concentrate on first.

_____ 1. Understand what accounting is—what it does, what its purpose is.

_____ 2. Know the fundamental accounting equation. (This is important!)

_____ 3. Know examples of accounts that are included in each asset, liability, or owner's equity category.

Once you've learned these items, email me, and we'll move on! Good luck.

Amy

As we stated in the Introduction, accounting is the process of analyzing, classifying, recording, summarizing, and interpreting business transactions. In this chapter, we will introduce the analyzing, classifying, and recording steps in the accounting process.

1-1 ASSETS, LIABILITIES, AND OWNER'S EQUITY

1-1a The Fundamental Accounting Equation

Assets are properties or things of value, such as cash, equipment, copyrights, buildings, and land, owned and controlled by an economic unit or a business entity. By the term **business entity**, we mean that the business is an economic unit in itself, and the assets or properties of the business are completely separate from the owner's personal assets. However, the owner has a claim on the assets of the business and generally has a responsibility for its debts. **The owner's right, claim, or financial interest in the business is expressed by the word equity.** Another term that can be used is **capital**. Whenever you see the term **owner's equity**, it means the owner's right to or investment in the business.

Assets	=	Owner's Equity
Properties or things of value owned by the business	=	Owner's *right* to or investment in the business

Suppose the total value of the assets is $80,000, and the business entity does not owe any amount against the assets. Then,

Assets	=	Owner's Equity
$80,000	=	$80,000

Learning Objective

 1 Define and identify *asset*, *liability*, and *owner's equity* accounts

Or suppose the assets consist of a truck that costs $35,000. The owner has invested $12,000 for the truck, and the business entity has borrowed the remainder from the bank, which is a **creditor** (one to whom money is owed). This business transaction or event can be shown as follows:

Assets	=	Liabilities	+	Owner's Equity
Items owned		*Amounts owed to creditors*		*Owner's investment*
$35,000	=	$23,000	+	$12,000

FYI

Even if the truck is not completely paid for (for example, a loan was taken out to pay for the truck), the truck is still considered an asset. The truck would be recorded at the total cost, and a liability would be recorded for the amount of the loan.

We have now introduced a new classification, **liabilities**, which represent debts. They are the amounts that the business entity owes its creditors. The debts may originate because the business bought goods or services on credit, borrowed money, or otherwise created an obligation to pay. The creditors' claims to the assets have priority over the claims of the owner.

An equation expressing the relationship of assets, liabilities, and owner's equity is called the **fundamental accounting equation**.

Assets	=	Liabilities	+	Owner's Equity

We'll deal with this equation constantly from now on. If we know two parts of this equation, we can determine the third. Let's look at some examples.

DETERMINE ASSETS

Fundamental Accounting Equation Example 1: Millie Adair has $17,000 invested in her travel agency, and the agency owes creditors $5,000; that is, the agency has liabilities of $5,000. Then,

Assets	=	Liabilities	+	Owner's Equity
?	=	$5,000	+	$17,000

We can find the amount of the business's assets by adding the liabilities and the owner's equity.

```
$  5,000 Liabilities
+ 17,000 Owner's Equity
$ 22,000 Assets
```

The completed equation now reads as follows:

Assets	=	Liabilities	+	Owner's Equity
$22,000	=	$5,000	+	$17,000

DETERMINE OWNER'S EQUITY

Fundamental Accounting Equation Example 2: Larry Roland owns a car repair shop. His business has assets of $40,000, and it owes creditors $16,000; that is, it has liabilities of $16,000. Then,

Assets	=	Liabilities	+	Owner's Equity
$40,000	=	$16,000	+	?

We find the owner's equity by subtracting the liabilities from the assets.

$40,000 Assets
−16,000 Liabilities
$24,000 Owner's Equity

The completed equation now reads as follows:

Assets	=	Liabilities	+	Owner's Equity
$40,000	=	$16,000	+	$24,000

DETERMINE LIABILITIES

Fundamental Accounting Equation Example 3: Theo Viero's insurance agency has assets of $86,000. His investment (his equity) amounts to $46,000. Then,

Assets	=	Liabilities	+	Owner's Equity
$86,000	=	?	+	$46,000

To find the firm's total liabilities, we subtract the equity from the assets.

$86,000 Assets
−46,000 Owner's Equity
$40,000 Liabilities

The completed equation reads as follows:

Assets	=	Liabilities	+	Owner's Equity
$86,000	=	$40,000	+	$46,000

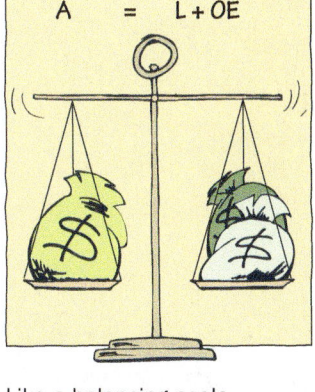

Like a balancing scale, the equation stays in balance by making equal or offsetting increases and decreases to one side or both sides.

To: Amy Roberts, CPA
Subject: **Assets, Liabilities, and Owner's Equity**

Hi Amy,
Thanks for your help! I have purchased QuickBooks Online. Do you have any tips for getting started? I am also doing really well with learning the fundamental accounting equation and identifying accounts. I can now identify most accounts as an asset, liability, or owner's equity. How does this knowledge apply to the transactions of my business?
Thanks,
Janie

To: Janie Conner
Subject: RE: Asset, Liabilities, and Owner's Equity

Hi Janie,
I'm glad to hear you have purchased QuickBooks Online, and I'll provide you with some tips to get started. Once you have learned a few more of the accounting basics, you will be ready to apply these in QuickBooks Online. Now that you know the fundamental accounting equation and also examples of accounts included in each asset, liability, or owners' equity category, you are ready to begin analyzing transactions. You will use your knowledge of accounts and apply this to the company's day-to-day transactions by recording these transactions in column form. This can be challenging, but I'll provide you with four easy steps to remember that will help you along the way. Let's get started!
Amy

1-2 RECORDING BUSINESS TRANSACTIONS

Learning Objective

2 Record, in column form, a group of business transactions involving changes in assets, liabilities, and owner's equity.

As explained in the Introduction, business transactions are events that have a direct effect on the operations of an economic unit or enterprise and are expressed in terms of money. Each business transaction must be recorded in the accounting records. As business transactions are recorded, the amounts listed under the headings Assets, Liabilities, and Owner's Equity change. However, **the total of one side of the fundamental accounting equation must equal the total of the other side.** The categories under these three main headings are called **accounts**.

Let's look at a group of business transactions. These transactions are typical of those seen in a service or professional business. In these transactions, let's assume that J. Conner establishes her own business and calls it Conner's Whitewater Adventures. Conner's Whitewater Adventures is a **sole proprietorship**, or a one-owner business.

TRANSACTION (a). Owner deposited $90,000 in a bank account in the name of the business. Conner deposits $90,000 cash in a separate bank account in the name of Conner's Whitewater Adventures. This separate bank account will help Conner keep her business investment separate from her personal funds. This is an example of the **separate entity concept**, which says a business is treated as a separate economic or accounting entity. (See Figure 1.) The business is independent, or stands by itself. It is separate from its owners, creditors, and customers.

The Cash account consists of bank deposits and money on hand. The business now has $90,000 more in cash than before, and Conner's investment has increased by $90,000.

Figure 1
Separate entity concept

Personal Entity   ≠   Business Entity

The account denoted by the owner's name followed by the word *Capital* indicates the amount of the owner's investment, or equity, in the business. The effect of this transaction on the fundamental accounting equation is as follows:

Assets	=	Liabilities	+	Owner's Equity
Items owned		*Amounts owed to creditors*		*Owner's investment*
Cash	=			J. Conner, Capital
(a) +90,000	=			+90,000

Besides cash, an investment may be in the form of goods, such as equipment. Therefore, the word *Capital* used under Owner's Equity does not always mean that cash was invested.

Accounting, as we said before, is the process of analyzing, classifying, recording, summarizing, and interpreting business transactions in terms of money. Look at transaction (a) above and see if you understand that we have gone through certain steps, which are stated below in question form.

STEP 1. What accounts are involved? Cash and J. Conner, Capital are involved.

STEP 2. What are the classifications of the accounts involved? Cash is an asset account, and J. Conner, Capital is an owner's equity account.

STEP 3. Are the accounts increased or decreased? Cash is increased because Conner's Whitewater Adventures has more cash now than it had before. J. Conner, Capital is increased because Conner has a greater investment now than she had before.

STEP 4. Is the equation in balance after the transaction has been recorded? Yes.

We will stress this step-by-step process throughout the text. This example serves as an introduction to **double-entry accounting**. The "double" entry method is demonstrated by the fact that each transaction must be recorded in at least two accounts, keeping the accounting equation in balance.

For example, transaction (a) resulted in a plus $90,000 and a plus $90,000 *on each side of the equation.* **The left side of the equation must always equal the right side of the equation.**

TRANSACTION (b). Company bought equipment, paying cash, $38,000. Conner's first task is to get her company ready for business. To do that, she needs the proper equipment. Accordingly, Conner buys equipment costing $38,000 and pays cash. **Note at this point that Conner does not invest any new money. She simply exchanges part of the business's cash for equipment.** Because equipment is a new type of property for the firm, a new account, Equipment, is created. Equipment is included under Assets because it is something of value owned by the business. As a result of this transaction, the accounting equation changes.

	Assets	=	Liabilities	+	Owner's Equity
	Items owned		*Amounts owed to creditors*		*Owner's investment*
	Cash + Equipment	=			J. Conner, Capital
Initial Investment	90,000	=			90,000
(b)	−38,000 + 38,000				
New balances	52,000 + 38,000	=			90,000
	90,000				90,000

STEP 1. What accounts are involved? Cash and Equipment are involved.

STEP 2. What are the classifications of the accounts involved? Cash is an asset account, and Equipment is an asset account.

STEP 3. Are the accounts increased or decreased? Cash is decreased because Conner used cash to purchase the equipment. Equipment is increased because Conner's Whitewater Adventures has more equipment now than it had before.

STEP 4. Is the equation in balance after the transaction is recorded? Yes.

Remember that the recording of each transaction must yield an equation that is in balance. In this example, the transaction was recorded on *the same side*. Is that okay? Yes! For example, transaction (b) resulted in a minus $38,000 and a plus $38,000 on the *same side*, with nothing recorded on the other side. This results in an overall change of $0 ($38,000 − $38,000) for each side. It does not matter whether you change one side or both sides. **The important point is that whenever a transaction is properly recorded, the accounting equation remains in balance.**

TRANSACTION (c). Company bought equipment on account from a supplier, $4,320. Conner's Whitewater Adventures buys equipment costing $4,320 on credit from Signal Products.

The Equipment account shows an increase because the business now owns $4,320 more in equipment. The terms *on credit* or *on account* mean that Conner's Whitewater Adventures does not pay cash for the equipment but instead will owe Signal Products money to be paid in the future. This causes an increase in liabilities because the business now owes $4,320. The liability account **Accounts Payable** is used for short-term obligations or charge accounts, usually due within 30 days. Because Conner's Whitewater Adventures owes money to Signal Products, Signal Products is called a creditor of Conner's Whitewater Adventures. A total of $94,320 is now on each side of the equal sign.

	Assets		=	Liabilities	+	Owner's Equity
	Items owned			Amounts owed to creditors		Owner's investment
	Cash +	Equipment	=	Accounts Payable	+	J. Conner, Capital
Previous balances	52,000 +	38,000	=			90,000
(c)		+4,320		+4,320		
New balances	52,000 +	42,320	=	4,320	+	90,000
	94,320				94,320	

STEP 1. What accounts are involved? Equipment and Accounts Payable are involved.

STEP 2. What are the classifications of the accounts involved? Equipment is an asset account, and Accounts Payable is a liability account.

STEP 3. Are the accounts increased or decreased? Equipment is increased because Conner's Whitewater Adventures has more equipment now than it had before. Accounts Payable is increased because Conner's owes more to creditors than it owed before.

STEP 4. Is the equation in balance after the transaction is recorded? Yes.

TRANSACTION (d). **Company paid a creditor on account, $2,000.** Conner's Whitewater Adventures pays $2,000 to Signal Products to be applied against the firm's liability of $4,320.

	Assets		=	**Liabilities**	+	**Owner's Equity**
		Items owned		*Amounts owed to creditors*		*Owner's investment*
	Cash	+ Equipment	=	Accounts Payable	+	J. Conner, Capital
Previous balances	52,000 +	42,320	=	4,320	+	90,000
(d)	−2,000			−2,000		
New balances	50,000 +	42,320	=	2,320	+	90,000
		92,320			92,320	

STEP 1. **What accounts are involved?** Cash and Accounts Payable are involved.

STEP 2. **What are the classifications of the accounts involved?** Cash is an asset account, and Accounts Payable is a liability account.

STEP 3. **Are the accounts increased or decreased?** Cash is decreased because Conner used cash to pay Signal Products. Accounts Payable is decreased because Conner's owes less now than it owed before.

STEP 4. **Is the equation in balance after the transaction is recorded?** Yes.

TRANSACTION (e). **Owner invested equipment in the business.** Conner invested her own computer equipment, having a **fair market value** of $5,200, in Conner's Whitewater Adventures. **Fair market value is the present worth of an asset.** It is the amount that would be received if the asset were sold on the open market. Examples of additional investments by owners may be in the form of equipment, cash, tools, or real estate.

	Assets		=	**Liabilities**	+	**Owner's Equity**
		Items owned		*Amounts owed to creditors*		*Owner's investment*
	Cash	+ Equipment	=	Accounts Payable	+	J. Conner, Capital
Previous balances	50,000 +	42,320	=	2,320	+	90,000
(e)		+5,200				+5,200
New balances	50,000 +	47,520	=	2,320	+	95,200
		97,520			97,520	

STEP 1. **What accounts are involved?** Equipment and J. Conner, Capital are involved.

STEP 2. **What are the classifications of the accounts involved?** Equipment is an asset account, and J. Conner, Capital is an owner's equity account.

STEP 3. Are the accounts increased or decreased? Equipment is increased because Conner's Whitewater Adventures now has more equipment than it had before. J. Conner, Capital is increased because Conner has a greater investment now than she had before.

STEP 4. Is the equation in balance after the transaction is recorded? Yes.

1-2a Summary of Transactions

Let's summarize the business transactions of Conner's Whitewater Adventures in column form. To test your understanding of the recording procedure, describe the nature of the transactions that have taken place.

	Assets		=	Liabilities	+	Owner's Equity
	Items owned			*Amounts owed to creditors*		*Owner's investment*
	Cash	+ Equipment	=	Accounts Payable	+	J. Conner, Capital
Transaction (a)	+90,000					+90,000
Transaction (b)	−38,000	+38,000				
Balance	52,000 +	38,000	=			90,000
Transaction (c)		+4,320		+4,320		
Balance	52,000 +	42,320	=	4,320	+	90,000
Transaction (d)	−2,000			−2,000		
Balance	50,000 +	42,320	=	2,320	+	90,000
Transaction (e)		+5,200				+5,200
Balance	50,000 +	47,520	=	2,320	+	95,200

97,520   97,520

The following observations apply to all types of business transactions:

1. Every transaction is recorded as an increase and/or decrease in two or more accounts.
2. One side of the equation is always equal to the other side of the equation.

In this chapter, we are using a column arrangement as a practical device to show how transactions are recorded. This arrangement is useful for showing increases and decreases in various accounts as a result of the transactions. We also show new balances after each transaction is recorded.

ACCOUNTING IN YOUR FUTURE

ACCOUNTING SKILLS

You may wonder why taking an accounting class is important. One possible career for students who study accounting is as an entry-level accounting clerk for a company. As an accounting clerk, you would be the financial recordkeeper for the business. Your responsibilities would include maintaining accounting records, such as those you are learning about in this chapter. You might also be responsible for preparing financial statements, making bank deposits, and handling payroll.

Many businesses require that an accounting clerk have a high school diploma and some accounting course work. An associate degree in accounting is highly recommended. Minimum requirements are a knowledge of basic accounting terminology, concepts, and processes, and using a manual accounting system or an automated accounting system such as general ledger accounting software. Skills related to Microsoft® Word® , Excel® , and Outlook® also are helpful.* You need to be able to work with others in the accounting department and be attentive to detail and accuracy. Accounting clerks, sometimes called bookkeepers, can become certified bookkeepers by meeting the requirements of the American Institute of Professional Bookkeepers (www.aipb.org). The U.S. Department of Labor's Bureau of Labor Statistics (www.bls.gov) provides information about this field, including job locations and pay scales.

Microsoft, Encarta, MSN, and Windows are either registered trademarks or trademarks of Microsoft Corporation in the United States and/or other countries.

1-3 REVENUE AND EXPENSE ACCOUNTS

Revenues are the amounts earned by a business. Examples of revenues are fees earned for performing services, income from selling merchandise, rent income from tenants for the use of property, and interest income for lending money. Revenues may be in the form of cash or credit card receipts. Revenues may also result from credit sales to charge customers, in which case cash will be received at a later time.

Expenses (or the costs of doing business) are the costs that relate to earning revenue. Examples of expenses are wages expense for labor performed, rent expense for the use of property, interest expense for the use of money, and advertising expense for the use of various media (for example, newspapers, radio, direct mail, and the Internet). Expenses may be paid in cash either when incurred or at a later time. Expenses to be paid at a later time involve Accounts Payable.

Revenues and expenses directly affect owner's equity. **If a business earns revenue, an increase in owner's equity occurs. When a business incurs expenses, owner's equity decreases.** For the present, think of it this way: If the company makes money, the owner's

 3 Define and identify *revenue* and *expense* accounts.

Learning Objective

FYI

Incurred is another word for *being responsible for* or *having taken place.*

equity is increased. If the company has to pay out money for the costs of doing business, the owner's equity is decreased. Revenues and expenses fall under the umbrella of owner's equity: Revenue increases owner's equity; expenses decrease owner's equity.

Figure 2
The umbrella of owner's equity

1-3a Chart of Accounts

The **chart of accounts** is the official list of accounts *tailor-made* for the business. All of the company's transactions must be recorded using the official account titles. The numbers preceding the account titles are the **account numbers**.

We now present the chart of accounts for Conner's Whitewater Adventures. Some of the accounts are new to you, but they will be explained as we move along. In the numbering of account titles, the 100s are used for assets, the 200s are used for liabilities, the 300s are used for owner's equity accounts, the 400s are used for revenue accounts, and the 500s are used for expense accounts.

CHART OF ACCOUNTS

Assets (100–199)
111 Cash
113 Accounts Receivable
115 Supplies
117 Prepaid Insurance
124 Equipment

Liabilities (200–299)
221 Accounts Payable

Owner's Equity (300–399)
311 J. Conner, Capital
312 J. Conner, Drawing

Revenue (400–499)
411 Income from Tours

Expenses (500–599)
511 Wages Expense
512 Rent Expense
514 Advertising Expense
515 Utilities Expense

While charts of accounts vary from business to business, the beginning numbers for assets, liabilities, owner's equity, revenues, and expenses are standard for a service business. Some account numbers are much longer than three digits. In any case, use the exact account titles listed in the company's chart of accounts.

For merchandising businesses selling goods (versus services), expenses will start with the 600s because accounts starting with the 500s are reserved for accounts related to the cost of the goods being sold.

Most accounting programs, such as QuickBooks Online, include a standard chart of accounts set up for many different types of businesses.

Rose Carson/Shutterstock.com

In the Real World

Every company must have a chart of accounts. For example, the mobile application and social media website Facebook has a chart of accounts similar to but much bigger than the example we're using. What might be some names of some accounts Facebook might have in its chart of accounts? Why is a listing of accounts so important?

1-4 RECORDING BUSINESS TRANSACTIONS

Let's examine more transactions of Conner's Whitewater Adventures for the first month of operations. Soon after the opening of Conner's Whitewater Adventures, the first customers arrive, beginning a flow of revenue for the business.

4 Record, in column form, a group of business transactions involving all five elements of the fundamental accounting equation.

Learning Objective

TRANSACTION (f). Company sold services for cash, $8,000. Conner's Whitewater Adventures receives cash revenue of $8,000 in return for providing whitewater rafting tours for customers over a two-week period. In other words, the company earns $8,000 for services performed for cash customers. Revenue has the effect of increasing owner's equity, but because the company wants to know how much revenue is earned, we set up a special column for revenue. The revenue account for Conner's Whitewater Adventures is called Income from Tours. The accounting equation is affected as follows: (1) PB stands for previous balance, and (2) NB stands for new balance.

	Assets		=	Liabilities	+	Owner's Equity		
	Cash	+ Equipment	=	Accounts Payable	+	J. Conner, Capital	+	Revenue
PB	50,000	+ 47,520	=	2,320	+	95,200		
(f)	+8,000							+8,000 (Income from Tours)
NB	58,000	+ 47,520	=	2,320	+	95,200	+	8,000
	105,520					105,520		

Let's review the mental process for formulating the entry.

STEP 1. **What accounts are involved?** In this transaction, they are Cash and Income from Tours.

STEP 2. **What are the classifications of the accounts involved?** Cash is an asset account, and Income from Tours is a revenue account and part of owner's equity.

STEP 3. Are the accounts increased or decreased? Cash is increased because Conner's Whitewater Adventures received cash. Income from Tours (revenue) is increased.

STEP 4. Is the equation in balance after the transaction has been recorded? Yes.

TRANSACTION (g). Company paid rent (an expense) for the month, $1,250. Shortly after opening the business, Conner's Whitewater Adventures pays the month's rent of $1,250. Rent is payment for the privilege of occupying property.

It seems logical that if revenue is added to owner's equity, expenses (the opposite of revenue) must be subtracted from owner's equity. To be consistent, a separate column is set up for expenses.

Because the time period represented by the rent payment is one month or less, we record the $1,250 as an expense. If the payment covered a period longer than one month, we would record the amount under an asset called Prepaid Rent.

	Assets		=	Liabilities	+		Owner's Equity		
	Cash	+ Equip.	=	Accounts Payable	+	J. Conner, Capital	+ Revenue	−	Expenses
PB	58,000	+ 47,520	=	2,320	+	95,200	+ 8,000		
(g)	−1,250								+1,250 (Rent Expense)
NB	56,750	+ 47,520	=	2,320	+	95,200	+ 8,000	−	1,250
		104,270					104,270		

STEP 1. What accounts are involved? Cash and Rent Expense are involved.

STEP 2. What are the classifications of the accounts involved? Cash is an asset account, and Rent Expense is an owner's equity account.

STEP 3. Are the accounts increased or decreased? Cash is decreased because after the payment, Conner's Whitewater Adventures has less cash than before. Rent Expense is increased because now Conner's Whitewater Adventures has more rent expense than before.

STEP 4. Is the equation in balance after the transaction is recorded? Yes. Notice that in this equation, it looks as though the account doesn't balance— there is a negative entry on the left and a positive entry on the right. This is deceiving. The entry to Rent Expense is a positive entry in a negative column, thus creating an overall negative entry. It looks like this: − (+1,250) = −1,250.

TRANSACTION (h). Company bought supplies on credit, $675. Conner's Whitewater Adventures buys office supplies costing $675 on credit from Fineman Company. Computer paper, ink cartridges, invoice pads, pens and pencils, folders, filing cabinets, and calculators are considered supplies to be used by Conner's Whitewater Adventures for the business. Supplies are recorded as an asset until they are used. When supplies are used, they are taken from the asset account and placed in the expense account. We'll talk more about this later. For the time being, because Conner hasn't used the supplies yet, we will record them as an asset.

	Assets		=	Liabilities	+		Owner's Equity		
				Accounts		J. Conner,			
Cash	+ Equip.	+ Supplies =		Payable	+	Capital	+ Revenue	− Expenses	
PB 56,750	+ 47,520		=	2,320	+	95,200	+ 8,000	− 1,250	
(h)		+675		+675					
NB 56,750	+ 47,520	+ 675	=	2,995	+	95,200	+ 8,000	− 1,250	
	104,945					104,945			

STEP 1. What accounts are involved? Supplies and Accounts Payable are involved.

STEP 2. What are the classifications of the accounts involved? Supplies is an asset account, and Accounts Payable is a liability account.

STEP 3. Are the accounts increased or decreased? Supplies is increased because Conner's Whitewater Adventures now has more supplies than before. Accounts Payable is increased because Conner's Whitewater Adventures now owes money for the purchase of supplies.

STEP 4. Is the equation in balance after the transaction has been recorded? Yes.

TRANSACTION (i). Company paid cash for insurance, $1,875. Conner's Whitewater Adventures paid $1,875 for a three-month liability insurance policy. At the time of payment, the company has not used up the insurance; thus, it is not yet an expense. As the insurance expires (is used), it will become an expense. **However, because it is paid in advance for a period longer than one month, it has value over that longer period and is, therefore, recorded as Prepaid Insurance, an asset.**

At the end of the year or accounting period, an adjustment will have to be made to take out the expired portion (that is, coverage for the months that have been used up) and record it as an expense. We discuss this adjustment in a later chapter.

	Assets				=	Liabilities	+		Owner's Equity		
				Ppd.		Accounts		J. Conner,			
Cash	+ Equip.	+ Supplies	+	Ins.	=	Payable	+	Capital	+ Revenue	− Expenses	
PB 56,750	+ 47,520	+ 675			=	2,995	+	95,200	+ 8,000	− 1,250	
(i) −1,875				+1,875							
NB 54,875	+ 47,520	+ 675	+	1,875	=	2,995	+	95,200	+ 8,000	− 1,250	
	104,945						104,945				

STEP 1. What accounts are involved? Cash and Prepaid Insurance are involved.

STEP 2. What are the classifications of the accounts involved? Cash and Prepaid Insurance are both asset accounts.

STEP 3. Are the accounts increased or decreased? Cash is decreased because Conner's Whitewater Adventures is paying money, and Prepaid Insurance is increased because Conner's Whitewater Adventures has more insurance than before.

STEP 4. Is the equation in balance after the transaction is recorded? Yes.

Remember that each time a transaction is recorded, the total amount on one side of the equation **remains equal** to the total amount on the other side. As proof of this equality, look at the following computation:

Cash	$ 54,875	**Accounts Payable**	$ 2,995
Equipment	47,520	**J. Conner, Capital**	95,200
Supplies	675	**Revenue**	8,000
Prepaid Insurance	1,875	**Expenses**	−1,250
	$104,945		$104,945

1-4a Steps in Analyzing Transactions

Now that we have recorded transactions in all five classifications of accounts, let's review the steps we followed.

STEP 1. Read the transaction to understand what is happening and how it affects the business. For example, the business has more revenue or has more expenses or has more cash or owes less to creditors. Identify the accounts involved. Look for Cash first. You will quickly recognize whether cash is coming in or going out.

STEP 2. Decide on the classifications of the accounts involved. For example, Equipment is something the business owns, and it's an asset. Accounts Payable is an amount the business owes, and it's a liability.

STEP 3. Decide whether the accounts are increased or decreased.

STEP 4. After recording the transaction, make sure the accounting equation is in balance.

FYI

Think through these steps each time you are presented with a transaction. We'll work through several more examples for Conner's Whitewater Adventures. However, we won't continue to show the steps. If you need extra help, write the steps in the margin.

SMALL BUSINESS **SUCCESS**

Tools to Success—The U.S. Small Business Administration

Throughout the pages of this text, you will occasionally find a feature labeled Small Business Success. This feature is designed to provide insight into accounting issues surrounding small businesses. Some of you may own a small business when you graduate. Maybe you are thinking of starting your own small bookkeeping firm. Many of you will work in small businesses such as a local or regional accounting firm. These features contain information that is useful to small and large businesses and will be helpful if you are thinking about owning your own business.

The U.S. Small Business Administration website (www.sba.gov) is a great place to find information about managing, accounting for, and running a small business. Take a moment to go to the website and review the tools that are available

to small businesses. Click on the Starting & Managing link, and you will find information that deals with starting a new business, managing a business, and financing a business.

You can also find audio and video podcasts on the website that provide information about business success. If you are interested in hearing about successful small businesses, you can find a series on small business features. The series discusses various small businesses that have used the tools provided by the Small Business Administration and have grown to be successful and profitable entities.

Keep an eye out for the Small Business Success feature! It will give you insight into how businesses use the accounting information you are learning in this course.

TRANSACTION (j). Company received a bill for an expense, $620. Conner's Whitewater Adventures receives a bill from *The Times* for newspaper advertising, $620. **Conner's Whitewater Adventures has received the bill for advertising, but it has not paid any cash.** Previously, we described an expense as cash paid or to be paid for the cost of doing business. An expense of $620 has now been incurred (or has taken place), and it should be recorded as an increase in expenses (Advertising Expense). Also, because the company owes $620 more than it did before and it intends to pay at a later time, this amount should be recorded as an increase in Accounts Payable. Notice that Cash is not used because the bill has not been paid.

	Assets						=	Liabilities	+		Owner's Equity			
	Cash	+	Equip.	+	Supplies	+	Ppd. Ins.	=	Accounts Payable	+	J. Conner, Capital	+ Revenue	−	Expenses
PB	54,875	+	47,520	+	675	+	1,875	=	2,995	+	95,200	+ 8,000	−	1,250
(j)									+620					+620 (Advertising Expense)
NB	54,875	+	47,520	+	675	+	1,875	=	3,615	+	95,200	+ 8,000	−	1,870

104,945   104,945

TRANSACTION (k). Company sold services on account, $6,750. Conner's Whitewater Adventures signs a contract with Crystal River Lodge to provide rafting adventures for guests. Conner's Whitewater Adventures provides 27 one-day rafting tours and bills Crystal River Lodge for $6,750.

A company uses the **Accounts Receivable** account to record the amounts due from (legal claims against) charge customers. Because Conner's Whitewater Adventures' claim of $6,750 against Crystal River Lodge is promised to be paid, it is recorded in Accounts Receivable. Revenue is earned or recognized when the service is performed, even though the $6,750 has not been received in cash. We count the $6,750 as an increase in revenue and an increase in Accounts Receivable. Keep in mind that Accounts Receivable is an asset, or something that is owned. Conner's Whitewater Adventures owns a claim of $6,750 against Crystal River Lodge.

	Assets								=	Liabilities	+		Owner's Equity	
	Cash	+ Equip.	+ Supplies	+	Ppd. Ins.	+	Accts. Rec.	=	Accounts Payable	+	J. Conner, Capital	+ Revenue	− Expenses
PB	54,875	+ 47,520	+ 675	+	1,875			=	3,615	+	95,200	+ 8,000	− 1,870
(k)							+6,750					+6,750 (Income from Tours)	
NB	54,875	+ 47,520	+ 675	+	1,875	+	6,750	=	3,615	+	95,200	+ 14,750	− 1,870

111,695   111,695

When Crystal River Lodge pays the $6,750 bill in cash, Conner's Whitewater Adventures records this transaction as an increase in Cash and a decrease in Accounts Receivable. At that time, Conner's Whitewater Adventures will *not* have to make an entry for the revenue because the **revenue was earned and recorded when the service was performed.**

TRANSACTION (l). Company paid creditor on account. Conner's Whitewater Adventures pays $1,500 to Signal Products, its creditor (the party to whom it owes money), as partial payment on account for the liability recorded in transaction (c).

	Assets					=	Liabilities +		Owner's Equity			
				Ppd.	Accts.		Accounts		J. Conner,			
	Cash	+ Equip.	+ Supplies	+ Ins.	+ Rec.	=	Payable	+	Capital	+ Revenue	− Expenses	
PB	54,875	+ 47,520	+ 675	+ 1,875	+ 6,750	=	3,615	+	95,200	+ 14,750	− 1,870	
(l)	−1,500						−1,500					
NB	53,375	+ 47,520	+ 675	+ 1,875	+ 6,750	=	2,115	+	95,200	+ 14,750	− 1,870	
			110,195							110,195		

TRANSACTION (m). Company paid an expense in cash, $225. Conner's Whitewater Adventures receives a bill from Solar Power, Inc., for $225. Because the bill was not previously recorded as a liability and is to be paid immediately, we record the amount directly as an expense.

	Assets					=	Liabilities +		Owner's Equity			
				Ppd.	Accts.		Accounts		J. Conner,			
	Cash	+ Equip.	+ Supplies	+ Ins.	+ Rec.	=	Payable	+	Capital	+ Revenue	− Expenses	
PB	53,375	+ 47,520	+ 675	+ 1,875	+ 6,750	=	2,115	+	95,200	+ 14,750	− 1,870	
(m)	−225										+225 (Utilities Expense)	
NB	53,150	+ 47,520	+ 675	+ 1,875	+ 6,750	=	2,115	+	95,200	+ 14,750	− 2,095	
			109,970							109,970		

TRANSACTION (n). Company paid creditor on account, $620. Conner's Whitewater Adventures pays $620 to *The Times* for advertising. Recall that this bill had previously been recorded as a liability in transaction (j).

	Assets					=	Liabilities +		Owner's Equity			
				Ppd.	Accts.		Accounts		J. Conner,			
	Cash	+ Equip.	+ Supplies	+ Ins.	+ Rec.	=	Payable	+	Capital	+ Revenue	− Expenses	
PB	53,150	+ 47,520	+ 675	+ 1,875	+ 6,750	=	2,115	+	95,200	+ 14,750	− 2,095	
(n)	−620						−620					
NB	52,530	+ 47,520	+ 675	+ 1,875	+ 6,750	=	1,495	+	95,200	+ 14,750	− 2,095	
			109,350							109,350		

TRANSACTION (o). Company paid an expense in cash, $2,360. Conner's Whitewater Adventures pays wages of a part-time employee, $2,360.

	Assets					=	Liabilities +		Owner's Equity		
	Cash	+ Equip.	+ Supplies	+ Ppd. Ins.	+ Accts. Rec.	=	Accounts Payable	+ J. Conner, Capital	+ Revenue	− Expenses
PB	52,530	+ 47,520	+ 675	+ 1,875	+ 6,750	=	1,495	+ 95,200	+ 14,750	− 2,095
(o)	−2,360									+2,360 (Wages Expense)
NB	50,170	+ 47,520	+ 675	+ 1,875	+ 6,750	=	1,495	+ 95,200	+ 14,750	− 4,455
	106,990							106,990		

TRANSACTION (p). Company buys equipment on account for $3,780, making a cash down payment of $1,850 and charging $1,930. Conner's Whitewater Adventures buys additional equipment from Signal Products for $3,780, paying $1,850 down with the remaining $1,930 on account. Because buying an item *on account* is the same as buying it *on credit,* both terms are used to describe such transactions and involve Accounts Payable.

	Assets					=	Liabilities +		Owner's Equity		
	Cash	+ Equip.	+ Supplies	+ Ppd. Ins.	+ Accts. Rec.	=	Accounts Payable	+ J. Conner, Capital	+ Revenue	− Expenses
PB	50,170	+ 47,520	+ 675	+ 1,875	+ 6,750	=	1,495	+ 95,200	+ 14,750	− 4,455
(p)	−1,850	+3,780					+1,930			
NB	48,320	+ 51,300	+ 675	+ 1,875	+ 6,750	=	3,425	+ 95,200	+ 14,750	− 4,455
	108,920							108,920		

Again, because the equipment is expected to last for years, Conner's Whitewater Adventures lists this $3,780 as an increase in the assets. Note that three accounts are involved in this transaction: Cash because cash was paid out, Equipment because the company has more equipment than it had before, and Accounts Payable because the company owes more now than it owed before.

TRANSACTION (q). Company receives cash on account from credit customer, $2,500. Conner's Whitewater Adventures receives $2,500 from Crystal River Lodge to apply against the amount billed in transaction (k). Because Crystal River Lodge now owes Conner's Whitewater Adventure less than it did before, Conner's Whitewater Adventures deducts the $2,500 from Accounts Receivable. An exchange of assets has no effect on the totals of the equation.

	Assets					=	Liabilities +		Owner's Equity		
	Cash	+ Equip.	+ Supplies	+ Ppd. Ins.	+ Accts. Rec.	=	Accounts Payable	+ J. Conner, Capital	+ Revenue	− Expenses
PB	48,320	+ 51,300	+ 675	+ 1,875	+ 6,750	=	3,425	+ 95,200	+ 14,750	− 4,455
(q)	+2,500				−2,500					
NB	50,820	+ 51,300	+ 675	+ 1,875	+ 4,250	=	3,425	+ 95,200	+ 14,750	− 4,455
	108,920							108,920		

Conner's Whitewater Adventures previously listed the amount as revenue [see transaction (k)], so it should *not* be recorded as revenue again.

TRANSACTION (r). Company sells services for cash, $8,570. Conner's Whitewater Adventures receives revenue from cash customers during the rest of the month, $8,570.

	Assets					=	Liabilities +		Owner's Equity		
	Cash	+ Equip.	+ Supplies	+ Ppd. Ins.	+ Accts. Rec.	=	Accounts Payable	+ J. Conner, Capital	+ Revenue	− Expenses
PB	50,820	+ 51,300	+ 675	+ 1,875	+ 4,250	=	3,425	+ 95,200	+ 14,750	− 4,455
(r)	+8,570								+8,570 (Income from Tours)	
NB	59,390	+ 51,300	+ 675	+ 1,875	+ 4,250	=	3,425	+ 95,200	+ 23,320	− 4,455
			117,490						117,490	

TRANSACTION (s). Owner makes a cash withdrawal, $3,500. At the end of the month, Conner withdraws $3,500 in cash from the business for her personal living costs. A **withdrawal** (or drawing) may be considered the opposite of an investment in cash by the owner and is treated as a decrease in owner's equity. Withdrawals are different from expenses. Expenses are paid to someone else for the cost of goods or services used in the business. On the other hand, withdrawals are paid directly to the owner and do not involve the cost of goods or services used in the business. A withdrawal may consist of cash or other assets.

Because the owner takes cash out of the business, there is a decrease of $3,500 in Cash. This withdrawal of cash also decreases owner's equity and is denoted in the account labeled with the owner's name followed by the word *Drawing*. We record $3,500 under J. Conner, Drawing.

	Assets					=	Liabilities +			Owner's Equity		
	Cash	+ Equip.	+ Supplies	+ Ppd. Ins.	+ Accts. Rec.	=	Accounts Payable	+ J. Conner, Capital	− J. Conner, Drawing	+ Revenue	− Expenses
PB	59,390	+ 51,300	+ 675	+ 1,875	+ 4,250	=	3,425	+ 95,200		+ 23,320	− 4,455
(s)	−3,500								+3,500		
NB	55,890	+ 51,300	+ 675	+ 1,875	+ 4,250	=	3,425	+ 95,200	− 3,500	+ 23,320	− 4,455
			113,990						113,990		

1-4b Summary of Transactions (f) through (s)

Figure 3 summarizes business transactions (f) through (s) of Conner's Whitewater Adventures, with the transactions identified by letter. To test your understanding of the recording procedure, describe the nature of the transactions.

Figure 3
Summary of transactions (f) through (s)

	Cash	+ Equip.	+ Supplies	+ Ppd. Ins.	+ Accts. Rec.	=	Accounts Payable	+ J. Conner, Capital	− J. Conner, Drawing	+ Revenue	− Expenses
			Assets			=	Liabilities +		Owner's Equity		
Bal.	50,000	+ 47,520				=	2,320	+ 95,200			
(f)	+8,000									+8,000 (Income from Tours)	
Bal.	58,000	+ 47,520				=	2,320	+ 95,200		+ 8,000	
(g)	−1,250										+1,250 (Rent Exp.)
Bal.	56,750	+ 47,520				=	2,320	+ 95,200		+ 8,000 −	1,250
(h)			+675				+675				
Bal.	56,750	+ 47,520 +	675			=	2,995	+ 95,200		+ 8,000 −	1,250
(i)	−1,875			+1,875							
Bal.	54,875	+ 47,520 +	675	+ 1,875		=	2,995	+ 95,200		+ 8,000 −	1,250
(j)							+620				+620 (Adv. Exp.)
Bal.	54,875	+ 47,520 +	675	+ 1,875		=	3,615	+ 95,200		+ 8,000 −	1,870
(k)					+6,750					+6,750 (Income from Tours)	
Bal.	54,875	+ 47,520 +	675	+ 1,875 +	6,750	=	3,615	+ 95,200		+ 14,750 −	1,870
(l)	−1,500						−1,500				
Bal.	53,375	+ 47,520 +	675	+ 1,875 +	6,750	=	2,115	+ 95,200		+ 14,750 −	1,870
(m)	−225										+225 (Util. Exp.)
Bal.	53,150	+ 47,520 +	675	+ 1,875 +	6,750	=	2,115	+ 95,200		+ 14,750 −	2,095
(n)	−620						−620				
Bal.	52,530	+ 47,520 +	675	+ 1,875 +	6,750	=	1,495	+ 95,200		+ 14,750 −	2,095
(o)	−2,360										+2,360 (Wages Exp.)
Bal.	50,170	+ 47,520 +	675	+ 1,875 +	6,750	=	1,495	+ 95,200		+ 14,750 −	4,455
(p)	−1,850	+3,780					+1,930				
Bal.	48,320	+ 51,300 +	675	+ 1,875 +	6,750	=	3,425	+ 95,200		+ 14,750 −	4,455
(q)	+2,500				−2,500						
Bal.	50,820	+ 51,300 +	675	+ 1,875 +	4,250	=	3,425	+ 95,200		+ 14,750 −	4,455
(r)	+8,570									+8,570 (Income from Tours)	
Bal.	59,390	+ 51,300 +	675	+ 1,875 +	4,250	=	3,425	+ 95,200		+ 23,320 −	4,455
(s)	−3,500								+3,500		
Bal.	55,890	+ 51,300 +	675	+ 1,875 +	4,250	=	3,425	+ 95,200 −	3,500	+ 23,320 −	4,455

Left Side of Equals Sign:		Right Side of Equals Sign:	
Cash	$ 55,890	Accounts Payable	$ 3,425
Equipment	51,300	J. Conner, Capital	95,200
Supplies	675	J. Conner, Drawing	−3,500
Prepaid Insurance	1,875	Revenue	23,320
Accounts Receivable	4,250	Expenses	−4,455
	$113,990		$113,990

YOU Make the Call

You've just been hired as an accounting clerk. The other accounting clerk, Sam, has asked you to check some transactions he analyzed. Use the transaction-analysis steps presented earlier in the chapter (see page 26) to determine the accuracy of the following transactions and write your own analysis.

SAM'S ANALYSES—FIND THE ERRORS

TRANSACTION 1. Received a bill for the month's rent, $1,000.

STEP 1. Cash and Rent Expense are the accounts involved.

STEP 2. Cash is an asset, and Rent Expense is an expense.

STEP 3. Cash is decreased, and Rent Expense is decreased.

TRANSACTION 2: Bought equipment on account for $1,800.

STEP 1. Equipment and Accounts Receivable are the accounts involved.

STEP 2. Equipment is an asset, and Accounts Receivable is an asset.

STEP 3. Equipment is decreased, and Accounts Receivable is increased.

SOLUTION

Sam's analyses for both transactions are incorrect.

TRANSACTION 1:

STEP 1. Accounts Payable and Rent Expense are the accounts involved.

STEP 2. The bill was received but not paid, therefore creating a liability. Cash is not involved because the business has not paid the monthly rent.

Accounts Payable is a liability, and Rent Expense is an expense.

STEP 3. Accounts Payable is increased, and Rent Expense is increased. Remember, the bill was only received, not paid; therefore, no cash is involved. Rent Expense increases, but its ultimate effect is a subtraction in the fundamental accounting equation.

TRANSACTION 2:

STEP 1. Equipment and Accounts Payable are the accounts involved.

STEP 2. Accounts Payable is involved because the business owes money to the seller. Accounts Payable is the account used to manage short-term liabilities. Accounts Receivable is the account used to keep track of what customers owe the business.

Equipment is an asset, and Accounts Payable is a liability.

STEP 3. Equipment is increased, and Accounts Payable is increased.

Chapter Review

Study and Practice

 1 Define and identify *asset, liability,* and *owner's equity* accounts.

Learning Objective

Assets are cash, properties, or things of value owned by the business. **Liabilities** are amounts the business owes to creditors. **Owner's equity** is the owner's investment in or rights to the business. The **fundamental accounting equation** expresses the relationship of assets, liabilities, and owner's equity and is represented as:

$$\text{Assets} = \text{Liabilities} + \text{Owner's Equity}$$

 PRACTICE EXERCISE 1

Complete the fundamental accounting equation:

Assets	=	Liabilities	+	Owner's Equity
Items owned		Amounts owed to creditors		Owner's investment
$50,000	=	$12,000	+	?

PRACTICE EXERCISE 1 • SOLUTION

$50,000 Assets
−12,000 Liabilities
$38,000 Owner's Equity

2 Record, in column form, a group of business transactions involving changes in assets, liabilities, and owner's equity.

Learning Objective

The accounting equation is stated as assets equals liabilities plus owner's equity. Under the appropriate classification, a separate column is set up for each **account**. Transactions are recorded by listing amounts as additions to or deductions from the various accounts. The equation must remain in balance.

 PRACTICE EXERCISE 2

Write the corresponding amounts for each transaction where you see question marks. Compute the balance to make sure the equation is in balance before proceeding to the next transaction.

(Continued)

	Assets		=	Liabilities	+	Owner's Equity
	Items owned			*Amounts owed to creditors*		*Owner's investment*
	Cash	+ Equipment =		Accounts Payable	+	J. Lawson, Capital
Transaction (a)	+90,000					?
Transaction (b)	?	+53,000				
Balance	? +	?	=			?
Transaction (c)		?		+9,000		
Balance	? +	?	=	?	+	?
Transaction (d)	?			−4,000		
Balance	? +	?	=	?	+	?
Transaction (e)		?				+5,200
Balance	? +	?	=	?	+	?
		?			?	

PRACTICE EXERCISE 2 • SOLUTION

	Assets		=	Liabilities	+	Owner's Equity
	Items owned			*Amounts owed to creditors*		*Owner's investment*
	Cash	+ Equipment =		Accounts Payable	+	J. Lawson, Capital
Transaction (a)	+90,000					+90,000
Transaction (b)	−53,000	+53,000				
Balance	37,000 +	53,000	=			90,000
Transaction (c)		+9,000		+9,000		
Balance	37,000 +	62,000	=	9,000	+	90,000
Transaction (d)	−4,000			−4,000		
Balance	33,000 +	62,000	=	5,000	+	90,000
Transaction (e)		+5,200				+5,200
Balance	33,000 +	67,200	=	5,000	+	95,200
		100,200			100,200	

3 Define and identify *revenue* and *expense* accounts.

Learning Objective

Revenues consist of amounts earned by a business, such as fees earned for performing services, income from selling merchandise, rent income from tenants for the use of property, and interest earned for lending money. **Expenses** are the costs of earning revenue—that is, of doing business—such as wages expense, rent expense, interest expense, and advertising expense.

 PRACTICE EXERCISE 3

Identify the revenue and expense accounts from the following list of accounts. If the account is a revenue account, write R. If the account is an expense account, write E. If it is neither, leave blank.

___	Accounts Payable	___	Service Income
___	Rent Expense	___	Utilities Expense
___	J. Martin, Drawing	___	Professional Fees Earned
___	Wages Expense	___	Accounts Receivable

PRACTICE EXERCISE 3 • SOLUTION

___	Accounts Payable	_R_	Service Income
_E_	Rent Expense	_E_	Utilities Expense
___	J. Martin, Drawing	_R_	Professional Fees Earned
_E_	Wages Expense	___	Accounts Receivable

4 Record, in column form, a group of business transactions involving all five elements of the fundamental accounting equation.

Learning Objective

The accounting equation has been expanded and should appear as follows:

Assets = Liabilities + Capital − Drawing + Revenue − Expenses

Accounts are classified and listed under each heading. Transactions are recorded by listing amounts as additions to or deductions from the various accounts. The equation must remain in balance.

 PRACTICE EXERCISE 4

Record the following transactions in the grid provided below.

Transaction (a).   Company bought equipment for $8,000 on account.
Transaction (b).   Company sold services on account for $6,200.
Transaction (c).   Customer paid $3,000 on account.
Transaction (d).   Company owner invested personal computer system in the business, fair market value, $3,400 (Equipment).

(Continued)

CHAPTER REVIEW

	Assets			=	Liabilities	+	Owner's Equity			
	Cash	+ Equipment +	Accounts Receivable	=	Accounts Payable	+ Capital	− Drawing	+ Revenue	− Expenses
(a)									
(b)									
Bal.									
(c)									
Bal.									
(d)									
Bal.									

PRACTICE EXERCISE 4 • SOLUTION

	Assets			=	Liabilities	+	Owner's Equity			
	Cash	+ Equipment +	Accounts Receivable	=	Accounts Payable	+ Capital	− Drawing	+ Revenue	− Expenses
(a)		+8,000			+8,000				
(b)			+6,200					+6,200	
Bal.		+8,000	+6,200	=	+8,000			+6,200	
(c)	+3,000		−3,000						
Bal.	+3,000	+8,000	+3,200	=	+8,000			+6,200	
(d)		+3,400				+3,400			
Bal.	3,000	+ 11,400	+ 3,200	=	8,000	+ 3,400		+ 6,200	

17,600   17,600

Glossary

Account numbers The numbers assigned to accounts according to the chart of accounts. (*p. 22*)

Accounts The categories under the Assets, Liabilities, and Owner's Equity headings. (*p. 16*)

Accounts Payable A liability account used for short-term obligations or charge accounts, usually due within 30 days. (*p. 18*)

Accounts Receivable An account used to record the amounts due from (legal claims against) charge customers. (*p. 27*)

Assets Cash, properties, and other things of value owned by an economic unit or a business entity. (*p. 13*)

Backups Procedures that store company data files in a safe place, such as online or on a flash drive. (*p. 48*)

Business entity A business enterprise, separate and distinct from the persons who supply the assets it uses. (*p. 13*)

Capital The owner's investment, or equity, in an enterprise. (*p. 13*)

Chart of accounts The official list of account titles to be used to record the transactions of a business. (*p. 22*)

Cloud computing Software that is used via the Internet instead of from a local computer. Software and data can be accessed anywhere there is an Internet connection. (*p. 48*)

Computerized accounting system An accounting system that records transactions using a computer and an accounting cloud-based application like QuickBooks Online. (*p. 47*)

Creditor One to whom money is owed. (*p. 14*)

Double-entry accounting The system by which each business transaction is recorded in at least two accounts and the accounting equation is kept in balance. (*p. 17*)

Equity The value of a right or claim to or financial interest in an asset or group of assets. (*p. 13*)

Expenses The costs that relate to earning revenue (the costs of doing business); examples are wages, rent, interest, and advertising. They may be paid in cash immediately or at a future time (Accounts Payable). (*p. 21*)

Fair market value The present worth of an asset or the amount that would be received if the asset were sold to an outsider on the open market. (*p. 19*)

Fundamental accounting equation (Assets = Liabilities + Owner's Equity) An equation expressing the relationship of assets, liabilities, and owner's equity. (*p. 14*)

Liabilities Debts or amounts owed to creditors. (*p. 14*)

Manual accounting system An accounting system in which transactions are recorded by hand. (*p. 47*)

Owner's equity The owner's right to or investment in the business. (*p. 13*)

QuickBooks Online A cloud-based subscription accounting software for small to medium-sized businesses. (*p. 47*)

Revenues The amounts a business earns; examples are fees earned for performing services, sales of merchandise, rent income, and interest income. They may be in the form of cash, credit card receipts, or Accounts Receivable (charge accounts). (*p. 21*)

Separate entity concept The concept by which a business is treated as a separate economic or accounting entity. The business stands by itself, separate from its owners, creditors, and customers. (*p. 16*)

Sole proprietorship A one-owner business. (*p. 16*)

Withdrawal The taking of cash or other assets out of a business by the owner for his or her own use. (This is also referred to as *drawing*.) A withdrawal is treated as a decrease in owner's equity. (*p. 30*)

Quiz Yourself

____ 1. ____ are properties or things of value owned and controlled by a business entity.
    a. Liabilities   c. Assets
    b. Owner's Equity   d. None of the above

____ 2. Parish Tutoring Services has assets of $25,000 and liabilities of $10,000. What is the amount of owner's equity?
    a. $35,000   c. $12,500
    b. $15,000   d. $10,000

____ 3. Which of the following accounts would increase owner's equity?
    a. Cash
    b. Accounts Payable
    c. Accounts Receivable
    d. Income from Tutoring

(*Continued*)

CHAPTER REVIEW

_____ 4. Which of the following statements is true?
   a. Every transaction is recorded as an increase and/or decrease in only one account.
   b. One side of the equation does not need to equal the other side of the equation.
   c. Double-entry accounting is demonstrated by the fact that each transaction must be recorded in at least two accounts.
   d. When a business earns revenue, owner's equity decreases.

_____ 5. M. Parish purchased supplies on credit. What is the impact on the accounting equation?
   a. Increase Supplies and decrease Cash.
   b. Increase Supplies Expense and increase Accounts Payable.
   c. Increase Supplies Expense and increase Accounts Receivable.
   d. Increase Supplies and increase Accounts Payable.

Answers: 1.c 2.b 3.d 4.c 5.d

Chapter Assignments

Discussion Questions

1. Define *assets*, *liabilities*, *owner's equity*, *revenues*, and *expenses*.
2. Explain the separate entity concept.
3. How do Accounts Payable and Accounts Receivable differ?
4. Describe two ways to increase owner's equity and two ways to decrease owner's equity.
5. What is the effect on the fundamental accounting equation if supplies are purchased on account? How will the fundamental accounting equation change if supplies are purchased with cash? Explain how this purchase will or will not change the owner's equity.
6. When an owner withdraws cash or goods from the business, why is this considered an increase to the Drawing account and not an increase to the Wages Expense account?
7. Define *chart of accounts* and identify the categories of accounts.
8. What account titles would you suggest for the chart of accounts for a city touring company owned by W. Sanders? List the accounts by account category and include an appropriate account number for each.

Exercises

LO 1

Practice Exercise 1

EXERCISE 1-1 Complete the following equations:
   a. Assets of $40,000 = Liabilities of $17,200 + Owner's Equity of $_____
   b. Assets of $_____ − Liabilities of $18,000 = Owner's Equity of $22,000
   c. Assets of $27,000 − Owner's Equity of $15,000 = Liabilities of $_____

LO 1

Practice Exercise 1

EXERCISE 1-2 Determine the following amounts:
a. The amount of the liabilities of a business that has $60,800 in assets and in which the owner has $34,500 equity.
b. The equity of the owner of a tour bus that cost $57,000 and on which is owed $21,800 on an installment loan payable to the bank.
c. The amount of the assets of a business that has $11,780 in liabilities and in which the owner has $28,500 equity.

LO 1

Practice Exercise 1

EXERCISE 1-3 Dr. L. M. Patton is an ophthalmologist. As of December 31, Dr. Patton owned the following property that related to his professional practice, Patton Eye Clinic:

Cash, $2,995
Professional Equipment, $63,000
Office Equipment, $8,450

On the same date, he owed the following business creditors:

Munez Supply Company, $3,816
Martin Equipment Sales, $3,728

Compute the following amounts in the accounting equation:

Assets $_____ = Liabilities $_____ + Owner's Equity $_____

LO 1, 3

Practice Exercises 1, 3

EXERCISE 1-4 Describe a business transaction that will do the following:
a. Increase an asset and increase a liability
b. Decrease an asset and decrease a liability
c. Decrease an asset and increase an expense
d. Increase an asset and increase owner's equity
e. Increase an asset and decrease an asset
f. Increase an asset and increase revenue

LO 2

Practice Exercise 2

EXERCISE 1-5 Describe a transaction that resulted in each of the following entries affecting the accounting equation.

	Assets			=	Liabilities	+	Owner's Equity
Cash	+	Office Equipment	+	Professional Equipment =	Accounts Payable	+	B. Lake, Capital
(a) +18,200							+18,200
(b) −1,375				+1,375			
Bal. 16,825			+	1,375 =			18,200
(c)		+640			+640		
Bal. 16,825	+	640	+	1,375 =	640	+	18,200
(d) −2,200				+7,000	+4,800		
Bal. 14,625	+	640	+	8,375 =	5,440	+	18,200
(e) −1,000					−1,000		
Bal. 13,625	+	640	+	8,375 =	4,440	+	18,200
		22,640				22,640	

CHAPTER ASSIGNMENTS

CHAPTER ASSIGNMENTS

LO **1, 3**

Practice Exercises 1, 3

EXERCISE 1-6 Label each of the following accounts as asset (A), liability (L), owner's equity (OE), revenue (R), or expense (E).

a. Supplies
b. Professional Fees
c. Prepaid Insurance
d. M. Jones, Drawing
e. Accounts Payable

f. Service Income
g. M. Jones, Capital
h. Office Equipment
i. Accounts Receivable
j. Salary Expense

LO **2, 4**

Practice Exercises 2, 4

EXERCISE 1-7 Describe a transaction that resulted in the following changes in accounts:

a. Rent Expense is increased by $1,050, and Cash is decreased by $1,050.
b. Advertising Expense is increased by $835, and Accounts Payable is increased by $835.
c. Accounts Receivable is increased by $372, and Service Income is increased by $372.
d. Cash is decreased by $410, and C. Tryon, Drawing, is increased by $410.
e. Equipment is increased by $1,850, Cash is decreased by $850, and Accounts Payable is increased by $1,000.
f. Cash is increased by $1,650, and Accounts Receivable is decreased by $1,650.

LO **2, 4**

Practice Exercises 2, 4

EXERCISE 1-8 Describe the transactions that are recorded in the following equation:

	Assets			= Liabilities +		Owner's Equity			
	Cash +	Accounts Receivable +	Equipment =	Accounts Payable +	J. Onyx, Capital −	J. Onyx, Drawing +	Revenue −	Expenses
(a)	+25,000		+4,500		+29,500			
(b)	−1,250							+1,250 (Rent Expense)
Bal.	23,750		+ 4,500 =		29,500			− 1,250
(c)		+2,000					+2,000 (Income from Services)	
Bal.	23,750 +	2,000 +	4,500 =		29,500		+ 2,000 −	1,250
(d)	−3,700		+16,000	+12,300				
Bal.	20,050 +	2,000 +	20,500 =	12,300 +	29,500		+ 2,000 −	1,250
(e)	−2,500					+2,500		
Bal.	17,550 +	2,000 +	20,500 =	12,300 +	29,500 −	2,500 +	2,000 −	1,250
		40,050				40,050		

Problem Set A

LO   1, 2, 3, 4

PROBLEM 1-1A On June 1 of this year, J. Larkin, Optometrist, established the Larkin Eye Clinic. The clinic's account names are presented below. Transactions completed during the month follow.

Assets			=	Liabilities	+	Owner's Equity				
Cash	+ Supplies	+ Office Equipment	=	Accounts Payable	+	Capital	− Drawing	+ Revenue	− Expenses

a. Larkin deposited $25,000 in a bank account in the name of the business.
b. Paid the office rent for the month, $950, Ck. No. 1001.
c. Bought supplies for cash, $357, Ck. No. 1002.
d. Bought office equipment on account from NYC Office Equipment Store, $8,956.
e. Bought a computer from Warden's Office Outfitters, $1,636, paying $750 in cash and placing the balance on account, Ck. No. 1003.
f. Sold professional services for cash, $3,482.
g. Paid on account to Warden's Office Outfitters, $886, Ck. No. 1004.
h. Received and paid the bill for utilities, $382, Ck. No. 1005.
i. Paid the salary of the assistant, $1,050, Ck. No. 1006.
j. Sold professional services for cash, $3,295.
k. Larkin withdrew cash for personal use, $1,250, Ck. No. 1007.

Required

1. Record the transactions and the balance after each transaction.
2. Total the left side of the accounting equation (left side of the equal sign), then total the right side of the accounting equation (right side of the equal sign). If the two totals are not equal, check the addition and subtraction. If you still cannot find the error, re-analyze each transaction.

Check Figure
Left side of equals sign total, $37,101

LO   1, 2, 3, 4

PROBLEM 1-2A On July 1 of this year, R. Green established the Green Rehab Clinic. The organization's account headings are presented below. Transactions completed during the month of July follow.

Assets				=	Liabilities	+	Owner's Equity				
Cash	+ Supplies	+ Office Equipment	+ Professional Equipment	=	Accounts Payable	+	Capital	− Drawing	+ Revenue	− Expenses

a. Green deposited $30,000 in a bank account in the name of the business.
b. Paid the office rent for the month, $1,800, Ck. No. 2001.
c. Bought supplies for cash, $362, Ck. No. 2002.
d. Bought professional equipment on account from Rehab Equipment Company, $18,000.
e. Bought office equipment from Hi-Tech Computers, $2,890, paying $890 in cash and placing the balance on account, Ck. No. 2003.
f. Sold professional services for cash, $4,600.
g. Paid on account to Rehab Equipment Company, $700, Ck. No. 2004.
h. Received and paid the bill for utilities, $367, Ck. No. 2005.
i. Paid the salary of the assistant, $1,150, Ck. No. 2006.
j. Sold professional services for cash, $3,868.
k. Green withdrew cash for personal use, $1,800, Ck. No. 2007.

(Continued)

CHAPTER ASSIGNMENTS

Check Figure
Cash, $31,399

Required

1. **R**ecord the transactions and the balance after each transaction.
2. Total the left side of the accounting equation (left side of the equal sign), then total the right side of the accounting equation (right side of the equal sign). If the two totals are not equal, check the addition and subtraction. If you still cannot find the error, re-analyze each transaction.

LO **1, 2, 3, 4** ·

PROBLEM 1-3A S. Davis, a graphic artist, opened a studio for her professional practice on August 1. The account headings are presented below. Transactions completed during the month follow.

Assets					=	Liabilities	+	Owner's Equity			
Cash +	Supplies +	Prepaid Insurance +	Office Equipment +	Photo Equipment =		Accounts Payable +		Capital −	Drawing +	Revenue −	Expenses

a.   Davis deposited $20,000 in a bank account in the name of the business.
b.   Bought office equipment on account from Starkey Equipment Company, $4,120.
c.   Davis invested her personal photographic equipment, $5,370, in the business.
d.   Paid the rent for the month, $1,500, Ck. No. 1000.
e.   Bought supplies for cash, $215, Ck. No. 1001.
f.   Bought insurance for two years, $1,840, Ck. No. 1002.
g.   Sold graphic services for cash, $3,616.
h.   Paid the salary of the part-time assistant, $982, Ck. No. 1003.
i.   Received and paid the bill for telephone service, $134, Ck. No. 1004.
j.   Paid cash for minor repairs to graphics equipment, $185, Ck. No. 1005.
k.   Sold graphic services for cash, $3,693.
l.   Paid on account to Starkey Equipment Company, $650, Ck. No. 1006.
m.   Davis withdrew cash for personal use, $1,800, Ck. No. 1007.

Check Figure
Right side of equals sign total, $31,548

Required

1. Record the transactions and the balance after each transaction.
2. Total the left side of the accounting equation (left side of the equal sign), then total the right side of the accounting equation (right side of the equal sign). If the two totals are not equal, check the addition and subtraction. If you still cannot find the error, re-analyze each transaction.

LO **1, 2, 3, 4** ·

PROBLEM 1-4A On March 1 of this year, B. Gervais established Gervais Catering Service. The account headings are presented below. Transactions completed during the month follow.

Assets						=	Liabilities	+	Owner's Equity			
Cash +	Accounts Receivable +	Supplies +	Prepaid Insurance +	Truck +	Catering Equipment =		Accounts Payable +		Capital −	Drawing +	Revenue −	Expenses

a.   Gervais deposited $25,000 in a bank account in the name of the business.
b.   Bought a truck from Kelly Motors for $26,329, paying $8,000 in cash and placing the balance on account, Ck. No. 500.
c.   Bought catering equipment on account from Luigi's Equipment, $3,795.
d.   Paid the rent for the month, $1,255, Ck. No. 501.
e.   Bought insurance for the truck for one year, $400, Ck. No. 502.
f.   Sold catering services for cash for the first half of the month, $3,012.

g.   Bought supplies for cash, $185, Ck. No. 503.
h.   Sold catering services on account, $4,307.
i.   Received and paid the heating bill, $248, Ck. No. 504.
j.   Received a bill from GC Gas and Lube for gas and oil for the truck, $128.
k.   Sold catering services for cash for the remainder of the month, $2,649.
l.   Gervais withdrew cash for personal use, $1,550, Ck. No. 505.
m.   Paid the salary of the assistant, $1,150, Ck. No. 506.

Required

1.   Record the transactions and the balance after each transaction.
2.   Total the left side of the accounting equation (left side of the equal sign), then total the right side of the accounting equation (right side of the equal sign). If the two totals are not equal, check the addition and subtraction. If you still cannot find the error, re-analyze each transaction.

Check Figure
Cash, $17,873

PROBLEM 1-5A   In April, J. Rodriguez established an apartment rental service. The account headings are presented below. Transactions completed during the month of April follow.

Assets					=	Liabilities +		Owner's Equity			
Cash +	Accounts Receivable +	Supplies +	Prepaid Insurance +	Truck +	Office Equipment =	Accounts Payable	+ Capital −	Drawing +	Revenue −	Expenses	

a.   Rodriguez deposited $70,000 in a bank account in the name of the business.
b.   Paid the rent for the month, $2,000, Ck. No. 101 (Rent Expense).
c.   Bought supplies on account, $150.
d.   Bought a truck for $23,500, paying $2,500 in cash and placing the remainder on account.
e.   Bought insurance for the truck for the year, $2,400, Ck. No. 102.
f.   Sold services on account, $4,700.
g.   Bought office equipment on account from Stern Office Supply, $1,250.
h.   Sold services for cash for the first half of the month, $8,250.
i.   Received and paid the bill for utilities, $280, Ck. No. 103.
j.   Received a bill for gas and oil for the truck, $130.
k.   Paid wages to the employees, $2,680, Ck. Nos. 104–106.
l.   Sold services for cash for the remainder of the month, $3,500.
m.   Rodriguez withdrew cash for personal use, $4,000, Ck. No. 107.

Required

1.   Record the transactions and the balance after each transaction.
2.   Total the left side of the accounting equation (left side of the equal sign), then total the right side of the accounting equation (right side of the equal sign). If the two totals are not equal, check the addition and subtraction. If you still cannot find the error, re-analyze each transaction.

Check Figure
Cash, $67,890

Problem Set B

LO 1, 2, 3, 4

PROBLEM 1-1B In July of this year, M. Wallace established a business called Wallace Realty. The account headings are presented below. Transactions completed during the month follow.

Assets			=	Liabilities	+	Owner's Equity				
		Office		Accounts		——— ,	——— ,			
Cash +	Supplies +	Equipment =		Payable	+	Capital −	Drawing +	Revenue −	Expenses	

a. Wallace deposited $24,000 in a bank account in the name of the business.
b. Paid the office rent for the current month, $650, Ck. No. 1000.
c. Bought office supplies for cash, $375, Ck. No. 1001.
d. Bought office equipment on account from Dellos Computers, $6,300.
e. Received a bill from the *City Crier* for advertising, $455.
f. Sold services for cash, $3,944.
g. Paid on account to Dellos Computers, $1,500, Ck. No. 1002.
h. Received and paid the bill for utilities, $340, Ck. No. 1003.
i. Paid on account to the *City Crier*, $455, Ck. No. 1004.
j. Paid truck expenses, $435, Ck. No. 1005.
k. Wallace withdrew cash for personal use, $1,500, Ck. No. 1006.

Check Figure
Left side of equals sign total, $29,364

Required

1. Record the transactions and the balance after each transaction.
2. Total the left side of the accounting equation (left side of the equal sign), then total the right side of the accounting equation (right side of the equal sign). If the two totals are not equal, check the addition and subtraction. If you still cannot find the error, re-analyze each transaction.

LO 1, 2, 3, 4

PROBLEM 1-2B In March, K. Haas, M.D., established the Haas Sports Injury Clinic. The clinic's account headings are presented below. Transactions completed during the month of March follow.

Assets				=	Liabilities	+	Owner's Equity			
		Office	Professional		Accounts		——— ,	——— ,		
Cash +	Supplies +	Equipment +	Equipment =		Payable	+	Capital −	Drawing +	Revenue −	Expenses

a. Haas deposited $48,000 in a bank account in the name of the business.
b. Paid the rent for the month, $2,200, Ck. No. 1000.
c. Bought supplies for cash from Medco Co., $2,138.
d. Bought professional equipment on account from Med-Tech Company, $18,000.
e. Bought office equipment on account from Equipment Depot, $1,955.
f. Sold professional services for cash, $8,960.
g. Paid on account to Med-Tech Company, $3,000, Ck. No. 1001.
h. Received and paid the bill for utilities, $472, Ck. No. 1002.
i. Paid the salary of the assistant, $1,738, Ck. No. 1003.
j. Sold professional services for cash, $10,196.
k. Haas withdrew cash for personal use, $3,500, Ck. No. 1004.

Required

1. Record the transactions and the balance after each transaction.
2. Total the left side of the accounting equation (left side of the equal sign), then total the right side of the accounting equation (right side of the equal sign). If the two totals are not equal, check the addition and subtraction. If you still cannot find the error, re-analyze each transaction.

Check Figure
Cash, $54,108

LO **1, 2, 3, 4**

PROBLEM 1-3B P. Schwartz, Attorney at Law, opened his office on October 1. The account headings are presented below. Transactions completed during the month follow.

			Assets		=	Liabilities +			Owner's Equity		
Cash +	Supplies +	Prepaid Insurance +	Office Equipment +	Library =		Accounts Payable +	Capital −	Drawing +	Revenue −	Expenses	

a. Schwartz deposited $25,000 in a bank account in the name of the business.
b. Bought office equipment on account from QuipCo, $9,670.
c. Schwartz invested his personal law library, which cost $2,800.
d. Paid the office rent for the month, $1,700, Ck. No. 2000.
e. Bought office supplies for cash, $418, Ck. No. 2001.
f. Bought insurance for two years, $944, Ck. No. 2002.
g. Sold legal services for cash, $8,518.
h. Paid the salary of the part-time receptionist, $1,820, Ck. No. 2003.
i. Received and paid the telephone bill, $388, Ck. No. 2004.
j. Received and paid the bill for utilities, $368, Ck. No. 2005.
k. Sold legal services for cash, $9,260.
l. Paid on account to QuipCo, $2,670, Ck. No. 2006.
m. Schwartz withdrew cash for personal use, $2,500, Ck. No. 2007.

Required

1. Record the transactions and the balance after each transaction.
2. Total the left side of the accounting equation (left side of the equal sign), then total the right side of the accounting equation (right side of the equal sign). If the two totals are not equal, check the addition and subtraction. If you still cannot find the error, re-analyze each transaction.

Check Figure
Right side of equals sign total, $45,802

LO **1, 2, 3, 4**

PROBLEM 1-4B In March, T. Carter established Carter Delivery Service. The account headings are presented below. Transactions completed during the month of March follow.

			Assets			=	Liabilities +			Owner's Equity		
Cash +	Accounts Receivable +	Supplies +	Prepaid Insurance +	Truck +	Equipment =		Accounts Payable +	Capital −	Drawing +	Revenue −	Expenses	

a. Carter deposited $25,000 in a bank account in the name of the business.
b. Bought a used truck from Degroot Motors for $15,140, paying $5,140 in cash and placing the remainder on account.
c. Bought equipment on account from Flemming Company, $3,450.
d. Paid the rent for the month, $1,000, Ck. No. 3001.
e. Sold services for cash for the first half of the month, $6,927.

(Continued)

f. Bought supplies for cash, $301, Ck. No. 3002.
g. Bought insurance for the truck for the year, $1,200, Ck. No. 3003.
h. Received and paid the bill for utilities, $349, Ck. No. 3004.
i. Received a bill for gas and oil for the truck, $218.
j. Sold services on account, $3,603.
k. Sold services for cash for the remainder of the month, $4,612.
l. Paid wages to the employees, $3,958, Ck. Nos. 3005–3007.
m. Carter withdrew cash for personal use, $1,250, Ck. No. 3008.

Check Figure
Cash, $23,341

Required

1. Record the transactions and the balance after each transaction
2. Total the left side of the accounting equation (left side of the equal sign), then total the right side of the accounting equation (right side of the equal sign). If the two totals are not equal, check the addition and subtraction. If you still cannot find the error, re-analyze each transaction.

LO 1, 2, 3, 4

PROBLEM 1-5B In October, A. Nguyen established an apartment rental service. The account headings are presented below. Transactions completed during the month of October follow.

Assets						=	Liabilities	+			Owner's Equity		
Cash +	Accounts Receivable +	Supplies +	Prepaid Insurance +	Truck +	Office Equipment =		Accounts Payable	+ Capital −		Drawing +	Revenue −	Expenses

a. Nguyen deposited $25,000 in a bank account in the name of the business.
b. Paid the rent for the month, $1,200, Ck. No. 2015.
c. Bought supplies on account, $225.
d. Bought a truck for $18,000, paying $1,000 in cash and placing the remainder on account.
e. Bought insurance for the truck for the year, $1,400, Ck. No. 2016.
f. Sold services on account, $5,000.
g. Bought office equipment on account from Henry Office Supply, $2,300.
h. Sold services for cash for the first half of the month, $6,050.
i. Received and paid the bill for utilities, $150, Ck. No. 2017.
j. Received a bill for gas and oil for the truck, $80.
k. Paid wages to the employees, $1,400, Ck. Nos. 2018–2020.
l. Sold services for cash for the remainder of the month, $4,200.
m. Nguyen withdrew cash for personal use, $2,000, Ck. No. 2021.

Check Figure
Cash, $28,100

Required

1. Record the transactions and the balance after each transaction.
2. Total the left side of the accounting equation (left side of the equal sign), then total the right side of the accounting equation (right side of the equal sign). If the two totals are not equal, check the addition and subtraction. If you still cannot find the error, re-analyze each transaction.

Accounting with 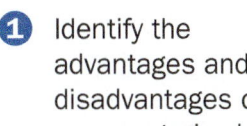 QuickBooks® Online

In this text, you will learn how to record transactions and prepare financial reports for various companies using a **manual accounting system**. You will also have an opportunity to use **QuickBooks Online**, a cloud-based, **computerized accounting system**. QuickBooks Online offers small to medium-sized businesses accounting software on a subscription basis. In a manual accounting system, accounting transactions are recorded and financial reports are prepared by hand, rather than on a computer. Using the featured *Accounting with QuickBooks Online* section throughout this text as well as the QuickBooks Online Appendix, located on the Cengage Learning companion site (Cengage.com), you will learn how to record transactions and process financial reports in a computerized accounting system using QuickBooks Online.

Characteristics of Computerized Accounting Systems

A computerized accounting system records accounting transactions using a computer and accounting software. There are many types of accounting software. QuickBooks Online is a cloud-based application that is often used by small to medium-sized businesses.

Learning Objective

After you have completed this section, you will be able to do the following:

1 Identify the advantages and disadvantages of a computerized accounting system.

 Identify the advantages and disadvantages of a computerized accounting system.

Learning Objective

A majority of companies use some form of a computerized accounting system. They do so because the advantages of a computerized accounting system far outweigh the disadvantages. Some of the advantages of a computerized accounting system are as follows:

- **Automatic**—Computerized accounting systems automatically complete many parts of the accounting cycle. Once a user enters a transaction, the software posts the transaction to the ledger and updates the financial statements. In addition, computerized accounting systems perform financial calculations, such as totaling revenue and expenses and determining net income.

- **Timeliness**—Computerized accounting systems allow companies to prepare up-to-date financial reports quickly. Also, accountants can easily locate specific transactions they want to review or investigate.

- **Accuracy**—Errors, such as out-of-balance transactions, are eliminated using a computerized accounting system. The software alerts the user when a transaction is out of balance and will not let the user proceed until the transaction is balanced.

- **Ease of use**—Basic accounting systems, like QuickBooks Online, are easy to use and often require the user to have little previous accounting knowledge.

- **Security measures**—Computerized accounting systems provide a series of security measures that include passwords to restrict access and built-in error checks.

- **Analysis**—Companies can easily analyze their financial statements to identify performance measurements, including determining which services are and are not profitable, the percentage of cash spent on expenses, and comparisons between the current and previous fiscal periods.

- **Inexpensive**—Basic accounting systems like QuickBooks Online are relatively inexpensive to purchase and use.

There are also disadvantages to using computerized accounting systems. These include:

- **Security risks**—Even with the security measures accounting software provides, in-house computer systems can still be hacked, and data can be compromised. In addition, data stored on these systems can be lost through power and/or computer failures. Some risks can be lessened by using a virus protection program and by performing routine **backups**. Backups store company data files in a safe place, such as online, or on an external backup device such as a USB flash drive, CD, or external hard drive. Security risks can also be minimized by using cloud-based accounting software such as QuickBooks Online. QuickBooks Online stores data on servers, which protect data from hardware and software failures as well as hackers and viruses.

- **User error**—Although QuickBooks Online and other computerized accounting systems are designed to help reduce certain input errors, such as out-of-balance transactions, errors can still occur. Transactions can be recorded incorrectly, and valuable information can be lost or deleted.

Getting Started with QuickBooks Online

QuickBooks® Online Tip

QuickBooks Online protects user data with the same technology implemented by many banks and brokerage firms.

In the associated QuickBooks Online Appendix at Cengage.com, we use Magnolia Spa to demonstrate how to record transactions and process reports in a computerized accounting system. We will be using the accounting program QuickBooks Online. Intuit, the company that offers various versions of QuickBooks Desktop software packages also offers QuickBooks Online. The online version of QuickBooks is an example of **cloud computing**. This version is used via the Internet, rather than a local computer. With cloud computing, authorized users can access software and data anywhere they have an Internet connection and from multiple types of devices. Data and software are not stored on an actual computer. QuickBooks Online provides a variety of advantages over QuickBooks Desktop software packages, such as anywhere/anytime access, automatic backups, secured data protection, access through multiple devices and the ability to use various web browers. To compare the different QuickBooks financial software packages, you can visit www.intuit.com.

An additional benefit of QuickBooks Online is the automatic update feature. Every time you log into QuickBooks Online, you will be using the latest version available. While this feature is helpful to companies in the real world, it also means that the "look and feel" of QuickBooks Online may change from time to time. Most of the updates will be minor, and you can use the Intuit weblink (www.qbo.intuit.com) to review the most recent releases. However, sometimes there may be major QuickBooks Online updates deployed. Therefore, this text will utilize the Cengage Learning companion site at Cengage.com for the QuickBooks Online Appendix, which includes *Accounting with QuickBooks Online* (a step-by-step guide to using QuickBooks Online) and a *Try It with QuickBooks Online* activity. The QuickBooks Online Appendix will be arranged by chapter, similar to the text. To get started with QuickBooks Online, go to the Cengage Learning companion site at Cengage.com.

Activities

Why Does It Matter?

MAC'S CUSTOM CATERING, Eugene, Oregon

Mac's Custom Catering, an award-winning catering business located in Eugene, Oregon, specializes in providing "only the best for you and your guest." Mac's Custom Catering has been in business for over 30 years and is experienced in providing catering services at weddings, corporate events, and large sit-down events. It offers several signature buffet options, including "Northwest Bounty," "Hawaiian Luau," and "Italian Fest."

Imagine that you have been hired to set up the accounting system for a catering business such as Mac's. What accounts would be included in the chart of accounts? As you list the accounts, identify the type of account. Is the account an asset, a liability, or owner's equity?

What Would You Say?

A friend of yours wants to start her own pet-sitting business. She already has a business license that is required in her city. She has had a personal checking account for years. You have told her that she also needs to open a separate account for her business needs, but she does not understand why she needs to have two separate accounts. Explain to her why she should have a business account separate from her personal account. Use some of the language of business you have learned in your text's Introduction and in this chapter.

What Do You Think?

Read the following memorandum and provide the requested information.

MEMORANDUM

TO: Your Name

FROM: J. Perrault, Supervisor

DATE: July 31, 20--

SUBJECT: Calculations for Richter Co.

Please provide the following information ASAP (as soon as possible).

1. The balance of cash in Richter Company's checkbook shows $13,364. I need to know if this ties to or matches the Cash account balance. I do know that total assets amount to $43,560; Office Equipment amounts to $3,896; and other non-cash assets are Professional Equipment, $24,375 and Prepaid Insurance, $1,925.

2. D. Richter, the owner, wants to know the amount of his owner's equity. I pulled the outstanding bills, which amount to $7,942.

Please put the information in a memo addressed to me. Thank you for your prompt response.

chapter 2

T Accounts, Debits and Credits, Trial Balance, and Financial Statements

Learning Objectives

After you have completed this chapter, you will be able to do the following:

1. Determine balances of T accounts.

2. Present the fundamental accounting equation using the T account form and label the plus and minus sides.

3. Present the fundamental accounting equation using the T account form and label the debit and credit sides.

4. Record directly in T accounts a group of business transactions involving changes in asset, liability, owner's equity, revenue, and expense accounts for a service business.

5. Prepare a trial balance.

6. Prepare (a) an income statement, (b) a statement of owner's equity, and (c) a balance sheet.

7. Recognize the effect of errors on account balances.

To: Amy Roberts, CPA
Subject: What's Next?

Hi Amy,

I feel as though I have a good understanding of what accounting is and what the different types of accounts are. I found some flashcards online and have been quizzing myself with the account names and types. I'm getting pretty good! I've also been practicing recording transactions in the column form. I think I'm now ready to learn something new. After I record transactions in the column form, what happens next? Am I ready to start using QuickBooks Online?

Thanks,

Janie

To: Janie Conner
Subject: RE: What's Next?

Hi Janie,

Using the flashcards was a great idea! It's very important that you recognize the accounts and know whether each is an asset, a liability, or an owner's equity account. We're going to use that knowledge for this next challenge. So here's your list of things to tackle:

_____ 1. Understand what debits and credits are and be able to apply each to the fundamental accounting equation.

_____ 2. Begin recording transactions in T accounts using debits and credits.

This is a lot to learn, but I know that with practice, you'll be successful! You are not quite ready to record entries in QuickBooks Online yet, but you can start setting up your new company and chart of accounts.

Amy

iStockPhoto.com/Mark Bowden

Accounting Language

Balance sheet (p. 70)
Compound entry (p. 63)
Credit (p. 54)
Debit (p. 54)
Financial position (p. 70)
Financial statement (p. 68)
Footings (p. 52)
Income statement (p. 68)
Net income (p. 68)
Net loss (p. 68)
Normal balance (p. 52)
Report form (p. 70)
Slide (p. 72)
Statement of
owner's equity (p. 69)
T account form (p. 51)
Transposition (p. 72)
Trial balance (p. 67)

In the previous chapter, we introduced the fundamental accounting equation as *Assets = Liabilities + Owner's Equity*. We learned that the fundamental accounting equation includes five account classifications: Assets, Liabilities, Owner's Equity, Revenue, and Expenses. These are the only five classifications in accounting; so whether you are dealing with a small, one-owner business or a large corporation, you will encounter only these five major classifications of accounts. We also discussed the recording of transactions in the column form.

In this chapter, we will record the same transactions from Chapter 1 in T account form and prove the equality of both sides of the fundamental accounting equation using a trial balance. Before we begin, take a moment to review the transactions from Chapter 1 on pages 16–31.

2-1 THE T ACCOUNT FORM

In Chapter 1, we recorded business transactions in a column arrangement, which had the following advantages:

1. **In the process of analyzing the transaction, you**
   a. Recognized the need to determine which accounts were involved.
   b. Determined the classification of the accounts involved.
   c. Decided whether the transaction resulted in an increase or a decrease in each of these accounts.

2. **You further realized that after each transaction was recorded, the two sides of the fundamental accounting equation were in balance. In other words, the total of one side of the accounting equation equaled the total of the other side.**

Now instead of recording transactions in a column for each account, we will use a **T account form** for each account. *The T account form has the advantage of providing two sides for each account. One side is used to record increases in the account, and the other side is used to record decreases.* Notice that the Cash account column in the books

1 Determine balances of T accounts.

Learning Objective

of Conner's Whitewater Adventures (used in Chapter 1) and the new Cash T account are presented below. The results are identical. It's just a different way of presenting the same information.

Cash Account Column:		
		Cash
Transaction	**(a)**	90,000
Transaction	**(b)**	−38,000
Balance		52,000
Transaction	**(d)**	−2,000
Balance		50,000
Transaction	**(f)**	+8,000
Balance		58,000
Transaction	**(g)**	−1,250
Balance		56,750
Transaction	**(i)**	−1,875
Balance		54,875
Transaction	**(l)**	−1,500
Balance		53,375
Transaction	**(m)**	−225
Balance		53,150
Transaction	**(n)**	−620
Balance		52,530
Transaction	**(o)**	−2,360
Balance		50,170
Transaction	**(p)**	−1,850
Balance		48,320
Transaction	**(q)**	+2,500
Balance		50,820
Transaction	**(r)**	+8,570
Balance		59,390
Transaction	**(s)**	−3,500
		55,890

Cash T Account:

Cash			
+		**−**	
(a)	90,000	**(b)**	38,000
(f)	8,000	**(d)**	2,000
(q)	2,500	**(g)**	1,250
(r)	8,570	**(i)**	1,875
	109,070	**(l)**	1,500
		(m)	225
		(n)	620
Footings		**(o)**	2,360
		(p)	1,850
		(s)	3,500
			53,180
Bal.	**55,890**		

Steps to calculate balance in T Accounts:

STEP 1. Add each side separately and record the totals (called footings).

90,000 + 8,000 + 2,500 + 8,570 = 109,070

38,000 + 2,000 + 1,250 + 1,875 + 1,500 + 225 + 620 + 2,360 + 1,850 + 3,500 = 53,180

STEP 2. Large footing − Small footing = Balance

109,070 − 53,180 = 55,890

STEP 3. Place the balance (from Step 2) on the large footing side and double-underline it.

55,890 goes on the same side as 109,070.

After we record a group of transactions in a T account, we add both sides and record the totals, called **footings**. Next, we subtract one footing from the other to determine the balance of the account. For the Cash account, shown previously, the balance is $55,890 ($109,070 − $53,180).

We now record the balance on the side of the account having the larger footing, which, with a few minor exceptions, is the plus (+) side. The plus side of a T account is the side that represents the **normal balance** of that account. However, depending on the type of account, the normal balance may fall on either the left or right side of an account.

2-2 THE T ACCOUNT FORM WITH PLUS AND MINUS SIDES

To review, we presented the T account for Cash. Cash is classified as an asset account, and all asset accounts look like the following T account:

Assets

+	−
Left	Right

However, **not all classifications of accounts have the increase side on the left.** Liability accounts are on the other side of the fundamental accounting equation. So their increase and decrease are opposite those of assets. Liabilities are increased on the right side and decreased on the left side. All liabilities look like the following T account:

Liabilities

−	+
Left	Right

Owner's equity is similar to liabilities. Increases in owner's equity are recorded on the right side of the account. Decreases in owner's equity are recorded on the left side of the account.

Owner's Equity

−	+
Left	Right

Recall that we placed capital, drawing, revenue, and expenses under the umbrella of owner's equity. Capital and revenue increase owner's equity, and drawing and expenses decrease owner's equity. The T accounts for this situation are as follows:

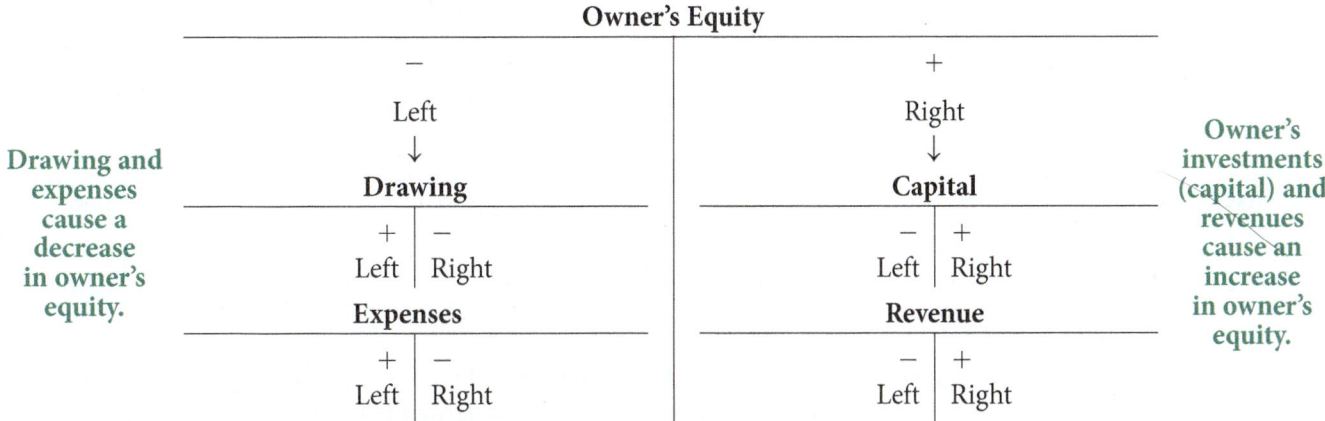

Increases in owner's equity are recorded on the right side of the account. Because capital and revenue increase owner's equity, additions are recorded on the right side.

Decreases in owner's equity are recorded on the left side of the account. Because drawing and expenses decrease owner's equity, additions to drawing and expenses are recorded on the left side.

We can now restate the equation with the T account forms and plus and minus signs for each account classification.

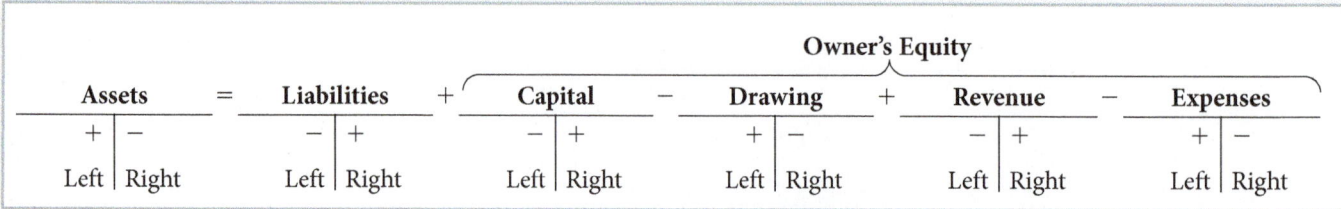

Assets	The *left* side is the *increase* side.
Liabilities	The *right* side is the *increase* side.
Capital	The *right* side is the *increase* side.
Drawing	The *left* side is the *increase* side.
Revenue	The *right* side is the *increase* side.
Expenses	The *left* side is the *increase* side.

Your accounting background up to this point has taught you to analyze business transactions to determine which accounts are involved and to recognize that each amount should be recorded as an increase or a decrease in these accounts. Now the recording process becomes a simple matter of knowing which side of the T accounts should be used to record increases and which should be used to record decreases. **Generally, you will not be using the minus side of the capital, drawing, revenue, and expense accounts because transactions involving these accounts usually result in increases in the accounts.** An exception to this statement is where errors have been made and require correction. Now let's add the last element to the T account before we record the familiar Conner's Whitewater Adventures transactions.

Learning Objective

3 Present the fundamental accounting equation using the T account form and label the debit and credit sides.

2-3 THE T ACCOUNT FORM WITH DEBITS AND CREDITS

The left side of a T account is called the **debit** side; the right side is called the **credit** side. The T accounts representing the accounting equation now contain both the signs and the words *Debit* and *Credit*.

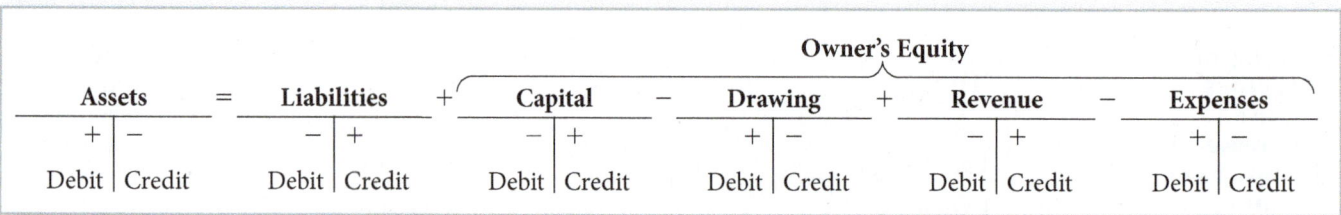

The following table summarizes debits and credits and the way they are affected by increases and decreases. **The critical rule to remember is that the amount placed on the debit side of one or more accounts *must* equal the amount placed on the credit side of another account or other accounts.**

Debits Signify		Credits Signify	
Increases in	{ Assets Drawing Expenses	Decreases in	{ Assets Drawing Expenses
Decreases in	{ Liabilities Capital Revenue	Increases in	{ Liabilities Capital Revenue

Debit is always the left side of the account, and credit is always the right side of the account. However, the + or − changes with the type of account.

2-4 RECORDING BUSINESS TRANSACTIONS IN T ACCOUNTS

Our task now is to learn how to record business transactions in the T account form. First, let's review the steps we've learned so far (Steps 1–3) in analyzing a business transaction. Then we will introduce a new step (Step 4).

STEP 1. What accounts are involved?

STEP 2. What are the classifications of the accounts involved (asset, liability, capital, drawing, revenue, expense)?

STEP 3. Are the accounts increased or decreased?

STEP 4. Write the transaction as a debit to one account (or accounts) and a credit to another account (or accounts).

STEP 5. Is the equation in balance after the transaction has been recorded?

For example, let's analyze the first transaction of the Conner's Whitewater Adventures transactions using this new five-step process. To formulate the entry, you must be able to visualize the fundamental accounting equation in the form of T accounts. With that in mind, the first transaction is as follows:

In transaction (a), Conner deposited $90,000 in a bank account in the name of the business. This transaction results in an increase to Cash with a debit and an increase in the Capital account with a credit.

STEP 1. What accounts are involved? The two accounts involved are Cash and J. Conner, Capital.

STEP 2. What are the classifications of the accounts involved? Cash is an asset account, and J. Conner, Capital, is an owner's equity account.

STEP 3. Are the accounts increased or decreased? Cash is being deposited in the bank account, an increase to Cash. The owner has invested that cash in the business and has increased J. Conner, Capital.

STEP 4. Write the transaction as a debit to one account (or accounts) and a credit to another account (or accounts). Because Cash is an asset account and Cash is increased, Cash is debited. We now need an off-setting credit. J. Conner, Capital, is an owner's equity account and is increased. Thus, J. Conner, Capital, is credited.

4 Record directly in T accounts a group of business transactions involving changes in asset, liability, owner's equity, revenue, and expense accounts for a service business.

Learning Objective

Remember

A business is always treated as a separate economic entity—separate and independent from its owner(s). Notice that we only say "J. Conner" for transactions involving owner investments or drawing. For all other transactions, it is Conner's Whitewater Adventures that is involved in the transaction.

STEP 5. Is the equation in balance after the transaction has been recorded? At least one account is debited, and at least one account is credited. And the total amount(s) debited equals the total amount(s) credited. You now have a debit equal to a credit, a $90,000 debit to Cash and a $90,000 credit to J. Conner, Capital.

The resulting transaction in T account form follows.

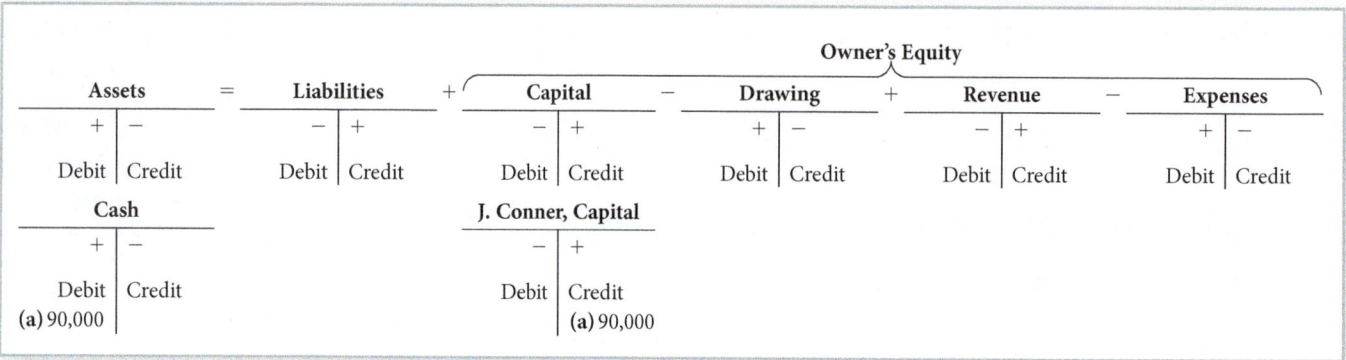

Let's go through the rest of the transactions for Conner's Whitewater Adventures. Because we already worked through Steps 1–3 in Chapter 1, we will discuss only Steps 4 and 5. In transaction (b), Conner's Whitewater Adventures bought equipment, paying cash, $38,000.

STEP 4. Write the transaction as a debit to one account (or accounts) and a credit to another account (or accounts).

This transaction results in an increase to Equipment with a debit and a decrease to Cash with a credit.

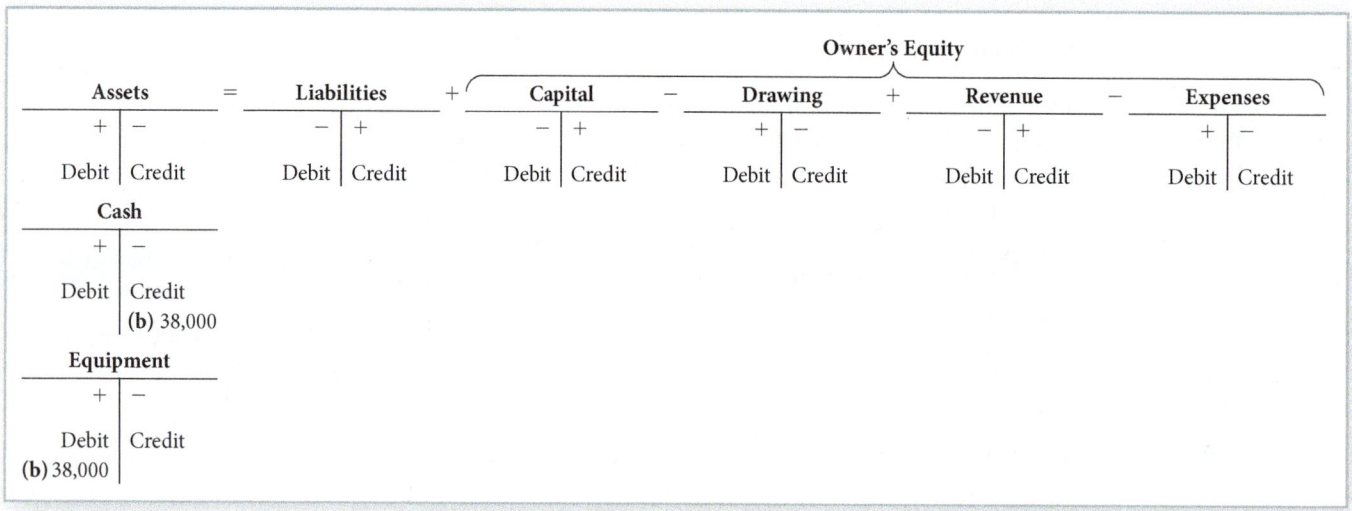

In transaction (c), Conner's Whitewater Adventures bought equipment on account from Signal Products, $4,320.

STEP 4. Write the transaction as a debit to one account (or accounts) and a credit to another account (or accounts).

This transaction results in an increase to Equipment with a debit and an increase to Accounts Payable with a credit.

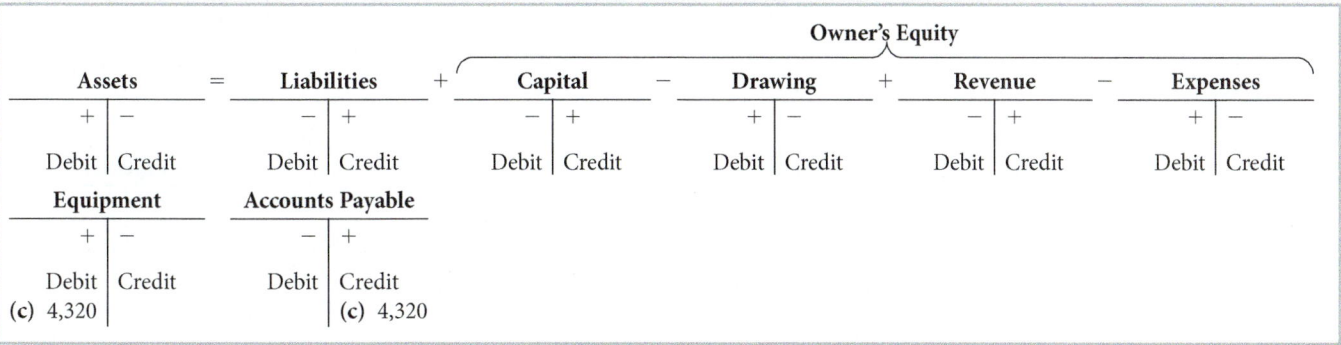

In transaction (d), Conner's Whitewater Adventures paid Signal Products, a creditor, $2,000.

STEP 4. Write the transaction as a debit to one account (or accounts) and a credit to another account (or accounts).

This transaction results in a decrease to Cash with a credit and a decrease to Accounts Payable with a debit.

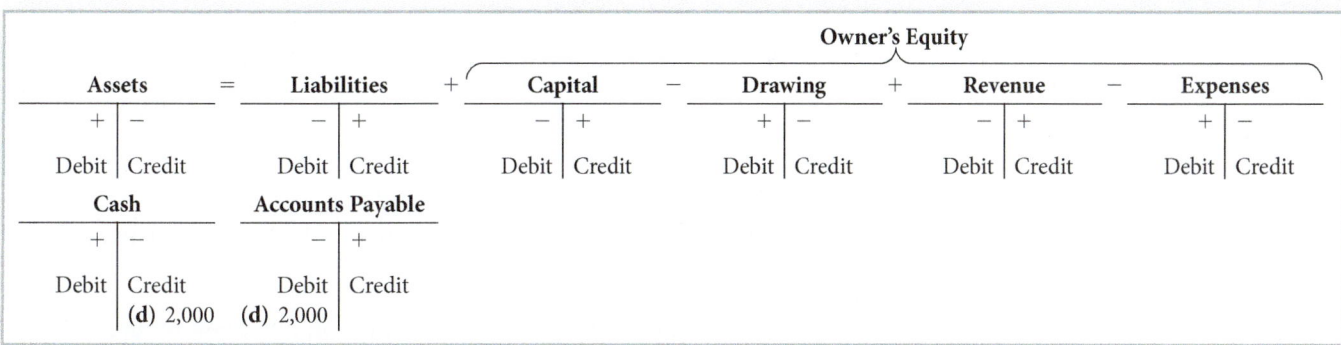

In transaction (e), J. Conner invests her personal computer, with a fair market value of $5,200, in the business.

STEP 4. Write the transaction as a debit to one account (or accounts) and a credit to another account (or accounts).

Equipment, an asset account, increases and is recorded with a debit. J. Conner, Capital, owner's equity, increases and is recorded with a credit.

Here is a restatement of the accounts after recording transactions (a) through (e). To test your understanding of the process, look at each transaction and describe what happened.

Footings or subtotals are required to compute the balances of the accounts. The balances are written in the accounts on the side with the larger total.

						Owner's Equity				

Assets	=	Liabilities	+	Capital	−	Drawing	+	Revenue	−	Expenses
+ | −		− | +		− | +		+ | −		− | +		+ | −
Debit | Credit		Debit | Credit		Debit | Credit		Debit | Credit		Debit | Credit		Debit | Credit

Cash

+	−
Debit	Credit
(a) 90,000	(b) 38,000
	(d) 2,000
	40,000

Bal. 50,000

Equipment

+	−
Debit	Credit
(b) 38,000	
(c) 4,320	
(e) 5,200	

Bal. 47,520

Accounts Payable

−	+
Debit	Credit
(d) 2,000	(c) 4,320
	Bal. 2,320

J. Conner, Capital

−	+
Debit	Credit
	(a) 90,000
	(e) 5,200
	Bal. 95,200

Let's pause to see if the debits are equal to the credits by listing the balances of the accounts.

STEP 5. Is the equation in balance after the transaction has been recorded?

Yes, the equation is in balance as shown below.

Account Name	Accounts with Normal Balances on the Left, or Debit, Side	Accounts with Normal Balances on the Right, or Credit, Side
	Assets Drawing Expenses	Liabilities Capital Revenue
Cash	$50,000	
Equipment	47,520	
Accounts Payable		$ 2,320
J. Conner, Capital		95,200
	$97,520	$97,520

In transaction (f), Conner's Whitewater Adventures sold rafting tours for cash, $8,000.

STEP 4. Write the transaction as a debit to one account (or accounts) and a credit to another account (or accounts).

This transaction results in an increase to Cash with a debit and an increase to Income from Tours with a credit.

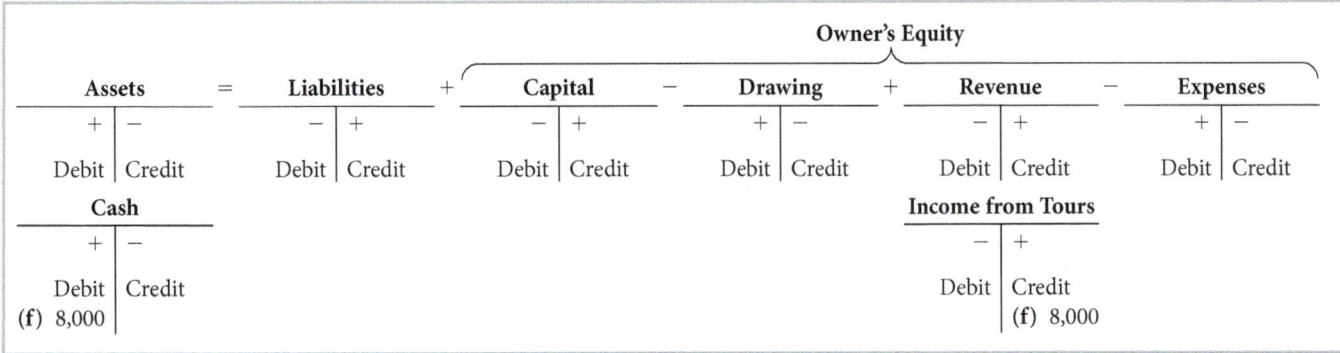

In transaction (g), Conner's Whitewater Adventures paid rent for the month, $1,250.

STEP 4. Write the transaction as a debit to one account (or accounts) and a credit to another account (or accounts).

This transaction results in an increase to Rent Expense with a debit and a decrease to Cash with a credit.

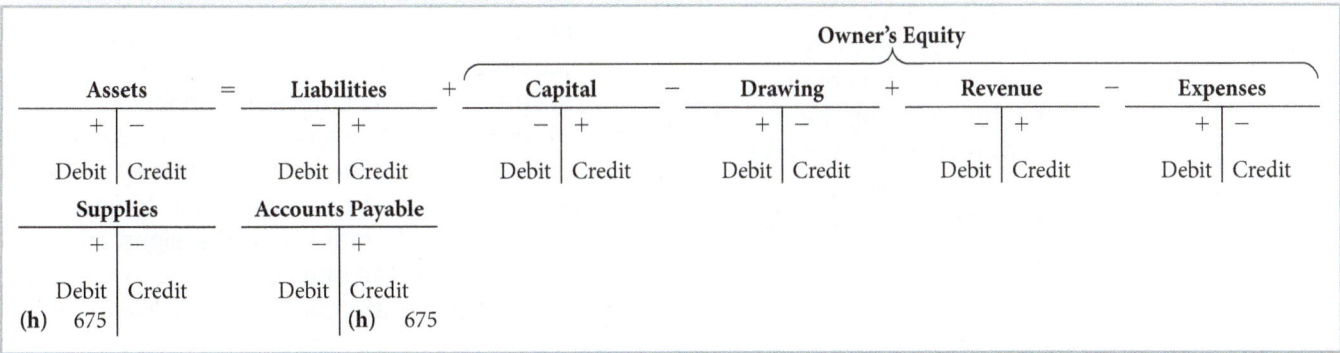

In transaction (h), Conner's Whitewater Adventures bought computer paper, ink cartridges, invoice pads, pens and pencils, folders, filing cabinets, and calculators on account from Fineman Company, $675.

STEP 4. Write the transaction as a debit to one account (or accounts) and a credit to another account (or accounts).

These items are considered supplies to be used by Conner's Whitewater Adventures and are recorded as an asset for $675 on account from Fineman Company. Remember, supplies are considered assets until they are used. When they are used, they are recorded as an expense. This transaction results in an increase to Supplies with a debit and an increase to Accounts Payable with a credit.

In transaction (i), Conner's Whitewater Adventures bought a three-month liability insurance policy, $1,875.

STEP 4. Write the transaction as a debit to one account (or accounts) and a credit to another account (or accounts).

This transaction results in an increase to the asset account Prepaid Insurance with a debit and a decrease to Cash with a credit.

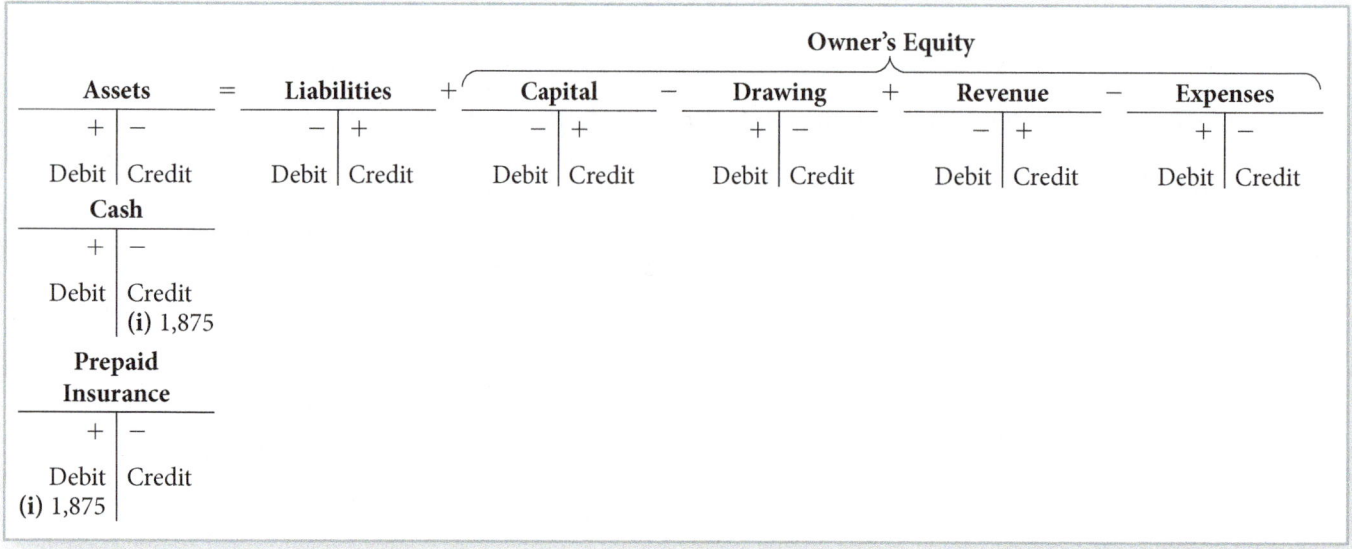

In transaction (j), Conner's Whitewater Adventures received a bill for newspaper advertising from *The Times*, $620.

STEP 4. Write the transaction as a debit to one account (or accounts) and a credit to another account (or accounts).

 YOU Make the Call

One of your fellow students is having trouble getting his accounting equation to balance after transaction (g). No matter how many times he computes the numbers, he can't get it to balance. When you look at his T accounts, you see that he has been crediting the expenses. He claims that expenses take away from owner's equity, so why should they be under the plus sign? How can you explain that he is partly correct?

SOLUTION

Your fellow student is correct in saying that expenses do take away from owner's equity, but the expense itself is increasing, which requires a debit, or increase, to the expense account. Expenses have the opposite signs of revenues—they are the costs of doing business and act in an opposite way to revenues. So the quick response to your classmate is to make sure the signs on expenses are the opposite of revenues and that expenses are debited when they happen.

This results in an increase to Advertising Expense with a debit and an increase to Accounts Payable with a credit.

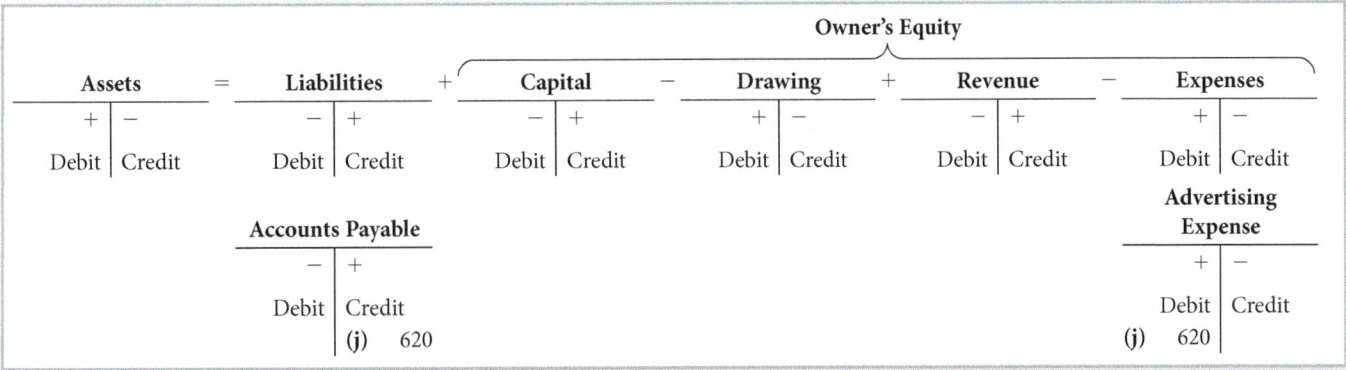

In transaction (k), Conner's Whitewater Adventures signs a contract with Crystal River Lodge to provide rafting adventures for guests. Conner's Whitewater Adventures provides 27 one-day rafting tours and bills Crystal River Lodge for $6,750.

STEP 4. **Write the transaction as a debit to one account (or accounts) and a credit to another account (or accounts).**

This results in an increase to Accounts Receivable with a debit and an increase to Income from Tours with a credit.

In transaction (l), Conner's Whitewater Adventures pays on account to Signal Products, $1,500.

STEP 4. **Write the transaction as a debit to one account (or accounts) and a credit to another account (or accounts).**

This transaction results in a decrease to Accounts Payable with a debit and a decrease to Cash with a credit.

In transaction (m), Conner's Whitewater Adventures received and paid Solar Power, Inc., for the electric bill, $225.

STEP 4. Write the transaction as a debit to one account (or accounts) and a credit to another account (or accounts).

The result of this transaction is an increase to Utilities Expense with a debit and a decrease to Cash with a credit.

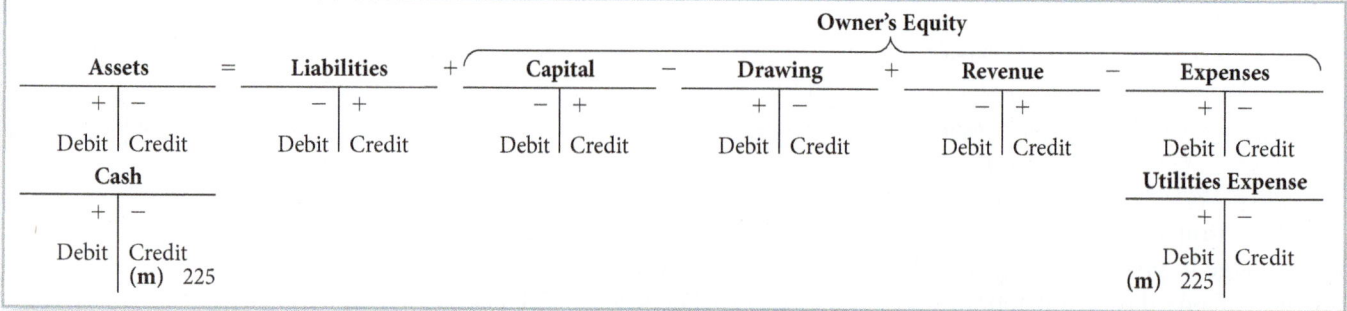

In transaction (n), Conner's Whitewater Adventures paid on account to *The Times*, $620.

STEP 4. Write the transaction as a debit to one account (or accounts) and a credit to another account (or accounts).

This transaction results in a decrease to Accounts Payable with a debit and a decrease to Cash with a credit. **Recall that this bill had previously been recorded as a liability in transaction (j).**

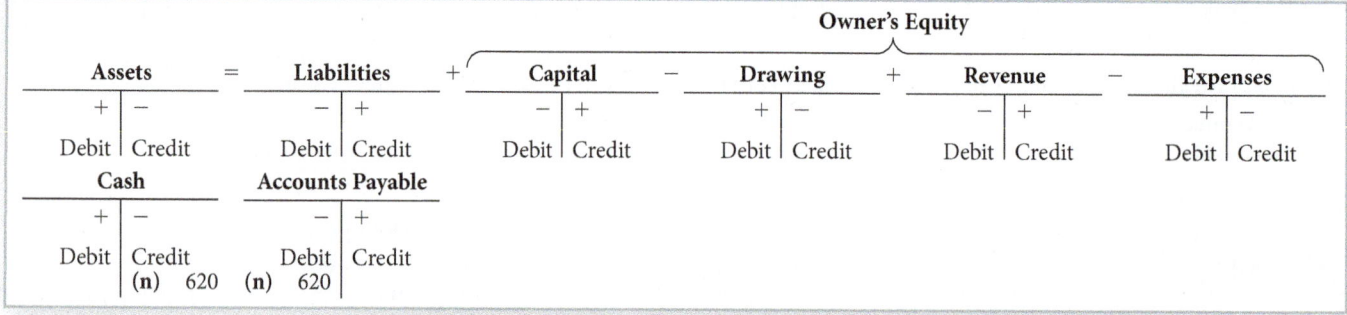

In transaction (o), Conner's Whitewater Adventures paid the wages of a part-time employee, $2,360.

STEP 4. Write the transaction as a debit to one account (or accounts) and a credit to another account (or accounts).

This transaction results in an increase to Wages Expense with a debit and a decrease to Cash with a credit.

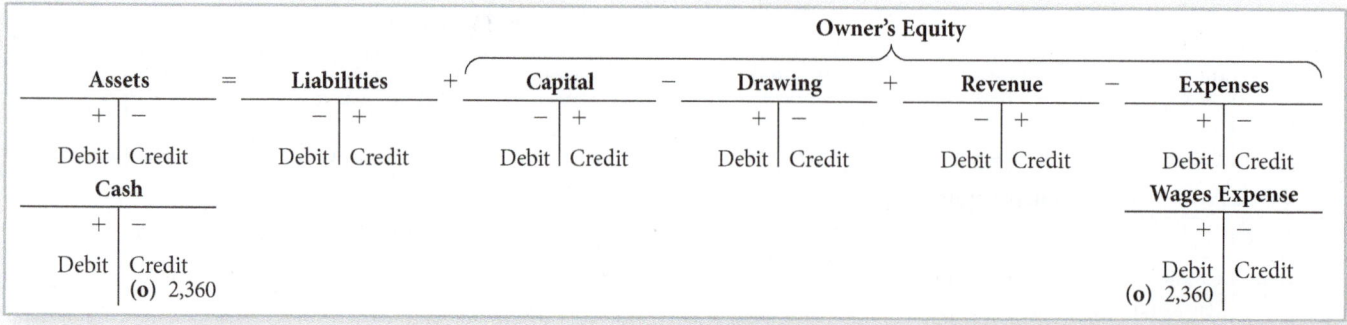

In transaction (p), Conner's Whitewater Adventures bought additional equipment from Signal Products, $3,780, paying $1,850 in cash and placing the balance on account.

STEP 4. **Write the transaction as a debit to one account (or accounts) and a credit to another account (or accounts).**

This transaction results in an increase to Equipment with a debit, an increase to Accounts Payable with a credit, and a decrease to Cash with a credit. This is called a **compound entry**, which always involves more than one debit or more than one credit.

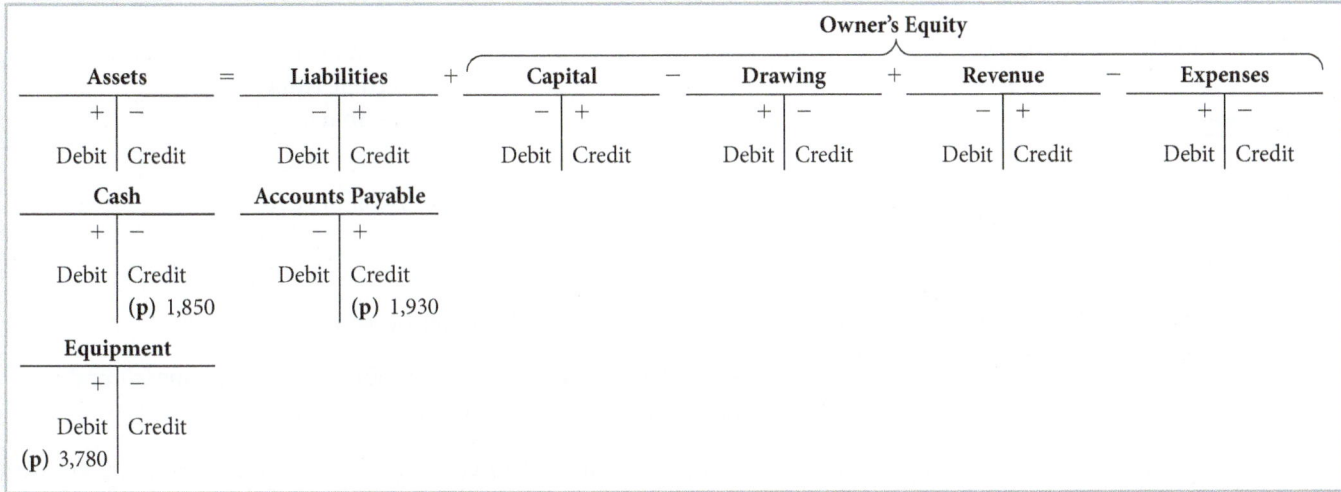

In transaction (q), Conner's Whitewater Adventures received $2,500 cash from Crystal River Lodge to apply against the amount billed in transaction (k).

STEP 4. **Write the transaction as a debit to one account (or accounts) and a credit to another account (or accounts).**

This transaction results in an increase to Cash with a debit and a decrease to Accounts Receivable with a credit.

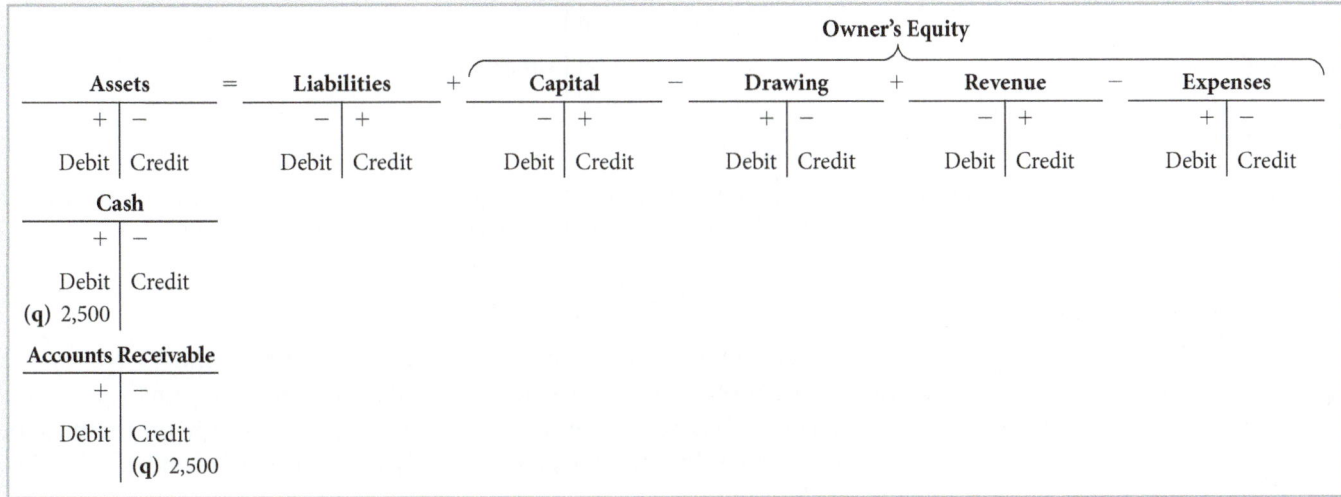

In transaction (r), Conner's Whitewater Adventures sold tours for cash, $8,570.

STEP 4. Write the transaction as a debit to one account (or accounts) and a
credit to another account (or accounts).

This transaction results in an increase to Cash with a debit and an increase to Income
from Tours with a credit.

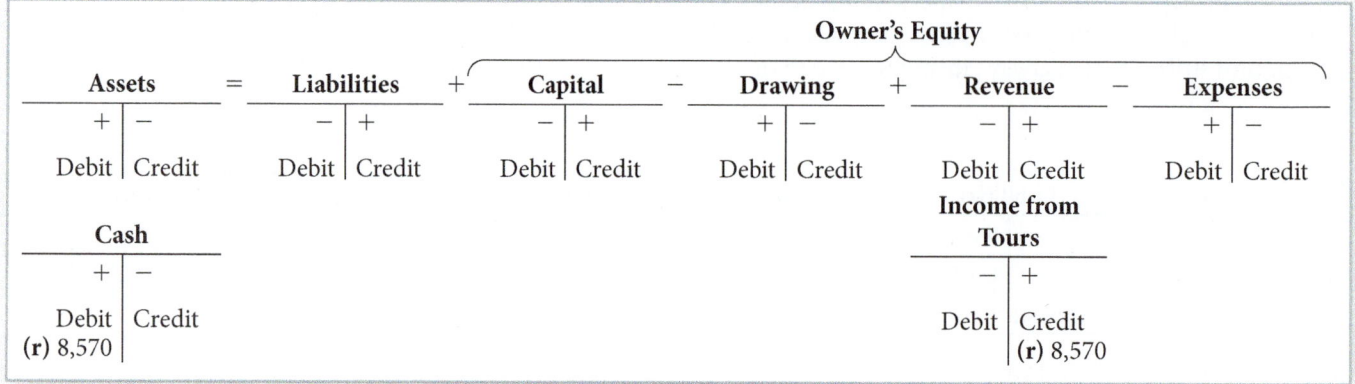

In transaction (s), J. Conner withdrew cash for her personal use, $3,500.

STEP 4. Write the transaction as a debit to one account (or accounts) and a
credit to another account (or accounts).

This transaction increases J. Conner, Drawing with a debit and decreases Cash with
a credit.

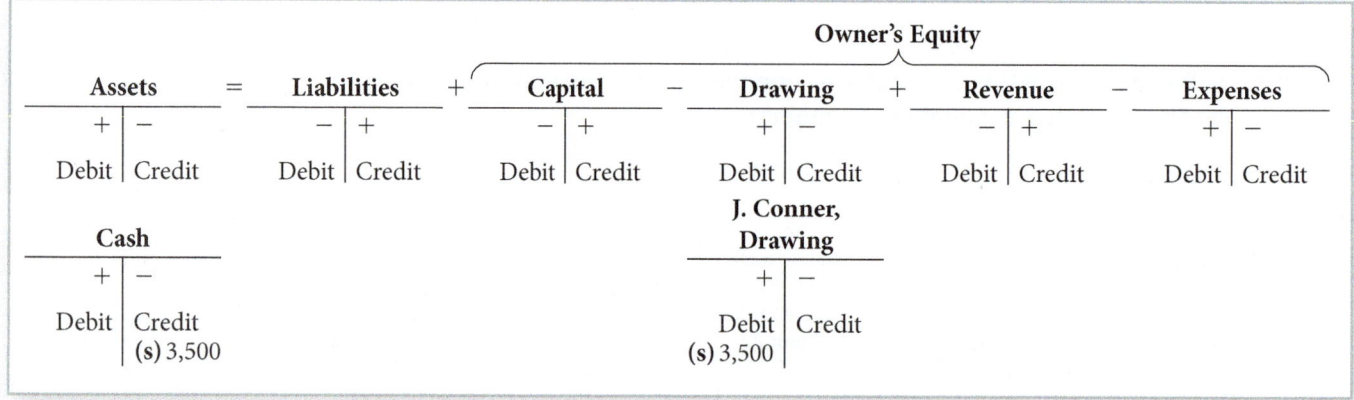

Remember that the Drawing account is used to record any withdrawals by the owner
from the business. The Drawing account always decreases owner's equity.

FYI

Traditionally, accountants
use the abbreviations
Dr. for Debit and Cr. for
Credit.

2-4a Summary of Transactions

The following T accounts provide a summary of all transactions for Conner's Whitewater
Adventures. You will notice that the balance of each account is normally on the plus side.
Note that in recording expenses, you normally place the entries only on the plus, or
debit, side. Also, in recording revenue, you normally place the entries only on the plus,
or credit, side.

Figure 1 describes a memory tool that may help you remember which accounts have normal debit balances, and which accounts have normal credit balances.

Figure 1

Account memory tool

A memory tool that helps some students memorize debits and credits in T accounts is the equation A + D + E = L + C + R. All accounts on the left side of the equation have normal debit balances, and all accounts on the right side have normal credit balances. You can make up a memorable sentence or use this one—All Drippy Eels Love Curly Radishes. Picture an eel dripping with water devouring curly radishes.

Account Memory Tool

Normal Debit Balance	Normal Credit Balance
Assets	Liabilities
Drawings	Capital
Expenses	Revenues

To: Amy Roberts, CPA
Subject: Debits equal credits?

Hi Amy,

I've recorded all of my transactions in T accounts using debits and credits. I know that my debits and credits need to equal. Is there an easy way to check this?

Thanks,

Janie

To: Janie Conner
Subject: RE: Debits equal credits?

Hi Janie,

You're correct! The total debits in the T accounts must always equal the total credits. One way to prove this is by preparing a trial balance. After the trial balance is prepared, you'll be able to prepare financial statements for your business. Financial statements will help you summarize the financial affairs of your business.

Let me know if you have any questions on these next two tasks:

    _____ 1. Prepare a trial balance.

    _____ 2. Prepare financial statements.

Thanks.

Amy

2-5 THE TRIAL BALANCE

After recording the transactions in the T accounts, you can prepare a trial balance by simply recording the balances of the T accounts in two columns. The **trial balance** is a listing of account balances in two columns—one labeled "Debit" and one labeled "Credit"—and is not considered a financial statement. It is, as the name implies, a trial run by the accountant to prove that the total of the debit balances equals the total of the credit balances. This is evidence of the equality of the two sides of the fundamental accounting equation. The accountant must prove that the accounts are in balance before preparing the company's financial statements.

⑤ Prepare a trial balance.

Learning Objective

In preparing a trial balance, shown in Figure 2, record the accounts with balances in the same order they are listed in the chart of accounts.

- Assets
- Liabilities
- Owner's Equity
- Revenue
- Expenses

Figure 2
Trial balance

Conner's Whitewater Adventures
Trial Balance
June 30, 20--

Column headings identify information in each column

Account Name	Debit	Credit
Cash	55,890	
Accounts Receivable	4,250	
Supplies	675	
Prepaid Insurance	1,875	
Equipment	51,300	
Accounts Payable		3,425
J. Conner, Capital		95,200
J. Conner, Drawing	3,500	
Income from Tours		23,320
Wages Expense	2,360	
Rent Expense	1,250	
Advertising Expense	620	
Utilities Expense	225	
	121,945	121,945

Accounts listed in order of the chart of accounts

Dollar signs not used on a trial balance

Single underline beneath figures to be added

Double underline beneath column totals

Remember, the normal balance of each account is on its plus side. The following table indicates where each of the account balances would normally be shown in a trial balance.

	TRIAL BALANCE	
Account Titles	**Left, or Debit, Balances**	**Right, or Credit, Balances**
Assets	Assets	
Liabilities		Liabilities
Capital		Capital
Drawing	Drawing	
Revenue		Revenue
Expenses	Expenses	
Totals		

2-6 MAJOR FINANCIAL STATEMENTS

Learning Objective

6a Prepare an income statement.

Earlier we listed summarizing as one of the five basic tasks of the accounting process. To accomplish this task, accountants use financial statements. A **financial statement** is a report prepared by accountants to summarize the financial affairs of a business for managers and others (both inside and outside the business).

Note that the headings of all financial statements require three lines:

1. Name of the company (or owner if there is no company name)
2. Title of the financial statement
3. Period of time covered by the financial statement, or its date

Also note that dollar signs are placed at the head of each column and with each total. Single lines are used to show that the figures above are being added or subtracted. Lines should be drawn across the entire column. A double line is drawn under the final total in a column.

The financial statements are all interconnected. The income statement must be prepared first, followed by the statement of owner's equity and then the balance sheet.

2-6a The Income Statement

The **income statement** shows total revenue minus total expenses, which yields the net income or net loss. The income statement reports the results of business transactions involving revenue and expense accounts—in other words, how the business has performed—over a period of time, usually a month or a year. When total revenue exceeds total expenses over the period, the result is **net income**, or profit. When the total revenue is less than total expenses, the result is a **net loss**.

The income statement in Figure 3 shows the results of the first month of operations for Conner's Whitewater Adventures.

For convenience, the individual expense amounts are recorded in the first amount column. Thus, the total expenses ($4,455) may be subtracted directly from the total revenue ($23,320).

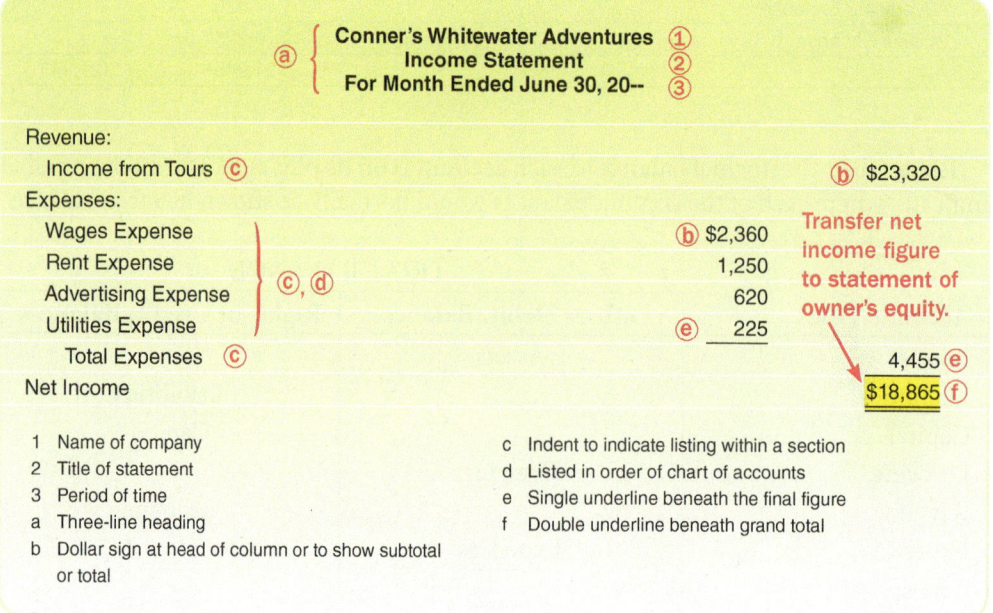

Conner's Whitewater Adventures ①		
Income Statement ②		
For Month Ended June 30, 20-- ③		
Revenue:		
Income from Tours ⓒ		ⓑ $23,320
Expenses:		
Wages Expense	ⓑ $2,360	
Rent Expense	1,250	
Advertising Expense	620	
Utilities Expense	ⓔ 225	
Total Expenses ⓒ		4,455 ⓔ
Net Income		$18,865 ⓕ

Transfer net income figure to statement of owner's equity.

1 Name of company
2 Title of statement
3 Period of time
a Three-line heading
b Dollar sign at head of column or to show subtotal or total

c Indent to indicate listing within a section
d Listed in order of chart of accounts
e Single underline beneath the final figure
f Double underline beneath grand total

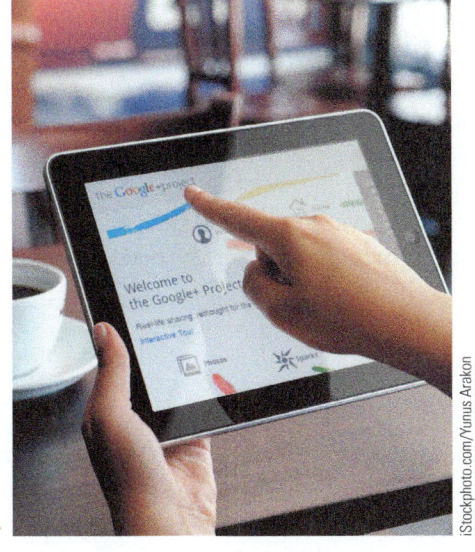

iStockphoto.com/Yunus Arakon

In the Real World

Where to open a new location is an important business decision. For companies such as Apple, a manufacturer and seller of computers, iPads, iPods, and iPhones, the decision to expand to a new retail store location—as well as other operating decisions—is made from financial statements such as the income statement. You can find a copy of Apple's financial statements on the Internet at http://investor.apple.com. For fiscal year ended September 26, 2015, Apple reported net income of $53,394,000,000 on its income statement. Dell is a competitor of Apple. Would you expect the financial statements of Dell to look similar to Apple's? If so, why might this be beneficial to users of the financial statements?

The income statement covers a period of time, whereas the balance sheet has only one date: the end of the financial period. On the income statement, the revenue for June less the expenses for June shows the results of operations—a net income of $18,865. To the accountant, the term *net income* means "clear" income, or profit after all expenses have been deducted. Expenses are usually listed in the same order as in the chart of accounts. Revenue and expense amounts are taken directly from the trial balance. If total expenses were greater than the revenue, then a net loss would be recorded.

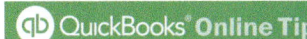 **QuickBooks® Online Tip**

The statement of owner's equity is not a standard report in QuickBooks Online. A customized report can be created if desired.

2-6b The Statement of Owner's Equity

In the previous chapter, we said that revenue and expenses are connected with owner's equity through the financial statements. Now let's demonstrate this using a statement of owner's equity, shown in Figure 4, which the accountant prepares after he or she has determined the net income or net loss on the income statement.

The **statement of owner's equity** shows how—and why—the owner's equity, or Capital account, has changed over a stated period of time (in this case, the month of June). Notice the third line in the heading of Figure 4. It shows that the statement of owner's equity covers the same period of time as the income statement.

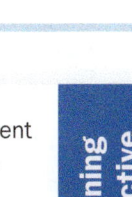 **6b** Prepare a statement of owner's equity.

Learning Objective

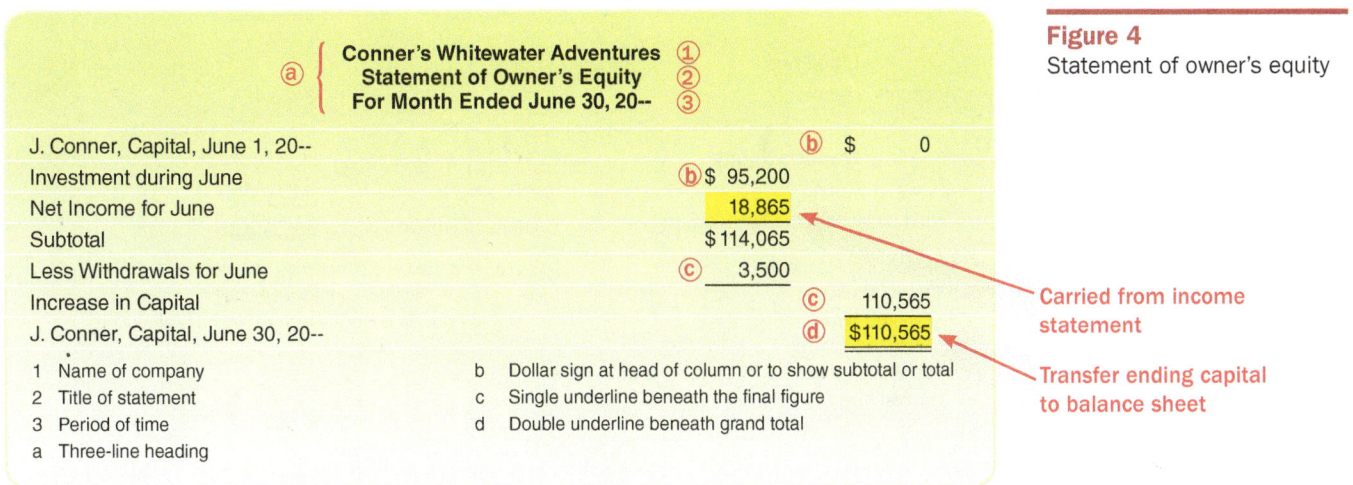

Figure 4
Statement of owner's equity

ⓐ {	**Conner's Whitewater Adventures** ① **Statement of Owner's Equity** ② **For Month Ended June 30, 20--** ③		
J. Conner, Capital, June 1, 20--		ⓑ $	0
Investment during June	ⓑ $ 95,200		
Net Income for June	18,865		
Subtotal	$ 114,065		
Less Withdrawals for June	ⓒ 3,500		
Increase in Capital		ⓒ	110,565
J. Conner, Capital, June 30, 20--		ⓓ	$110,565

Carried from income statement

Transfer ending capital to balance sheet

1 Name of company	b	Dollar sign at head of column or to show subtotal or total
2 Title of statement	c	Single underline beneath the final figure
3 Period of time	d	Double underline beneath grand total
a Three-line heading		

Look at the body of the statement. The first line shows the zero balance in the Capital account at the beginning of the month. The beginning balance is zero because this is a new business. All new businesses start with a zero beginning balance in the Capital account. An investment of $95,200 was made by J. Conner: total investment, $95,200. Two other items have affected owner's equity during the month: A net income of $18,865 was earned, and the owner withdrew $3,500. To perform the calculations, move to the left-hand column and add the total investments and the net income ($95,200 + $18,865 = $114,065). Then subtract the withdrawals from the subtotal ($114,065 − $3,500 = $110,565). The difference ($110,565) represents an increase in capital. This difference is placed in the right-hand column to be added to the beginning capital. The final figure is the ending amount in the owner's Capital account.

2-6c The Balance Sheet

After preparing the statement of owner's equity, we prepare a balance sheet. The **balance sheet** shows the **financial position**, or the condition of a business's assets offset by claims against them *as of one particular date*. It summarizes the balances of the asset, liability, and owner's equity accounts on a given date (usually the end of a month or year). Thus, the balance sheet is like a snapshot—a picture of the financial condition of the business at that particular date.

The ending capital balance on the balance sheet is taken from the statement of owner's equity. Note that the accounts appear in the same order as in the chart of accounts.

In the **report form** of the balance sheet, the elements in the accounting equation are presented one on top of the other. A balance sheet prepared on June 30 for Conner's Whitewater Adventures in report form is shown in Figure 5.

Figure 5
Balance sheet

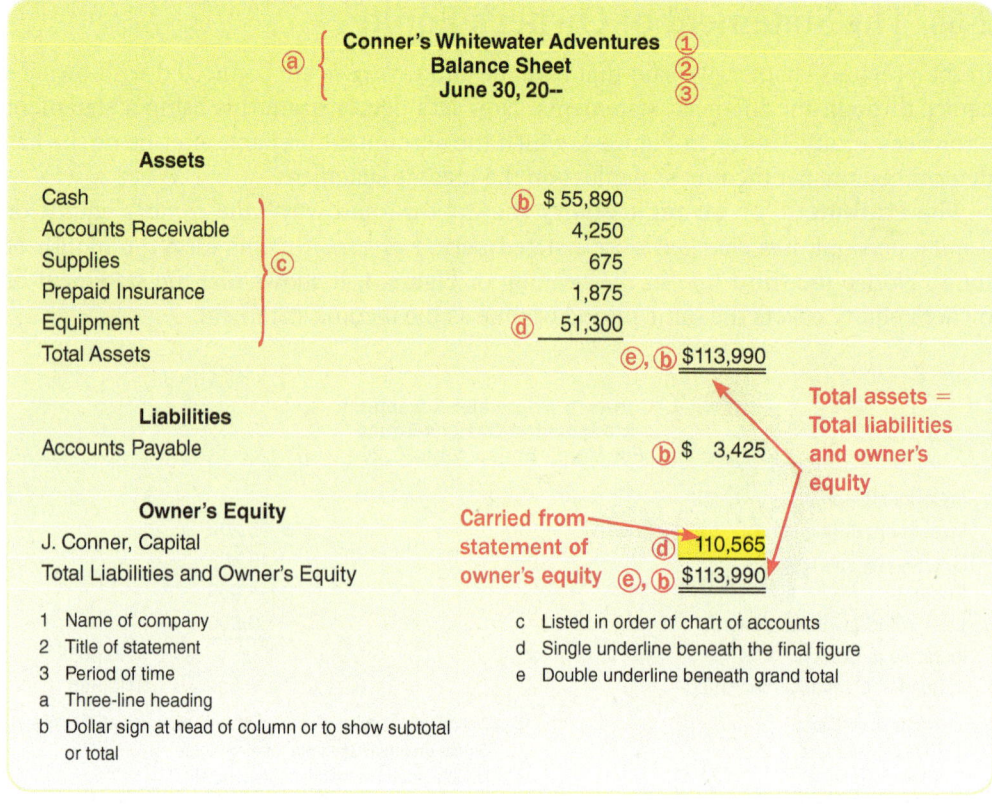

2-7 ERRORS EXPOSED BY THE TRIAL BALANCE

If the debit and credit columns in a trial balance are not equal, it is evident that we have made an error. Possible mistakes include the following:

- Making errors in arithmetic, such as errors in adding the trial balance columns or in finding the balances of the accounts.
- Recording only half an entry, such as a debit without a corresponding credit or vice versa.
- Recording both halves of the entry on the same side, such as two debits rather than a debit and a credit.
- Recording one or more amounts incorrectly.

It's important to note that even when debits equal credits, this does not necessarily mean that no errors were made in recording the transactions. For example, a transaction may have been forgotten, it may have been included twice, or it may have been written for an incorrect amount. Although using a computer greatly reduces the occurrence of addition and subtraction errors, it does not prevent the occurrence of other kinds of errors, such as an incorrect amount being recorded.

 7 Recognize the effect of errors on account balances.

Learning Objective

QuickBooks® Online Tip

Computerized accounting software, like QuickBooks Online, prevents out-of-balance errors by requiring transactions to balance before updating.

ACCOUNTING IN YOUR FUTURE

ACCOUNTING CLERK

One of many variations in accounting jobs you might find is an accounting clerk. Responsibilities might include invoicing for customers' fees, collecting fees, and maintaining customer accounts. The job might also include some marketing and customer service activities; therefore, people skills would be vital.

As the accounting clerk, you would be required to provide the accountant with weekly reports so that the accountant could correctly report revenue. You would also need to manage financial information regarding collection expenses and marketing expenses, as well as any expenses related to customer service. Consider how knowing the accounting cycle would be beneficial in this position.

2-7a Procedure for Locating Errors

Suppose you are in a business situation where you have recorded transactions for a month in the account books and the accounts do not balance. To save yourself time, you need to have a definite procedure for tracking down the errors. The best method is to do everything in reverse, as follows:

STEP 1. Look at the pattern of balances to see if a normal balance was placed in the wrong column on the trial balance.

STEP 2. Re-add the trial balance columns.

STEP 3. Check the transferring of the figures from the accounts to the trial balance.

STEP 4. Verify the footings and balances of the accounts.

As an added precaution, form the habit of verifying all addition and subtraction as you go along. You can then correct many mistakes *before* the time comes to prepare a trial balance.

When the trial balance totals do not balance, the difference might indicate that you forgot to record half an entry in the accounts. For example, if the difference in the trial balance totals is $20, you may have recorded $20 on the debit side of one account without recording $20 on the credit side of another account.

Another possibility is to divide the difference by 2. This may provide a clue that you accidentally recorded half an entry twice. For example, if the difference in the trial balance is $600, you may have recorded $300 on the debit side of one account and an additional $300 on the debit side of another account. Look for a transaction that involved $300 and see if you recorded both a debit and a credit. By knowing which transactions to check, you can save a lot of time.

2-7b Transpositions and Slides

If the difference is evenly divisible by 9, the discrepancy may be either a transposition or a slide. A **transposition** means that the digits have been transposed, or switched around, when the numbers were copied from one place to another. For example, one transposition of digits in 916 can be written as 619.

Correct Number	Number Copied	Difference	Difference Divided by 9
$916	$619	$297	$297 ÷ 9 = $33

A **slide** is an error in placing the decimal point (in other words, a slide in the decimal point). For example, $27,000 could be inadvertently written as $2,700.

Correct Number	Number Copied	Difference	Difference Divided by 9
$27,000	$2,700	$24,300	$24,300 ÷ 9 = $2,700

Or the error may be a combination of a transposition and a slide, as when $450 is written as $54.

Correct Number	Number Copied	Difference	Difference Divided by 9
$450	$54	$396	$396 ÷ 9 = $44

Again, the difference is evenly divisible by 9 (with no remainder).

Chapter Review

Study and Practice

 1 Determine balances of T accounts.

Learning Objective

To determine balances of T accounts, add the amounts listed on each side of the T account. The totals are called **footings**. To get the account balance, subtract the total of the smaller side from the total of the larger side. Record the account balance on the larger side.

 PRACTICE EXERCISE 1

Using the T accounts presented below, determine the balances.

	Cash				Accounts Payable				J. Jay, Capital			J. Jay, Drawing	
(a)	90,000	(b)	38,000	(d)	1,500	(c)	4,500	(a)	90,000	(f)	1,200		
		(f)	1,200					(e)	5,000				

	Equipment		
(b)	38,000	(d)	1,500
(c)	4,500		
(e)	5,000		

PRACTICE EXERCISE 1 • SOLUTION

	Cash				Accounts Payable				J. Jay, Capital			J. Jay, Drawing	
(a)	90,000	(b)	38,000	(d)	1,500	(c)	4,500	(a)	90,000	(f)	1,200		
		(f)	1,200			Bal.	3,000	(e)	5,000	Bal.	1,200		
			39,200					Bal.	95,000				
Bal.	50,800												

	Equipment		
(b)	38,000	(d)	1,500
(c)	4,500		
(e)	5,000		
	47,500		
Bal.	46,000		

 2 Present the fundamental accounting equation using the T account form and label the plus and minus sides.

Learning Objective

The fundamental accounting equation can be restated in **T account form** using plus and minus sides. The following table summarizes the rules:

Assets	The *left* side is the *increase* side.
Liabilities	The *right* side is the *increase* side.
Capital	The *right* side is the *increase* side.

Drawing	The *left* side is the *increase* side.
Revenue	The *right* side is the *increase* side.
Expenses	The *left* side is the *increase* side.

 PRACTICE EXERCISE 2

Using the fundamental accounting equation in T account form, label each side with plus and minus.

PRACTICE EXERCISE 2 • SOLUTION

				Owner's Equity			
Assets	=	Liabilities	+	Capital	−	Drawing	+	Revenue	−	Expenses
+ | −		− | +		− | +		+ | −		− | +		+ | −

Learning Objective   Present the fundamental accounting equation using the T account form and label the debit and credit sides.

Each account category in the fundamental accounting equation has a debit and credit. The left side of a T account, regardless of the account category, is called the **debit** side. The right side is called the **credit** side. A debit or credit could signify either an increase or a decrease—it depends on the account category. The following table summarizes these rules:

Debits Signify		**Credits Signify**	
Increases in	Assets / Drawing / Expenses	Decreases in	Assets / Drawing / Expenses
Decreases in	Liabilities / Capital / Revenue	Increases in	Liabilities / Capital / Revenue

 PRACTICE EXERCISE 3

Using the fundamental accounting equation in T account form, label each side as debit and credit.

PRACTICE EXERCISE 3 • SOLUTION

				Owner's Equity			
Assets	=	Liabilities	+	Capital	−	Drawing	+	Revenue	−	Expenses
+ | −		− | +		− | +		+ | −		− | +		+ | −
Debit | Credit		Debit | Credit		Debit | Credit		Debit | Credit		Debit | Credit		Debit | Credit

Learning Objective   Record directly in T accounts a group of business transactions involving changes in asset, liability, owner's equity, revenue, and expense accounts for a service business.

Transactions can be recorded directly into the T accounts. When analyzing a business transaction, follow these steps:

STEP 1. What accounts are involved?

STEP 2. What are the classifications of the accounts involved (asset, liability, capital, drawing, revenue, expense)?

STEP 3. Are the accounts increased or decreased?

STEP 4. Write the transaction as a debit to one account (or accounts) and a credit to another account (or accounts).

STEP 5. Is the equation in balance after the transaction has been recorded?

 PRACTICE EXERCISE 4

Record the following transactions directly into the appropriate T accounts and determine the balance in each account.

a. J. Molson deposited $90,000 in the name of the business.

b. Bought equipment for cash, $38,000.

c. Bought advertising on account, $4,320.

d. Paid $2,000 on account.

e. J. Molson invested his personal equipment, valued at $5,200, in the business.

f. The business received cash from customers, $4,000.

g. J. Molson withdrew $1,200 from the business for personal use.

PRACTICE EXERCISE 4 • SOLUTION

Assets	=	Liabilities	+	Capital	–	Drawing	+	Revenue	–	Expenses
+ –		– +		– +		+ –		– +		+ –
Debit Credit		Debit Credit		Debit Credit		Debit Credit		Debit Credit		Debit Credit

Cash

	+ Debit	– Credit	
(a)	90,000	(b) 38,000	
(f)	4,000	(d) 2,000	
	94,000	(g) 1,200	
		41,200	

Bal. 52,800

Equipment

	+ Debit	– Credit
(b)	38,000	
(e)	5,200	

Bal. 43,200

Accounts Payable

– Debit	+ Credit
(d) 2,000	(c) 4,320
	Bal. 2,320

J. Molson, Capital

– Debit	+ Credit
	(a) 90,000
	(e) 5,200
	Bal. 95,200

J. Molson, Drawing

+ Debit	– Credit
(g) 1,200	
Bal. 1,200	

Fees Earned

– Debit	+ Credit
	(f) 4,000
	Bal. 4,000

Advertising Expense

+ Debit	– Credit
(c) 4,320	
Bal. 4,320	

 5 Prepare a trial balance.

Learning Objective

A **trial balance** is a list of all account balances in two columns—one labeled "Debit" and one labeled "Credit." The trial balance shows that both sides of the accounting equation are equal. The heading consists of the company name, the title of the form (trial balance), and the date.

PRACTICE EXERCISE 5

Using the following account balances, prepare a trial balance for Collins's Backpack Adventures as of July 31, 20--.

Accounts Payable	$ 3,325	J. Collins, Drawing	$3,400
Accounts Receivable	4,150	Prepaid Insurance	1,675
Advertising Expense	680	Rent Expense	1,350
Cash	55,830	Supplies	575
Equipment	51,500	Utilities Expense	325
Income from Treks	23,220	Wages Expense	2,460
J. Collins, Capital	95,400		

PRACTICE EXERCISE 5 • SOLUTION

Collins's Backpack Adventures
Trial Balance
July 31, 20—

Account Name	Debit	Credit
Cash	55,830	
Accounts Receivable	4,150	
Supplies	575	
Prepaid Insurance	1,675	
Equipment	51,500	
Accounts Payable		3,325
J. Collins, Capital		95,400
J. Collins, Drawing	3,400	
Income from Treks		23,220
Wages Expense	2,460	
Rent Expense	1,350	
Advertising Expense	680	
Utilities Expense	325	
	121,945	121,945

Learning Objective   Present the fundamental accounting equation using the T account form and label the debit and credit sides.

(a) An **income statement** shows the results of operations of a business for a period of time. It includes revenue and expense accounts and reports either a **net income** or a **net loss**. (b) A **statement of owner's equity** shows the activity in the owner's equity, or Capital account, for a period of time. It includes the balance in the Capital account at the beginning of the period plus any additional investments and any increase or decrease in capital as the result of a net income (or a net loss) minus any withdrawals. (c) A **balance sheet** shows the financial condition of a business at a particular date in time. It summarizes the balances of the asset, liability, and owner's equity accounts on a given date.

 PRACTICE EXERCISE 6

Use the trial balance in Practice Exercise 5 to prepare (a) an income statement, (b) a statement of owner's equity, and (c) a balance sheet. Assume that Collins's Backpack Adventures started business on July 1, 20--.

PRACTICE EXERCISE 6 • SOLUTION

(a)

Collins's Backpack Adventures
Income Statement
For Month Ended July 31, 20--

Revenue:		
Income from Treks		$23,220
Expenses:		
Wages Expense	$2,460	
Rent Expense	1,350	
Advertising Expense	680	
Utilities Expense	325	
Total Expenses		4,815
Net Income		$18,405

(b)

Collins's Backpack Adventures
Statement of Owner's Equity
For Month Ended July 31, 20--

J. Collins, Capital, July 1, 20--		$ 0
Investments during July	$ 95,400	
Net Income for July	18,405	
Subtotal	$113,805	
Less Withdrawals for July	3,400	
Increase in Capital		110,405
J. Collins, Capital, July 31, 20--		$ 110,405

(c)

Collins's Backpack Adventures
Balance Sheet
July 31, 20--

Assets		
Cash	$55,830	
Accounts Receivable	4,150	
Supplies	575	
Prepaid Insurance	1,675	
Equipment	51,500	
Total Assets		$ 113,730
Liabilities		
Accounts Payable		$ 3,325
Owner's Equity		
J. Collins, Capital		110,405
Total Liabilities and Owner's Equity		$ 113,730

| **Learning Objective** | 7 | Recognize the effect of errors on account balances. |

Transpositions and slides account for many trial balance errors. The clue is whether the difference in account balances or trial balance totals is evenly divisible by 9.

    a. A **transposition** occurs when digits are switched around, such as 541 written as 415.
    b. A **slide** is an error in placing the decimal point (in other words, a *slide* in the decimal point). For example, $62,000 could be inadvertently written as $6,200.
    c. An error in a trial balance may be a combination of a transposition and a slide, as when $230 is written as $32.

 PRACTICE EXERCISE 7

Identify the following errors as transpositions or slides and indicate the amount of the difference and whether it is divisible by 9.

    a. The amount of supplies bought totaled $341, but it was written as $431.
    b. Equipment was purchased for $3,500, but it was written as $35.
    c. An error was made in the trial balance because $35 was written as $530.

PRACTICE EXERCISE 7 • SOLUTION

a. Transposition: The difference is $90 and can be evenly divided by 9.

Correct Number	Number Copied	Difference	Difference Divided by 9
$341	$431	$90	$90 ÷ 9 = $10

b. Slide: The difference is $3,465 and can be evenly divided by 9.

Correct Number	Number Copied	Difference	Difference Divided by 9
$3,500	$35	$3,465	$3,465 ÷ 9 = $385

c. Transposition and slide: The difference is $495 and can be evenly divided by 9.

Correct Number	Number Copied	Difference	Difference Divided by 9
$35	$530	$495	$495 ÷ 9 = $55

Glossary

Balance sheet A financial statement showing the financial position of an organization on a given date, such as June 30 or December 31. The balance sheet lists the balances in the asset, liability, and owner's equity accounts. (*p. 70*)

Compound entry A transaction that requires more than one debit or more than one credit to be recorded. (*p. 63*)

Credit The right side of a T account; to credit is to record an amount on the right side of a T account. Credits represent increases in liability, capital, or revenue accounts and decreases in asset, drawing, or expense accounts. (*p. 54*)

Debit The left side of a T account; to debit is to record an amount on the left side of a T account. Debits represent increases in asset, drawing, or expense accounts and decreases in liability, capital, or revenue accounts. (*p. 54*)

Financial position The resources or assets owned by an organization at a point in time, offset by the claims against those resources and owner's equity; shown on a balance sheet. (*p. 70*)

Financial statement A report prepared by accountants that summarizes the financial affairs of a business. (*p. 68*)

Footings The totals of each side of a T account. (*p. 52*)

Income statement A financial statement showing the results of business transactions involving revenue and expense accounts over a period of time. (*p. 68*)

Net income The result when total revenue exceeds total expenses over a period of time. (*p. 68*)

Net loss The result when total expenses exceed total revenue over a period of time. (*p. 68*)

Normal balance The plus side of a T account. (*p. 52*)

Report form The form of the balance sheet in which assets are placed at the top and liabilities and owner's equity are placed below. (*p. 70*)

Slide An error in placing the decimal point in a number. (*p. 72*)

Statement of owner's equity A financial statement showing the activity in the owner's equity, or Capital account, over the financial period. (*p. 69*)

T account form A form of account shaped like the letter *T* in which increases and decreases in the account may be recorded. One side of the *T* is for entries on the debit or left side. The other side of the *T* is for entries on the credit or right side. (*p. 51*)

Transposition An error that involves interchanging, or switching around, digits during the recording of a number. (*p. 72*)

Trial balance A list of all account balances to prove that the total of all debit balances equals the total of all credit balances. (*p. 67*)

Quiz Yourself

_____ 1. Determine the balance of the following T account:

Cash	
90,000	38,000
3,500	1,200
600	

    a. 94,100 debit
    b. 54,900 debit
    c. 133,300 credit
    d. 54,900 credit
    e. 133,300 debit

_____ 2. Which of the following statements is correct?
    a. Increases to cash are shown on the right side of the account.
    b. Decreases to accounts payable are shown on the right side of the account.
    c. Decreases to supplies are shown on the right side of the account.
    d. Increases to rent expense are shown on the right side of the account.

_____ 3. Which of the following statements is false?
    a. R. Flores, Capital is increased with a credit.
    b. Prepaid Insurance is decreased with a credit.
    c. Professional Fees is increased with a debit.
    d. Rent Expense is increased with a debit.

_____ 4. R. Nelson invests his personal computer, with a fair market value of $2,500, in the business. How would this transaction be recorded?
    a. A debit to R. Nelson, Capital, $2,500.
    b. A credit to Cash, $2,500.
    c. A credit to Professional Fees, $2,500
    d. A debit to Computer, $2,500.

_____ 5. When preparing a trial balance, which of the following is correct?
    a. The purpose of the trial balance is to prove that the total of all debit balances equals the total of all credit balances.
    b. Advertising Expense would normally be recorded as a credit.
    c. The trial balance is considered to be a financial statement.
    d. Supplies would normally be recorded as a credit.

(Continued)

Use the following information for questions 6–8:

Flores's Catering
Trial Balance
February 28, 20—

Account Name	Debit	Credit
Cash	20,500	
Accounts Receivable	2,300	
Supplies	500	
Equipment	13,000	
Accounts Payable		3,500
R. Flores, Capital		22,000
R. Flores, Drawing	6,000	
Professional Fees		20,000
Rent Expense	2,400	
Advertising Expense	800	
	45,500	45,500

_____ 6. What would be the net income for Flores's
Catering?
a. $45,500
b. $16,800
c. $19,800
d. $10,800

_____ 7. On which financial statement(s) would
R. Flores, Drawing appear?
a. Income statement
b. Balance sheet
c. Statement of owner's equity
d. Income statement and statement of owner's
equity

_____ 8. What is the amount of ending capital shown on
the balance sheet for Flores's Catering?
a. $22,000
b. $20,000
c. $45,500
d. $32,800

_____ 9. Flores's Catering purchased equipment that cost
$2,500, but it was recorded as $520. Which of the
following is correct?
a. This is a transposition error.
b. This is a slide error.
c. This is neither a transposition error nor a slide
error.
d. Both a and b are correct.

Chapter Assignments

Discussion Questions

1. Explain how a trial balance and a balance sheet differ.
2. Explain why the term *debit* doesn't always mean "increase" and why the term *credit* doesn't always mean "decrease."
3. What are footings in accounting?
4. How are the three financial statements shown in this chapter connected?
5. What is a compound entry?
6. List two reasons why the debits and credits in the trial balance might not balance.
7. Give an example of a slide and an example of a transposition. Explain how you might decide whether an error is a slide or a transposition.
8. What do we mean when we say that capital, drawing, revenue, and expense accounts are under the umbrella of owner's equity?

Exercises

LO **2, 3**

Practice Exercises 2, 3

EXERCISE 2-1 On a sheet of paper, draw the fundamental accounting equation with T accounts under each of the account classifications, with plus and minus signs and debit and credit on the appropriate side of each account. Under each of the classifications, draw T accounts, again with the correct plus and minus signs and debit and credit, for each of the following accounts of Davie Engine Repair.

Cash	J. Davie, Drawing
Accounts Receivable	Income from Repairs
Supplies	Salary Expense
Equipment	Rent Expense
Accounts Payable	Utilities Expense
J. Davie, Capital	Miscellaneous Expense

LO **2, 3**

Practice Exercises 2, 3

EXERCISE 2-2 List the classification of each of the following accounts as A (asset), L (liability), OE (owner's equity), R (revenue), or E (expense). Write *Debit* or *Credit* to indicate the increase side, the decrease side, and the normal balance side.

(Continued)

Account	Classification	Increase Side	Normal Balance Side	Decrease Side
0. Cash	A	Debit	Debit	Credit
1. Salary Expense				
2. Office Equipment				
3. J. Samuels, Capital				
4. Service Revenue				
5. J. Samuels, Drawing				
6. Accounts Receivable				
7. Insurance Expense				
8. Fees Earned				
9. Accounts Payable				

LO 2, 3, 4

Practice Exercise 4

EXERCISE 2-3 R. Dalberg operates Dalberg's Tours. The company has the following chart of accounts:

Assets
Cash
Accounts Receivable
Supplies
Prepaid Insurance
Display Equipment
Van
Office Equipment

Liabilities
Accounts Payable

Owner's Equity
R. Dalberg, Capital
R. Dalberg, Drawing

Revenue
Income from Tours

Expenses
Wages Expense
Gas Expense
Advertising Expense
Utilities Expense

Using the chart of accounts, record the following transactions in pairs of T accounts. Give the T account to be debited first and the account to be credited to the right. Show debit and credit and plus and minus signs. (Example: Received and paid the bill for the month's rent, $480.)

Rent Expense			Cash	
+	−		+	−
Debit	Credit		Debit	Credit
480				480

a. Received and paid the electric bill, $175.
b. Bought supplies on account, $135.
c. Paid for insurance for one year, $580.
d. Made a payment on account to a creditor, $65.
e. Received and paid the telephone bill, $186.
f. Sold services on account, $1,375.
g. Received and paid the gasoline bill for the van, $130.
h. Received cash on account from customers, $1,458.
i. Dalberg withdrew cash for personal use, $700.

LO 4

Practice Exercise 4

EXERCISE 2-4 During the first month of operation, Graham Expeditions recorded the following transactions. Describe what has happened in each of the transactions (a) through (k).

Cash		Accounts Payable		J. D. Rakes, Capital		J.D. Rakes, Drawing		Income from Tours		Rent Expense	
(a) 5,000	(b) 600		(d) 720		(a) 5,000	(j) 750			(h) 1,015	(b) 600	
(k) 2,025	(c) 100		(g) 1,000		(f) 4,000				(k) 2,025		
	(e) 50										
	(g) 500										
	(i) 250										
	(j) 750										

Advertising Expense
(c) 100

Accounts Receivable
(h) 1,015

Utilities Expense
(i) 250

Supplies
(d) 720

Miscellaneous Expense
(e) 50

Equipment
(f) 4,000
(g) 1,500

LO 5

Practice Exercise 5

EXERCISE 2-5 Speedy Sewing Services, owned by T. Nguyen, hired a new bookkeeper who is not entirely familiar with the process of preparing a trial balance. All of the accounts have normal balances. Find the errors and prepare a corrected trial balance for December 31 of this year.

Speedy Sewing Services
Trial Balance
December 31, 20—

Account Name	Debit	Credit
Accounts Receivable		10,700
Cash	3,200	
Accounts Payable		9,500
Equipment	24,000	
T. Nguyen, Capital		22,800
T. Nguyen, Drawing		1,900
Prepaid Insurance		1,300
Income from Services		36,000
Wages Expense	17,500	
Rent Expense		4,500
Supplies	1,800	
Utilities Expense	3,400	
	49,900	86,700

CHAPTER ASSIGNMENTS

LO **5, 6**

Practice Exercises 5, 6

EXERCISE 2-6 During the first month of operations, Landish Modeling Agency recorded transactions in T account form. Foot and balance the accounts. Then prepare a trial balance, an income statement, a statement of owner's equity, and a balance sheet dated March 31, 20--.

	Cash				Accounts Payable				Salary Expense	
(a)	8,200	(b)	350			(k)	2,800	(g)	3,400	
(c)	8,400	(d)	1,600			(j)	82			
(i)	7,580	(f)	175							
		(g)	3,400		R. Landish, Capital				Rent Expense	
		(h)	2,200			(a)	8,200	(d)	1,600	

	Accounts Receivable			R. Landish, Drawing	
(e)	2,600		(h)	2,200	

	Supplies			Modeling Fees			Utilities Expense	
(j)	82			(c)	8,400	(f)	175	
				(e)	2,600			

	Office Furniture				
(b)	350		(i)	7,580	

	Office Equipment	
(k)	2,800	

LO **7**

Practice Exercise 7

EXERCISE 2-7 The following errors were made in journalizing transactions. In each case, calculate the amount of the error and indicate whether the debit or the credit column of the trial balance will be understated or overstated.

	Amount of Difference	Debit or Credit Column of Trial Balance Understated or Overstated
0. Example: A $149 debit to Accounts Receivable was not recorded.	$149	Debit column understated
a. A $42 debit to Supplies was recorded as $420.		
b. A $155 debit to Accounts Receivable was recorded twice.		
c. A $179 debit to Prepaid Insurance was not recorded.		
d. A $65 credit to Cash was not recorded.		
e. A $190 debit to Equipment was recorded twice.		
f. A $57 debit to Utilities Expense was recorded as $75.		

LO **7**

Practice Exercise 7

EXERCISE 2-8 Would the following errors cause the trial balance to have equal or unequal totals? As a result of the errors, which accounts are overstated (by how much) or understated (by how much)?

a. A purchase of office equipment for $380 was recorded as a debit to Office Equipment for $38 and a credit to Cash for $38.

b. A payment of $280 to a creditor was debited to Accounts Receivable and credited to Cash for $280 each.

c. A purchase of supplies for $245 was recorded as a debit to Equipment for $245 and a credit to Cash for $245.

d. A payment of $76 to a creditor was recorded as a debit to Accounts Payable for $76 and a credit to Cash for $67.

Problem Set A

 LO 1, 2, 3, 4

PROBLEM 2-1A   During December of this year, G. Elden established Ginny's Gym. The following asset, liability, and owner's equity accounts are included in the chart of accounts:

Cash	Accounts Payable
Exercise Equipment	G. Elden, Capital
Store Equipment	Income from Services
Office Equipment	Advertising Expense

During December, the following transactions occurred:

a. Elden deposited $35,000 in a bank account in the name of the business.
b. Bought exercise equipment for cash, $8,150, Ck. No. 1001.
c. Bought advertising on account from Hazel Company, $105.
d. Bought a display rack on account from Cyber Core, $790.
e. Bought office equipment on account from Office Aids, $185.
f. Elden invested her exercise equipment with a fair market value of $1,200 in the business.
g. Made a payment to Cyber Core, $200, Ck. No. 1002.
h. Sold services for the month of December for cash, $800.

Required

1. Write the account classifications (Assets, Liabilities, Capital, Drawing, Revenue, Expense) in the fundamental accounting equation, as well as the plus and minus signs and *Debit* and *Credit*.
2. Write the account names on the T accounts under the classifications, place the plus and minus signs for each T account, and label the debit and credit sides of the T accounts.
3. Record the amounts in the proper positions in the T accounts. Write the letter next to each entry to identify the transaction.
4. Foot and balance the accounts.

Check Figure
Balance of Cash, $27,450

 LO 1, 2, 3, 4, 5

PROBLEM 2-2A   B. Kelso established Computer Wizards during November of this year. The accountant prepared the following chart of accounts:

Assets	**Owner's Equity**	**Expenses**
Cash	B. Kelso, Capital	Wages Expense
Supplies	B. Kelso, Drawing	Rent Expense
Computer Software		Advertising Expense
Office Equipment	**Revenue**	Utilities Expense
Neon Sign	Income from Services	Miscellaneous Expense

Liabilities
Accounts Payable

(Continued)

The following transactions occurred during the month:

a.   Kelso deposited $45,000 in a bank account in the name of the business.
b.   Paid the rent for the current month, $1,800, Ck. No. 2001.
c.   Bought office desks and filing cabinets for cash, $790, Ck. No. 2002.
d.   Bought a computer and printer from Cyber Center for use in the business, $2,700, paying $1,700 in cash and placing the balance on account, Ck. No. 2003.
e.   Bought a neon sign on account from Signage Co., $1,350.
f.   Kelso invested her personal computer software with a fair market value of $600 in the business.
g.   Received a bill from *Country News* for newspaper advertising, $365.
h.   Sold services for cash, $1,245.
i.   Received and paid the electric bill, $345, Ck. No. 2004.
j.   Paid on account to *Country News,* a creditor, $285, Ck. No. 2005.
k.   Sold services for cash, $1,450.
l.   Paid wages to an employee, $925, Ck. No. 2006.
m.   Received and paid the bill for the city business license, $75, Ck. No. 2007.
n.   Kelso withdrew cash for personal use, $850, Ck. No. 2008.
o.   Bought printer paper and letterhead stationery on account from Office Aids, $115.

Check Figure
Trial balance total,
$50,840

Required

1.   Record the owner's name in the Capital and Drawing T accounts.
2.   Correctly place the plus and minus signs for each T account and label the debit and credit sides of the accounts.
3.   Record the transactions in T accounts. Write the letter of each entry to identify the transaction.
4.   Foot the T accounts and show the balances.
5.   Prepare a trial balance, with a three-line heading, dated November 30, 20--.

LO   **1, 2, 3, 4, 5, 6** ....

PROBLEM 2-3A S. Myers, a speech therapist, opened a clinic in the name of Myers Clinic. Her accountant prepared the following chart of accounts:

Assets	**Owner's Equity**	**Expenses**
Cash	S. Myers, Capital	Salary Expense
Accounts Receivable	S. Myers, Drawing	Rent Expense
Office Equipment		Utilities Expense
Office Furniture	**Revenue**	Miscellaneous Expense
	Professional Fees	
Liabilities		
Accounts Payable		

The following transactions occurred during June of this year:

a.   Myers deposited $40,000 in a bank account in the name of the business.
b.   Bought waiting room chairs and tables on account, $1,330.
c.   Bought a fax/copier/scanner combination from Max's Equipment for $595, paying $200 in cash and placing the balance on account, Ck. No. 1001.
d.   Bought an intercom system on account from Regan Office Supply, $375.
e.   Received and paid the telephone bill, $155, Ck. No. 1002.
f.   Sold professional services on account, $1,484.
g.   Received and paid the electric bill, $190, Ck. No. 1003.
h.   Received and paid the bill for the state speech therapy convention, $450, Ck. No. 1004.

i. Sold professional services for cash, $2,575.
j. Paid on account to Regan Office Supply, $300, Ck. No. 1005.
k. Paid the rent for the current month, $940, Ck. No. 1006.
l. Paid salary of the receptionist, $880, Ck. No. 1007.
m. Myers withdrew cash for personal use, $800, Ck. No. 1008.
n. Received $885 on account from patients who were previously billed.

Required

1. Record the owner's name in the Capital and Drawing T accounts.
2. Correctly place the plus and minus signs for each T account and label the debit and credit sides of the accounts.
3. Record the transactions in the T accounts. Write the letter of each entry to identify the transaction.
4. Foot the T accounts and show the balances.
5. Prepare a trial balance as of June 30, 20--.
6. Prepare an income statement for June 30, 20--.
7. Prepare a statement of owner's equity for June 30, 20--.
8. Prepare a balance sheet as of June 30, 20--.

Check Figure
Net Income, $1,444

LO 1, 2, 3, 4, 5, 6

PROBLEM 2-4A On May 1, B. Bangle opened Self-Wash Laundry. His accountant listed the following chart of accounts:

Cash	B. Bangle, Drawing
Supplies	Laundry Revenue
Prepaid Insurance	Wages Expense
Equipment	Rent Expense
Furniture and Fixtures	Utilities Expense
Accounts Payable	Miscellaneous Expense
B. Bangle, Capital	

The following transactions were completed during May:

a. Bangle deposited $35,000 in a bank account in the name of the business.
b. Bought chairs and tables, paying cash, $1,870, Ck. No. 1000.
c. Bought supplies on account from Barnes Supply Company, $225.
d. Paid the rent for the current month, $875, Ck. No. 1001.
e. Bought washing machines and dryers from Lara Equipment Company, $12,500, paying $3,600 in cash and placing the balance on account, Ck. No. 1002.
f. Sold services for cash for the first half of the month, $1,925.
g. Bought insurance for one year, $1,560, Ck. No. 1003.
h. Paid on account to Lara Equipment Company, $1,800, Ck. No. 1004.
i. Received and paid electric bill, $285, Ck. No. 1005.
j. Sold services for cash for the second half of the month, $1,835.
k. Paid wages to an employee, $940, Ck. No. 1006.
l. Bangle withdrew cash for his personal use, $800, Ck. No. 1007.
m. Paid on account to Barnes Supply Company, $225, Ck. No. 1008.
n. Received and paid bill from the county for sidewalk repair assessment, $280, Ck. No. 1009.

(Continued)

Check Figure
Trial balance total,
$45,860

Required

1. Record the owner's name in the Capital and Drawing T accounts.
2. Correctly place the plus and minus signs for each T account and label the debit and credit sides of the accounts.
3. Record the transactions in the T accounts. Write the letter of each entry to identify the transaction.
4. Foot the T accounts and show the balances.
5. Prepare a trial balance as of May 31, 20--.
6. Prepare an income statement for May 31, 20--.
7. Prepare a statement of owner's equity for May 31, 20--.
8. Prepare a balance sheet as of May 31, 20--.

LO 6

PROBLEM 2-5A The financial statements for Daniels' Custom Haircuts for the month of October follow.

Daniels' Custom Haircuts
Income Statement
(a)

Revenue:		
Professional Fees		$25,000
Expenses:		
Salary Expense	$1,200	
Rent Expense	3,000	
Utilities Expense	600	
Miscellaneous Expense	450	
Total Expenses		(b)
Net Income		$19,750

(c)
Statement of Owner's Equity
(d)

Q. Daniels, Capital, October 1, 20--		$ 0
Investments during October	$ (e)	
Net Income for October	(f)	
Subtotal	$29,750	
Less Withdrawals for October	4,000	
Increase in Capital		(g)
Q. Daniels, Capital, October 31, 20--		$25,750

Daniels' Custom Haircuts
Balance Sheet
(h)

Assets		
Cash	$16,000	
Accounts Receivable	2,400	
Office Equipment	10,000	
Office Furniture	8,000	
Total Assets		$ (i)
Liabilities		
Accounts Payable		$ 10,650
Owner's Equity		
Q. Daniels, Capital		(j)
Total Liabilities and Owner's Equity		$ (k)

Required

Solve for the missing information.

Problem Set B

LO **1, 2, 3, 4**

PROBLEM 2-1B During February of this year, H. Rose established Rose Shoe Hospital. The following asset, liability, and owner's equity accounts are included in the chart of accounts:

Cash	Accounts Payable
Shop Equipment	H. Rose, Capital
Store Equipment	Income from Services
Office Equipment	Advertising Expense

The following transactions occurred during the month of February:

a.   Rose deposited $25,000 cash in a bank account in the name of the business.
b.   Bought shop equipment for cash, $1,525, Ck. No. 1000.
c.   Bought advertising on account from Milland Company, $325.
d.   Bought store shelving on account from Inger Hardware, $750.
e.   Bought office equipment from Shara's Office Supply, $625, paying $225 in cash and placing the balance on account, Ck. No. 1001.
f.   Paid on account to Inger Hardware, $750, Ck. No. 1002.
g.   Rose invested his personal leather working tools with a fair market value of $800 in the business.
h.   Sold services for the month of February for cash, $250.

(Continued)

Check Figure
Cash balance,
$22,750

Required

1. Write the account classifications (Assets, Liabilities, Capital, Drawing, Revenue, Expense) in the fundamental accounting equation, as well as the plus and minus signs and *Debit* and *Credit*.
2. Write the account names on the T accounts under the classifications, place the plus and minus signs for each T account, and label the debit and credit sides of the T accounts.
3. Record the amounts in the proper positions in the T accounts. Write the letter next to each entry to identify the transaction.
4. Foot and balance the accounts.

LO 1, 2, 3, 4, 5 ·

PROBLEM 2-2B J. Carrie established Carrie's Photo Tours during June of this year. The accountant prepared the following chart of accounts:

Assets	**Owner's Equity**	**Expenses**
Cash	J. Carrie, Capital	Wages Expense
Supplies	J. Carrie, Drawing	Rent Expense
Computer Software		Advertising Expense
Office Equipment	**Revenue**	Utilities Expense
Neon Sign	Income from Services	Miscellaneous Expense

Liabilities
Accounts Payable

The following transactions occurred during the month of June:

a. Carrie deposited $30,000 cash in a bank account in the name of the business.
b. Bought office equipment for cash, $1,850, Ck. No. 1001.
c. Bought computer software from Morey's Computer Center, $640, paying $350 in cash and placing the balance on account, Ck. No. 1002.
d. Paid current month's rent, $950, Ck. No. 1003.
e. Sold services for cash, $1,575.
f. Bought a neon sign from The Sign Company, $1,335, paying $435 in cash and placing the balance on account, Ck. No. 1004.
g. Received bill from *The Gossiper* for advertising, $445.
h. Bought supplies on account from City Supply, $460.
i. Received and paid the electric bill, $380, Ck. No. 1005.
j. Paid on account to *The Gossiper,* $245, Ck. No. 1006.
k. Sold services for cash, $3,474.
l. Paid wages to an employee, $930, Ck. No. 1007.
m. Carrie invested his personal computer with a fair market value of $1,000 in the business.
n. Carrie withdrew cash for personal use, $800, Ck. No. 1008.
o. Received and paid the bill for city business license, $75, Ck. No. 1009.

Check Figure
Trial balance total,
$37,899

Required

1. Record the owner's name in the Capital and Drawing T accounts.
2. Correctly place the plus and minus signs for each T account and label the debit and credit sides of the accounts.
3. Record the transactions in the T accounts. Write the letter of each entry to identify the transaction.
4. Foot the T accounts and show the balances.
5. Prepare a trial balance, with a three-line heading, dated June 30, 20--.

LO 1, 2, 3, 4, 5, 6

PROBLEM 2-3B D. Johnston, a physical therapist, opened Johnston's Clinic. His accountant provided the following chart of accounts:

Assets
Cash
Accounts Receivable
Office Equipment
Office Furniture

Liabilities
Accounts Payable

Owner's Equity
D. Johnston, Capital
D. Johnston, Drawing

Revenue
Professional Fees

Expenses
Salary Expense
Rent Expense
Utilities Expense
Miscellaneous Expense

The following transactions occurred during July of this year:

a. Johnston deposited $35,000 in a bank account in the name of the business.
b. Bought filing cabinets on account from Muller Office Supply, $560.
c. Paid cash for chairs and carpeting for the waiting room, $835, Ck. No. 1000.
d. Bought a photocopier from Rob's Office Equipment, $650, paying $250 in cash and placing the balance on account, Ck. No. 1001.
e. Received and paid the telephone bill, which included installation charges, $185, Ck. No. 1002.
f. Sold professional services on account, $2,255.
g. Received and paid the bill for the state physical therapy convention, $445, Ck. No. 1003.
h. Received and paid the electric bill, $335, Ck. No. 1004.
i. Received cash on account from credit customers, $1,940.
j. Paid on account to Muller Office Supply, $250, Ck. No. 1005.
k. Paid the office rent for the current month, $1,245, Ck. No. 1006.
l. Sold professional services for cash, $1,950.
m. Paid the salary of the receptionist, $960, Ck. No. 1007.
n. Johnston withdrew cash for personal use, $1,200, Ck. No. 1008.

Required

1. Record the owner's name in the Capital and Drawing T accounts.
2. Correctly place the plus and minus signs for each T account and label the debit and credit sides of the accounts.
3. Record the transactions in the T accounts. Write the letter of each entry to identify the transaction.
4. Foot the T accounts and show the balances.
5. Prepare a trial balance as of July 31, 20--.
6. Prepare an income statement for July 31, 20--.
7. Prepare a statement of owner's equity for July 31, 20--.
8. Prepare a balance sheet as of July 31, 20--.

Check Figure
Net Income, $1,035

CHAPTER ASSIGNMENTS

LO **1, 2, 3, 4, 5, 6** ....

PROBLEM 2-4B On July 1, K. Resser opened Resser's Business Services. Resser's accountant listed the following chart of accounts:

Cash	K. Resser, Drawing
Supplies	Business Services Revenue
Prepaid Insurance	Wages Expense
Equipment	Rent Expense
Furniture and Fixtures	Utilities Expense
Accounts Payable	Miscellaneous Expense
K. Resser, Capital	

The following transactions were completed during July:

a. Resser deposited $25,000 in a bank account in the name of the business.
b. Bought tables and chairs for cash, $725, Ck. No. 1200.
c. Paid the rent for the current month, $1,750, Ck. No. 1201.
d. Bought computers and copy machines from Ferber Equipment, $15,700, paying $4,000 in cash and placing the balance on account, Ck. No. 1202.
e. Bought supplies on account from Wiggins's Distributors, $535.
f. Sold services for cash, $1,742.
g. Bought insurance for one year, $1,375, Ck. No. 1203.
h. Paid on account to Ferber Equipment, $700, Ck. No. 1204.
i. Received and paid the electric bill, $438, Ck. No. 1205.
j. Paid on account to Wiggins's Distributors, $315, Ck. No. 1206.
k. Sold services to customers for cash for the second half of the month, $820.
l. Received and paid the bill for the business license, $75, Ck. No. 1207.
m. Paid wages to an employee, $1,200, Ck. No. 1208.
n. Resser withdrew cash for personal use, $700, Ck. No. 1209.

Check Figure
K. Resser, Capital,
July 31, 20--, $23,399

Required

1. Record the owner's name in the Capital and Drawing T accounts.
2. Correctly place the plus and minus signs for each T account and label the debit and credit sides of the accounts.
3. Record the transactions in the T accounts. Write the letter of each entry to identify the transaction.
4. Foot the T accounts and show the balances.
5. Prepare a trial balance as of July 31, 20--.
6. Prepare an income statement for July 31, 20--.
7. Prepare a statement of owner's equity for July 31, 20--.
8. Prepare a balance sheet as of July 31, 20--.

LO 6

PROBLEM 2-5B The financial statements for Baker Custom Catering for the month of April are presented below.

Baker Custom Catering
Income Statement
(a)

Revenue:		
Professional Fees		$12,000
Expenses:		
Salary Expense	$ 800	
Rent Expense	1,200	
Utilities Expense	360	
Miscellaneous Expense	80	
Total Expenses		(b)
Net Income		$ 9,560

(c)
Statement of Owner's Equity
(d)

L. Baker, Capital, April 1, 20--		$ 0
Investments during April	$ (e)	
Net Income for April	(f)	
Subtotal	$14,560	
Less Withdrawals for April	1,000	
Increase in Capital		(g)
L. Baker, Capital, April 30, 20--		$13,560

Baker Custom Catering
Balance Sheet
(h)

Assets		
Cash	$8,000	
Accounts Receivable	800	
Office Equipment	4,000	
Office Furniture	2,000	
Total Assets		$ (i)
Liabilities		
Accounts Payable		$ 1,240
Owner's Equity		
L. Baker, Capital		(j)
Total Liabilities and Owner's Equity		$ (k)

Required

Solve for the missing information.

Accounting with qb QuickBooks® Online

Go to the QuickBooks Online Chapter 2 Appendix located on the Cengage Learning companion site at **Cengage.com**. Review the *Accounting with QuickBooks Online* (step-by-step guide to using QuickBooks Online). *Accounting with QuickBooks Online*, Chapter 2, will introduce you to (1) setting up a new company, including establishing company settings, (2) modifying the chart of accounts, and (3) adding new customers, vendors, and employees.

Activities

Why Does It Matter?

SOLID ROCK GYM, San Diego, California

Individuals and groups of all ages come to Solid Rock Gym for fun and fitness. Services include several types of indoor rock-climbing experiences such as individual and group instruction, team development, and fitness programs. Solid Rock Gym also offers bouldering (climbing close to the bottom—no rope or hardware), top-roping (climbing while protected by a rope running through anchors above the intended route), and lead climbing (climbing while protected by a rope clipped to anchors as the climber ascends a route).

List five transactions that Solid Rock Gym might record during the month. Determine what accounts are involved and whether the accounts are debited or credited.

Example: Transaction 0. Owner invested cash in the business. Accounts involved: Cash and Capital. Cash is debited, and Capital is credited.

What Would You Say?

A fellow accounting student has difficulty understanding how the fundamental accounting equation stays in balance when a compound entry with one debit and two credits is recorded. Consider, for example, that a business bought equipment for $15,000, paid $5,000 in cash, and placed the remainder on account.

This means that there are two credits and one debit—one debit and one credit on the left side of the equation and the other credit on the right side of the equation. Explain to your fellow student how the equation stays in balance.

What Would You Do?

A new bookkeeper can't find the errors that are causing the company's month-end trial balance to be out of balance. The bookkeeper is too shy to ask for help at the office, so she takes the financial records home and asks her uncle, a retired bookkeeper, to help her locate the errors. Even with the help of her uncle, the trial balance is still out of balance, and now she is too embarrassed to return to the office and ask for help. The bookkeeper decides to show the trial balance is in balance and hope no one notices. Explain if there is anything wrong with this practice.

3

The General Journal and the General Ledger

Learning Objectives

After you have completed this chapter, you will be able to do the following:

1 Record a group of transactions pertaining to a service business in a two-column general journal.

2 Post entries from a two-column general journal to general ledger accounts.

3 Prepare a trial balance from the ledger accounts.

4 Explain the importance of source documents.

5 Correct entries using the ruling or correcting entry method.

To: Amy Roberts, CPA
Subject: Recording Transactions

Hi Amy,

This accounting stuff can be tough! But I think I am finally getting the hang of recording transactions using T accounts. Is this how accountants actually record transactions? As I have been looking around in QuickBooks Online, I don't see T accounts anywhere! Help!

Thanks,

Janie

To: Janie Conner
Subject: RE: Recording Transactions

Hi Janie,

You're right—you won't find T accounts in QuickBooks Online. That's because recording transactions using T accounts is a beginning step. Are you ready to learn how accountants actually record transactions—in journal entries? Using what you've learned so far about T accounts and debits and credits, you're ready to move on. Here's what you'll need to do:

_____ 1. Begin recording transactions using journal entries.

_____ 2. Learn how to post journal entries into the ledger.

Your knowledge of T accounts and debits and credits is very important for this next challenge and will help you prepare the journal entries correctly. Before you get started, take some time to review the rules of debits and credits. This will really help! You are now ready to start using QuickBooks Online to record transactions and prepare financial reports, such as the trial balance, income statement, and balance sheet. I will send you some hints to help you get started.

Amy

Gpointstudio/Shutterstock.com

In Chapter 2, we learned how to use T accounts as a tool for practicing debits and credits. We also used the trial balance as a means of making sure the debits equal the credits. In this chapter, we will further formalize our accounting procedures by learning about the general journal and the posting procedure.

Recall that *recording* is a step in the definition of accounting. Here we introduce the journal as the official record of business transactions. We have recorded business transactions as debits and credits to T accounts because it's easier to visualize these debits and credits as the plus and minus sides of the T accounts involved. **Determining the appropriate transaction debits and credits is the most important element in the accounting process.** It represents the very basic foundation of accounting, and all of the structure represented by financial statements and other reports is entirely dependent upon it. After determining the debits and credits, the accountant records the transactions in a journal.

The initial steps in the accounting process are as follows:

STEP 1. Record business transactions in a journal.

STEP 2. Post entries to accounts in the ledger.

STEP 3. Prepare a trial balance.

In this chapter, we explain all three steps.

3-1 THE GENERAL JOURNAL

We have seen that an accountant must keep a record of each transaction. In Chapter 2, we recorded the transactions directly in T accounts; however, only part of the transaction would be listed in each T account. A **journal** is a book in which business transactions are recorded as they happen. In the journal, both the debits and the credits of the entire transaction are recorded in one place. Actually, the journal is a diary for the business in which you record in day-by-day or chronological order all the events involving financial affairs. A journal is called a *book of original entry*. In other words, a transaction is always recorded first in the journal. The process of recording a business transaction

Accounting Language

Cost principle (p. 101)
Cross-reference (p. 106)
General ledger (p. 104)
Journal (p. 97)
Journalizing (p. 98)
Ledger account (p. 104)
Posting (p. 106)
Source documents (p. 98)
Two-column general journal (p. 99)

1 Record a group of transactions pertaining to a service business in a two-column general journal.

Learning Objective

in the journal is called **journalizing**. The information about transactions comes from **source documents** such as checks, invoices, receipts, letters, and memos. These source documents furnish proof (objective evidence) that a transaction has taken place, and they should be identified in the journal entry whenever possible.

Remember the first transaction for Conner's Whitewater Adventures?

TRANSACTION (a). June 1: Conner deposited $90,000 in a bank account in the name of the business.

When the business receives the cash from J. Conner, the accountant creates a source document—in this case, a receipt. See Figure 1 for an example of the source document that would be created.

Figure 1
Source document

Receipt	Date *June 1*	20 __	No.
Received From *J. Conner*			90,000.00
Ninety thousand and 00/100 Dollars			
For *Owner investment*			

Next, the accountant needs to analyze this transaction. We already know how to do this by following the steps presented in Chapter 2.

STEP 1. **What accounts are involved?** Cash and J. Conner, Capital are involved.

STEP 2. **What are the classifications of the accounts involved?** Cash is an asset account, and J. Conner, Capital is an owner's equity account.

STEP 3. **Are the accounts increased or decreased?** Cash is increased because Conner's Whitewater Adventures has more cash now than it had before. J. Conner, Capital is increased because Conner has a greater investment now than it had before.

STEP 4. **Write the transaction as a debit to one account (or accounts) and a credit to another account (or accounts).** Cash is increased, and the increase side of Cash is the left, or debit, side. J. Conner, Capital is an owner's equity account and is increased. The increase side of Capital is the right, or credit, side.

STEP 5. **Is the equation in balance after the transaction has been recorded?** Yes.

Let's show these entries by referring to our reliable fundamental accounting equation with the accompanying T accounts.

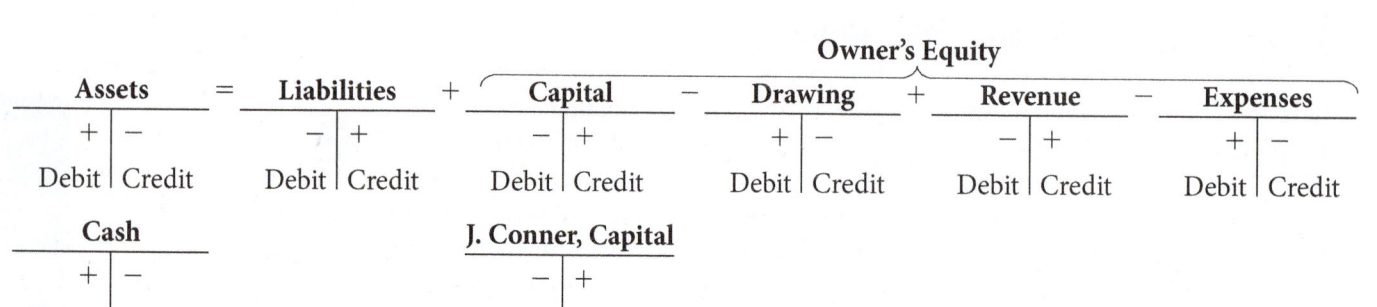

Now the accountant is ready to journalize the transaction. He or she records the business transaction in the journal. The basic form of the journal is the **two-column general journal**. The term *two-column* refers to the two columns used for debit and credit amounts. The pages of the journal are numbered in consecutive order.

Let's take a look at completed transaction (a) in the journal.

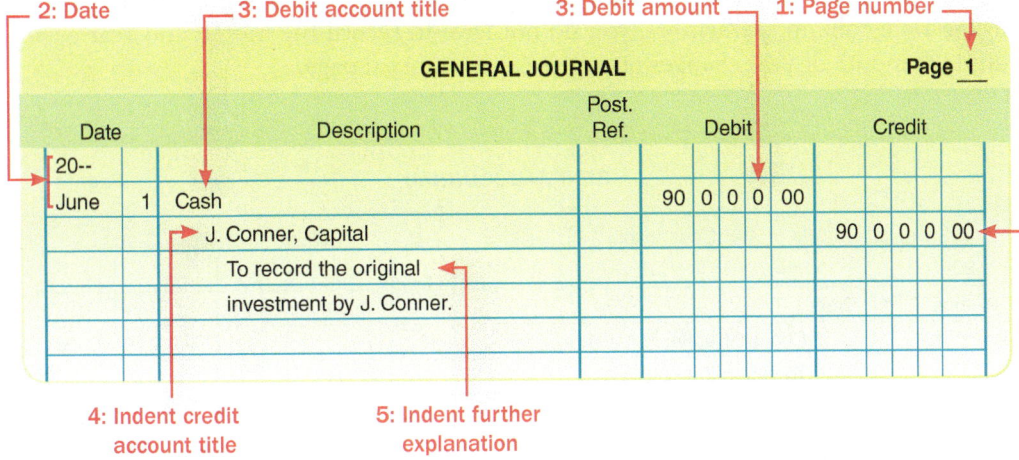

To explain the entry, we will break it down line by line. All journal entries contain the following:

STEP 1. *Page Number:* At the top of the page, record the page number.

STEP 2. *Date:* On the first line, record the year in the left part of the Date column. On the second line, record the month in the left part of the Date column and the day of the month in the right part of the Date column. *You don't have to repeat the year and month until you start a new page or until the year or month changes.*

STEP 3. *Debit:* **The debit part of the entry is always recorded first.** Insert the account title in the Description column and the dollar amount in the Debit column.

STEP 4. *Credit:* **The credit part of the entry is always indented and inserted on the line below the debit entry.** Insert the account title in the Description column and the dollar amount in the Credit column.

STEP 5. *Explanation:* **The explanation, indented further, is inserted on the line below the last line of the entry.** The explanation should refer to source documents, providing information such as check numbers, receipt numbers, or invoice numbers. You may also list names of charge customers or creditors or terms of payment.

For an entry in the general journal to be complete, it must contain (1) the date, (2) a debit entry, (3) a credit entry, and (4) an explanation. To anyone thoroughly familiar with the accounts, the explanation may seem obvious. Nevertheless, record the explanation as a required, integral part of the entry. To make the journal entries easier to read, leave one blank line between each transaction in your homework.

TRANSACTION (b). June 2: Conner's Whitewater Adventures bought equipment, paying cash, $38,000. Decide which accounts are involved. Then determine which of the five possible classifications each part of the transaction applies to. Visualize the plus and minus signs for each classification. Decide whether the accounts are increased or decreased. When you use T accounts to analyze the transaction, the results are as follows:

	Equipment		Cash	
	+	−	+	−
	Debit	Credit	Debit	Credit
	38,000			38,000

Now journalize this analysis below the first transaction. Record the day of the month in the Date column. Remember, you do not have to record the month and year again until the month or year changes or you use a new journal page.

GENERAL JOURNAL   Page 1

Date		Description	Post. Ref.	Debit	Credit
20--					
June	1	Cash		90 0 0 0 00	
		J. Conner, Capital			90 0 0 0 00
		To record the original			
		investment by J. Conner.			
	2	Equipment		38 0 0 0 00	
		Cash			38 0 0 0 00
		Bought equipment for cash.			

Skip a line between entries in your homework → (arrow pointing to blank line between entries)

TRANSACTION (c). **June 3: Conner's Whitewater Adventures bought equipment on account from Signal Products, $4,320.** Again, start with the T accounts.

	Equipment		Accounts Payable	
	+	−	−	+
	Debit	Credit	Debit	Credit
	4,320			4,320

After skipping a line in the journal, record the day of the month and then the entry. In journalizing a transaction involving Accounts Payable, state the name of the creditor in the explanation. Similarly, in journalizing a transaction involving Accounts Receivable, in the explanation, state the name of the customer who charged the amount.

Remember

In trying to figure out how a transaction should be recorded, first decide on the accounts involved. Then classify the accounts as A, L, OE, R, or E. Finally, ask yourself whether the accounts are increased or decreased and think of the related accounts with their plus and minus sides. This process will make the debits and credits of the transaction fall into place.

GENERAL JOURNAL   Page 1

Date		Description	Post. Ref.	Debit	Credit
	3	Equipment		4 3 2 0 00	
		Accounts Payable			4 3 2 0 00
		Bought equipment on account			
		from Signal Products.			

When a business buys an asset, the asset should be recorded at the actual cost (the agreed amount of a transaction). This is called the **cost principle**. For example, suppose that the $4,320 that Conner's Whitewater Adventures paid for the equipment from Signal Products was a bargain price, as Signal Products had been asking $7,500 for the equipment. Conner's Whitewater Adventures *should record the cost of the equipment as the actual amount paid ($4,320) in the transaction that occurred.* This is true even though the asking price was $7,500.

TRANSACTION (d). June 4: Conner's Whitewater Adventures paid Signal Products, a creditor, $2,000. Picture the T accounts like this:

Cash		Accounts Payable	
+	−	−	+
Debit	Credit	Debit	Credit
	2,000	2,000	

In this case, we see that cash is decreasing, so we record it on the minus side. We now have a credit to Cash and have completed half of the entry. Next, we recognize that Accounts Payable is involved. We ask ourselves, "Do we owe more or less as a result of this transaction?" The answer is "less," so we record it on the minus, or debit, side of the account.

ACCOUNTING IN YOUR FUTURE

ACCOUNTING SKILLS

If you decide to work in the field of accounting, there are a number of skills that you need to bring to the position. Of course, you will need to be able to write well and have solid communication and interpersonal skills—those skills are assumed capabilities for nearly every job. However, if you are in the accounting department, you will be expected to be skilled at analyzing transactions, debiting and crediting accounts accurately as you journalize, and posting those transactions too.

You may also be required to prepare a trial balance and financial statements. While your work will be primarily on a computer, using general ledger software, or in a cloud-based accounting application, like QuickBooks Online, you still need to understand what goes on behind the screen. This is especially important when totals don't balance or some other error needs to be uncovered and corrected. That is why the first three chapters in this textbook are particularly critical to building your accounting skills.

GENERAL JOURNAL — Page 1

Date		Description	Post. Ref.	Debit	Credit
	4	Accounts Payable		2 0 0 0 00	
		Cash			2 0 0 0 00
		Paid Signal Products on account.			

Because you have already determined the debits and credits in Chapter 2, we will now simply list the transactions for June for Conner's Whitewater Adventures with the date of each transaction. The journal entries are illustrated in Figures 2, 3, and 4.

June 1 Conner deposited $90,000 in a bank account in the name of her business.
2 Conner's Whitewater Adventures buys equipment, paying cash, $38,000.
3 Buys equipment on account from Signal Products, $4,320.
4 Pays $2,000 on account to Signal Products, a creditor.
4 Conner invests her personal computer, with a fair market value of $5,200, in the business.
7 Conner's Whitewater Adventures sells rafting tours for cash, $8,000.

Figure 2
Journal entries for Conner's Whitewater Adventures, June 1–7

GENERAL JOURNAL — Page 1

Date		Description	Post. Ref.	Debit	Credit
20--					
June	1	Cash		90 0 0 0 00	
		J. Conner, Capital			90 0 0 0 00
		To record the original			
		investment by J. Conner.			
	2	Equipment		38 0 0 0 00	
		Cash			38 0 0 0 00
		Bought equipment for cash.			
	3	Equipment		4 3 2 0 00	
		Accounts Payable			4 3 2 0 00
		Bought equipment on account			
		from Signal Products.			
	4	Accounts Payable		2 0 0 0 00	
		Cash			2 0 0 0 00
		Paid Signal Products on account.			
	4	Equipment		5 2 0 0 00	
		J. Conner, Capital			5 2 0 0 00
		To record the investment by J. Conner			
		in Conner's Whitewater Adventures.			
	7	Cash		8 0 0 0 00	
		Income from Tours			8 0 0 0 00
		Received cash for rafting tour sales.			

June 8   Conner's Whitewater Adventures pays rent for the month, $1,250.
      10   Buys supplies on account from Fineman Company, $675.
      10   Buys a three-month liability insurance policy, $1,875.
      14   Receives a bill for newspaper advertising from *The Times,* $620.
      15   Signs a contract with Crystal River Lodge to provide rafting adventures for guests. Conner's Whitewater Adventures provides 27 one-day rafting tours and bills Crystal River Lodge for $6,750.
      15   Pays on account to Signal Products, $1,500.
      18   Receives and pays Solar Power, Inc., for the electric bill, $225.

Remember

In recording business transactions in the journal, you must use the exact account titles as listed in the company's chart of accounts.

GENERAL JOURNAL Page 2

Date		Description	Post. Ref.	Debit	Credit
20--					
June	8	Rent Expense		1 2 5 0 00	
		Cash			1 2 5 0 00
		Paid rent for June.			
	10	Supplies		6 7 5 00	
		Accounts Payable			6 7 5 00
		Bought supplies on account			
		from Fineman Company.			
	10	Prepaid Insurance		1 8 7 5 00	
		Cash			1 8 7 5 00
		Paid premium for three-month			
		liability insurance policy.			
	14	Advertising Expense		6 2 0 00	
		Accounts Payable			6 2 0 00
		Received bill from			
		advertising with *The Times.*			
	15	Accounts Receivable		6 7 5 0 00	
		Income from Tours			6 7 5 0 00
		Billed Crystal River Lodge for			
		services performed.			
	15	Accounts Payable		1 5 0 0 00	
		Cash			1 5 0 0 00
		Paid Signal Products on account.			
	18	Utilities Expense		2 2 5 00	
		Cash			2 2 5 00
		Paid Solar Power, Inc., bill for utilities.			

Figure 3
Journal entries for Conner's Whitewater Adventures, June 8–18

June 20 Conner's Whitewater Adventures pays on account to *The Times*, $620. (This bill was recorded previously.)

24 Pays wages of part-time employee, $2,360.

26 Buys additional equipment from Signal Products for $3,780, paying $1,850 in cash and placing the balance on account.

30 Receives $2,500 cash from Crystal River Lodge to apply against amount billed on June 15.

30 Sells tours for cash, $8,570.

30 J. Conner withdraws cash for her personal use, $3,500.

Figure 4
Journal entries for Conner's Whitewater Adventures, June 20–30

									Page 3

GENERAL JOURNAL

Date		Description	Post. Ref.	Debit	Credit
20--					
June	20	Accounts Payable		6 2 0 00	
		Cash			6 2 0 00
		Paid *The Times* in full.			
	24	Wages Expense		2 3 6 0 00	
		Cash			2 3 6 0 00
		Paid wages of part-time employee.			
	26	Equipment		3 7 8 0 00	
		Cash			1 8 5 0 00
		Accounts Payable			1 9 3 0 00
		Bought equipment			
		from Signal Products.			
	30	Cash		2 5 0 0 00	
		Accounts Receivable			2 5 0 0 00
		Received from Crystal River Lodge			
		to apply on account.			
	30	Cash		8 5 7 0 00	
		Income from Tours			8 5 7 0 00
		Receiving cash for rafting tour sales.			
	30	J. Conner, Drawing		3 5 0 0 00	
		Cash			3 5 0 0 00
		Withdrew cash for personal use.			

Remember

In each journal entry, debits must equal credits.

3-2 POSTING TO THE GENERAL LEDGER

You know that the journal is the *book of original entry.* Each transaction must first be recorded in the journal in full. However, it is difficult to determine the balance of any one account, such as Cash, from the general journal entries. So the **ledger account** has been devised to give a complete record of the transactions recorded in each account. The **general ledger** contains all of the ledger accounts and contains detailed information about the increases and decreases in each of those accounts.

The journal is like a diary of the business's financial changes written in chronological or date order. = Diary of the business

The ledger is like sorted laundry—grouped information about each account is summarized in one place. =

$$A = L + Cap - Draw + R - E$$

3-2a The Ledger Account Form (Running Balance Format)

We have been looking at accounts in the simple T account form primarily because T accounts illustrate situations so well. The debit and credit sides are specifically labeled, making the T account form a good way to picture account activity. However, determining the balance of an account using the T account form is difficult. You must add both columns and subtract the smaller total from the larger. To overcome this disadvantage, accountants generally use the four-column account form with Balance columns in the general ledger. Let's look at the Cash account of Conner's Whitewater Adventures in four-column form (Figure 5) compared with the T account form. *Leave the Post. Ref. column blank for now.*

GENERAL LEDGER

ACCOUNT Cash   ACCOUNT NO. 111

Date	Item	Post. Ref.	Debit	Credit	Balance Debit	Balance Credit
20--						
June 1			90 0 0 0 00		90 0 0 0 00	
2				38 0 0 0 00	52 0 0 0 00	
4				2 0 0 0 00	50 0 0 0 00	
7			8 0 0 0 00		58 0 0 0 00	
8				1 2 5 0 00	56 7 5 0 00	
10				1 8 7 5 00	54 8 7 5 00	
15				1 5 0 0 00	53 3 7 5 00	
18				2 2 5 00	53 1 5 0 00	
20				6 2 0 00	52 5 3 0 00	
24				2 3 6 0 00	50 1 7 0 00	
26				1 8 5 0 00	48 3 2 0 00	
30			2 5 0 0 00		50 8 2 0 00	
30			8 5 7 0 00		59 3 9 0 00	
30				3 5 0 0 00	55 8 9 0 00	

Transaction amount   Running balance

Figure 5
General ledger for Conner's Whitewater Adventures

Cash

+	−
(a) 90,000	(b) 38,000
(f) 8,000	(d) 2,000
(q) 2,500	(g) 1,250
(r) 8,570	(i) 1,875
109,070	(l) 1,500
	(m) 225
	(n) 620
	(o) 2,360
	(p) 1,850
Footings	(s) 3,500
	53,180
Bal. 55,890	

Note the calculation of the running balance. In the abbreviated form, it looks like this:

GENERAL LEDGER

ACCOUNT Cash   ACCOUNT NO. **111**

Date		Item	Post. Ref.	Debit	Credit	Balance Debit	Balance Credit
20--							
June	1			90 0 0 0 00		90 0 0 0 00	
	2				38 0 0 0 00	52 0 0 0 00	
	4				2 0 0 0 00	50 0 0 0 00	

90,000 − 38,000 = 52,000
52,000 − 2,000 = 50,000

3-2b The Posting Process

2 Post entries from a two-column general journal to general ledger accounts.

Learning Objective

The process of transferring information from the journal to the ledger accounts is called **posting**. In the posting process, you must transfer the following information from the journal to the ledger accounts: the *date of the transaction*, the *debit and credit amounts*, and the *page number* of the journal. **Post each account separately**, using the following steps. Post the debit part of the entry first.

STEP 1. Write the date of the transaction in the account's Date column.

STEP 2. Write the amount of the transaction in the Debit or Credit column and enter the new balance in the Balance columns under *Debit* or *Credit*.

STEP 3. Write the page number of the journal in the Post. Ref. column of the ledger account. (This is a **cross-reference**; it tells where the amount came from.)

STEP 4. Record the ledger account number in the Post. Ref. column of the journal. (This is also a cross-reference; it tells where the amount was posted.)

Entering the account number in the Post. Ref. column of the journal should be the last step. It acts as a verification of the three preceding steps.

The June 1 transaction for Conner's Whitewater Adventures is illustrated in Figure 6. Let's look at the posting of the debit part of the entry.

QuickBooks® Online Tip

The Post Reference column is not used with cloud-based accounting applications like QuickBooks Online.

Figure 6
Posting from the general journal to the general ledger—debit entry (June 1 transaction)

① Date of transaction
② Amount of transaction
③ Page number of the journal
④ Ledger account number

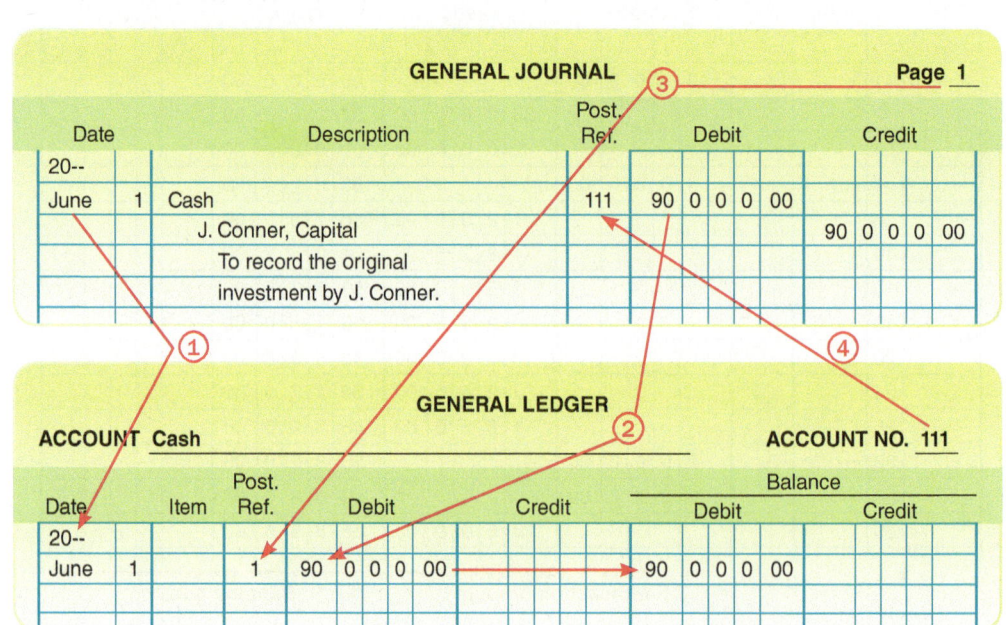

Next, we post the credit part of the entry, as shown in Figure 7.

The accountant normally uses the Item column only at the end of a financial period. The following words may appear in this column: *balance, closing, adjusting,* and *reversing.* We will explain the use of these terms later.

Incidentally, some accountants use running balance-type ledger account forms that have only one balance column. However, we have used the two-balance-column arrangement to show clearly the appropriate balance of an account. For example, in Figure 6, Cash has a $90,000 balance recorded in the Debit column (normal balance). In Figure 7, J. Conner, Capital, has a $90,000 balance recorded in the Credit column (normal balance).

In the recording of the June 2 transaction, shown in Figure 8, see if you can identify in order the four steps in the posting process.

GENERAL JOURNAL Page 1

Date	Description	Post. Ref.	Debit	Credit
2	Equipment	124	38 0 0 0 00	
	Cash	111		38 0 0 0 00
	Bought equipment for cash.			

GENERAL LEDGER

ACCOUNT Cash   ACCOUNT NO. 111

Date	Item	Post. Ref.	Debit	Credit	Balance Debit	Credit
20--						
June 1		1	90 0 0 0 00		90 0 0 0 00	
2		1		38 0 0 0 00	52 0 0 0 00	

ACCOUNT Equipment   ACCOUNT NO. 124

Date	Item	Post. Ref.	Debit	Credit	Balance Debit	Credit
20--						
June 2		1	38 0 0 0 00		38 0 0 0 00	

Figure 8
Posting from the general journal to the general ledger (June 2 transaction)

Remember
Posting is simply transferring or copying the same date and the debits and credits listed in the journal entry from the journal to the ledger.

QuickBooks Online Tip
Posting from the journal to the ledger is done automatically in QuickBooks Online.

If the temporary balance of an account happens to be zero, insert long dashes through both the Debit Balance and the Credit Balance columns. **We'll use another business, the Becker Company, in this example.** Its Accounts Receivable ledger account follows. Notice that the zero balance on October 29 is represented by long dashes in the Debit and Credit columns.

GENERAL LEDGER

ACCOUNT Accounts Receivable   ACCOUNT NO. 113

Date	Item	Post. Ref.	Debit	Credit	Balance Debit	Credit
20--						
Oct. 7		96	1 5 0 00		1 5 0 00	
19		97	2 4 8 00		3 9 8 00	
21		97		1 5 0 00	2 4 8 00	
29		98		2 4 8 00	——	
31		98	1 8 2 00		1 8 2 00	

Returning to Conner's Whitewater Adventures, let's look at the journal entries for the first month of operation. As you can see in Figure 9, the Post. Ref. column has been filled in because the posting was completed. Immediately after the journal entries, the ledger accounts and entries for Conner's Whitewater Adventures are shown in Figure 10. Take a moment to review all of the journal entries and the related postings.

Figure 9
Journal entries for Conner's Whitewater Adventures (first month of operation)

GENERAL JOURNAL   Page 1

Date	Description	Post. Ref.	Debit	Credit
20--				
June 1	Cash	111	90 0 0 0 00	
	J. Conner, Capital	311		90 0 0 0 00
	To record the original			
	investment by J. Conner.			
2	Equipment	124	38 0 0 0 00	
	Cash	111		38 0 0 0 00
	Bought equipment for cash.			
3	Equipment	124	4 3 2 0 00	
	Accounts Payable	221		4 3 2 0 00
	Bought equipment on account			
	from Signal Products.			
4	Accounts Payable	221	2 0 0 0 00	
	Cash	111		2 0 0 0 00
	Paid Signal Products on account.			

Figure 9
(Continued)

		Description	Post. Ref.	Debit	Credit
	4	Equipment	124	5 2 0 0 00	
		J. Conner, Capital	311		5 2 0 0 00
		To record the investment by J. Conner			
		in Conner's Whitewater Adventures.			
	7	Cash	111	8 0 0 0 00	
		Income from Tours	411		8 0 0 0 00
		Received cash for rafting tour sales.			

GENERAL JOURNAL   Page 2

Date		Description	Post. Ref.	Debit	Credit
20--					
June	8	Rent Expense	512	1 2 5 0 00	
		Cash	111		1 2 5 0 00
		Paid rent for June.			
	10	Supplies	115	6 7 5 00	
		Accounts Payable	221		6 7 5 00
		Bought supplies on account			
		from Fineman Company.			
	10	Prepaid Insurance	117	1 8 7 5 00	
		Cash	111		1 8 7 5 00
		Paid premium for three-month			
		liability insurance policy.			
	14	Advertising Expense	514	6 2 0 00	
		Accounts Payable	221		6 2 0 00
		Received bill from			
		advertising with *The Times*.			
	15	Accounts Receivable	113	6 7 5 0 00	
		Income from Tours	411		6 7 5 0 00
		Billed Crystal River Lodge for			
		services performed.			
	15	Accounts Payable	221	1 5 0 0 00	
		Cash	111		1 5 0 0 00
		Paid Signal Products on account.			
	18	Utilities Expense	515	2 2 5 00	
		Cash	111		2 2 5 00
		Paid Solar Power, Inc., bill for utilities.			

Figure 9
(Concluded)

GENERAL JOURNAL   Page 3

Date		Description	Post. Ref.	Debit	Credit
20--					
June	20	Accounts Payable	221	6 2 0 00	
		Cash	111		6 2 0 00
		Paid *The Times* in full.			
	24	Wages Expense	511	2 3 6 0 00	
		Cash	111		2 3 6 0 00
		Paid wages of part-time employee.			
	26	Equipment	124	3 7 8 0 00	
		Cash	111		1 8 5 0 00
		Accounts Payable	221		1 9 3 0 00
		Bought equipment			
		from Signal Products.			
	30	Cash	111	2 5 0 0 00	
		Accounts Receivable	113		2 5 0 0 00
		Received from Crystal River Lodge			
		to apply on account.			
	30	Cash	111	8 5 7 0 00	
		Income from Tours	411		8 5 7 0 00
		Received cash for rafting tour sales.			
	30	J. Conner, Drawing	312	3 5 0 0 00	
		Cash	111		3 5 0 0 00
		Withdrew cash for personal use.			

Figure 10
General ledger for Conner's Whitewater Adventures (first month of operation)

GENERAL LEDGER

ACCOUNT Cash   ACCOUNT NO. 111

Date		Item	Post. Ref.	Debit	Credit	Balance Debit	Balance Credit
20--							
June	1		1	90 0 0 0 00		90 0 0 0 00	
	2		1		38 0 0 0 00	52 0 0 0 00	
	4		1		2 0 0 0 00	50 0 0 0 00	
	7		1	8 0 0 0 00		58 0 0 0 00	
	8		2		1 2 5 0 00	56 7 5 0 00	
	10		2		1 8 7 5 00	54 8 7 5 00	
	15		2		1 5 0 0 00	53 3 7 5 00	
	18		2		2 2 5 00	53 1 5 0 00	
	20		3		6 2 0 00	52 5 3 0 00	
	24		3		2 3 6 0 00	50 1 7 0 00	
	26		3		1 8 5 0 00	48 3 2 0 00	
	30		3	2 5 0 0 00		50 8 2 0 00	
	30		3	8 5 7 0 00		59 3 9 0 00	
	30		3		3 5 0 0 00	55 8 9 0 00	

Figure 10
(Continued)

ACCOUNT **Accounts Receivable**   ACCOUNT NO. 113

Date		Item	Post. Ref.	Debit	Credit	Balance Debit	Balance Credit
20--							
June	15		2	6 7 5 0 00		6 7 5 0 00	
	30		3		2 5 0 0 00	4 2 5 0 00	

ACCOUNT **Supplies**   ACCOUNT NO. 115

Date		Item	Post. Ref.	Debit	Credit	Balance Debit	Balance Credit
20--							
June	10		2	6 7 5 00		6 7 5 00	

ACCOUNT **Prepaid Insurance**   ACCOUNT NO. 117

Date		Item	Post. Ref.	Debit	Credit	Balance Debit	Balance Credit
20--							
June	10		2	1 8 7 5 00		1 8 7 5 00	

ACCOUNT **Equipment**   ACCOUNT NO. 124

Date		Item	Post. Ref.	Debit	Credit	Balance Debit	Balance Credit
20--							
June	2		1	38 0 0 0 00		38 0 0 0 00	
	3		1	4 3 2 0 00		42 3 2 0 00	
	4		1	5 2 0 0 00		47 5 2 0 00	
	26		3	3 7 8 0 00		51 3 0 0 00	

ACCOUNT **Accounts Payable**   ACCOUNT NO. 221

Date		Item	Post. Ref.	Debit	Credit	Balance Debit	Balance Credit
20--							
June	3		1		4 3 2 0 00		4 3 2 0 00
	4		1	2 0 0 0 00			2 3 2 0 00
	10		2		6 7 5 00		2 9 9 5 00
	14		2		6 2 0 00		3 6 1 5 00
	15		2	1 5 0 0 00			2 1 1 5 00
	20		3	6 2 0 00			1 4 9 5 00
	26		3		1 9 3 0 00		3 4 2 5 00

Figure 10
(Continued)

ACCOUNT J. Conner, Capital   ACCOUNT NO. 311

Date		Item	Post. Ref.	Debit	Credit	Balance Debit	Balance Credit
20--							
June	1		1		90 0 0 0 00		90 0 0 0 00
	4		1		5 2 0 0 00		95 2 0 0 00

ACCOUNT J. Conner, Drawing   ACCOUNT NO. 312

Date		Item	Post. Ref.	Debit	Credit	Balance Debit	Balance Credit
20--							
June	30		3	3 5 0 0 00		3 5 0 0 00	

ACCOUNT Income from Tours   ACCOUNT NO. 411

Date		Item	Post. Ref.	Debit	Credit	Balance Debit	Balance Credit
20--							
June	7		1		8 0 0 0 00		8 0 0 0 00
	15		2		6 7 5 0 00		14 7 5 0 00
	30		3		8 5 7 0 00		23 3 2 0 00

ACCOUNT Wages Expense   ACCOUNT NO. 511

Date		Item	Post. Ref.	Debit	Credit	Balance Debit	Balance Credit
20--							
June	24		3	2 3 6 0 00		2 3 6 0 00	

ACCOUNT Rent Expense   ACCOUNT NO. 512

Date		Item	Post. Ref.	Debit	Credit	Balance Debit	Balance Credit
20--							
June	8		2	1 2 5 0 00		1 2 5 0 00	

Figure 10
(Continued)

ACCOUNT Advertising Expense   **ACCOUNT NO.** 514

Date	Item	Post. Ref.	Debit	Credit	Balance Debit	Balance Credit
20--						
June 14		2	6 2 0 00		6 2 0 00	

ACCOUNT Utilities Expense   **ACCOUNT NO.** 515

Date	Item	Post. Ref.	Debit	Credit	Balance Debit	Balance Credit
20--						
June 18		2	2 2 5 00		2 2 5 00	

3-3 THE TRIAL BALANCE

3-3a Preparation of the Trial Balance

After the journal entries have been posted, a trial balance must be prepared. The trial balance is simply a list of the ledger accounts that have balances. A trial balance is presented in Figure 11.

Remember that the trial balance proves only that the total ledger debit balances equal the total ledger credit balances. Even when the debit and credit balances are equal, other types of errors may slip through such as:

1. Posting the correct debit or credit amounts to the incorrect account or
2. Neglecting to journalize or post an entire transaction.

3 Prepare a trial balance from the ledger accounts.

Learning Objective

Conner's Whitewater Adventures Trial Balance June 30, 20—		
Account Name	**Debit**	**Credit**
Cash	55,890	
Accounts Receivable	4,250	
Supplies	675	
Prepaid Insurance	1,875	
Equipment	51,300	
Accounts Payable		3,425
J. Conner, Capital		95,200
J. Conner, Drawing	3,500	
Income from Tours		23,320
Wages Expense	2,360	
Rent Expense	1,250	
Advertising Expense	620	
Utilities Expense	225	
	121,945	121,945

Figure 11
Trial balance for Conner's Whitewater Adventures

3-3b Steps in the Accounting Process

So far, you have learned the first three steps in the accounting process.

STEP 1. Record the transactions of a business in a journal (book of original entry or day-by-day record of the transactions of a firm). An entry should be based on some source document or evidence that a transaction has occurred, such as an invoice, a receipt, or a check.

STEP 2. Post entries to the accounts in the ledger. Transfer the amounts from the journal to the Debit or Credit columns of the specified accounts in the ledger. Use a cross-reference system. Accounts are organized in the ledger according to the account numbers assigned to them in the chart of accounts.

STEP 3. Prepare a trial balance. Record the balances of the ledger accounts in the appropriate column, Debit or Credit, of the trial balance form. Prove that the total of the debit balances equals the total of the credit balances.

3-4 SOURCE DOCUMENTS

Learning Objective

4 Explain the importance of source documents.

As mentioned earlier, a source document can be an invoice, a receipt, or a check, for example. We now add an important detail in the recording of a journal entry. This detail consists of listing the related source document number, which is used as a reference for the proof of a transaction. For example, Figure 12 is an example of a source document followed by the journal entry (Figure 13) and ledger accounts (Figure 14).

Using the source document, the accountant records the entry in the journal (Figure 13). Note how the explanation includes important information from the source document. The explanation now includes the invoice number.

Figure 12
Source document

INVOICE				
FINEMAN COMPANY				No. 4-962
220 East Ames Street, Denver CO 80012				
Sold By: 203 Date: 6/10/20--				
Name: Conner's Whitewater Adventures				
Address: 1701 East Delaware Street Colorado Springs, CO 80902				
Terms: Net 30 days				

Quantity	Description	Unit Price		Amount	
10 bx	Invoice forms	12	00	120	00
5 bx	Ink cartridges	32	00	160	00
3 bx	8 x 11 copy paper	20	00	60	00
2	File cabinets, 2-drawer	32	00	64	00
4 bx	3-tab folders	12	00	48	00
3	10-key electric calculators	24	00	72	00
5 bx	12-count black ink pens	12	00	60	00
5 bx	10-count mechanical pencils	10	00	50	00
	SUBTOTAL			634	00
	SALES TAX			41	00
	SHIPPING—free			0	00
	TOTAL			675	00

GENERAL JOURNAL							Page 1			
Date	Description	Post. Ref.	Debit				Credit			
10	Supplies	115	6	7	5	00				
	Accounts Payable	221					6	7	5	00
	Bought supplies on account									
	from Fineman Company,									
	Invoice No. 4-962.									

Figure 13
Journal entry related to source document

SMALL BUSINESS **SUCCESS**

Paperwork—Why It's Worth Keeping Track of!

As you analyze transactions for a business, you learned that each transaction must be evidenced by a source document. Source documents, or the paperwork for transactions, are very important to all businesses. This is because all accounting transactions are developed from source documents. What are some examples of source documents? Bills from vendors, checks from customers, deposit slips, credit card receipts, bank statements, and customer invoices are all examples of source documents.

Many times businesses use accounting software to create source documents that can be printed for the businesses' or customers' records. Source documents should include the name and address of the business, as well as the date, amount, and description of the transaction. The documents should also include any customer information. The detail provided on the source documents will help the accountant record the transactions.

Source documents are also needed to substantiate the transactions should the business be audited. Internal and external auditors will review the paperwork when determining whether the transactions recorded by the business are accurate. The Internal Revenue Service (IRS) will also require the business to provide proof of transactions for income and deductions shown on the entity's tax return.

Is it necessary for the business to keep source documents forever? Well, that depends on what the source document is and to whom you talk with. Most accountants agree on the following guidelines:

Source Document	Time Period
Support for your tax return	3 years
Related to assets purchased, such as a business vehicle or computer	Keep until you sell or dispose
Documents such as accounts receivable or accounts payable ledgers, bank statements, canceled checks, and invoices	7 years
Items such as legal documents, tax returns, general ledgers, and financial statements	Indefinitely

Source documents are an important part of the accounting cycle. Take a moment to make sure you are comfortable with the information provided on the documents and that you are familiar with the most common documents used in accounting, such as invoices, deposit slips, receipts, and bills from vendors. As you work through the chapters of the textbook, you will be introduced to many types of source documents. Be sure to review them—important information is included on these documents!

The journal entry is then posted to the ledger (Figure 14).

Figure 14
Ledger posting

ACCOUNT Supplies   **ACCOUNT NO.** 115

Date	Item	Post. Ref.	Debit	Credit	Balance Debit	Balance Credit
20--						
June 10		2	6 7 5 00		6 7 5 00	

ACCOUNT Accounts Payable   **ACCOUNT NO.** 221

Previous Postings {

Date	Item	Post. Ref.	Debit	Credit	Balance Debit	Balance Credit
20--						
June 3		1		4 3 2 0 00		4 3 2 0 00
4		1	2 0 0 0 00			2 3 2 0 00
10		2		6 7 5 00		2 9 9 5 00

To: Amy Roberts, CPA
Subject: Errors?

Hi Amy,

I was thinking about recording transactions and wondered what happens if I make an error? Do I simply delete the error and then correct the entry?
Thanks,
Janie

To: Janie Conner
Subject: RE: Errors?

Hi Janie,

Errors happen even when you are extra careful. Once you find an error, it's important that you don't delete the error, but instead correct it using specific procedures. Using these procedures will ensure that you are properly documenting the error and the corresponding correction.
Amy

3-5 CORRECTION OF ERRORS—MANUAL AND COMPUTERIZED

Errors are occasionally made in recording journal entries and posting to the ledger accounts whether recording them manually or on a computer. Never erase or delete the errors because it may look as if you were trying to hide something. The method for correcting errors depends on how and when the errors were made. The two methods for correcting errors are as follows:

5 Correct entries using the ruling or correcting entry method.

1. The ruling method (can be used only for manual entry).
2. The correcting entry method (can be used for manual and computerized entry).

3-5a The Ruling Method

You can use the ruling method to correct an error in the journal before posting or to correct an error in the ledger after an entry has been posted, but only if the entry was recorded manually (with paper and pencil).

CORRECTING ERRORS BEFORE POSTING HAS TAKEN PLACE

When an error has been made in recording an account title in a journal entry, draw a line through the incorrect account title in the journal entry and write the correct account title immediately above it. Include your initials with the correction. For example, an entry to record payment of $1,500 rent was incorrectly debited to Salary Expense.

	GENERAL JOURNAL							Page 1	
Date	Description	Post. Ref.		Debit			Credit		
20--	*Rent Expense*								
Mar. 1	~~Salary Expense~~ *DJM*		1 5 0 0	00					
	Cash					1 5 0 0	00		
	Paid rent for the month.								

When an error has been made in recording an amount, draw a line through the incorrect amount in the journal entry and write the correct amount immediately above it. For example, an entry for a $120 payment for office supplies was recorded as $210. Include your initials with the correction.

	GENERAL JOURNAL						Page 1	
Date	Description	Post. Ref.		Debit			Credit	
20--			*DJM* 1 2 0 00					
Apr. 6	Supplies		~~2 1 0 00~~	*DJM* 1 2 0 00				
	Cash			~~2 1 0 00~~				
	Bought office supplies.							

CORRECTING ERRORS AFTER POSTING HAS TAKEN PLACE

When an entry was journalized correctly but one of the amounts was posted incorrectly, correct the error by drawing a single line through the amount and recording the correct amount above it. For example, an entry to record cash received for professional fees was correctly journalized as $400. However, it was posted as a debit to Cash for $400 and a credit to Professional Fees for $4,000. In the Professional Fees account, draw

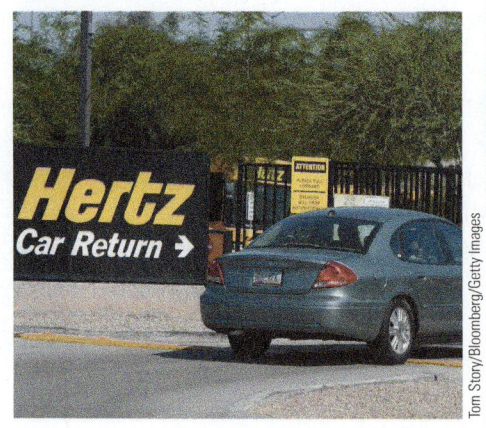

Tom Story/Bloomberg/Getty Images

In the Real World

Even large businesses make accounting errors. When a large corporation makes an error and discovers it after the financial statements have been published, the corporation is required to restate its financial statements. Some of these restatements can be huge. For example, Hertz, the rental car company, once announced that it was restating its financial statements for errors made in previous years. There were errors reported in the amount of $46.3 million in just one year!

a line through $4,000 and insert $400 above or next to the incorrect amount. Change the running balance of the account and initial the corrections.

ACCOUNT	Professional Fees					ACCOUNT NO. 411	
		Post.				Balance	
Date	Item	Ref.	Debit	Credit		Debit	Credit
				DJM 4 0 0 00		*DJM* 25 6 0 0 00	
6		94		~~4 0 0 0 00~~		~~29 2 0 0 00~~	

3-5b Correcting Entry Method—Manual or Computerized

If the transaction was journalized incorrectly and the amounts were posted, you should use the correcting entry method.

Use this entry when working with computerized accounting software. **Never delete or "fix" the original incorrect entry in a computerized accounting program.**

Following are the two correcting entry methods:

1. *One-step method.* One entry undoes the error and provides the correct account.
2. *Two-step method.* The first step reverses the error made by the original entry. The second step includes the correct entry.

When recording a correcting entry using either the one-step or two-step method, you must include an explanation. For example, on January 9, a $620 payment for advertising was incorrectly journalized and posted as a debit to Miscellaneous Expense for $620 and a credit to Cash for $620. The error was discovered and corrected on January 27 as follows using the one-step method.

		GENERAL JOURNAL				Page 1	
Date		Description	Post. Ref.	Debit		Credit	
20--							
Jan.	27	Advertising Expense		6 2 0 00			
		Miscellaneous Expense				6 2 0 00	
		To correct error of January 9 in which					
		a payment for Advertising Expense					
		was debited to Miscellaneous Expense.					

Following the two-step method, if the original entry was recorded as a debit to Miscellaneous Expense and a credit to Cash, reverse this entry by debiting Cash and crediting Miscellaneous Expense, then record the correct entry.

GENERAL JOURNAL				Page 1	
Date	Description	Post. Ref.	Debit	Credit	
20--					
Jan. 27	Cash		6 2 0 00		
	Miscellaneous Expense			6 2 0 00	
	To reverse out an incorrect				
	entry recorded January 9.				
27	Advertising Expense		6 2 0 00		
	Cash			6 2 0 00	
	To correct error of January 9				
	in which a payment for				
	Advertising Expense was				
	debited to Miscellaneous Expense.				

YOU Make the Call

Imagine you are an accounting clerk. You find that your trial balance balances, but something doesn't seem quite right. The amount of Miscellaneous Expense is much higher than it was last month, but you don't recall making an entry that would cause this discrepancy. In checking the journal entries, you find that an entry for $724 was accidentally debited to Miscellaneous Expense and credited to Accounts Payable. The $724 should have been debited to Utilities Expense. Explain how you would correct this entry and why you chose that method.

SOLUTION

Because this is a correction after the information was posted, two methods can be used to make the correction.

1. The first method is to simply make a journal entry to correct the original error. In this case, make a journal entry to debit Utilities Expense for $724 and credit Miscellaneous Expense for $724. This is called the one-step method.

2. Another method is to "back out," or reverse, the entry that contains the error and journalize the correct entry. That is, debit Accounts Payable for $724 and credit Miscellaneous Expense for $724. Finally, the correct journal entry is to debit Utilities Expense for $724 and credit Accounts Payable for $724.

These two methods can be used in a manual or computerized system.

Chapter Review

Study and Practice

Learning Objective	Record a group of transactions pertaining to a service business in a two-column general journal.

Based on **source documents**, the transactions are analyzed to determine what accounts are involved and whether the accounts are debited or credited. For each transaction, total debits must equal total credits. The **journal** is a book of original entry in which a day-by-day record of business transactions is maintained. The parts of a journal entry consist of the transaction date, the title of the account(s) debited, the title of the account(s) credited, the amounts recorded in the Debit and Credit columns, and an explanation.

 PRACTICE EXERCISE 1

Journalize the following transactions for the month of June:

June 1   J. Jonah deposited $35,000 in the bank in the name of the business (Jonah Company).

2   The business purchased $8,000 in equipment, paying $2,000 in cash and placing the remainder on account.

4   The business purchased supplies for cash, $250.

10   The business received cash revenue, $3,250.

20   The business paid the monthly rent, $1,800.

24   J. Jonah withdrew $500 for personal use.

PRACTICE EXERCISE 1 • SOLUTION

	GENERAL JOURNAL				Page 1
Date	Description	Post. Ref.	Debit	Credit	
20--					
June 1	Cash		35 0 0 0 00		
	J. Jonah, Capital			35 0 0 0 00	
	Jonah invested cash.				
2	Equipment		8 0 0 0 00		
	Cash			2 0 0 0 00	
	Accounts Payable			6 0 0 0 00	
	Purchased equipment.				
4	Supplies		2 5 0 00		
	Cash			2 5 0 00	
	Purchased supplies.				
10	Cash		3 2 5 0 00		
	Income from Services			3 2 5 0 00	
	Cash revenue.				

	20	Rent Expense		1	8	0	0	00					
		Cash							1	8	0	0	00
		Paid the monthly rent.											
	24	J. Jonah, Drawing			5	0	0	00					
		Cash								5	0	0	00
		Withdrawal for personal use.											

2 Post entries from a two-column general journal to general ledger accounts.

Learning Objective

The **general ledger** is a book that contains all of the accounts, arranged according to the chart of accounts. **Posting** is the process of transferring information from the journal to the **ledger accounts**. The posting process consists of four steps:

STEP 1. Write the date of the transaction in the account's Date column.

STEP 2. Write the amount of the transaction in the Debit or Credit column and enter the new balance in the Balance columns under *Debit* or *Credit*.

STEP 3. Write the page number of the journal in the Post. Ref. column of the ledger account.

STEP 4. Record the ledger account number in the Post. Ref. column of the journal.

 PRACTICE EXERCISE 2

Post the journal entries from Practice Exercise 1 to the following general ledger accounts:

Assets
111 Cash
115 Supplies
124 Equipment

Liabilities
221 Accounts Payable

Owner's Equity
311 J. Jonah, Capital
312 J. Jonah, Drawing

Revenue
411 Income from Services

Expenses
512 Rent Expense

PRACTICE EXERCISE 2 • SOLUTION

GENERAL LEDGER

ACCOUNT Cash   ACCOUNT NO. 111

Date		Item	Post. Ref.	Debit						Credit					Balance								
															Debit					Credit			
20--																							
June	1		1	35	0	0	0	00							35	0	0	0	00				
	2		1							2	0	0	0	00	33	0	0	0	00				
	4		1								2	5	0	00	32	7	5	0	00				
	10		1		3	2	5	0	00						36	0	0	0	00				
	20		1							1	8	0	0	00	34	2	0	0	00				
	24		1								5	0	0	00	33	7	0	0	00				

(Continued)

ACCOUNT Supplies   **ACCOUNT NO. 115**

Date		Item	Post. Ref.	Debit	Credit	Balance Debit	Balance Credit
20--							
June	4		1	2 5 0 00		2 5 0 00	

ACCOUNT Equipment   **ACCOUNT NO. 124**

Date		Item	Post. Ref.	Debit	Credit	Balance Debit	Balance Credit
20--							
June	2		1	8 0 0 0 00		8 0 0 0 00	

ACCOUNT Accounts Payable   **ACCOUNT NO. 221**

Date		Item	Post. Ref.	Debit	Credit	Balance Debit	Balance Credit
20--							
June	2		1		6 0 0 0 00		6 0 0 0 00

ACCOUNT J. Jonah, Capital   **ACCOUNT NO. 311**

Date		Item	Post. Ref.	Debit	Credit	Balance Debit	Balance Credit
20--							
June	1		1		35 0 0 0 00		35 0 0 0 00

ACCOUNT J. Jonah, Drawing   **ACCOUNT NO. 312**

Date		Item	Post. Ref.	Debit	Credit	Balance Debit	Balance Credit
20--							
June	24		1	5 0 0 00		5 0 0 00	

ACCOUNT Income from Services   **ACCOUNT NO. 411**

Date		Item	Post. Ref.	Debit	Credit	Balance Debit	Balance Credit
20--							
June	10		1		3 2 5 0 00		3 2 5 0 00

ACCOUNT Rent Expense   **ACCOUNT NO. 512**

Date		Item	Post. Ref.	Debit	Credit	Balance Debit	Balance Credit
20--							
June	20		1	1 8 0 0 00		1 8 0 0 00	

3 Prepare a trial balance from the ledger accounts.

The trial balance consists of a listing of account balances in two columns—one labeled Debit and one labeled Credit. The balances come from the ledger accounts.

PRACTICE EXERCISE 3

Prepare a trial balance from the ledger accounts in Practice Exercise 2.

PRACTICE EXERCISE 3 • SOLUTION

Jonah Company
Trial Balance
June 30, 20--

Account Name	Debit	Credit
Cash	33,700	
Supplies	250	
Equipment	8,000	
Accounts Payable		6,000
J. Jonah, Capital		35,000
J. Jonah, Drawing	500	
Income from Services		3,250
Rent Expense	1,800	
	44,250	44,250

 4 Explain the importance of source documents.

Source documents provide proof of a transaction. Examples of source documents include invoices, receipts, checks, and deposit slips.

PRACTICE EXERCISE 4

What is a possible source document for each of the following transactions?

June 1 J. Jonah deposited $35,000 in the bank in the name of the business (Jonah Company).
2 The business purchased $8,000 in equipment, paying $2,000 in cash and placing the remainder on account.
4 The business purchased supplies for cash, $250.
10 The business received cash revenue, $3,250.
20 The business paid the monthly rent, $1,800.
24 J. Jonah withdrew $500 for personal use.

PRACTICE EXERCISE 4 • SOLUTION

June 1 Deposit slip and receipt
2 Receipt
4 Vendor invoice (bill) and check
10 Customer receipt and deposit slip
20 Vendor invoice (bill) and check
24 Withdrawal slip or ATM receipt

| Learning Objective | 5 | Correct entries using the ruling or correcting entry method. |

The ruling method can be used if an error is discovered before or after an entry was posted. A line is drawn through the incorrect account title or amount and the correct account title or amount written immediately above. The person making the correction also includes his or her initials with the correction.

The correcting entry method is used if an error is discovered after an incorrectly journalized entry was posted. If the error consists of the wrong account(s), an entry is made to cancel out or reverse the incorrect account(s) and insert the correct account(s). The correcting entry must include an explanation.

 PRACTICE EXERCISE 5

On July 9, a $380 payment for Supplies was incorrectly journalized and posted as a debit to Supplies Expense for $380 and a credit to Cash for $380. Provide the correcting entry following the one-step method.

PRACTICE EXERCISE 5 • SOLUTION

		GENERAL JOURNAL			Page 1	
Date		Description	Post. Ref.	Debit	Credit	
20--						
July	9	Supplies		3 8 0 00		
		Supplies Expense			3 8 0 00	
		To correct error of July 9				
		in which a payment for Supplies				
		was debited to Supplies Expense.				

Glossary

Cost principle The principle that a purchased asset should be recorded at its actual cost. (*p. 101*)

Cross-reference The ledger account number in the Post. Ref. column of the journal and the journal page number in the Post. Ref. column of the ledger account. (*p. 106*)

General ledger A book or file containing the activity (by accounts), either manual or computerized, of a business. (*p. 104*)

Journal The book in which a person makes the original record of a business transaction; commonly referred to as a *book of original entry*. (*p. 97*)

Journalizing The process of recording a business transaction in a journal. (*p. 98*)

Ledger account A complete record of the transactions recorded in an individual account. (*p. 104*)

Posting The process of transferring figures from the journal to the ledger accounts. (*p. 106*)

Source documents Business papers, such as checks, invoices, receipts, letters, and memos, that furnish proof that a transaction has taken place. (*p. 98*)

Two-column general journal A general journal in which there are two amount columns, one used for debit amounts and one used for credit amounts. (*p. 99*)

Quiz Yourself

_____ 1. A _____ is a book in which business transactions are recorded.
  a. journal
  b. ledger
  c. trial balance
  d. balance sheet

_____ 2. Transferring information from the journal to the ledger is called
  a. preparing the financial statements.
  b. journalizing.
  c. posting.
  d. tracking.

_____ 3. For a journal entry to be complete, it must contain
  a. the date.
  b. a debit entry.
  c. a credit entry.
  d. an explanation.
  e. all of the above.

_____ 4. The _____ is used to determine where the amount in the ledger comes from.
  a. debit amount
  b. posting reference (or cross-reference)
  c. journal
  d. none of the above

_____ 5. Which of the following is an example of source documents?
  a. Canceled checks
  b. Vendor invoices
  c. Receipts
  d. All of the above

_____ 6. A $250 payment for salaries expense was incorrectly journalized and posted as a debit to Salaries Expense for $2,500 and a credit to Cash for $2,500. Using the one-step method, how would the entry be corrected?

a. Cash	2,500	
Salaries Expense		2,500
b. Salaries Expense	250	
Cash		250
c. Cash	2,250	
Salaries Expense		2,250
d. Salaries Expense	2,250	
Cash		2,250

Answers:
1. a 2. c 3. e 4. b 5. d 6. c

Chapter Assignments

Discussion Questions

1. Why is the journal called a book of original entry?
2. How does the journal differ from the ledger?
3. What is the purpose of providing a ledger account for each account?
4. List by account classification the order of the accounts in the general ledger.
5. Arrange the following steps in the posting process in correct order:
   a. Write the ledger account number in the Post. Ref. column of the journal.
   b. Write the amount of the transaction.
   c. Write the date of the transaction.
   d. Write the page number of the journal in the Post. Ref. column of the ledger account.
6. What does cross-referencing mean in the posting process?
7. Why is a source document important? List some examples of source documents.

Exercises

EXERCISE 3-1 In the following two-column journal, the capital letters represent where parts of a journal entry appear. Write the numbers 1 through 8 on a sheet of paper. After each number, match the capital letter where these items appear with the number of the item. (Not all letters will be used.)

GENERAL JOURNAL					Page 1
Date	Description	Post. Ref.	Debit		Credit
G					
H I	J	O	M		
	K	P			N
	L				

1. Year	4. Title of account debited	6. Amount of debit
2. Month	5. Ledger account number of account credited	7. Day of the month
3. Explanation		8. Title of account credited

EXERCISE 3-2 Decor Services completed the following transactions. Journalize the transactions in general journal form, including brief explanations.

Oct.   7   Received cash on account from Randy Hill, a customer, Inv. No. 312, $970.
       15   Paid on account to Miller Ideas, a creditor, $725, Ck. No. 2242.
       20   B. Brown, the owner, withdrew cash for personal use, $1,200, Ck. No. 2243.
       23   Bought store supplies for $150 and office supplies for $70 on account from Williams Office Supply, Inv. No. 1040.
       29   B. Brown, the owner, invested $3,000 cash and $1,500 of his personal equipment.

EXERCISE 3-3 Montoya Tutoring Service completed the following transactions. Journalize the transactions in general journal form, including brief explanations.

Mar.   1   Bought equipment for $5,798 from Teaching Suppliers, paying $3,798 in cash and placing the balance on account, Ck. No. 3230.
       10   Paid the wages for the first week of March, $1,536, Ck. No. 3231.
       15   Sold services for cash to Mason District, $1,481, Sales Inv. 121.
       26   Sold services on account to Tempe School, $1,400, Sales Inv. 122.
       31   Paid on account to Teaching Suppliers, $725, Ck. No. 3232.

EXERCISE 3-4 The following February journal entries all involved cash.

Increases to Cash—Debits		Decreases to Cash—Credits	
2/1	6,400	2/3	640
2/9	1,748	2/6	952
2/16	4,600	2/12	1,200
2/21	980	2/25	3,842
2/28	5,900		

Post the amounts to the ledger account for Cash, Account No. 111. Assume that all transactions appeared on page 1 of the general journal.

EXERCISE 3-5 Arrange the following steps in the posting process in correct order:

a. The amount of the balance of the ledger account is recorded in the Debit Balance or Credit Balance column.
b. The amount of the transaction is recorded in the Debit or Credit column of the ledger account.
c. The ledger account number is recorded in the Post. Ref. column of the journal.
d. The date of the transaction is recorded in the Date column of the ledger account.
e. The page number of the journal is recorded in the Post. Ref. column of the ledger account.

Practice Exercise 2

Practice Exercise 3

EXERCISE 3-6 The bookkeeper for Nevado Company has prepared the following trial balance:

Nevado Company Trial Balance June 30, 20--		
Account Name	**Debit**	**Credit**
Cash		2,500
Accounts Receivable	8,300	
Supplies	600	
Prepaid Insurance	650	
Equipment	15,300	
Accounts Payable		2,700
M. Nevado, Capital		12,500
M. Nevado, Drawing	4,890	
Professional Fees		17,540
Rent Expense	500	
Miscellaneous Expense	1,800	
	32,040	35,240

The bookkeeper has asked for your help. In examining the company's journal and ledger, you discover the following errors. Use this information to construct a corrected trial balance.

a. The debits to the Cash account total $8,000, and the credits total $3,300.
b. A $500 payment to a creditor was entered in the journal correctly but was not posted to the Accounts Payable account.
c. The first two numbers in the balance of the Accounts Receivable account were transposed when the balance was copied from the ledger to the trial balance.
d. The $1,500 amount withdrawn by the owner for personal use was debited to Miscellaneous Expense by mistake—it was correctly credited to Cash.

Practice Exercise 5

EXERCISE 3-7 Determine the effect of the following errors on a company's total revenue, total expenses, and net income. Indicate the effect by writing O for Overstated (too much), U for Understated (too little), or NA for Not Affected.

Transactions	Total Revenue	Total Expenses	Net Income
Example: A check for $325 was written to pay on account. The accountant debited Rent Expense for $325 and credited Cash for $325.	NA	O	U
a. $615 was received on account from customers. The accountant debited Cash for $615 and credited Professional Fees for $615.			

(*Continued*)

Transactions	Total Revenue	Total Expenses	Net Income

b. The owner withdrew $1,500 for personal use. The accountant debited Salary Expense for $1,500 and credited Cash for $1,500.

c. A check was written for $1,265 to pay the rent. The accountant debited Rent Expense for $1,625 and credited Cash for $1,625.

d. $2,100 was received on account from customers. The accountant debited Cash for $2,100 and credited the Capital account for $2,100.

e. A check was written for $525 to pay the phone bill received and recorded earlier in the month. The accountant debited Phone Expense for $525 and credited Cash for $525.

LO 5

EXERCISE 3-8 Journalize correcting entries for each of the following errors and include a brief explanation.

a. A cash purchase of office equipment for $680 was journalized as a cash purchase of store equipment for $680. (Use the ruling method; assume that the entry has not been posted.)

b. An entry for a $180 payment for office supplies was journalized as $810. (Use the ruling method; assume that the entry has not been posted.)

c. A $620 payment for repairs was journalized and posted as a debit to Equipment instead of a debit to Repair Expense. (Use the correcting entry method to journalize the correction.)

d. A $750 bill for vehicle insurance was received and immediately paid. It was journalized and posted as $660. (Use the correcting entry method to journalize the correction.)

Problem Set A

LO 1

PROBLEM 3-1A The chart of accounts of the Barnes School is shown here, followed by the transactions that took place during October of this year.

Assets
111 Cash
113 Accounts Receivable
115 Prepaid Insurance
124 Equipment
127 Furniture

Liabilities
221 Accounts Payable

Owner's Equity
311 R. Barnes, Capital
312 R. Barnes, Drawing

Revenue
411 Tuition Income

Expenses
511 Salary Expense
512 Rent Expense
513 Gas and Oil Expense
514 Advertising Expense
515 Repair Expense
516 Telephone Expense
517 Utilities Expense
529 Miscellaneous Expense

Oct.	1	Bought liability insurance for one year, $1,850, Ck. No. 1527.
	3	Received a bill for advertising from *Business Summary*, $415.
	4	Paid the rent for the current month, $1,870, Ck. No. 1528.
	7	Received a bill for equipment repair from Fix-It Service, $318, Inv. No. 436.
	10	Received and deposited tuition from students, $6,375.
	11	Received and paid the telephone bill $312, Ck. No. 1529.
	15	Bought desks and chairs from The Oak Center, $1,980, paying $980 in cash and placing the balance on account, Ck. No. 1530.
	18	Paid on account to *Business Summary*, $415, Ck. No. 1531.
	21	R. Barnes withdrew $1,000 for personal use, Ck. No. 1532.
	24	Received a bill for gas and oil from Wagner Oil Company, $225, Inv. No. 682.
	25	Received and deposited tuition from students, $6,380.
	27	Paid the salary of the part-time office assistant, $1,150. Ck. No. 1533.
	28	Bought a photocopier on account from Gorst Office Machines, $1,950, Inv. No. 417.
	29	Received $950 tuition from a student who had charged the tuition on account in September.
	30	Received and paid the bill for utilities, $623, Ck. No. 1534.
	31	Paid for flower arrangements for front office, $87, Ck. No. 1535.
	31	R. Barnes invested his personal computer and printer, with a fair market value of $1,549, in the business.

Required

Record these transactions in the general journal, including a brief explanation for each entry. If you are using working papers, number the journal pages 31 and 32.

Check Figure
Equipment increased by
$3,499 in October

LO 2, 3

PROBLEM 3-2A The journal entries for August, Carley's Car Care's second month of business, have been journalized in the general journal in the Working Papers and in CengageNow. The balances of the accounts as of July 31 have been recorded in the general ledger in the Working Papers and in CengageNow. Notice the word *Balance* in the Item column, the check mark in the Post. Ref. column, and the fact that the amount is in the Balance column only. This indicates a balance brought forward from a prior page or month.

Required

1. If you are using working papers, write the owner's name, M. Carley, in the Capital and Drawing accounts.
2. Post the general journal entries to the general ledger accounts.
3. Prepare a trial balance as of August 31, 20--.
4. Prepare an income statement for the two months ended August 31, 20--.
5. Prepare a statement of owner's equity for the two months ended August 31, 20--.
6. Prepare a balance sheet as of August 31, 20--.

Check Figure
Net Income. $11,649

LO 1, 2, 3

PROBLEM 3-3A Following is the chart of accounts of the C. Lucern Clinic:

Assets
111 Cash
113 Accounts Receivable
115 Supplies
117 Prepaid Insurance
124 Equipment

Revenue
411 Professional Fees

Expenses
511 Salary Expense
512 Rent Expense
513 Laboratory Expense
514 Utilities Expense

(Continued)

Liabilities

221 Accounts Payable

Owner's Equity

311 C. Lucern, Capital

312 C. Lucern, Drawing

Dr. Lucern completed the following transactions during July:

July	1	Bought laboratory equipment on account from Laser Surgical Supply Company, $3,660, paying $1,660 in cash and placing the remainder on account, Ck. No. 1730.
	3	Paid the office rent for the current month, $1,300, Ck. No. 1731.
	5	Received cash on account from patients, $360.
	6	Bought supplies on account from McRae Supply Company, $315, Inv. No. 3455.
	7	Received and paid the bill for laboratory services, $1,380, Ck. No. 1732.
	8	Bought insurance for one year, $2,650, Ck. No. 1733.
	12	Performed medical services for patients on account, $5,886.
	15	Performed medical services for patients for cash, $4,793.
	16	The equipment purchased on July 1 was found to be broken. Dr. Lucern returned the damaged part and received a reduction in his bill, $518, Inv. No. 3162, Credit Memo No. 141.
	18	Paid the salary of the part-time nurse, $2,100, Ck. No. 1734.
	24	Received and paid the telephone bill for the month, $624, Ck. No. 1735.
	28	Performed medical services for patients on account, $7,381.
	29	Dr. Lucern withdrew cash for his personal use, $2,000, Ck. No. 1736.

Check Figure

Trial balance total, $62,679

Required

1. Journalize the transactions for July in the general journal. If you are using working papers, number the pages beginning with page 21.
2. If you are using working papers, write the name of the owner next to the Capital and Drawing accounts in the general ledger. The balances of the accounts as of June 30 have been recorded in the general ledger in the Working Papers and in Cengage-Now. Notice the word *Balance* in the Item column, the check mark in the Post. Ref. column, and the fact that the amount is in the Balance column only. This indicates a balance brought forward from a prior page or month.
3. Post the entries to the general ledger accounts.
4. Prepare a trial balance.

LO **1, 2, 3** ···

CLGL

PROBLEM 3-4A Lara's Landscaping Service has the following chart of accounts:

Assets

111 Cash

113 Accounts Receivable

115 Supplies

117 Prepaid Insurance

124 Equipment

Liabilities

221 Accounts Payable

Owner's Equity

311 J. Lara, Capital

312 J. Lara, Drawing

Revenue

411 Landscaping Income

Expenses

511 Salary Expense

512 Rent Expense

513 Gas and Oil Expense

514 Utilities Expense

The following transactions were completed by Lara's Landscaping Service:

Mar. 1 Lara deposited $35,000 in a bank account in the name of the business.

4 Lara invested his personal landscaping equipment, with a fair market value of $1,325, in the business.

6 Bought a used trailer on account from Tow Sales, $915, Inv. No. 314.

7 Paid the rent for the current month, $950, Ck. No. 1000.

9 Bought a used backhoe from Digger's Equipment, $5,300, paying $3,000 in cash and placing the balance on account, Inv. No. 4166, Ck. No. 1001.

10 Bought liability insurance for one year, $1,800, Ck. No. 1002.

13 Sold landscaping services on account to Fredkey's, $3,895, Inv. No. 100.

14 Bought supplies on account from Office Requip, $380, Inv. No. 5172.

15 Sold landscaping services on account to C. Endel, $2,832, Inv. No. 101.

17 Received and paid the bill from Commercial Services for gas and oil for the equipment, $180, Ck. No. 1003.

19 Sold landscaping services for cash to Riston Company, $1,864, Inv. No. 102.

22 Paid on account to Tow Sales, $500, Inv. No. 314, Ck. No. 1004.

24 Received on account from Fredkey's, $800, Inv. No. 100.

28 Sold landscaping services on account to Stevens, Inc., $1,830, Inv. No. 103.

29 Received and paid the telephone bill, $260, Ck. No. 1005.

30 Paid the salary of the employee, $1,850, Ck. No. 1006.

31 Lara withdrew cash for his personal use, $1,500, Ck. No. 1007.

Required

1. Journalize the transactions in the general journal. Provide a brief explanation for each entry.
2. If you are using working papers, write the name of the owner on the Capital and Drawing accounts. (Skip this step if you are using CLGL.)
3. Post the journal entries to the general ledger accounts. (Skip this step if you are using CLGL.)
4. Prepare a trial balance dated March 31, 20--.

*If you are using CLGL, use the year 2020 when recording transactions and preparing reports.

Check Figure
Trial balance total,
$49,841

LO **1, 2, 3**

PROBLEM 3-5A Following is the chart of accounts of Sanchez Realty Company:

Assets
111 Cash
113 Accounts Receivable
115 Supplies
117 Prepaid Insurance
124 Office Furniture

Liabilities
221 Accounts Payable

Owner's Equity
311 T. Sanchez, Capital
312 T. Sanchez, Drawing

Revenue
411 Professional Fees

Expenses
511 Salary Expense
512 Rent Expense
513 Advertising Expense
514 Utilities Expense

Sanchez completed the following transactions during April (the first month of business):

Apr. 1 Sanchez deposited $20,000 in a bank account in the name of the business.

5 Sold realty services on account to R. Miller, $7,500, Inv. No. 100.

7 Paid a bill for advertising, $250, Ck. No. 1001.

(Continued)

Apr.   8   Bought supplies on account from Taylor Supply, $420, Inv. No. 2340.
       9   Performed realty services for clients for cash, $2,530.
      15   Received and paid the bill for utilities, $280, Ck. No. 1002.
      17   Bought a desk and chair from Lewis Furniture, $1,800, paying $300 in cash and placing the balance on account, Ck. No. 1003.
      20   Bought liability insurance for one year, $1,800, Ck. No. 1004.
      21   Paid the rent for the current month, $1,000, Ck. No. 1005.
      25   Paid on account to Taylor Supply, $420, for supplies purchased on April 8, Ck. No. 1006.
      27   Received $7,500 from R. Miller for services performed on April 5.
      28   Received and paid the telephone bill for the month, $150, Ck. No. 1007.
      29   Paid the salary of the office assistant, $1,030, Ck. No. 1008.
      30   Sanchez withdrew cash for his personal use, $3,000, Ck. No. 1009.

Check Figure
Trial balance total,
$31,530

Required

1. Journalize the transactions for April in the general journal.
2. Post the entries to the general ledger accounts. (Skip this step if you are using CLGL.)
3. Prepare a trial balance as of April 30, 20--.
4. Prepare an income statement for the month ended April 30, 20--.
5. Prepare a statement of owner's equity for the month ended April 30, 20--.
6. Prepare a balance sheet as of April 30, 20--.

*If you are using CLGL, use the year 2020 when preparing all reports.

Problem Set B

LO 1

PROBLEM 3-1B   The chart of accounts of Ethan Academy is shown here, followed by the transactions that took place during December of this year.

Assets
111 Cash
113 Accounts Receivable
114 Supplies
115 Prepaid Insurance
124 Equipment
127 Furniture

Liabilities
221 Accounts Payable

Owner's Equity
311 R. Ethan, Capital
312 R. Ethan, Drawing

Revenue
411 Tuition Income

Expenses
511 Salary Expense
512 Rent Expense
513 Gas and Oil Expense
514 Advertising Expense
515 Repair Expense
516 Telephone Expense
517 Utilities Expense
529 Miscellaneous Expense

Dec.   1   Bought liability insurance for one year, $2,260, Ck. No. 1627.
      11   Received a bill for advertising from the *City News*, $415, Statement No. 4267.
      12   Paid the rent for the current month, $1,850, Ck. No. 1628.
      13   Received a bill for equipment repair from Electronic Services, $345, Inv. No. 547.
      16   Received and deposited tuition from students, $5,850.
      17   Received and paid the telephone bill, $305, Ck. No. 1629.

Dec. 18   Bought desks and chairs from School Furniture, $1,625, paying $625 in cash and placing the balance on account, Ck. No. 1630.

     20   Paid on account to the *City News,* $415, Statement No. 4267, Ck. No. 1631.

     21   R. Ethan withdrew $1,000 for personal use, Ck. No. 1632.

     26   Received a bill for gas and oil from Discount Oil Company, $210, Inv. No. 591.

     27   Received and deposited tuition from students, $6,045.

     31   Paid the salary of the office assistant, $1,375, Ck. No. 1633.

     31   Bought a fax machine on account from EquipCo, $118, Inv. No. 529.

     31   Received $1,150 tuition from a student who had charged the tuition on account last month.

     31   Received and paid the bill for utilities, $470, Ck. No. 1634.

     31   R. Ethan invested her personal computer and printer, with a fair market value of $1,150, in the business.

     31   Bought supplies, $295, Ck. No. 1635.

Required

Record these transactions in the general journal, including a brief explanation for each entry. If you are using working papers, number the journal pages 31 and 32.

Check Figure
Equipment increased by $1,268 in December

PROBLEM 3-2B The journal entries for May, Kiddy Day Care's second month of business, have been journalized in the general journal in the Working Papers and in CengageNow. The balances of the accounts as of April 30 have been recorded in the general ledger in the Working Papers and in CengageNow. Notice the word *Balance* in the Item column, the check mark in the Post. Ref. column, and the fact that the amount is in the Balance column only. This indicates a balance brought forward from a prior page or month.

Required

1. If you are using working papers, write the owner's name, R. Ramirez, in the Capital and Drawing accounts.
2. Post the general journal entries to the general ledger accounts.
3. Prepare a trial balance as of May 31, 20--.
4. Prepare an income statement for the two months ended May 31, 20--.
5. Prepare a statement of owner's equity for the two months ended May 31, 20--.
6. Prepare a balance sheet as of May 31, 20--.

Check Figure
Net Income, $12,261

PROBLEM 3-3B Following is the chart of accounts of Vance Rehab Clinic:

Assets
111 Cash
113 Accounts Receivable
115 Supplies
117 Prepaid Insurance
124 Equipment

Liabilities
221 Accounts Payable

Owner's Equity
311 J. Vance, Capital
312 J. Vance, Drawing

Revenue
411 Professional Fees

Expenses
511 Salary Expense
512 Rent Expense
513 Laboratory Expense
514 Utilities Expense

(Continued)

Vance completed the following transactions during July:

July 1 Bought laboratory equipment on account from Sage Surgical Supply Company, $6,520, paying $1,520 in cash and placing the remainder on account, Inv. No. 2071, Ck. No. 1930.

3 Paid the office rent for the current month, $1,550, Ck. No. 1931.

5 Received cash on account from patients, $3,045.

6 Bought supplies on account from Allround Supply, $320, Inv. No. 3455.

9 Received and paid the bill for laboratory services, $1,484, Ck. No. 1932.

10 Bought insurance for one year, $2,600, Ck. No. 1933.

12 Performed rehab services for patients on account, $5,185.

14 Performed rehab services for patients for cash, $5,050.

18 Part of the equipment purchased on July 1 was found to be broken. Vance returned the damaged part and received a reduction in her bill, $410, Inv. No. 2071, Credit Memo No. 218.

20 Paid the salary of the part-time nurse, $2,200, Ck. No. 1934.

22 Received and paid the telephone bill for the month, $380, Ck. No. 1935.

24 Performed rehab services for patients on account, $4,235.

30 Vance withdrew cash for her personal use, $2,000, Ck. No. 1936.

Check Figure
Trial balance total, $46,028

Required

1. Journalize the transactions for July in the general journal. If you are using working papers, number the pages beginning with 21.

2. If you are using working papers, write the name of the owner next to the Capital and Drawing accounts in the general ledger. The balances of the accounts as of June 30 have been recorded in the general ledger in the Working Papers and in CengageNow. Notice the word *Balance* in the Item column, the check mark in the Post. Ref. column, and the fact that the amount is in the Balance column only. This indicates a balance brought forward from a prior page or month.

3. Post the entries to the general ledger accounts.

4. Prepare a trial balance.

LO 1, 2, 3 •••

PROBLEM 3-4B Leander's Landscaping Service maintains the following chart of accounts:

Assets
111 Cash
113 Accounts Receivable
117 Prepaid Insurance
124 Equipment

Liabilities
221 Accounts Payable

Owner's Equity
311 O. Leander, Capital
312 O. Leander, Drawing

Revenue
411 Landscaping Income

Expenses
511 Salary Expense
512 Rent Expense
513 Gas and Oil Expense
514 Utilities Expense
515 Supplies Expense

The following transactions were completed by Leander:

Apr. 1 Leander deposited $30,000 in a bank account in the name of the business.

4 Leander invested his personal landscaping equipment, with a fair market value of $1,750, in the business.

6 Bought a used trailer on account from Used Mart, $1,450, Inv. No. 415.

Apr.   7   Paid the rent for the current month, $925, Ck. No. 100.

       9   Bought a used bulldozer from Dray's Equipment, $5,100, paying $2,100 in cash and placing the balance on account, Inv. No. 3255, Ck. No. 101.

      10   Bought liability insurance for one year, $2,800, Ck. No. 102.

      13   Sold landscaping services on account to Fulton Homes, $4,595, Inv. No. 100.

      14   Bought supplies on account from Perry's Supply, $427, Inv. No. 4281.

      15   Sold landscaping services on account to D. D. Mau Inc., $3,997, Inv. No. 101.

      17   Received and paid the bill from Pumpers for gas and oil for the equipment, $227, Ck. No. 103.

      19   Sold landscaping services for cash to Cliff's House, $1,437, Inv. No. 102.

      22   Paid on account to Used Mart, $450, Inv. No. 415, Ck. No. 104.

      24   Received on account from Fulton Homes, $800, Inv. No. 100.

      28   Sold landscaping services on account to H. Ron, $1,785, Inv. No. 103.

      29   Received and paid the telephone bill, $321, Ck. No. 105.

      30   Paid the salary of the employee, $1,836, Ck. No. 106.

      30   Leander withdrew cash for his personal use, $1,500, Ck. No. 107.

Required

1. Journalize the transactions in the general journal. Prepare a brief explanation for each entry.

2. If you are using working papers, write the name of the owner on the Capital and Drawing accounts.

3. Post the journal entries to the general ledger accounts. (Skip this step if you are using CLGL.)

4. Prepare a trial balance dated April 30, 20--.

*If you are using CLGL, use the year 2020 when recording transactions and preparing reports.

Check Figure
Trial balance total, $47,991

LO **1, 2, 3**

PROBLEM 3-5B Following is the chart of accounts of Smith Financial Services:

Assets
111 Cash
113 Accounts Receivable
115 Supplies
117 Prepaid Insurance
124 Office Furniture

Liabilities
221 Accounts Payable

Owner's Equity
311 A. Smith, Capital
312 A. Smith, Drawing

Revenue
411 Professional Fees

Expenses
511 Salary Expense
512 Rent Expense
513 Advertising Expense
514 Utilities Expense

Smith completed the following transactions during June (the first month of business):

June   1   Smith deposited $10,000 in a bank account in the name of the business.

       3   Sold financial services on account to W. Johnson, $3,030, Inv. No. 001.

       8   Paid a bill for advertising, $100, Ck. No. 200.

       9   Bought supplies on account from Jones Supply, $75, Inv. No. 405.

      13   Performed financial services for clients for cash, $3,200.

      17   Received and paid the bill for utilities, $104, Ck. No. 201.

      19   Bought a desk and chair from Davis Furniture, $600, paying $50 in cash and placing the balance on account, Ck. No. 202.

(Continued)

June 20   Bought liability insurance for one year, $600, Ck. No. 203.
      23   Paid the rent for the current month, $400, Ck. No. 204.
      27   Paid on account to Jones Supply, $75, for supplies purchased on June 9, Ck. No. 205.
      29   Received $3,030 from W. Johnson for services performed on June 3.
      29   Received and paid the telephone bill for the month, $80, Ck. No. 206.
      30   Paid the salary of the office assistant, $600, Ck. No. 207.
      30   Smith withdrew cash for her personal use, $800, Ck. No. 208.

Check Figure
Trial balance total,
$16,780

Required

1. Journalize the transactions for June in the general journal.
2. Post the entries to the general ledger accounts. (Skip this step if you are using CLGL.)
3. Prepare a trial balance as of June 30, 20--.
4. Prepare an income statement for the month ended June 30, 20--.
5. Prepare a statement of owner's equity for the month ended June 30, 20--.
6. Prepare a balance sheet as of June 30, 20--.

*If you are using CLGL, use the year 2020 when recording transactions and preparing reports.

Accounting with QuickBooks® Online

Go to the QuickBooks Online Chapter 3 Appendix located on the Cengage Learning companion site at Cengage.com. Review the *Accounting with QuickBooks Online* (step-by-step guide to using QuickBooks Online). *Accounting with QuickBooks Online,* Chapter 3, will introduce you to preparing journal entries to reflect checkbook entries, record purchases on account, and record sales on account. Additionally, you will prepare a trial balance, income statement, and balance sheet.

Activities

Why Does It Matter?

ECOTOUR EXPEDITIONS, INC., Jamestown, Rhode Island

You probably have never imagined the possibility of being an accountant who could have a direct impact on improving global ecosystems. Accountants who work for Ecotour Expeditions, Inc., an ecotourism company, might manage accounting details for guest air travel and accommodations, tour guide compensation, expedition

(Continued)

revenue, and a variety of expenses. What type of accounting transactions would Ecotour Expeditions have? List 3 to 4 transactions and then record the journal entry for each transaction.

Example: *Purchase safari jeep with cash, $42,500.*

Safari Jeep	42,500	
Cash		42,500

What Would You Say?

You are the new bookkeeper for a small business. The bookkeeper whose job you are taking is training you on the business's manual system. As he journalizes, he writes the account number in the Post. Ref. column because he believes it's easier. His thinking is that, when he posts, he won't be bothered writing the account numbers. How would you explain why he should *not* write the account number in the Post. Ref. column immediately and instead should enter the account number after he has posted the amount to the ledger?

What Do You Think?

You work as an accounting clerk. You have received the following information supplied by a client, S. Winston, from the client's bank statement, the client's tax returns, and a variety of other July documents. The client wants you to prepare an income statement, a statement of owner's equity, and a balance sheet for the month of July for Winston Company.

Income from Services	$ 9,570	Utilities Expense	$ 388
Beginning Capital	50,000	Drawing	2,500
Cash	24,940	Supplies	635
Truck	?	Equipment	16,148
Accounts Payable	?	Total Liabilities and Owner's	
Rent Expense	1,200	Equity	57,473
Wages Expense	4,200		

What Would You Do?

You are responsible for preparing all of the journal entries for Regional Financial Services. You have correctly prepared the following entry for financial services provided on December 15:

Dec. 15	Cash	10,000	
	Fees Earned		10,000

Your boss has asked you to change the date from December 15 to January 15 so that the business's profit, and thus taxes, would be lower. Are you allowed to do this? What is your response to your boss? How should you handle this situation?

Before a Test Check: Chapters 1–3

PART I: Multiple-Choice Questions

_____ **1.** Which of the following is not considered an account?
a. Cash
b. Prepaid Insurance
c. Equipment
d. Assets
e. Accounts Receivable

_____ **2.** In which of the following transactions would an expense be recorded?
a. Received a bill for advertising.
b. Paid on an account payable for the utility bill.
c. Received and paid a bill for repairs.
d. All of these should be recorded as an expense.
e. Only a and c should be recorded as an expense.

_____ **3.** The ending capital balance appears on which of the following statements?
a. Statement of owner's equity
b. Balance sheet
c. Income statement
d. Statement of owner's equity and balance sheet
e. Statement of owner's equity and income statement

_____ **4.** On a statement of owner's equity, if beginning capital is $42,000 and there is an additional investment of $5,000, a net loss of $9,000, and owner withdrawals of $15,000, the ending capital amount would be
a. $70,000.
b. $23,000.
c. $40,000.
d. $54,000.
e. none of these.

_____ **5.** If a $260 payment of rent is recorded as a $620 debit to Rent Expense and a $620 credit to Cash, what will the result be?
a. The trial balance will be in balance.
b. The Rent Expense account will be overstated.
c. The Cash account will be understated.
d. Rent Expense will be overstated and Cash will be understated.
e. All of the above are true.

_____ **6.** A person who wanted to know the balance of an account would look in
a. the ledger.
b. the chart of accounts.
c. the journal.
d. the source documents.
e. none of these.

PART II: The Accounting Cycle
Journalizing, Posting, Trial Balance, and Financial Statements

The accounts and their balances as of December 1 of this year for Antec Services are as follows:

111 Cash	$18,900		311 J. Dunn, Capital	$49,590
113 Accounts Receivable	6,300		312 J. Dunn, Drawing	11,200
115 Supplies	870			
116 Prepaid Insurance	1,230		411 Service Income	39,600
124 Equipment	31,200			
			511 Wages Expense	10,450
221 Accounts Payable	6,340		512 Utilities Expense	2,760
			513 Rent Expense	12,620

Check Figure
Net Income,
$22,315

Required

1. Journalize the following December transactions in general journal form on journal page 31.

Dec.   1   Sold services for cash, $9,500.
         4   Received and paid the bill for the rent for December, $1,000, Ck. No. 2331.

(Continued)

Dec. 11 Received $1,750 on account from customers, Cash Receipt Nos. 1430–1438.
    19 Sold services on account, $2,075, Sales Inv. No. 2591.
    22 Received and paid the bill for utilities, $255, Ck. No. 2332.
    23 Bought supplies on account from Office Works, $292, Inv. No. 2606.
    31 Paid the wages for the month, $1,775, Ck. No. 2333.
    31 Dunn withdrew $1,500 for personal use, Ck. No. 2334.

2. Label T accounts with the above account names.
3. Correctly place the plus and minus signs under all T accounts and label the debit and credit sides of each T account.
4. Post the entries to the T accounts by date and foot and balance the accounts.
5. Prepare a trial balance as of December 31.
6. Prepare an income statement for the year ended December 31.
7. Prepare a statement of owner's equity for the year ended December 31.
8. Prepare a balance sheet as of December 31.

Answers: Part I

1. d **2.** e **3.** d **4.** b **5.** e **6.** a

Answers: Part II

1.

GENERAL JOURNAL   Page 3

Date		Description	Post. Ref.	Debit	Credit
20--					
Dec.	1	Cash	111	9 5 0 0 00	
		Service Income	411		9 5 0 0 00
		Sold services for cash.			
	4	Rent Expense	513	1 0 0 0 00	
		Cash	111		1 0 0 0 00
		Ck. No. 2331.			
	11	Cash	111	1 7 5 0 00	
		Accounts Receivable	113		1 7 5 0 00
		Cash on account from customers,			
		Cash Receipt Nos. 1430–1438.			
	19	Accounts Receivable	113	2 0 7 5 00	
		Service Income	411		2 0 7 5 00
		Sales Inv. No. 2591.			
	22	Utilities Expense	512	2 5 5 00	
		Cash	111		2 5 5 00
		Ck. No. 2332.			
	23	Supplies	115	2 9 2 00	
		Accounts Payable	221		2 9 2 00
		Office Works, Inv. No. 2606.			
	31	Wages Expense	511	1 7 7 5 00	
		Cash	111		1 7 7 5 00
		Paid month's wages, Ck. No. 2333.			
	31	J. Dunn, Drawing	312	1 5 0 0 00	
		Cash	111		1 5 0 0 00
		Ck. No. 2334.			

(Continued)

BEFORE A TEST CHECK

2., 3., and 4.

Owner's Equity

Assets = Liabilities + (Capital − Drawing + Revenue − Expenses)

Assets

Cash — 111

Debit (+)		Credit (−)	
Bal.	18,900	12/4	1,000
12/1	9,500	12/22	255
12/11	1,750	12/31	1,775
	30,150	12/31	1,500
			4,530
Bal. 25,620			

Accounts Receivable — 113

Debit (+)		Credit (−)	
Bal.	6,300	12/11	1,750
12/19	2,075		
	8,375		
Bal. 6,625			

Supplies — 115

Debit (+)		Credit (−)	
Bal.	870		
12/23	292		
Bal. 1,162			

Prepaid Insurance — 116

Debit (+)		Credit (−)	
Bal.	1,230		

Equipment — 124

Debit (+)		Credit (−)	
Bal.	31,200		

Liabilities

Accounts Payable — 221

Debit (−)		Credit (+)	
		Bal.	6,340
		12/23	292
		Bal. 6,632	

Capital

J. Dunn, Capital — 311

Debit (−)		Credit (+)	
		Bal. 49,590	

Drawing

J. Dunn, Drawing — 312

Debit (+)		Credit (−)	
Bal.	11,200		
12/31	1,500		
Bal. 12,700			

Revenue

Service Income — 411

Debit (−)		Credit (+)	
		Bal.	39,600
		12/1	9,500
		12/19	2,075
		Bal. 51,175	

Expenses

Wages Expense — 511

Debit (+)		Credit (−)	
Bal.	10,450		
12/31	1,775		
Bal. 12,225			

Utilities Expense — 512

Debit (+)		Credit (−)	
Bal.	2,760		
12/22	255		
Bal. 3,015			

Rent Expense — 513

Debit (+)		Credit (−)	
Bal.	12,620		
12/4	1,000		
Bal. 13,620			

(Continued)

5.

Antec Services Trial Balance December 31, 20--		
Account Name	**Debit**	**Credit**
Cash	25,620	
Accounts Receivable	6,625	
Supplies	1,162	
Prepaid Insurance	1,230	
Equipment	31,200	
Accounts Payable		6,632
J. Dunn, Capital		49,590
J. Dunn, Drawing	12,700	
Service Income		51,175
Wages Expense	12,225	
Utilities Expense	3,015	
Rent Expense	13,620	
	107,397	107,397

6.

Antec Services Income Statement For Year Ended December 31, 20--		
Revenue:		
Service Income		$51,175
Expenses:		
Wages Expense	$12,225	
Utilities Expense	3,015	
Rent Expense	13,620	
Total Expenses		28,860
Net Income		$22,315

7.

Antec Services Statement of Owner's Equity For Year Ended December 31, 20--		
J. Dunn, Capital, January 1, 20--		$49,590
Investments during Year	$ 0	
Net Income for Year	22,315	
Subtotal	$22,315	
Less Withdrawals for Year	12,700	
Increase in Capital		9,615
J. Dunn, Capital, December 31, 20--		$59,205

(Continued)

8.

Antec Services Balance Sheet December 31, 20--	
Assets	
Cash	$25,620
Accounts Receivable	6,625
Supplies	1,162
Prepaid Insurance	1,230
Equipment	31,200
Total Assets	$65,837
Liabilities	
Accounts Payable	$ 6,632
Owner's Equity	
J. Dunn, Capital	59,205
Total Liabilities and Owner's Equity	$65,837

Journalizing, Posting, and Preparing a Trial Balance

A friend of yours, Anika Valli, has decided to open a spa to serve her small resort town of about 7,000 people and 4 million tourists annually. She has named the business All About You Spa to convey the idea that the business intends to pamper those who enter its doors. She will operate the spa five days a week, Tuesday through Saturday, but a phone line will always be available to answer questions and schedule appointments. Hours will be from 8 A.M. to 8 P.M. She has asked you to be the bookkeeper for this new business. At the end of the month of October, the owner, Anika Valli, would like you to provide the following:

1. General journal
2. General ledger
3. Trial balance
4. Income statement
5. Statement of owner's equity
6. Balance sheet

She has kept a checkbook and a file folder with summary evidence of October's spa activity: a check register, a summary report of charges by customers for services provided, all receipts that were issued, and a summary of charges made by All About You Spa. Most of the income from services is received in cash and as charges to credit cards. No checks are accepted, except from approved clients (primarily conference planners and other organizations that book packages as prizes for attendees or gifts for employees, speakers, or other people they want to thank with a spa service or package of services). Anika deposits cash receipts on customer's accounts on the 7th, 14th, 21st, and last day of each month.

The first page in the file folder contains the following chart of accounts. Currently, you will not use or may not be familiar with some of the accounts listed here. Ignore those accounts for now; we will use them later.

CHART OF ACCOUNTS FOR ALL ABOUT YOU SPA

Assets
111 Cash
113 Accounts Receivable
114 Office Supplies
115 Spa Supplies
117 Prepaid Insurance
124 Office Equipment
125 Accum. Depr.—Office Equipment
128 Spa Equipment
129 Accum. Depr.—Spa Equipment

Liabilities
211 Accounts Payable
212 Wages Payable

Owner's Equity
311 A. Valli, Capital
312 A. Valli, Drawing
313 Income Summary

Revenue
411 Income from Services

Expenses
611 Wages Expense
612 Rent Expense
613 Office Supplies Expense
614 Spa Supplies Expense
615 Laundry Expense

616 Advertising Expense
617 Utilities Expense
618 Insurance Expense
619 Depr. Expense—Office Equipment
620 Depr. Expense—Spa Equipment
630 Promotional Expense

(Continued)

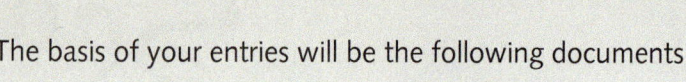

The basis of your entries will be the following documents:

Checkbook Entries
(Deposits made and checks written)

Check No.	Date	Explanation	√	Deposits	Check Amount
	10/1	Invested cash in business.		25,000.00	
2011	10/3	Bought 6-month liability insurance policy.			840.00
2012	10/3	Bought spa equipment from Spa Equipment, Inc., for $5,550, putting $3,000 cash down.			3,000.00
2013	10/3	Paid June rent.			1,000.00
2014	10/5	Bought office supplies.			230.00
2015	10/5	Purchased promotional items (flowers and balloons) for grand opening.			115.00
2016	10/7	Paid first week's wages.			2,075.00
	10/7	Deposited first week's cash revenue.		3,465.00	
2017	10/11	Paid on account payable for spa equipment (October 3).			1000.00
	10/14	Deposited second week's cash revenue.		3,307.00	
2018	10/14	Paid second week's wages.			2,075.00
2019	10/18	Paid on account for spa equipment (October 3).			1,200.00
	10/21	Deposited third week's cash revenue.		4,587.00	
2020	10/21	Paid third week's wages.			2,075.00
2021	10/25	Paid on account for spa equipment (October 3).			350.00
2022	10/28	Paid fourth week's wages.			2,075.00
2023	10/28	Paid month's laundry bill.			105.00
	10/31	Deposited end of month's cash revenue.		6,588.00	
2024	10/31	A. Valli withdrew $1,500 for personal use.			1,500.00
2025	10/31	Paid October telephone bill.			325.00
2026	10/31	Paid October power and water bill.			385.00

Other information that require journal entries:

Receipt	
10/1 A. Valli, owner of All About You Spa, invested her personal spa equipment	$3,575.00

(Continued)

All About You
Spa

October Accounts Payable Charges Summary Report

10/3 Bought spa supplies on account from Spa Supplies, Inc., Inv. No. 904	$685.00
10/5 Bought office equipment on account from Office Equipment Company, Inv. No. 4315	$520.00
10/5 Bought advertising pamphlets on account from Adco, Inc., Inv. No. 215	$415.00
10/5 Bought office equipment on account from Office Equipment, Company, Inv. No. 4445	$825.00
10/5 Bought office supplies on account from Office Staples, Inv. No. 222	$125.00

October Sales to Customers on Account Summary Report

10/7	Jill Anson	$350.00
10/14	Jack Morgan	$468.00
10/21	Tory Ligman	$345.00
10/31	Judy Wilcox	$110.00

Required

1. Journalize the transactions for October (in date order) in the general journal.
   — If you are using GL, review the instructions for the program on the textbook website. If you are preparing the journal entries manually, enter your transactions beginning on page 1.

2. Post the entries to the general ledger accounts.

   — Ignore this step if you are using CLGL.

3. Prepare a trial balance as of October 31, 20--.

4. Prepare an income statement for the month ended October 31, 20--.

5. Prepare a statement of owner's equity for the month ended October 31, 20--.

6. Prepare a balance sheet as of October 31, 20--.

*If you are using CLGL, use the year 2020 when recording journal entries and preparing reports.

Note: The trial balance and financial statements are unadjusted. In the next chapter, you will learn that certain accounts need to be adjusted. These adjustments will change some of the figures in these reports.

4

Adjusting Entries and the Work Sheet

Learning Objectives

After you have completed this chapter, you will be able to do the following:

1 *Define* fiscal period *and* fiscal year and explain the accounting cycle.

2 List the classifications of the accounts that occupy each column of a ten-column work sheet.

3 Complete a work sheet for a service enterprise, involving adjustments for supplies, expired insurance, depreciation, and accrued wages.

4 Journalize and post the adjusting entries.

5 Prepare an income statement, a statement of owner's equity, and a balance sheet for a service business directly from the work sheet. Prepare (a) an income statement involving more than one revenue account and a net loss, (b) a statement of owner's equity with an additional investment and either a net income or a net loss, and (c) a balance sheet for a business having more than one accumulated depreciation account.

To: **Amy Roberts, CPA**
Subject: **What's Next?**

Hi Amy,

I've recorded all of my transactions for the month of June. So now I need to prepare the financial statements for the bank—I'm thinking about applying for a loan. Am I ready to prepare the financial statements that the bank requested, because I have all of the transactions recorded?

Thanks,

Janie

To: **Janie Conner**
Subject: **RE: What's Next?**

Hi Janie,

One more step needs to take place before you can prepare the financial statements for the bank. You need to prepare and record adjusting entries. Adjusting entries update the accounts for any internal transactions that haven't yet been recorded, such as usage of supplies, expiration of prepaid insurance, and wages that are owed. Adjusting entries need to be recorded before you prepare the financial statements for the bank, to ensure that your accounts are up to date. The easiest way to learn how to prepare adjusting entries is by using a work sheet. This will also help you learn how to prepare the financial statements. So here's what you need to know before you're ready to prepare your financial statements for the bank:

_____ 1. Prepare a work sheet to help in recording adjusting entries

_____ 2. Record adjusting entries in the journal

Let me know if you need help!

Amy

iStockPhoto.com/asiseeit

As part of the *summarizing* step in the definition of accounting, we now introduce the work sheet and the financial statements. Now that you are familiar with the classifying and recording phases of accounting for a service business, let's look at the remaining steps in the accounting process.

4-1 FISCAL PERIOD

A **fiscal period** is any period of time covering a complete accounting cycle. A **fiscal year** is a fiscal period consisting of 12 consecutive months. It does not have to coincide with the calendar year. If a business has seasonal peaks, it is a good idea to complete the accounting operations at the end of the most active season. At that time, management wants to know what the results of the year are and where the business stands financially. The fiscal year of a resort that operates during the summer may be from October 1 of one year to September 30 of the next year. The government has a fiscal year from October 1 of one year to September 30 of the following year. Department stores often use a fiscal period from February 1 of one year to January 31 of the next year.

4-1a The Accounting Cycle

The **accounting cycle** represents the sequence of steps in the accounting process completed during the fiscal period. Figure 1 shows how we introduce these steps on a chapter-by-chapter basis. This outline brings you up to date on what we have accomplished so far, as well as what will be covered in Chapter 5, and how each chapter fits into the steps in the accounting cycle.

4-1b The Work Sheet

The **work sheet** is an optional working paper used by accountants, in a manual accounting system, to record necessary adjustments and provide up-to-date account balances needed to prepare the financial statements. **The work sheet is a tool that accountants use to help in preparing the financial statements.** As a tool, the work sheet serves as a central place for bringing together the information needed to

Accounting Language

Accounting cycle (p. 147)
Accrual (p. 155)
Accrued wages (p. 155)
Adjusting entries (p. 161)
Adjustments (p. 150)
Book value (carrying value) (p. 153)
Contra account (p. 152)
Depreciation (p. 151)
Fiscal period (p. 147)
Fiscal year (p. 147)
Matching principle (p. 161)
Mixed accounts (p. 155)
Straight-line depreciation (p. 152)
Work sheet (p. 147)

 1 *Define* fiscal period *and* fiscal year and explain the accounting cycle.

Learning Objective

Figure 1
The accounting cycle
by chapter

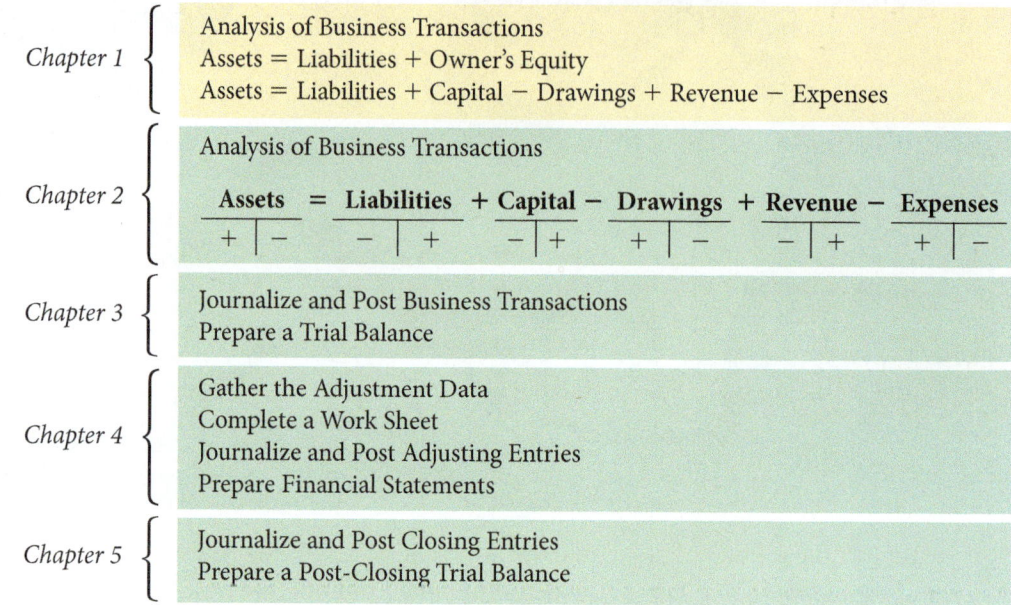

| Chapter 1 | Analysis of Business Transactions
Assets = Liabilities + Owner's Equity
Assets = Liabilities + Capital − Drawings + Revenue − Expenses |

Chapter 2

Analysis of Business Transactions

Assets	=	**Liabilities**	+	**Capital**	−	**Drawings**	+	**Revenue**	−	**Expenses**
+ | −		− | +		− | +		+ | −		− | +		+ | −

| Chapter 3 | Journalize and Post Business Transactions
Prepare a Trial Balance |

| Chapter 4 | Gather the Adjustment Data
Complete a Work Sheet
Journalize and Post Adjusting Entries
Prepare Financial Statements |

| Chapter 5 | Journalize and Post Closing Entries
Prepare a Post-Closing Trial Balance |

QuickBooks® Online Tip

When using accounting software or a cloud-based accounting application like QuickBooks Online, the work sheet is not needed.

Remember

Accounting steps:
Analyzing: *Which accounts are involved?*
Classifying: *assets, liabilities, capital, drawing, revenue, and expenses*
Recording: *journalizing*
Summarizing: *financial statements*
Interpreting: *drawing conclusions*

record the adjustments. With up-to-date account balances, the accountant can then prepare the financial statements.

First, we present the work sheet form so that you can see the big picture. Then, we describe and show examples of adjustments. Finally, we show how the adjustments are entered on the work sheet and how the work sheet is completed.

We will use a ten-column work sheet—so called because two amount columns are provided for each of the work sheet's five major sections. Work sheets are most often prepared using a spreadsheet program, such as Microsoft Excel®. We will explain the function of each of these sections, again basing our discussion on the accounting activities of Conner's Whitewater Adventures. But first we need to fill in the heading, which consists of three lines: (1) the name of the company, (2) the title of the working paper, and (3) the period of time covered.

	A	B	C	D	E	F	G	H	I	J	K
1					Conner's Whitewater Adventures						
2					Work Sheet						
3					For Month Ended June 30, 20--						
4											
5		TRIAL BALANCE		ADJUSTMENTS		ADJUSTED TRIAL BALANCE		INCOME STATEMENT		BALANCE SHEET	
6	ACCOUNT NAME	DEBIT	CREDIT	DEBIT	CREDIT	DEBIT	CREDIT	DEBIT	CREDIT	DEBIT	CREDIT
7											

Next, we want to point out the account classifications that are placed in each column. We start with the Trial Balance columns and then move across the work sheet, discussing each pair of columns separately.

4-2 THE COLUMNS OF THE WORK SHEET

TRIAL BALANCE COLUMNS

When you use a work sheet, you do not have to prepare a trial balance on a separate sheet of paper. Instead, you enter the account balances from the general ledger in the first two amount columns of the work sheet. List the accounts that have balances in the Account Name column in the same order in which they appear in the chart of accounts. Assuming **normal balances,** the amount of each account is listed in the Trial Balance Debit and Credit columns of the work sheet according to its classification, as shown on page 149.

Learning Objective

2 List the classifications of the accounts that occupy each column of a ten-column work sheet.

	A	B	C	D	E	F	G	H	I	J	K
					Conner's Whitewater Adventures						
					Work Sheet						
					For Month Ended June 30, 20--						
5		TRIAL BALANCE		ADJUSTMENTS		ADJUSTED TRIAL BALANCE		INCOME STATEMENT		BALANCE SHEET	
6	ACCOUNT NAME	DEBIT	CREDIT	DEBIT	CREDIT	DEBIT	CREDIT	DEBIT	CREDIT	DEBIT	CREDIT
7		Assets ———————————→				Assets					
8			Liabilities ———————→				Liabilities				
9			Capital ————————→				Capital				
10		Drawing ——————————→				Drawing					
11			Revenue ———————→				Revenue				
12		Expenses ————————→				Expenses					

As we move along in this chapter, we will discuss the adjustments. The Adjusted Trial Balance columns contain the same account classifications as the Trial Balance columns. **The Adjusted Trial Balance columns are merely extensions of the Trial Balance columns, plus or minus any adjustment amounts.** If an adjustment is required, the amounts are carried from the Trial Balance columns through the Adjustments columns and into the Adjusted Trial Balance columns.

INCOME STATEMENT COLUMNS

An income statement contains the revenues minus the expenses. Revenue accounts have credit balances, so they are recorded in the Income Statement Credit column. Expense accounts have debit balances, so they are recorded in the Income Statement Debit column.

	A	B	C	D	E	F	G	H	I	J	K
					Conner's Whitewater Adventures						
					Work Sheet						
					For Month Ended June 30, 20--						
5		TRIAL BALANCE		ADJUSTMENTS		ADJUSTED TRIAL BALANCE		INCOME STATEMENT		BALANCE SHEET	
6	ACCOUNT NAME	DEBIT	CREDIT	DEBIT	CREDIT	DEBIT	CREDIT	DEBIT	CREDIT	DEBIT	CREDIT
7		Assets ———————————→				Assets					
8			Liabilities ———————→				Liabilities				
9			Capital ————————→				Capital				
10		Drawing ——————————→				Drawing					
11			Revenue ———————→				Revenue ———————→		Revenue		
12		Expenses ————————→				Expenses ————————→		Expenses			

BALANCE SHEET COLUMNS

As you may recall, the balance sheet is a statement showing assets, liabilities, and owner's equity. Asset accounts have debit balances, so they are recorded in the Balance Sheet Debit column. Liability accounts have credit balances, so they are recorded in the Balance Sheet Credit column. The Capital account has a credit balance, so it is recorded in the Balance Sheet Credit column. Because the Drawing account is a deduction from Capital, it has a debit balance and is recorded in the Balance Sheet Debit column (the opposite column from that in which Capital is recorded).

	A	B	C	D	E	F	G	H	I	J	K
					Conner's Whitewater Adventures						
					Work Sheet						
					For Month Ended June 30, 20--						
5		TRIAL BALANCE		ADJUSTMENTS		ADJUSTED TRIAL BALANCE		INCOME STATEMENT		BALANCE SHEET	
6	ACCOUNT NAME	DEBIT	CREDIT	DEBIT	CREDIT	DEBIT	CREDIT	DEBIT	CREDIT	DEBIT	CREDIT
7		Assets ———————————→				Assets ———————————→				Assets	
8			Liabilities ———————→				Liabilities ———————→				Liabilities
9			Capital ————————→				Capital ————————→				Capital
10		Drawing ——————————→				Drawing ——————————→				Drawing	
11			Revenue ———————→				Revenue ———————→		Revenue		
12		Expenses ————————→				Expenses ————————→		Expenses			

4-3 ADJUSTMENTS

Adjustments are a way of updating the ledger accounts. They may be considered *internal transactions*. They have not been recorded in the accounts up to this time because no outside party has been involved. Adjustments are determined after the trial balance has been prepared. Adjustments fine-tune the accounts to present a more accurate report of the accounts.

Only a few accounts are adjusted. To describe the reasons for making adjustments, let's return to Conner's Whitewater Adventures. First, we select the accounts that require adjustments. Then, we show the adjustments recorded in T accounts so that you can see the effect on the accounts. **However, bear in mind that the adjustments**

The Financial Picture Before Adjustments

The Financial Picture After Adjustments

Without adjustments, the financial statements would be unclear.

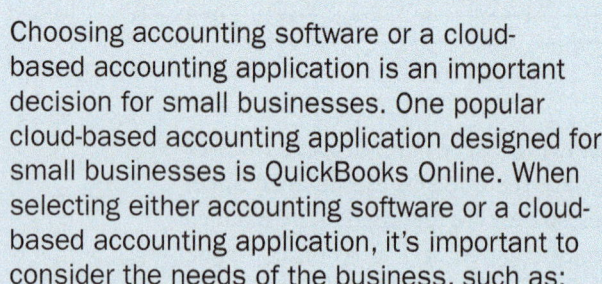

SMALL BUSINESS **SUCCESS**

Choosing Accounting Software or a Cloud-based Accounting Application

Choosing accounting software or a cloud-based accounting application is an important decision for small businesses. One popular cloud-based accounting application designed for small businesses is QuickBooks Online. When selecting either accounting software or a cloud-based accounting application, it's important to consider the needs of the business, such as:

- How many individuals will use the software or cloud-based application?
- What tools are available?
- Can the software or cloud-based application handle inventory?
- Is it easy to use?
- What is the cost?
- Can the software or cloud-based application be used from any type of computer or mobile device?

QuickBooks Online can handle most basic small business accounting transactions. This cloud-based application includes a general ledger, subsidiary ledgers, and financial statements. QuickBooks Online also has the ability to export data into Excel and Word. Differences in general ledger software packages and cloud-based accounting applications typically relate to their look and how transactions are entered. For example, QuickBooks Online uses a more *forms-based* approach, which is identified by different "centers," such as vendors, customers, employees, company, and banking.

It is highly recommended that all small business owners and accounting majors take at least one course in how to use accounting software and/or a cloud-based accounting application, such as QuickBooks Online. Knowledge of accounting cloud-based applications, such as QuickBooks Online, can easily be applied to other accounting software packages or cloud-based applications, and is a skill needed for success in the business world.

are first recorded on the work sheet when using a manual accounting system. When using general ledger software, adjustments are recorded in the general journal. The adjustments are made at the end of the company's accounting period—in the case of Conner's Whitewater Adventures, June 30.

4-3a Supplies

Remember that when a business buys supplies for cash or on credit, the supplies account is debited. An asset is recorded because the supplies have not yet been used. At the end of the accounting period, the amount of supplies that have been used during the period must be deducted from the Supplies account and added to Supplies Expense. During June, Conner's Whitewater Adventures purchased $675 of supplies. At the end of the time period, the company counted its supplies and determined that it had $215 worth of supplies remaining. Thus, $460 ($675 − $215) worth of supplies were used during the period. The amount used, $460, must be deducted from the Supplies account and added to the Supplies Expense account.

		Supplies					**Supplies Expense**	
		+	−				+	−
(Old)	Balance	675	**Adjusting**	460	**Adjusting**	460		
(New)	Balance	215						

Notice that the new balance of the Supplies account is the amount remaining, $215 ($675 − $460). The $460 amount in Supplies Expense represents the cost of supplies used during the time period.

4-3b Prepaid Insurance

The $1,875 balance in Prepaid Insurance represents the premium paid in advance for a three-month liability insurance policy. One month ($625) of the three months of premium has now expired.

$$\$1,875 \text{ premium} \div 3 \text{ months} = \$625 \text{ per month}$$

In the adjustment, Conner's Whitewater Adventures deducts the expired, or used, portion from Prepaid Insurance and adds it to Insurance Expense.

		Prepaid Insurance					**Insurance Expense**	
		+	−				+	−
(Old)	Balance	1,875	**Adjusting**	625	**Adjusting**	625		
(New)	Balance	1,250						

The new balance of Prepaid Insurance, $1,250 ($1,875 − $625), represents the cost of insurance that remains paid in advance and should therefore appear in the Balance Sheet Debit column. The $625 amount in Insurance Expense represents the cost of insurance that has expired and should appear in the Income Statement Debit column.

4-3c Depreciation of Equipment

We have recorded durable items, such as appliances and fixtures, under Equipment because they will last longer than one year. The benefits of these assets will eventually be used up. (The assets will either wear out or become obsolete.) Therefore, we should systematically spread the cost of these assets over their useful lives. That is, we allocate the cost of the equipment as an expense *over its estimated useful life* and call this **depreciation** because, over time, such equipment loses its usefulness. A part of this depreciation expense is allotted to each

> **Remember**
>
> For the adjustment of insurance, you are given the amount used (expired). So in the adjusting entry, take the amount used directly out of Prepaid Insurance and put it into Insurance Expense.

fiscal period. In the case of Conner's Whitewater Adventures, the Equipment account has a balance of $51,300. Suppose we estimate that the equipment will have a useful life of seven years, with a trade-in (salvage) value of $8,292 at the end of that time. Using **straight-line depreciation**, we can allocate the cost of an asset, less any trade-in value, evenly over the useful life of the asset. Depreciation for one month is figured like this:

STEP 1. Cost − Trade-in (salvage) value = Full depreciation
$51,300 − $8,292 = $43,008 full depreciation

STEP 2. Full depreciation ÷ Number of years in the asset's useful life = Depreciation for one year
$43,008 full depreciation ÷ 7 years = $6,144 per year

STEP 3. Depreciation for one year ÷ 12 = Depreciation for one month
$6,144 per year ÷ 12 months = $512 per month

When depreciation is recorded, we do not subtract it directly from the asset account. In asset accounts, such as Equipment and Building, we must keep the original cost recorded in the account. Instead, a **contra account** is used. Such accounts are contrary to, or deducted from, other accounts and are used to provide more information to financial statement users. In this case, the amount of depreciation must be recorded in another account; that account is Accumulated Depreciation. If you were to record depreciation incorrectly by crediting the asset account, the balance of your asset account would eventually reach zero or the trade-in value, which is not correct. You would still have the equipment and need to maintain the original cost in the account. The credit should be to the contra-asset account, Accumulated Depreciation. Accumulated Depreciation, Equipment is contrary to, or a deduction from, Equipment.

Always record the adjusting entry for depreciation as a debit to Depreciation Expense (an income statement item) and a credit to Accumulated Depreciation (a balance sheet item), which increases both accounts. The adjustment in T account form would appear as follows:

Depreciation Expense, Equipment			Accumulated Depreciation, Equipment	
+	−		−	+
Adjusting 512				Adjusting 512

To show the accounts under their proper headings, let's look at the fundamental accounting equation. Brackets indicate that Accumulated Depreciation, Equipment is a deduction from the Equipment account. Note that the plus and minus signs are opposite.

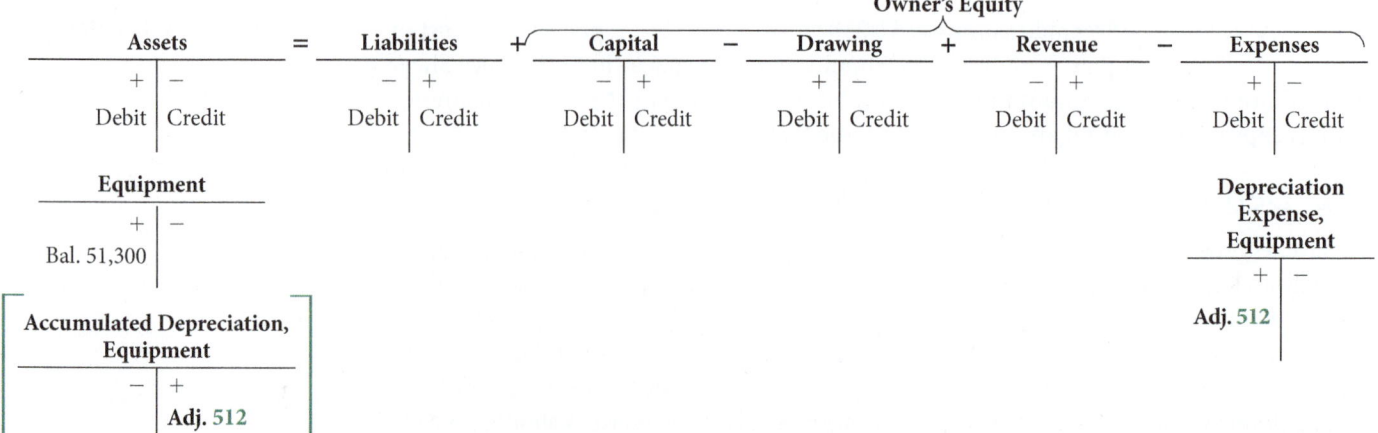

On the work sheet, Equipment (an asset) appears in the Balance Sheet Debit column. Accumulated Depreciation (a deduction from an asset) appears in the opposite column, which is the Balance Sheet Credit column.

Accumulated Depreciation, Equipment, as the title implies, is the total depreciation the company has taken since the original purchase of the asset. Rather than crediting the Equipment account, Conner's Whitewater Adventures uses a separate account to keep track of the total depreciation taken since it first acquired the asset. The maximum depreciation it could take would be the cost of the equipment, $51,300, less the trade-in value of $8,292. So for the first year, Accumulated Depreciation, Equipment will increase at the rate of $512 per month, assuming that no additional equipment has been purchased. For example, at the end of the second month, Accumulated Depreciation, Equipment will amount to $1,024 ($512 + $512).

On the balance sheet, the balance of Accumulated Depreciation is deducted from the balance of the related asset account, as illustrated on the following partial balance sheet for Conner's Whitewater Adventures. The net amount shown, $50,788, is referred to as the book value of the asset. Thus, **book value** (or **carrying value**) is the cost of an asset minus its accumulated depreciation ($51,300 − $512).

Conner's Whitewater Adventures
Partial Balance Sheet
June 30, 20--

Assets

Equipment	$51,300	
Less Accumulated Depreciation	512	$50,788

4-3d Wages Expense

The end of the fiscal period and the end of the employees' payroll period rarely fall on the same day. A diagram of the situation looks like this:

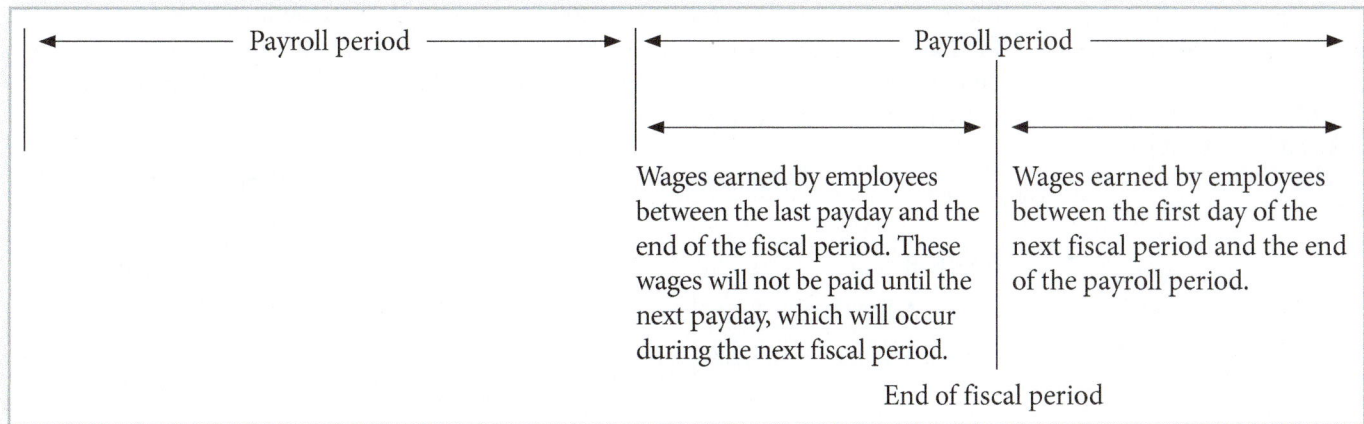

Because the last day of the fiscal period falls in the middle of the payroll period, we must split up the wages earned in that payroll period between the fiscal period just ended and the next fiscal period. We will use another company for this example.

Assume that Brown Company pays its employees $400 per day and that payday falls on Friday. The employees work a five-day week. When employees pick up their paychecks on Friday, the amount of the checks includes their wages for that day and for the preceding four days. Suppose that the last day of the fiscal period falls on Wednesday, December 31. The diagram below illustrates this situation.

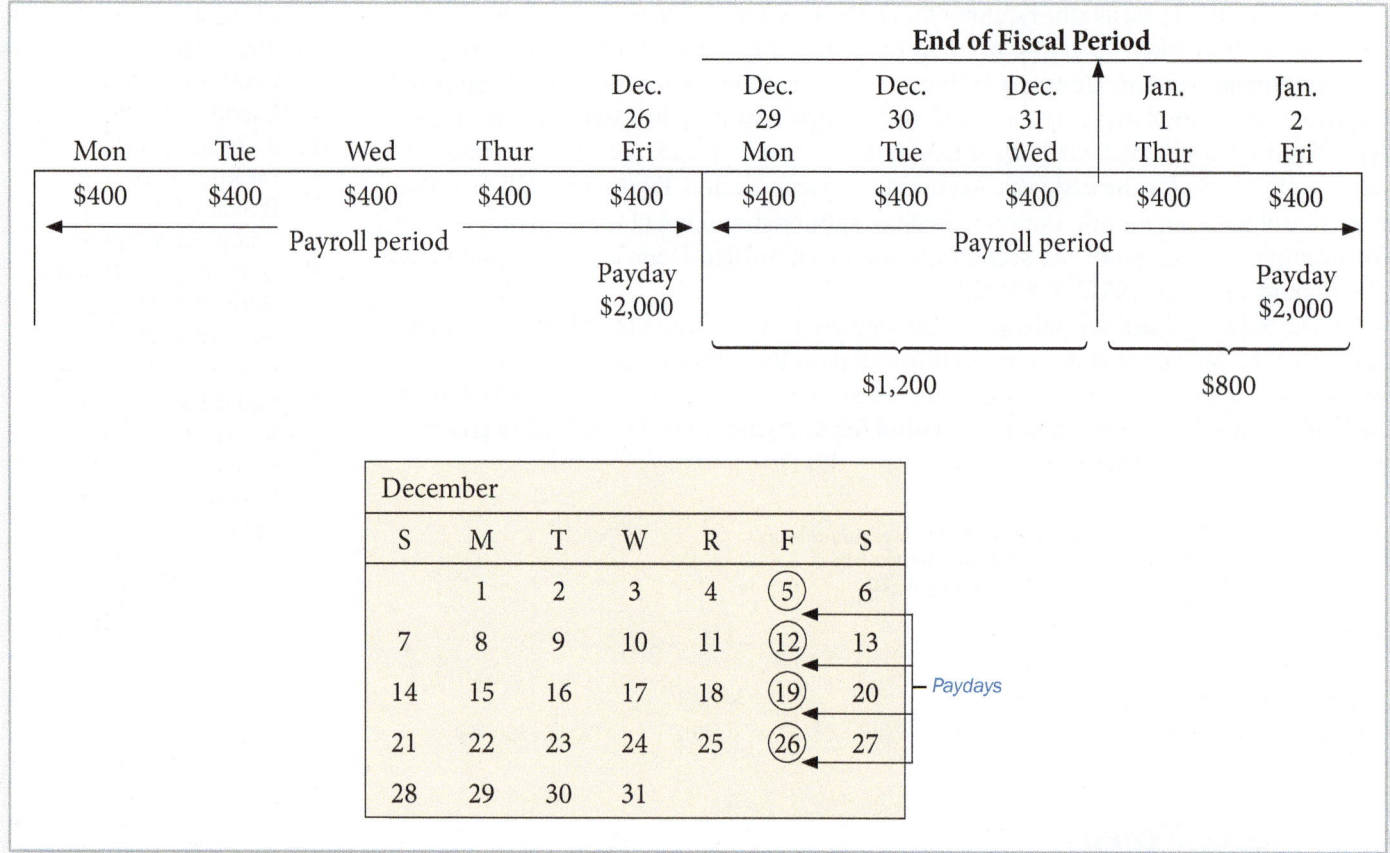

Remember

If the end of the fiscal period (or end of the fiscal year) occurs during the middle of a payroll period, Wages Expense must be adjusted to bring it up to date. In the adjusting entry, add the amount employees have earned between the end of the last payroll period and the end of the fiscal period.

So that the Wages Expense account shows an accurate balance for the fiscal period, you need to add $1,200 for the cost of labor between the last payday, December 26, and the end of the year, December 31 ($400 for December 29; $400 for December 30; $400 for December 31). Because the $1,200 will not be paid at this time but is owed to the employees as of December 31, you also need to add $1,200 to Wages Payable, a liability account, because the company owes this amount to employees.

Wages Expense				Wages Payable	
	+	−		−	+
(Old) Balance	104,000				**Adjusting 1,200**
Adjusting	**1,200**				
(New) Balance	105,200				

Returning to our illustration of Conner's Whitewater Adventures, the amount of wages that has been paid so far for the month of June is $2,360. However, the last payday was June 24. Between June 24 and the end of the month, Conner's Whitewater Adventures has determined that it owes an additional $472 in wages to its employees. The additional $472 will need to be added to the Wages Expense account and also the Wages Payable.

It might be tempting to decrease cash in this adjustment, but cash is not used in this case because the wages have yet not been paid.

Accountants refer to this extra amount that has not been recorded at the end of the month as **accrued wages**. In accounting terms, **accrual** means recognition of an expense or a revenue that has been incurred (expense) or earned (revenue) but has not yet been recorded.

	Wages Expense				Wages Payable	
	+	−			−	+
(Old) Balance	2,360					Adjusting 472
Adjusting	472					
(New) Balance	2,832					

MIXED ACCOUNTS

At this point, take special notice of the fact that each **adjusting entry contains an income statement account (revenue or expense) and a balance sheet account (asset, contra asset, or liability).** Accountants refer to these accounts as **mixed accounts**—accounts with balances that are partly income statement amounts and partly balance sheet amounts. The income statement and balance sheet accounts involved are separate accounts having a part of their name in common, such as Prepaid Insurance and Insurance Expense. Prepaid Insurance is recorded as $1,875 in the Trial Balance columns but is apportioned as $625 in Insurance Expense in the Income Statement columns and $1,250 in Prepaid Insurance in the Balance Sheet columns. In other words, portions of these trial balance amounts are recorded in each section.

4-3e Placement of Accounts on the Work Sheet

We now have to enter the adjustments on the work sheet, but before doing so, let's briefly discuss the Drawing and Accumulated Depreciation accounts, as well as net income, and their effect on the work sheet.

CAPITAL AND DRAWING ACCOUNT BALANCES

The Drawing account is a contra account (contrary to Capital). In the statement of owner's equity, Drawing is deducted from Capital. To show one account as a deduction from another, the plus and minus signs are switched. The T accounts look like this:

	J. Conner, Capital			J. Conner, Drawing	
	−	+		+	−
	Debit	Credit		Debit	Credit
		Balance		Balance	

The normal balance for the Capital account is recorded in the Credit columns of the Trial Balance, the Adjusted Trial Balance, and the Balance Sheet sections. The normal balance for the Drawing account is recorded in the Debit columns of the Trial Balance, the Adjusted Trial Balance, and the Balance Sheet sections.

EQUIPMENT AND ACCUMULATED DEPRECIATION, EQUIPMENT ACCOUNT BALANCES

The Accumulated Depreciation, Equipment account is a contra account (contrary to Equipment). On the balance sheet, Accumulated Depreciation, Equipment is deducted from Equipment. The T accounts look like this:

	Equipment		Accumulated Depreciation, Equipment	
	+	−	−	+
	Debit	Credit	Debit	Credit
	Balance			Balance

The normal balance for the Equipment account is recorded in the Debit columns of the Trial Balance, the Adjusted Trial Balance, and the Balance Sheet sections. The normal balance for the Accumulated Depreciation, Equipment account is recorded in the Credit columns of the Trial Balance, the Adjusted Trial Balance, and the Balance Sheet sections.

NET INCOME

Net income (or net loss) is the difference between revenue and expenses. It is used to balance the Income Statement columns. Because revenue is normally larger than expenses, the balancing amount must be added to the expense side. Net income (or net loss) is also used to balance the Balance Sheet columns. On the statement of owner's equity, you add net income to the owner's beginning Capital balance. Because the Capital balance is located in the Balance Sheet Credit column, net income must also be added to that side. The following diagram shows these relationships:

	A	B	C	D	E	F	G	H	I	J	K
1					Conner's Whitewater Adventures						
2					Work Sheet						
3					For Month Ended June 30, 20--						
4											
5			TRIAL BALANCE		ADJUSTMENTS		ADJUSTED TRIAL BALANCE		INCOME STATEMENT		BALANCE SHEET	
6	ACCOUNT NAME	DEBIT	CREDIT	DEBIT	CREDIT	DEBIT	CREDIT	DEBIT	CREDIT	DEBIT	CREDIT
7		Assets	Accum. Depr.			Assets	Accum. Depr.			Assets	Accum. Depr.
8		+	+			+	+			+	+
9		Drawing	Liabilities			Drawing	Liabilities			Drawing	Liabilities
10		+	+			+	+				+
11		Expenses	Capital			Expenses	Capital	Expenses			Capital
12			+				+				
13			Revenue				Revenue		Revenue		
14		Total	Total			Total	Total	Total	Total	Total	Total
15	Net Income							(NI) ←		→	(NI)
16								Total =	Total	Total =	Total
17											
18								Totals equal each other.		Totals equal each other.	
19											

On the other hand, if expenses are larger than revenue, the result is a net loss. You must add net loss to the revenue side to balance the Income Statement columns.

Also, because a net loss is deducted from the owner's beginning Capital balance, you must include net loss on the debit side of the Balance Sheet columns, thereby balancing these columns. To show this, let's look at the Income Statement and Balance Sheet columns diagrammed here.

		INCOME STATEMENT			BALANCE SHEET	
5						
6	ACCOUNT NAME	DEBIT	CREDIT		DEBIT	CREDIT
7					Assets	Accum. Depr.
8					+	+
9					Drawing	Liabilities
10						+
11		Expenses				Capital
12						
13			Revenue			
14		Total	Total		Total	Total
15	Net Loss		(NL) ←	→ (NL)		
16		Total =	Total		Total =	Total
17						
18		Totals equal each other.			Totals equal each other.	
19						
20						
21						

4-3f Steps in the Completion of the Work Sheet

The recommended steps to complete the work sheet are as follows:

STEP 1. Complete the Trial Balance columns, total, and rule (single-underline before double-underlining totals).

STEP 2. Complete the Adjustments columns, total, and rule.

STEP 3. Complete the Adjusted Trial Balance columns, total, and rule.

STEP 4. Record balances in the Income Statement and Balance Sheet columns and total each column.

STEP 5. Record net income or net loss in the Income Statement columns by subtracting the smaller side from the larger side and adding the difference to the smaller side, total, and rule.

STEP 6. Record net income or net loss in the Balance Sheet columns by subtracting the smaller side from the larger side and adding the difference to the smaller side (the amount should be the same as the difference between the Income Statement column totals—if not, there is an error), total, and rule.

The work sheet can be prepared using a computer spreadsheet program, such as Microsoft Excel®, or the work sheet can be prepared manually. Whether the work sheet is prepared manually or on a computer, the columns must be completed, totaled, and ruled.

STEP 1: TRIAL BALANCE COLUMNS

Note that the trial balance in Figure 2 is the same trial balance presented earlier for Conner's Whitewater Adventures. You will be able to follow the completion of the entire work sheet for Conner's Whitewater Adventures in Figure 3.

STEP 2: ADJUSTMENTS COLUMNS

When we write the adjustments, we identify them as (a), (b), (c), and (d) to indicate the relationships between the debit and credit sides and the sequence of the individual adjusting entries. (See Figures 2 and 3.)

Note that Supplies Expense; Insurance Expense; Depreciation Expense, Equipment; Accumulated Depreciation, Equipment; and Wages Payable did not appear in the trial balance because there were no balances in the accounts at that time. We wrote them below the Trial Balance totals to complete the work sheet. In this chapter, the business is in its first accounting period. Therefore, these accounts had no balance until the end of the fiscal period adjustments, which means they were not in the trial balance prior to adjustments. After the first fiscal period, these accounts could have a balance and would be listed in the Trial Balance columns in the order of the chart of accounts.

Here is a brief review of the adjustments:

a. To record $460 worth of supplies used during June.
b. To record the $625 cost of insurance expired during June.
c. To record $512 depreciation for the month of June.
d. To record $472 of accrued wages owed at the end of June.

Again, we emphasize that the work sheet is strictly a tool used to gather all of the up-to-date information needed to prepare the financial statements. **The adjustments must still be recorded in the journal.**

Figure 2

Partial work sheet for Conner's Whitewater Adventures

	A	B	C	D	E
1					Conner's
2					
3			Step 1		Step 2	
4					
5		TRIAL BALANCE		ADJUSTMENTS	
6	ACCOUNT NAME	DEBIT	CREDIT	DEBIT	CREDIT
7			*Accum. Depr.*		
8		*A + Draw. + E*	*+ L + Cap. + R*		
9	Cash	55,890.00			
10	Accounts Receivable	4,250.00			
11	Supplies	675.00			(a) 460.00
12	Prepaid Insurance	1,875.00			(b) 625.00
13	Equipment	51,300.00			
14	Accounts Payable		3,425.00		
15	J. Conner, Capital		95,200.00		
16	J. Conner, Drawing	3,500.00			
17	Income from Tours		23,320.00		
18	Wages Expense	2,360.00		(d) 472.00	
19	Rent Expense	1,250.00			
20	Advertising Expense	620.00			
21	Utilities Expense	225.00			
22		121,945.00	121,945.00		
23	Supplies Expense			(a) 460.00	
24	Insurance Expense			(b) 625.00	
25	Depr. Exp., Equip.			(c) 512.00	
26	Accum. Depr., Equip.				(c) 512.00
27	Wages Payable				(d) 472.00
28				2,069.00	2,069.00

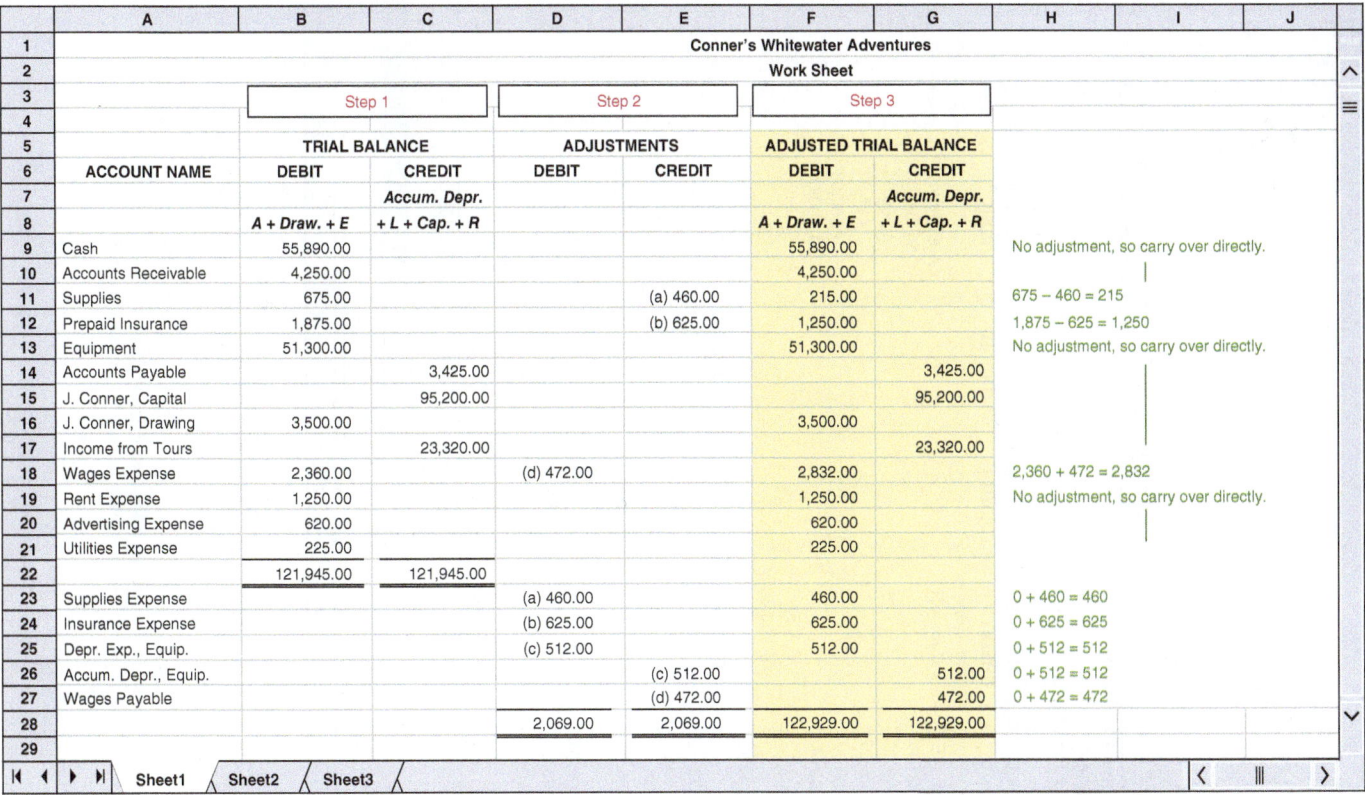

	A	B	C	D	E	F	G	H	I	J
1						Conner's Whitewater Adventures				
2						Work Sheet				
3			Step 1		Step 2		Step 3			
4										
5		TRIAL BALANCE		ADJUSTMENTS		ADJUSTED TRIAL BALANCE				
6	ACCOUNT NAME	DEBIT	CREDIT	DEBIT	CREDIT	DEBIT	CREDIT			
7			*Accum. Depr.*				*Accum. Depr.*			
8		*A + Draw. + E*	*+ L + Cap. + R*			*A + Draw. + E*	*+ L + Cap. + R*			
9	Cash	55,890.00				55,890.00		No adjustment, so carry over directly.		
10	Accounts Receivable	4,250.00				4,250.00				
11	Supplies	675.00			(a) 460.00	215.00		675 − 460 = 215		
12	Prepaid Insurance	1,875.00			(b) 625.00	1,250.00		1,875 − 625 = 1,250		
13	Equipment	51,300.00				51,300.00		No adjustment, so carry over directly.		
14	Accounts Payable		3,425.00				3,425.00			
15	J. Conner, Capital		95,200.00				95,200.00			
16	J. Conner, Drawing	3,500.00				3,500.00				
17	Income from Tours		23,320.00				23,320.00			
18	Wages Expense	2,360.00		(d) 472.00		2,832.00		2,360 + 472 = 2,832		
19	Rent Expense	1,250.00				1,250.00		No adjustment, so carry over directly.		
20	Advertising Expense	620.00				620.00				
21	Utilities Expense	225.00				225.00				
22		121,945.00	121,945.00							
23	Supplies Expense			(a) 460.00		460.00		0 + 460 = 460		
24	Insurance Expense			(b) 625.00		625.00		0 + 625 = 625		
25	Depr. Exp., Equip.			(c) 512.00		512.00		0 + 512 = 512		
26	Accum. Depr., Equip.				(c) 512.00		512.00	0 + 512 = 512		
27	Wages Payable				(d) 472.00		472.00	0 + 472 = 472		
28				2,069.00	2,069.00	122,929.00	122,929.00			
29										

Sheet1 / Sheet2 / Sheet3

Figure 3
Work sheet with steps
of completion explained
for Conner's Whitewater
Adventures

STEP 3: ADJUSTED TRIAL BALANCE COLUMNS

Once the Adjustments columns are totaled and ruled, extend each Trial Balance amount, plus or minus any adjustment from the Adjustments columns, to the Adjusted Trial Balance columns as shown in Figure 3.

STEP 4: INCOME STATEMENT AND BALANCE SHEET COLUMNS

Extend the balances in the Adjusted Trial Balance columns to either the Income Statement or the Balance Sheet columns. (See Figure 4.)

STEP 5: NET INCOME OR NET LOSS—INCOME STATEMENT COLUMNS

Total each of the two Income Statement columns. Subtract the smaller side from the larger side, write the difference under the smaller Income Statement column total, and total and rule as shown in Figure 4.

If there is a net income, the credit side of the Income Statement columns will be larger than the debit side—more revenue than expenses. In this case, write *Net Income* in the Account Name column on the same line as the difference you calculated. If there is a net loss, the debit side of the Income Statement columns will be larger than the credit side—more expenses than revenue. In that case, write *Net Loss* in the Account Name column on the same line as the difference you calculated.

STEP 6: NET INCOME OR NET LOSS—BALANCE SHEET COLUMNS

Total the two Balance Sheet columns. Subtract the smaller side from the larger side, write the difference under the smaller Balance Sheet column total (the amount should equal the difference between the Income Statement column totals—if not, there is an error), and total and rule as shown in Figure 4.

Figure 4
Work sheet for Conner's Whitewater Adventures—Excel version

Conner's Whitewater Adventures
Work Sheet
For Month Ended June 30, 20--

ACCOUNT NAME	TRIAL BALANCE DEBIT	TRIAL BALANCE CREDIT	ADJUSTMENTS DEBIT	ADJUSTMENTS CREDIT	ADJUSTED TRIAL BALANCE DEBIT	ADJUSTED TRIAL BALANCE CREDIT	INCOME STATEMENT DEBIT	INCOME STATEMENT CREDIT	BALANCE SHEET DEBIT	BALANCE SHEET CREDIT
	A + Draw. + E	+ L + Cap. + R (Accum. Depr.)			A + Draw. + E	+ L + Cap. + R (Accum. Depr.)	E	R	A + Draw.	+ L + Cap. (Accum. Depr.)
Cash	55,890.00				55,890.00				55,890.00	
Accounts Receivable	4,250.00				4,250.00				4,250.00	
Supplies	675.00			(a) 460.00	215.00				215.00	
Prepaid Insurance	1,875.00			(b) 625.00	1,250.00				1,250.00	
Equipment	51,300.00				51,300.00				51,300.00	
Accounts Payable		3,425.00				3,425.00				3,425.00
J. Conner, Capital		95,200.00				95,200.00				95,200.00
J. Conner, Drawing	3,500.00				3,500.00				3,500.00	
Income from Tours		23,320.00				23,320.00		23,320.00		
Wages Expense	2,360.00		(d) 472.00		2,832.00		2,832.00			
Rent Expense	1,250.00				1,250.00		1,250.00			
Advertising Expense	620.00				620.00		620.00			
Utilities Expense	225.00				225.00		225.00			
Supplies Expense			(a) 460.00		460.00		460.00			
Insurance Expense			(b) 625.00		625.00		625.00			
Depr. Exp., Equip.			(c) 512.00		512.00		512.00			
Accum. Depr., Equip.				(c) 512.00		512.00				512.00
Wages Payable				(d) 472.00		472.00				472.00
	121,945.00	121,945.00	2,069.00	2,069.00	122,929.00	122,929.00	6,524.00	23,320.00	116,405.00	99,609.00
Net Income							16,796.00			16,796.00
							23,320.00	23,320.00	116,405.00	116,405.00

Step 1
Step 2
Step 3
Steps 4, 5, and 6

Sheet1 / Sheet2 / Sheet3

Step 1
In the Account name column, lists the accounts that have balances. Enter the account balances in the Trial Balance columns. Total and rule the columns.

Step 2
Enter the adjustments, labeling each adjustment as (a), (b), (c), and so on. Total and rule the columns.
(a) Supplies used, $460
(b) Insurance expired, $625
(c) Depr. of equip., $512
(d) Accrued wages, $472

Step 3
Carry amounts across from the Trial Balance columns, plus or minus any amounts appearing in the Adjustments columns. Total and rule the columns.

Step 4
From the top of the Adjusted Trial Balance columns, go down line by line, carrying each amount over to the Income Statement or Balance Sheet columns. Total the columns.

Step 5
Write Net Income or Net Loss in the Account Name column and the amount in the appropriate Income Statement column. Total and rule the columns.

Step 6
Enter the net income or loss amount in the appropriate Balance Sheet column. Total, balance, and rule the columns.

4-3g Finding Errors in the Income Statement and Balance Sheet Columns

As you have seen, the amount of the net income or net loss must be recorded in both an Income Statement column and a Balance Sheet column. Suppose that after the net income is added to the Balance Sheet Credit column, the Balance Sheet columns are not equal. To find the error, follow this procedure:

STEP 1. Check that the amount of the net income or loss is recorded in the correct columns. For example, net income is placed in the Income Statement Debit column and the Balance Sheet Credit column.

STEP 2. Verify the addition of all columns.

STEP 3. Check that the appropriate amounts have been recorded in the Income Statement and Balance Sheet columns. For example, asset amounts should be listed in the Balance Sheet Debit column, expense amounts should be listed in the Income Statement Debit column, and so on.

STEP 4. Verify by adding or subtracting across each line that the amounts carried over from the Trial Balance columns through the Adjustments columns into the Adjusted Trial Balance columns are correct.

STEP 5. Verify that the correct amounts of the revenue and expense accounts are transferred to the Income Statement columns.

STEP 6. Verify that the correct amounts of assets, liabilities, and owner's equity accounts are transferred to the Balance Sheet columns.

Generally, one of these steps will expose the error.

4-4 JOURNALIZING ADJUSTING ENTRIES

To change the balance of a ledger account, you need a journal entry as evidence of the change. So far, we have been listing adjustments only in the Adjustments columns of the work sheet. The work sheet is not a journal, so we must journalize **adjusting entries** to update the ledger accounts. **Take the information for these entries directly from the Adjustments columns of the work sheet, debiting and crediting the same accounts and amounts in the journal entries.**

4 Journalize and post the adjusting entries.

Learning Objective

In the Description column of the general journal, write *Adjusting Entries* before you begin making these entries. This eliminates the need to write an explanation for each entry. The adjusting entries for Conner's Whitewater Adventures are shown in Figure 5 on page 162.

When you post the adjusting entries to the ledger accounts, write the abbreviation *Adj.* in the Item column of the ledger account. The adjusting entry for Prepaid Insurance is posted below the adjusting entries on page 162.

In the adjusted accounts for Conner's Whitewater Adventures, notice that the intent is to make sure that the expenses recorded match up or are reported with the revenues for the same period of time. In other words, for the month of June, we record all of the revenues for June and all of the expenses for June. Thus, the revenues and expenses for the same time period are matched. This is called the **matching principle**.

Figure 5
Adjusting entries for Conner's Whitewater Adventures

GENERAL JOURNAL — Page 4

Date		Description	Post. Ref.	Debit	Credit
20--		Adjusting Entries			
June	30	Supplies Expense	513	4 6 0 00	
		Supplies	115		4 6 0 00
	30	Insurance Expense	516	6 2 5 00	
		Prepaid Insurance	117		6 2 5 00
	30	Depr. Expense, Equipment	517	5 1 2 00	
		Accum. Depr., Equipment	125		5 1 2 00
	30	Wages Expense	511	4 7 2 00	
		Wages Payable	222		4 7 2 00

ACCOUNT Prepaid Insurance **ACCOUNT NO. 117**

Date		Item	Post. Ref.	Debit	Credit	Balance Debit	Balance Credit
20--							
June	10		2	1 8 7 5 00		1 8 7 5 00	
	30	Adj.	4		6 2 5 00	1 2 5 0 00	

ACCOUNT Insurance Expense **ACCOUNT NO. 516**

Date		Item	Post. Ref.	Debit	Credit	Balance Debit	Balance Credit
20--							
June	30	Adj.	4	6 2 5 00		6 2 5 00	

Visions/Shutterstock.com

In the Real World

Do companies such as Snapchat, Inc., a company that developed the popular photo messaging application for mobile devices, need to make adjusting entries? You bet! All companies, regardless of size, are required to make adjusting entries so that their financial statements are reported accurately. Snapchat, Inc. makes similar adjusting entries to the ones we made in this chapter (for example, Prepaid Insurance, Depreciation, and Wages). So regardless of the company, adjusting entries are an important part of the accounting cycle.

YOU Make the Call

Imagine that you have just been hired as an accounting clerk for a local tour bus company. Part of your job is to prepare adjusting entries prior to producing the financial statements. You have spent the week familiarizing yourself with the accounting system. You find the following preliminary adjusting notes left by the prior accounting clerk:

(a) The tour bus company pays weekly salaries of $606.65 for a five-day workweek. The end of the accounting period is on a Thursday. The amount of wages per day was computed to be $121.33.

(b) The depreciation for the buses, using the straight-line method, is $33,392.86 per year and $2,782.74 per month. (The buses cost $275,000, with an estimated useful life of seven years and a trade-in value of $41,250 at the end of that time.)

(c) The balance of the Prepaid Insurance account is $2,480, which covers one year. The amount of the adjusting entry for Insurance Expense for this one-month period is $206.67.

As the new accounting clerk, your job is to review these figures for accuracy and then record the appropriate adjusting entries in the general journal.

SOLUTION

(a) $606.65 ÷ 5 = $121.33
$121.33 × 4 days = $485.32 adjustment amount

(b) 1. $275,000 − $41,250 = $233,750 full depreciation
2. $233,750 full depreciation ÷ 7 years = $33,392.86 per year
3. $33,392.86 per year ÷ 12 months = $2,782.74 per month

(c) $2,480 per year ÷ 12 months = $206.67 per month

		GENERAL JOURNAL				Page ___	
Date		Description	Post. Ref.	Debit		Credit	
		Adjusting Entries					
	(a)	Wages Expense		4 8 5 32			
		Wages Payable				4 8 5 32	
	(b)	Depreciation Expense, Equipment		2 7 8 2 74			
		Accumulated Depreciation, Equipment				2 7 8 2 74	
	(c)	Insurance Expense		2 0 6 67			
		Prepaid Insurance				2 0 6 67	

To: Amy Roberts, CPA
Subject: **Financial Statements Review**

Hi Amy,
I have completed the adjusting entries using the work sheet, recorded them in the general journal, and posted them to the ledger. I know we've talked before about financial statements, but I probably need a short review. Can you help?
Thanks,
Janie

To: Janie Conner
Subject: **RE: Financial Statements Review**

Hi Janie,
I am glad that you have the adjusting entries recorded in the general journal and also posted to the ledger. Now that the accounts are up to date, you are ready to prepare the financial statements. Remember, from what we talked about earlier, the income statement is prepared first, followed by the statement of owner's equity, and then the balance sheet. Let's review each of these statements so that you are ready to give them to the bank. Let me know if you need help.
Amy

4-5 COMPLETION OF THE FINANCIAL STATEMENTS

As we stated, the purpose of the work sheet is to help the accountant prepare the financial statements. Now that we have recorded the adjusting entries, we can use the work sheet to prepare the income statement, the statement of owner's equity, and the balance sheet. The figures for the financial statements are taken directly from the work sheet. These statements are shown in Figure 6.

Note that you record Accumulated Depreciation, Equipment in the asset section of the balance sheet as a direct deduction from Equipment. As we have said, accountants refer to this as a contra account because it is contrary to its companion asset account. The difference, $50,788, is called the book value or carrying value because it represents the cost of the asset after Accumulated Depreciation has been deducted.

When preparing the statement of owner's equity, remember to check the beginning balance of Capital against the balance shown in the Capital account in the general ledger. An additional investment may have been made during the fiscal period, and you need to report any such investment in the statement of owner's equity.

Conner's Whitewater Adventures
Income Statement
For Month Ended June 30, 20--

Revenue:		
Income from Tours		$23,320
Expenses:		
Wages Expense	$2,832	
Rent Expense	1,250	
Supplies Expense	460	
Advertising Expense	620	
Utilities Expense	225	
Insurance Expense	625	
Depreciation Expense, Equipment	512	
Total Expenses		6,524
Net Income		$16,796

Conner's Whitewater Adventures
Statement of Owner's Equity
For Month Ended June 30, 20--

J. Conner, Capital, June 1, 20--		$ 0
Investment during June	$ 95,200	
Net Income for June	16,796	
Subtotal	$111,996	
Less Withdrawals for June	3,500	
Increase in Capital		108,496
J. Conner, Capital, June 30, 20--		$108,496

Conner's Whitewater Adventures
Balance Sheet
June 30, 20--

Assets		
Cash		$ 55,890
Accounts Receivable		4,250
Supplies		215
Prepaid Insurance		1,250
Equipment	$51,300	
Less Accumulated Depreciation	512	50,788
Total Assets		$112,393
Liabilities		
Accounts Payable	$ 3,425	
Wages Payable	472	
Total Liabilities		$ 3,897
Owner's Equity		
J. Conner, Capital		108,496
Total Liabilities and Owner's Equity		$112,393

Figure 6

Financial statements for Conner's Whitewater Adventures

Remember

The columns shown on the financial statements do not represent Debit or Credit. Each column simply shows account balances. Amounts in these columns are either added or subtracted.

Remember

Total assets must always equal total liabilities and owner's equity.

5a Prepare an income statement involving more than one revenue account and a net loss

4-5a Income Statement Involving More Than One Revenue Account and a Net Loss

When an organization has more than one distinct source of revenue, a separate revenue account is set up for each source. See, for example, the income statement of Harris Miniature Golf presented in Figure 7. Also note that expenses are greater than revenues, resulting in a net loss.

Figure 7
Income statement for Harris Miniature Golf

Harris Miniature Golf Income Statement For Month Ended September 30, 20--		
Revenues:		
Admissions Fees	$2,624	
Concession Fees	1,512	
Total Revenues		$ 4,136
Expenses:		
Wages Expense	$3,123	
Supplies Expense	317	
Advertising Expense	1,000	
Rent Expense	1,900	
Miscellaneous Expense	128	
Total Expenses		6,468
Net Loss		$(2,332)

4-5b Statement of Owner's Equity with an Additional Investment and Either a Net Income or a Net Loss

5b Prepare a statement of owner's equity with an additional investment and either a net income or a net loss.

Any additional investment by the owner during the period covered by the financial statements is shown on the statement of owner's equity because such a statement should show everything that has affected the Capital account from the *beginning* until the *end* of the period covered by the financial statements. For example, in Figure 8, assume that the following information is true for L. A. Grand Company, which has a net income:

Balance of L. A. Grand, Capital, on April 1	$86,000
Additional investment by L. A. Grand on April 12	8,000
Net income for the month (from income statement)	6,200
Total withdrawals for the month	4,000

Figure 8
Statement of owner's equity for L. A. Grand Company

L. A. Grand Company Statement of Owner's Equity For Month Ended April 30, 20--		
L. A. Grand, Capital, April 1, 20--		$86,000
Investment during April	$ 8,000	
Net Income for April	6,200	
Subtotal	$14,200	
Less Withdrawals for April	4,000	
Increase in Capital		10,200
L. A. Grand, Capital, April 30, 20--		$96,200

Now assume the following for J. D. Ross Company, which has a net loss:

J. D. Ross, Capital, on Oct. 1	$75,000
Additional investment by J. D. Ross on Oct. 25	10,000
Net loss for the month (from income statement)	1,500
Total withdrawals for the month	5,100

The statement of owner's equity in Figure 9 shows this information. Notice that the net loss is subtracted from the additional investment during October.

FYI

The information normally shown on the statement of owner's equity is sometimes included as part of the owner's equity section of the balance sheet in computerized general ledger systems.

J. D. Ross Company
Statement of Owner's Equity
For Month Ended October 31, 20--

J. D. Ross, Capital, October 1, 20--		$75,000
Investment during October	$10,000	
Net Loss for October	1,500	
Subtotal	$ 8,500	
Less Withdrawals for October	5,100	
Increase in Capital		3,400
J. D. Ross, Capital, October 31, 20--		$78,400

Figure 9
Statement of owner's equity for J. D. Ross Company

4-5c Businesses with More Than One Depreciation Expense Account and More Than One Accumulated Depreciation Account

Figures 10 and 11 show the income statement and the balance sheet for Molen Veterinary Clinic. In Figure 11, note that the company has two assets subject to depreciation: Building and Equipment. In the financial statements, Depreciation Expense and Accumulated Depreciation must be listed for each asset.

5c Prepare a balance sheet for a business having more than one accumulated depreciation account.

Learning Objective

Molen Veterinary Clinic
Income Statement
For Month Ended December 31, 20--

Revenue:		
Professional Fees	$332,300	
Boarding Fees	65,270	
Total Revenue		$397,570
Expenses:		
Salary Expense	$250,000	
Depreciation Expense, Building	19,450	
Depreciation Expense, Equipment	11,500	
Supplies Expense	11,380	
Insurance Expense	2,240	
Miscellaneous Expense	4,420	
Total Expenses		298,990
Net Income		$ 98,580

Figure 10
Income statement for Molen Veterinary Clinic

Figure 11
Balance sheet for Molen
Veterinary Clinic

Molen Veterinary Clinic		
Balance Sheet		
December 31, 20--		
Assets		
Cash		$ 21,320
Land		15,200
Building	$349,100	
Less Accumulated Depreciation	112,200	236,900
Equipment	$124,800	
Less Accumulated Depreciation	87,600	37,200
Total Assets		$310,620
Liabilities		
Accounts Payable		$ 7,400
Owner's Equity		
R. N. Molen, Capital		303,220
Total Liabilities and Owner's Equity		$310,620

Chapter Review

Study and Practice

Learning Objective   **1**   *Define* fiscal period *and* fiscal year *and explain the accounting cycle.*

A **fiscal period** is any period of time covering a complete accounting cycle. A **fiscal year** consists of 12 consecutive months. The accounting cycle represents the sequence of the accounting process steps completed during the fiscal period.

 PRACTICE EXERCISE 1

Which of the following would be considered a fiscal year?

(a) July 1, 20-- to June 30, 20--
(b) October 1, 20-- to August 31, 20--
(c) April 1, 20-- to January 31, 20--
(d) January 1, 20-- to December 31, 20--

PRACTICE EXERCISE 1 • SOLUTION
(a) and (d)

2 List the classifications of the accounts that occupy each column of a ten-column work sheet.

Learning Objective

Trial Balance Debit	Assets + Drawing + Expenses
Trial Balance Credit	Accum. Depr. + Liabilities + Capital + Revenue
Adjusted Trial Balance Debit	Assets + Drawing + Expenses
Adjusted Trial Balance Credit	Accum. Depr. + Liabilities + Capital + Revenue
Income Statement Debit	Expenses
Income Statement Credit	Revenue
Balance Sheet Debit	Assets + Drawing
Balance Sheet Credit	Accum. Depr. + Liabilities + Capital

 PRACTICE EXERCISE 2

Using a ten-column work sheet, list the classifications of accounts that are found in each column, with the exception of the Adjustments columns (Trial Balance, Adjusted Trial Balance, Income Statement, and Balance Sheet).

PRACTICE EXERCISE 2 • SOLUTION

	A	B	C	D	E	F	G	H	I	J	K
4											
5		TRIAL BALANCE		ADJUSTMENTS		ADJUSTED TRIAL BALANCE		INCOME STATEMENT		BALANCE SHEET	
6	ACCOUNT NAME	DEBIT	CREDIT	DEBIT	CREDIT	DEBIT	CREDIT	DEBIT	CREDIT	DEBIT	CREDIT
7		Assets	Accum. Depr.			Assets	Accum. Depr.			Assets	Accum. Depr.
8		Drawing	Liabilities			Drawing	Liabilities			Drawing	Liabilities
9		Expenses	Capital			Expenses	Capital	Expenses			Capital
10			Revenue				Revenue		Revenue		
11											

Sheet1 / Sheet2 / Sheet3

3 Complete a work sheet for a service enterprise, involving adjustments for supplies, expired insurance, depreciation, and accrued wages.

Learning Objective

Adjustment for supplies used: debit Supplies Expense and credit Supplies.
Adjustment for expired insurance: debit Insurance Expense and credit Prepaid Insurance.
Adjustment for **depreciation**: debit Depreciation Expense and credit Accumulated Depreciation.
Adjustment for accrued wages: debit Wages Expense and credit Wages Payable.

 PRACTICE EXERCISE 3

Complete the work sheet on page 170 for Fun and Games for the month of September. Adjustment information:

(a) Supplies used during September, $500.
(b) Insurance expired during September, $175.
(c) Depreciation of equipment for the month of September, $540.
(d) Accrued wages owed at the end of September, $260.

PRACTICE EXERCISE 3 • SOLUTION
See the completed work sheet on page 171.

Fun and Games
Work Sheet
For Month Ended September 30, 20–

ACCOUNT NAME	TRIAL BALANCE DEBIT	TRIAL BALANCE CREDIT	ADJUSTMENTS DEBIT	ADJUSTMENTS CREDIT	ADJUSTED TRIAL BALANCE DEBIT	ADJUSTED TRIAL BALANCE CREDIT	INCOME STATEMENT DEBIT	INCOME STATEMENT CREDIT	BALANCE SHEET DEBIT	BALANCE SHEET CREDIT
Cash	24,770.00									
Accounts Receivable	5,750.00									
Supplies	630.00									
Prepaid Insurance	2,100.00									
Equipment	36,000.00									
Accum. Depr., Equip.		540.00								
Accounts Payable		3,985.00								
J. Jay, Capital		54,075.00								
J. Jay, Drawing	5,000.00									
Income from Services		21,000.00								
Wages Expense	2,670.00									
Rent Expense	1,950.00									
Advertising Expense	450.00									
Utilities Expense	280.00									
	79,600.00	79,600.00								
Supplies Expense										
Insurance Expense										
Depr. Exp., Equip.										
Wages Payable										
Net Income										

Sheet1 Sheet2 Sheet3

Fun and Games
Work Sheet
For Month Ended September 30, 20–

ACCOUNT NAME	TRIAL BALANCE DEBIT	TRIAL BALANCE CREDIT	ADJUSTMENTS DEBIT	ADJUSTMENTS CREDIT	ADJUSTED TRIAL BALANCE DEBIT	ADJUSTED TRIAL BALANCE CREDIT	INCOME STATEMENT DEBIT	INCOME STATEMENT CREDIT	BALANCE SHEET DEBIT	BALANCE SHEET CREDIT
Cash	24,770.00				24,770.00				24,770.00	
Accounts Receivable	5,750.00				5,750.00				5,750.00	
Supplies	630.00			(a) 500.00	130.00				130.00	
Prepaid Insurance	2,100.00			(b) 175.00	1,925.00				1,925.00	
Equipment	36,000.00				36,000.00				36,000.00	
Accum. Depr., Equip.		540.00		(c) 540.00		1,080.00				1,080.00
Accounts Payable		3,985.00				3,985.00				3,985.00
J. Jay, Capital		54,075.00				54,075.00				54,075.00
J. Jay, Drawing	5,000.00				5,000.00				5,000.00	
Income from Services		21,000.00				21,000.00		21,000.00		
Wages Expense	2,670.00		(d) 260.00		2,930.00		2,930.00			
Rent Expense	1,950.00				1,950.00		1,950.00			
Advertising Expense	450.00				450.00		450.00			
Utilities Expense	280.00				280.00		280.00			
	79,600.00	79,600.00								
Supplies Expense			(a) 500.00		500.00		500.00			
Insurance Expense			(b) 175.00		175.00		175.00			
Depr. Exp., Equip.			(c) 540.00		540.00		540.00			
Wages Payable				(d) 260.00		260.00				260.00
			1,475.00	1,475.00	80,400.00	80,400.00	6,825.00	21,000.00	73,575.00	59,400.00
Net Income							14,175.00			14,175.00
							21,000.00	21,000.00	73,575.00	73,575.00

Sheet1 / Sheet2 / Sheet3

Learning Objective   **4** Journalize and post the adjusting entries.

Adjustments are a way of updating the ledger accounts. They are determined after the trial balance has been prepared. To change the balance of the ledger accounts, **adjusting entries** are needed in the general journal as evidence of the changes. The information for these entries is taken directly from the Adjustments columns of the work sheet, debiting and crediting the same accounts and amounts in the journal entries. Therefore, each adjusting entry consists of an income statement account and a balance sheet account. When the adjusting entries are posted to the ledger accounts, the abbreviation *Adj.* is written in the Item column of the ledger account.

 PRACTICE EXERCISE 4

Journalize and post the adjusting entries for Fun and Games from Practice Exercise 3.

PRACTICE EXERCISE 4 • SOLUTION

GENERAL JOURNAL — Page 4

Date		Description	Post. Ref.	Debit	Credit
20--		Adjusting Entries			
Sept.	30	Supplies Expense	513	5 0 0 00	
		Supplies	115		5 0 0 00
	30	Insurance Expense	516	1 7 5 00	
		Prepaid Insurance	117		1 7 5 00
	30	Depr. Expense, Equipment	517	5 4 0 00	
		Accum. Depr., Equipment	125		5 4 0 00
	30	Wages Expense	511	2 6 0 00	
		Wages Payable	222		2 6 0 00

ACCOUNT Supplies — ACCOUNT NO. 115

Date		Item	Post. Ref.	Debit	Credit	Balance Debit	Balance Credit
20--							
Sept.	30	Bal.		6 3 0 00		6 3 0 00	
		Adj.			5 0 0 00	1 3 0 00	

ACCOUNT Prepaid Insurance — ACCOUNT NO. 117

Date		Item	Post. Ref.	Debit	Credit	Balance Debit	Balance Credit
20--							
Sept.	15		2	2 1 0 0 00		2 1 0 0 00	
	30	Adj.	4		1 7 5 00	1 9 2 5 00	

ACCOUNT Accumulated Depreciation, Equipment   **ACCOUNT NO. 125**

Date		Item	Post. Ref.	Debit	Credit	Balance Debit	Balance Credit
20--							
Sept.		Bal.			5 4 0 00		5 4 0 00
	30	Adj.	4		5 4 0 00		1 0 8 0 00

ACCOUNT Wages Payable   **ACCOUNT NO. 222**

Date		Item	Post. Ref.	Debit	Credit	Balance Debit	Balance Credit
20--							
Sept.	30	Adj.	4		2 6 0 00		2 6 0 00

ACCOUNT Wages Expense   **ACCOUNT NO. 511**

Date		Item	Post. Ref.	Debit	Credit	Balance Debit	Balance Credit
20--							
Sept.	15		2	2 6 7 0 00		2 6 7 0 00	
	30	Adj.	4	2 6 0 00		2 9 3 0 00	

ACCOUNT Supplies Expense   **ACCOUNT NO. 513**

Date		Item	Post. Ref.	Debit	Credit	Balance Debit	Balance Credit
20--							
Sept.	30	Adj.	4	5 0 0 00		5 0 0 00	

ACCOUNT Insurance Expense   **ACCOUNT NO. 516**

Date		Item	Post. Ref.	Debit	Credit	Balance Debit	Balance Credit
20--							
Sept.	30	Adj.	4	1 7 5 00		1 7 5 00	

ACCOUNT Depreciation Expense, Equipment   **ACCOUNT NO. 517**

Date		Item	Post. Ref.	Debit	Credit	Balance Debit	Balance Credit
20--							
Sept.	30	Adj.	4	5 4 0 00		5 4 0 00	

 5 Prepare an income statement, a statement of owner's equity, and a balance sheet for a service business directly from the work sheet.

Learning Objective

The income statement is prepared directly from the amounts listed in the Income Statement Debit and Credit columns. The net income should equal the net income previously determined on the **work sheet.** For the statement of owner's equity, use the amount of the beginning capital listed in the Balance Sheet Credit column after checking the general ledger for any additional investment(s), the amount of the net income from the Balance Sheet Credit column, and the amount of Drawing from the Balance Sheet Debit column. Prepare the balance sheet directly from the amounts listed in the Balance Sheet Debit and Credit columns (except Drawing and Capital).

 PRACTICE EXERCISE 5

Prepare an income statement, a statement of owner's equity, and a balance sheet for Fun and Games using the information from Practice Exercise 3.

PRACTICE EXERCISE 5 • SOLUTION

Fun and Games
Income Statement
For Month Ended September 30, 20--

Revenue:		
Income from Services		$21,000
Expenses:		
Wages Expense	$2,930	
Rent Expense	1,950	
Supplies Expense	500	
Advertising Expense	450	
Utilities Expense	280	
Insurance Expense	175	
Depreciation Expense, Equipment	540	
Total Expenses		6,825
Net Income		$14,175

Fun and Games
Statement of Owner's Equity
For Month Ended September 30, 20--

J. Jay, Capital, September 1, 20--		$54,075
Investment during September	$ 0	
Net Income for September	14,175	
Subtotal	$14,175	
Less Withdrawals for September	5,000	
Increase in Capital		9,175
J. Jay, Capital, September 30, 20--		$63,250

Fun and Games
Balance Sheet
September 30, 20--

Assets

Cash		$24,770
Accounts Receivable		5,750
Supplies		130
Prepaid Insurance		1,925
Equipment	$36,000	
Less Accumulated Depreciation	1,080	34,920
Total Assets		$67,495

Liabilities

Accounts Payable	$ 3,985	
Wages Payable	260	
Total Liabilities		$ 4,245

Owner's Equity

J. Jay, Capital		63,250
Total Liabilities and Owner's Equity		$67,495

 5 **(cont.)** Prepare (a) an income statement involving more than one revenue account and a net loss, (b) a statement of owner's equity with an additional investment and either a net income or a net loss, and (c) a balance sheet for a business having more than one accumulated depreciation account.

Learning Objective

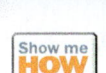

(a) An income statement containing more than one revenue account requires an additional line for each type of revenue, followed by a total amount of revenue.
(b) A statement of owner's equity involving an additional investment requires a line for each additional investment beneath the beginning capital amount, followed by a total amount of investment.
(c) Businesses that have more than one type of asset subject to depreciation must show a separate account for each asset on the balance sheet.

 ### PRACTICE EXERCISE 5a

Using the following information, prepare an income statement for the month of September for The Swim Shack:

Depreciation Expense, Equipment	$ 525
Income from Concessions	4,000
Income from Services	1,500
Insurance Expense	200
Rent Expense	1,950
Utilities Expense	790
Wages Expense	3,580
Supplies Expense	100

CHAPTER REVIEW

PRACTICE EXERCISE 5a • SOLUTION

The Swim Shack Income Statement For Month Ended September 30, 20--		
Revenue:		
Income from Concessions	$4,000	
Income from Services	1,500	
Total Revenue		$ 5,500
Expenses:		
Wages Expense	$3,580	
Rent Expense	1,950	
Supplies Expense	100	
Utilities Expense	790	
Insurance Expense	200	
Depreciation Expense, Equipment	525	
Total Expenses		7,145
Net Loss		$(1,645)

PRACTICE EXERCISE 5b

Using the following information, prepare a statement of owner's equity for the month of July for Stanley's Computers and Electronics.

P. Stanley, Capital, on July 1	$205,077
Additional investment by P. Stanley on July 21	15,500
Net loss for the month (from income statement)	1,850
Total withdrawals for the month	3,500

PRACTICE EXERCISE 5b • SOLUTION

Stanley's Computers and Electronics Statement of Owner's Equity For Month Ended July 31, 20--		
P. Stanley, Capital, July 1, 20--		$205,077
Investment during July	$15,500	
Net Loss for July	1,850	
Subtotal	$13,650	
Less Withdrawals for July	3,500	
Increase in Capital		10,150
P. Stanley, Capital, July 31, 20--		$215,227

PRACTICE EXERCISE 5c

Using the following information, prepare a year-end balance sheet for Moreland Clinic as of December 31.

Accounts Payable	$ 7,380
Accumulated Depreciation, Building	112,200
Accumulated Depreciation, Equipment	87,600
Building	339,100
Cash	31,345
Equipment	114,800
Land	25,000
Supplies	175
W. Moreland, Capital	303,240

PRACTICE EXERCISE 5c • SOLUTION

Moreland Clinic
Balance Sheet
December 31, 20--

Assets		
Cash		$ 31,345
Supplies		175
Land		25,000
Building	$339,100	
Less Accumulated Depreciation	112,200	226,900
Equipment	$114,800	
Less Accumulated Depreciation	87,600	27,200
Total Assets		$310,620
Liabilities		
Accounts Payable		$ 7,380
Owner's Equity		
W. Moreland, Capital		303,240
Total Liabilities and Owner's Equity		$310,620

Glossary

Accounting cycle The sequence of steps in the accounting process completed during the fiscal period. (*p. 147*)

Accrual Recognition of an expense or a revenue that has been incurred or earned but has not yet been recorded. (*p. 155*)

Accrued wages Unpaid wages owed to employees for the time between the end of the last pay period and the end of the fiscal period. (*p. 155*)

Adjusting entries Entries that bring the books up to date at the end of the fiscal period. (*p. 161*)

Adjustments Internal transactions that bring ledger accounts up to date as a planned part of the accounting procedure. (*p. 150*)

Book value/carrying value The cost of an asset minus the accumulated depreciation. (*p. 153*)

Contra account An account that is contrary to, or a deduction from, another account. For example, Accumulated Depreciation, Equipment is listed as a deduction from Equipment. (*p. 152*)

Depreciation An expense based on the expectation that an asset will gradually decline in usefulness due to time, wear and tear, or obsolescence. The cost of the asset is therefore spread out over its estimated useful life. A part of depreciation expense is apportioned to each fiscal period. (*p. 151*)

Fiscal period Any period of time covering a complete accounting cycle, generally consisting of 12 consecutive months. (*p. 147*)

Fiscal year A fiscal period consisting of 12 consecutive months. (*p. 147*)

Matching principle The principle that the expenses for one time period are matched up with the related revenues for the same time period. (*p. 161*)

Mixed accounts Certain accounts that appear on the trial balance with balances that are partly income statement amounts and partly balance sheet amounts—for example, Prepaid Insurance and Insurance Expense. (*p. 155*)

Straight-line depreciation A means of calculating depreciation in which the cost of an asset, less any trade-in value, is allocated evenly over the useful life of the asset. (*p. 152*)

Work sheet A working paper used by accountants to record necessary adjustments and provide up-to-date account balances needed to prepare the financial statements. (*p. 147*)

Quiz Yourself

_____ 1. The _____ represents the sequence of steps in the accounting process.
  a. fiscal year
  b. fiscal period
  c. accounting cycle
  d. work sheet

_____ 2. The _____ is a working paper used by accountants to record necessary adjustments and provide up-to-date account balances needed to prepare the financial statements.
  a. journal
  b. balance sheet
  c. accounting cycle
  d. work sheet

_____ 3. On the work sheet, assets are recorded in which of the following columns?
  a. Trial Balance, Credit
  b. Income Statement, Debit
  c. Balance Sheet, Debit
  d. Adjusted Trial Balance, Credit

_____ 4. Rainy Day Services had $430 of supplies reported on its unadjusted trial balance as of March 31. During the month of March, Rainy Day Services used $175 worth of supplies. What is the entry to adjust supplies?
  a. Supplies Expense   175
     Cash   175
  b. Supplies   430
     Supplies Expense   430

  c. Supplies Expense   255
     Supplies   255
  d. Supplies Expense   175
     Supplies   175

_____ 5. On the work sheet, Accumulated Depreciation, Equipment would be recorded in which of the following columns?
  a. Adjusted Trial Balance, Credit
  b. Income Statement, Debit
  c. Balance Sheet, Debit
  d. Income Statement, Credit

_____ 6. The _____ requires that expenses be matched up with revenue for the same period of time.
  a. matching principle
  b. expense principle
  c. revenue recognition principle
  d. separate entity concept

_____ 7. Accumulated Depreciation, Equipment is reported
  a. on the income statement as an expense.
  b. on the balance sheet as an addition to total assets.
  c. on the income statement as a revenue.
  d. on the balance sheet as a subtraction from the related asset account.

Answers:
1. c 2. d 3. c 4. d 5. a 6. a 7. d

Chapter Assignments

Discussion Questions

1. What is the purpose of a work sheet?
2. What is the purpose of adjusting entries?
3. What is a mixed account? A contra account? Give an example of each.
4. In which column of the work sheet—Income Statement (IS) or Balance Sheet (BS)— would the adjusted balances of the following accounts appear?

Account	IS or BS?	Account	IS or BS?
a. Prepaid Insurance		e. Accumulated Depreciation, Equipment	
b. Wages Expense		f. J. Karl, Drawing	
c. Wages Payable		g. Insurance Expense	
d. Income from Services		h. Depreciation Expense, Equipment	

5. Why is it necessary to make an adjustment if wages for work performed for the pay period Monday through Friday are paid on Friday and the accounting period ends on a Wednesday?
6. Define depreciation as it relates to a van you bought for your business.
7. Define an internal transaction and provide an example.
8. Why is it necessary to journalize and post adjusting entries?

Exercises

LO 2

EXERCISE 4-1

1. List the following classifications of accounts in all of the columns in which they appear on the work sheet, with the exception of the Adjustments columns. (Example: Assets)

Practice Exercise 2

Show me HOW

Assets	Capital
Accumulated Depreciation (with previous balance)	Drawing
	Revenue
Liabilities	Expenses

2. List *Net Income* in the appropriate columns.

	A	B	C	D	E	F	G	H	I	J	K
4											
5		TRIAL BALANCE		ADJUSTMENTS		ADJUSTED TRIAL BALANCE		INCOME STATEMENT		BALANCE SHEET	
6	ACCOUNT NAME	DEBIT	CREDIT	DEBIT	CREDIT	DEBIT	CREDIT	DEBIT	CREDIT	DEBIT	CREDIT
7		Assets				Assets				Assets	
8											
9											
10											
11											
12											
13											
14											
15	Net Income										
16											

Sheet1 / Sheet2 / Sheet3

CHAPTER ASSIGNMENTS

LO 2

Practice Exercise 2

EXERCISE 4-2 Classify each of the accounts listed below as assets (A), liabilities (L), owner's equity (OE), revenue (R), or expenses (E). Indicate the normal debit or credit balance of each account. Indicate whether each account will appear in the Income Statement columns (IS) or the Balance Sheet columns (BS) of the work sheet. Item 0 is given as an example.

Account	Classification	Normal Balance	IS or BS Columns
0. Example: Wages Expense	E	Debit	IS
a. Prepaid Insurance			
b. Accounts Payable			
c. Office Supplies Expense			
d. T. Bristol, Capital			
e. Accumulated Depreciation, Building			
f. T. Bristol, Drawing			
g. Income from Services			
h. Equipment			
i. Depreciation Expense, Equipment			
j. Wages Payable			

LO 3

EXERCISE 4-3 Place a check mark next to any account(s) requiring adjustment. Explain why those accounts must be adjusted.

✓	Account Name (in trial balance order)	Reason for Adjusting This Account
	a. Cash	
	b. Prepaid Insurance	
	c. Equipment	
	d. Accumulated Depreciation, Equipment	
	e. Wages Payable	
	f. R. Wesley, Capital	
	g. R. Wesley, Drawing	
	h. Wages Expense	

LO 3

Practice Exercise 3

EXERCISE 4-4 A partial work sheet for Marge's Place is shown below. Prepare the following adjustments on this work sheet for the month ended June 30, 20--.
a. Expired or used-up insurance, $450.
b. Depreciation expense on equipment, $750.
c. Wages accrued or earned since the last payday, $380 (owed and to be paid on the next payday).
d. Supplies used, $110.

	A	B	C	D	E
1	Marge's Place				
2	Work Sheet				
3	For Month Ended June 30, 20--				
4					
5		TRIAL BALANCE		ADJUSTMENTS	
6	ACCOUNT NAME	DEBIT	CREDIT	DEBIT	CREDIT
7	Cash	4,370.00			
8	Supplies	250.00			
9	Prepaid Insurance	1,800.00			
10	Equipment	4,880.00			
11	Accumulated Depreciation, Equipment		1,350.00		
12	Accounts Payable		2,539.00		
13	M. Benson, Capital		4,544.00		
14	M. Benson, Drawing	2,000.00			
15	Income from Services		6,937.00		
16	Rent Expense	1,086.00			
17	Supplies Expense	256.00			
18	Wages Expense	660.00			
19	Miscellaneous Expense	68.00			
20		15,370.00	15,370.00		
21					

Sheet1 / Sheet2 / Sheet3

EXERCISE 4-5 Complete the work sheet for Ramey Company, dated December 31, 20--, through the adjusted trial balance using the following adjustment information:

a. Expired or used-up insurance, $460.

b. Depreciation expense on equipment, $870. (Remember to credit the Accumulated Depreciation account for equipment, not Equipment.)

c. Wages accrued or earned since the last payday, $120 (owed and to be paid on the next payday).

d. Supplies remaining, $80.

LO 3

Practice Exercise 3

	A	B	C	D	E	F	G
1	Ramey Company						
2	Work Sheet						
3	For Month Ended December 31, 20--						
4							
5		TRIAL BALANCE		ADJUSTMENTS		ADJUSTED TRIAL BALANCE	
6	ACCOUNT NAME	DEBIT	CREDIT	DEBIT	CREDIT	DEBIT	CREDIT
7	Cash	5,190.00					
8	Supplies	430.00					
9	Prepaid Insurance	1,200.00					
10	Equipment	4,678.00					
11	Accumulated. Depr., Equip.		1,556.00				
12	Accounts Payable		1,875.00				
13	S. Ramey, Capital		6,026.00				
14	S. Ramey, Drawing	1,700.00					
15	Service Fees		5,836.00				
16	Rent Expense	965.00					
17	Supplies Expense	267.00					
18	Wages Expense	765.00					
19	Miscellaneous Expense	98.00					
20		15,293.00	15,293.00				
21							

Sheet1 / Sheet2 / Sheet3

EXERCISE 4-6 Journalize the adjusting entries from the partial work sheet on the next page for Brady Company for the month ended May 31.

LO 4

Practice Exercise 4

(Continued)

	A	H	I	J	K
1		Brady Company			
2		Work Sheet			
3		For Month Ended May 31, 20--			
4					
5		INCOME STATEMENT		BALANCE SHEET	
6	ACCOUNT NAME	DEBIT	CREDIT	DEBIT	CREDIT
7	Cash			5,501.00	
8	Supplies			230.00	
9	Prepaid Insurance			841.00	
10	Equipment			4,832.00	
11	Accumulated Depreciation, Equipment				1,720.00
12	Accounts Payable				1,085.00
13	S. Brady, Capital				6,800.00
14	S. Brady, Drawing			2,150.00	
15	Professional Fees		9,673.00		
16	Salaries Expense	3,787.00			
17	Rent Expense	1,484.00			
18	Miscellaneous Expense	134.00			
19					
20	Insurance Expense	200.00			
21	Depreciation Expense, Equipment	364.00			
22	Salaries Payable				330.00
23	Supplies Expense	85.00			
24		6,054.00	9,673.00	13,554.00	9,935.00
25	Net Income	3,619.00			3,619.00
26		9,673.00	9,673.00	13,554.00	13,554.00
27					

H ◀ ▶ H Sheet1 / Sheet2 / Sheet3

LO 4

Practice Exercise 4

EXERCISE 4-7 Journalize the adjusting entries from the partial work sheet for Newkirk Company as of September 30.

	A	B	C	D	E
1		Newkirk Company			
2		Work Sheet			
3		For Month Ended September 30, 20--			
4					
5		TRIAL BALANCE		ADJUSTMENTS	
6	ACCOUNT NAME	DEBIT	CREDIT	DEBIT	CREDIT
7	Cash	3,526.00			
8	Supplies	345.00			(d) 95.00
9	Prepaid Insurance	3,973.00			(a) 350.00
10	Equipment	3,678.00			
11	Accumulated Depreciation, Equipment		645.00		(b) 260.00
12	Accounts Payable		1,843.00		
13	J. Newkirk, Capital		10,752.00		
14	J. Newkirk, Drawing	3,000.00			
15	Service Fees		5,683.00		
16	Rent Expense	2,458.00			
17	Wages Expense	1,865.00		(c) 286.00	
18	Miscellaneous Expense	78.00			
19		18,923.00	18,923.00		
20	Insurance Expense			(a) 350.00	
21	Depreciation Expense, Equipment			(b) 260.00	
22	Wages Payable				(c) 286.00
23	Supplies Expense			(d) 95.00	
24				991.00	991.00
25					

H ◀ ▶ H Sheet1 / Sheet2 / Sheet3

LO 4

Practice Exercise 4

EXERCISE 4-8 Journalize the following adjusting entries that were included on the work sheet for the month ended December 31.

Dec. 31   Salaries for three days are unpaid at December 31, $2,700. Salaries are $4,500 for a five-day week.

31   Insurance was bought on September 1 for $3,600 for 12 months' coverage. Four months' coverage has expired, $1,200.

31   Depreciation for the month on equipment, $50, based on an asset costing $3,200 with a trade-in value of $200 and an estimated life of five years.

31   The balance in supplies before adjustment totaled $154. The amount of supplies on hand at the end of the year is $72.

LO 5

EXERCISE 4-9 Determine on which financial statement each account listed below is reported. Use the following abbreviations: Income Statement (IS), Statement of Owner's Equity (OE), and Balance Sheet (BS).

a. M. James, Capital
b. Cash
c. Rent Expense
d. Accumulated Depreciation, Equipment
e. Wages Payable
f. M. James, Drawing

g. Equipment
h. Office Supplies
i. Depreciation Expense
j. Office Supplies
k. Income from Services
l. Accounts Receivable

Problem Set A

LO 3

PROBLEM 4-1A The trial balance of Morgan's Insurance Agency as of September 30, after the firm has completed its first month of operations, is as follows:

Morgan's Insurance Company Trial Balance September 30, 20—		
Account Name	**Debit**	**Credit**
Cash	3,337	
Accounts Receivable	1,428	
Supplies	487	
Prepaid Insurance	775	
Office Equipment	5,146	
Accounts Payable		1,367
S. Morgan, Capital		9,528
S. Morgan, Drawing	1,000	
Commissions Earned		2,843
Rent Expense	885	
Travel Expense	388	
Utilities Expense	227	
Miscellaneous Expense	65	
	13,738	13,738

Required

1. Record the amounts in the Trial Balance columns of the work sheet.
2. Complete the work sheet by making the following adjustments and lettering each adjustment:
   a. Expired or used-up insurance, $300.
   b. Depreciation expense on office equipment, $600.
   c. Supplies used, $150.

Check Figure
Net Income, $228

CHAPTER ASSIGNMENTS

LO 3, 4

PROBLEM 4-2A The trial balance of Clayton Cleaners for the month ended September 30 is as follows:

Clayton Cleaners Trial Balance September 30, 20—		
Account Name	**Debit**	**Credit**
Cash	2,589	
Supplies	652	
Prepaid Insurance	1,136	
Equipment	21,752	
Accumulated Depreciation, Equipment		14,357
Accounts Payable		2,647
K. Clayton, Capital		28,169
K. Clayton, Drawing	21,359	
Income from Services		40,850
Wages Expense	23,983	
Rent Expense	11,673	
Utilities Expense	1,254	
Telephone Expense	1,144	
Miscellaneous Expense	481	
	86,023	86,023

Data for the adjustments are as follows:

a. Expired or used-up insurance, $800.
b. Depreciation expense on equipment, $2,700.
c. Wages accrued or earned since the last payday, $585 (owed and to be paid on the next payday).
d. Supplies remaining at the end of month, $230.

Check Figure
Net Loss, $2,192

Required

1. Complete a work sheet. (Skip this step if using CLGL.)
2. Journalize the adjusting entries.

*If you are using CLGL, use the year 2020 when recording transactions.

LO 4, 5

PROBLEM 4-3A The completed work sheet for Chelsey Decorators for the month of March is in the Working Papers, CengageNow or CLGL.

Check Figure
Total Assets, $15,003

Required

1. Journalize the adjusting entries.
2. If using CLGL, prepare an adjusted trial balance.
3. Prepare an income statement.
4. Prepare a statement of owner's equity. Assume that no additional investments were made in March.
5. Prepare a balance sheet.

*If you are using CLGL, use the year 2020 when recording transactions and preparing reports.

LO **3, 4, 5**

PROBLEM 4-4A The trial balance for Game Time on July 31 is as follows:

Game Time Trial Balance July 31, 20—		
Account Name	**Debit**	**Credit**
Cash	14,721	
Supplies	257	
Prepaid Insurance	1,295	
Equipment	17,642	
Accumulated Depreciation, Equipment		2,287
Repair Equipment	1,265	
Accumulated Depreciation, Repair Equipment		880
Accounts Payable		942
B. Ryan, Capital		23,871
B. Ryan, Drawing	2,000	
Game Fees		7,954
Concession Fees		3,752
Wages Expense	1,068	
Rent Expense	980	
Utilities Expense	246	
Repair Expense	180	
Miscellaneous Expense	32	
	39,686	39,686

Data for month-end adjustments are as follows:

a. Expired or used-up insurance, $480.
b. Depreciation expense on equipment, $850.
c. Depreciation expense on repair equipment, $120.
d. Wages accrued or earned since the last payday, $525 (owed and to be paid on the next payday).
e. Supplies used, $70.

Required

1. Complete a work sheet for the month. (Skip this step if using CLGL.)
2. Journalize the adjusting entries.
3. If using CLGL prepare an adjusted trial balance.
4. Prepare an income statement, a statement of owner's equity, and a balance sheet. Assume that no additional investments were made during July.

*If you are using CLGL, use the year 2020 when recording transactions and preparing reports.

Check Figure
Net Income, $7,155

LO   3, 4, 5 ....

PROBLEM 4-5A The trial balance for Benner Hair Salon on March 31 is as follows:

Benner Hair Salon Trial Balance March 31, 20—		
Account Name	**Debit**	**Credit**
Cash	4,440	
Supplies	150	
Prepaid Insurance	2,354	
Equipment	10,507	
Accumulated Depreciation, Equipment		1,000
Accounts Payable		240
A. Benner, Capital		13,449
A. Benner, Drawing	1,500	
Salon Fees		6,230
Wages Expense	1,036	
Rent Expense	650	
Utilities Expense	130	
Repair Expense	65	
Miscellaneous Expense	87	
	20,919	20,919

Data for month-end adjustments are as follows:

a. Expired or used-up insurance, $300.
b. Depreciation expense on equipment, $500.
c. Wages accrued or earned since the last payday, $235 (owed and to be paid on the next payday).
d. Supplies remaining at the end of the month, $65.

Check Figure
Net Income, $3,142

Required
1. Complete a work sheet for the month. (Skip this step if using CLGL.)
2. Journalize the adjusting entries.
3. Prepare an income statement, a statement of owner's equity, and a balance sheet. Assume that no additional investments were made during March.

*If you are using CLGL, use the year 2020 when recording transactions and preparing reports.

Problem Set B

LO   3 ....

PROBLEM 4-1B The trial balance for Mason's Insurance Agency as of August 31, after the firm has completed its first month of operations, is shown on the next page.

Mason's Insurance Company
Trial Balance
August 31, 20—

Account Name	Debit	Credit
Cash	3,527	
Accounts Receivable	1,219	
Supplies	492	
Prepaid Insurance	1,362	
Office Equipment	3,939	
Accounts Payable		2,071
C. Mason, Capital		9,020
C. Mason, Drawing	1,900	
Commissions Earned		3,520
Rent Expense	1,695	
Travel Expense	225	
Utilities Expense	198	
Miscellaneous Expense	54	
	14,611	14,611

Required

1. Record amounts in the Trial Balance columns of the work sheet.
2. Complete the work sheet by making the following adjustments and lettering each adjustment:
   a. Expired or used-up insurance, $260.
   b. Depreciation expense on office equipment, $900.
   c. Supplies used, $200.

Check Figure
Net Loss, $12

LO 3, 4

PROBLEM 4-2B The trial balance of The New Decors for the month ended September 30 is as follows:

The New Decors
Trial Balance
September 30, 20—

Account Name	Debit	Credit
Cash	4,378	
Supplies	1,864	
Prepaid Insurance	1,345	
Equipment	30,978	
Accumulated Depreciation, Equipment		15,235
Accounts Payable		3,751
R. Becker, Capital		44,208
R. Becker, Drawing	20,445	
Income from Services		44,791
Wages Expense	29,761	
Rent Expense	15,932	
Utilities Expense	1,573	
Telephone Expense	1,271	
Miscellaneous Expense	438	
	107,985	107,985

(Continued)

Data for the adjustments are as follows:
a. Expired or used-up insurance, $425.
b. Depreciation expense on equipment, $2,750.
c. Wages accrued or earned since the last payday, $475 (owed and to be paid on the next payday).
d. Supplies remaining at end of month, $215.

Check Figure
Net Loss, $9,483

Required
1. Complete a work sheet. (Skip this step if using GL.)
2. Journalize the adjusting entries.

*If you are using CLGL, use the year 2020 when recording transactions.

PROBLEM 4-3B The completed work sheet for Juarez Design for the month of March is in your Working Papers, CengageNow or CLGL.

Check Figure
Total Assets, $21,997

Required
1. Journalize the adjusting entries.
2. Prepare an income statement.
3. Prepare a statement of owner's equity. Assume that no additional investments were made in March.
4. Prepare a balance sheet.

PROBLEM 4-4B The trial balance for Harris Pitch and Putt on June 30 is as follows:

Harris Pitch and Putt Trial Balance June 30, 20—		
Account Name	**Debit**	**Credit**
Cash	5,532	
Supplies	246	
Prepaid Insurance	1,284	
Equipment	21,687	
Accumulated Depreciation, Equipment		1,478
Repair Equipment	5,289	
Accumulated Depreciation, Repair Equipment		1,285
Accounts Payable		860
W. Harris, Capital		23,110
W. Harris, Drawing	2,565	
Golf Fees		11,487
Concession Fees		3,763
Wages Expense	3,163	
Rent Expense	1,350	
Utilities Expense	457	
Repair Expense	171	
Miscellaneous Expense	239	
	41,983	41,983

Data for month-end adjustments are as follows:
a. Expired or used-up insurance, $380.
b. Depreciation expense on equipment, $1,950.
c. Depreciation expense on repair equipment, $1,650.

d.   Wages accrued or earned since the last payday, $585 (owed and to be paid on the next payday).
e.   Supplies remaining at end of month, $120.

Required

1. Complete a work sheet for the month. (Skip this step if using CLGL.)
2. Journalize the adjusting entries.
3. If using CLGL, prepare an adjusted trial balance.
4. Prepare an income statement, a statement of owner's equity, and a balance sheet. Assume that no additional investments were made during June.

Check Figure
Net Income, $5,179

*If you are using CLGL, use the year 2020 when recording transactions.

PROBLEM 4-5B The trial balance for Wilson Financial Services on January 31 is as follows:

LO **3, 4, 5**

CLGL

Wilson Financial Services Trial Balance January 31, 20—		
Account Name	**Debit**	**Credit**
Cash	17,910	
Supplies	650	
Prepaid Insurance	4,500	
Equipment	15,400	
Accumulated Depreciation, Equipment		3,500
Accounts Payable		2,450
L. Wilson, Capital		25,800
L. Wilson, Drawing	3,000	
Financial Services Fees		15,550
Wages Expense	4,025	
Rent Expense	1,200	
Utilities Expense	430	
Repair Expense	110	
Miscellaneous Expense	75	
	47,300	47,300

Data for month-end adjustments are as follows:
a.   Expired or used-up insurance, $750.
b.   Depreciation expense on equipment, $300.
c.   Wages accrued or earned since the last payday, $1,055 (owed and to be paid on the next payday).
d.   Supplies used, $535.

Required

1. Complete a work sheet for the month. (Skip this step if using CLGL.)
2. Journalize the adjusting entries.
3. If using CLGL, prepare an adjusted trial balance.
4. Prepare an income statement, a statement of owner's equity, and a balance sheet. Assume that no additional investments were made during January.

Check Figure
Net Income, $7,070

*If you are using CLGL, use the year 2020 when recording transactions and preparing reports.

Accounting with QuickBooks® Online

Go to the QuickBooks Online Chapter 4 Appendix located on the Cengage Learning companion site at Cengage.com. Review the *Accounting with QuickBooks Online* (step-by-step guide to using QuickBooks Online). *Accounting with QuickBooks Online,* Chapter 4 will introduce you to preparing journal entries to account for prepaid insurance, depreciation on equipment, accrued wages, and consumptions of supplies. Additionally, you will prepare an adjusted trial balance, an income statement (after adjusting entries), and a balance sheet (after adjusting entries).

Activities

Why Does It Matter?

RIDE THE DUCKS OF SEATTLE, Seattle, Washington

Ride the Ducks of Seattle may seem like an unlikely name for a thriving business—but it is the name of a real business! The year-round Seattle tour company uses vehicles that can be providing a road tour one minute and plying the waters of Elliott Bay the next. One of Ride the Ducks' employees is a bookkeeper who also serves as a reservationist, tour vehicle cleaner, and computer specialist. In addition to recording and posting journal entries each month, he makes adjusting entries. What are some of the adjusting entries this bookkeeper might make for Ride the Ducks of Seattle?

What Would You Say?

You are the bookkeeper for a small but thriving business. You have asked the owner for the information you need to make adjusting entries for depreciation, supplies, insurance, and wages. He says that he's really busy and that what you've done so far is "close enough." Explain the need for adjusting entries and their effect on the owner's balance sheet and the "bottom line" on the income statement.

What Do You Think?

Your supervisor just finished a work sheet for the month of June, but all of the columns except those shown on the next page were left unreadable because of a spilled latte. You have been asked to journalize the adjusting entries using the surviving partial work sheet.

ACCOUNT NAME	INCOME STATEMENT		BALANCE SHEET	
	DEBIT	CREDIT	DEBIT	CREDIT
Cash			8,476.00	
Accounts Receivable			1,486.00	
Equipment			12,367.00	
Accumulated Depreciation, Equipment				3,610.00
Accounts Payable				2,813.00
G. Kramer, Capital				11,707.00
G. Kramer, Drawing			1,100.00	
Income from Services		11,216.00		
Rent Expense	2,510.00			
Wages Expense	2,467.00			
Insurance Expense	210.00			
Depreciation Expense, Equipment	750.00			
Wages Payable				620.00
	5,937.00	11,216.00	24,029.00	18,750.00
Net Income	5,279.00			5,279.00
	11,216.00	11,216.00	24,029.00	24,029.00

What Would You Do?

Your client is preparing financial statements to show the bank. You know that he has incurred a refrigeration repair expense during the month, but you see no such expense on the books. When you question the client, he tells you that he has not yet paid the $1,255 bill. Your client is on the accrual basis of accounting. He does not want the refrigeration repair expense on the books as of the end of the month because he wants his profits to look good for the bank. Is your client behaving ethically by suggesting that the refrigeration repair expense not be booked until the $1,255 is paid? Are you behaving ethically if you agree to the client's request? What principle is involved here?

CONTINUING PROBLEM

Adjustments

Although you printed the trial balance and financial statements to get an idea of how All About You Spa is doing financially, some accounts are not accurate. You need to make adjusting entries to provide a clearer picture of how the spa is doing.

HOW TO COMPUTE THE ADJUSTMENTS

Compute the adjustment amounts for the month of October, using the following information:

Adjustment (a): Liability insurance for six months was purchased during the first days of the month. That protection for one month has been used or expended.

Adjustments (b) and (c): Office equipment and spa equipment have depreciated. That means they have been in use for a month and have, for accounting purposes, lost some usefulness. This is an estimate, of course, which allows us to expense the depreciation and, in effect, lowers the book value (value on the books) of both types of equipment.

(b): The owner, Anika Valli, purchased office equipment totaling $1,345. The office equipment will be depreciated using the straight-line method. The office equipment is estimated to have a salvage (trade-in) value of $550 and is expected to last five years. Remember, you want to compute the depreciation for one month, not one year.

(c): Anika Valli invested spa equipment totaling $9,125 in the business ($3,575 of her own spa equipment plus $5,550 of new spa equipment purchased). The spa equipment will be depreciated using the straight-line method. The spa equipment is estimated to have a trade-in, or salvage, value of $125 and is expected to last five years. Remember, you want to compute the depreciation for one month, not one year.

Adjustment (d): All About You Spa owes one day of wages to its employees. The month's total wages paid in October amounted to $8,300. The employees worked 21 days but were paid for only 20 days because the payday for the last day worked is in the next pay period.

Adjustments (e) and (f): After a count of supplies at the end of the month, All About You Spa has $125 remaining in Office Supplies and $255 remaining in Spa Supplies.

Required

1. Complete a work sheet for the month (if required by your instructor).

2. Journalize the adjusting entries in the general journal.

   - If you are preparing the adjusting entries manually, using Working Papers, enter your transactions beginning on page 4.

All About You
Spa

3. Post the adjusting entries to the general ledger accounts.

- Ignore this step if you are using CLGL.

4. Prepare an adjusted trial balance as of October 31, 20--.

5. Prepare an income statement (after adjustment) for the month ended October 31, 20--.

6. Prepare a statement of owner's equity (after adjustment) for the month ended October 31, 20--.

7. Prepare a balance sheet (after adjustment) as of October 31, 20--.

*If you are using CLGL, use the year 2020 when recording transactions and preparing reports.

Check Figures
4. Adjusted trial balance total, $50,943.25
5. Net income, $7,196.75
6. A. Valli, Capital, ending balance, $34,271.75
7. Total assets, $37,256.75

5 Closing Entries and the Post-Closing Trial Balance

Learning Objectives

After you have completed this chapter, you will be able to do the following:

1 List the steps in the accounting cycle.

2 Journalize and post closing entries for a service enterprise.

3 Prepare a post-closing trial balance.

4 Define cash basis and accrual basis accounting.

5 Prepare interim statements.

To: Amy Roberts, CPA
Subject: It's the End of the Year!

Hi Amy,

Well, I made it! The business has been successful this year, and I am even earning a profit! I can't begin to thank you enough for all the help you've given me. I guess I'll just continue to record transactions using everything we've talked about so far. Is there anything else that still needs to be completed?

Thanks,

Janie

To: Janie Conner
Subject: RE: It's the End of the Year!

Hi Janie,

I'm glad to hear the business has been successful! At the end of each fiscal period, two more steps need to take place to finish the accounting work: closing entries and post-closing trial balance. Let's start with closing entries. Closing entries are completed to prepare the accounts for next year. Like last time, we'll be looking at the work sheet to help us prepare closing entries. Here are the steps to learn:

_____ 1. Understand the steps of the accounting cycle (which is what you've been learning all along).

_____ 2. Learn how to record and post closing entries.

Let me know if you need help!

Amy

5-1 STEPS IN THE ACCOUNTING CYCLE

Let's review the steps in the accounting cycle for an entire fiscal period. Remember that a fiscal period is generally 12 consecutive months.

STEP 1. Analyze source documents and record business transactions in a journal.

STEP 2. Post journal entries to the accounts in the ledger.

STEP 3. Prepare a trial balance.

STEP 4. Gather adjustment data and record the adjusting entries on a work sheet.

STEP 5. Complete the work sheet.

STEP 6. Journalize and post the adjusting entries from the data on the work sheet.

STEP 7. Prepare financial statements from the data on the work sheet.

STEP 8. Journalize and post the closing entries.

STEP 9. Prepare a post-closing trial balance.

This chapter explains the procedure for completing the final steps in the accounting cycle: journalizing and posting the closing entries, and preparing the post-closing trial balance. To introduce you to these final steps in the accounting cycle, we assume that the fiscal period for Conner's Whitewater Adventures ends after one month. We make this assumption so that we can thoroughly cover the material and give you a chance to practice its application. The entire accounting cycle is outlined in Figure 1 on the next page.

5-2 CLOSING ENTRIES

To help you understand the reason for the closing entries, let's take a look at a version of the fundamental accounting equation.

$$\text{Assets} = \text{Liabilities} + \text{Capital} - \text{Drawing} + \text{Revenue} - \text{Expenses}$$

Accounting Language

Accrual basis
of accounting (p. 207)

Cash basis
of accounting (p. 206)

Closing entries (p. 196)

Income Summary
account (p. 197)

Interim statements (p. 207)

Nominal (temporary-
equity) accounts (p. 201)

Post-closing
trial balance (p. 205)

Real (permanent)
accounts (p. 201)

1 List the steps in the accounting cycle.

Learning Objective

2 Journalize and post closing entries for a service enterprise.

Learning Objective

Figure 1
The accounting cycle

We know that the income statement, as stated in the third line of its heading, covers a period of time. The income statement consists of revenue minus expenses for this period of time only. So when the next fiscal period begins, we should start with zero balances. We start over again each period.

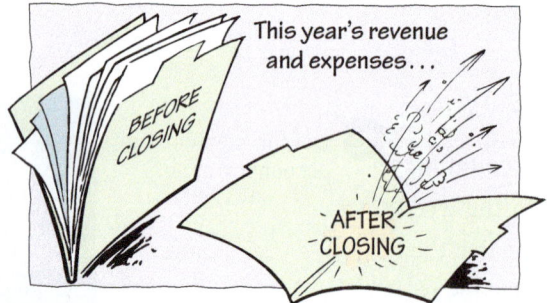

Closing entries empty, or zero out, temporary owner's equity accounts and prepare the accounts for the new accounting period—much like when you empty the information from your tax folders for one year so that you can fill the folders with the new year's revenue and expense receipts.

5-2a Purpose of Closing Entries

This brings us to the *purpose* of the **closing entries**, which is to close (or zero out) revenue, expense, and Drawing accounts. We do this because their balances apply to only one fiscal period. Closing entries are made after the last adjusting entry and after the financial statements have been prepared. With the coming of the next fiscal period, we want to start from zero, recording revenue and expenses for the new fiscal period. The closing entries also update the owner's Capital account.

Accountants also refer to closing the accounts as *clearing the accounts*. For income tax purposes, this is certainly understandable. No one wants to pay income tax more than once on the same income, and the Internal Revenue Service doesn't allow you to count an expense more than once. So now we have this:

$$\text{Assets} = \text{Liabilities} + \text{Capital} - \underset{\text{(closed)}}{\cancel{\text{Drawing}}} + \underset{\text{(closed)}}{\cancel{\text{Revenue}}} - \underset{\text{(closed)}}{\cancel{\text{Expenses}}}$$

The assets, liabilities, and owner's Capital accounts remain open. The balance sheet gives the present balances of these accounts. The accountant carries the asset, liability, and Capital account balances over to the next fiscal period.

5-2b Procedure for Closing

The procedure for closing is simply to balance off the account (in other words, to make the balance *equal to zero*). This meets our objective, which is to start from zero in the next fiscal period. Let's illustrate this first with T accounts. Suppose an account to be closed has a debit balance of $870. To make the balance equal to zero, we *credit* the account for $870.

	Debit		Credit	
Balance	870	Closing		**870**
New Balance	0			

Now suppose an account to be closed has a credit balance of $1,400. To make the balance equal to zero, we *debit* the account for $1,400.

	Debit		Credit	
Closing	**1,400**	Balance		1,400
		New Balance		0

Remember, every entry must have at least one debit and one credit. So to record the other half of the closing entry, we bring into existence the **Income Summary account**. The Income Summary account does not have plus and minus signs and does not have a normal balance, just debit and credit.

There are four steps in the closing procedure:

STEP 1. Close the revenue account(s) into Income Summary.

STEP 2. Close the expense account(s) into Income Summary.

STEP 3. Close the Income Summary account into the Capital account, transferring the net income or net loss to the Capital account.

STEP 4. Close the Drawing account into the Capital account.

To illustrate, we return to Conner's Whitewater Adventures. For the purpose of the illustration, assume that Conner's Whitewater Adventures' fiscal period ends after one month. We have the following T account balances in the revenue and expense accounts after the adjustments have been posted.

Income from Tours				Advertising Expense		
−	+			+	−	
	Balance	23,320		Balance	620	

Wages Expense				Utilities Expense		
+	−			+	−	
Balance	2,832			Balance	225	

Rent Expense				Insurance Expense		
+	−			+	−	
Balance	1,250			Balance	625	

Supplies Expense				Depreciation Expense, Equipment		
+	−			+	−	
Balance	460			Balance	512	

STEP 1. Close the revenue account(s) into Income Summary.

To make the balance of Income from Tours equal to zero, we *balance it off*, or debit it, in the amount of $23,320. Because we need an offsetting credit, we credit Income Summary for the same amount. Notice that there are no signs in Income Summary, only debit and credit.

QuickBooks® Online Tip

QuickBooks Online automatically closes revenues and expenses. No journal entry is required.

Income from Tours					Income Summary		
	−	+					
Closing	23,320	Balance	23,320			(Revenue)	23,320

The balance of Income from Tours is transferred to Income Summary.

STEP 2. Close the expense account(s) into Income Summary.

To make the balances of the expense accounts equal to zero, we need to *balance them off*, or credit them. Again, the T accounts are useful for formulating this journal entry.

Wages Expense					Income Summary			
	+	−						
Balance	2,832	Closing	2,832	(Expenses)	6,524	(Revenue)	23,320

Rent Expense			
	+	−	
Balance	1,250	Closing	1,250

Supplies Expense			
	+	−	
Balance	460	Closing	460

Advertising Expense			
	+	−	
Balance	620	Closing	620

Utilities Expense			
	+	−	
Balance	225	Closing	225

Insurance Expense			
	+	−	
Balance	625	Closing	625

Depreciation Expense, Equipment			
	+	−	
Balance	512	Closing	512

STEP 3. Close the Income Summary account into the Capital account, transferring the net income or net loss to the Capital account.

Recall that we created Income Summary so that we could have a debit and a credit in each closing entry. Now that it has done its job, we close it out. We use the same procedure as before, making the balance equal to zero, or balancing off the account. We transfer, or close, the balance of the Income Summary account into the Capital account, as shown in the T accounts below. In addition, Figure 2 shows the closing entries recorded in the general journal for steps 1 through 3.

Income Summary

(Expenses)	6,524	(Revenue)	23,320
Closing	**16,796**	Balance	16,796

J. Conner, Capital

	−	+	
		Balance	95,200
		Closing	**16,796**

Figure 2

Closing entries for Conner's Whitewater Adventures

		GENERAL JOURNAL				Page 4				
Date		Description	Post. Ref.	Debit			Credit			
		Closing Entries								
Step 1	30	Income from Tours		23 3 2 0	00					
		Income Summary					23 3 2 0	00		
	30	Income Summary		6 5 2 4	00					
		Wages Expense					2 8 3 2	00		
		Rent Expense					1 2 5 0	00		
Step 2		Supplies Expense					4 6 0	00		
		Advertising Expense					6 2 0	00		
		Utilities Expense					2 2 5	00		
		Insurance Expense					6 2 5	00		
		Depreciation Expense, Equipment					5 1 2	00		
Step 3	30	Income Summary		16 7 9 6	00					
		J. Conner, Capital					16 7 9 6	00		

Income Summary is always closed into the Capital account by the amount of revenue minus expenses (the net income or the net loss). Comparing net income or net loss on the work sheet with the closing entry for Income Summary can serve as a checkpoint or verification for you.

Net income is added (credited) to the Capital account because, as shown in the statement of owner's equity, net income is treated as an addition. Net loss, on the other hand, is subtracted from (debited to) the Capital account, because net loss is treated as a deduction in the statement of owner's equity. Assuming that J. Doe Company had a net loss of $600, here's how to close Income Summary:

Income Summary

(Expenses)	3,000	(Revenue)	**2,400**
Balance	600	Closing	**600**

J. Doe, Capital

(Net Loss)	**600**	−	+	
			Balance	42,000

The entry to close Income Summary into J. Doe's Capital account for a net loss would look like the following:

		GENERAL JOURNAL														Page 3	
Date		Description	Post. Ref.		Debit						Credit						
		Closing Entries															
	31	J. Doe, Capital				6	0	0	00								
		Income Summary											6	0	0	00	

STEP 4. Close the Drawing account into the Capital account.

Let's return to the example of Conner's Whitewater Adventures. The Drawing account applies to only one fiscal period, so it too must be closed. Drawing is not an expense because it did not help the business generate revenue. **And because Drawing is not an expense, it cannot affect net income or net loss.** It appears in the statement of owner's equity as a deduction from the Capital account, so it is closed directly into the Capital account. We balance off the Drawing account, or make its balance equal to zero, by transferring the balance of Drawing to the Capital account.

J. Conner, Drawing				J. Conner, Capital		
+	−		−	+		
Balance 3,500	Closing **3,500**	(Drawing) **3,500**	Balance 95,200			
			(Net Inc.) 16,796			
			Balance 108,496			

The entire set of journal entries in the closing procedure for Conner's Whitewater Adventures is shown below.

Figure 3
Closing entries for Conner's Whitewater Adventures

		GENERAL JOURNAL														Page 4	
Date		Description	Post. Ref.		Debit						Credit						
		Closing Entries															
Step 1	30	Income from Tours		23	3	2	0	00									
		Income Summary									23	3	2	0	00		
	30	Income Summary			6	5	2	4	00								
		Wages Expense										2	8	3	2	00	
		Rent Expense										1	2	5	0	00	
		Supplies Expense											4	6	0	00	
Step 2		Advertising Expense											6	2	0	00	
		Utilities Expense											2	2	5	00	
		Insurance Expense											6	2	5	00	
		Depreciation Expense, Equipment											5	1	2	00	
	30	Income Summary			16	7	9	6	00								
Step 3		J. Conner, Capital									16	7	9	6	00		
Step 4	30	J. Conner, Capital			3	5	0	0	00								
		J. Conner, Drawing									3	5	0	0	00		

These closing entries show that Conner's Whitewater Adventures has net income of $16,796, the owner has withdrawn $3,500 for personal expenses, and $13,296 ($16,796 − $3,500) has been retained in the business, thereby increasing capital.

5-2c Closing Entries Using Cloud-based Accounting Applications

Making closing entries using accounting software or cloud-based accounting applications, such as QuickBooks Online, is frequently an automatic procedure. Most accounting software or cloud-based applications, like QuickBooks Online, automatically update the capital account or at a minimum automatically close the revenue and expense accounts, based on the company's fiscal year settings. If you are using accounting software, or a cloud-based accounting application, be sure to review and understand the automated closing process involved.

5-2d Closing Entries Using the Work Sheet

You can gather the information for the closing entries directly from the ledger accounts or from the work sheet. Because the Income Statement columns of the work sheet consist entirely of revenues and expenses, you can pick up the figures for three of the four closing entries from these columns. Figure 4, on page 202, shows a partial work sheet for Conner's Whitewater Adventures.

You can plan the closing entries by balancing off all of the figures that appear in the Income Statement columns. For example, in the Income Statement Credit column, there is a credit for $23,320 (Income from Tours), so we debit that account for $23,320 and credit Income Summary for $23,320.

There are debits for $2,832, $1,250, $620, $225, $460, $625, and $512 (expense accounts). So now we *credit* these accounts for the same amounts and debit Income Summary for the total ($6,524).

Next, we close Income Summary into Capital, using the net income figure ($16,796) already shown on the work sheet in Figure 4.

We do, of course, have to get the last closing entry from the Balance Sheet columns to close Drawing.

Incidentally, accountants call the accounts that are to be closed (such as revenue, expenses, and Drawing) **nominal (temporary-equity) accounts**. These accounts are temporary in that their balances apply to only one fiscal period. The *equity* aspect pertains because all of these accounts come under the umbrella of owner's equity.

On the other hand, accountants call the accounts that remain open (such as assets, liabilities, and Capital) **real (permanent) accounts**. These accounts have balances that will be carried over to the next fiscal period. They are *permanent* because as long as the company exists, these accounts will retain their balances.

5-2e Posting the Closing Entries

In the Item column of the ledger account, we write the word *Closing*. To show that the balance of an account is zero, we draw a line through both the Debit Balance and the Credit Balance columns.

Figure 4

Partial work sheet for Conner's Whitewater Adventures

Conner's Whitewater Adventures

Work Sheet

For Month Ended June 30, 20--

ACCOUNT NAME	TRIAL BALANCE DEBIT A + Draw. + E	TRIAL BALANCE CREDIT Accum. Depr. + L + Cap. + R	ADJUSTMENTS DEBIT	ADJUSTMENTS CREDIT	ADJUSTED TRIAL BALANCE DEBIT A + Draw. + E	ADJUSTED TRIAL BALANCE CREDIT Accum. Depr. + L + Cap. + R	INCOME STATEMENT DEBIT E	INCOME STATEMENT CREDIT R	BALANCE SHEET DEBIT A + Draw.	BALANCE SHEET CREDIT Accum. Depr. + L + Cap.
Cash	55,890.00				55,890.00				55,890.00	
Accounts Receivable	4,250.00				4,250.00				4,250.00	
Supplies	675.00			(a) 460.00	215.00				215.00	
Prepaid Insurance	1,875.00			(b) 625.00	1,250.00				1,250.00	
Equipment	51,300.00				51,300.00				51,300.00	
Accounts Payable		3,425.00				3,425.00				3,425.00
J. Conner, Capital		95,200.00				95,200.00				95,200.00
J. Conner, Drawing	3,500.00				3,500.00				3,500.00	
Income from Tours		23,320.00				23,320.00		23,320.00		
Wages Expense	2,360.00		(d) 472.00		2,832.00		2,832.00			
Rent Expense	1,250.00				1,250.00		1,250.00			
Advertising Expense	620.00				620.00		620.00			
Utilities Expense	225.00				225.00		225.00			
Supplies Expense			(a) 460.00		460.00		460.00			
Insurance Expense			(b) 625.00		625.00		625.00			
Depr. Exp., Equip.			(c) 512.00		512.00		512.00			
Accum. Depr., Equip.				(c) 512.00		512.00				512.00
Wages Payable				(d) 472.00		472.00				472.00
	121,945.00	121,945.00	2,069.00	2,069.00	122,929.00	122,929.00	6,524.00	23,320.00	116,405.00	99,609.00
Net Income							16,796.00			16,796.00
							23,320.00	23,320.00	116,405.00	116,405.00

Sheet1 | Sheet2 | Sheet3

After we have posted the closing entries, the Capital, Drawing, Income Summary, revenue, and expense accounts of Conner's Whitewater Adventures appear as follows:

GENERAL LEDGER

ACCOUNT J. Conner, Capital   **ACCOUNT NO. 311**

Date		Item	Post. Ref.	Debit	Credit	Balance Debit	Balance Credit
20--							
June	1		1		90 0 0 0 00		90 0 0 0 00
	4		1		5 2 0 0 00		95 2 0 0 00
	30	Closing	4		16 7 9 6 00		111 9 9 6 00
	30	Closing	4	3 5 0 0 00			108 4 9 6 00

ACCOUNT J. Conner, Drawing   **ACCOUNT NO. 312**

Date		Item	Post. Ref.	Debit	Credit	Balance Debit	Balance Credit
20--							
June	30		3	3 5 0 0 00		3 5 0 0 00	
	30	Closing	4		3 5 0 0 00	——	——

ACCOUNT Income Summary   **ACCOUNT NO. 313**

Date		Item	Post. Ref.	Debit	Credit	Balance Debit	Balance Credit
20--							
June	30	Closing	4		23 3 2 0 00		23 3 2 0 00
	30	Closing	4	6 5 2 4 00			16 7 9 6 00
	30	Closing	4	16 7 9 6 00		——	——

ACCOUNT Income from Tours   **ACCOUNT NO. 411**

Date		Item	Post. Ref.	Debit	Credit	Balance Debit	Balance Credit
20--							
June	7		1		8 0 0 0 00		8 0 0 0 00
	15		2		6 7 5 0 00		14 7 5 0 00
	30		3		8 5 7 0 00		23 3 2 0 00
	30	Closing	4	23 3 2 0 00		——	——

ACCOUNT Wages Expense   **ACCOUNT NO. 511**

Date		Item	Post. Ref.	Debit	Credit	Balance Debit	Balance Credit
20--							
June	24		2	2 3 6 0 00		2 3 6 0 00	
	30	Adj.	4	4 7 2 00		2 8 3 2 00	
	30	Closing	4		2 8 3 2 00	——	——

ACCOUNT Rent Expense   **ACCOUNT NO. 512**

Date		Item	Post. Ref.	Debit	Credit	Balance Debit	Balance Credit
20--							
June	8		1	1 2 5 0 00		1 2 5 0 00	
	30	Closing	4		1 2 5 0 00		

ACCOUNT Supplies Expense   **ACCOUNT NO. 513**

Date		Item	Post. Ref.	Debit	Credit	Balance Debit	Balance Credit
20--							
June	30	Adj.	4	4 6 0 00		4 6 0 00	
	30	Closing	4		4 6 0 00		

ACCOUNT Advertising Expense   **ACCOUNT NO. 514**

Date		Item	Post. Ref.	Debit	Credit	Balance Debit	Balance Credit
20--							
June	14		2	6 2 0 00		6 2 0 00	
	30	Closing	4		6 2 0 00		

ACCOUNT Utilities Expense   **ACCOUNT NO. 515**

Date		Item	Post. Ref.	Debit	Credit	Balance Debit	Balance Credit
20--							
June	18		2	2 2 5 00		2 2 5 00	
	30	Closing	4		2 2 5 00		

ACCOUNT Insurance Expense   **ACCOUNT NO. 516**

Date		Item	Post. Ref.	Debit	Credit	Balance Debit	Balance Credit
20--							
June	30	Adj.	4	6 2 5 00		6 2 5 00	
	30	Closing	4		6 2 5 00		

ACCOUNT Depreciation Expense, Equipment   **ACCOUNT NO. 517**

Date		Item	Post. Ref.	Debit	Credit	Balance Debit	Balance Credit
20--							
June	30	Adj.	4	5 1 2 00		5 1 2 00	
	30	Closing	4		5 1 2 00		

To: Amy Roberts, CPA
Subject: **Closing Entries Recorded and Posted**

Hi Amy,
I have recorded and posted the closing entries. Last time we talked, you mentioned that we need to prepare a post-closing trial balance after the closing entries. What's the purpose of that trial balance?
Thanks,
Janie

To: Janie Conner
Subject: **RE: Closing Entries Recorded and Posted**

Hi Janie,
That's right. The post-closing trial balance is the next step. It is prepared after the closing entries have been recorded and posted, and it will help ensure the debit balances equal the credit balances. Let's take a look at the post-closing trial balance. As always, email me back if you have questions.
Amy

5-3 THE POST-CLOSING TRIAL BALANCE

After posting the closing entries and before going on to the next fiscal period, it is important to verify the balances of the accounts that remain open. To do so, prepare a **post-closing trial balance** using the final balance figures from the ledger accounts. The purpose of the post-closing trial balance is to make sure the debit balances equal the credit balances.

Note that the accounts listed in the post-closing trial balance (assets, liabilities, and Capital) are the *real*, or *permanent*, *accounts*. (See Figure 5.) The accountant carries the balances of the permanent accounts forward from one fiscal period to another.

3 Prepare a post-closing trial balance.

Learning Objective

Figure 5
Post-closing trial balance for Conner's Whitewater Adventures

Conner's Whitewater Adventures Post-Closing Trial Balance June 30, 20—		
Account Name	**Debit**	**Credit**
Cash	55,890	
Accounts Receivable	4,250	
Supplies	215	
Prepaid Insurance	1,250	
Equipment	51,300	
Accumulated Depreciation, Equipment		512
Accounts Payable		3,425
Wages Payable		472
J. Conner, Capital		108,496
	112,905	112,905

Notice that the *nominal*, or *temporary-equity*, *accounts* (revenue, expenses, Income Summary, and Drawing), which are closed at the end of each fiscal period, are not shown on the post-closing trial balance. These accounts are not shown because they have zero balances.

If the total debits and total credits of the post-closing trial balance are not equal, here's a recommended procedure for tracking down the error.

1. Re-add the trial balance columns.
2. Check that the figures were correctly transferred from the ledger accounts to the post-closing trial balance.
3. Verify the posting of the adjusting entries and the recording of the new balances.
4. Check that the closing entries have been posted and that all revenue, expense, Income Summary, and Drawing accounts have zero balances.

5-4 THE BASES OF ACCOUNTING: CASH AND ACCRUAL

The basis of accounting that a company chooses has a direct effect on the company's net income and the company's income tax. The business must use the same basis of accounting from year to year, and the basis of accounting must clearly reflect the net income of the business.

Under the **cash basis of accounting**, revenue is recorded when it is received in cash and expenses are recorded when they are paid in cash. Many small businesses' and individuals' personal income taxes are recorded on the cash basis.

SMALL BUSINESS **SUCCESS**

Do I Need an Accountant?

If you are not taking this class because you want to be an accountant or a bookkeeper, you might be taking the class because you plan on owning and operating a small business. Many new small business owners take on the responsibilities of being the accountant for their business. However, at some point, your business will begin to grow, and you may need to consider hiring someone to manage your accounting books so that your time is free to run the business.

An accountant can help you in many areas of your small business, such as:

• What should my business structure be—sole proprietorship, partnership, S corporation, or corporation?

• What software should I use for my accounting?
• How do I handle the payroll for employees?
• What are my requirements for filing taxes?
• What expenses are deductible for tax purposes?
• How do I prepare financial statements when applying for a loan?

So how do you find an accountant? The best way is by referrals. Ask other businesses in your industry for references or visit. Find AICPA at www.aicpa.org/ForThePublic/Pages/ForthePublic.aspx for more recommendations.

Under the **accrual basis of accounting**, revenue is recorded when it is earned and expenses are recorded when they are incurred (when they occur or when the bill is received). For example, in the sale of goods, revenue is counted by the seller when the buyer accepts delivery of the goods. Expenses are recorded by the seller of the goods when the costs are incurred. Recall that this is called the matching principle because revenue in one fiscal period is matched to expenses incurred in the same period. If your business produces, purchases, or sells merchandise, the business must keep an inventory and use the accrual method for sales and purchases of merchandise.

Let's look at this example of the differences between cash and accrual. Roby Hair Salon pays $6,000 cash in July for the current month (July) and the following five months of rent (August–December). If Roby uses the cash basis of accounting, the full $6,000 will be recorded as rent expense in July. If Roby uses the accrual basis of accounting instead, the expense will be spread over the six months. The amount of $1,000 ($6,000/6) will be recorded each month.

	Cash Basis	Accrual Basis
July	$6,000	$1,000
August		1,000
September		1,000
October		1,000
November		1,000
December		1,000
TOTAL	$6,000	$6,000

Notice that the total expense recorded under both methods is the same, $6,000. The difference between the cash and the accrual basis is simply an issue of *when* the expense is recorded.

Most businesses use the same method of accounting for their financial statements and income tax reporting. Some businesses, though, are not allowed to use the cash basis method for reporting income tax. For example, corporations that average annual gross receipts of more than $5 million may not use the cash basis method. However, there are some important exceptions to this general rule. A business may use a combination of cash and accrual bases of accounting, called the *hybrid method*. Selecting a basis of accounting can often be complicated and confusing. IRS Publication 538, Accounting Periods and Methods, provides information that makes this decision less confusing. Publication 538 is available on the IRS website at www.irs.gov.

5-5 INTERIM STATEMENTS

The owner of a business understandably does not want to wait until the end of the 12-month fiscal period to determine whether the company is making a profit or a loss. Instead, most owners want financial statements at the end of each month. Financial statements prepared during the fiscal year, for periods of less than 12 months, are called **interim statements**. (They are given this name because they are prepared within the fiscal period.) For example, a business may prepare the income statement, the statement of owner's equity, and the

5 Prepare interim statements.

Learning Objective

YOU Make the Call

Using the information you know about the cash basis versus the accrual basis, review the four types of businesses listed below. Consider the type of accounting transactions the following businesses might make. Then suggest whether the cash basis or the accrual basis would be a logical fit for the business.

1. An investment advisory corporation owned by outside investors with $12 million in annual gross receipts

2. A crane sales company with $1 million in annual gross receipts

3. A travel agency owned by one individual with $60,000 in annual gross receipts

4. A tractor sales company with $6 million in annual gross receipts

SOLUTION

The travel agency would probably be on the cash basis because it is a sole proprietorship. However, the investment advisory corporation would likely be on the accrual basis because its annual gross receipts exceed $5 million. The crane sales company and the tractor sales company would also use the accrual basis because both companies have inventory.

balance sheet *monthly.* These statements provide up-to-date information about the results and status of operations. A company might have the following interim statements:

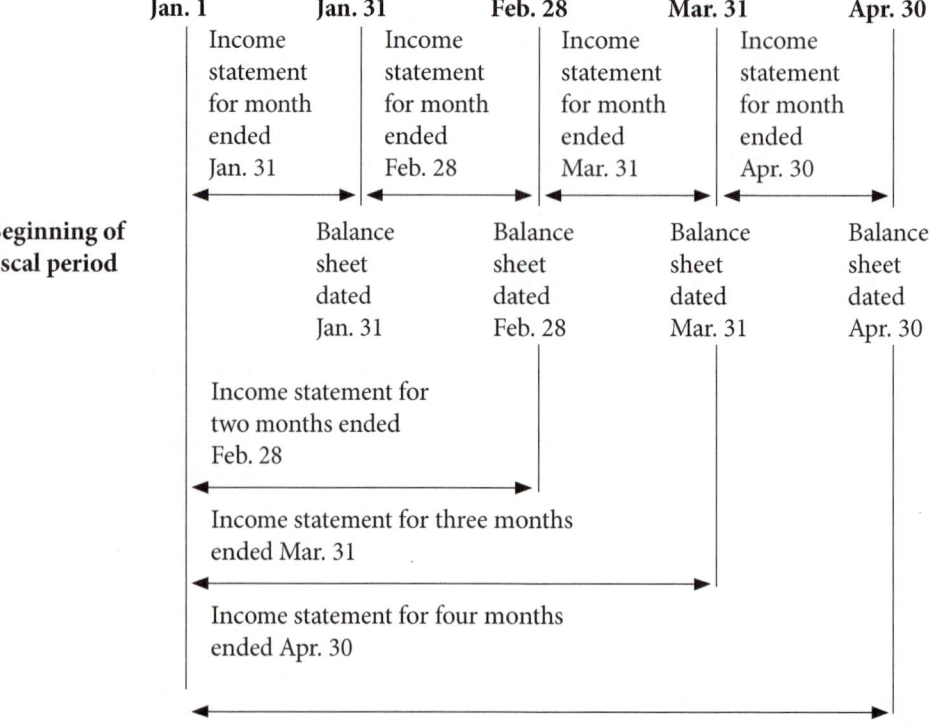

In this case, the accountant would prepare a work sheet at the end of each month. Next, based on these work sheets, he or she would journalize and post the adjusting entries and prepare the financial statements. However, the remaining steps—preparing closing entries and the post-closing trial balance—would be performed only at the end of the year.

In the Real World

Publicly traded corporations such as Apple, Inc., are required to file interim financial statements. These interim financial statements are filed using Form 10-Q and present the quarterly (every three months) financial position of the corporation. The interim financial statements are similar to the annual financial statements but are not as detailed and are typically not verified by an auditor.

AR Pictures/Shutterstock.com

Chapter Review

Study and Practice

1 List the steps in the accounting cycle.

Learning Objective

STEP 1. Analyze source documents and record business transactions in a journal.

STEP 2. Post journal entries to the accounts in the ledger.

STEP 3. Prepare a trial balance.

STEP 4. Gather adjustment data and record the adjusting entries on a work sheet.

STEP 5. Complete the work sheet.

STEP 6. Journalize and post the adjusting entries from the data on the work sheet.

STEP 7. Prepare financial statements from the data on the work sheet.

STEP 8. Journalize and post the **closing entries**.

STEP 9. Prepare a post-closing trial balance.

 PRACTICE EXERCISE 1

Match the steps of the accounting cycle to their corresponding number.

____ 1. Step 1   a. Journalize and post the closing entries.
____ 2. Step 2   b. Prepare a trial balance.

(Continued)

CHAPTER REVIEW

	3. Step 3	c. Analyze source documents and record business transactions in a journal.
	4. Step 4	
	5. Step 5	d. Prepare a post-closing trial balance.
	6. Step 6	e. Prepare financial statements from the data on the work sheet.
	7. Step 7	f. Post journal entries to the accounts in the ledger.
	8. Step 8	g. Complete the work sheet.
	9. Step 9	h. Journalize and post the adjusting entries from the data on the work sheet.
		i. Gather adjustment data and record the adjusting entries on a work sheet.

PRACTICE EXERCISE 1 • SOLUTION

1. c   2. f   3. b   4. i   5. g   6. h   7. e   8. a   9. d

Learning Objective   Journalize and post closing entries for a service enterprise.

The four steps in the closing procedure are as follows:

STEP 1. Close the revenue account(s) into Income Summary.

STEP 2. Close the expense account(s) into Income Summary.

STEP 3. Close the **Income Summary account** into the Capital account, transferring the net income or net loss to the Capital account.

STEP 4. Close the Drawing account into the Capital account.

 PRACTICE EXERCISE 2

The adjusted trial balance for Larson Floral is listed below. Using this information, journalize the four closing entries.

Larson Floral
Adjusted Trial Balance
June 30, 20—

Account Name	Debit	Credit
Cash	14,600	
Accounts Receivable	500	
Supplies	335	
Prepaid Insurance	320	
Delivery Van	28,275	
Accumulated Depreciation, Delivery Van		810
Accounts Payable		750
Wages Payable		300
E. Larson, Capital		37,435
E. Larson, Drawing	1,500	
Income from Services		12,170
Wages Expense	3,600	
Rent Expense	775	
Supplies Expense	710	
Advertising Expense	270	
Utilities Expense	250	
Insurance Expense	30	
Depreciation Expense, Delivery Van	300	
	51,465	51,465

PRACTICE EXERCISE 2 • SOLUTION

GENERAL JOURNAL											Page 4			
Date		Description	Post. Ref.		Debit					Credit				
20--		Closing Entries												
June	30	Income from Services		12	1	7	0	00						
		Income Summary							12	1	7	0	00	
	30	Income Summary		5	9	3	5	00						
		Wages Expense							3	6	0	0	00	
		Rent Expense								7	7	5	00	
		Supplies Expense								7	1	0	00	
		Advertising Expense								2	7	0	00	
		Utilities Expense								2	5	0	00	
		Insurance Expense									3	0	00	
		Depreciation Expense, Delivery Van								3	0	0	00	
	30	Income Summary		6	2	3	5	00						
		E. Larson, Capital							6	2	3	5	00	
	30	E. Larson, Capital		1	5	0	0	00						
		E. Larson, Drawing							1	5	0	0	00	

---

3 Prepare a post-closing trial balance.   **Learning Objective**

A **post-closing trial balance** consists of the final balances of the accounts remaining open. It is the final proof that the debit balances equal the credit balances before the posting for the new fiscal period begins.

PRACTICE EXERCISE 3

Using the information in Practice Exercise 2, prepare a post-closing trial balance for Larson Floral.

PRACTICE EXERCISE 3 • SOLUTION

Larson Floral
Post-Closing Trial Balance
June 30, 20—

Account Name	Debit	Credit
Cash	14,600	
Accounts Receivable	500	
Supplies	335	
Prepaid Insurance	320	
Delivery Van	28,275	
Accumulated Depreciation, Delivery Van		810
Accounts Payable		750
Wages Payable		300
E. Larson, Capital		42,170
	44,030	44,030

CHAPTER REVIEW

Under the **cash basis of accounting**, revenue is recorded when it is received in cash, and expenses are recorded when they are paid in cash. Under the **accrual basis of accounting**, revenue is recorded when earned, even if cash is received at an earlier or a later date, and expenses are recorded when incurred, even if cash is to be paid at an earlier or a later date.

PRACTICE EXERCISE 4

Considering the following events, determine which month the revenue or expenses would be recorded using the accounting method specified.

a.   Crane Company uses the *accrual basis of accounting.* Crane prepays cash in June for insurance that covers the following month, July, only.

b.   Loggins & Rogers Tax Services uses the *cash basis of accounting.* Loggins & Rogers receives cash from customers in January for services to be performed in March.

c.   Red Tractor Supplies Company uses the *accrual basis of accounting.* Red Tractor Supplies makes a sale to a customer in September but does not expect payment until November.

d.   Norton Company uses the *cash basis of accounting.* Norton prepays cash in February for insurance that covers the following month, March, only.

PRACTICE EXERCISE 4 • SOLUTION

a.   July
b.   January
c.   September
d.   February

Interim statements consist of year-to-date income statements, statements of owner's equity, and balance sheets as of various dates during the fiscal period.

PRACTICE EXERCISE 5

Assume that Larson Floral's fiscal period does not end on June 30 but rather December 31. Using the information from Practice Exercise 2, complete an interim balance sheet for June for Larson Floral.

PRACTICE EXERCISE 5 • SOLUTION

Larson Floral
Balance Sheet
June 30, 20--

Assets

Cash		$14,600
Accounts Receivable		500
Supplies		335
Prepaid Insurance		320
Delivery Van	$28,275	
Less Accumulated Depreciation	810	27,465
Total Assets		$43,220

Liabilities

Accounts Payable	$ 750	
Wages Payable	300	
Total Liabilities		$ 1,050

Owner's Equity

E. Larson, Capital	42,170
Total Liabilities and Owner's Equity	$43,220

Glossary

Accrual basis of accounting An accounting method under which revenue is recorded when it is earned, regardless of when it is received, and expenses are recorded when they are incurred, regardless of when they are paid. (*p. 207*)

Cash basis of accounting An accounting method under which revenue is recorded only when it is received in cash, and expenses are recorded only when they are paid in cash. (*p. 206*)

Closing entries Entries made at the end of a fiscal period to close off the revenue, expense, and Drawing accounts—that is, to make the balances of the temporary-equity accounts equal to zero. Closing is also called *clearing the accounts*. (*p. 196*)

Income Summary account An account brought into existence as a debit to balance expense accounts or as a credit to balance revenue accounts in the closing entry process. The revenue and expense account

balances are transferred to this account to allow calculations of net income or net loss. (*p. 197*)

Interim statements Financial statements that cover a period of less than 12 months and are prepared during the fiscal year. (*p. 207*)

Nominal (temporary-equity) accounts Accounts that apply to only one fiscal period and that are to be closed at the end of that fiscal period. These are the revenue, expense, and Drawing accounts. This category may also be described as all accounts except assets, liabilities, and the Capital account. (*p. 201*)

Post-closing trial balance The listing of the final balances of the real accounts at the end of the fiscal period. (*p. 205*)

Real (permanent) accounts The accounts that remain open (assets, liabilities, and the Capital account in owner's equity) and have balances that will be carried over to the next fiscal period. (*p. 201*)

Quiz Yourself

_____ 1. What is the third step in the accounting cycle?
   a. Analyze source documents and record business transactions in a journal.
   b. Prepare a post-closing trial balance.
   c. Journalize and post the closing entries.
   d. Prepare a trial balance.

_____ 2. Which of the following accounts would be closed during the closing process?
   a. Service Revenue
   b. Cash
   c. B. Williams, Capital
   d. Accumulated Depreciation, Equipment

_____ 3. If Income from Services had a $20,400 credit balance before closing entries, which of the following would be the appropriate closing entry to close revenues?

a. Income from Services	20,400	
Cash		20,400
b. Income from Services	20,400	
Income Summary		20,400
c. Income Summary	20,400	
J. Crestview, Capital		20,400
d. J. Crestview, Capital	20,400	
Income from Services		20,400

_____ 4. Which of the following accounts would appear on a post-closing trial balance?
   a. Depreciation Expense, Equipment
   b. Income from Services
   c. R. McDonald, Drawing
   d. R. McDonald, Capital

_____ 5. Under the cash basis of accounting, which of the following statements is true?
   a. Revenue is recorded when it is earned, regardless of when the cash is received.
   b. Expenses are recorded when they are paid.
   c. Expenses are recorded when they are incurred, regardless of when the cash is paid.
   d. The cash basis of accounting is allowed for all corporations.

_____ 6. _____ are prepared during the fiscal year for periods of less than 12 months.
   a. Work sheets
   b. Intermediary statements
   c. Interim statements
   d. In-between statements

Answers: 1. d 2. a 3. b 4. d 5. b 6. c

Chapter Assignments

Discussion Questions

1. Number in order the following steps in the accounting cycle:
   a. Prepare a trial balance.
   b. Post journal entries to the accounts in the ledger.
   c. Journalize and post the adjusting entries from the data on the work sheet.
   d. Analyze source documents and record business transactions in a journal.
   e. Prepare financial statements from the data on the work sheet.
   f. Gather adjustment data and record the adjusting entries on a work sheet.
   g. Journalize and post the closing entries.
   h. Prepare a post-closing trial balance.
   i. Complete the work sheet.
2. List the steps in the closing procedure in the correct order.
3. What is the purpose of closing entries? What is a consequence of forgetting to make closing entries?

4. What are real accounts? What are nominal accounts? Give examples of each.
5. What is the purpose of the Income Summary account? How does it relate to the revenue and expense accounts?
6. What is the purpose of the post-closing trial balance? What is the difference between a trial balance and a post-closing trial balance?
7. Write the third closing entry to transfer the net income or net loss to the P. Hernandez, Capital account, assuming the following:
   a. A net income of $3,842 during the first quarter (Jan.–Mar.)
   b. A net loss of $1,781 during the second quarter (Apr.–Jun.)
8. When would revenue and expenses be recorded if a business used the cash basis of accounting? If a business used the accrual basis of accounting?
9. What are interim financial statements? Why would a business want to prepare them?

Exercises

LO 2

Practice Exercise 2

EXERCISE 5-1 Classify the following accounts as real (permanent) or nominal (temporary) and indicate with an X whether the account is closed. Also indicate the financial statement in which each account will appear. The Building account is given as an example.

Account Title	Real	Nominal	Closed Yes	Closed No	Income Statement	Balance Sheet
0. Example: Building	X			X		X
a. Prepaid Insurance						
b. Accounts Payable						
c. Wages Payable						
d. Income from Services						
e. Rent Expense						
f. Office Supplies Expense						
g. Accum. Depr., Equipment						

LO 2

Practice Exercise 2

EXERCISE 5-2 The ledger accounts after adjusting entries for Cruz Services are presented below.
a. Journalize the following closing entries and number as steps 1 through 4.
b. What is the new balance of A. Cruz, Capital after closing? Show your calculations.

(Continued)

CHAPTER ASSIGNMENTS

							Owner's Equity					
Assets	=	Liabilities	+	Capital	−	Drawing	+	Revenue	−	Expenses		

Assets		=	Liabilities		+	Capital		−	Drawing		+	Revenue		−	Expenses	
+	−		−	+		−	+		+	−		−	+		+	−
Debit	Credit		Debit	Credit		Debit	Credit		Debit	Credit		Debit	Credit		Debit	Credit

Cash

Bal. 10,200	

Wages Payable

	(a) 540

A. Cruz, Capital

	Bal. 24,000

A. Cruz, Drawing

Bal. 500	

Professional Fees

	Bal. 5,875

Wages Expense

Bal. 3,100	
(a) 540	
Bal. 3,640	

Prepaid Insurance

Bal. 990	(c) 420
Bal. 570	

Insurance Expense

(c) 420	

Equipment

Bal. 18,125	

Depr. Expense, Equipment

(b) 725	

Accum. Depr., Equipment

	Bal. 3,200
	(b) 725
	Bal. 3,925

Misc. Expense

Bal. 160	

LO 2

Practice Exercise 2

Show me
HOW
👁

EXERCISE 5-3 As of December 31, the end of the current year, the ledger of Harris Company contained the following account balances after adjustment. All accounts have normal balances. Journalize the closing entries.

Cash	$ 8,440	C. Harris, Drawing	$1,498
Equipment	11,586	Professional Fees	7,075
Accumulated Depreciation, Equipment	2,587	Wages Expense	1,268
		Rent Expense	1,090
Accounts Payable	1,674	Depreciation Expense, Equipment	1,143
Wages Payable	658	
C. Harris, Capital	13,376	Miscellaneous Expense	345

CHAPTER ASSIGNMENTS

LO 2

Practice Exercise 2

EXERCISE 5-4 The Income Statement columns of the work sheet of Dunn Company for the fiscal year ended June 30 follow. During the year, K. Dunn withdrew $4,000. Journalize the closing entries.

	A	H	I
5		INCOME STATEMENT	
6	**ACCOUNT NAME**	**DEBIT**	**CREDIT**
7	Service Revenue		6,797.00
8	Rental Revenue		3,576.00
9	Rent Expense	2,800.00	
10	Wages Expense	1,854.00	
11	Utilities Expense	465.00	
12	Miscellaneous Expense	59.00	
13		5,178.00	10,373.00
14	Net Income	5,195.00	
15		10,373.00	10,373.00
16			

Sheet1 / Sheet2 / Sheet3

LO 2

Practice Exercise 2

EXERCISE 5-5 The Income Statement columns of the work sheet of Redfax Company for the fiscal year ended December 31 follow. During the year, D. Redfax withdrew $12,000. Journalize the closing entries.

	A	H	I
5		INCOME STATEMENT	
6	**ACCOUNT NAME**	**DEBIT**	**CREDIT**
7	Income from Services		32,750.00
8	Rental Revenue		18,000.00
9	Wages Expense	36,725.00	
10	Utilities Expense	8,650.00	
11	Miscellaneous Expense	2,415.00	
12		47,790.00	50,750.00
13	Net Income	2,960.00	
14		50,750.00	50,750.00
15			

Sheet1 / Sheet2 / Sheet3

LO 2

Practice Exercise 2

EXERCISE 5-6 After all revenue and expenses have been closed at the end of the fiscal period ended December 31, Income Summary has a debit of $45,550 and a credit of $36,520. On the same date, D. Mau, Drawing has a debit balance of $12,000 and D. Mau, Capital had a beginning credit balance of $63,410.
a. Journalize the entries to close the remaining temporary accounts.
b. What is the new balance of D. Mau, Capital after closing the remaining temporary accounts? Show your calculations.

CHAPTER ASSIGNMENTS

LO 3

Practice Exercise 3

EXERCISE 5-7 Identify whether the following accounts would be included on a post-closing trial balance.

	Post-Closing Trial Balance	
Account Title	**Yes**	**No**
0. Example: Cash	X	
a. Service Revenue		
b. Prepaid Insurance		
c. Supplies		
d. Accounts Payable		
e. D. Hughes, Drawing		
f. Depreciation Expense, Equipment		
g. Wages Payable		
h. Accounts Receivable		
i. Wages Expense		
j. Accumulated Depreciation, Equipment		
k. D. Hughes, Capital		

LO 4

Practice Exercise 4

EXERCISE 5-8 Considering the following events, determine which month the revenue or expenses would be recorded using the accounting method specified.
a.   Gerber Company uses the *cash basis of accounting*. Gerber prepays cash in May for insurance that only covers the following month, (June).
b.   Matthews and Dudley Attorneys uses the *accrual basis of accounting*. Matthews and Dudley Attorneys receives cash from customers in June for services to be performed in July.
c.   Eckstein Company uses the *accrual basis of accounting*. Eckstein prepays cash in October for rent that covers the following month, (October).
d.   Gerbino Company uses the *cash basis of accounting*. Gerbino makes a sale to a customer in February but does not expect payment until March.

LO 5

Practice Exercise 5

EXERCISE 5-9 Indicate with an X whether each of the following would appear on the income statement, statement of owner's equity, or balance sheet. An item may appear on more than one statement. The first item is provided as an example.

Item	Income Statement	Statement of Owner's Equity	Balance Sheet
0. Example: The total liabilities of the business at the end of the year.			X
a. The amount of the owner's Capital balance at the end of the year.			
b. The amount of depreciation expense on equipment during the year.			
c. The amount of the company's net income for the year.			
d. The book value of the equipment.			
e. Total insurance expired during the year.			
f. Total accounts receivable at the end of the year.			
g. Total withdrawals by the owner.			
h. The cost of utilities used during the year.			
i. The amount of the owner's Capital balance at the beginning of the year.			

 LO 5

EXERCISE 5-10 Prepare a statement of owner's equity for The Lindal Clinic for the year ended December 31. P. Lindal's capital amount on January 1 was $124,000, and there was an additional investment of $7,000 on May 12 and withdrawals of $31,500 for the year. Net income for the year was $20,418.

Practice Exercise 5

Problem Set A

 LO 1, 3

PROBLEM 5-1A After the accountant posted the adjusting entries for B. Lyon, Designer, the work sheet contained the following account balances on May 31:

	A	F	G
5		ADJUSTED TRIAL BALANCE	
6	ACCOUNT NAME	DEBIT	CREDIT
7	Cash	2,018.00	
8	Supplies	300.00	
9	Accounts Receivable	1,408.00	
10	Prepaid Insurance	987.00	
11	Office Equipment	5,790.00	
12	Accumulated Depreciation, Office Equipment		1,372.00
13	Accounts Payable		880.00
14	B. Lyon, Capital		7,520.00
15	B. Lyon, Drawing	1,550.00	
16	Commissions Earned		4,679.00
17	Rent Expense	995.00	
18	Supplies Expense	575.00	
19	Depreciation Expense, Office Equipment	462.00	
20	Utilities Expense	269.00	
21	Miscellaneous Expense	97.00	
22		14,451.00	14,451.00
23			

Sheet1 / Sheet2 / Sheet3

(Continued)

CHAPTER ASSIGNMENTS

Check Figure
Net Income, $2,281

Required

If you are using working papers, complete the following:

1. a. Write the owner's name on the Capital and Drawing T accounts.
   b. Record the account balances in the T accounts for owner's equity, revenue, and expenses.
2. Journalize the closing entries using the four steps in correct order. Number the closing entries 1 through 4.
3. Post the closing entries to the T accounts immediately after you journalize each one to see the effect of the closing entries. Number the closing entries 1 through 4.

*Skip Step 1 if using CengageNow or CLGL.

LO 2 ....

PROBLEM 5-2A The partial work sheet for Ho Consulting for May follows:

	A	H	I	J	K
5		INCOME STATEMENT		BALANCE SHEET	
6	ACCOUNT NAME	DEBIT	CREDIT	DEBIT	CREDIT
7	Cash			5,710.00	
8	Supplies			209.00	
9	Prepaid Insurance			1,123.00	
10	Equipment			5,731.00	
11	Accumulated Depreciation, Equipment				1,444.00
12	Accounts Payable				1,841.00
13	G. Ho, Capital				4,302.00
14	G. Ho, Drawing			2,400.00	
15	Consulting Revenue		13,060.00		
16	Rent Expense	2,200.00			
17	Wages Expense	1,828.00			
18	Supplies Expense	422.00			
19	Miscellaneous Expense	230.00			
20					
21	Insurance Expense	325.00			
22	Depreciation Expense, Equipment	835.00			
23	Wages Payable				366.00
24		5,840.00	13,060.00	15,173.00	7,953.00
25	Net Income	7,220.00			7,220.00
26		13,060.00	13,060.00	15,173.00	15,173.00
27					

Sheet1 / Sheet2 / Sheet3

Check Figure
Debit to Income Summary, second entry, $5,840

Required

If you are using working papers, complete the following:

1. a. Write the owner's name on the Capital and Drawing T accounts.
   b. Record the account balances in the T accounts for owner's equity, revenue, and expenses.
2. Journalize the closing entries using the four steps in correct order. Number the closing entries 1 through 4.
3. Post the closing entries to the T accounts immediately after you journalize each one to see the effect of the closing entries. Number the closing entries 1 through 4.

*Skip Step 1 if using CengageNow or CLGL.

LO 1,2,3

PROBLEM 5-3A The completed work sheet for Valerie Insurance Agency as of December 31 is presented in your Working Papers or in CengageNow, along with the general ledger as of December 31 before adjustments.

Required

If you are using working papers, complete the following:

1. a. Write the owner's name on the Capital and Drawing T accounts.
   b. Write the balances from the unadjusted trial balance in the general ledger.
2. Journalize and post the adjusting entries.
3. Journalize and post the closing entries in the correct order.
4. Prepare a post-closing trial balance.

*Skip Step 1 if using CengageNow or CLGL.

Check Figure
Post-closing trial balance total, $10,170

LO 1,2,3

CLGL

PROBLEM 5-4A The account balances of Bryan Company as of June 30, the end of the current fiscal year, are as follows:

	A	B	C	
5		**TRIAL BALANCE**		
6	**ACCOUNT NAME**	**DEBIT**	**CREDIT**	
7	Cash	5,491.00		
8	Accounts Receivable	624.00		
9	Supplies	397.00		
10	Prepaid Insurance	1,280.00		
11	Equipment	6,497.00		
12	Accumulated Depreciation, Equipment		2,672.00	
13	Van	10,989.00		
14	Accumulated Depreciation, Van		4,368.00	
15	Accounts Payable		1,036.00	
16	B. Bryan, Capital		18,583.00	
17	B. Bryan, Drawing	18,000.00		
18	Fees Earned		38,417.00	
19	Salaries Expense	18,600.00		
20	Advertising Expense	1,887.00		
21	Van Operating Expense	462.00		
22	Utilities Expense	685.00		
23	Miscellaneous Expense	164.00		
24		65,076.00	65,076.00	
25				

Sheet1 / Sheet2 / Sheet3

Required

1. Data for the adjustments are as follows:
   a. Expired or used up insurance, $495
   b. Depreciation expense on equipment, $670.
   c. Depreciation expense on the van, $1,190.
   d. Salary accrued (earned) since the last payday, $540 (owed and to be paid on the next payday).
   e. Supplies used during the period, $97.

   Your instructor may want you to use a work sheet for these adjustments.
2. Journalize the adjusting entries.
3. Prepare an income statement.
4. Prepare a statement of owner's equity. Assume that there was an additional investment of $2,000 on June 10.
5. Prepare a balance sheet.
6. Journalize the closing entries using the four steps in the correct sequence.

*If you are using CLGL, use the year 2020 when recording transactions and preparing reports.

Check Figure
Net Income, $13,627

LO 2,3,5

PROBLEM 5-5A Williams Mechanic Services prepared the following work sheet for the year ended March 31, 20--.

	A	B	C	D	E	F	G
1		Williams Mechanic Services					
2		Work Sheet					
3		For Year Ended March 31, 20—					
4							
5		TRIAL BALANCE		ADJUSTMENTS		ADJUSTED TRIAL BALANCE	
6	ACCOUNT NAME	DEBIT	CREDIT	DEBIT	CREDIT	DEBIT	CREDIT
7	Cash	6,500.00				6,500.00	
8	Accounts Receivable	1,250.00				1,250.00	
9	Supplies	415.00			(e) 200.00	215.00	
10	Prepaid Insurance	2,175.00			(a) 175.00	2,000.00	
11	Equipment	3,500.00				3,500.00	
12	Accumulated Depreciation, Equipment		1,200.00		(b) 75.00		1,275.00
13	Truck	18,300.00				18,300.00	
14	Accumulated Depreciation, Truck		4,000.00		(c) 300.00		4,300.00
15	Accounts Payable		800.00				800.00
16	J. Williams, Capital		16,940.00				16,940.00
17	J. Williams, Drawing	3,000.00				3,000.00	
18	Fees Earned		15,000.00				15,000.00
19	Salary Expense	1,200.00		(d) 125.00		1,325.00	
20	Advertising Expense	600.00				600.00	
21	Truck Operating Expense	250.00				250.00	
22	Utilities Expense	600.00				600.00	
23	Miscellaneous Expense	150.00				150.00	
24		37,940.00	37,940.00				
25	Insurance Expense			(a) 175.00		175.00	
26	Depreciation Expense, Equipment			(b) 75.00		75.00	
27	Depreciation Expense, Truck			(c) 300.00		300.00	
28	Salaries Payable				(d) 125.00		125.00
29	Supplies Expense			(e) 200.00		200.00	
30				875.00	875.00	38,440.00	38,440.00
31							

Sheet1 / Sheet2 / Sheet3

Required

1. Complete the work sheet. (Skip this step if using CLGL.)
2. Prepare an income statement.
3. Prepare a statement of owner's equity. Assume that there was an additional investment of $5,000 on March 13.
4. Prepare a balance sheet.
5. Journalize the closing entries using the four steps in the correct sequence.
6. Prepare a post-closing trial balance.

Check Figure
Post-closing trial balance total,
$31,765

*If you are using CLGL, use the year 2020 when recording transactions and preparing reports.

Problem Set B

 LO 2

PROBLEM 5-1B After the accountant posted the adjusting entries for M. Wally, Designer, the work sheet contained the following account balances on May 31:

	A	F	G
5		ADJUSTED TRIAL BALANCE	
6	**ACCOUNT NAME**	**DEBIT**	**CREDIT**
7	Cash	2,029.00	
8	Accounts Receivable	886.00	
9	Supplies	400.00	
10	Prepaid Insurance	1,460.00	
11	Office Equipment	4,672.00	
12	Accumulated Depreciation, Office Equipment		1,170.00
13	Accounts Payable		943.00
14	M. Wally, Capital		9,221.00
15	M. Wally, Drawing	1,600.00	
16	Commissions Earned		1,997.00
17	Rent Expense	990.00	
18	Supplies Expense	480.00	
19	Depreciation Expense, Office Equipment	420.00	
20	Utilities Expense	286.00	
21	Miscellaneous Expense	108.00	
22		13,331.00	13,331.00
23			

Sheet1 / Sheet2 / Sheet3

Required

Check Figure
Net Loss, $287

If you are using Working Papers, complete the following:

1. a. Write the owner's name on the Capital and Drawing T accounts.
   b. Record the account balances in the T accounts for owner's equity, revenue, and expenses.
2. Journalize the closing entries using the four steps in correct order. Number the closing entries 1 through 4.
3. Post the closing entries to the T accounts immediately after you journalize each one to see the effect of the closing entries. Number the closing entries 1 through 4.

*Skip Step 1 if using CengageNow or CLGL.

 LO 2

PROBLEM 5-2B The partial work sheet for Emil Consulting for June is as follows:

	A	H	I	J	K
5		INCOME STATEMENT		BALANCE SHEET	
6	**ACCOUNT NAME**	**DEBIT**	**CREDIT**	**DEBIT**	**CREDIT**
7	Cash			6,000.00	
8	Supplies			104.00	
9	Prepaid Insurance			1,344.00	
10	Equipment			6,751.00	
11	Accumulated Depreciation, Equipment				4,212.00
12	Accounts Payable				1,356.00
13	W. Emil, Capital				5,367.00
14	W. Emil, Drawing			1,700.00	
15	Consulting Fees		9,546.00		
16	Rent Expense	1,800.00			
17	Wages Expense	1,533.00			
18	Miscellaneous Expense	168.00			
19					
20	Supplies Expense	365.00			
21	Insurance Expense	364.00			
22	Depreciation Expense, Equipment	700.00			
23	Wages Payable				348.00
24		4,930.00	9,546.00	15,899.00	11,283.00
25	Net Income	4,616.00			4,616.00
26		9,546.00	9,546.00	15,899.00	15,899.00
27					

Sheet1 / Sheet2 / Sheet3

(Continued)

Check Figure
Debit to Income Summary,
second entry,
$4,930

Required

If you are using Working Papers, complete the following:

1. a. Write the owner's name on the Capital and Drawing T accounts.
   b. Record the account balances in the T accounts for owner's equity, revenue, and expenses.
2. Journalize the closing entries using the four steps in correct order. Number the closing entries 1 through 4.
3. Post the closing entries to the T accounts immediately after you journalize each one to see the effect of the closing entries. Number closing entries 1 through 4.

*Skip Step 1 if using CengageNow or CLGL.

LO 1,2,3 ....

Check Figure
Post-closing trial balance
total, $9,147

PROBLEM 5-3B The completed work sheet for Oliver Tour Company as of December 31 is presented in your Working Papers or in CengageNow, along with the general ledger as of December 31 before adjustments.

Required

If you are using Working Papers, complete the following:

1. a. Write the owner's name on the Capital and Drawing T accounts.
   b. Write the balances from the unadjusted trial balance in the general ledger.
2. Journalize and post the adjusting entries.
3. Journalize and post the closing entries in the correct order.
4. Prepare a post-closing trial balance.

*Skip Step 1 if using CengageNow or CLGL.

LO 1,2,3 ....

PROBLEM 5-4B The account balances of Miss Beverly's Tutoring Service as of June 30, the end of the current fiscal year, are as follows:

	A	B	C
		TRIAL BALANCE	
	ACCOUNT NAME	**DEBIT**	**CREDIT**
7	Cash	6,491.00	
8	Accounts Receivable	624.00	
9	Supplies	527.00	
10	Prepaid Insurance	1,280.00	
11	Equipment	5,497.00	
12	Accumulated Depreciation, Equipment		2,472.00
13	Van	13,674.00	
14	Accumulated Depreciation, Van		4,168.00
15	Accounts Payable		1,436.00
16	B. Morrow, Capital		14,848.00
17	B. Morrow, Drawing	18,000.00	
18	Fees Earned		43,680.00
19	Salaries Expense	16,000.00	
20	Advertising Expense	2,200.00	
21	Van Operating Expense	705.00	
22	Utilities Expense	1,248.00	
23	Miscellaneous Expense	358.00	
24		66,604.00	66,604.00
25			

Sheet1 / Sheet2 / Sheet3

Check Figure
Net income, $19,567

Required

1. Data for the adjustments are as follows:
   a. Expired or used up insurance, $470.
   b. Depreciation expense on equipment, $948.

c. Depreciation expense on the van, $1,490.

d. Salary accrued (earned) since the last payday, $574 (owed and to be paid on the next payday).

e. Supplies remaining as of June 30, $407.

Your instructor may want you to use a work sheet for these adjustments.

2. Journalize the adjusting entries.

3. Prepare an income statement.

4. Prepare a statement of owner's equity. Assume that there was an additional investment of $3,000 on June 10.

5. Prepare a balance sheet.

6. Journalize the closing entries using the four steps in the proper sequence.

*If you are using CLGL, use the year 2020 when recording transactions and preparing reports.

LO **2,3,5**

PROBLEM 5-5B Tom's Catering Services prepared the following work sheet for the year ended December 31, 20--.

	A	B	C	E	G	I	K
1		Tom's Catering Services					
2		Work Sheet					
3		For Year Ended December 31, 20--					
4			TRIAL BALANCE		ADJUSTMENTS		ADJUSTED TRIAL BALANCE	
5		DEBIT	CREDIT	DEBIT	CREDIT	DEBIT	CREDIT
6	ACCOUNT NAME	DEBIT	CREDIT	DEBIT	CREDIT	DEBIT	CREDIT
7	Cash	2,400.00				2,400.00	
8	Accounts Receivable	800.00				800.00	
9	Supplies	225.00			(e) 80.00	145.00	
10	Prepaid Insurance	1,200.00			(a) 100.00	1,100.00	
11	Equipment	2,220.00				2,220.00	
12	Accumulated Depreciation, Equipment		370.00		(b) 185.00		555.00
13	Truck	25,000.00				25,000.00	
14	Accumulated Depreciation, Truck		5,000.00		(c) 1,000.00		6,000.00
15	Accounts Payable		250.00				250.00
16	Y. Tom, Capital		26,500.00				26,500.00
17	Y. Tom, Drawing	1,500.00				1,500.00	
18	Fees Earned		2,400.00				2,400.00
19	Salaries Expense	640.00		(d) 80.00		720.00	
20	Advertising Expense	130.00				130.00	
21	Truck Operating Expense	125.00				125.00	
22	Utilities Expense	200.00				200.00	
23	Miscellaneous Expense	80.00				80.00	
24		34,520.00	34,520.00				
25	Insurance Expense			(a) 100.00		100.00	
26	Depreciation Expense, Equipment			(b) 185.00		185.00	
27	Depreciation Expense, Truck			(c) 1,000.00		1,000.00	
28	Salaries Payable				(d) 80.00		80.00
29	Supplies Expense			(e) 80.00		80.00	
30				1,445.00	1,445.00	35,785.00	35,785.00
31							

Sheet1 / Sheet2 / Sheet3

Required

1. Complete the work sheet. (Skip this step if using CLGL.)

2. Prepare an income statement.

3. Prepare a statement of owner's equity. Assume that there was an additional investment of $2,500 on December 1.

4. Prepare a balance sheet.

5. Journalize the closing entries with the four steps in the correct sequence.

6. Prepare a post-closing trial balance.

*If you are using CLGL, use the year 2020 when recording transactions and preparing reports.

Check Figure
Post-closing trial balance total, $31,665

Accounting with **qb** QuickBooks® Online

Go to the QuickBooks Online Chapter 5 Appendix located on the Cengage Learning companion site at Cengage.com. Review the *Accounting with QuickBooks Online* (step-by-step guide to using QuickBooks Online). *Accounting with QuickBooks Online*, Chapter 5 will introduce you to preparing closing entries and a post-closing trial balance.

Activities

Why Does It Matter?

REAL GAP EXPERIENCE, Tunbridge Wells, Kent (UK)

Rather than going directly to college, some students take time off to travel abroad, learn new skills, or volunteer. This period is known as a "gap year." Real Gap Experience provides hundreds of gap year traveling opportunities in over 45 countries around the world. The company offers everything from volunteering to building houses in Guatemala to teaching in China (for pay) to taking a year-long, around-the-world trip. What does this have to do with accounting, and why is it important? Every company needs to keep a record of its financial activities so that financial statements can be presented and used for decision making. Real Gap Experience's accounting records are most likely computerized, but the company still needs to go through the closing process. Why is the closing process important to a company such as Real Gap Experience? What types of accounts would be used during the closing process for this company?

What Would You Say?

Your uncle owns a small sole proprietorship. He does his own bookkeeping, although he didn't finish the chapter on closing entries before he opened his business. He mentions to you that closing entries look like they take a long time. He wonders why he should bother to do them because all he really looks at is the checkbook. What would you say to convince him that closing entries are necessary?

What Do You Think?

The post-closing trial balance submitted to you by the bookkeeper of Tafoya Consulting Company is shown below. Assume that the debit total ($41,048) is correct.
a.   Analyze the work and prepare a response to what you have reviewed.
b.   Journalize the closing entries.
c.   What is the net income or net loss?
d.   Is there an increase or a decrease in Capital?
e.   What would be the ending amount of Capital?
f.   What is the new balance of the post-closing trial balance?

Tafoya Consulting Company
Post-Closing Trial Balance
December 31, 20--

Account Name	Debit	Credit
Cash	3,412	
Accounts Receivable	1,693	
Prepaid Insurance	2,147	
Accounts Payable		?
C. Tafoya, Capital		13,818
C. Tafoya, Drawing	6,360	
Consulting Fees		25,603
Wages Expense	11,994	
Rent Expense	9,600	
Advertising Expense	2,582	
Supplies Expense	914	
Insurance Expense	1,610	
Miscellaneous Expense	736	
	41,048	41,048

What Would You Do?

You are preparing a post-closing trial balance for the company where you work, but it doesn't balance. You are tired, and besides, you don't think the company pays you for this much hassle and extra time. You decide to increase the balance of an asset account to make the totals balance. Discuss this action and explain whether it is ethical or illegal.

What's Wrong with This Picture?

The bookkeeper has completed a work sheet and has journalized and posted the closing entries, but he forgot to journalize and post the adjusting entries from the work sheet. What are the effects of these actions and omissions? How would these actions and omissions affect the accounting records and the resulting financial statements?

Before a Test Check: Chapters 4–5

PART 1: Multiple-Choice Questions

_____ 1. The net income appears on all of the following statements except
   a. the statement of owner's equity.
   b. the balance sheet.
   c. the income statement.
   d. all of the above.
   e. none of the above.

_____ 2. Which of the following entries records the withdrawal of cash for personal use by Dolan, the owner of a business firm?
   a. Debit Cash and credit Drawing.
   b. Debit Salary Expense and credit Cash.
   c. Debit Cash and credit Salary Expense.
   d. Debit Drawing and credit Cash.
   e. None of the above.

_____ 3. Which of the following errors, considered individually, would cause the trial balance totals to be unequal?
   a. A payment of $25 for supplies was posted as a debit of $25 to Supplies Expense and a credit of $52 to Cash.
   b. A payment of $555 to a creditor was posted as a debit of $555 to Accounts Payable and a debit of $555 to Cash.
   c. Cash received from customers on account was posted as a debit of $160 to Cash and a credit of $16 to Accounts Receivable.
   d. All of the above.
   e. None of the above.

_____ 4. The balance in the Prepaid Insurance account before adjustment at the end of the year is $1,200. This represents six months' insurance paid on November 1. No adjusting entry was made on November 30. The adjusting entry required on December 31 is
   a. debit Insurance Expense, $400; credit Prepaid Insurance, $400.
   b. debit Prepaid Insurance, $200; credit Insurance Expense, $200.
   c. debit Prepaid Insurance, $1,200; credit Insurance Expense, $1,200.
   d. debit Insurance Expense, $1,200; credit Prepaid Insurance, $1,200.
   e. none of the above.

_____ 5. If an accountant fails to make an adjusting entry to record expired insurance at the end of a fiscal period, the omission will cause
   a. total expenses to be understated.
   b. total revenue to be understated.
   c. total assets to be understated.
   d. all of the above.
   e. none of the above.

_____ 6. Farmer Company bought equipment on January 2 of this year for $10,000. At the time of purchase, the equipment was estimated to have a useful life of five years and no ending trade-in value. The depreciation of equipment for the year is $2,000. The adjusting entry required on December 31 is
   a. debit Accumulated Depreciation, Equipment, $2,000; credit Depreciation Expense, $2,000.
   b. debit Depreciation Expense, $2,000; credit Accumulated Depreciation, $2,000.
   c. debit Accumulated Depreciation, Equipment, $166.67; credit Depreciation Expense, $166.67.
   d. debit Depreciation Expense, $166.67; credit Accumulated Depreciation, $166.67.
   e. none of the above.

_____ 7. If expenses are greater than revenue, the Income Summary account will be closed by a debit to
   a. Cash and a credit to Income Summary.
   b. Income Summary and a credit to Cash.
   c. Capital and a credit to Income Summary.
   d. Income Summary and a credit to Capital.
   e. none of the above.

_____ 8. In preparing closing entries, it is helpful to refer to which of the following columns of the work sheet first?
   a. The Balance Sheet columns
   b. The Adjusted Trial Balance columns
   c. The Income Statement columns
   d. Both the Adjusted Trial Balance and the Income Statement columns
   e. None of the above

PART II: Practical Application

On December 31, the ledger accounts of Alexander's Upholstery Shop have the following balances after all adjusting entries have been posted.

Cash	$ 8,300
Supplies	1,400
Equipment	12,000
Accumulated Depreciation, Equipment	1,200
Accounts Payable	500
L. Alexander, Capital	15,600
L. Alexander, Drawing	14,600
Income Summary	
Service Revenue	39,500
Wages Expense	10,250
Rent Expense	3,650
Supplies Expense	4,100
Utilities Expense	900
Depreciation Expense, Equipment	700
Miscellaneous Expense	1,800

Required

Journalize the four closing entries in the proper order.

PART III: Matching Questions

_____ 1. Creditor

_____ 2. Business entity

_____ 3. Fundamental accounting equation

_____ 4. Income statement

_____ 5. Owner's equity

_____ 6. Accounts Receivable

_____ 7. Net loss

_____ 8. Ledger

_____ 9. Credit

_____ 10. Compound entry

_____ 11. Trial balance

_____ 12. Journalizing

_____ 13. Posting

_____ 14. Cross-reference

_____ 15. Journal

_____ 16. Work sheet

_____ 17. Book value

_____ 18. Depreciation

_____ 19. Accounting cycle

_____ 20. Fiscal year

_____ 21. Contra account

_____ 22. Mixed accounts

_____ 23. Temporary-equity accounts

_____ 24. Real accounts

_____ 25. Debit

a. The book of original entry

b. One to whom money is owed.

c. Accounts that are partly income statement and partly balance sheet accounts

d. Assets − Liabilities

e. A listing of the ending balances of all ledger accounts that proves the equality of total debits and total credits

f. The process of recording transactions in a journal

g. The left side of a T account

h. A business enterprise, separate and distinct from the person who owns its assets.

i. The process of transferring accounts and amounts from the journal to the ledger

j. An account that is deducted from another account

k. Amounts owed by charge customers

l. Balance sheet accounts

m. Assets = Liabilities + Owner's Equity

n. A bookkeeping device for referring from journal to ledger or ledger to journal

o. The right side of a T account

(Continued)

p. Allocation of the cost of a plant asset over its estimated life

q. Financial statement that shows the net results of operations

r. Accounts that belong to only one fiscal period and are closed out at the end of each fiscal period

s. A transaction that has two or more debits and/or credits

t. Spreadsheet used to record adjustments and provide balances to prepare financial statements

u. Excess of total expenses over total revenues

v. A period of 12 consecutive months

w. A book containing all of the accounts of a business

x. The cost of an asset minus its accumulated depreciation

y. Steps in the accounting process, completed during the fiscal period

Answers: Part I

1. b   **2.** d   **3.** d   **4.** a   **5.** a   **6.** b   **7.** c   **8.** c

Answers: Part II

Date		Description	Post. Ref.	Debit	Credit
20--		Closing Entries			
Dec.	31	Service Revenue		39 5 0 0 00	
		Income Summary			39 5 0 0 00
	31	Income Summary		21 4 0 0 00	
		Wages Expense			10 2 5 0 00
		Rent Expense			3 6 5 0 00
		Supplies Expense			4 1 0 0 00
		Utilities Expense			9 0 0 00
		Depreciation Expense, Equipment			7 0 0 00
		Miscellaneous Expense			18 0 0 0 00
	31	Income Summary		18 1 0 0 00	
		L. Alexander, Capital			18 1 0 0 00
	31	L. Alexander, Capital		14 6 0 0 00	
		L. Alexander, Drawing			14 6 0 0 00

GENERAL JOURNAL — Page 4

Answers: Part III

1. b   **2.** h   **3.** m   **4.** q   **5.** d   **6.** k   **7.** u   **8.** w   **9.** o   **10.** s   **11.** e   **12.** f   **13.** i
14. n   **15.** a   **16.** t   **17.** x   **18.** p   **19.** y   **20.** v   **21.** j   **22.** c   **23.** r   **24.** l   **25.** g

Accounting Cycle Review: Problem A

This problem is designed to enable you to apply the knowledge you have acquired in the preceding chapters. In accounting, the ultimate test is being able to handle data in real-life situations. This problem will give you valuable experience.

CHART OF ACCOUNTS

Assets

111	Cash
112	Accounts Receivable
114	Prepaid Insurance
121	Land
122	Building
123	Accumulated Depreciation, Building
124	Pool/Slide Facility
125	Accumulated Depreciation, Pool/Slide Facility
126	Pool Furniture
127	Accumulated Depreciation, Pool Furniture

Liabilities

221	Accounts Payable
222	Wages Payable
223	Mortgage Payable

Owner's Equity

311	L. Judar, Capital
312	L. Judar, Drawing
313	Income Summary

Revenue

| 411 | Income from Services |
| 412 | Concessions Income |

Expenses

511	Pool Maintenance Expense
512	Wages Expense
513	Advertising Expense
514	Utilities Expense
515	Interest Expense
517	Insurance Expense
518	Depreciation Expense, Building
519	Depreciation Expense, Pool/Slide Facility
520	Depreciation Expense, Pool Furniture
522	Miscellaneous Expense

You are to record transactions in a two-column general journal. Assume that the fiscal period is one month. You will then be able to complete all of the steps in the accounting cycle.

When you are analyzing the transactions, think them through by visualizing the T accounts or by writing them down on scratch paper. For unfamiliar types of transactions, specific instructions for recording them are included. However, reason them out for yourself as well. Check off each transaction as it is recorded.

July   1   Judar deposited $135,000 in a bank account for the purpose of buying Blast Off! The business is a recreation area offering three large waterslides (called "tubes")—one children's slide, an inner tube run, and a looping extreme slide.

2   Bought Blast Off! in its entirety for a total price of $540,800. The assets include pool furniture, $3,800; the pool/slide facility (includes filter system, pools, pump, and slides), $148,800; building, $96,200; and land, $292,000. Paid $120,000 down and signed a mortgage note for the remainder.

2   Received and paid the bill for a one-year premium for insurance, $12,240.

(Continued)

July	2	Bought 125 inner tubes from Worn Tires for $1,225, paying $500 down, with the remainder due in 20 days.
	3	Signed a contract with a video game company to lease space for video games and to provide a food concession. The rental income agreed upon is 10 percent of the revenues generated from the machines and food, with the estimated monthly rental income paid in advance. Received cash payment for July, $250.
	5	Received bills totaling $1,320 for the grand opening/Fourth of July party. The bill from Party Rentals for the promotional handouts, balloons, decorations, and prizes was $620, and the newspaper advertising bills from the *City Star* were $700.
	6	Signed a one-year contract for the pool maintenance with All-Around Maintenance and paid the maintenance fee for July of $1,600.
	6	Paid cash for employee picnic food and beverages, $128. (Miscellaneous Expense.)
	7	Received $12,086 in cash as income for the use of the facilities.
	9	Bought parts to repair the filter system on account from Arlen's Pool Supply, $646.
	14	Received $10,445 in cash as income for the use of the facilities.
	15	Paid wages to employees for the period ended July 14, $9,460.
	16	Paid $1,150 cash as partial payment on account for promotional expenses recorded on July 5. Party Rentals was paid $620 and City Star was paid the remainder of $530.
	16	Judar withdrew cash for personal use, $2,500.
	17	Bought additional pool furniture from Pool Suppliers for $2,100; payment due in 30 days.
	18	Paid cash to seamstress for alterations and repairs to the character costumes, $328. (Miscellaneous Expense.)
	21	Received $10,330 in cash as income for the use of the facilities.
	21	Paid cash to Worn Tires as partial payment on account, $600.
	23	Received a $225 reduction of our account from Pool Suppliers for lawn chairs received in damaged condition.
	25	Received and paid telephone bill, $292.
	29	Paid wages for the period July 15 through 28 of $8,227.
	31	Received $11,870 in cash as income for the use of the facilities.
	31	Paid cash to Arlen's Pool Supply to apply on account, $360.
	31	Received and paid water bill, $684.
	31	Paid cash as an installment payment on the mortgage, $3,890. Of this amount, $1,910 represents a reduction in the principal and the remainder is interest.
	31	Received and paid electric bill, $942.
	31	Bought additional inner tubes from Worn Tires for $480, paying $100 down, with the remainder due in 30 days.
	31	Judar withdrew cash for personal use, $3,200.
	31	Sales for the video and food concessions amounted to $4,840, and 10 percent of $4,840 equals $484. Because you have already recorded $250 as concessions income, record the additional $234 revenue due from the concessionaire. (Cash was not received.)

Check Figure

Trial balance total, $601,941; net income, $16,293; post-closing trial balance total, $569,614

Required

1. Journalize the transactions. (Start on page 1 of the general journal if using Excel or Working Papers.)
2. Post the transactions to the ledger accounts. (Skip this step if using CLGL.)

3. Prepare a trial balance. (If using a work sheet, use the first two columns.)
4. Data for the adjustments are as follows:
   a. Insurance expired during the month, $1,020.
   b. Depreciation of building for the month, $480.
   c. Depreciation of pool/slide facility for the month, $675.
   d. Depreciation of pool furniture for the month, $220.
   e. Wages accrued at July 31, $920.
   Your instructor may want you to use a work sheet for these adjustments.
5. Journalize adjusting entries.
6. Post adjusting entries to the ledger accounts. (Skip this step if using CLGL.)
7. Prepare an adjusted trial balance.
8. Prepare the income statement.
9. Prepare the statement of owner's equity.
10. Prepare the balance sheet.
11. Journalize closing entries.
12. Post closing entries to the ledger accounts. (Skip this step if using CLGL.)
13. Prepare a post-closing trial balance.

*If you are using CLGL, use the year 2020 when recording transactions and preparing reports.

Accounting Cycle Review: Problem B

This problem is designed to enable you to apply the knowledge you have acquired in the preceding chapters. In accounting, the ultimate test is being able to handle data in real-life situations. This problem will give you valuable experience.

CHART OF ACCOUNTS

Assets
111 Cash
112 Accounts Receivable
114 Prepaid Insurance
121 Land
125 Pool Structure
126 Accumulated Depreciation, Pool Structure
127 Fan System
128 Accumulated Depreciation, Fan System
129 Sailboats
130 Accumulated Depreciation, Sailboats

Liabilities
221 Accounts Payable
222 Wages Payable
223 Mortgage Payable

Owner's Equity
311 R. Cury, Capital
312 R. Cury, Drawing
313 Income Summary

Revenue
411 Income from Services
412 Concessions Income

Expenses
511 Sailboat Rental Expense
512 Wages Expense
513 Advertising Expense
514 Utilities Expense
515 Interest Expense
516 Insurance Expense
517 Depreciation Expense, Pool Structure
518 Depreciation Expense, Fan System
519 Depreciation Expense, Sailboats
522 Miscellaneous Expense

You are to record transactions in a two-column general journal. Assume that the fiscal period is one month. You will then be able to complete all of the steps in the accounting cycle.

When you are analyzing the transactions, think them through by visualizing the T accounts or by writing them down on scratch paper. For unfamiliar types of transactions, specific instructions for recording them are included. However, reason them out for yourself as well. Check off each transaction as it is recorded.

June	1	Cury deposited $95,000 in a bank account for the purpose of buying Wind In Your Sails, a business offering the use of small sailboats to the public at a large indoor pool with a fan system that provides wind.
	2	Bought Wind In Your Sails in its entirety for a total price of $216,100. The assets include sailboats, $25,800; fan system, $13,300; pool structure, $140,000; and land, $37,000. Paid $60,000 down and signed a mortgage note for the remainder.
	3	Received and paid bill for newspaper advertising, $350.
	3	Received and paid bill for a one-year premium for insurance, $12,000.
	3	Bought additional boats from Louis Manufacturing Co. for $7,200, paying $3,200 down, with the remainder due in 30 days.
	3	Signed a contract with a vending machine service to lease space for vending machines. The rental income agreed upon is 10 percent of the sales generated from the machines, with the estimated total rental income payable in advance. Received estimated cash payment for June, $150.
	3	Received bill from Quick Printing for promotional handouts, $540.
	3	Signed a contract for leasing sailboats from K. Einstein Boat Co. and paid rental fee for June, $700.
	5	Paid cash for miscellaneous expenses, $104.
	8	Received $2,855 in cash as income for the use of the boats.
	9	Bought an addition for the fan system on account from Stark Pool Supply, $745.
	15	Paid wages to employees for the period ended June 14, $3,900.
	16	Paid on account for promotional handouts already recorded on June 3, $540.
	16	Cury withdrew cash for personal use, $2,500.
	16	Bought additional sails from Canvas Products, Inc., $850; payment due in 30 days.
	16	Received $6,850 in cash as income for the use of the boats.
	19	Paid cash for miscellaneous expenses, $40.
	20	Paid cash to Louis Manufacturing Co. as part payment on account, $1,300.
	22	Received $8,260 in cash for the use of the boats.
	23	Received a reduction in the outstanding bill from Louis Manufacturing Co. for a boat received in damaged condition, $380.
	24	Received and paid telephone bill, $324.
	29	Paid wages for period June 15 through 28, $4,973.
	30	Paid cash to Stark Pool Supply to apply on account, $475.
	30	Received and paid electric bill, $345.
	30	Paid cash as an installment payment on the mortgage, $1,848. Of this amount, $497 represents a reduction in the principal and the remainder is interest.
	30	Received and paid water bill, $590.
	30	Bought additional boats from Riddle and Son for $5,320, paying $1,550 down, with the remainder due in 30 days.

June 30   Cury withdrew cash for personal use, $1,800.

     30   Received $5,902 in cash as income for the use of the boats.

     30   Sales from vending machines for the month amounted to $1,780. Ten percent of $1,780 equals $178. Because you have already recorded $150 as concessions income, list the additional $28 revenue earned from the vending machine operator. (Cash was not received.)

Required

1. Journalize the transactions. (Start on page 1 of the general journal if using Excel or Working Papers.)
2. Post the transactions to the ledger accounts. (Skip this step if using CLGL.)
3. Prepare a trial balance. (If using a work sheet, use the first two columns.)
4. Data for the adjustments are as follows:
   a. Insurance expired during the month, $1,000.
   b. Depreciation of pool structure for the month, $715.
   c. Depreciation of fan system for the month, $260.
   d. Depreciation of sailboats for the month, $900.
   e. Wages accrued at June 30, $810.

   Your instructor may want you to use a work sheet for these adjustments.
5. Journalize adjusting entries.
6. Post adjusting entries to the ledger accounts. (Skip this step if using CLGL.)
7. Prepare an adjusted trial balance.
8. Prepare the income statement.
9. Prepare the statement of owner's equity.
10. Prepare the balance sheet.
11. Journalize closing entries.
12. Post closing entries to the ledger accounts. (Skip this step if using CLGL.)
13. Prepare a post-closing trial balance.

*If you are using CLGL, use the year 2020 when recording transactions and preparing reports.

Check Figure

Trial balance total, $281,858; net income, $7,143; post-closing trial balance total, $263,341

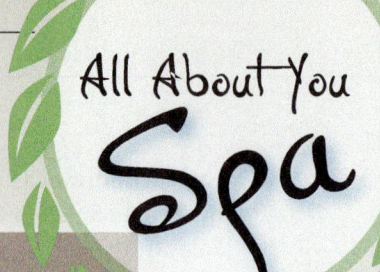

All About You
Spa

CLGL

Closing Entries

After the adjusting entries are recorded and posted and the financial statements have been prepared, you are ready to record the closing entries. Closing entries zero out the temporary owner's equity accounts (revenue(s), expenses(s), and Drawing). This process transfers the net income or net loss and the withdrawals to the Capital account. In addition, the closing process prepares the records for the new fiscal period.

Required

1. Journalize the closing entries in the general journal.
   (If you are using Working Papers to prepare the closing entries, enter your transactions beginning on page 5.)
2. Post the closing entries to the general ledger accounts.
   (Skip this step if you are using CLGL.)
3. Prepare a post-closing trial balance as of October 31, 20--.

*If you are using CLGL, use the year 2020 when recording transactions and preparing reports.

Check Figures
1. Debit to Income Summary second entry, $12,023.25
2. Post-closing trial balance total, $37,420.00

chapter 6

Bank Accounts, Cash Funds, and Internal Controls

Learning Objectives

After you have completed this chapter, you will be able to do the following:

1. List internal controls for cash receipts and cash payments.

2. Describe the procedures for recording deposits and withdrawals.

3. Reconcile a bank statement.

4. Record the required journal entries from the bank reconciliation.

5. (a) Record journal entries to establish a Petty Cash Fund. (b) Complete petty cash vouchers, (c) petty cash payments record, and (d) reimburse the petty cash fund.

6. Record the journal entries to establish a Change Fund.

7. Record journal entries for transactions involving Cash Short and Over.

To: Amy Roberts, CPA
Subject: Protecting My Cash

Hi Amy,

Well, I'm definitely more comfortable with the accounting procedures you helped me set up in my business, but I feel like I'm missing something. Today I heard about a company that lost a lot of money to embezzlement. This made me think about how little I know about managing my cash or setting up controls to prevent this from happening. In fact, I'm not even sure I know how often to reconcile my bank account. Can you give me some advice on how I can manage my cash and prevent fraud? I've worked hard to get my business started, and I don't want to lose money.
Thanks,

Janie

To: Janie Conner
Subject: RE: Protecting My Cash

Hi Janie,

You have certainly worked hard and learned a lot about accounting. It is smart to start thinking about the steps you need to take to manage your cash and prevent fraud. There is a lot to consider when we talk about cash and internal controls, so let's break things down into smaller steps. Below are a couple of items to get you started. Once you are comfortable with the following, I can send you the rest.

_____ 1. Set up internal control guidelines. Keeping cash handling duties and accounting activities separate is a priority.

_____ 2. Reconcile the bank balance and ledger balance for your cash accounts regularly. At a minimum, you should complete this process monthly. QuickBooks Online actually has a bank reconciliation application that simplifies the reconciliation process. After you understand how to reconcile a bank statement manually, you can learn how to use this wonderful QuickBooks Online feature.

Let me know if you have any questions as you work through the steps.
Good luck! You are doing great!

Amy

Lester Lefkowitz/Getty Images

6-1 INTERNAL CONTROLS

A very important aspect of any financial accounting system, for an individual or for a business enterprise, is the accurate and efficient management of assets. To protect assets, a company sets up a system of policies and procedures known as **internal control**. The system is designed to:

1. Protect assets against fraud and waste.

2. Provide for accurate accounting data.

3. Promote efficient operation.

4. Encourage adherence to management policies.

Cash is one of the key assets internal control procedures are established to protect. When we talk about cash, we mean currency, coins, checks, money orders, traveler's checks, and bank drafts or bank cashier's checks. Personal checks are accepted conditionally—that is, based on the condition that they are valid. In other words, we consider checks to be good until they are otherwise proven not to be good.

Managing cash is an important aspect of business. All embezzlement starts with an employee or employees failing to follow internal control procedures. The following are some simple internal control guidelines for better management of cash receipts and payments:

Cash receipts
- Maintain separation of duties between cash handling and cash recording.
- Designate someone other than the bookkeeper to open mail.
- Make a record of cash received.
- Endorse checks immediately upon receipt with the stamp "For Deposit Only."
- Deposit cash daily.
- Journalize cash receipts as soon as possible, preferably by someone different from the person who first received the cash.
- Post cash receipts to the Accounts Receivable account as soon as possible.

Cash payments
- Make sure all cash payments are made by check (with the exception of petty cash).
- Make certain all checks are prenumbered.
- Keep check supplies in a secured area.

1 List internal controls for cash receipts and cash payments.

Learning Objective

239

- Assign someone different from the check signer to prepare the checks.
- Appoint someone other than the person preparing checks to prepare the bank reconciliations. (How to prepare a bank reconciliation is explained later in this chapter.)
- Keep petty cash under lock and limit access to one person other than the bookkeeper.

When cash register drawers are involved, additional security measures are required. For instance, cashiers should have their register drawer totals verified by a designated employee, manager, or owner when their shifts end. Later, we will see how the bank deposit amount is determined, considering the cash in the till at the start of business.

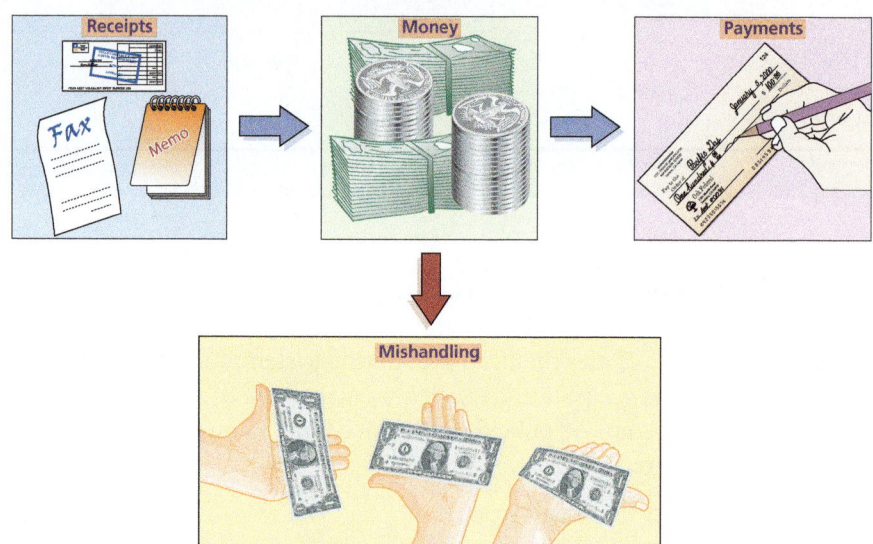

In this chapter, besides discussing bank accounts, we are going to talk about **cash funds**—Petty Cash Funds and Change Funds—which are separate cash accounts used for specific purposes.

SMALL BUSINESS **SUCCESS**

What Is Fraud?

Fraud is defined as an intentional misrepresentation of the truth. In a recent report, the Association of Certified Fraud Examiners (ACFE) estimated that "small businesses are especially vulnerable to occupational fraud, and it has become a global problem. The median loss suffered by organizations, including small businesses, was $145,000. Approximately one-fifth of all fraud cases are in excess of one million dollars." The ACFE is an organization that provides anti-fraud training and education (www.acfe.com).

A common type of fraud that occurs in small businesses involves theft of assets by employees. Theft of assets involves stealing of cash, supplies, inventory, and so on. Employees will go to such extent as to create fake employees who receive payroll and falsify invoices for payment.

The ACFE suggests several strategies to prevent fraud in small business, such as promoting honesty in the workplace and removing opportunities to commit fraud by maintaining internal controls on accounting records. In addition, companies should be especially careful when hiring employees and always conduct background checks.

6-2 USING A CHECKING ACCOUNT

Although you may be familiar with the process of opening a checking account, making deposits, and writing checks, let's review these and other procedures associated with opening and maintaining a business checking account. We will discuss signature cards, deposit slips, automated teller machines, online banking, Electronic Funds Transfer, night deposits, and endorsements.

6-2a Signature Card

When Melinda B. Roland founded Roland's Delivery Services, she opened a checking account in the name of the business. When she opened the account, she filled out a **signature card** for the bank's files. Because Roland gave her assistant, Sheila R. Bayes, the right to sign checks too, the assistant also signed the card. The signature card gives the bank a copy of the official signatures of any persons authorized to sign checks. The bank can use it to verify the signatures on any checks Roland's Delivery Services presents for payment. This card helps the bank detect forgeries. Each banking entity has its own signature card. Figure 1 shows a typical signature card.

> **FYI**
>
> As a means of preventing employee theft, many companies require more than one signature on checks over a certain dollar amount.

2 Describe the procedures for recording deposits and withdrawals.

Learning Objective

Title **Roland's Delivery Services**			Account number 5008-3007

In consideration of the acceptance by   COMPASS BANK   of my/our account of the type indicated below, I/we agree to be bound by such rules and regulations and/or such schedules of interest, fees and charges applicable to such account as may now or hereafter be adopted by and in effect at said Bank, and also by the provisions printed hereon. It is understood that the acceptance by said Bank of my/our account is subject to the receipt by said Bank of satisfactory credit information.

(1) Sign Here   *Melinda B. Roland*

(2) Sign Here   *Sheila R. Bayes*

Address **951 Bay Road**	City	State	Zip
	San Diego	**California**	**92109**

☑ CHECKING   ☐ MULTIPLE MATURITY   ☐ CASH MANAGER

☐ SAVINGS   ☐ GUARANTEED INTEREST (Multiple Maturity)   ☐ SAFE DEPOSIT   ☐ OTHER_____

IF THIS IS A JOINT ACCOUNT, BOTH OWNERS MUST SIGN ABOVE

Each of the signers guarantees the genuineness of the signature of the other. Each signer also agrees with the other and the Bank that deposits now or hereafter made to this account may be withdrawn in whole or part by either or survivor, and that each may endorse for deposit to this account any instrument payable to the order of either or both. Provisions respecting this agreement shall be modified only upon receipt by the Bank of written notice, signed by both.

Figure 1
Signature card for Roland's Delivery Services

6-2b Deposit Slips

The bank provides printed **deposit slips** on which customers record the amount of coins, currency, and checks they are depositing. Checks being deposited are listed individually. A typical deposit slip is shown in Figure 2.

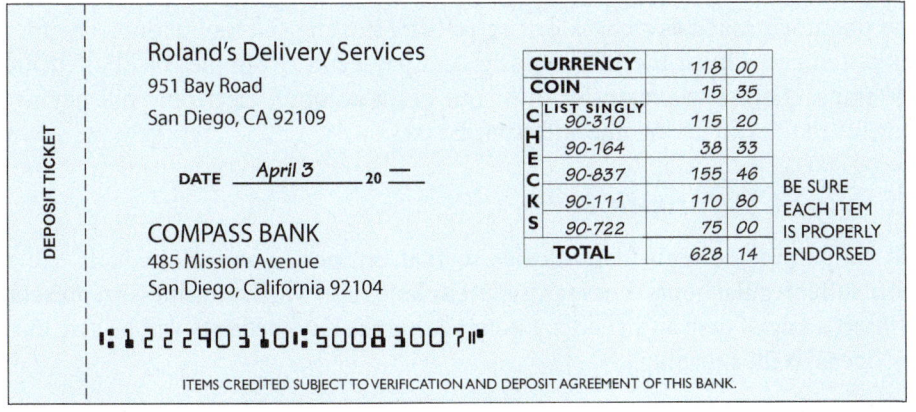

Figure 2
Deposit slip for Roland's Delivery Service

DEPOSIT TICKET

Roland's Delivery Services
951 Bay Road
San Diego, CA 92109

DATE _____April 3_____ 20 __

COMPASS BANK
485 Mission Avenue
San Diego, California 92104

⑆122290310⑆5008300 7⑈

CURRENCY	118	00
COIN	15	35
CHECKS LIST SINGLY 90-310	115	20
90-164	38	33
90-837	155	46
90-111	110	80
90-722	75	00
TOTAL	628	14

BE SURE EACH ITEM IS PROPERLY ENDORSED

ITEMS CREDITED SUBJECT TO VERIFICATION AND DEPOSIT AGREEMENT OF THIS BANK.

For a business account, the depositor fills out the deposit slip in duplicate, giving the original to the bank teller and keeping the copy. (This procedure may vary from bank to bank or company to company.)

A 2004 federal law, called The Check Clearing for the 21st Century Act (or Check 21 Act), allows banks that receive a check from a depositor to create a two-sided digital version of the original check, called a **substitute check**. This substitute check eliminates the need to handle a paper check through the banking system. One of several effects of the Check 21 Act is that consumers are no longer able to require a bank to return to them their original canceled checks with their monthly statement. Another side effect of the law is that it is now legal for anyone to use a computer scanner to capture images of checks and deposit them electronically, a process known as **remote deposit**. The Federal Reserve's website (www.federalreserve.gov/pubs/check21/consumer_guide.htm) provides more information about the Check 21 Act.

6-2c Automated Teller Machines

Deposits, withdrawals, and transfers can be made 24 hours a day, 7 days a week with **ATMs (automated teller machines)**. Each depositor uses a plastic card that contains a coded number and has a **personal identification number (PIN)**. The amount to be deposited, withdrawn, or transferred is keyed by the depositor. To make a deposit, the customer inserts into the ATM an envelope containing cash and/or checks and, if required, a copy of the deposit slip. To make a withdrawal, the customer requests an amount, the ATM dispenses it, and the customer removes the cash. In addition to deposits and withdrawals, a customer may transfer amounts from one account to another (for example, from savings to checking) as well as check the balance of his or her accounts.

6-2d Online Banking

Most transactions that can be handled at a bank location can also be completed online. With **online banking**, banks provide secure websites where customers can process transactions, such as pay bills, transfer funds, and review bank statements. Most banks also allow online banking customers to download banking transactions to a spreadsheet or accounting software. Strong internal controls are required for online banking. It is important that user names and passwords be protected. As an additional security measure, many lenders also require online banking customers to change their passwords on a regular basis.

6-2e Electronic Funds Transfer

A transfer of funds initiated through an electronic terminal, such as a telephone, a computer, or magnetic tape, is an **Electronic Funds Transfer (EFT)**. There is no paper document, such as a check or deposit slip, starting the transaction. The monthly bank statement will list the EFT deposits and payments. Examples of EFTs include an ATM transaction, a wire transfer in or out of an account, electronic bill paying, and payments to the IRS for income and payroll taxes.

6-2f Night Deposits

Most banks provide night depositories so that businesses and individuals can make deposits after regular hours. These are secured chutes into which a business's representative can insert a bag of cash and checks, knowing that the day's receipts will be safe until the bank opens in the morning.

6-2g Endorsements

The bank does not accept for deposit a check made out to a business until someone from the business has endorsed the check by signature or by stamp. The endorsement should appear on the back of the left end of a check, as it does in Figure 3. The **endorsement** (1) transfers title to the money and (2) authorizes payment of the check.

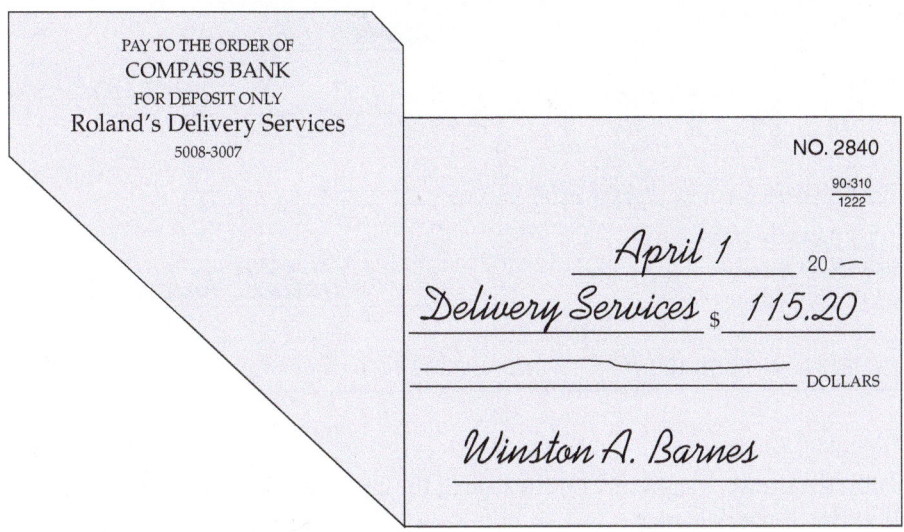

Figure 3
Endorsement for Roland's Delivery Services

6-2h Writing Checks

Most people generally use a check to make payments for bills and other items. The party writing the check is called the **drawer**. A check represents an order by the drawer, directing the bank to pay a designated person or company. The party to whom payment is to be made is the **payee**.

Manual checks may be attached to check stubs. Each stub has spaces for recording the check number and amount, the date and payee, the purpose of the check, and the beginning and ending balances of cash. *Note: The information recorded on the check stub is the basis for the journal entry, so check stubs are vitally important.* A person in a hurry or under pressure sometimes neglects to fill in the check stubs. Therefore, it is best to record all information on the check stub *before making out the check*. Businesses that use computerized checks do not need check stubs. One of the benefits of computerized accounting is that checks are automatically entered into the accounting system when generated.

Checks should be written carefully so that no one can successfully alter them. Figure 4 is a manual check, with the accompanying stub, drawn on the account of Roland's Delivery Services.

Follow these steps to write a manual check:

STEP 1. Write the payee's name on the first long line.

STEP 2. Write the amount of the check in figures close to the dollar sign.

STEP 3. Write the amount in words at the extreme left of the line provided for this information. Write cents as a fraction of 100. Legally, if there is a discrepancy between the amount in figures and the written amount, the written amount prevails. However, generally, the bank gets in touch with the drawer and asks what the correct amount should be.

Figure 4

Manual check with accompanying stub for Roland's Delivery Services

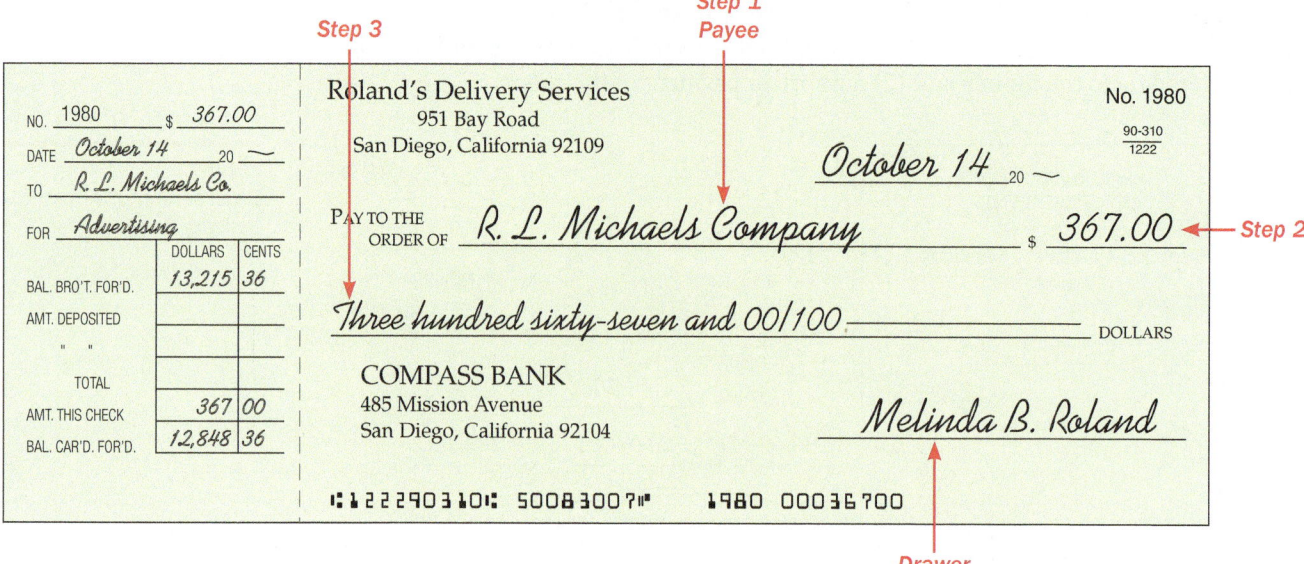

Figure 5

Description of the script from Ck. No. 1980 in Figure 4

Finally, the drawer's signature on the face of the check should match the signature card on file at the drawer's bank.

The bottom of a check contains some important information such as the **bank routing number** (a nine-digit number used by the Federal Reserve Bank to identify the financial institution), the depositor account number, and the check number, which are all pre-printed on the check before being sent to the account holder. Figure 5 shows where the numbers are located and what they mean.

6-2i Positive Pay

A fraud prevention cash management program offered by banks in an attempt to protect customers and the bank is called **positive pay**. Before the bank will allow payment, positive pay programs require companies to submit an authorized list of checks written. This authorized list includes information such as the payee, check number, and check amount. Many banks now require business customers to enroll in the positive pay program if they expect fraud protection from the bank. Businesses that fail to enroll in this program often do not have fraud protection coverage through the bank.

6-3 **BANK STATEMENTS**

The bank prepares the **bank statement**, which is created from the bank's viewpoint. Keep in mind that a customer's account is a liability to the bank and, therefore, has a credit balance. Once a month, the bank sends each of its customers the following information with the bank statement:

- The balance at the beginning of the month
- Additions in the form of deposits and credit memos
- Deductions in the form of checks and debit memos
- Electronic transactions
- The final balance at the end of the month

A bank statement for Roland's Delivery Services is shown in Figure 6 (see page 246). The legend of symbols listed on the bottom of the statement include:

CM (credit memo) Increases or credits to the account, such as notes or accounts collected by the bank and/or interest income earned.

DM (debit memo) Decreases or debits to the account, such as NSF checks (discussed later in this chapter) and service charges. Service charges are based on the number of items processed and the average account balance. Special charges may also be levied against the account for collections and other services performed, including check printing.

OD (overdraft) The withdrawal of more than the cash balance in the account, resulting in a negative balance.

EC (error correction) Corrections of errors made by the bank, such as encoding mistakes.

Neirfy/Shutterstock.com

In the Real World

Internet businesses, such as eBay, Inc., understand the importance of implementing controls that protect the integrity of the service they offer. The success of eBay relies on the number of transactions between buyers and sellers; therefore, it is important that eBay users feel comfortable trading in this online marketplace.

An example of one control used by eBay to protect the integrity of the system is their feedback forum. The feedback forum helps eBay and their members uncover sellers that are misrepresenting items for sale or who fail to deliver promised goods. It also lets sellers know which buyers are not promptly paying for the items they purchased. eBay uses the feedback forum to help buyers and sellers monitor fellow users of the system. Those users who don't follow eBay's policies and procedures end up with negative feedback, which eventually hurts their reputation and may cause eBay to suspend or cancel their user access.

Figure 6

Bank statement for Roland's Delivery Services

COMPASS BANK
485 Mission Avenue
San Diego, CA 92104

STATEMENT OF ACCOUNT

Roland's Delivery Services
951 Bay Road
San Diego, CA 92109

ACCOUNT NUMBER
5008-3007
STATEMENT DATE
September 30, 20-- to October 31, 20--
TAX ID NUMBER
83-5249862

SUMMARY		
Balance Last Statement		$10,403.57
Amount of Checks and Debits		$37,947.06
Number of Checks		69
Amount of Deposits and Credits		$44,793.10
Number of Deposits		21
Balance This Statement		$17,249.61

CHECKS/ OTHER DEBITS

CHECKS	CHECK NUMBER	DATE POSTED	AMOUNT	CHECK NUMBER	DATE POSTED	AMOUNT
	1952	10-01	55.00	1988	10-17	65.22
	1953	10-01	210.40	1989	10-17	465.30
	1954	10-01	440.00	1990	10-18	560.00
	1955	10-02	146.80	1991	10-19	114.57
	1956	10-02	186.25	1992	10-19	24.90
	1957	10-02	651.75	1993	10-19	135.36
	1958	10-03	742.20	1994	10-20	118.36
	1984	10-14	564.55	2018	10-30	120.75
	1985	10-15	617.00	2019	10-30	843.54
	1986	10-16	60.64	2020	10-31	743.20
	1987	10-16	481.85	2021	10-31	123.92

OTHER DEBITS

DESCRIPTION	DATE POSTED	AMOUNT
DM NSF check from B. R. Rumson	10-15	283.00
DM Automated Teller Trans. 092349 customer M3272348 at terminal 30962—cash	10-16	100.00
DM Service charge	10-31	19.50

DEPOSITS/ OTHER CREDITS

DEPOSITS	DATE POSTED	AMOUNT	DATE POSTED	AMOUNT
	10-01	832.00	10-17	973.22
	10-02	1,567.20	10-18	836.79
	10-03	451.63	10-21	438.49
	10-04	790.46	10-22	1,217.25
	10-07	1,048.15	10-23	814.15
	10-08	1,399.00	10-26	377.82
	10-14	872.25	10-28	559.47
	10-15	760.42	10-29	713.14
	10-16	636.34	10-30	854.32

OTHER CREDITS

DESCRIPTION	DATE POSTED	AMOUNT
CM Note collected, principal $1,000, interest $10	10-29	1,010.00

PLEASE EXAMINE THIS STATEMENT CAREFULLY. REPORT ANY POSSIBLE ERRORS WITHIN 10 DAYS.

CODE SYMBOLS

CM Credit Memo
DM Debit Memo

OD Overdraft
EC Error Correction

The bank statement is a valuable aid to efficiency and accuracy because it provides a double record of the Cash account. If a business entity deposits all cash receipts in the bank and makes all payments by check, the bank is keeping an independent record of the business's cash. You might think that the two balances—the company's and the bank's—should be equal, but this is unlikely. Some transactions may have been recorded in the company's account before being entered in the bank's records. In addition, there are unavoidable delays (by the business or the bank) in recording transactions. Ordinarily, there is a delay of one or more days between the date on which a check is written and the date it is presented to the bank for payment. Also, banks may not record deposits until the following business day. During this time lag, deposits made or checks written are recorded in the company's check register, but they are not yet listed on the bank statement.

Each month, the bank sends statements, either by mail or electronically via the Internet, to its depositors. The **canceled checks** (checks that have been paid or cleared by the bank) are listed on the bank statement. Debit or credit memos are also described on the bank statement.

6-3a Recording Deposits or Withdrawals

Each business entity keeps its accounts from its own point of view. As far as the bank is concerned, each customer's deposits are liabilities because the bank owes the customer the amount of the deposits. Using T accounts, it looks like this:

Liabilities

−	+
Debits	Credits

Deposits Payable

−	+
Debits	Credits

Debit memos	Checks written	Deposits	**Credit memos**
	Service charges	Notes collected	
	NSF checks	Interest income	
	ATM withdrawals	Wire transfers received	
	Electronic payments made		

> **Remember**
>
> Debit memos represent deductions from and credit memos represent additions to a bank account.

When the bank receives a cash deposit from a customer, the bank credits Deposits Payable because it owes more to its customer. When the bank cashes a check (pays out) for a customer, the bank debits Deposits Payable because it owes less to its customer.

The customer, on the other hand, uses the account titled Cash or Cash in Bank or simply the name of the bank. Deposits are recorded as debits and withdrawals are recorded as credits in the account. On a bank reconciliation, the balance of the account is listed as the **ledger balance of cash** before reconciliation with the bank statement.

6-3b Need for Reconciling Bank Balance and Ledger Balance

Because the bank statement balance and the ledger balance of cash are not always equal, a business prepares a **bank reconciliation**. The bank reconciliation process uncovers the reasons for the difference between the two balances and corrects any errors that may have been made by the bank or the business. This makes it possible to arrive at the same balance in each account, which is called the *adjusted balance*, or *true balance*, of the Cash account.

> **3** Reconcile a bank statement.
>
> **Learning Objective**

Because identity theft and white-collar crimes are potential problems for a business, another purpose of the bank reconciliation is to make sure all of the amounts paid out from the account are proper disbursements for the business. As stated earlier, a mark of good internal control is to have the bank reconciliation prepared by someone other than the check signer (if someone other than the business owner is signing checks). The person performing the bank reconciliation will be making sure (1) the dollar amount of each canceled check matches the check entry in the ledger balance of the company's cash account, (2) all of the charges, checks, and electronic transfers belong to the company, and (3) deposits are made in a timely manner.

There are a variety of reasons for differences between the bank statement balance and the customer's cash balance. Here are some of the more common ones:

Deposit in transit A deposit made after the bank statement was issued. The depositor has already added the amount to the Cash account in his or her books, but the deposit has not been recorded by the bank. (This is also called a *late deposit*.)

Outstanding checks Checks that have been written by the company but not yet received for payment by the time the bank sends out its statement. The company employee, when preparing the checks, deducted the amounts from the Cash account in the company's books, which explains the difference.

Collections Money collected by the bank for the customer. When the bank acts as a collection point for its customers by accepting payments on their behalf, it adds the proceeds to the customer's bank account and either immediately sends a credit memorandum to notify the customer of the transaction or includes it on the next bank statement.

Interest income Interest earned for keeping cash in the bank account. Some checking accounts are interest-bearing or interest-earning. The depositor will not learn how much interest the bank has credited to the bank account until he or she receives the bank statement.

NSF (non-sufficient funds) check A deposited check that the bank cannot process because the check writer's account does not contain enough money. When a bank customer deposits a check, it is recorded as cash on the customer's books. Occasionally, however, a check is not paid (bounces). When the bank notifies the customer of this, the customer must make a deduction from the Cash account. Simultaneously, the depositor records an increase in accounts receivable because the client's debt to the depositor remains unpaid. An NSF check is also called a *dishonored check*.

Service charge A bank charge for services rendered: for handling checks, for collecting money, for collecting payments on notes for its customers, for printing checks, and for providing other such services. The bank immediately deducts the fee from the balance of the bank account and identifies the charges on the bank statement.

Errors Mistakes made by the customer or the bank. In spite of internal controls and systems that are designed to double-check the process to prevent errors, sometimes the customer or the bank makes a mistake. Often these errors do not become evident until the bank reconciliation is performed.

6-3c Steps in Reconciling the Bank Statement

Follow these steps to reconcile a bank statement:

STEP 1. **Canceled checks.** Compare the amount of each canceled check on the bank statement with the ledger entries in the company's cash account. Any differences between the amount on the bank statement and the amount on the company's books should be noted.

FYI

When a bank agrees to accept payments on behalf of a customer, the fee the bank charges does not necessarily mean that the bank will follow up on collection of a payment or notify the customer that the payment is late.

FYI

When a company's Cash account has a credit balance in the general ledger, the account is overdrawn.

STEP 2. Deposits.

    a. Compare the deposits in transit (deposits not recorded by the bank at the time of the statement) listed on last month's bank reconciliation with the deposits shown on the bank statement. All of last month's deposits in transit should be listed on this month's bank statement. If they are not, notify the bank immediately.

    b. Compare the remaining deposits listed on this month's bank statement with deposits written in the company's accounting records. Consider any deposits not shown on the bank statement as *deposits in transit*.

STEP 3. Outstanding checks.

    a. Review the list of outstanding checks left over from last month's bank reconciliation and note the checks that have since been returned or cleared.

    b. For each canceled check, compare the amount recorded on the bank statement with the amount recorded in the checkbook or general ledger cash account. Use a check mark (✔) to indicate that the check has been paid and that the amount is correct. Any payments that have not been marked off, including the outstanding checks from last month's bank reconciliation, are the present *outstanding checks*.

STEP 4. Bank memoranda. Trace the credit memos and debit memos to the journal. If the memos have not been recorded, make separate entries for them.

> **qb QuickBooks® Online Tip**
>
> QuickBooks Online provides users with an account reconciliation feature, which can be used to reconcile the bank statement.

Many businesses now have computerized check registers, so the bank reconciliation will be done primarily on the computer. The procedures are similar, as there is still the need to compare canceled check information, compare deposits, identify outstanding checks and deposits, and record adjustments.

6-3d Examples of Bank Reconciliations

Let's go through the reconciliation process for two businesses, W. Carson Company and Roland's Delivery Services.

W. CARSON COMPANY

The bank statement of W. Carson Company indicates a balance of $6,446 as of March 31. The balance of the Cash account in Carson's ledger as of that date is $4,650. Carson's accountant has taken the following steps:

STEP 1. Verified that canceled checks were recorded correctly on the bank statement.

STEP 2. Noted that the deposit made on March 31 was not recorded on the bank statement, $2,174.

STEP 3. Noted outstanding checks: no. 920, $1,695; no. 975, $325; no. 976, $1,279.

STEP 4. Noted credit memo: Note collected by the bank from T. Landon, $700, not recorded in the journal. Noted debit memo: Collection charge and service charge not recorded in the journal, $29.

The note received from T. Landon is called a *promissory note*. A **promissory note** is a written promise to pay a specific amount at a specific future time. Let's assume that W. Carson Company received the 60-day non-interest-bearing note from T. Landon for services performed. In recording the transaction, Carson's accountant debited Notes Receivable and credited Income from Services. (The account Notes Receivable is similar to Accounts Receivable. However, Accounts Receivable is reserved for customer charge accounts, with payments usually due in 30 days.) Then W. Carson Company turned the note over to its bank for collection.

The bank will use a credit memo form to notify W. Carson Company that the note has been collected and that the company's bank account has been increased by the amount of the note. Based on the credit memo, Carson's accountant will make a journal entry debiting Cash and crediting Notes Receivable.

Think of the bank reconciliation in terms of the following:

1. It brings the bank statement balance up to date by recognizing the activities or transactions we knew about but the bank did not know about when it prepared the statement (deposits in transit and outstanding checks as shown in our checkbook, for example).

2. It brings the balance of the Cash account up to date by recognizing the activities or transactions the bank knew about but we did not know about until we received the statement (bank fees, NSF checks, notes collected, checks cleared, interest income, debit memos, and credit memos as shown on the bank statement, for example).

Figure 7 shows W. Carson Company's bank reconciliation. The reconciliation items in Figure 7 that require journal entries are shown in color.

Figure 7

Bank reconciliation for W. Carson Company

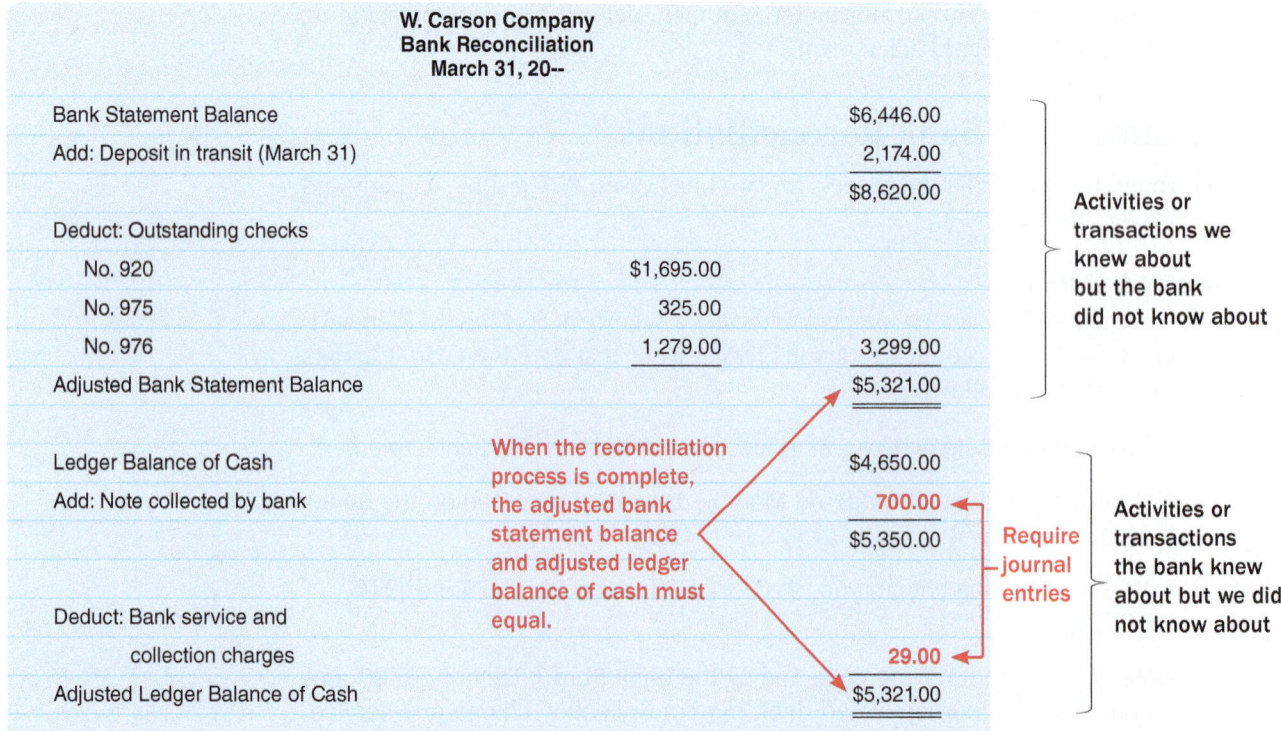

W. Carson Company Bank Reconciliation March 31, 20--			
Bank Statement Balance			$6,446.00
Add: Deposit in transit (March 31)			2,174.00
			$8,620.00
Deduct: Outstanding checks			
No. 920		$1,695.00	
No. 975		325.00	
No. 976		1,279.00	3,299.00
Adjusted Bank Statement Balance			$5,321.00
Ledger Balance of Cash			$4,650.00
Add: Note collected by bank			700.00
			$5,350.00
Deduct: Bank service and			
collection charges			29.00
Adjusted Ledger Balance of Cash			$5,321.00

Activities or transactions we knew about but the bank did not know about

When the reconciliation process is complete, the adjusted bank statement balance and adjusted ledger balance of cash must equal.

Require journal entries

Activities or transactions the bank knew about but we did not know about

YOU Make the Call

Assume that you manage a service business that has three employees: a bookkeeper, an office manager, and a salesperson. You are so busy growing your business that you have turned over all bookkeeping and cash activities to the bookkeeper, including check-writing and signing privileges, bank reconciliation, and data entry. Your time has been so limited that you have not looked at any reports or reviewed any bank statements. Today is payday, and to your utter surprise, you are informed that there is not enough cash to make this week's payroll. When you look at the last three bank statements and compare the deposits to your cash receipts and cash payments journal, you see that things are not matching up, leading you to the conclusion that embezzlement (theft) of cash has taken place. Thinking back to how you assigned duties for your employees, what could you have done differently to have prevented this disaster?

SOLUTION

There should have been a better segregation of duties to prevent this occurrence. First, the bookkeeper should not have been assigned all cash activities, especially check-writing and signing privileges. Only you or the office manager should write and sign checks. You and no other employee in the business should mail the checks. The office manager should have the responsibility of opening and endorsing each check by stamping on the back of the check "For Deposit Only." This restricts, or limits, any further transfer of the check and forces the deposit of the check because the endorsement is not valid for any other purpose. The office manager, not the bookkeeper, should do the bank reconciliation, with you reviewing the completed statements. The bookkeeper's primary responsibilities should be to make journal entries for cash received for the general ledger as well as for the Accounts Receivable and Accounts Payable accounts.

6-4 JOURNAL ENTRIES FROM THE BANK RECONCILIATION

Note that the journal entries are based on the items used to adjust the ledger balance of Cash. These items represent the transactions that the bank has knowledge of but the business does not. According to the bank reconciliation, the true balance of Cash is $5,321, which is the balance we want to show on the company's books. We can't change the balance of an account unless we make a journal entry and then post the entry to the accounts involved. **Consequently, we have to make journal entries for items in the Ledger Balance of Cash section of the bank reconciliation.** The additions are debited to the Cash account, and the deductions are credited to the Cash account. W. Carson Company records the entries in its general journal as follows:

 Record the required journal entries from the bank reconciliation.

Learning Objective

GENERAL JOURNAL						Page ___	
Date	Description	Post. Ref.	Debit		Credit	
20--						
Mar.	31	Cash		7 0 0 00		
		Notes Receivable			7 0 0 00	
		Non-interest-bearing note signed by				
		T. Landon was collected by the bank.				
	31	Miscellaneous Expense		2 9 00		
		Cash			2 9 00	
		Service charge and collection				
		charge levied by bank.				

Here bank service and collection charges are recorded in Miscellaneous Expense because the amounts are relatively small. Some accountants may use a separate expense account, such as Bank Charge Expense. After the entries have been posted, the T account for Cash looks like this:

Cash

Balance	4,650	Mar. 31	29
Mar. 31	700		
Bal.	**5,321**		

Note that the balance in the T account is now equal to both the adjusted bank statement balance and the adjusted ledger balance of cash.

6-4a Form of Bank Reconciliation

Now that you have seen an example of a bank reconciliation, let's look at the standard form of a bank reconciliation for an imaginary company.

Bank Statement Balance (last figure on the statement) $4,000

Add:

Deposits in transit (deposits made after the bank statement was issued and already added to the ledger balance of Cash) $300

Bank errors (that understate balance)   20   320

   $4,320

Deduct:

Outstanding checks and transfers (they have already been deducted from the Cash account) $960

Bank errors (that overstate balance)   40   1,000

Adjusted Bank Statement Balance (the true balance of Cash) $3,320

Ledger Balance of Cash (The latest balance of the Cash account if it has been posted up to date. Otherwise, take the beginning balance of Cash plus cash receipts minus cash payments) $2,850

Add:

Credit memos (additions by the bank not recorded in the Cash account, such as collections of notes and interest income earned) $500

Book errors (that understate balance)   40   540

   $3,390

Deduct:

Debit memos (deductions by the bank not recorded in the Cash account, such as service charges or collection charges and NSF checks)	$ 20	
Book errors (that overstate balance)	50	70
Adjusted Ledger Balance of Cash (the true balance of Cash)		$3,320

ROLAND'S DELIVERY SERVICES

The bank statement of Roland's Delivery Services shows a final balance of $17,249.61 as of October 31. (See Figure 6, on page 246.) The present balance of the Cash account in the ledger, after Roland's Delivery Services' accountant has posted from the journal, is $16,296.11. The accountant took the following steps:

STEP 1. Verified that canceled checks were recorded correctly on the bank statement.

STEP 2. Discovered that a deposit of $1,012 made on October 31 was not recorded on the bank statement.

STEP 3. Noted outstanding checks: no. 1951, $687; no. 2022, $185; no. 2023, $367; no. 2024, $110.

STEP 4. Noted that a credit memo for a note collected by the bank from Lawson and Richards, $1,000 principal plus $10 interest, was not recorded in the journal. Found that check no. 2002 for $745, payable to Sanders, Inc., on account, was recorded in the journal as $754. (The correct amount is $745.) Noted that a debit memo for a collection charge and service charge of $19.50 was not recorded in the journal. Noted that a debit memo for an NSF check for $283 from B. R. Rumson was not recorded. Noted that a $100 personal withdrawal by Melinda B. Roland, the owner, using an ATM, was not recorded.

Look at Figure 8 (page 254) to see how each step relates to the bank reconciliation.

The accountant makes journal entries for the items indicated in Figure 8 to change the balance of the Cash account from its present balance of $16,296.11 to the true balance of $16,912.61. Again, those items that require journal entries are highlighted in Figure 8 and shown in Figure 9 on page 254.

Interest Income is classified as a revenue account. It represents the amount received on the promissory note that is over and above the face value of the note.

As for the NSF check, upon being notified by the bank, Roland's Delivery Services calls its customer (B. R. Rumson). Rumson can now take steps to cover the check. Let's review Roland's Delivery Services' transaction with B. R. Rumson: In return for services provided, Roland's Delivery Services received Rumson's check for $283. At that time, Roland's Delivery Services' accountant recorded the transaction as a debit to Cash for $283 and a credit to Income from Services for $283. Later, the bank, through its debit memorandum, notified Roland's Delivery Services about Rumson's NSF check. Then, to avoid overdrawing its own bank account, Roland's Delivery Services makes an entry crediting Cash (to correct its earlier debit to Cash) and debiting Accounts Receivable (to put the amount into Accounts Receivable). Because B. R. Rumson owes the money, it is logical to add the amount to Accounts Receivable for future collection.

> **Remember**
>
> When you are reconciling a bank statement, always double-check for any outstanding checks or deposits from previous statements that have been carried forward. Also double-check for any bank service charges.

Figure 8

Bank reconciliation for Roland's Delivery Services

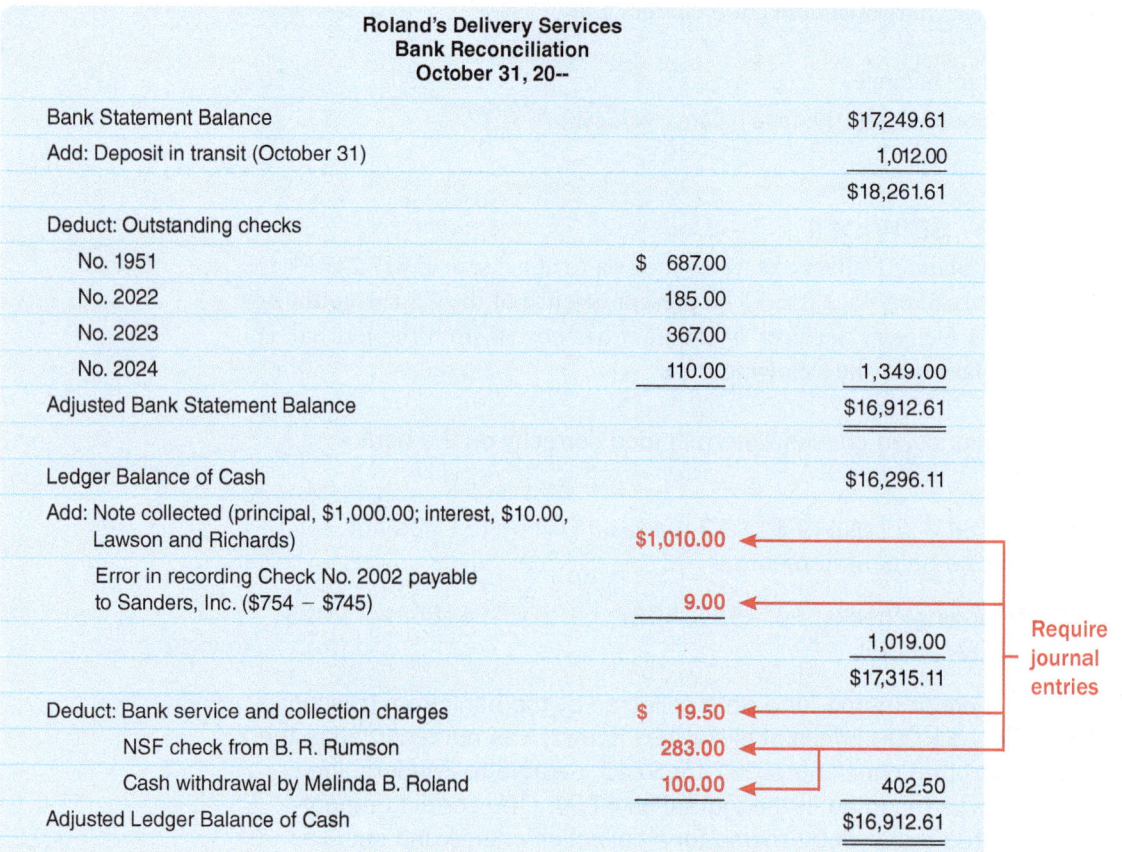

Roland's Delivery Services
Bank Reconciliation
October 31, 20--

Bank Statement Balance		$17,249.61
Add: Deposit in transit (October 31)		1,012.00
		$18,261.61
Deduct: Outstanding checks		
No. 1951	$ 687.00	
No. 2022	185.00	
No. 2023	367.00	
No. 2024	110.00	1,349.00
Adjusted Bank Statement Balance		$16,912.61
Ledger Balance of Cash		$16,296.11
Add: Note collected (principal, $1,000.00; interest, $10.00, Lawson and Richards)	$1,010.00	
Error in recording Check No. 2002 payable to Sanders, Inc. ($754 − $745)	9.00	
		1,019.00
		$17,315.11
Deduct: Bank service and collection charges	$ 19.50	
NSF check from B. R. Rumson	283.00	
Cash withdrawal by Melinda B. Roland	100.00	402.50
Adjusted Ledger Balance of Cash		$16,912.61

Require journal entries

Figure 9

Journal entries for Roland's Delivery Services

GENERAL JOURNAL   Page ___

Date		Description	Post. Ref.	Debit	Credit
20--					
Oct.	31	Cash		1 0 1 0 00	
		Notes Receivable			1 0 0 0 00
		Interest Income			1 0 00
		Bank collected note signed			
		by Lawson and Richards.			
	31	Cash		9 00	
		Accounts Payable			9 00
		Error in recording Ck. No. 2002			
		payable to Sanders, Inc.			
	31	Miscellaneous Expense		1 9 50	
		Cash			1 9 50
		Bank service charge and			
		collection charge.			

	31	Accounts Receivable		2 8 3 00	
		Cash			2 8 3 00
		NSF check received from			
		B. R. Rumson.			
	31	M. B. Roland, Drawing		1 0 0 00	
		Cash			1 0 0 00
		Withdrawal for personal use.			

Figure 9
(Concluded)

A bank reconciliation form is ordinarily printed on the back of the bank statement. The adjusted balance for the ledger balance of cash has already been determined. Consequently, the bank form is provided only for calculating the adjusted bank statement balance of the bank reconciliation. The bank form for Roland's Delivery Services is shown in Figure 10.

Figure 10
Bank form for Roland's Delivery Services

THIS FORM IS PROVIDED TO HELP YOU BALANCE YOUR BANK STATEMENT

CHECKS OUTSTANDING—NOT CHARGED TO ACCOUNT

NO. 1951	$ 687	00
2022	185	00
2023	367	00
2024	110	00
TOTAL	$ 1,349	00

BEFORE YOU START

PLEASE BE SURE YOU HAVE ENTERED IN YOUR CHECKBOOK ALL AUTOMATIC TRANSACTIONS SHOWN ON THE FRONT OF YOUR STATEMENT.

YOU SHOULD HAVE ADDED IF ANY OCCURRED:
1. Loan advances.
2. Credit memos.
3. Other automatic deposits.

YOU SHOULD HAVE SUBTRACTED IF ANY OCCURRED:
1. Automatic loan payments.
2. Automatic savings transfers.
3. Service charges.
4. Debit memos.
5. Other automatic deductions and payments.

BANK BALANCE SHOWN
ON THIS STATEMENT $ 17,249.61

ADD
DEPOSITS NOT SHOWN
ON THIS STATEMENT
(IF ANY) $ 1,012.00

TOTAL $ 18,261.61

SUBTRACT

CHECKS OUTSTANDING $ 1,349.00

BALANCE $ 16,912.61

SHOULD AGREE WITH YOUR CHECKBOOK
BALANCE AFTER DEDUCTING SERVICE CHARGE
(IF ANY) SHOWN ON THIS STATEMENT.

Please examine immediately and report if incorrect. If no reply
is received within 10 days, the account will be considered correct.

To: **Amy Roberts, CPA**
Subject: **Protecting My Cash**

Hi Amy,

I've set up my internal control guidelines and have made sure to separate the cash handling duties from the accounting activities. I have also set up a bank reconciliation schedule, so I'm sure this activity is done on a regular basis. I think I am ready for the rest of the steps you talked about. What should I look for or do next?

Thanks,

Janie

To: **Janie Conner**
Subject: **RE: Protecting My Cash**

Hi Janie,

It sounds like you are right on track. Below is a checklist for the rest of the items you should set up or monitor on a regular basis. Let me know if you have any questions.

    _____ 1. Set up a Petty Cash fund for smaller purchases.

    _____ 2. Set up a Change Fund to oversee your cash register funds.

    _____ 3. Use the Cash Short and Over account to monitor shortages and overages when they occur.

Amy

6-5 THE PETTY CASH FUND

Day after day businesses are confronted with transactions requiring small, immediate payments, such as paying for delivery charges, birthday cards, or pizza for after-hours workers. If the business had to make all payments by check, the time required would be frustrating and the whole process would be unduly expensive. For many businesses, the cost of writing each check is more than $10. This includes the cost of an employee's time for writing and reconciling the check. Suppose you buy a few stamps from an employee for $2.20 and you want to reimburse her. To write a check would not be practical.

It makes more sense to pay in cash using the **Petty Cash Fund**. *Petty* means "small," so the business sets a maximum amount that can be paid immediately out of petty cash. Payments that exceed this maximum must be processed by regular check through the journal.

ACCOUNTING IN YOUR FUTURE

FORENSIC ACCOUNTANT

If the super detective Sherlock Holmes was around today and needed to investigate corporate financial crimes, he would need to rely on not only his detective skills but also his accounting knowledge. The combination of accounting and detective skills is what makes accountants such good investigators in today's financial world. Many public accountants specialize in forensic accounting—investigating and interpreting white-collar crimes such as securities fraud and embezzlement, bankruptcies and contract disputes, as well as other complex and possibly criminal financial transactions such as money laundering. Forensic accountants combine their knowledge of accounting and finance with law and investigative techniques to determine whether an activity is illegal. Many forensic accountants work closely with law enforcement personnel and lawyers during investigations and often appear as expert witnesses during trials.

Increased focus on financial crimes such as embezzlement, bribery, and securities fraud, in addition to the growing number of these occurrences, will increase the demand for forensic accountants. Computer technology has made these crimes easier to commit. At the same time, the development of new computer software and electronic surveillance technology has made tracking down financial criminals easier, thus increasing the likelihood of discovery. As success rates of investigations grow, demand for forensic accountants will increase. *U.S. News & World Report* listed forensic accounting as one of the eight most secure career tracks in America.

The Association of Certified Fraud Examiners offers the Certified Fraud Examiner (CFE) designation for forensic or public accountants involved in fraud prevention, detection, deterrence, and investigation. To obtain the designation, individuals must have a bachelor's degree and two years of relevant experience, pass a four-part exam, and abide by a code of ethics. Therefore, if you take the additional steps of securing your CPA status as well as education leading to your becoming a CFE, you can feed your taste for detective work while still enjoying your life as an accountant!

6-5a Establishing the Petty Cash Fund

5 (a) Record journal entries to establish a Petty Cash Fund.

Learning Objective

After the business has set the maximum amount of a payment allowed from petty cash, the next step is to estimate how much cash will be needed during a given period of time, such as a month. It is also important to consider the element of security when keeping cash in the office. If the risk is great, the amount kept in the fund should be small. Roland's Delivery Services decides to establish a Petty Cash Fund of $100 and put it under the control of the accounting assistant. Accordingly, Roland's Delivery Services' accountant writes a check, cashes it at the bank, and records this transaction in the journal as follows:

Date		Description	Post. Ref.	Debit	Credit
20--					
Sept.	1	Petty Cash Fund		1 0 0 00	
		Cash			1 0 0 00
		Established a Petty Cash Fund,			
		Ck. No. 1880.			

GENERAL JOURNAL — Page ___

T accounts for the entry look like this:

Petty Cash Fund			**Cash**	
+	−		+	−
100				100

Because the Petty Cash Fund is an asset account, it is listed on the balance sheet immediately below Cash.

Once the fund has been created, it is not debited again unless the original amount is not large enough to handle the necessary transactions. In that case, the accountant has to increase the Petty Cash Fund—perhaps from $100 to $200. **However, if no change is made in the size of the fund, the Petty Cash Fund is debited only once, when the fund is first established.**

The check is written to the accounting assistant, "Sheila R. Bayes, Petty Cash Fund." She converts it into convenient **denominations**, which are varieties of coins and currency, such as quarters and dimes and $1 and $5 bills. Then, the accounting assistant puts the money in a locked drawer and will not pay anything larger than $20 (or whatever the company determines as the agreed-upon amount) out of petty cash.

> **Remember**
>
> If no change is made in the size of the fund, the Petty Cash Fund account is debited only once, when the fund is first established.

6-5b Payments from the Petty Cash Fund

5 (cont.) (b) Complete petty cash vouchers, (c) petty cash payments record, and (d) reimburse the petty cash fund.

Learning Objective

The accounting assistant is designated as the only person who can make payments from the Petty Cash Fund. In case of her illness, another employee should be named as a backup. A **petty cash voucher** must be used to account for every payment from the fund. The voucher represents a receipt signed by the person who authorized the payment and by the person who received the payment. The voucher also explains the purpose for the payment. Thus, even for small payments of $20 or less, there would have to be collusion between the payee and the assistant for any theft to occur. Figure 11 shows an example of a petty cash voucher.

```
                    PETTY CASH VOUCHER

No.   1                            Date   September 2, 20--

Paid to  Mason Delivery Squad               $  10.00

For     Delivery

Account  Delivery Expense

Approved by                    Payment received by

        S. Bayes                      R. Bates
```

Figure 11
Petty cash voucher

6-5c Petty Cash Payments Record

Some businesses prefer to have a written record on one sheet of paper, so they keep a **petty cash payments record**. In a petty cash payments record, petty cash vouchers and the accounts that are to be charged are listed. The purpose of the expenditure is also listed. Special columns for frequent types of expenditures are included in the Distribution of Payments section. The petty cash payments record is not a journal.

Roland's Delivery Services made the following payments from its Petty Cash Fund during September:

Sept. 2   Paid $10 for flowers for the front counter to Mason Delivery Squad, voucher no. 1.

3   Bought pencils and pens, $8.59, voucher no. 2.

5   Bought local newspapers for article related to Roland's Delivery Services, $2.50, voucher no. 3.

7   Paid postage on incoming packages, $3.70, voucher no. 4.

10   Melinda B. Roland, the owner, withdrew $10 for personal use, voucher no. 5.

14   Reimbursed employee for stamps, $2.20, voucher no. 6.

21   Bought stick-on tabs, $4.10, voucher no. 7.

22   Paid $14 for gift for retiring employee, voucher no. 8.

26   Paid for mailing packages, $3.60, voucher no. 9.

27   Paid $9 for Girl Scout cookies, voucher no. 10.

29   Bought memo pads, $4.40, voucher no. 11.

29   Paid for making duplicate keys, $8.20, voucher no. 12.

30   Paid $8 to have parking area swept, voucher no. 13.

30   Paid for trash removal, $5, voucher no. 14.

Figure 12, on page 260, shows how these payments are recorded.

6-5d Reimbursement of the Petty Cash Fund

To bring the fund back up to the original amount when it is nearly exhausted (for instance, at the end of the month), the accountant reimburses the fund for expenditures made. Consequently, the Petty Cash Fund may be considered a revolving fund. If the amount initially put in the Petty Cash Fund is $100 and at the end of the month only $6.71 is left, the accountant puts $93.29 back into the fund as a reimbursement. This will bring the fund back to the original $100 to start the new month.

Bear in mind that the petty cash payments record is only a supplementary record for gathering information. A less formal way of compiling the information concerning petty cash payments might consist of collecting one month's petty cash vouchers, then sorting them by accounts (for example, Office Supplies and Delivery Expense). After the vouchers have been sorted by account, a calculator tape can be run to update account totals.

> **Remember**
>
> The petty cash payments record is not a journal. It is simply used as a basis for compiling information for the journal entry. Remember, to change the amount of an account, we have to make a journal entry.

Figure 12

Petty cash payments record for Roland's Delivery Services

Petty Cash Payments Record
Month of September 20--

Distribution of payments

Date	Vou. No.	Explanation	Payments	Office Supplies	Maintenance Expense	Miscellaneous Expense	Other Accounts Account	Amount
Sept. 1		Establish fund, Ck. No. 1880, $100						
2	1	Mason Delivery Squad	10.00			10.00		
3	2	Pencils and pens	8.59	8.59				
5	3	Local newspapers	2.50			2.50		
7	4	Postage on incoming packages	3.70			3.70		
10	5	Withdrawal by M. B. Roland	10.00				M.B. Roland, Drawing	10.00
14	6	Reimburse employee for stamps	2.20			2.20		
21	7	Stick-on tabs	4.10	4.10				
22	8	Gift for retiring employee	14.00			14.00		
26	9	Postage for mailings	3.60			3.60		
27	10	Girl Scout cookies	9.00			9.00		
29	11	Memo pads	4.40	4.40				
29	12	Making duplicate keys	8.20		8.20			
30	13	Sweeping of parking area	8.00		8.00			
30	14	Trash removal	5.00		5.00			
30		Totals	93.29	17.09	21.20	45.00		10.00
		Balance in Fund	$ 6.71					
		Reimburse fund, Ck. No. 1950	93.29					
		Total	$100.00					

Sheet1 | Sheet2 | Sheet3

At the end of the month, the accountant makes a summarizing entry to officially journalize the transactions that have taken place. The general journal and T accounts of Roland's Delivery Services are shown below.

Note that in the summarizing entry, the accountant debits the accounts for which the payments were made and credits the Cash account. No entry is made to the Petty Cash Fund account. Then, the accounting assistant cashes a check for $93.29 and puts the cash in the locked Petty Cash box. The Petty Cash Fund is now restored to the original $100.

		GENERAL JOURNAL				Page ___	
Date		Description	Post. Ref.	Debit		Credit	
20--							
Sept.	30	Office Supplies		17 09			
		Maintenance Expense		21 20			
		Miscellaneous Expense		45 00			
		M. B. Roland, Drawing		10 00			
		Cash				93 29	
		Reimbursed the Petty Cash					
		Fund, Ck. No. 1950.					

Cash		Office Supplies		M. B. Roland, Drawing	
+	−	+	−	+	−
	93.29	17.09		10.00	

Maintenance Expense		Miscellaneous Expense	
+	−	+	−
21.20		45.00	

6-6 THE CHANGE FUND

Anyone who has tried to pay for a small item with a $20 bill knows that any business that carries out numerous cash transactions needs a **Change Fund**.

6 Record the journal entries to establish a Change Fund.

Learning Objective

6-6a Establishing the Change Fund

Before setting up a Change Fund, you have to decide two things: (1) how much money needs to be in the fund and (2) what denominations of bills and coins are needed. Like the Petty Cash Fund, **the Change Fund is debited only once: when it is established.** It is left at the initial figure unless the person in charge decides to make it larger. The Change Fund account, like the Petty Cash Fund account, is an asset. It is recorded in the balance sheet immediately below Cash. If the Petty Cash Fund account is larger than the Change Fund account, it precedes the Change Fund.

The owner of Roland's Delivery Services, Melinda B. Roland, decides to establish a Change Fund. She decides this at the same time she sets up the company's Petty Cash Fund. The entries for the two transactions look like this:

Date		Description	Post. Ref.	Debit	Credit
20--					
Sept.	1	Petty Cash Fund		1 0 0 00	
		Cash			1 0 0 00
		Established a Petty Cash Fund,			
		Ck. No. 1880.			
	1	Change Fund		1 5 0 00	
		Cash			1 5 0 00
		Established a Change Fund,			
		Ck. No. 1881.			

GENERAL JOURNAL — Page ___

The T accounts for establishing the Change Fund are as follows:

Change Fund			Cash	
+	−		+	−
150				150

Roland cashes a check for $150 and gets the money in several denominations. She is now prepared to make change for any normal business transactions.

6-6b Depositing Cash

At the end of each business day, Roland's Delivery Services' accountant deposits the cash taken in during the day, less the amount of the Change Fund, which should be in small denominations for the next day's business. Let's assume that on September 1, Roland's Delivery Services had $1,575 on hand at the end of the day.

$1,575	Total cash count
− 150	Change Fund
$1,425	New cash deposit

The day's receipts are journalized as follows:

GENERAL JOURNAL — Page ___

Date		Description	Post. Ref.	Debit	Credit
20--					
Sept.	1	Cash		1 4 2 5 00	
		Income from Services			1 4 2 5 00
		To record revenue earned			
		during the day.			

The T accounts look like this:

Cash		Income from Services	
+	−	−	+
1,425			1,425

The amount of the cash deposit is the total cash count less the amount of the Change Fund. This should be equal to the income earned.

On September 9, the cash count is $1,672. So the accountant deposits $1,522 ($1,672 − $150). Roland's Delivery Services' accountant makes the following entry to record the day's receipts:

GENERAL JOURNAL											Page ___			
Date		Description	Post. Ref.		Debit					Credit				
20--														
Sept.	9	Cash		1	5	2	2	00						
		Income from Services							1	5	2	2	00	
		To record revenue earned												
		during the day.												

Some businesses label the Cash account *Cash in Bank* and label the Change Fund *Cash on Hand*.

6-7 CASH SHORT AND OVER

There is an inherent danger in making change: Human beings make mistakes, especially when many customers need to be waited on or when the business is temporarily short-handed. Because mistakes do happen, accounting records must be set up to cope with the situation. One reason a business uses a cash register is to detect mistakes in handling cash. **If, after the Change Fund is removed, the day's receipts are less than the register reading, a cash shortage exists. Conversely, when the day's receipts are greater than the register reading, a cash overage exists.** Both shortages and overages are recorded in the same account, which is called Cash Short and Over. Shortages are considered an expense of operating a business; therefore, shortages are recorded on the debit side of the account. Overages are treated as another form of revenue; therefore, overages are recorded on the credit side of the account.

Let's assume that on September 14, Roland's Delivery Services is faced with the following situation:

Cash Register Tape	Cash Count	Amount of the Change Fund
$1,515	$1,663	$150

After deducting the $150 in the Change Fund, Roland will deposit $1,513 ($1,663 − $150). Note that this amount is $2 less than the amount indicated by the cash register tape ($1,515 − $1,513); therefore, a $2 cash shortage exists. The following T accounts show how the accountant entered this transaction in the books.

 7 Record journal entries for transactions involving Cash Short and Over.

Learning Objective

FYI

The Cash Short and Over account may also be used to handle shortages and overages in the Petty Cash Fund.

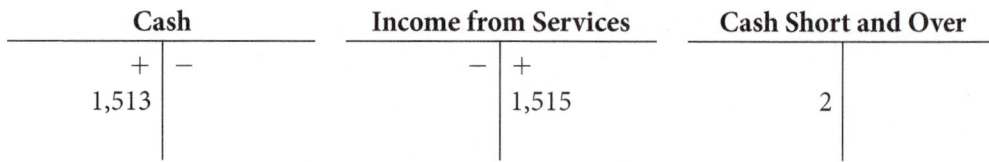

Cash	Income from Services	Cash Short and Over
+ −	− +	
1,513	1,515	2

The next day, September 15, the pendulum happens to swing in the other direction, as follows:

Cash Register Tape	Cash Count	Amount of the Change Fund
$1,578	$1,732	$150

The amount to be deposited is $1,582 ($1,732 − $150). This figure is $4 greater than the $1,578 in income from services indicated by the cash register tape. Thus, there is a $4 cash overage ($1,582 − $1,578). The analysis of this transaction is shown in the following T accounts:

Cash	Income from Services	Cash Short and Over
+ −	− +	
1,582	1,578	4

Roland's Delivery Services' revenue for September 14 and 15 is recorded in the general journal as follows:

GENERAL JOURNAL   Page ___

Date		Description	Post. Ref.	Debit	Credit
20--					
Sept.	14	Cash		1 5 1 3 00	
		Cash Short and Over		2 00	
		Income from Services			1 5 1 5 00
		To record revenue earned for the day,			
		involving a cash shortage of $2.00.			
	15	Cash		1 5 8 2 00	
		Income from Services			1 5 7 8 00
		Cash Short and Over			4 00
		To record revenue earned for the day,			
		involving a cash overage of $4.00.			

As far as errors are concerned, one would think that shortages would be offset by overages. However, customers receiving change are more likely to report shortages than overages. **Consequently, the business usually experiences a greater number of shortages.** A business may set a tolerance level for the cashiers. If the shortages consistently exceed the level of tolerance, either fraud is being committed or somebody is making entirely too many careless mistakes. In the world of accounting, both cash shortages and cash overages are areas of concern.

Now let's summarize our discussion of the Cash Short and Over account by drawing the following conclusions from the illustration:

1. At the close of the business day, the business deposits the difference between the amount in the cash drawer and the amount in the Change Fund.

2. The business records the amount shown on the cash register tape as its income from services.

3. If the amount of the cash deposit disagrees with the record of receipts, Cash Short and Over makes up the difference. In the first situation just described, there was a shortage of $2, so the Cash Short and Over account was debited. In the second situation, there was an overage of $4, so the Cash Short and Over account was credited. It is apparent that as a result of these transactions, the account looks like this:

Cash Short and Over

Shortage	2	Overage	4

Throughout any fiscal period, the accountant must continually record shortages and overages in the Cash Short and Over account. Let's assume that Roland's Delivery Services' final balance is $18 on the debit side. Roland's Delivery Services winds up with a net shortage of $18. The T account would look like this:

Cash Short and Over

Shortage	2	Overage	4
	4		1
	3		1
	7		2
	5		1
	2		2
	3		1
	4		
Bal.	**18**		

At the end of the fiscal period, **if the account has a debit balance, or net shortage, the accountant classifies it as an expense, crediting Cash Short and Over and debiting Miscellaneous Expense. The amount is then reported on the income statement under Miscellaneous Expense.**

Conversely, **if the account has a credit balance, or net overage, the accountant classifies it as a revenue account and debits Cash Short and Over and credits Miscellaneous Income. The amount is then reported on the income statement under Miscellaneous Income.** This is an exception to the policy of recording accounts under their exact account title in financial statements. Rather than attaching plus and minus signs to the Cash Short and Over account immediately, we wait until we find out its final balance, then make a journal entry to send the balance to the correct account classification.

Chapter Review

Study and Practice

Learning Objective   List internal controls for cash receipts and cash payments.

An important aspect of any financial accounting system, for an individual or for a business enterprise, is the accurate and efficient management of assets. The handling of assets in a manner that will protect them from fraud and waste is known as **internal control**. Management of cash is especially important, as embezzlement starts with an employee or employees failing to follow internal control procedures.

 PRACTICE EXERCISE 1

What are the internal control system policies and procedures designed to do?

PRACTICE EXERCISE 1 • SOLUTION

1. Protect assets against fraud and waste
2. Provide for accurate accounting data
3. Promote efficient operations
4. Encourage adherence to management policies

Learning Objective   Describe the procedures for recording deposits and withdrawals.

When a customer deposits money in a bank, the transaction is recorded on the company books as a debit to Cash, Cash in Bank, or simply the name of the bank. Withdrawals from the customer's account is recorded on the company books as a credit to the specified Cash account.

 PRACTICE EXERCISE 2

Each business entity keeps its accounts from its own point of view. Determine the point of view. Then answer (T) or (F) for the following statements:

___ 1. When the bank receives a deposit from a customer, the bank debits the Cash account.

___ 2. When the bank cashes a check (pays out) for a customer, the bank credits the Cash account.

___ 3. When the bank receives an NSF check on a customer's account, the bank debits the customer's account.

___ 4. When a customer deposits money into the bank, the customer debits his or her Cash account to record the transaction.

PRACTICE EXERCISE 2 • SOLUTION

1. F
2. F
3. T
4. T

3   Reconcile a bank statement.

The standard form for a **bank reconciliation** is as follows:

Bank Statement Balance

Add:
Deposits in transit
Bank errors that understate the **bank statement** balance

Deduct:
Outstanding checks or electronic transfers
Bank errors that overstate the bank statement balance

Adjusted Bank Statement Balance

Ledger Balance of Cash

Add:
Notes collected
Interest income earned
Checkbook errors that understate the ledger balance of cash
Bank credit memos

Deduct:
Bank service charges
Checkbook errors that overstate the ledger balance of cash
NSF checks
Bank debit memos

Adjusted Ledger Balance of Cash

 PRACTICE EXERCISE 3

The bank statement of M. C. Johnson Company indicates a balance of $7,428 as of July 31. The balance of the Cash account in Johnson's ledger as of that date is $6,872. Johnson's accountant has taken the following steps:

STEP 1. Verified that canceled checks were recorded correctly on the bank statement.

STEP 2. Noted that the deposit made on July 31 was not recorded on the bank statement, $2,071.

STEP 3. Noted outstanding checks: no. 1066, $1,075; no. 1099, $462; no. 1100, $605.

STEP 4. Noted credit memo: Non-interest-bearing note collected by the bank from L. Stewart, $500, not recorded in the journal. Noted debit memo: Collection charge and service charge not recorded in the journal, $15.

Based on the preceding information, prepare a bank reconciliation for M. C. Johnson Company.

(Continued)

CHAPTER REVIEW

PRACTICE EXERCISE 3 • SOLUTION

M. C. Johnson Company
Bank Reconciliation
July 31, 20--

Bank Statement Balance		$7,428.00
Add: Deposit in transit (July 31)		2,071.00
		$9,499.00
Deduct: Outstanding checks		
No. 1066	$1,075.00	
No. 1099	462.00	
No. 1100	605.00	2,142.00
Adjusted Bank Statement Balance		$7,357.00
Ledger Balance of Cash		$6,872.00
Add: Note collected by bank (L. Stewart)		500.00
		$7,372.00
Deduct: Bank service and collection charges		15.00
Adjusted Ledger Balance of Cash		$7,357.00

Learning Objective   **4**   Record the required journal entries from the bank reconciliation.

Journal entries for the Ledger Balance of Cash section are required. The entry for notes and interest collected is a debit to Cash and credits to Notes Receivable and Interest Income. The entry for a bank service charge is a debit to Miscellaneous Expense and a credit to Cash. The entry for an NSF check is a debit to Accounts Receivable and a credit to Cash.

 4 ### PRACTICE EXERCISE 4
Prepare the necessary journal entries from the bank reconciliation in Practice Exercise 3 for M. C. Johnson Company.

PRACTICE EXERCISE 4 • SOLUTION

GENERAL JOURNAL								Page ___	
Date		Description	Post. Ref.	Debit			Credit		
20--									
July	31	Cash		5 0 0	00				
		Notes Receivable					5 0 0	00	
		Non-interest-bearing note							
		signed by L. Stewart was							
		collected by the bank.							
	31	Miscellaneous Expense		1 5	00				
		Cash					1 5	00	
		Service charge and collection							
		charge levied by bank.							

5   (a) Record journal entries to establish a Petty Cash Fund.

Learning Objective

The entry to establish a **Petty Cash Fund** is a debit to Petty Cash Fund and a credit to Cash.

 ## PRACTICE EXERCISE 5a

A Petty Cash Fund of $100 was established on October 1. At the end of the month, the following accounts were charged for expenditures from the Petty Cash Fund: Office Supplies, $13.75; Delivery Expense, $15.00; Miscellaneous Expense, $36.00; B. Thomas, Drawing, $25.00. Record the journal entries for the establishment of the Petty Cash Fund.

PRACTICE EXERCISE 5a • SOLUTION

		GENERAL JOURNAL				Page ___	
Date		Description	Post. Ref.	Debit		Credit	
20--							
Oct.	1	Petty Cash Fund		1 0 0 00			
		Cash				1 0 0 00	
		Established a Petty Cash Fund.					

5   (b) Complete petty cash vouchers, (c) petty cash payments record, and (d) reimburse the petty cash fund.

Learning Objective (cont.)

A **petty cash voucher** is made out for each payment from the Petty Cash Fund. In the **petty cash payments record**, each voucher is listed and a notation is made concerning the accounts involved. In addition, an explanation of why the money was paid out is recorded. The petty cash payments record is used as a source of information for making the journal entry to reimburse the Petty Cash Fund. The entry to reimburse the Petty Cash Fund consists of debits to the items for which payments from the Petty Cash Fund were made and one credit to Cash for the total payments.

PRACTICE EXERCISE 5b, c, d (cont.)

Using the information from Practice Exercise 5a, record the journal entry for the reimbursement of the Petty Cash Fund.

PRACTICE EXERCISE 5b, c, d (cont.) • SOLUTION

		GENERAL JOURNAL				Page ___	
Date		Description	Post. Ref.	Debit		Credit	
20--							
Oct.	31	Office Supplies		1 3 75			
		Delivery Expense		1 5 00			
		Miscellaneous Expense		3 6 00			
		B. Thomas, Drawing		2 5 00			
		Cash				8 9 75	
		Reimbursed the Petty Cash Fund.					

CHAPTER REVIEW

Learning Objective

6   Record the journal entries to establish a Change Fund.

The entry to establish the **Change Fund** is a debit to Change Fund and a credit to Cash.

6 **PRACTICE EXERCISE 6**

Journalize the entry to establish a Change Fund amounting to $150 on July 1.

PRACTICE EXERCISE 6 • SOLUTION

			GENERAL JOURNAL				Page ___
Date		Description	Post. Ref.	Debit		Credit	
20--							
July	1	Change Fund		1 5 0 00			
		Cash				1 5 0 00	
		Established a Change Fund.					

Learning Objective

7   Record journal entries for transactions involving Cash Short and Over.

The Cash Short and Over account provides a way to keep a record of errors in making change. A debit balance in Cash Short and Over denotes a shortage, which is listed as Miscellaneous Expense. The entry is a debit to Miscellaneous Expense and a credit to Cash Short and Over. A credit balance in Cash Short and Over denotes an overage, which becomes Miscellaneous Income. The entry is a debit to Cash Short and Over and a credit to Miscellaneous Income.

7 **PRACTICE EXERCISE 7**

Journalize the entries to account for two bank deposits on June 29 and June 30. The amount of the Change Fund is $100.

a. On June 29, the cash register tape showed $950.86 in income from sales. The amount in the cash drawer was $1,051.86.

b. On June 30, the cash register tape showed $1,327.44 in income from sales. The amount in the cash drawer was $1,426.12.

PRACTICE EXERCISE 7 • SOLUTION

		GENERAL JOURNAL				Page ___	
Date		Description	Post. Ref.	Debit		Credit	
20--							
June	29	Cash		9 5 1	86		
		Income from Sales				9 5 0	86
		Cash Short and Over				1	00
		To record revenue earned					
		involving a cash overage					
		of $1.00 for the day.					
	30	Cash		1 3 2 6	12		
		Cash Short and Over		1	32		
		Income from Sales				1 3 2 7	44
		To record revenue earned					
		involving a cash shortage					
		of $1.32 for the day.					

Glossary

ATMs (automated teller machines) Machines that enable depositors to make deposits, withdrawals, and transfers using a coded plastic card. (*p. 242*)

Bank reconciliation A process by which an accountant determines whether and why there is a difference between the balance shown on the bank statement and the balance of the Cash account in the business's general ledger. The object is to determine the adjusted (or true) balance of the Cash account. (*p. 247*)

Bank routing number A nine-digit number used by the Federal Reserve Bank to identify the financial institution of the account holder. (*p. 244*)

Bank statement A periodic statement that a bank sends to the drawer/depositor of a checking account, listing deposits received and checks paid by the bank, debit and credit memos, electronic transactions, and beginning and ending balances. (*p. 244*)

Canceled checks Checks issued by the depositor that have been paid (cleared) by the bank and listed on the bank statement. They are called canceled checks because they are canceled by a stamp, indicating that they have been paid. (*p. 247*)

Cash funds Separately held reserves of cash set aside for specific purposes. (*p. 240*)

Change Fund A cash fund used by a business to make change for customers who pay cash for goods or services. (*p. 261*)

Collections Payments collected by the bank and added to the customer's bank account in the form of a credit memorandum. (*p. 248*)

Denominations Varieties of coins and currency, such as quarters, dimes, and nickels and $1 and $5 bills. (*p. 258*)

Deposit in transit A deposit not recorded on the bank statement because the deposit was made between the time of the bank's closing date for compiling items for its statement and the time the statement is received by the depositor; also known as a *late deposit*. (*p. 248*)

Deposit slips Printed forms provided by a bank, on which customers can list all items being deposited; also known as *deposit tickets*. (*p. 241*)

Drawer The party who writes the check. (*p. 243*)

Electronic Funds Transfer (EFT) A transfer of funds initiated through an electronic terminal, such as a telephone, computer, or magnetic tape. (*p. 242*)

Endorsement The process by which the payee transfers ownership of the check to a bank or another party. A check must be endorsed when deposited in a bank, because the bank must have legal title to it in order to collect payment from the drawer of the check (the person or firm who wrote the check). (*p. 243*)

Errors Mistakes made by a customer or the bank. (*p. 248*)

Interest income The amount earned from lending money to another person or business. (*p. 248*)

Internal control Plans and procedures built into the accounting system with the following objectives: (1) to protect assets against fraud and waste, (2) to provide accurate accounting data, (3) to promote efficient operation, and (4) to encourage adherence to management policies. (*p. 239*)

Ledger balance of cash The balance of the Cash account in the general ledger before it is reconciled with the bank statement. (*p. 247*)

NSF (non-sufficient funds) check Check drawn against an account in which there are *not sufficient funds* and returned by the payee's bank to the drawer's bank because of nonpayment; also known as a *dishonored check*. (*p. 248*)

Online banking Customers conduct banking transactions, such as pay bills, transfer funds, and review bank statements through a secure website. (*p. 242*)

Outstanding checks Checks that have been written by the drawer and deducted on his or her records but have not reached the bank for payment and are not deducted from the bank balance by the time the bank issues its statement. (*p. 248*)

Payee The person to whom a check is payable. (*p. 243*)

Petty Cash Fund A cash fund used to make small, immediate cash payments. (*p. 257*)

Petty cash payments record A record indicating the amount of each petty cash voucher, the accounts to which it should be charged, and the purpose of the expenditure. (*p. 259*)

Petty cash voucher A form stating who requested cash from the Petty Cash Fund, signed by (1) the person in charge of the fund and (2) the person who received the cash, and indicating the purpose of the petty cash payment. (*p. 258*)

Personal identification number (PIN) A unique *personal identification number* that is entered by the user to protect access to the user's account. (*p. 242*)

Positive pay A fraud prevention cash management program offered by banks in an attempt to protect customers and the bank. (*p. 244*)

Promissory note A written promise to pay a specific sum at a definite future time. (*p. 250*)

Remote deposit The process of capturing checks and deposits electronically for presentation to a financial institution. (*p. 242*)

Service charge The fee the bank charges for handling checks, collections, and other items. It is in the form of a debit memorandum. (*p. 248*)

Signature card The form a depositor signs to give the bank a copy of the official signatures of any persons authorized to sign checks. The bank can use it to verify the depositors' signatures on checks. (*p. 241*)

Substitute check The creation of a two-sided digital version of an original check. (*p. 242*)

Quiz Yourself

_____ 1. Which of the following is *not* an example of an internal control system?
   a. Maintain separate duties between cash handling and cash recording.
   b. Make weekly deposits.
   c. Keep petty cash locked up and under one person's control.
   d. Prenumber checks.
   e. Endorse checks immediate upon receipt.

_____ 2. Which of the following does *not* affect the bank statement?
   a. Credit memo
   b. Debit memo
   c. Overdraft
   d. Electronic transactions
   e. Endorsements

_____ 3. Which of the following does *not* explain the differences between the bank statement balance and the customer's cash balance?
   a. Deposit in transit
   b. Canceled checks
   c. An NSF check
   d. Errors
   e. Interest income

_____ 4. What is the journal entry to record an NSF check, from J. Smith for $250, that is returned with the bank statement?
   a. Cash $250 DR; NSF Check $250 CR
   b. Accounts Receivable $250 DR; Cash $250 CR
   c. NSF Check $250 DR; Accounts Receivable $250 CR
   d. Cash $250 DR; Accounts Receivable $250 CR
   e. Cash $250 DR; Miscellaneous Expense $250 DR

_____ 5. The Petty Cash account is a(n) _____.
   a. Liability
   b. Expense
   c. Asset
   d. Owner's Equity
   e. Prepaid Account

_____ 6. When the Petty Cash account is replenished at the end of the month, the journal entry includes which of the following?
   a. Debit to Cash
   b. Debit to Petty Cash
   c. Credit to Cash
   d. Credit to an Expense Account
   e. Credit to a Revenue Account

_____ 7. The entry to establish the Change Fund includes which of the following?
   a. Debit to Cash
   b. Debit to Change Fund
   c. Credit to Change Fund
   d. Debit to Petty Cash
   e. Credit to Petty Cash

_____ 8. The Cash Short and Over account covers both shortages and overages that occur in a business. What is the correct entry to record a shortage in the Cash Short and Over account? Where will the account appear on the income statement?
   a. DR Cash Short and Over; Expense
   b. CR Cash Short and Over; Income
   c. DR Cash Short and Over; Income
   d. CR Cash Short and Over; Expense
   e. None of the above; the Cash Short and Over account appears on the balance sheet.

Answers: 1.b 2.e 3.b 4.b 5.c 6.c 7.b 8.a

Chapter Assignments

Discussion Questions

1. What are internal controls designed to do?
2. Why does a bank keep a signature card on file for customers' accounts?
3. What is the purpose of endorsing a check?
4. Why is there generally a difference between the balance in the Cash account on the company's books and the balance on the bank statement?
5. Indicate whether the following items in a bank reconciliation should be (1) added to the Cash account balance, (2) deducted from the Cash account balance, (3) added to the bank statement balance, or (4) deducted from the bank statement balance.
   a. NSF check
   b. Deposit in transit
   c. Outstanding check
   d. Bank error charging the business's account with another company's check
   e. Bank service charge

6. Why is it necessary to make general journal entries for the ledger balance side of the bank reconciliation?

7. a. Why would a business use a Petty Cash Fund?

   b. Describe the entry needed to establish a $50 Petty Cash Fund and an entry to reimburse the fund.

8. a. What does a debit balance in Cash Short and Over mean?

   b. Where does a debit balance in Cash Short and Over appear in the financial statements?

   c. What does a credit balance in Cash Short and Over mean?

   d. Where does a credit balance in Cash Short and Over appear in the financial statements?

Exercises

LO 3

Practice Exercise 3

EXERCISE 6-1 Fill in the missing amounts for the following bank reconciliation:

Bank Reconciliation March 31, 20--		
Bank Statement Balance		$3,764.00
Add: Deposit in transit		(a)
		$4,031.00
Deduct: Outstanding checks	$212.00	
No. 211	(b)	
No. 225	318.00	
No. 228		850.00
Adjusted Bank Statement Balance		(c)
Ledger Balance of Cash		$2,837.00
Add: Note collected by bank		430.00
		(d)
Deduct: Bank service and collection charges	(e)	
NSF check from customer	74.00	86.00
Adjusted Ledger Balance of Cash		(f)

LO 4

Practice Exercise 4

EXERCISE 6-2 The Ledger Balance of Cash section of the bank reconciliation for Virtual Net Company for August 31 follows.

Ledger Balance of Cash		$6,536.00
Add: Note collected (principal, $600.00; interest, $15.75, signed by S. Sambey)	$615.75	
Error in recording Ck. No. 3351 payable to Fairview Company (recorded check for $16.00 too much)	16.00	631.75
		$ 7,167.75
Deduct: NSF check from R. Leswick	$ 176.00	
Bank service and collection charges	25.00	201.00
Adjusted Ledger Balance of Cash		$6,966.75

Journalize the entries required to bring the general ledger up to date as of August of this year.

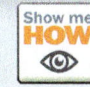

EXERCISE 6-3 When the bank statement is received on July 3, it shows a balance, before reconciliation, of $5,200 as of June 30. After reconciliation, the adjusted balance is $3,100. If one deposit in transit amounted to $1,200, what was the total of the outstanding checks, assuming that no other adjustments would be made to the bank statement?

EXERCISE 6-4 Place a check mark in the column that indicates the location of each item that would be found on a bank reconciliation. Assume that the checks written by the company are written correctly.

Item	Add to Bank Statement Balance	Subtract from Bank Statement Balance	Add to Ledger Balance of Cash	Subtract from Ledger Balance of Cash
a. A check-printing charge				
b. An outstanding check				
c. A deposit for $198 listed incorrectly on the bank statement as $189				
d. A collection charge the bank made for a note it collected for its depositor				
e. A check written for $51.74 and recorded incorrectly in the checkbook as $51.47				
f. A deposit in transit				
g. An NSF check received from a customer				
h. A check written for $75.60 and recorded incorrectly in the checkbook as $750.60				

EXERCISE 6-5 Hosung Company's Cash account shows a balance of $801.65 as of August 31 of this year. The balance on the bank statement on that date is $1,383. Checks for $260.50, $425.10, and $331.00 are outstanding. The bank statement shows a check issued by another depositor for $237.25. (In other words, the bank made an error and charged Hosung Company for a check written by another company.) The bank statement also shows an NSF check for $180 received from one of Hosung's customers. Service charges for the month were $18. What is the adjusted ledger balance of cash as of August 31?

EXERCISE 6-6 Record entries in general journal form to record the following:
a. Established a Petty Cash Fund, $100. Issued Ck. No. 587.
b. Reimbursed the Petty Cash Fund for expenditures of $89: Store Supplies, $39; Office Supplies, $20; Miscellaneous Expense, $30. Issued Ck. No. 595.
c. Increased the amount of the fund by an additional $75. Issued Ck. No. 597.
d. Reimbursed the Petty Cash Fund for expenditures of $97.50: Store Supplies, $36.50; Delivery Expense, $41.00; Miscellaneous Expense, $20.00. Issued Ck. No. 599.

EXERCISE 6-7 At the end of the day, the cash register tape lists $881.40 as total income from services. Cash on hand consists of $18.25 in coins, $433.60 in currency, $100.00 in traveler's checks, and $427.00 in customers' checks. The amount of the Change Fund is $100. In general journal form, record the entry to record the day's cash revenue.

CHAPTER ASSIGNMENTS

LO   6, 7 ···

Practice Exercises 6, 7

EXERCISE 6-8

a. Describe the entries that have been posted to the following accounts after the Change Fund was established.

Change Fund			Sales			Cash		
150				Mar. 4 1,472	Mar. 4 1,475		
				16 1,398	16 1,397		
				27 1,545	27 1,541		

Cash Short and Over			
Mar. 16	1	Mar. 4	3
27	4		

b. How will the balance of Cash Short and Over be reported on the income statement?

Problem Set A

LO   3, 4 ···

PROBLEM 6-1A Arthur's Men's Shop deposits all receipts in the bank each evening and makes all payments by check. On November 30, its ledger balance of cash is $2,375.05. The bank statement balance of cash as of November 30 is $2,784.77. Use the following information to reconcile the bank statement:

a. The reconciliation for October, the previous month, showed three checks outstanding on October 31: no. 1417 for $95.00, no. 1420 for $125.87, and no. 1422 for $136.00. Check no. 1417 and no. 1422 were returned with the November bank statement; however, check no. 1420 was not returned.

b. Check no. 1500 for $155.00, no. 1517 for $132.00, no. 1518 for $218.00, and no. 1519 for $128.85 were written during November and have not been returned by the bank.

c. A deposit of $945 was placed in the night depository on November 30 and did not appear on the bank statement.

d. The canceled checks were compared with the entries in the checkbook, and it was observed that check no. 1487, for $89, was written correctly, payable to M. A. Golden, the owner, for personal use, but was recorded in the checkbook as $98.

e. Included in the bank statement was a bank debit memo for service charges, $29.

f. A bank credit memo was also enclosed for the collection of a note signed by C.G. Tolson, $615, including $600 principal and $15 interest.

Check Figure
Adjusted ledger balance of cash, $2,970.05

Required

1. Prepare a bank reconciliation as of November 30, assuming that the debit and credit memos have not been recorded.

2. Record the necessary entries in general journal form.

LO 5

PROBLEM 6-2A On May 1 of this year, Ellsworth and Company established a Petty Cash Fund. The following petty cash transactions took place during the month:

May   1   Cashed check no. 956 for $150 to establish a Petty Cash Fund, and put the $150 in a locked drawer in the office.

3   Bought postage stamps, $8.80, voucher no. 1 (Miscellaneous Expense).

4   Issued voucher no. 2 for taxi fare, $12 (Miscellaneous Expense).

6   Issued voucher no. 3 for delivery charges on outgoing parts, $15.

9   B. Ellsworth, the owner, withdrew $25 for personal use, voucher no. 4.

13   Paid $8.29 for postage, voucher no. 5 (Miscellaneous Expense).

19   Bought pens for office, $6, voucher no. 6.

23   Paid $3.59 for a box of staples, voucher no. 7.

28   Paid $15 for window cleaning service, voucher no. 8 (Miscellaneous Expense).

29   Paid $2 for pencils for office, voucher no. 9.

31   Issued for cash check no. 1098 for $95.68 to reimburse Petty Cash Fund.

Required

1. Journalize the entry establishing the Petty Cash Fund in the general journal.
2. Record the disbursements of petty cash in the petty cash payments record.
3. Journalize the summarizing entry to reimburse the Petty Cash Fund.

Check Figure
Office Supplies, $11.59

LO 7

PROBLEM 6-3A Ellie Harrod, owner of Harrod's Dry Cleaners, makes bank deposits in the night depository at the close of each business day. The following information for the last four days of July is available.

	July			
	28	**29**	**30**	**31**
Cash register tape	$895.20	$ 977.40	$884.50	$1,027.25
Cash count	993.50	1,075.80	986.60	1,124.40

Required

In general journal form, record the cash deposit for each day, assuming that there is a $100 Change Fund.

Check Figure
Cash Short and Over, July 31, $2.85 cash shortage

LO 3, 4

PROBLEM 6-4A On August 31, Baginski and Company receives its bank statement (shown on the next page). The company deposits its receipts in the bank and makes all payments by check. The debit memo for $95 is for an NSF check written by L. Pitts. Check no. 925 for $47, payable to Jardin Company (a creditor), was recorded in the checkbook and journal as $74.

The ledger balance of cash as of August 31, is $1,563. Outstanding checks as of August 31 are no. 928, $150 and no. 929, $292. The accountant notes that the deposit of August 31 for $599 did not appear on the bank statement.

Required

1. Prepare a bank reconciliation as of August 31, assuming that the debit memos have not been recorded.
2. Record the necessary journal entries.
3. Complete the bank form to determine the adjusted balance of cash.

Check Figure
Adjusted ledger balance of cash, $1,480

(Continued)

PEABODY NATIONAL BANK

STATEMENT OF ACCOUNT	Baginski and Company 416 Seneca Avenue Kansas City, Missouri 64102	ACCOUNT NO. 152-655-217 STATEMENT DATE August 1 to 31, 20--

SUMMARY		
	Balance Last Statement	$961.00
	Amount of Checks and Debits	$2,289.00
	Number of Checks	11
	Amount of Deposits and Credits	$2,651.00
	Number of Deposits	7
	Balance This Statement	$1,323.00

CHECKS/ OTHER DEBITS	CHECKS	CHECK NUMBER	DATE POSTED	AMOUNT	CHECK NUMBER	DATE POSTED	AMOUNT
		917	8-04	172.00	923	8-09	621.00
		918	8-04	76.00	924	8-17	37.00
		919	8-05	146.00	925	8-17	47.00
		920	8-07	206.00	926	8-23	441.00
		921	8-07	139.00	927	8-28	94.00
		922	8-07	200.00			

OTHER DEBITS	DESCRIPTION	DATE POSTED	AMOUNT
	DM NSF check	8-31	95.00
	DM Service charge	8-31	15.00

DEPOSITS/ OTHER CREDITS	DEPOSITS	DATE POSTED	AMOUNT	DATE POSTED	AMOUNT
		8-02	326.00	8-18	419.00
		8-05	412.00	8-24	398.00
		8-09	437.00	8-28	291.00
		8-14	368.00		

PLEASE EXAMINE THIS STATEMENT CAREFULLY. REPORT ANY POSSIBLE ERRORS WITHIN 10 DAYS.

CODE SYMBOLS

CM Credit Memo   DM Debit Memo   OD Overdraft   EC Error Correction

*If you are using CLGL, use the year 2020 when recording transactions and preparing reports.

LO 3, 4

PROBLEM 6-5A The Quilt Shop deposits all receipts in the bank each evening and makes all payments by check. On July 31, its ledger balance of cash is $2,830.15. The bank statement balance of cash as of July 31 is $3,215.20. Use the following information to reconcile the bank statement:

a.   The reconciliation for June, the previous month, showed three checks outstanding on June 30: no. 1820 for $85.00, no. 1822 for $115.20, and no. 1823 for $120.00. Check no. 1820 and no. 1822 were returned with the July bank statement; however, check no. 1823 was not returned.

b.   Check no. 2500 for $255.00, no. 2517 for $332.00, no. 2518 for $115.00, and no. 2519 for $28.85 were written during July and have not been returned by the bank.

c.   A deposit of $446.80 was placed in the night depository on July 31 and did not appear on the bank statement.

(*Continued*)

d. The canceled checks were compared with the entries in the checkbook, and it was observed that check no. 2587, for $26, was written correctly, payable to J. L. Lang, the owner, for personal use, but was recorded in the checkbook as $62.

e. Included in the bank statement was a bank debit memo for service charges, $25.

f. Included in the bank statement was an NSF check from Jeremy Jones in the amount of $30.

Required

1. Prepare a bank reconciliation as of July 31, assuming that the debit memo and NSF check have not been recorded.

2. Record the necessary entries in general journal form.

Check Figure
Adjusted ledger balance
of cash $2,811.15

Problem Set B

PROBLEM 6-1B Merkle Company deposits all receipts in the bank each evening and makes all payments by check. On November 30, its ledger balance of cash is $3,219.72. The bank statement balance of cash as of November 30, is $3,490.72. You are given the following information with which to reconcile the bank statement:

a. A deposit of $525.30 was placed in the night depository on November 30 and did not appear on the bank statement.

b. The reconciliation for October, the previous month, showed three checks outstanding on October 31: no. 728 for $80.20, no. 731 for $129.00, and no. 732 for $145.34. Check no. 728 and no. 731 were returned with the November bank statement; however, check no. 732 was not returned.

c. Check no. 743 for $42.00, no. 744 for $16.20, no. 745 for $119.00, and no. 746 for $35.26 were written during November but were not returned by the bank.

d. A $150 personal withdrawal by C. R. Merkle, the owner, using an ATM, was not recorded.

e. Included in the bank statement was a bank debit memo for service charges, $19.

f. A bank credit memo was also enclosed for the collection of a note signed by O. L. Leland, $607.50, including $600.00 principal and $7.50 interest.

Required

1. Prepare a bank reconciliation as of November 30, assuming that the debit and credit memos have not been recorded.

2. Record the necessary entries in general journal form.

Check Figure
Adjusted ledger balance of
cash $3,658.22

LO **5**

PROBLEM 6-2B On March 1 of this year, Stowe Company established a Petty Cash Fund, and the following petty cash transactions took place during the month:

Mar. 1 Cashed check no. 314 for $100 to establish a Petty Cash Fund, and put the $100 in a locked drawer in the office.

4 Issued voucher no. 1 for taxi fare, $7.60 (Miscellaneous Expense).

7 Issued voucher no. 2 for memo pads, $6.50 (Office Supplies).

9 Paid $21.50 for an advertisement in a college basketball program, voucher no. 3.

16 Bought postage stamps, $8.80, voucher no. 4 (Miscellaneous Expense).

20 Paid $10 to have snow removed from office front sidewalk, voucher no. 5 (Miscellaneous Expense).

25 Issued voucher no. 6 for delivery charge, $12.

(Continued)

28   R. C. Stowe, the owner, withdrew $20 for personal use, voucher no. 7.

29   Paid $4.20 for postage, voucher no. 8 (Miscellaneous Expense).

30   Paid $5.90 for delivery charge, voucher no. 9.

31   Issued for cash check no. 372 for $96.50 to reimburse Petty Cash Fund.

Check Figure
Office Supplies, $6.50

Required

1. Journalize the entry establishing the Petty Cash Fund in the general journal.
2. Record the disbursements of petty cash in the petty cash payments record.
3. Journalize the summarizing entry to reimburse the Petty Cash Fund.

LO 7

PROBLEM 6-3B Roberta Felino, owner of Roberta's Beauty Salon, makes bank deposits in the night depository at the close of each business day. The following information for the first four days of April is available.

	April			
	1	2	3	4
Cash register tape	$386.75	$582.65	$586.65	$623.25
Cash count	485.50	685.75	685.75	726.15

Check Figure
Cash Short and Over, April 3, $0.90 cash shortage

Required

In general journal form, record the cash deposit for each day, assuming that there is a $100 Change Fund.

LO 3, 4

PROBLEM 6-4B On August 2, Northern Motel receives its bank statement (shown on the next page). The company deposits its receipts in the bank and makes all payments by check. The debit memo for $37 is for an NSF check written by T. R. Royce. Check no. 1617 for $75.50, payable to Mitchel Company (a creditor), was incorrectly recorded in the checkbook and journal as $57.50.

The ledger balance of Cash as of July 31 is $1,909.30. Outstanding checks as of July 31 are no. 1631, $118.20; no. 1632, $78.20; and no. 1633, $178.36. The accountant notes that the July 31 deposit of $630 did not appear on the bank statement.

(Continued)

STANTON NATIONAL BANK

STATEMENT OF ACCOUNT	Northern Motel 423 E. Long Avenue Rockford, IL 61104	ACCOUNT NO. 750-135-772 STATEMENT DATE July 1 to 31, 20--

SUMMARY		
	Balance Last Statement	$1,153.80
	Amount of Checks and Debits	$2,105.91
	Number of Checks	14
	Amount of Deposits and Credits	$2,528.17
	Number of Deposits	7
	Balance This Statement	$1,576.06

CHECKS/ OTHER DEBITS	CHECKS	CHECK NUMBER	DATE POSTED	AMOUNT	CHECK NUMBER	DATE POSTED	AMOUNT
		1617	7-03	75.50	1624	7-08	120.00
		1618	7-03	164.00	1625	7-09	409.70
		1619	7-03	124.20	1626	7-12	37.40
		1620	7-05	137.20	1627	7-14	38.49
		1621	7-06	236.25	1628	7-22	182.71
		1622	7-06	159.89	1629	7-25	96.87
		1623	7-08	244.50	1630	7-26	19.20

OTHER DEBITS	DESCRIPTION	DATE POSTED	AMOUNT
	DM NSF check	7-22	37.00
	DM Service charge	7-31	23.00

DEPOSITS/ OTHER CREDITS	DEPOSITS	DATE POSTED	AMOUNT	DATE POSTED	AMOUNT
		7-03	491.50	7-15	291.76
		7-06	415.72	7-18	142.90
		7-09	439.16	7-28	368.93
		7-11	378.20		

PLEASE EXAMINE THIS STATEMENT CAREFULLY. REPORT ANY POSSIBLE ERRORS WITHIN 10 DAYS.

CODE SYMBOLS

CM Credit Memo   DM Debit Memo   OD Overdraft   EC Error Correction

Required

1. Prepare a bank reconciliation as of July 31, assuming that the debit memos have not been recorded.
2. Record the necessary journal entries.
3. Complete the bank form to determine the adjusted balance of cash.

*If you are using CLGL, use the year 2020 when recording transactions and preparing reports.

Check Figure
Adjusted ledger balance of cash, $1,831.30

 3, 4

PROBLEM 6-5B Jim's Fitness Center deposits all receipts in the bank each evening and makes all payments by check. On April 30, its ledger balance of cash is $1,515.10. The bank statement balance of cash as of April 30 is $1,920.42. Use the following information to reconcile the bank statement:

a. The reconciliation for March, the previous month, showed three checks outstanding on March 31: no. 555 for $56.00, no. 556 for $428.25, and no. 557 for $20.00. Check no. 555 and no. 557 were returned with the April bank statement; however, check no. 556 was not returned.

(Continued)

b. Check no. 565 for $120.00, no. 567 for $45.00, no. 569 for $15.00, and no. 570 for $18.15 were written during April and have not been returned by the bank.

c. A deposit of $119.08 was placed in the night depository on April 30 and did not appear on the bank statement.

d. The canceled checks were compared with the entries in the checkbook, and it was observed that check no. 561, for $46, was written correctly, payable to J. L. Lang, the owner, for personal use, but was recorded in the checkbook as $64.

e. Included in the bank statement was a bank debit memo for service charges, $25.

f. Included in the bank statement was an NSF check from Millie Smith in the amount of $95.

Check Figure
Adjusted ledger balance of
cash $1,413.10

Required

1. Prepare a bank reconciliation as of April 30, assuming that the debit memo and NSF check have not been recorded.
2. Record the necessary entries in general journal form.

Accounting with QuickBooks® Online

Go to the QuickBooks Online Chapter 6 Appendix located on the Cengage Learning companion site at Cengage.com. Review the *Accounting with QuickBooks Online* (step-by-step guide to using QuickBooks Online). *Accounting with QuickBooks Online*, Chapter 6, will introduce you to reconciling a bank account and creating a bank reconciliation report.

Activities

Why Does It Matter?

BDO USA, LLP and Grant Thornton, LLP

BDO USA, LLP and Grant Thornton, LLP are full-service consulting and forensic accounting firms. These firms offer services ranging from determining contract damages to overseeing fraud examination. Their forensic accountants are experts at finding even the cleverest trails of fraudulent financial data and then providing the hard numbers needed to prove a case of fraud. The forensic accountants look beyond the numbers to analyze and reveal all relevant aspects of the situation.

BDO USA, LLP and Grant Thornton, LLP have extensive experience in information technology for consulting audits and assessments. They also deliver complete data analysis of electronic business records and files, including e-mails, financial spreadsheets, hard drives, and tape backups.

Assume that you are a business owner concerned about preventing fraud. Explain how hiring a firm specializing in forensic accounting such as BDO USA, LLP or Grant Thornton, LLP can help you stop fraud from occurring.

What Would You Say?

As the new bookkeeper for a small business, you find that several people access the Petty Cash Fund, usually without anyone leaving a written explanation of what the money was used for. The amount of cash does not match the recorded amount of the fund. Explain how operation of the Petty Cash Fund can be made more efficient to maintain an accurate accounting of how the money is used.

What Do You Think?

You work as a cashier for a service business. Some days you are short of cash at the end of the day, and some days you have more cash than the cash register tape says was earned. You are embarrassed when your cash is short and don't want the owner to know, so you use your own money to make up the difference. On days when you are over, you keep the difference to help pay back what you paid to cover your shortages. What do you think of this practice? Explain.

Employee Earnings and Deductions

Learning Objectives

After you have completed this chapter, you will be able to do the following:

1. Recognize the role of income tax laws that affect payroll deductions and contributions.

2. Calculate total earnings based on an hourly, salary, piece-rate, or commission basis.

3. Determine deductions from gross pay, such as federal income tax withheld, Social Security tax, and Medicare tax, to calculate net pay.

4. Complete a payroll register.

5. Journalize the payroll entry from a payroll register.

6. Maintain employees' individual earnings records.

To: **Amy Roberts, CPA**
Subject: **Employee Earnings and Deductions**

Hi Amy,

Thanks for all of your help with setting up my accounting system. Now I need some guidance on how to calculate and account for earnings, payroll taxes, and any other important deductions. I've been told that handling payroll in a timely and accurate manner is extremely important. Therefore, I want to make sure I know what to do. What do I need to know to calculate employee earnings and deductions?

Thanks,

Janie

To: **Janie Conner**
Subject: **RE: Employee Earnings and Deductions**

Hi Janie,

You are right. Handling payroll in a timely and accurate manner is extremely important to your employees and your company. To gain an accurate understanding of payroll, you'll need to know the following:

_____ 1. What tax laws affect payroll deductions and contributions

_____ 2. How to calculate total earnings based on hourly, salary, piece-rate, or commission basis

_____ 3. How to determine deductions and net pay

_____ 4. How to set up and use a payroll register

_____ 5. How to journalize payroll entries

_____ 6. How to maintain individual employee earnings records

Give me a call tomorrow and we can set up a meeting to discuss these items further.

Amy

Until now, we have been recording employees' earnings as a debit to Salary or Wages Expense and a credit to Cash, but we have been talking only about **gross pay**—the total amount of an employee's pay before deductions. We have not mentioned the various deductions that are taken out of gross pay to arrive at take-home pay, or **net pay**. In this chapter, we will talk about types of deductions and explain how to enter them in the payroll records. We also will cover the journal entries to record payroll and pay the employees.

7-1 LAWS AFFECTING EMPLOYEES' PAY DEDUCTIONS AND EMPLOYER'S PAYROLL TAXES

There are two primary reasons we need to maintain accurate payroll records: First, we must collect the data necessary to compute the compensation for each employee by payroll period. Second, we must provide the information needed to complete the various government reports—federal and state—required of all employers.

All business enterprises, both large and small, are required by law to (1) withhold certain amounts from employees' pay for taxes, (2) make payments to government agencies by specific deadlines, and (3) submit reports on official forms. Because governments impose penalties if the requirements are not met, employers are vitally concerned with payroll accounting.

The employer is required to keep records of the following information:

1. **Personal data on employee:** Name, address, Social Security number, date of birth
2. **Data on wage payments:** Dates, amounts of payments, and payroll periods
3. **Amount of taxable wages paid:** Dates and amount earned (year-to-date) for the calendar year involved
4. **Amount of tax withheld from each employee's earnings by pay period**

Many companies use software, such as Excel®; QuickBooks®; QuickBooks Online, a cloud-based accounting application; or an outside payroll services, such as ADP® or Paychex®, to assist with their payroll accounting.

Payroll accounting involves employee compensation, withholdings, records, reports, and taxes. Therefore, it is important to determine who is an employee and who is an independent contractor. An **employee** is one who is under the direction and control of the employer, such as a salesperson, an administrative assistant, a vice president, and a controller. An **independent contractor** is engaged for a definite job or service and may choose his or her own means of doing the work. Payments made to independent contractors are in the form of fees or charges. Independent contractors submit bills or invoices for the work they do. The payment is not subject to withholding or payroll taxes by the person or firm paying the invoice. Such taxes are the responsibility of the independent contractor. **Businesses are required to give an independent contractor an IRS Form 1099-MISC for the year if the fees paid are $600 or more.** The IRS has published guidelines for employers to use in determining worker classification. If a worker is classified as an independent contractor and should be an employee, the IRS will impose substantial penalties on the employer. For more information about employee versus independent contractor status, go to www.irs.gov.

Both federal and state laws require the employer to act as a collecting agent and deduct specified amounts from employees' gross earnings. The employer sends the withholdings to the appropriate government agencies, along with reports substantiating the figures. Certain payroll taxes are also levied on the employer. These taxes are based on the total wages paid to employees. Let's look at some of the more important laws that pertain to payroll.

7-1a Fair Labor Standards Act

The **Fair Labor Standards Act** of 1938 is referred to as "the Act" or "FLSA." The Act provides minimum standards for both wages and overtime. Also included in the Act are provisions related to child labor and equal pay for equal work. In addition, the Act exempts specified employees or groups of employees from some of its provisions. Details of the Act may be found at www.opm.gov.

In the Real World

In the real world, many companies (especially small businesses, such as this street cafe) outsource their payroll processing activities. According to Paychex®, Inc., a payroll and human resource company, businesses outsource their payroll to improve accuracy, to increase security, and to maintain compliance with tax laws and regulations. B. Thomas Golisano started Paychex in 1971 with just one employee and a $3,000 investment. In 1983, the company went public and is currently traded on the NASDAQ stock exchange.

7-1b Federal Income Tax Withholding

The **Current Tax Payment Act**, passed in 1943, requires employers not only to withhold the tax and pay it to the U.S. Treasury but also to keep records of the names and addresses of persons employed, their earnings, withholdings, and the amounts and dates of payment. The employer must submit reports to the Internal Revenue Service on a quarterly basis (Form 941) and to the employee on an annual basis (W-2 form). We will discuss these reports and the related deposits in Chapter 8.

7-1c FICA Taxes (Employees' Share)

The **Social Security Act of 1935** began as an attempt to provide retired workers with benefits based on their work history. Several amendments have been added (for example, benefits for spouses and minor children of retired workers, disability insurance, an increase in the age as to when benefits may be collected, Medicare, and supplemental security income).

Currently, **FICA taxes** consists of **Social Security taxes** and **Medicare taxes**. At the writing of this text, employees contribute 6.2 percent (0.062) on the first $118,500 earned in a calendar year for Social Security. Employees contribute 1.45 percent (0.0145) on all earnings in a calendar year for Medicare, with no earnings limit. Throughout this chapter, we will use these percentages and earnings limitations for our calculations.

7-1d FICA Taxes (Employer's Share)

As of the writing of this text, the employer is required to match the amount of FICA taxes withheld from the employee's wages. The employer pays 6.2% (0.062) on the first $118,500 earned by the employee for Social Security taxes and also matches the amount of Medicare taxes (1.45%, or 0.0145) withheld from the employees' wages. The employer's share of these taxes is recorded under Payroll Tax Expense. Every three months the employer must submit reports to the U.S. Treasury, using Form 941, which is the same form used to report income tax withheld. The employer's payment to the Internal Revenue Service consists of (1) the employee's share of the FICA taxes, (2) the employer's matching portion of the FICA taxes, and (3) the employee's income tax withheld. We will talk about this in detail in Chapter 8.

7-1e State Unemployment Taxes (SUTA)

Each state is responsible for paying its own unemployment compensation benefits. The revenue provided by state unemployment taxes is used exclusively for this purpose. However, there is considerable variation among the states concerning the tax rates and the amount of taxable income. **This tax is paid by employers only.** A few states, under their State Unemployment Tax Act, charge their employers a percentage on the first $7,000 an employee earns. This is similar to the taxable income stipulated in the Federal Unemployment Tax Act. However, most states have a much higher taxable wage base. As of the writing of this text, Washington State, with a taxable wage base of $44,000, is the highest. In this text, we will use 5.4 percent (0.054) of the first $7,000. Most states require employers to file reports and payments on a quarterly, or three-month, basis. Included in these reports are a listing of employees' names, Social Security numbers, amounts of wages paid to each employee, and computations of unemployment taxes.

FYI

For employees who are paid wages in excess of $200,000, an additional 0.9 percent must be withheld. Employers do not have to match the additional Medicare withholding.

FYI

Certain employees, such as railroad workers and some teachers, may be exempt from FICA Social Security tax.

7-1f Federal Unemployment Tax Act (FUTA)

The purpose of the Federal Unemployment Tax Act is to financially support government-run employment offices, pay half of extended unemployment benefits when unemployment is high, and provide a fund that states can borrow from to pay benefits if needed. **FUTA taxes are paid by employers only**. Generally, this includes all employers except nonprofit schools and charities.

The federal unemployment tax is based on the total earnings of each employee during the **calendar year** (January 1–December 31). For the examples and problems in this text, we will use the current federal unemployment tax rate of 0.6 percent (0.006) on the first $7,000 of each employee's earnings during the calendar year. Reports to the federal government must be submitted annually on Form 940. We will discuss the SUTA and FUTA reports in Chapter 8.

7-1g Workers' Compensation Laws

Workers' compensation laws protect employees and their dependents against losses due to death or injury incurred on the job. Most states require employers to contribute to a state compensation insurance fund or to buy similar insurance from a private insurance company. The employer ordinarily pays the cost of the insurance premiums. The premium rates vary according to the degree of danger inherent in each job category and the employer's number of accidents. The employer must keep records of job descriptions and classification, as well as claims of insured persons.

The following table presents a summary of the various payroll taxes and identifies who is responsible for each.

Employee Pays	Employer Pays
Federal income tax withholding (based on income tax rates) FICA taxes – Social Security (6.2% of earnings up to $118,500) – Medicare (1.45% of all earnings)	FICA taxes – Social Security (6.2% of earnings up to $118,500) – Medicare (1.45% of all earnings) Federal and state unemployment taxes Workers' compensation

Employees may be paid salaries or wages, depending on the type of work and the period of time covered. Money paid to a person for managerial or administrative services is usually called a salary, and the time period covered is generally a month or a year. Money paid for skilled or unskilled labor is usually called wages, and the time period covered is hours or weeks. Wages may also be paid on a piecework basis (or per-unit basis, such as number of boxes of strawberries picked). A company may also supplement an employee's salary or wage with other benefits (for example, commissions, bonuses, cost-of-living adjustments, and profit-sharing plans). As a rule, employees are paid by check or by direct deposit to their bank account. However, their compensation may also include amounts for items such as personal use of company automobiles, athletic club dues, or holiday gift cards. When the compensation is in these forms, the employer must determine the fair value of the property or service given in payment for an employee's labor. For more information on what fringe benefits are taxable and how to value them, see Publication 15-B, Employer's Tax Guide to Fringe Benefits, located on the IRS website at www.irs.gov.

7-2 CALCULATING TOTAL EARNINGS

When compensation is based on the amount of time worked, the accountant must have a record of the number of hours that each employee worked. When there are only a few employees, this can be accomplished by means of a time book. When there are many employees, time clocks or other electronic time-keeping systems are used.

Employees may be paid weekly, biweekly, semimonthly, or monthly. Biweekly is every two weeks. Semimonthly is twice a month.

② Calculate total earnings based on an hourly, salary, piece-rate, or commission basis.

Learning Objective

7-2a Wages

Consider Mark Anderson, who works for Green Sales Company. His regular rate of pay is $22.95 per hour. The company pays time-and-a-half for hours worked in excess of 40 per week. In addition, the company pays him double time for any work he does on Sundays and holidays. Anderson has a ½-hour lunch break during an 8½-hour day. He is not paid for the lunch break, nor is he paid for minutes before 8:00 A.M. or after 4:30 P.M., unless hours of overtime are authorized in advance. His time card for the week is shown in Figure 1.

TIME CARD

Name	Anderson, Mark					
Week ended	Oct. 11, 20--					

Day	In	Out	In	Out	Hours Worked Regular	Hours Worked Overtime
Mon	7 57	12 00	12 20	4 32	8	
Tue	7 56	12 06	12 36	4 37	8	
Wed	7 57	12 02	12 31	4 31	8	
Thu	8 00	12 11	12 40	6 32	8	2
Fri	8 00	12 03	12 33	5 33	8	1
Sat	7 59	11 02				3
Sun						

Figure 1
Time card for Mark Anderson

Anderson's gross wages can be computed by one of two methods. The first method works like this:

40 hours at straight time	40 × $22.95 per hour =	$ 918.00
2 hours overtime on Thursday	2 × $34.43 per hour =	68.86
($22.95 × 1.5 = $34.43)		
1 hour overtime on Friday	1 × $34.43 per hour =	34.43
3 hours overtime on Saturday	3 × $34.43 per hour =	103.29
Total hours and gross wages	46	$1,124.58

The second method of calculating gross wages is often used when it is necessary to identify or track overtime premium.

46 hours at straight time	46 × $22.95 per hour =	$1,055.70
Overtime premium:		
6 hours overtime ($22.95 × 0.5 = $11.48)	6 × $11.48 per hour =	68.88
Total gross wages		$1,124.58

FYI

Minimum wages are set by Congress or the state legislature—whichever is higher. Originally, in 1938, the minimum wage was $0.25 per hour.

7-2b Salaries

Employees who are paid a regular salary may also be entitled to extra pay for overtime. It is necessary to figure out their regular hourly rate of pay before you can determine their overtime rate. Consider Madeline Huan, who receives a salary of $4,350 per month. She is entitled to overtime pay for all hours worked in excess of 40 during a week at time-and-a-half her regular hourly rate. This past week she worked 44 hours, so we calculate her gross pay as follows:

$4,350 per month × 12 months = $52,200 per year
$52,200 per year ÷ 52 weeks   = $1,003.85 per week
$1,003.85 per week ÷ 40 hours = $25.10 per regular hour
$25.10 per regular hour × 1.5 = $37.65 per overtime hour

Earnings for 44 hours:
   40 hours at straight time (as calculated above)   = $1,003.85
   4 hours overtime   (4 × $37.65) =   150.60
Total gross earnings $1,154.45

A shortcut to determine the hourly rate is to divide the annual salary by 2,080 (the standard work hours in a year). In this case, the calculation would be ($4,350 × 12) ÷ 2,080 = $25.10.

7-2c Piece-Rate

Workers under the piece-rate system are paid at the rate of so much per unit of production. For example, John Joseph, a strawberry picker, is paid $3 for each box of strawberries picked. If he picks 24 boxes during the day, his total earnings are 24 × $3 = $72.

7-2d Commissions

Some salespeople are paid on a purely commission basis. However, a more common arrangement is a salary plus a commission or bonus. Assume that Lora Brown receives an annual salary of $44,000. Her employer agrees to pay her a 5 percent commission on all sales during the year in excess of $200,000. Her sales for the year total $445,000. Her commission is $12,250 [($445,000 − $200,000) × 0.05]. Therefore, her total earnings are $56,250 ($44,000 + $12,250).

7-3 DEETUCTIONS FROM TOTAL EARNINGS

Anyone who has ever earned a paycheck has encountered some type of deductions. As discussed previously in this chapter, gross pay minus deductions equals net pay. Following are the most common deductions:

- Federal income tax withholding
- State income tax withholding
- FICA taxes (Social Security and Medicare), employee's share
- Union dues
- Medical insurance premiums and medical expenses under a flexible spending plan
- Contributions to a charitable organization such as United Way
- Repayment of personal loans from the company

- Savings through the company 401(k) plan
- Dependent care expenses under a flexible spending plan (subject to a $5,000 limit)

Medical insurance premiums, medical expenses, and dependent care expenses under a flexible spending plan and 401(k) deductions are usually **pre-tax deductions**. If a deduction is pre-tax, the employee does not have to pay income tax on the amount of federal income tax withheld. In certain circumstances, FICA tax also may be exempt when calculating federal income tax withholding. For example, if Lynn Langseth has a weekly salary of $4,000 and the company deducts $200 for medical premiums paid for Lynn's dependents, her payroll subject to income tax is $3,800, not $4,000. If Lynn also contributes $100 to charity, her payroll subject to income tax is still $3,800. The charitable deduction is not a pre-tax deduction.

7-3a Employees' Federal Income Tax Withholding

Employers are required not only to withhold employees' taxes and then pay them to the U.S. Treasury but also to keep records of the names and addresses of persons employed, their **taxable earnings** (the earnings subject to tax) and withholdings, and the amounts and dates of payment.

The amount of federal income tax withheld from an employee's earnings depends on the amount of his or her total earnings, marital status, and number of withholding allowances claimed. A **withholding allowance** is used by employers to calculate the amount of income tax withheld from an employee's paycheck. The more withholding allowances an employee claims, the less income tax an employer withholds from the employee's paycheck. An employee is entitled to one personal allowance for the taxpayer, one for his or her spouse, and one for each dependent. An **exemption** is an amount of an employee's annual earnings not subject to income tax. Each employee has to fill out an **Employee's Withholding Allowance Certificate (Form W-4)**, shown in Figure 2. The employer retains this form as authorization to withhold money for the employee's federal income tax.

Figure 2

Employee's Withholding Allowance Certificate (Form W-4) for Mark Anderson

Form W-4 — Employee's Withholding Allowance Certificate   OMB No. 1545-0074   20--

Department of the Treasury Internal Revenue Service

▶ Whether you are entitled to claim a certain number of allowances or exemption from withholding is subject to review by the IRS. Your employer may be required to send a copy of this form to the IRS.

1 Type or print your first name and middle initial. **Mark E.**   Last name **Anderson**   2 Your social security number **543 24 1680**

Home address (number and street or rural route) **1104 Rosewood Street**

3 ☐ Single ☒ Married ☐ Married, but withhold at higher Single rate.
Note. If married, but legally separated, or spouse is a nonresident alien, check the "Single" box.

City or town, state, and ZIP code **Bangor, Maine 04401**

4 If your last name differs from that shown on your social security card, check here. You must call 1-800-772-1213 for a new card. ▶ ☐

5 Total number of allowances you are claiming (from line **H** above **or** from the applicable worksheet on page 2)   **5 1**

6 Additional amount, if any, you want withheld from each paycheck   **6 $**

7 I claim exemption from withholding for 20--, and I certify that I meet **both** of the following conditions for exemption.
   - Last year I had a right to a refund of **all** federal income tax withheld because I had **no** tax liability **and**
   - This year I expect a refund of **all** federal income tax withheld because I expect to have **no** tax liability.
   If you meet both conditions, write "Exempt" here   ▶ **7**

Under penalties of perjury, I declare that I have examined this certificate and to the best of my knowledge and belief, it is true, correct, and complete.

Employee's signature
(Form is not valid unless you sign it.) ▶ *Mark E. Anderson*   Date ▶ *January 2, 20--*

8 Employer's name and address (Employer: Complete lines 8 and 10 only if sending to the IRS.)   9 Office code (optional)   10 Employer identification number (EIN)

For Privacy Act and Paperwork Reduction Act Notice, see page 2.   Cat. No. 10220Q   Form **W-4** (20--)

7-3b Publication 15 (Circular E), Employer's Tax Guide

Publication 15 (Circular E) contains the rules for depositing federal income, Social Security, and Medicare taxes, and contains the withholding tables for these taxes. This publication is regularly updated to reflect changes in tax laws and withholding rates. Publication 15 (Circular E) also describes filing requirements for official employer reports and is provided free of charge by the Internal Revenue Service (available on the Internet at www.irs.gov). Accountants responsible for preparation of payroll registers and forms should be familiar with the content in this publication.

The **wage-bracket tax tables** (found in Publication 15) cover monthly, semimonthly, biweekly, weekly, and daily payroll periods. The tables are also subdivided on the basis of marital status. To determine the federal income tax withheld, perform the following steps:

STEP 1. Locate the wage bracket in the first two columns of the table.

STEP 2. Find the column for the number of allowances claimed and read down this column until you get to the appropriate wage-bracket line.

A portion of the weekly federal income tax withholding table for married persons is reproduced in Figure 3 on pages 293–294.

Assume that Mark Anderson, who claims one allowance as of the October 11 payroll, has gross wages of $1,124.58 for the week. As $1,124.58 falls in the $1,120–$1,130 bracket, you can see from the table that $115 should be withheld.

Note the headings of the bracket columns: "At least" and "But less than." A strict interpretation of the $1,120–$1,130 bracket really means $1,120–$1,129.99. Therefore, if Anderson's salary were $1,130, it would fall into the $1,130–$1,140 bracket.

7-3c Employees' State Income Tax Withholding

Many states that levy state income taxes also furnish employers with withholding tables. Other states use a fixed percentage of the federal income tax withholding as the amount to be withheld for state taxes. In our illustration, we assume that the amount of each employee's state income tax deduction is 20 percent (0.20) of that employee's federal income tax deduction.

7-3d Employees' FICA Taxes Withholding (Social Security and Medicare)

The Federal Insurance Contributions Act provides for early retirement benefits after a worker reaches age 62. Currently, full retirement benefits are available at age 66, and the age will eventually increase to 68. FICA also provides disability benefits for any worker who becomes disabled (including dependents), and a health insurance program after age 65 (Medicare). Both the employee and the employer must pay FICA taxes, which are commonly referred to as Social Security taxes and Medicare taxes. The employer withholds FICA taxes from employees' wages and pays them to the U.S. Treasury.

FICA tax rates apply to the gross earnings of an employee during the calendar year. After an employee has paid Social Security tax on the maximum taxable earnings, the employer stops deducting Social Security tax until the next calendar year begins. Congress has frequently changed the schedule of rates and taxable incomes. **As explained earlier, in this text, we assume a Social Security rate of 6.2 percent (0.062) of the first $118,500 for each employee and a Medicare rate of 1.45 percent (0.0145) of all earnings for each employee. Both tax rates apply to earnings during the calendar year.** (Tables for Social Security and Medicare tax withholdings are available in the Internal Revenue Service Publication 15.)

FYI

Federal tax rates change frequently, but the procedure generally stays the same. We will use the tax table given in this chapter for all computations.

FYI

At one time, Social Security and Medicare were not separated for tax computation and there was a limit on Medicare taxable earnings. Now all earnings are taxable for Medicare.

Figure 3
2016 federal income tax withholding table for married persons (weekly payroll period)

Wage Bracket Method Tables for Income Tax Withholding
MARRIED Persons—WEEKLY Payroll Period
(For Wages Paid through December 31, 20--)

And the wages are—		And the number of withholding allowances claimed is—										
At least	But less than	0	1	2	3	4	5	6	7	8	9	10
		The amount of income tax to be withheld is—										
$0	$170	$0	$0	$0	$0	$0	$0	$0	$0	$0	$0	$0
170	175	1	0	0	0	0	0	0	0	0	0	0
175	180	1	0	0	0	0	0	0	0	0	0	0
180	185	2	0	0	0	0	0	0	0	0	0	0
185	190	2	0	0	0	0	0	0	0	0	0	0
190	195	3	0	0	0	0	0	0	0	0	0	0
195	200	3	0	0	0	0	0	0	0	0	0	0
200	210	4	0	0	0	0	0	0	0	0	0	0
210	220	5	0	0	0	0	0	0	0	0	0	0
220	230	6	0	0	0	0	0	0	0	0	0	0
230	240	7	0	0	0	0	0	0	0	0	0	0
240	250	8	0	0	0	0	0	0	0	0	0	0
250	260	9	1	0	0	0	0	0	0	0	0	0
260	270	10	2	0	0	0	0	0	0	0	0	0
270	280	11	3	0	0	0	0	0	0	0	0	0
280	290	12	4	0	0	0	0	0	0	0	0	0
290	300	13	5	0	0	0	0	0	0	0	0	0
300	310	14	6	0	0	0	0	0	0	0	0	0
310	320	15	7	0	0	0	0	0	0	0	0	0
320	330	16	8	0	0	0	0	0	0	0	0	0
330	340	17	9	1	0	0	0	0	0	0	0	0
340	350	18	10	2	0	0	0	0	0	0	0	0
350	360	19	11	3	0	0	0	0	0	0	0	0
360	370	20	12	4	0	0	0	0	0	0	0	0
370	380	21	13	5	0	0	0	0	0	0	0	0
380	390	22	14	6	0	0	0	0	0	0	0	0
390	400	23	15	7	0	0	0	0	0	0	0	0
400	410	24	16	8	1	0	0	0	0	0	0	0
410	420	25	17	9	2	0	0	0	0	0	0	0
420	430	26	18	10	3	0	0	0	0	0	0	0
430	440	27	19	11	4	0	0	0	0	0	0	0
440	450	28	20	12	5	0	0	0	0	0	0	0
450	460	29	21	13	6	0	0	0	0	0	0	0
460	470	30	22	14	7	0	0	0	0	0	0	0
470	480	31	23	15	8	0	0	0	0	0	0	0
480	490	32	24	16	9	1	0	0	0	0	0	0
490	500	33	25	17	10	2	0	0	0	0	0	0
500	510	34	26	18	11	3	0	0	0	0	0	0
510	520	35	27	19	12	4	0	0	0	0	0	0
520	530	36	28	20	13	5	0	0	0	0	0	0
530	540	38	29	21	14	6	0	0	0	0	0	0
540	550	39	30	22	15	7	0	0	0	0	0	0
550	560	41	31	23	16	8	0	0	0	0	0	0
560	570	42	32	24	17	9	1	0	0	0	0	0
570	580	44	33	25	18	10	2	0	0	0	0	0
580	590	45	34	26	19	11	3	0	0	0	0	0
590	600	47	35	27	20	12	4	0	0	0	0	0
600	610	48	37	28	21	13	5	0	0	0	0	0
610	620	50	38	29	22	14	6	0	0	0	0	0
620	630	51	40	30	23	15	7	0	0	0	0	0
630	640	53	41	31	24	16	8	0	0	0	0	0
640	650	54	43	32	25	17	9	1	0	0	0	0
650	660	56	44	33	26	18	10	2	0	0	0	0
660	670	57	46	34	27	19	11	3	0	0	0	0
670	680	59	47	35	28	20	12	4	0	0	0	0
680	690	60	49	37	29	21	13	5	0	0	0	0
690	700	62	50	38	30	22	14	6	0	0	0	0
700	710	63	52	40	31	23	15	7	0	0	0	0
710	720	65	53	41	32	24	16	8	1	0	0	0
720	730	66	55	43	33	25	17	9	2	0	0	0
730	740	68	56	44	34	26	18	10	3	0	0	0
740	750	69	58	46	35	27	19	11	4	0	0	0
750	760	71	59	47	36	28	20	12	5	0	0	0
760	770	72	61	49	37	29	21	13	6	0	0	0
770	780	74	62	50	39	30	22	14	7	0	0	0
780	790	75	64	52	40	31	23	15	8	0	0	0
790	800	77	65	53	42	32	24	16	9	1	0	0

Figure 3
(Concluded)

Wage Bracket Method Tables for Income Tax Withholding
MARRIED Persons—WEEKLY Payroll Period
(For Wages Paid through December 31, 20--)

And the wages are—		And the number of withholding allowances claimed is—										
At least	But less than	0	1	2	3	4	5	6	7	8	9	10
		The amount of income tax to be withheld is—										
$800	$810	$78	$67	$55	$43	$33	$25	$17	$10	$2	$0	$0
810	820	80	68	56	45	34	26	18	11	3	0	0
820	830	81	70	58	46	35	27	19	12	4	0	0
830	840	83	71	59	48	36	28	20	13	5	0	0
840	850	84	73	61	49	38	29	21	14	6	0	0
850	860	86	74	62	51	39	30	22	15	7	0	0
860	870	87	76	64	52	41	31	23	16	8	0	0
870	880	89	77	65	54	42	32	24	17	9	1	0
880	890	90	79	67	55	44	33	25	18	10	2	0
890	900	92	80	68	57	45	34	26	19	11	3	0
900	910	93	82	70	58	47	35	27	20	12	4	0
910	920	95	83	71	60	48	36	28	21	13	5	0
920	930	96	85	73	61	50	38	29	22	14	6	0
930	940	98	86	74	63	51	39	30	23	15	7	0
940	950	99	88	76	64	53	41	31	24	16	8	0
950	960	101	89	77	66	54	42	32	25	17	9	1
960	970	102	91	79	67	56	44	33	26	18	10	2
970	980	104	92	80	69	57	45	34	27	19	11	3
980	990	105	94	82	70	59	47	35	28	20	12	4
990	1,000	107	95	83	72	60	48	37	29	21	13	5
1,000	1,010	108	97	85	73	62	50	38	30	22	14	6
1,010	1,020	110	98	86	75	63	51	40	31	23	15	7
1,020	1,030	111	100	88	76	65	53	41	32	24	16	8
1,030	1,040	113	101	89	78	66	54	43	33	25	17	9
1,040	1,050	114	103	91	79	68	56	44	34	26	18	10
1,050	1,060	116	104	92	81	69	57	46	35	27	19	11
1,060	1,070	117	106	94	82	71	59	47	36	28	20	12
1,070	1,080	119	107	95	84	72	60	49	37	29	21	13
1,080	1,090	120	109	97	85	74	62	50	38	30	22	14
1,090	1,100	122	110	98	87	75	63	52	40	31	23	15
1,100	1,110	123	112	100	88	77	65	53	41	32	24	16
1,110	1,120	125	113	101	90	78	66	55	43	33	25	17
1,120	1,130	126	115	103	91	80	68	56	44	34	26	18
1,130	1,140	128	116	104	93	81	69	58	46	35	27	19
1,140	1,150	129	118	106	94	83	71	59	47	36	28	20
1,150	1,160	131	119	107	96	84	72	61	49	37	29	21
1,160	1,170	132	121	109	97	86	74	62	50	39	30	22
1,170	1,180	134	122	110	99	87	75	64	52	40	31	23
1,180	1,190	135	124	112	100	89	77	65	53	42	32	24
1,190	1,200	137	125	113	102	90	78	67	55	43	33	25
1,200	1,210	138	127	115	103	92	80	68	56	45	34	26
1,210	1,220	140	128	116	105	93	81	70	58	46	35	27
1,220	1,230	141	130	118	106	95	83	71	59	48	36	28
1,230	1,240	143	131	119	108	96	84	73	61	49	38	29
1,240	1,250	144	133	121	109	98	86	74	62	51	39	30
1,250	1,260	146	134	122	111	99	87	76	64	52	41	31
1,260	1,270	147	136	124	112	101	89	77	65	54	42	32
1,270	1,280	149	137	125	114	102	90	79	67	55	44	33
1,280	1,290	150	139	127	115	104	92	80	68	57	45	34
1,290	1,300	152	140	128	117	105	93	82	70	58	47	35
1,300	1,310	153	142	130	118	107	95	83	71	60	48	36
1,310	1,320	155	143	131	120	108	96	85	73	61	50	38
1,320	1,330	156	145	133	121	110	98	86	74	63	51	39
1,330	1,340	158	146	134	123	111	99	88	76	64	53	41
1,340	1,350	159	148	136	124	113	101	89	77	66	54	42
1,350	1,360	161	149	137	126	114	102	91	79	67	56	44
1,360	1,370	162	151	139	127	116	104	92	80	69	57	45
1,370	1,380	164	152	140	129	117	105	94	82	70	59	47
1,380	1,390	165	154	142	130	119	107	95	83	72	60	48
1,390	1,400	167	155	143	132	120	108	97	85	73	62	50
1,400	1,410	168	157	145	133	122	110	98	86	75	63	51
1,410	1,420	170	158	146	135	123	111	100	88	76	65	53
1,420	1,430	171	160	148	136	125	113	101	89	78	66	54
1,430	1,440	173	161	149	138	126	114	103	91	79	68	56
1,440	1,450	174	163	151	139	128	116	104	92	81	69	57
1,450	1,460	176	164	152	141	129	117	106	94	82	71	59
1,460	1,470	177	166	154	142	131	119	107	95	84	72	60
1,470	1,480	179	167	155	144	132	120	109	97	85	74	62
1,480	1,490	180	169	157	145	134	122	110	98	87	75	63

| $1,490 and over | Use Table 1(b) for a **MARRIED person** on page 44. Also see the instructions on page 42. |

ACCOUNTING IN YOUR FUTURE

PAYROLL DEPARTMENT

The payroll department is an important part of the accounting and finance functions at companies. Payroll personnel are responsible for ensuring that all company employees receive compensation and benefits critical to maintaining a productive and motivated workforce. Some payroll departments work closely with Information Technology, Human Resources, and other departments to ensure that the company's payroll is accurate, is up-to-date, and is serving the company's current business objectives. For these reasons, it is important to understand how payroll is determined, whether you are directly responsible for processing payroll or you are employed in another business department.

Let's return to the example of Mark Anderson, who had gross wages of $1,124.58 for the week ending October 11. Suppose his total accumulated gross wages earned this year prior to this payroll period are $44,960. Anderson's total gross wages including this payroll period were $46,084.58 ($44,960 + $1,124.58). Because the Social Security tax applies to the first $118,500 and the Medicare tax applies to all earnings, Anderson's earnings are subject to both taxes. For Anderson's Social Security tax, multiply $1,124.58 by 6.2 percent ($1,124.58 × 0.062 = $69.72). For Anderson's Medicare tax, multiply $1,124.58 by 1.45 percent ($1,124.58 × 0.0145 = $16.31).

Here's another example. At the beginning of the pay period, Grace Wallace had cumulative earnings of $115,600, which is $2,900 less than $118,500. During this pay period, she earned $3,010.35, which is greater than $2,900. Thus, she must pay Social Security tax of $179.80 ($2,900 × 0.062) on $2,900. However, because the Medicare tax applies to all earnings, she is not exempt from any Medicare tax. Her Medicare tax is $43.65 ($3,010.35 × 0.0145). Because Grace's cumulative earnings after this pay period are over $118,500, any remaining pay will not be subject to Social Security tax.

To: **Amy Roberts, CPA**
Subject: **Employee Earnings and Deductions**

Hi Amy,
Thanks for your help with understanding how to calculate payroll. I never knew there was so much involved. I am now ready to record my payroll entries. Can you tell me what I need to do?
Thanks,
Janie

To: **Janie Conner**
Subject: **RE: Employee Earnings and Deductions**

Hi Janie,
I'm glad you have a basic understanding of how to calculate payroll. The next steps involve the recordkeeping aspects of the payroll process. Below is a checklist of what you need to know. We can discuss this information further tomorrow. Can you give me a call in the morning? Let's say 10 A.M.?

_____ 1. How to set up and use a payroll register
_____ 2. How to journalize payroll entries
_____ 3. How to maintain individual employee earnings records

Amy

7-4 PAYROLL REGISTER

Learning Objective

4 Complete a payroll register.

The **payroll register** is a manual or computerized schedule prepared for each payroll period. It lists the earnings, deductions, and net pay for each employee. In Figure 4, we see a payroll register using Excel®. It shows the data for each employee on a separate line. This would be suitable for a firm such as Green Sales Company, which has a small number of employees.

First, we'll show the entire payroll register. Then we'll break down the payroll register and explain it column by column. The number at the foot of each column refers to the related text description.

Figure 4
Payroll register for Green Sales Company

	A	B	C	D	E	F	G	H	I	J
1					EARNINGS					(7) TAXABLE EARNINGS
2-4	NAME	TOTAL HOURS	BEGINNING CUMULATIVE EARNINGS	REGULAR	OVERTIME	TOTAL	ENDING CUMULATIVE EARNINGS	UNEMPLOYMENT	SOCIAL SECURITY	MEDICARE
5	Anderson, Mark	46	44,960.00	918.00	206.58	1,124.58	46,084.58	0.00	1,124.58	1,124.58
6	Bodell, Anna	45	5,987.00	626.20	118.00	744.20	6,731.20	744.20	744.20	744.20
7	Dorn, David	49	6,786.00	686.00	230.00	916.00	7,702.00	214.00	916.00	916.00
8	Fields, Sarah	40	38,462.00	1,084.50	0.00	1,084.50	39,546.50	0.00	1,084.50	1,084.50
9	Graham, Jason	40	68,600.00	1,798.45	0.00	1,798.45	70,398.45	0.00	1,798.45	1,798.45
10	Lee, Jeremy	40	68,500.00	1,895.58	0.00	1,895.58	70,395.58	0.00	1,895.58	1,895.58
11	Mankowitz, Hanna	55	37,850.00	1,260.00	708.75	1,968.75	39,818.75	0.00	1,968.75	1,968.75
12	Olsen, Barbara	40	45,820.00	1,487.20	0.00	1,487.20	47,307.20	0.00	1,487.20	1,487.20
13	Parker, William	44	46,430.00	1,581.58	194.70	1,776.28	48,206.28	0.00	1,776.28	1,776.28
14	Raman, Soma	45	54,867.00	1,400.00	262.50	1,662.50	56,529.50	0.00	1,662.50	1,662.50
15	Tabor, Annette	40	42,740.00	1,168.83	0.00	1,168.83	43,908.83	0.00	1,168.83	1,168.83
16	Wallace, Grace	40	115,600.00	3,010.35	0.00	3,010.35	118,610.35	0.00	2,900.00	3,010.35
17			576,602.00	16,916.69	1,720.53	18,637.22	595,239.22	958.20	18,526.87	18,637.22
18		(1)	(2)	(3)	(4)	(5)	(6)	(7A)	(7B)	(7C)
19										

16,916.69 + 1,720.53 = 18,637.22

576,602.00 + 18,637.22 = 595,239.22

The payroll period shown in Figure 4 covers October 5 through October 11. The first part consists of employees' names, hours worked, beginning cumulative earnings, and taxable earnings.

(1) **Total Hours**—Taken from employees' time records (manual or computerized).

(2) **Beginning Cumulative Earnings**—The amount each employee has earned between January 1 and October 4 (the last day of the previous payroll period). It is taken from each employee's individual earnings record. (See Figure 7, page 302.)

(3) **Regular Earnings**—Earnings for hours worked up to and including 40. In other words, the first 40 hours multiplied by each employee's regular hourly rate.

(4) **Overtime Earnings**—Hours in excess of 40 (relative to a 40-hour week) that each employee worked, multiplied by that employee's overtime rate.

(5) **Total Earnings**—Regular earnings plus overtime earnings.

(6) **Ending Cumulative Earnings**—Beginning Cumulative Earnings plus Total Earnings.

(7) **Taxable Earnings**—The amount of earnings subject to taxation, **not the tax itself.** We will use these columns later to figure the amount of each tax. In other words, **Taxable Earnings is the base on which to figure the tax. Taxable Earnings multiplied by the tax rate equals the amount of the tax.**

(7A) **Unemployment Taxable Earnings**—In our illustration, we are using a maximum of $7,000 for unemployment tax liability on the employer for each employee. This column represents the previously untaxed portion remaining of the $7,000 for the individual employees. **Unemployment tax is paid only by the employer in most states. An unemployment tax is generally paid to both the state and federal government.** As of the writing of this text, most states use different maximum earnings and rates from the federal government's current earnings limit of $7,000. However, in this text, we will use $7,000 as the earnings limit for all federal and state unemployment

> **Remember**
>
> Taxable earnings are the base on which to figure the tax, not the tax itself.

Figure 4
(Concluded)

K	L	M	N	O	P	Q	R	S	T	U
		(8) DEDUCTIONS					(9) PAYMENTS		(10) EXPENSE ACCOUNT DEBITED	
FEDERAL INCOME TAX	STATE INCOME TAX	SOCIAL SECURITY TAX	MEDICARE TAX		OTHER DEDUCTIONS	TOTAL	NET AMOUNT	CK. NO.	SALES WAGES EXPENSE	OFFICE WAGES EXPENSE
115.00	23.00	69.72	16.31		0.00	224.03	900.55	832	1,124.58	
56.00	11.20	46.14	10.79	UW	35.00	159.13	585.07	833	744.20	
83.00	16.60	56.79	13.28	UW	25.00	194.67	721.33	834	916.00	
109.00	21.80	67.24	15.72	UW	10.00	223.76	860.74	835		1,084.50
226.39	45.88	111.50	26.08		0.00	409.85	1,388.60	836	1,798.45	
250.67	50.13	117.53	27.48	AR	20.00	465.81	1,429.77	837		1,895.58
268.96	53.79	122.06	28.55		0.00	473.36	1,495.39	838	1,968.75	
169.00	33.80	92.21	21.56		0.00	316.57	1,170.63	839		1,487.20
220.85	44.17	110.13	25.76		0.00	400.91	1,375.37	840	1,776.28	
195.24	39.05	103.08	24.11	AR	30.00	391.48	1,271.02	841	1,662.50	
121.00	24.20	72.47	16.95	UW	25.00	259.62	909.21	842	1,168.83	
529.36	105.87	179.80	43.65	UW	100.00	958.68	2,051.67	843		3,010.35
2,344.47	469.49	1,148.67	270.24		245.00	4,477.87	14,159.35		11,159.59	7,477.63
(8A)	(8B)	(8C)	(8D)		(8E)	(8F)	(9A)	(9B)	(10A)	(10B)

2,344.47 + 469.49 + 1,148.67 + 270.24 + 245.00 = 4,477.87

4,477.87 + 14,159.35 = 18,637.22

11,159.59 + 7,477.63 = 18,637.22

calculations. There are three possibilities for Unemployment Taxable Earnings, as follows:

a. **Employee's cumulative earnings, including this pay period, have not reached $7,000.** When an employee's cumulative earnings so far during the calendar year (since January 1) are less than $7,000, we record the total earnings for the payroll period in the Unemployment Taxable Earnings column. For example, Anna Bodell's cumulative earnings before this week were $5,987. Bodell's cumulative earnings after this week are $6,731.20 ($5,987 + $744.20). Because Bodell's cumulative earnings are still less than $7,000 (after the current check of $744.20), her entire $744.20 in wages earned during this pay period is listed in the Unemployment Taxable Earnings column.

b. **Employee's cumulative earnings were less than $7,000 before this week and are more than $7,000 after this week.** Look at the line for David Dorn and notice that his cumulative earnings before this week were $6,786. Dorn's new cumulative earnings (ending) are $7,702 ($6,786 + $916), putting him over the $7,000 maximum. Therefore, to bring Dorn up to the $7,000 limit, $214 ($7,000 − $6,786) of his earnings for the week are taxable. After this week, none of Dorn's earnings for the remainder of this calendar year will be taxable for unemployment.

c. **Employee's cumulative earnings before this week were more than $7,000.** After an employee's earnings top $7,000 during the calendar year, record a zero or a dash in the Unemployment Taxable Earnings column to indicate that the column has not been forgotten or overlooked. For example, Mark Anderson's total earnings before the payroll period ended October 11 (beginning) were $44,960 (as shown in his individual earnings record in Figure 7 on page 302. Because he had previously earned more than $7,000 this year, we record a zero in the Unemployment Taxable Earnings column.

(7B) **Social Security Taxable Earnings**—The first $118,500 for each employee. We assume a Social Security tax rate of 6.2 percent of the first $118,500 paid to each employee during the calendar year.

a. **Employee's cumulative earnings, including this pay period, have not reached $118,500.** When an employee's cumulative earnings so far during the year are less than $118,500, we record the total earnings for the payroll period in the Social Security Taxable Earnings column. For example, Anna Bodell's cumulative earnings so far this year amount to $6,731.20. Because Bodell's total earnings are less than $118,500, the entire $744.20 of wages earned during this pay period is listed in the Social Security Taxable Earnings column. Note that this is true of all of the employees except Grace Wallace.

b. **Employee's cumulative earnings were less than $118,500 before this week and are more than $118,500 after this week.** The line for Grace Wallace shows that her cumulative earnings before the payroll period ended October 11 were $115,600. However, the cumulative earnings, including those of this payroll period, total $118,610.35, which is greater than the $118,500 limit. This means that only $2,900 ($118,500 − $115,600) of her current pay period earnings is recorded in the Social Security Taxable Earnings column. After an employee's earnings top $118,500 during the calendar year, record a zero

Remember

Unemployment taxable earnings are used for calculating the amount of the unemployment tax, which is paid by the employer only.

FYI

Social Security and Medicare taxes are recorded separately in the payroll register because there is no limit on Medicare, like there is on Social Security.

or a dash to indicate that the column has not been forgotten or overlooked. (Use the same procedure as that for the Unemployment Taxable Earnings column.)

(7C) **Medicare Taxable Earnings**—All earnings for this period. We have assumed a Medicare tax rate of 1.45 percent (0.0145) on all earnings that are paid to each employee during the calendar year. Therefore, all earnings for this period are taxable and are recorded in the Medicare Taxable Earnings column.

(8) **Deductions**—Amounts taken away (withheld) from total earnings.

(8A) **Federal Income Tax Deductions**—The amount of the federal income tax deduction for each employee can be located directly on the wage-bracket tables or calculated on a percentage basis. We assumed that the employees are married and have one withholding allowance.

(8B) **State Income Tax Deductions**—States that impose income taxes also provide wage-bracket tables. The state tax deduction for each employee can be located in the appropriate table. As stated previously, we are assuming a rate of 20 percent of the federal income tax.

(8C) **Social Security Tax Deductions**—For each employee's Social Security tax deduction, we go to the Social Security Taxable Earnings column and note the amount subject to tax. Then, we multiply the Social Security taxable earnings by 6.2 percent (0.062). For example, Bodell's taxable earnings are $744.20 and her Social Security tax deduction is $46.14 ($744.20 × 0.062).

(8D) **Medicare Tax Deductions**—For each employee's Medicare tax deduction, we go to the Medicare Taxable Earnings column and note the amount subject to tax. Then, we multiply the Medicare taxable earnings by 1.45 percent. For example, Bodell's taxable earnings are $744.20 and her Medicare tax deduction is $10.79 ($744.20 × 0.0145).

(8E) **Other Deductions**—Employees' voluntary withholdings. In our illustration, UW represents the United Way and AR stands for Accounts Receivable (employee pays off a loan with the company). For example, Jeremy Lee paid $20 on his loan with the company.

(8F) **Total Deductions**—The combined total of each employee's deductions for taxes and other. For example, Bodell's total deduction is $159.13 ($56.00 + $11.20 + $46.14 + $10.79 + $35.00).

(9) **Payments**—The amount of each employee's payroll check (net pay or take-home pay).

(9A) **Net Amount**—Each employee's Total Earnings minus Total Deductions. For example, Bodell's net amount is $585.07 ($744.20 − $159.13).

(9B) **Ck. No.**—The number of each employee's payroll check.

(10) **Expense Account Debited**—Columns used for distributing each amount in the appropriate wages expense account. Green Sales Company uses Sales Wages Expense and Office Wages Expense. The sum of these two columns equals the total earnings.

(10A) **Sales Wages Expense**—Amounts earned by employees involved in sales activities.

(10B) **Office Wages Expense**—Amounts earned by employees involved in office activities.

Remember

Taxable earnings multiplied by the tax rate equals the tax.

7-5   THE PAYROLL ENTRY

Because the payroll register summarizes the payroll data for the period, it is used as the basis for recording the payroll in the journal. Because the payroll register does not have the status of a journal, a journal entry is necessary. Figure 5 shows the entry in general journal form.

Figure 5
Payroll journal entry for Green Sales Company

Date		Description	Post. Ref.	Debit	Credit
20--					
Oct.	11	Sales Wages Expense		11 1 5 9 59	
		Office Wages Expense		7 4 7 7 63	
		Employees' Federal Income Tax Payable			2 3 4 4 47
		FICA Social Security Tax Payable			1 1 4 8 67
		FICA Medicare Tax Payable			2 7 0 24
		Employees' State Income Tax Payable			4 6 9 49
		Employees' United Way Payable			1 9 5 00
		Accounts Receivable			5 0 00
		Wages Payable			14 1 5 9 35
		Payroll register for the week			
		ended October 11, 20--.			
Oct.	12	Wages Payable		14 1 5 9 35	
		Cash—M. Anderson			9 0 0 55
		Cash—A. Bodell			5 8 5 07
		Cash—D. Dorn			7 2 1 33
		Cash—S. Fields			8 6 0 74
		Cash—J. Graham			1 3 8 8 60
		Cash—J. Lee			1 4 2 9 77
		Cash—H. Mankowitz			1 4 9 5 39
		Cash—B. Olson			1 1 7 0 63
		Cash—W. Parker			1 3 7 5 37
		Cash—S. Raman			1 2 7 1 02
		Cash—A. Tabor			9 0 9 21
		Cash—G. Wallace			2 0 5 1 67

GENERAL JOURNAL   **Page 31**

FYI

A company with a small number of employees would probably use its regular bank account to issue a check to each employee.

Remember

The totals from the Payroll register are the amounts used in the payroll entry.

Remember

The amount shown as Wages Payable is the employees' take-home pay.

Note that the accountant records the total cost to the company for services of employees as debits to the Wages Expense accounts.

To pay the employees from the company's regular checking account, the accountant makes the journal entry as shown in Figure 5.

7-5a Special Payroll Bank Account—An Alternative

A firm with a large number of employees would probably open a special **payroll bank account** with its bank. One check drawn on the regular bank account is made payable to the special payroll account for the amount of the total net pay for a payroll period. All payroll checks for the period are then written on the special payroll account. To record this, the accountant makes the following journal entry. In this book, assume that the entry to debit Cash—Payroll Bank Account and to credit Cash has already been made.

		GENERAL JOURNAL			Page 31
Date	Description	Post. Ref.	Debit	Credit
Oct. 12	Wages Payable		14 1 5 9 35	
	Cash—Payroll Bank Account			14 1 5 9 35
	Paid wages for week ended			
	October 11.			

7-5b Paycheck

All of the data needed to make out a payroll check are available in the payroll register. Mark Anderson's paycheck is shown in Figure 6.

EMPLOYEE	TOTAL HOURS	O.T. HOURS	REG. PAY	O.T. PREM. PAY	GROSS PAY	FED INC. TAX	STATE INC. TAX	SOCIAL SECURITY TAX	MEDICARE TAX	OTHER	TOTAL DED.	NET PAY
Mark Anderson	46	6	918.00	206.58	1,124.58	115.00	23.00	69.72	16.31	—	224.03	900.55

Payroll Account

Green Sales Company
610 First Avenue
Bangor, Maine 04401

CENTRAL NATIONAL BANK

98-461
252

October 12 20 -- No. *832*

PAY TO THE ORDER OF *Mark Anderson* $ *900.55*

Nine hundred and 55/100 _____ DOLLARS

Eileen Green

⑆121000167⑆ 1234567890⑈ 832

Figure 6
Paycheck for Mark Anderson

7-6 EMPLOYEES' INDIVIDUAL EARNINGS RECORDS

6 Maintain employees' individual earnings records.

Learning Objective

To comply with government regulations, a firm has to keep current data on each employee's accumulated earnings, deductions, and net pay. The information contained in the payroll register is recorded each payday in each **employee's individual earnings record**. Figure 7, on page 302, shows a portion of the earnings record for Mark Anderson.

Figure 7

Employee's individual earnings record for Mark Anderson

	A	B	C	D	E	F	G	H	I	J
1	EMPLOYEE'S INDIVIDUAL EARNINGS RECORD									
2	NAME	Mark E. Anderson				EMPLOYEE NO.		55		
3	ADDRESS	1104 Rosewood Street				SOC. SEC. NO.		543-24-1680		
4		Bangor, Maine 04401				PAY RATE		$22.95		
5	MALE	X		FEMALE		EQUIVALENT HOURLY RATE		$22.95		
6	MARRIED	X		SINGLE		DATE TERMINATED				
7	PHONE NO.	207-555-2256		DATE OF BIRTH 9/17/72		CLASSIFICATION FOR WORKERS' COMPENSATION INSURANCE Sales floor				
8			HOURS WORKED			EARNINGS			DEDUCTIONS	
9/10/40	PERIOD ENDED	DATE PAID	REGULAR	OVERTIME	REGULAR	OVERTIME	TOTAL	ENDING CUMULATIVE EARNINGS	FEDERAL INCOME TAX	STATE INCOME TAX
41	9/6	9/7	40	8	918.00	275.44	1,193.44	40,771.55	125.00	25.00
42	9/13	9/14	40	2	918.00	68.86	986.86	41,758.41	94.00	18.80
43	9/20	9/21	40	2	918.00	68.86	986.86	42,745.27	94.00	18.80
44	9/27	9/28	40	5	918.00	172.15	1,090.15	43,835.42	110.00	22.00
45	10/4	10/5	40	6	918.00	206.58	1,124.58	44,960.00	115.00	23.00
46	10/11	10/12	40	6	918.00	206.58	1,124.58	46,084.58	115.00	23.00
47										

K		L	M	N	O	P	Q
DATE EMPLOYED	2/1/--						
NO. OF EXEMPTIONS	1						
PER HOUR	X		PER DAY _____				
PER WEEK			PER MONTH _____				
DEDUCTIONS						PAID	
SOCIAL SECURITY TAX		MEDICARE TAX	OTHER		TOTAL	NET AMOUNT	CK. NO.
			CODE	AMOUNT			
73.99		17.30	UW	5.00	246.29	947.15	771
61.19		14.31	UW	0.00	188.30	798.56	783
61.19		14.31	UW	5.00	193.30	793.56	795
67.59		15.81	UW	0.00	215.40	874.75	807
69.72		16.31	UW	5.00	229.03	895.55	819
69.72		16.31	UW	0.00	224.03	900.55	832

Chapter Review

Study and Practice

 1 Recognize the role of income tax laws that affect payroll deductions and contributions.

Learning Objective

Employees and employers involved in the computation and paying of employees for their work must understand the laws, know the percentages and limits involved, and know when and to whom to submit the funds deducted from employees and contributed by employees. The federal income tax withholding tables are provided by the IRS in Publication 15 (Circular E). FICA payroll taxes, withheld from the employee, are currently 6.2 percent (0.062) for the employee's portion of the Social Security tax, based on the first $118,500 of wages and 1.45 percent (0.0145) on all wages for Medicare.

 PRACTICE EXERCISE 1

Sally Quinn earns an annual salary of $150,000. How much does she pay in FICA payroll taxes this year?

PRACTICE EXERCISE 1 • SOLUTION

Social Security taxes (limited to first $118,500)	$118,500 × 0.062 =	$7,347.00
Medicare taxes	$150,000 × 0.0145 =	2,175.00
Total FICA taxes		$9,522.00

 2 Calculate total earnings based on an hourly, salary, piece-rate, or commission basis.

Learning Objective

Earnings calculated on an *hourly basis* equal the hourly rate multiplied by the number of hours worked. If an employee is paid on a *salary basis* and is entitled to extra pay for overtime, the overtime rate is the annual salary divided by 52 (weeks) divided by 40 (normal hours per week). Earnings calculated on a *piece-rate basis* equals the total number of products produced multiplied by the rate per unit of product. Earnings calculated on a *commission basis* equal the total number of units sold or the price of units sold multiplied by the commission rate.

 PRACTICE EXERCISE 2

Soma Raman worked 45 hours for the week ended November 7. His hourly rate is $41.85. Determine his gross wages if he is paid time-and-a-half for all overtime hours.

PRACTICE EXERCISE 2 • SOLUTION

40 hours at straight time	40 × $41.85 per hour =	$1,674.00
5 hours overtime ($41.85 × 1.5 = $62.78)	5 × $62.78 per hour =	313.90
Total hours and gross wages	45	$1,987.90

 3 Determine deductions from gross pay, such as federal income tax withheld, Social Security tax, and Medicare tax, to calculate net pay.

Learning Objective

Starting with **gross pay**, an employee's pay is reduced for federal and state income tax withholding, **FICA taxes** (**Social Security** and **Medicare taxes**), and other items such as retirement savings through a 401(k) plan and medical reimbursement plans to arrive at **net pay**.

PRACTICE EXERCISE 3

Using Figure 3 on pages 293–294, calculate the federal income tax withholding for an employee who is married and is paid weekly and whose wages are $1,360 with one withholding allowance. Then calculate the Social Security tax and Medicare tax for the employee, assuming the employee has cumulative earnings of less than $118,500 for the calendar year to date.

PRACTICE EXERCISE 3 • SOLUTION

According to Figure 3, $151 should be withheld for an employee who is married, paid weekly and whose wages are $1,360 with one withholding allowance. Social Security and Medicare taxes would be computed as follows:

$1,360 $\times$ 0.062 = $84.32 Social Security tax
$1,360 $\times$ 0.0145 = $19.72 Medicare tax

Learning Objective   **4**   Complete a payroll register.

To complete the **payroll register**, list the employees' names, hours worked, and beginning cumulative earnings. Add the total earnings to the beginning cumulative earnings to get ending cumulative earnings. The Unemployment Taxable Earnings column is used for the first $7,000 of each employee's earnings for FUTA and SUTA. The Social Security Taxable Earnings column is used for the first $118,500 paid to each employee during the **calendar year**. The Medicare Taxable Earnings column is used for all earnings. Under the Deductions columns, list the federal and state income taxes withheld, the Social Security taxes withheld, the Medicare taxes withheld, and other deductions. The Social Security tax deduction equals the Social Security **taxable earnings** multiplied by an assumed rate of 6.2 percent. The Medicare tax deduction equals the Medicare taxable earnings multiplied by an assumed rate of 1.45 percent. The Net Amount column equals Total Earnings minus Total Deductions.

PRACTICE EXERCISE 4

Complete the following payroll register. The employees are paid time-and-a-half for overtime.

	A	B	C	D	E	F	G	H
1					EARNINGS			
2			BEGINNING				ENDING	
3		TOTAL	CUMULATIVE				CUMULATIVE	
4	NAME	HOURS	EARNINGS	REGULAR	OVERTIME	TOTAL	EARNINGS	UNEMPLOYMENT
5	Abbott, Jack	40	55,820.00	1,487.20				0.00
6	Monohan, William	44	56,430.00	1,581.60				0.00
7	Romar, Sue	45	58,967.00	1,674.16				0.00
8	Williams, Emma	40	140,000.00	3,010.35				0.00
9			311,217.00	7,753.31				0.00
10								

I	J	K	L	M	N	O	P	Q
TAXABLE EARNINGS				DEDUCTIONS			PAYMENTS	
SOCIAL SECURITY	MEDICARE	FEDERAL INCOME TAX	STATE INCOME TAX	SOCIAL SECURITY TAX	MEDICARE TAX	TOTAL	NET AMOUNT	CK. NO.
		169.00	33.80					1520
		231.49	46.30					1521
		273.97	54.79					1522
		529.54	105.91					1523
		1,204.00	240.80					

PRACTICE EXERCISE 4 • SOLUTION

	A	B	C	D	E	F	G	H
				EARNINGS				
			BEGINNING				ENDING	
		TOTAL	CUMULATIVE				CUMULATIVE	
	NAME	HOURS	EARNINGS	REGULAR	OVERTIME	TOTAL	EARNINGS	UNEMPLOYMENT
5	Abbott, Jack	40	55,820.00	1,487.20	0.00	1,487.20	57,307.20	0.00
6	Monohan, William	44	56,430.00	1,581.60	237.24	1,818.84	58,248.84	0.00
7	Romar, Sue	45	58,967.00	1,674.16	313.90	1,988.06	60,955.06	0.00
8	Williams, Emma	40	140,000.00	3,010.35	0.00	3,010.35	143,010.35	0.00
9			311,217.00	7,753.31	551.14	8,304.45	319,521.45	0.00
10								

I	J	K	L	M	N	O	P	Q
TAXABLE EARNINGS		DEDUCTIONS					PAYMENTS	
				SOCIAL				CK.
SOCIAL		FEDERAL	STATE	SECURITY				CK.
SECURITY	MEDICARE	INCOME TAX	INCOME TAX	TAX	MEDICARE TAX	TOTAL	NET AMOUNT	NO.
1,487.20	1,487.20	169.00	33.80	92.21	21.56	316.57	1,170.63	1520
1,818.84	1,818.84	231.49	46.30	112.77	26.37	416.93	1,401.91	1521
1,988.06	1,988.06	273.97	54.79	123.26	28.83	480.85	1,507.21	1522
0.00	3,010.35	529.54	105.91	0.00	43.65	679.10	2,331.25	1523
5,294.10	8,304.45	1,204.00	240.80	328.24	120.41	1,893.45	6,411.00	

5 Journalize the payroll entry from a payroll register.

Learning Objective

Totals are taken directly from the payroll register. Refer to the general journal illustrations on pages 300–301 for an example of the first payroll entry and examples of two ways to journalize the payment of the payroll—one from the company's regular checking account and one from a special **payroll bank account**.

Show me
HOW

PRACTICE EXERCISE 5

Based on the payroll register created in Practice Exercise 4, prepare the journal entry to record the payroll for the week of December 8, 20--.

PRACTICE EXERCISE 5 • SOLUTION

GENERAL JOURNAL				Page 31	
Date	Description	Post. Ref.	Debit	Credit	
20--					
Dec. 8	Wages Expense		8 3 0 4 45		
	Employees' Federal Income				
	Tax Payable			1 2 0 4 00	
	FICA Social Security Tax Payable			3 2 8 24	
	FICA Medicare Tax Payable			1 2 0 41	
	Employees' State Income Tax				
	Payable			2 4 0 80	
	Wages payable			6 4 1 1 00	
	Payroll register for the				
	week ended December 8, 20--.				

Learning Objective **6** Maintain employees' individual earnings records.

In the **employees' individual earnings records**, list the personal data for each employee. Based on the information contained in the payroll register, record the earnings and deductions for each payroll period.

 PRACTICE EXERCISE 6

Update the following employee's individual earnings record for William Monohan for the December 8 payroll from the payroll register in Practice Exercise 4.

	A	B	C	D	E	F	G	H	I
1	EMPLOYEE'S INDIVIDUAL EARNINGS RECORD								
2	NAME	William Monohan				EMPLOYEE NO.		592	
3	ADDRESS	17058 SE 97th Court				SOC. SEC. NO.		544-64-8240	
4		Miami, Florida 33158				PAY RATE		$39.54	
5	MALE	X		FEMALE		OVERTIME PAY		1½x	
6	MARRIED	X		SINGLE					
7	PHONE NO.	305-999-9001		DATE OF BIRTH	6/17/73				
8			HOURS WORKED			EARNINGS			DEDUCTIONS
9								ENDING	FEDERAL
10	PERIOD ENDED	DATE PAID	REGULAR	OVERTIME	REGULAR	OVERTIME	TOTAL	CUMULATIVE EARNINGS	INCOME TAX
11	11/17	11/18	40	8	1,581.60	474.48	2,056.08	53,029.56	290.80
12	11/24	11/25	40	2	1,581.60	118.62	1,700.22	54,729.78	201.83
13	12/1	12/2	40	2	1,581.60	118.62	1,700.22	56,430.00	201.83
14									

J	K	L	M	N	O
	DATE EMPLOYED	2/1/--			
	NO. OF EXEMPTIONS	1			
	PER HOUR	X	PER DAY _____		
	PER WEEK		PER MONTH _____		
	DEDUCTIONS			PAID	
STATE INCOME TAX	SOCIAL SECURITY TAX	MEDICARE TAX	TOTAL	NET AMOUNT	CK. NO.
58.16	127.48	29.81	506.25	1,549.83	920
40.37	105.41	24.65	372.26	1,327.96	1120
40.37	105.41	24.65	372.26	1,327.96	1325

PRACTICE EXERCISE 6 • SOLUTION

	A	B	C	D	E	F	G	H	I
1	EMPLOYEE'S INDIVIDUAL EARNINGS RECORD								
2	NAME	William Monohan				EMPLOYEE NO.		592	
3	ADDRESS	17058 SE 97th Court				SOC. SEC. NO.		544-64-8240	
4		Miami, Florida 33158				PAY RATE		$39.54	
5	MALE	X		FEMALE		OVERTIME PAY		1½x	
6	MARRIED	X		SINGLE					
7	PHONE NO.	305-999-9001		DATE OF BIRTH 6/17/73					
8			HOURS WORKED			EARNINGS			DEDUCTIONS
9								ENDING CUMULATIVE EARNINGS	FEDERAL INCOME TAX
10	PERIOD ENDED	DATE PAID	REGULAR	OVERTIME	REGULAR	OVERTIME	TOTAL		
11	11/17	11/18	40	8	1,581.60	474.48	2,056.08	53,029.56	290.80
12	11/24	11/25	40	2	1,581.60	118.62	1,700.22	54,729.78	201.83
13	12/1	12/2	40	2	1,581.60	118.62	1,700.22	56,430.00	201.83
14	12/8	12/9	40	4	1,581.60	237.24	1,818.84	58,248.84	231.49
15									

J	K	L	M	N	O
	DATE EMPLOYED	2/1/—			
	NO. OF EXEMPTIONS	1			
	PER HOUR	X	PER DAY _____		
	PER WEEK		PER MONTH _____		
	DEDUCTIONS			PAID	
STATE INCOME TAX	SOCIAL SECURITY TAX	MEDICARE TAX	TOTAL	NET AMOUNT	CK. NO.
58.16	127.48	29.81	506.25	1,549.83	920
40.37	105.41	24.65	372.26	1,327.96	1120
40.37	105.41	24.65	372.26	1,327.96	1325
46.30	112.77	26.37	416.93	1,401.91	1521

Glossary

Calendar year A 12-month period beginning January 1 and ending December 31 of the same year. (*p. 288*)

Current Tax Payment Act (Income Tax Withholding) An act that requires employers to withhold and pay employee funds to the U.S. Treasury. (*p. 286*)

Employee One who works for compensation under the direction and control of the employer. (*p. 287*)

Employee's individual earnings record A supplementary record for each employee showing personal payroll data and yearly cumulative earnings, deductions, and net pay. (*p. 301*)

Employee's Withholding Allowance Certificate (Form W-4) A form that specifies the number of allowances claimed by each employee and gives the employer the authority to withhold money for an employee's federal income taxes. (*p. 291*)

Exemption An amount of an employee's annual earnings not subject to income tax for the taxpayer, taxpayer's spouse, and dependents (*usually children*). (*p. 291*)

Fair Labor Standards Act The act of 1938 that provides for minimum standards for wages and overtime, including provisions related to child labor and equal pay for equal work. (*p. 286*)

FICA taxes Social Security taxes plus Medicare taxes, paid by both employee and employer under the provisions of the Federal Insurance Contributions Act. The proceeds are used to pay old-age and disability pensions and to fund the Medicare program. (*p. 287*)

Gross pay The total amount of an employee's pay before any deductions. (*p. 285*)

Independent contractor Someone who is engaged for a definite job or service and who may choose his or her own means of doing the work. This person is not an employee of the firm for which the service is provided. (*p. 286*)

Medicare taxes Federal government taxes levied on employees and employers; proceeds are used for medical insurance for eligible people aged 65 and over. (*p. 287*)

Net pay Gross pay minus deductions. Also called *take-home pay*. (*p. 285*)

Payroll bank account A special checking account used to pay a company's employees. (*p. 301*)

Payroll register A manual or computerized schedule prepared for each payroll period listing the earnings, deductions, and net pay for each employee. (*p. 296*)

Pre-tax deductions Employee deductions that are not subject to income tax. The deductions include medical insurance premiums, medical and dependent care expenses under a flexible spending plan, and 401(k) contributions. (*p. 291*)

Social Security Act of 1935 An act that provides for worker retirement funding through deductions from workers' wages and matching amounts from their employers. (*p. 287*)

Social Security taxes Federal government taxes levied on employees and employers; proceeds are used for old-age pensions and disability benefits. (*p. 287*)

Taxable earnings The amount of an employee's earnings subject to a tax. (*p. 291*)

Wage-bracket tax tables A chart providing the amounts to be deducted for income taxes based on amount of earnings, marital status, and number of allowances claimed. (*p. 292*)

Withholding allowance An allowance claimed by an employee (on a W-4), which employers use to calculate the amount of income tax withheld from an employee's paycheck. (*p. 291*)

Workers' compensation laws Laws that protect employees and dependents against losses due to death or injury incurred on the job. (*p. 288*)

Quiz Yourself

_____ 1. Which of the following is *not* usually considered an independent contractor?
   a. Plumber   d. CPA
   b. Salesperson   e. Electrician
   c. Lawyer

_____ 2. Which of the following taxes are *not* withheld from an employee?
   a. FICA Social Security
   b. Federal Unemployment (FUTA)
   c. FICA Medicare
   d. Federal Income Tax
   e. All of the above are withheld

_____ 3. Calculate an employee's total earnings if the company pays time-and-a-half when Jill Smith works 41 hours at $15 per hour.
   a. $600.00   d. $635.00
   b. $615.00   e. None of the above
   c. $622.50

_____ 4. Which of the following is *not* a deduction from total earnings?
   a. Federal income tax
   b. Union dues
   c. 2.5 hours of overtime
   d. Medical insurance premiums
   e. State income tax

_____ 5. Which of the following is *not* included in the payroll register?
  a. Total hours
  b. Overtime earnings
  c. Unemployment taxable earnings
  d. Wage-bracket tax table
  e. Total earnings

_____ 6. Firms with a large number of employees generally use which of the following for disbursing payroll to employees?
  a. Payroll bank account
  b. General bank account
  c. Credit card account
  d. Accounts Receivable
  e. Accounts Payable

_____ 7. When is the payroll register updated?
  a. Annually
  b. Each payday
  c. Quarterly
  d. Monthly
  e. No set schedule—whenever there is time

Answers:
1.b 2.b 3.c 4.c 5.d 6.a 7.b

Chapter Assignments

Discussion Questions

1. Why must employers maintain employees' individual earnings records?
2. What information is included in an employee's individual earnings record?
3. What is the purpose of the payroll register?
4. Explain the difference between gross earnings and net earnings for a payroll period.
5. Describe how a special payroll bank account is useful in paying the wages and salaries of employees.
6. List three required deductions and four voluntary deductions from an employee's total earnings.
7. What is the difference between an employee and an independent contractor? List two examples of an independent contractor.
8. What information is needed to use the wage-bracket withholding table? Where is the table found?

Exercises

 1, 2

EXERCISE 7-1 Determine the gross pay for each employee listed below.

a. Clay Jones is paid time-and-a-half for all hours over 40. He worked 45 hours during the week. His regular pay rate is $25 per hour.

Practice Exercises 1, 2

b. Mary James worked 48 hours during the week. She is entitled to time-and-a-half for all hours in excess of 40 per week. Her regular pay rate is $20 per hour.

c. Lori Terry is paid a commission of 10 percent of her sales, which amounted to $23,650.

d. Nicole Smith's yearly salary is $95,500. During the week, she worked 46 hours, and she is entitled to time-and-a-half for all hours over 40.

LO 1, 2, 3

Practice Exercises 1, 2, 3

EXERCISE 7-2 Lisa Meilo works for Pacific Company, which pays its employees time-and-a-half for all hours worked in excess of 40 per week. Meilo's pay rate is $37 per hour. Her wages are subject to federal income tax, a Social Security tax deduction at the rate of 6.2 percent, and a Medicare tax deduction at the rate of 1.45 percent. She is married and claims three allowances. Meilo has an unpaid half-hour lunch break during an 8½-hour day. In the most recent pay period, she worked 50 hours. Meilo's beginning cumulative earnings are $73,654.

Complete the following:

a. _____ hours at straight time × $ _____ per hour $ _____

b. _____ hours overtime × $ _____ per hour   _____

c. Total gross pay $ _____

d. Federal income tax withholding $ 247.30

e. Social Security tax withholding at 6.2 percent   _____

f. Medicare tax withholding at 1.45 percent   _____

g. Total withholding   _____

h. Net pay $ _____

LO 1, 2, 3, 4

Practice Exercises 1, 2, 3, 4

EXERCISE 7-3 Using the income tax withholding table in Figure 3, pages 293–294, for each employee of Miller Company, determine the net pay for the week ended January 21. Assume a Social Security tax of 6.2 percent and a Medicare tax of 1.45 percent. All employees have cumulative earnings, including this pay period, of less than $118,500. Assume that all employees are married.

Employee	Allowances	Total Earnings	Federal Income Tax Withheld	Social Security Tax Withheld	Medicare Tax Withheld	Union Dues Withheld	United Way Contribution	Net Pay
a. Aston, F. B.	1	$ 900.00	$	$	$	$ 25.00	$ 35.00	$
b. Dwyer, S. J.	2	920.00				25.00	35.00	
c. Flynn, K. A.	3	1,110.00				25.00	40.00	
d. Harden, J. L.	0	1,025.00				25.00	40.00	
e. Nguyen, H.	2	925.00				25.00	35.00	
Totals		$4,880.00	$	$	$	$125.00	$185.00	$

LO **1, 4**

Practice Exercises 1, 4

EXERCISE 7-4 For the week ended September 7, the totals of the payroll register for Benton, Inc., are presented below. The regular and overtime earnings are correct. List six errors that exist. None of the employees have earned more than $118,500, so all earnings are subject to Social Security and Medicare taxes. Assume that amounts for taxable earnings (unemployment, Social Security, Medicare) and deductions (federal income tax, union dues, charity) are correct. Round amounts to the nearest penny.

	A	B	C	D	E	F	G	H	I
1					EARNINGS			TAXABLE EARNINGS	
2		BEGINNING				ENDING			
3		CUMULATIVE				CUMULATIVE		SOCIAL	
4	NAME	EARNINGS	REGULAR	OVERTIME	TOTAL	EARNINGS	UNEMPLOYMENT	SECURITY	MEDICARE
9		245,754.00	6,724.00	1,220.00	7,494.00	253,248.00	2,456.00	7,944.00	7,944.00
10									
11									

	J	K	L	M	N	O	P	Q	R
			DEDUCTIONS				PAYMENTS		
	FEDERAL	SOCIAL							WAGES
	INCOME	SECURITY	MEDICARE	UNION			NET	CK. NO.	EXPENSE
	TAX	TAX	TAX	DUES	CHARITY	TOTAL	AMOUNT		DEBIT
	949.00	314.75	115.19	193.00	292.00	1,863.94	5,630.06		7,494.00

LO **1, 4**

Practice Exercises 1, 4

EXERCISE 7-5 For tax purposes, assume that the maximum taxable earnings are $118,500 for Social Security and $7,000 for the unemployment tax and that all earnings are taxable for Medicare. For the payroll register for the month of November for Shelby, Inc., determine the taxable earnings for each employee.

	A	B	C	D	E	F	G
1					TAXABLE EARNINGS		
2		BEGINNING		ENDING			
3		CUMULATIVE		CUMULATIVE			
4	NAME	EARNINGS	TOTAL EARNINGS	EARNINGS	UNEMPLOYMENT	SOCIAL SECURITY	MEDICARE
5	Axton, C.	112,800.00	7,691.00	120,491.00			
6	Edgar, E.	145,465.00	10,900.00	156,365.00			
7	Gorman, L.	36,879.00	3,064.00	39,943.00			
8	Jolson, R.	24,634.00	2,325.00	26,959.00			
9	Nixel, P.	6,850.00	2,463.00	9,313.00			
10							
11							

LO **1, 4, 5**

Practice Exercises 1, 4, 5

EXERCISE 7-6 On January 21, the column totals of the payroll register for Great Products Company showed that its sales employees had earned $14,960, its truck driver employees had earned $10,692, and its office employees had earned $8,670. Social Security taxes were withheld at an assumed rate of 6.2 percent, and Medicare taxes were withheld at an assumed rate of 1.45 percent. Other deductions consisted of federal income tax, $3,975, and union dues, $560. Determine the amount of Social Security and Medicare taxes withheld and record the general journal entry for the payroll, crediting Salaries Payable for the net pay. All earnings were taxable. Round amounts to the nearest penny.

CHAPTER ASSIGNMENTS

LO 1, 2, 3

Practice Exercises 1, 2, 3

EXERCISE 7-7 Precision Labs has two employees. The following information was taken from its individual earnings records for the month of September. Determine the missing amounts assuming that the Social Security tax is 6.2 percent, the Medicare tax is 1.45 percent, and the state income tax is 20 percent of the federal income tax. Assume that the employees are married and have one withholding allowance. All earnings are subject to Social Security and Medicare taxes. Round amounts to the nearest penny.

	Brown	Ringness	Total
Regular earnings	$ 3,500.00	$?	$?
Overtime earnings	?	120.00	
Total earnings	$ 3,646.00	$?	$?
Federal income tax withheld	$ 312.08	$?	$?
State income tax withheld	?	35.18	?
Social Security tax withheld	226.05	169.76	?
Medicare tax withheld	52.87	39.70	?
Charity withheld	35.00	97.00	?
Total deductions	$ 688.42	$ 517.53	$?
Net pay	$?	$ 2,220.47	$?

LO 5

Practice Exercise 5

EXERCISE 7-8 Assume that the employees in Exercise 7–7 are paid from the company's regular bank account (check numbers 981 and 982). Prepare the entry to record and pay the payroll in general journal form, dated September 30.

Problem Set A

LO 1, 2, 3

PROBLEM 7-1A Jennifer Ross, an employee of Hampton Company, worked 44 hours during the week of February 9 through 15. Her rate of pay is $30 per hour, and she receives time-and-a-half for work in excess of 40 hours per week. She is married and claims two allowances on her W-4 form. Her wages are subject to the following deductions:

a. Federal income tax (use the table in Figure 3, pages 293–294).
b. Social Security tax at 6.2 percent.
c. Medicare tax at 1.45 percent.
d. Union dues, $30.

Check Figure
Net pay, $1,102.43

Required
Compute Ross's regular pay, overtime pay, gross pay, and net pay.

LO **1, 2, 3, 4, 5**

PROBLEM 7-2A Highridge Homes has the following payroll information for the week ended February 21:

| Name | Earnings at End of Previous Week | Daily Time | | | | | | | Pay Rate | Federal Income Tax |
		S	M	T	W	T	F	S		
Arthur, P.	7,800.00	8	8	8	8	8			45.00	226.78
Bills, D.	2,060.00			8	8	8	8	8	12.50	26.00
Carney, W.	2,085.00	8	8	8			8	8	12.95	27.00
Dorn, J.	748.00				8	8			22.00	11.00
Edgar, L.	2,687.00	8	8	8			8	8	15.00	37.00
Fitzwilson, G.	4,150.00	8	8		8	8	8	8	23.00	125.00

Taxable earnings for Social Security are based on the first $118,500. Taxable earnings for Medicare are based on all earnings. Taxable earnings for federal and state unemployment are based on the first $7,000. Employees are paid time-and-a-half for work in excess of 40 hours per week. Round amounts to the nearest penny.

Required

1. Complete the payroll register. The Social Security tax rate is 6.2 percent, and the Medicare tax rate is 1.45 percent. Begin payroll checks with No. 2080.
2. Prepare a general journal entry to record the payroll. The firm's general ledger contains a Wages Expense account and a Wages Payable account.
3. Assuming that the firm has transferred funds from its regular bank account to its special payroll bank account and that this entry has been made, prepare a general journal entry to record the payment of wages.

Check Figure
Net amount, $4,133.33

LO **1, 2, 3, 4, 5**

PROBLEM 7-3A Alpine Company pays its employees time-and-a-half for hours worked in excess of 40 per week. The information available from time cards and employees' individual earnings records for the pay period ended October 14 is shown in the following chart:

| Name | Earnings at End of Previous Week | Daily Time | | | | | | Pay Rate | Income Tax Allowances or Amount |
		M	T	W	T	F	S		
Bardin, J.	43,627.00	8	8	8	8	8	2	21.30	2
Caris, A.	44,340.00	8	8	8	8	8	8	21.60	1
Drew, W.	43,845.00	8	10	10	8	8	0	21.50	1
Garen, S.	117,600.00	8	8	8	8	8	0	49.00	$227.83
North, O.	43,875.00	8	8	8	8	8	5	21.40	3
Ovid, N.	40,150.00	8	8	8	8	8	0	21.50	1
Ross, J.	6,430.00	8	8	8	8	8	4	20.50	1
Springer, O.	44,175.00	8	8	8	8	8	3	21.25	2

Taxable earnings for Social Security are based on the first $118,500. Taxable earnings for Medicare are based on all earnings. Taxable earnings for federal and state unemployment are based on the first $7,000. *Round to the nearest penny.

(Continued)

Check Figure
Net amount, $7,326.50

Required

1. Complete the payroll register using the wage-bracket income tax withholding table in Figure 3 (pages 293–294). The Social Security tax rate is 6.2 percent, and the Medicare tax rate is 1.45 percent. Assume that all employees are married. In the payroll register, begin payroll checks with No. 3945.
2. Prepare a general journal entry to record the payroll. The firm's general ledger contains a Wages Expense account and a Wages Payable account.
3. Assuming that the firm has transferred funds from its regular bank account to its special payroll bank account and that this entry has been made, prepare a general journal entry to record the payment of wages.

LO   1, 3, 4, 5

PROBLEM 7-4A The information for Titan Company, shown in the following chart, is available from Titan's time records and the employees' individual earnings records for the pay period ended December 22.

Name	Hours Worked	Earnings at End of Previous Week	Total Earnings	Class.	Federal Income Tax	Other Deductions	
Albee, C.	44	63,340.00	1,650.00	Sales	193.37	UW	25.00
Don, V.	40	136,410.00	2,841.00	Sales	487.03	AR	95.00
Fine, J.	40	76,860.00	1,507.00	Sales	171.92	UW	25.00
Ginny, N.	46	33,590.00	660.00	Office	46.00	UW	35.00
Johnson, J.	47	56,980.00	1,117.00	Office	113.00	UW	25.00
Lund, D.	43	116,600.00	2,100.00	Sales	301.78	UW	20.00
Maya, R.	42	66,860.00	1,310.00	Sales	143.00	AR	70.00
Nord, P.	41	36,750.00	720.00	Sales	55.00	UW	20.00
Oscar, T.	43	93,480.00	1,832.00	Sales	234.78	UW	25.00
Troy, B.	40	47,250.00	930.00	Sales	86.00	UW	20.00

Taxable earnings for Social Security are based on the first $118,500. Taxable earnings for Medicare are based on all earnings. Taxable earnings for federal and state unemployment are based on the first $7,000. The company does not pay for overtime hours.

Check Figure
Net amount, $11,541.64

Required

1. Complete the payroll register using a Social Security tax rate of 6.2 percent and a Medicare tax rate of 1.45 percent. Concerning Other Deductions, AR refers to Accounts Receivable and UW refers to United Way. Begin payroll checks in the payroll register with No. 2914.
2. Prepare the general journal entry to record the payroll. The firm's general ledger contains a Salary Expense account and a Salaries Payable account.
3. Prepare the general journal entry to pay the payroll. Assume that funds for this payroll have been transferred to Cash—Payroll Bank Account and that this entry has been made.

LO   **2, 3**

Problem 7-5A Jim Moss, an employee of Jones International, worked 49 hours during the week of April 4 through 10. His rate of pay is $15 per hour, and he receives time and a half for work in excess of 40 hours per week. Jim is married and claims four allowances on his W-4 form. Jim's YTD earnings before this pay period are $7,600, and his wages are subject to the following deductions:

a. Federal income tax (use the table in Figure 3, pages 293–294).
b. Social Security tax at 6.2 percent, with a wage limit of $118,500.
c. Medicare tax at 1.45 percent.
d. Medical insurance premium (after tax), $50.
e. United Way contribution, $10.

Required
Compute Jim's regular pay, overtime pay, gross pay, and net pay.

Check Figure
Net pay, $648.10

Problem Set B

LO   **1, 2, 3**

PROBLEM 7-1B Erin Chang, an employee of Solutions Company, worked 48 hours during the week of October 12 through 18. Her rate of pay is $17.50 per hour, and she receives time-and-a-half for all work in excess of 40 hours per week. Chang is married and claims two allowances on her W-4 form. Her wages are subject to the following deductions:

a. Federal income tax (use the table in Figure 3, pages 293–294).
b. Social Security tax at 6.2 percent.
c. Medicare tax at 1.45 percent.
d. Union dues, $32.

Required
Compute Chang's regular pay, overtime pay, gross pay, and net pay.

Check Figure
Net pay, $737.38

LO   **1, 2, 3, 4, 5**

PROBLEM 7-2B Harvest Company has the following payroll information for the pay period ended April 14:

Name	Earnings at End of Previous Week	Daily Time M	T	W	T	F	S	Pay Rate	Federal Income Tax
Grant, L.	7,536.00	8	8	8	8	8	0	18.00	55.00
Hamn, R.	6,496.00	8	8	8	8	8	0	18.10	55.00
Lisk, J.	6,798.00	0	8	8	8	8	8	17.80	52.00
Myre, G.	9,589.00	8	8	8	0	8	8	19.25	62.00
Segel, T.	6,585.00	8	8	8	8	8	6	17.95	77.00
Torgel, I.	7,501.00	0	8	8	8	8	8	18.70	58.00

    Taxable earnings for Social Security are based on the first $118,500. Taxable earnings for Medicare are based on all earnings. Taxable earnings for federal and state unemployment are based on the first $7,000. Employees are paid time-and-a-half for work in excess of 40 hours per week.

(Continued)

Check Figure
Net amount, $3,846.23

Required

1. Complete the payroll register. The Social Security tax rate is 6.2 percent, and the Medicare tax rate is 1.45 percent. Begin payroll checks with No. 2944.
2. Prepare a general journal entry to record the payroll. The firm's general ledger contains a Wages Expense account and a Wages Payable account.
3. Assuming that the firm has transferred funds from its regular bank account to its special payroll bank account and that this entry has been made, prepare a journal entry to record the payment of wages.

 1, 2, 3, 4, 5

PROBLEM 7-3B Williams Company pays its employees time-and-a-half for hours worked in excess of 40 per week. The information available from time records and employees' individual earnings records for the pay period ended September 21 is shown in the following chart:

Name	Earnings at End of Previous Week	Daily Time						Pay Rate	Income Tax Allowances or Amount
		M	T	W	T	F	S		
Bolt, D.	6,745.00	8	8	8	10	8	0	25.00	1
Dore, C.	136,240.00	8	8	8	8	8	0	49.50	$252.30
Gayle, A.	32,730.00	8	10	8	8	8	0	24.50	2
Hale, R.	117,560.00	8	8	8	8	8	4	40.00	$195.50
Jilly, B.	35,154.00	8	8	8	8	8	0	49.50	$291.25
Karn, S.	29,938.00	8	8	9	8	8	0	20.50	2
Ober, N.	6,795.00	8	8	8	9	9	4	21.00	1
Wong, J.	27,252.00	8	8	10	8	8	0	20.00	2

Taxable earnings for Social Security are based on the first $118,500. Taxable earnings for Medicare are based on all earnings. Taxable earnings for federal and state unemployment are based on the first $7,000.

Check Figure
Net amount, 8,869.10

Required

1. Complete the payroll register using the wage-bracket income tax withholding table in Figure 3 (pages 293–294). The Social Security tax rate is 6.2 percent, and the Medicare tax rate is 1.45 percent. Assume that all employees are married. In the payroll register, begin payroll checks with No. 1863.
2. Prepare a general journal entry to record the payroll. The firm's general ledger contains a Wages Expense account and a Wages Payable account.
3. Assuming that the firm has transferred funds from its regular bank account to its special payroll bank account and that this entry has been made, prepare a general journal entry to record the payment of wages.

 1, 3, 4, 5

PROBLEM 7-4B The information for Best Sports Company, shown in the chart on the next page, is available from Best Sports' time records and employees' individual earnings records for the pay period ended December 29.

Name	Hours Worked	Earnings at End of Previous Week	Total Earnings	Class.	Federal Income Tax	Other Deductions	
Chang, C.	40	33,900.00	680.00	Sales	49.00	AR	80.00
Dugan, T.	42	38,270.00	2,841.00	Sales	487.03	UW	20.00
Fancher, K.	40	37,680.00	725.00	Sales	55.00	UW	25.00
Gannon, T.	40	33,245.00	660.00	Office	46.00		—
Jones, L.	40	37,789.00	750.00	Office	59.00	UW	25.00
Lange, M.	40	117,000.00	2,100.00	Office	301.78	UW	35.00
Milton, D.	40	37,684.00	1,310.00	Sales	143.00	UW	20.00
Naylor, B.	40	37,499.00	720.00	Sales	55.00		—
Orton, A.	44	94,338.00	1,780.00	Sales	221.78	AR	70.00
Tiosha, J.	42	48,120.00	1,065.00	Sales	106.00	UW	25.00

Taxable earnings for Social Security are based on the first $118,500. Taxable earnings for Medicare are based on all earnings. Taxable earnings for federal and state unemployment are based on the first $7,000. The company does not pay for overtime hours.

Required

1. Complete the payroll register using a Social Security tax rate of 6.2 percent and a Medicare tax rate of 1.45 percent. Concerning Other Deductions, AR refers to Accounts Receivable and UW refers to United Way. Begin payroll checks in the payroll register with No. 2914.
2. Prepare the general journal entry to record the payroll. The firm's general ledger contains a Salary Expense account and a Salaries Payable account.
3. Prepare the general journal entry to pay the payroll. Assume that funds for this payroll have been transferred to Cash—Payroll Bank Account and that this entry has been made.

Check Figure
Net amount, $9,934.14

LO 2, 3

Problem 7-5B Rick Davis, an employee of ABC Motors, worked 42 hours during the week of September 12 through 18. His rate of pay is $30 per hour, and he receives time-a-half for work in excess of 40 hours per week. Rick is married and claims zero allowances on his W-4 form. Rick's YTD earnings before this pay period are $47,250, and his wages are subject to the following deductions:

a. Federal income tax (use the table in Figure 3, pages 293–294).
b. Social Security tax at 6.2 percent, with a wage limit of $118,500.
c. Medicare tax at 1.45 percent.
d. Medical insurance premium (after tax), $75.
e. United Way contribution, $25.

Required

Compute Rick's regular pay, overtime pay, gross pay, and net pay.

Check Figure
Net pay, $939.31

Accounting with qb QuickBooks® Online

Go to the QuickBooks Online Chapter 7 Appendix located on the Cengage Learning companion site at Cengage.com. Review the *Accounting with QuickBooks Online* (step-by-step guide to using QuickBooks Online). *Accounting with QuickBooks Online*, Chapter 7 will introduce you to modifying a previously recorded journal entry to reflect employee payroll deductions and help you understand the effects employee payroll deductions have on the financial statements.

Activities

Why Does It Matter?

RECREATIONAL EQUIPMENT INC. (REI), Sumner, Washington

Attracting and retaining the best employees is crucial to operating a business. Employees will join a company based on opportunities for advancement, training, company culture, and salary and benefits provided.

One business that is often listed in *Fortune* magazine's "100 Best Companies to Work For" is Recreational Equipment Inc. (REI). REI is committed to inspiring, educating, and outfitting its customers for a lifetime of outdoor adventure. REI offers competitive salaries as well as benefits, including paid sabbaticals, an onsite fitness center, healthcare coverage, telecommuting, and a compressed workweek.

The accounting department at REI is responsible for determining salaries/wages and benefits for employees, calculating payroll deductions for taxes and other expenses, and ensuring that company payrolls are processed in a timely and accurate manner. In this chapter, you learned how companies such as REI complete the payroll records for their employees. Why do you think timely and accurate payroll information is so important to a company such as REI?

What Would You Say?

Southern Company pays its employees weekly by issuing checks on its regular bank account. The owner thinks it would be too much trouble to have a second checking account. Explain to the owner why having this account might be worth the additional effort.

What Would You Do?

An employee who is married and has three children submits a W-4 form to his employer. He checks the box that says "Single" and writes zero in the "Deductions Claimed" box. Is this action ethical, unethical, or illegal? Explain your reasoning.

CHAPTER ACTIVITIES

Employer Taxes, Payments, and Reports

Learning Objectives

After you have completed this chapter, you will be able to do the following:

1 Calculate the amount of payroll tax expense and journalize the entry.

2 Journalize the entry for the deposit of employees' federal income taxes withheld and FICA taxes (both employees' withheld and employer's share) and prepare the deposit.

3 Journalize the entries for the payment of employer's state and federal unemployment taxes.

4 Journalize the entry for the deposit of employees' state income taxes withheld.

5 Complete Employer's Quarterly Federal Tax Return, Form 941.

6 Prepare W-2 and W-3 forms and Form 940.

7 Calculate the premium for workers' compensation insurance and prepare the entry for payment in advance.

8 Determine the amount of the end-of-the-year adjustments for (a) workers' compensation insurance and (b) accrued salaries and wages and record the adjustments.

To: Amy Roberts, CPA
Subject: Employee Taxes, Payments, and Reporting

Hi Amy,

Thanks for helping me set up the payroll system for my company. I started paying my employees a few weeks ago and have been recording the payroll expenses and liabilities as you instructed. I think it is almost time to make my first payroll tax deposit(s), and I would like to review this process with you. I also am curious about how to record workers' compensation premium payments and how to handle the end-of-the-year adjustments for workers' compensation insurance and accrued salaries and wages. If you can help me better understand the payroll process, I would appreciate it. I know how important it is to handle the payroll for my company properly. I want to make sure that I'm in compliance with all tax laws, that I make deposits on time, and that I file my reports correctly when they are due. I certainly don't want to incur any penalties.

Thanks,

Janie

To: Janie Conner
Subject: RE: Employee Taxes, Payments, and Reporting

Hi Janie,

I'm glad you have a better understanding of how to handle paying your employees and recording the payroll liability. You are correct—it's time to start thinking about scheduling your payroll tax deposits and preparing for filing the appropriate reports. I would be happy to review the employer payroll taxes with you and help you set up a tax calendar to make sure you are making your deposits and filing your reports on time. Let's plan on meeting Friday to discuss the following:

_____ 1. How to calculate and record the employer payroll tax expense
_____ 2. How to prepare and record the FICA and Federal Employee Withholding payroll tax deposit
_____ 3. How to calculate and record the FUTA and SUTA liabilities and payments
_____ 4. How to journalize the payment of state income taxes withheld

Give me a call later today so that we can set up a time for our meeting.

Amy

We have talked about how to compute and record such payroll data as gross pay, employees' income tax withheld, employees' FICA taxes withheld, and various deductions requested by employees. Now we will learn how to record the transactions to pay these withholding liabilities and the taxes levied on the employer.

8-1 EMPLOYER'S PAYROLL TAXES

Everyone must have a Social Security number or an Individual Taxpayer Identification Number (ITIN), a vital part of federal income tax returns. An employer's counterpart to the Social Security number is the **Employer Identification Number (EIN)**, which is assigned by the Internal Revenue Service. Employers of one or more persons are required to have such a number, and it must be listed on all reports and payments of employees' federal income tax withholding and FICA taxes.

An employer's payroll taxes are based on the gross wages paid to employees. Payroll taxes—like property taxes—are an expense of doing business. Green Sales Company records these taxes in the **Payroll Tax Expense** account and debits the account for the company's portion of FICA taxes and for state and federal unemployment taxes. In T account form, Payroll Tax Expense for Green Sales Company would look like this:

Payroll Tax Expense

+	−
FICA taxes (employer's portion)	Closed at the end of the year
State unemployment tax	along with all other expense
Federal unemployment tax	accounts

As you can see, **FICA taxes (employer's share of Social Security and Medicare taxes), state unemployment tax, and federal unemployment tax are included under the Payroll Tax Expense heading.** In most states, the unemployment taxes are levied on the employer only.

1 Calculate the amount of payroll tax expense and journalize the entry

Learning Objective

8-1a Employer's Portion of FICA Taxes

FICA taxes (the combined Social Security and Medicare taxes) are imposed equally on both the employer and employees. The employer's share is determined the same way as the employee's by multiplying the employer's tax rates [6.2 percent (0.062) for Social Security and 1.45 percent (0.0145) for Medicare] by the taxable earnings (up to a maximum wage limit of $118,500 for Social Security and all earnings for Medicare).

The accountant obtains the Social Security and Medicare taxable earnings amounts from the payroll register. Figure 1 shows the Taxable Earnings columns taken from the payroll register for Green Sales Company as prepared in the previous chapter for the week ended October 11.

Figure 1

Partial payroll register for Green Sales Company

Amount of employees' earnings for the period that has not, as of yet, been taxed as part of the $7,000 maximum liability

Amount of employees' earnings that are less than $118,500 per employee for the year

Amount of all employees' earnings

	A	B	F	G	H	I	J
1						(7) TAXABLE EARNINGS	
2				ENDING			
3		TOTAL		CUMULATIVE		SOCIAL	
4	NAME	HOURS	TOTAL	EARNINGS	UNEMPLOYMENT	SECURITY	MEDICARE
5	Anderson, Mark	46	1,124.58	46,084.58	0.00	1,124.58	1,124.58
6	Bodell, Anna	45	744.20	6,731.20	744.20	744.20	744.20
7	Dorn, David	49	916.00	7,702.00	214.00	916.00	916.00
8	Fields, Sarah	40	1,084.50	39,546.50	0.00	1,084.50	1,084.50
9	Graham, Jason	40	1,798.45	70,398.45	0.00	1,798.45	1,798.45
10	Lee, Jeremy	40	1,895.58	70,395.58	0.00	1,895.58	1,895.58
11	Mankowitz, Hanna	55	1,968.75	39,818.75	0.00	1,968.75	1,968.75
12	Olsen, Barbara	40	1,487.20	47,307.20	0.00	1,487.20	1,487.20
13	Parker, William	44	1,776.28	48,206.28	0.00	1,776.28	1,776.28
14	Raman, Soma	45	1,662.50	56,529.50	0.00	1,662.50	1,662.50
15	Tabor, Annette	40	1,168.83	43,908.83	0.00	1,168.83	1,168.83
16	Wallace, Grace	40	3,010.35	118,610.35	0.00	2,900.00	3,010.35
17			18,637.22	595,239.22	958.20	18,526.87	18,637.22
18		(1)	(5)	(6)	(7A)	(7B)	(7C)
19							

Employer's state unemployment tax
$958.20 × 0.054 = **$51.74**
(7A)

Employer's federal unemployment tax
$958.20 × 0.006 = **$5.75**
(7A)

Employer's Social Security tax
$18,526.87 × 0.062 = **$1,148.67**
(7B)

Employer's Medicare tax
$18,637.22 × 0.0145 = **$270.24**
(7C)

Combined Employer's FICA taxes
(Social Security $1,148.67 + Medicare $270.24) = **$1,418.91**

Employees' Social Security tax
$18,526.87 × 0.062 = **$1,148.67**
(7B)

Employees' Medicare tax
$18,637.22 × 0.0145 = **$270.24**
(7C)

Combined Employees' FICA taxes
(Social Security $1,148.67 + Medicare $270.24) = **$1,418.91**

Before we look at the journal entry to record the employer's share of FICA taxes, let's look at the entry in T account form.

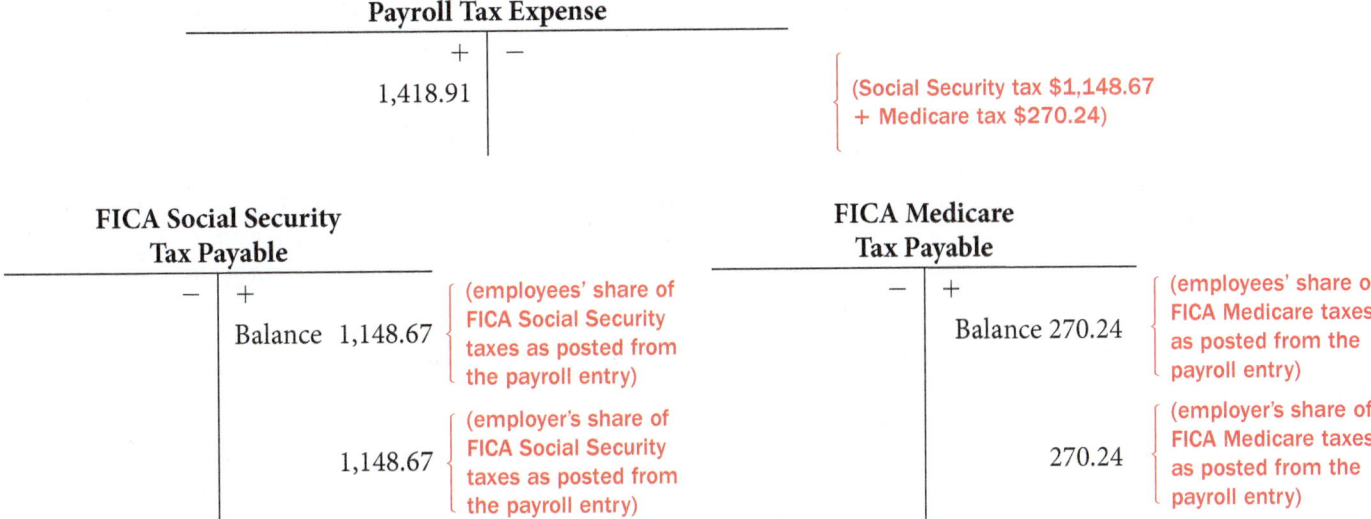

Note the FICA Social Security Tax Payable account and the FICA Medicare Tax Payable account are often used for both the tax liability of the employer and the amounts withheld from the employees. This is logical because both FICA taxes are paid at the same time and to the same place. There may be a slight difference between the employer's and the employees' share of FICA Medicare tax because of the rounding process. For the employees' FICA taxes, the accountant uses the total of the employees' Social Security and Medicare tax deductions. For the employer's share of FICA taxes, the accountant multiplies the total taxable earnings for all employees (Social Security and Medicare) by the employer's tax rates.

8-1b Employer's State Unemployment Tax

The proceeds of the **state unemployment tax (SUTA)**, which most states levy only on the employer, are used to pay subsistence benefits to unemployed workers. The rate of the state unemployment tax varies considerably among the states. Assume that Green Sales Company is subject to a rate of 5.4 percent (0.054) on the first $7,000 of each employee's earnings (the same base amount used for the federal unemployment tax). Looking at the payroll register (Figure 1), $958.20 of earnings are subject to the state unemployment tax. The following T accounts show how the state unemployment tax is calculated and posted.

Payroll Tax Expense		State Unemployment Tax Payable	
+	−	−	+
(958.20 × 0.054) 51.74			(958.20 × 0.054) 51.74

8-1c Employer's Federal Unemployment Tax

The federal unemployment tax (FUTA) is paid only by the employer. From time to time, Congress may change the rate. Let's assume a rate of 0.6 percent (0.006) on the first $7,000 earned by each employee during the calendar year. For the weekly payroll period, Green Sales Company shows a tax liability of $5.75 ($958.20 of unemployment taxable earnings, taken from the payroll register, multiplied by 0.006, the tax rate). The T account is as follows:

Payroll Tax Expense		Federal Unemployment Tax Payable	
+	−	−	+
(958.20 × 0.006) 5.75			(958.20 × 0.006) 5.75

Now let's combine figures for the employer's three payroll taxes, which were previously presented separately, into the following entry. Assume that Green Sales Company pays its employees weekly, so it also makes its Payroll Tax Expense entry weekly.

Date		Description	Post. Ref.	Debit	Credit
20--					
Oct.	11	Payroll Tax Expense		1 4 7 6 40	
		FICA Social Security Tax Payable			1 1 4 8 67
		FICA Medicare Tax Payable			2 7 0 24
		State Unemployment Tax Payable			5 1 74
		Federal Unemployment Tax Payable			5 75
		To record employer's share of FICA			
		taxes and employer's state and federal			
		unemployment taxes.			

8-1d Journal Entries for Recording Payroll

At this point, let's restate in general journal form the entries that have already been recorded. The sequence of steps for recording the payroll entries is as follows:

STEP 1. Record the payroll for the present period in the payroll register.

STEP 2. Based on the payroll register, record the payroll entry in the journal.

STEP 3. Based on the Taxable Earnings columns of the payroll register, record Payroll Tax Expense in the journal.

STEP 4. Record a journal entry to pay the employees.

Once the payroll for the present period is recorded in the payroll register (see Chapter 7), the entry to record the payroll, which was also presented in Chapter 7, is journalized.

Date		Description	Post. Ref.	Debit	Credit
20--					
Oct.	11	Sales Wages Expense		11 1 5 9 59	
		Office Wages Expense		7 4 7 7 63	
		Employees' Federal Income Tax Payable			2 3 4 4 47
		FICA Social Security Tax Payable			1 1 4 8 67
		FICA Medicare Tax Payable			2 7 0 24
		Employees' State Income Tax Payable			4 6 9 49
		Employees' United Way Payable			1 9 5 00
		Accounts Receivable			5 0 00
		Wages Payable			14 1 5 9 35
		Payroll register for the week ended			
		October 11, 20--.			

Next, the entry to record the employer's payroll taxes is journalized.

Date		Description	Post. Ref.	Debit					Credit				
20--													
Oct.	11	Payroll Tax Expense		1	4	7	6	40					
		FICA Social Security Tax Payable							1	1	4	8	67
		FICA Medicare Tax Payable								2	7	0	24
		State Unemployment Tax Payable									5	1	74
		Federal Unemployment Tax Payable										5	75
		To record employer's share of FICA											
		taxes and employer's state and											
		federal unemployment taxes.											

Finally, the entry to pay the employees is journalized. Green Sales Company issues one check payable to a payroll bank account. To pay its employees, it will draw separate payroll checks on this payroll account. (The entry to transfer cash to the payroll bank account is not shown here.)

Date		Description	Post. Ref.	Debit					Credit				
20--													
Oct.	12	Wages Payable		14	1	5	9	35					
		Cash—Payroll Bank Account							14	1	5	9	35
		Paid wages for week											
		ended October 11, 20--.											

As stated previously, in the first payroll entry, small employers will credit Cash directly instead of Wages Payable. These employers issue separate checks out of their regular bank accounts for each employee.

Next, we describe the entries for paying withholdings for employees' federal income tax and FICA taxes as well as the employer's share of FICA taxes. We also show the entries for paying the federal and state unemployment taxes and the withholdings for employees' state income taxes.

8-2 PAYMENTS OF FICA TAXES AND EMPLOYEES' FEDERAL INCOME TAX WITHHOLDING

After paying employees, the employer must make payments in the form of federal tax deposits. A deposit includes the combined total of three items:

- Employees' federal income taxes withheld
- Employees' FICA taxes (Social Security and Medicare) withheld
- Employer's share of FICA taxes (Social Security and Medicare)

The timing of when the deposits must be made depends on the amount of the payroll.

The IRS now requires all companies to make tax deposits electronically, using the **Electronic Federal Tax Payment System (EFTPS)**. Deposits can be submitted by

 Journalize the entry for the deposit of employees' federal income taxes withheld and FICA taxes (both employees' withheld and employer's share) and prepare the deposit.

Learning Objective

FYI

Substantial penalties are applied for late deposits of federal taxes.

FYI

We will show a Form 941 later in this chapter.

computer or telephone. EFTPS allows taxpayers to make payments 24 hours a day, 7 days a week and to schedule tax payments up to 120 days in advance of the due date. See IRS Publication 15 (Circular E), Employer's Tax Guide, at www.irs.gov for more information on deposit requirements.

Employers submit a return, Form 941, every **quarter** (three consecutive months). The due dates for filing this return are as follows:

Quarter	Ending Date of Quarter	Due Date for Forms 941/941e
January–February–March	March 31	April 30
April–May–June	June 30	July 31
July–August–September	September 30	October 31
October–November–December	December 31	January 31

8-2a Federal Tax Deposit

Let's go back to Green Sales Company, where tax payments were up-to-date. From the payroll of October 11, the following federal taxes are owed:

Employees' federal income taxes withheld	$2,344.47
Employees' FICA taxes withheld ($1,148.67 + $270.24)	1,418.91
Employer's share of FICA taxes ($1,148.67 + $270.24)	1,418.91
Total federal undeposited taxes	$5,182.29

Let's continue with the next payroll period, ended October 18. Assuming that the payroll information for the week is the same as it was for the week ended October 11, the two periods would be as follows:

	Oct. 11	Oct. 18	Total
Employees' federal income taxes withheld	$2,344.47	$2,344.47	$ 4,688.94
Employees' FICA taxes withheld	1,418.91	1,418.91	2,837.82
Employer's share of FICA taxes	1,418.91	1,418.91	2,837.82
Total federal undeposited taxes	$5,182.29	$5,182.29	$10,364.58

FYI

Because of rounding differences, the employee and employer amounts of FICA taxes may differ slightly. Line 7 of Form 941 accommodates this difference.

Green Sales Company, which deposits taxes semiweekly, will initiate an EFTPS tax deposit via computer or telephone. EFTPS tax deposits must be processed one calendar day in advance of the tax liability due date to be considered on time and to avoid penalties.

The following entry in general journal form records the deposit of two weeks' taxes:

Date		Description	Post. Ref.	Debit	Credit
20--					
Oct.	15	Employees' Federal Income Tax Payable		4 6 8 8 94	
		FICA Social Security Tax Payable		2 8 3 7 82	
		FICA Medicare Tax Payable		2 8 3 7 82	
		Cash			10 3 6 4 58
		Issued check for federal tax			
		deposit, Central National Bank.			

ACCOUNTING IN YOUR FUTURE

PAYROLL CLERK

Payroll clerks perform vital functions for businesses—ensuring that employees are paid on time and that their paychecks are accurate. If mistakes are made, such as monetary errors or incorrect amounts of vacation time, these clerks research and correct the records.

Payroll clerks also perform other clerical tasks:

- Screening time cards for calculating, coding, or other errors
- Computing pay by subtracting deductions, including federal and state taxes and contributions to retirement, insurance, and savings plans, from gross earnings
- Recording changes in employees' addresses
- Closing out files when workers retire, resign, or transfer
- Advising employees on income tax withholding and other mandatory deductions

For this reason, payroll clerks need to be aware of changes in tax and deduction laws so that they can implement them. Failure to do so can leave the organization exposed to penalties and other legal issues.

Payroll clerks are found in every industry. They train on the job, gaining skills by watching and learning from other workers. Those who have completed a certification program have an advantage in the job market.

As entering and recording payroll information becomes more simplified due to the increasing use of computers, the job itself is becoming more varied and complex. For example, companies now offer a greater variety of pension, 401(k), and other investment plans to their employees. These developments will contribute to job growth for payroll clerks in the years to come.

8-3a   Payments of State Unemployment Tax

As mentioned previously, states differ with regard to both the rate and the taxable base for unemployment insurance. In our example, we assume that the state tax is 5.4 percent (0.054) of the first $7,000 paid to each employee during the calendar year. **The state tax is usually paid quarterly and is due by the end of the month following the end of the quarter (the same as the due dates for Form 941).** The entry in general journal form made by Green Sales Company for the first quarter (covering January, February, and March) is on the next page. We assume that $70,325 was taxable for the quarter. The amount of the tax is $3,797.55 ($70,325 × 0.054).

 3   Journalize the entries for the payment of employer's state and federal unemployment taxes.

Learning Objective

Date		Description	Post. Ref.	Debit	Credit
20--					
Apr.	30	State Unemployment Tax Payable		3 7 9 7 55	
		Cash			3 7 9 7 55
		Issued check for payment of			
		state unemployment tax.			

The T accounts are as follows:

	Cash			State Unemployment Tax Payable	
+	−		−	+	
	Apr. 30 3,797.55		Apr. 30 3,797.55	Balance 3,797.55	

The balance in State Unemployment Tax Payable is the result of weekly entries recording the state unemployment portion of payroll tax expense and represents the balance on March 31. After the payment is made on April 30, the balance is shown as zero for illustrative purposes. However, throughout April, the company would be making weekly entries to record the tax liability and tax expense.

8-3b Payments of Federal Unemployment Tax

The FUTA tax is calculated quarterly, during the month following the end of each calendar quarter. **If the accumulated tax liability is greater than $500, the tax is deposited electronically,** similar to how deposits are handled for employees' federal income tax withholding and FICA taxes. The due date for this deposit is the last day of the month following the end of the quarter, the same as the due dates for the Employer's Quarterly Federal Tax Return and for state unemployment taxes.

Here is the entry in general journal form made by Green Sales Company for the first quarter. In our example, because the FUTA and state unemployment taxable earnings are the same (the first $7,000 for each employee), we assume that $70,325 was taxable for the quarter. The amount of the tax is $421.95 ($70,325 × 0.006).

Date		Description	Post. Ref.	Debit	Credit
20--					
Apr.	30	Federal Unemployment Tax Payable		4 2 1 95	
		Cash			4 2 1 95
		Issued check for payment of			
		federal unemployment tax.			

The T accounts are as follows:

Cash			Federal Unemployment Tax Payable		
+	–		–	+	
	Apr. 30 421.95		Apr. 30 421.95	Balance 421.95	

The balance in Federal Unemployment Tax Payable is the result of weekly entries recording the federal unemployment portion of payroll tax expense.

8-4 DEPOSITS OF EMPLOYEES' STATE INCOME TAX WITHHOLDING

Assume that the withholdings for employees' state income taxes are deposited on a quarterly basis, payable at the same time as state unemployment tax. Also, as of March 31, the credit balance of Employees' State Income Tax Payable is $1,674.10. The entry in general journal form to record the payment for the first quarter is as follows:

4 Journalize the entry for the deposit of employees' state income taxes withheld.

Learning Objective

Date		Description	Post. Ref.	Debit	Credit
20--					
Apr.	30	Employees' State Income Tax Payable		1 6 7 4 10	
		Cash			1 6 7 4 10
		Issued check for state income			
		tax deposit.			

The T accounts are as follows:

Cash			Employees' State Income Tax Payable		
+	–		–	+	
	Apr. 30 1,674.10		Apr. 30 1,674.10	Balance 1,674.10	

8-5 EMPLOYER'S QUARTERLY FEDERAL TAX RETURN (FORM 941)

If you are an employer, you must file a quarterly **Form 941**, Employer's Quarterly Federal Tax Return. The purpose of Form 941 is to report the tax liability for withholdings of employees' federal income tax and FICA taxes and the employer's share of FICA taxes. Total tax deposits made are also listed. As the title implies, the time period is three months. Remember that the due dates for the calendar year are first quarter, April 30; second quarter, July 31; third quarter, October 31; and fourth quarter, January 31.

A completed Form 941 for Green Sales Company is shown in Figure 2 (pages 332–333). There are five parts to this form. Figure 2 shows the information for Green Sales Company

5 Complete Employer's Quarterly Federal Tax Return, Form 941.

Learning Objective

To: **Amy Roberts, CPA**
Subject: **Employee Taxes, Payments, and Reporting**

Hi Amy,

I've calculated and recorded the payroll tax expenses for FICA, FUTA, and State Unemployment Taxes Payable. I've also made the appropriate tax payments and have journalized the state income taxes withheld. Is there anything else I'm missing?

Thanks,

Janie

To: **Janie Conner**
Subject: **RE: Employee Taxes, Payments, and Reporting**

Hi Janie,

Great! You are now ready to complete the payroll tax reports. We should also discuss workers' compensation insurance and adjusting for accrued salaries and wages. The following is a list of items for us to talk about when we get together:

_____ 1. Completing the 941 and 940 reports

_____ 2. Preparing W-2's and W-3's

_____ 3. Workers' Compensation Insurance

_____ 4. Adjusting for accrued salaries and wages

Can you meet on Wednesday at 1 pm?

Amy

for Parts 1 and 2. Part 3 is used when you close your business and stop paying wages—this will also stop the IRS from automatically sending 941 forms. Part 4 is for you to give the IRS permission—or not—to speak with your third-party designee (employee or paid tax preparer, for example). Part 5 is the signature, title, and date block for the paid preparer and/ or employer. You can find instructions or complete Form 941 online at www.irs.gov.

The top of the form contains basic information about the employer. Once an employer has secured an identification number and has filed the first return, the Internal Revenue Service automatically sends forms directly to the employer. These subsequent forms will have the employer's name, address, and identification number filled in.

Now let's look at a completed Employer's Quarterly Federal Tax Return (Form 941) on pages 332–333.

8-5a Questions Listed on Form 941 (Figure 2)

Tax forms can be somewhat intimidating. The best approach to completing a tax form is to have accurate and complete records and to read and complete the form line by line without skipping ahead. Green Sales Company's fourth-quarter form, shown in Figure 2, has been completed as follows. Note that the employees at Green Sales Company earn only wages. Had they also earned tips or other compensation, such as bonuses, those would have been included in the form.

Part 1:

Line 1 indicates the number of employees (12) who received wages.

Line 2 shows the total of those wages for the quarter ($197,622.00).

Line 3 shows the total income tax withheld from wages for the quarter ($35,572.00).

Line 4 is not checked because all wages during the quarter are subject to Medicare tax.

Lines 5a-d provide information that indicates how the total of the Social Security and Medicare taxes ($22,025.00 + $5,731.04 = $27,756.04) is calculated. Note that the multipliers represent the combined FICA employee and employer contributions [for Social Security, 0.062 (Employee FICA) + 0.062 (Employer FICA) = 0.124; for Medicare, $0.0145 \times 2 = 0.029$].

Line 5e Add column 2 on Form 941 for lines 5a-d. ($27,756.04).

Line 5f provides information about taxes due on unreported tips, which did not apply to Green Sales Company's employees.

Line 6 ($63,328.04) is the total of the income taxes withheld (line 3) plus the Social Security and Medicare taxes (line 5d), before adjustments.

Line 7 indicates tax adjustments for fraction of cents due to rounding.

Line 8 indicates adjustments for sick pay FICA taxes withheld from employees and deposited by a third-party payer.

Line 9 indicates adjustments for uncollected FICA taxes on tips and group-term life insurance.

Line 10 shows the total taxes after adjustments (lines 6–9 = $63,328.04).

Line 11 shows the total deposits ($63,328.04) made by Green Sales Company for this quarter and includes any overpayments from prior quarters. As indicated, the company has made deposits equaling the total due for this quarter.

Lines 12a and 12b disclose any premium assistance payments of COBRA for eligible individuals and the number of individuals who were provided COBRA premium assistance. COBRA provides certain former employees, retirees, spouses, former spouses, and dependent children the right to temporary continuation of health coverage at group rates when previous coverage is lost due to certain events. Qualifying events include activities such as reduction in the number of employment hours and voluntary or involuntary termination of employment for reasons other than gross misconduct. Green Sales Company did not have any COBRA payments this quarter.

Line 13 is the total of lines 11 and 12a ($63,328.04).

Lines 14 (underpayment) **and 15** (overpayment), which indicate the difference between lines 11 and 13, show that the company's balance for the quarter is zero.

Part 2:

Line 16 shows a checkmark in the third box because Green Sales Company was a semiweekly scheduled depositor for this quarter.

As stated earlier, the remaining parts of the 941 form require stating whether your business has closed (Part 3); giving permission to allow third-party inquires (Part 4); and providing signatures, titles of the preparer, and the date Form 941 is completed (Part 5). For instructions to assist you in filling out any IRS form, go to www.irs.gov and enter the name of the form or descriptive words into the search box.

Figure 2

Employer's Quarterly Federal Tax Return (Form 941) for Green Sales Company

Form **941 for 20--:** **Employer's QUARTERLY Federal Tax Return**   950113
(Rev. January 2013)   Department of the Treasury — Internal Revenue Service   OMB No. 1545-0029

Employer identification number (EIN)   9 1 – 7 2 2 8 1 6 2

Name *(not your trade name)*

Trade name *(if any)*   Green Sales Company

Address   610 First Avenue
Number   Street   Suite or room number

Bangor   ME   04401
City   State   ZIP code

Report for this Quarter of 20--
(Check one.)

☐ **1:** January, February, March

☐ **2:** April, May, June

☐ **3:** July, August, September

☒ **4:** October, November, December

Instructions and prior year forms are available at *www.irs.gov/form941*.

Read the separate instructions before you complete Form 941. Type or print within the boxes.

Part 1:   Answer these questions for this quarter.

1	Number of employees who received wages, tips, or other compensation for the pay period including: *Mar. 12* (Quarter 1), *June 12* (Quarter 2), *Sept. 12* (Quarter 3), or *Dec. 12* (Quarter 4) **1**	12
2	Wages, tips, and other compensation **2**	197,622.00.00
3	Income tax withheld from wages, tips, and other compensation **3**	35,572.00
4	If no wages, tips, and other compensation are subject to social security or Medicare tax ☐ Check and go to line 6.	

		Column 1		Column 2
5a	Taxable social security wages . .	177,621.00	× .124 =	22,025.00
5b	Taxable social security tips . . .	0.00	× .124 =	0.00
5c	Taxable Medicare wages & tips. .	197,622.00	× .029 =	5,731.00
5d	Taxable wages & tips subject to Additional Medicare Tax withholding	0.00	× .009 =	0.00

5e	Add Column 2 from lines 5a, 5b, 5c, and 5d **5e**	27,756.04
5f	Section 3121(q) Notice and Demand—Tax due on unreported tips (see instructions) . . **5f**	0.00
6	Total taxes before adjustments (add lines 3, 5e, and 5f) **6**	63,328.04
7	Current quarter's adjustment for fractions of cents **7**	0.00
8	Current quarter's adjustment for sick pay **8**	0.00
9	Current quarter's adjustments for tips and group-term life insurance **9**	0.00
10	Total taxes after adjustments. Combine lines 6 through 9 . . . . **10**	63,328.04
11	Total deposits for this quarter, including overpayment applied from a prior quarter and overpayment applied from Form 941-X or Form 944-X filed in the current quarter . . . **11**	63,328.04
12a	COBRA premium assistance payments (see instructions) **12a**	0.00
12b	Number of individuals provided COBRA premium assistance . . 0	
13	Add lines 11 and 12a **13**	63,328.04
14	Balance due. If line 10 is more than line 13, enter the difference and see instructions . . . **14**	0.00
15	Overpayment. If line 13 is more than line 10, enter the difference 0.00 Check one: ☐ Apply to next return. ☐ Send a refund.	

▶ **You MUST complete both pages of Form 941 and SIGN it.**   Next ▶

For Privacy Act and Paperwork Reduction Act Notice, see the back of the Payment Voucher.   Cat. No. 17001Z   Form **941** (Rev. 1-20--)

Figure 2 (continued)

Name (not your trade name)	Employer identification number (EIN)
Green Sales Company	91-7228162

950213

Part 2:   Tell us about your deposit schedule and tax liability for this quarter.

If you are unsure about whether you are a monthly schedule depositor or a semiweekly schedule depositor, see Pub. 15 (Circular E), section 11.

16   Check one: ☐   Line 10 on this return is less than $2,500 or line 10 on the return for the prior quarter was less than $2,500, and you did not incur a $100,000 next-day deposit obligation during the current quarter. If line 10 for the prior quarter was less than $2,500 but line 10 on this return is $100,000 or more, you must provide a record of your federal tax liability. If you are a monthly schedule depositor, complete the deposit schedule below; if you are a semiweekly schedule depositor, attach Schedule B (Form 941). Go to Part 3.

☐   **You were a monthly schedule depositor for the entire quarter.** Enter your tax liability for each month and total liability for the quarter, then go to Part 3.

Tax liability: Month 1 [.   ]

Month 2 [.   ]

Month 3 [.   ]

Total liability for quarter [.   ]   Total must equal line 10.

☒   **You were a semiweekly schedule depositor for any part of this quarter.** Complete Schedule B (Form 941), Report of Tax Liability for Semiweekly Schedule Depositors, and attach it to Form 941.

Part 3:   Tell us about your business. If a question does NOT apply to your business, leave it blank.

17   If your business has closed or you stopped paying wages . . . .   ☐ Check here, and

enter the final date you paid wages [/   /   ] .

18   If you are a seasonal employer and you do not have to file a return for every quarter of the year . .   ☐ Check here.

Part 4:   May we speak with your third-party designee?

Do you want to allow an employee, a paid tax preparer, or another person to discuss this return with the IRS? See the instructions for details.

☐ Yes.   Designee's name and phone number [   ] [   ]

Select a 5-digit Personal Identification Number (PIN) to use when talking to the IRS. ☐ ☐ ☐ ☐ ☐

☑ No.

Part 5:   Sign here. You MUST complete both pages of Form 941 and SIGN it.

Under penalties of perjury, I declare that I have examined this return, including accompanying schedules and statements, and to the best of my knowledge and belief, it is true, correct, and complete. Declaration of preparer (other than taxpayer) is based on all information of which preparer has any knowledge.

X   **Sign your name here**   [   ]   Print your name here [R. Jones]

Print your title here [Controller]

Date [/   /   ]   Best daytime phone [xxx-xxx-xxxx]

Paid Preparer Use Only   Check if you are self-employed . . . ☐

Preparer's name	[ ]	PTIN	[ ]
Preparer's signature	[ ]	Date	[/ /]
Firm's name (or yours if self-employed)	[ ]	EIN	[ ]
Address	[ ]	Phone	[ ]
City	[ ] State [ ]	ZIP code	[ ]

8-6 WAGE WITHHOLDING STATEMENTS FOR EMPLOYEES (FORM W-2)

After the end of a year (December 31) and by the following January 31, the employer must provide each employee a Wage and Tax Statement, known as **Form W-2**. This form contains information about the employee's earnings and tax deductions for the year. The source of the information used to complete Form W-2 is the employee's individual earnings record. The amounts used to complete Mark Anderson's W-2 form (in Figure 3) represent the amounts taken from his earnings record at the end of the calendar year, December 31.

Box 13 is used for miscellaneous items: statutory employees (workers who are independent contractors under the common-law rules but are treated by statute as employees, such as full-time life insurance sales agents and traveling salespeople), 401(k) plan contributions, or sick pay that is not included in income because the employee contributed to the sick pay plan. Box 14 may include the value of noncash fringe benefits, providing a vehicle for the employee, for example.

At least four copies of the W-2 form are required for each employee:

Copy A—Employer sends to the Social Security Administration.
Copy B—Employer gives to employee to be attached to the employee's individual federal income tax return.
Copy C—Employer gives to employee to be kept for his or her personal records.
Copy D—Employer keeps this copy as a record of payments made.

Figure 3
Wage and Tax Statement
(Form W-2) for Mark Anderson

a Employee's social security number 543-24-1680	OMB No. 1545-0008	Safe, accurate, FAST! Use IRS e~file	Visit the IRS website at www.irs.gov/efile

b Employer identification number (EIN) 91-7228162	1 Wages, tips, other compensation 58,404.58	2 Federal income tax withheld 10,920.00
c Employer's name, address, and ZIP code Green Sales Company 610 First Avenue Bangor, Maine 04401	3 Social security wages 58,404.58	4 Social security tax withheld 3,621.08
	5 Medicare wages and tips 58,404.58	6 Medicare tax withheld 846.87
	7 Social security tips 0	8 Allocated tips 0
d Control number	9	10 Dependent care benefits 0
e Employee's first name and initial Last name Suff.	11 Nonqualified plans 0	12a See instructions for box 12
Mark E. Anderson 1104 Rosewood Street Bangor, Maine 04401	13 Statutory employee ☐ Retirement plan ☐ Third-party sick pay ☐	12b
	14 Other 0	12c
		12d
f Employee's address and ZIP code		

15 State ME	Employer's state ID number 464-729	16 State wages, tips, etc. 58,404.58	17 State income tax 2,184.00	18 Local wages, tips, etc. 0	19 Local income tax 0	20 Locality name

Form **W-2** Wage and Tax Statement   20--   Department of the Treasury—Internal Revenue Service

Copy B—To Be Filed With Employee's **FEDERAL** Tax Return.
This information is being furnished to the Internal Revenue Service.

If state and local income taxes are withheld, the employer prepares additional copies to be sent to the appropriate tax agencies.

8-6a Employer's Annual Federal Income Tax Reports (Form W-3)

Along with Copy A of the employees' W-2 forms, Green Sales Company sends **Form W-3**, Transmittal of Wage and Tax Statements, to the Social Security Administration. This form is due on February 28 following the end of the calendar year.

Form W-3 shows (for all employees) the total wages and tips, total federal income taxes withheld, total FICA Social Security and Medicare taxable wages, total FICA Social Security and Medicare taxes withheld, and other tax-related information. These amounts must be the same as the grand totals of the W-2 forms and the four quarterly 941 forms for the year. Green Sales Company's completed Form W-3 is presented in Figure 4.

A few boxes deserve an explanation. Box d, Establishment number, may be used for a company that has separate establishments, with each establishment filing W-2 and W-3 forms separately. Box h is used by a company that had more than one employer identification number (EIN) during the year.

To summarize, the employer must submit the following at the end of the calendar year: (1) Employer's Quarterly Federal Tax Return (Form 941, for the fourth quarter by

> **FYI**
>
> A copy of the W-2 is also sent (if applicable) to the state and/or local tax department, and a copy is given to the employee to attach to the state/local tax return.

Figure 4

Transmittal of Wage and Tax Statements (Form W-3) for Green Sales Company

January 31); (2) Wage and Tax Statements (Form W-2, for all employees by January 31); and (3) Transmittal of Wage and Tax Statements (Form W-3 by February 28).

8-6b Reports and Payments of Federal Unemployment Tax

As we stated previously, generally all employers are subject to the Federal Unemployment Tax Act. These employers must submit an Employer's Annual Federal Unemployment (FUTA) Tax Return, Form 940, no later than January 31 following the close of the calendar year. This deadline may be extended until February 10 if the employer has made deposits paying the FUTA tax liability in full. **Form 940** shows total wages paid to employees, total wages subject to federal unemployment tax, and other information.

Using Green Sales Company as an example, federal unemployment taxable earnings by quarter are as follows:

Federal Unemployment Tax	1st Quarter	2nd Quarter	3rd Quarter	4th Quarter	Cumulative Total
Taxable earnings	$85,325	$ 4,485	$ 2,816	$ 1,020	$93,646
Tax rate	× 0.006	× 0.006	× 0.006	× 0.006	× 0.006
Tax liability	$511.95	$ 26.91	$ 16.90	$ 6.12	$561.88

We now repeat the journal entry for the first quarter, in which $511.95 was deposited on April 30.

Date		Description	Post. Ref.	Debit	Credit
20--					
Apr.	30	Federal Unemployment Tax Payable		5 1 1 95	
		Cash			5 1 1 95
		Issued check for deposit of			
		federal unemployment tax.			

During the second and third quarters, many employees' total earnings passed the $7,000 limit of taxable earnings, and the firm's tax liability was reduced accordingly. Because Green Sales Company's total accumulated liability of $43.81 ($26.91 + $16.90) was less than $500, deposits covering those quarters were not made.

By the end of the fourth quarter, each of the 12 employees' earnings passed the $7,000 mark. The total accumulated liability for the second, third, and fourth quarters is $49.93 ($26.91 + $16.90 + $6.12). This amount will be paid by January 31, accompanied by the completed Employer's Annual Federal Unemployment (FUTA) Tax Return, Form 940.

The T account for Federal Unemployment Tax Payable follows. The credits to the account were part of the entries to record the federal unemployment tax portion of Payroll Tax Expense for each payroll period.

Federal Unemployment Tax Payable

	−	+	
Apr. 30 deposit	511.95	1st quarter (liability)	511.95
		2nd quarter (liability)	26.91
		3rd quarter (liability)	16.90
Jan. 31 deposit	49.93	4th quarter (liability)	6.12

8-6c Employer's Annual Federal Unemployment (FUTA) Tax Return (Form 940)

Figure 5 (pages 338–339) shows a completed Form 940 for Green Sales Company. This form has seven parts. (Keep in mind that all forms change from time to time. Go to www.irs.gov for updates and detailed instructions.)

Part 1:

Line 1a indicates the abbreviation for the state in which the business was required to pay taxes, while **line 1b** is for multi-state employers.

Line 2 is for businesses that paid wages in a state that is subject to credit reduction. A credit reduction state is a state that has not repaid money it borrowed from the federal government to pay unemployment benefits. Let's assume the U.S. Department of Labor announced that there are no credit reduction states for the current tax year. In that case, Green Sales Company skips this line.

Part 2:

Line 3 lists the total wages paid during the calendar year ($861,530.00).

Line 4 lists the amount of wages exempt from FUTA tax—this includes such items as agricultural labor, family employment, and the value of meals and lodging. It is assumed that Green Sales Company had no such wages. If it had, the appropriate box or boxes on lines 4a-e would need to be checked to show the types of payments exempt from FUTA tax.

Line 5 shows the exempt wages paid ($767,884.00)—wages paid to each employee over and above $7,000 for the calendar year.

Line 6 is the total exempt payments ($767,884.00).

Line 7 shows the total taxable FUTA wages ($93,646.00), which is computed by subtracting the total amount of exempt payments (line 6) from the total wages paid (line 3).

Line 8 indicates the total amount of FUTA tax due before adjustments ($93,646.00 × 0.006 = $561.88).

Part 3:

Lines 9 and 10 are to be completed if all or some of the FUTA wages paid were excluded from state unemployment tax. These lines do not apply to Green Sales Company, so they are left blank.

Line 11 is also left blank because the U.S. Department of Labor announced that there are no credit reduction states for the current tax year.

Part 4:

Line 12 indicates the amount of total FUTA tax after adjustments ($561.88), which is the sum of line 8 + lines 9–11.

Line 13 shows the amount of total FUTA tax that was deposited for the year ($421.95).

Figure 5

Employer's Annual Federal Unemployment (FUTA) Tax Return (Form 940) for Green Sales Company

Form **940 for 20--:** **Employer's Annual Federal Unemployment (FUTA) Tax Return**   850108

Department of the Treasury — Internal Revenue Service

OMB No. 1545-0028

(EIN)
Employer identification number   9 1 – 7 2 2 8 1 6 2

Name *(not your trade name)*

Trade name *(if any)*   **Green Sales Company**

Address   **610 First Avenue**

Number   Street   Suite or room number

Bangor   **ME**   **04401**

City   State   ZIP code

Type of Return
(Check all that apply.)

☐ **a.** Amended
☐ **b.** Successor employer
☐ **c.** No payments to employees in 20--
☐ **d.** Final: Business closed or stopped paying wages

Read the separate instructions before you fill out this form. Please type or print within the boxes.

Part 1: Tell us about your return. If any line does NOT apply, leave it blank.

1   If you were required to pay your state unemployment tax in ...

   1a One state only, write the state abbreviation . . . **1a** | **ME** |
   - OR -
   1b More than one state (You are a multi-state employer) . . . . **1b** ☐ Check here. Fill out Schedule A.

    Skip line 2 for 20-- and go to line 3.

2   If you paid wages in a state that is subject to CREDIT REDUCTION . . . . **2** ☐ Check here. Fill out Schedule A (Form 940), Part 2.

Part 2: Determine your FUTA tax before adjustments for 20--. If any line does NOT apply, leave it blank.

3   Total payments to all employees . . . . **3**   861,530 . 00

4   Payments exempt from FUTA tax . . . . **4**   0 . 00

   Check all that apply: **4a** ☐ Fringe benefits   **4c** ☐ Retirement/Pension   **4e** ☐ Other
              4b ☐ Group-term life insurance   **4d** ☐ Dependent care

5   Total of payments made to each employee in excess of $7,000 . . **5**   767,884 . 00

6   Subtotal (line 4 + line 5 = line 6) . . . . **6**   767,884 . 00

7   Total taxable FUTA wages (line 3 – line 6 = line 7) . . . . **7**   93,646 . 00

8   FUTA tax before adjustments (line 7 × .006 = line 8) . . . . **8**   561 . 88

Part 3: Determine your adjustments. If any line does NOT apply, leave it blank.

9   If ALL of the taxable FUTA wages you paid were excluded from state unemployment tax, multiply line 7 by .054 (line 7 × .054 = line 9). Then go to line 12 . . . . **9**   0 . 00

10   If SOME of the taxable FUTA wages you paid were excluded from state unemployment tax, OR you paid ANY state unemployment tax late (after the due date for filing Form 940), fill out the worksheet in the instructions. Enter the amount from line 7 of the worksheet onto line 10 . **10**   0 . 00

    Skip line 11 for 20-- and go to line 12.

11   If credit reduction applies, enter the amount from line 3 of Schedule A (Form 940) . . . . **11** .

Part 4: Determine your FUTA tax and balance due or overpayment for 20--. If any line does NOT apply, leave it blank.

12   Total FUTA tax after adjustments (lines 8 + 9 + 10 + 11 = line 12) . . . . **12**   561 . 88

13   FUTA tax deposited for the year, including any payment applied from a prior year . . . **13**   421 . 95

14   Balance due (If line 12 is more than line 13, enter the difference on line 14.)
   ● If line 14 is more than $500, you must deposit your tax.
   ● If line 14 is $500 or less, you may pay with this return. For more information on how to pay, see the separate instructions . . . . **14**   139 . 93

15   Overpayment (If line 13 is more than line 12, enter the difference on line 15 and check a box below.) . . . . **15** .

▶ You **MUST** fill out both pages of this form and **SIGN** it.

Check one: ☐ Apply to next return.
        ☐ Send a refund.

Next ➡

For Privacy Act and Paperwork Reduction Act Notice, see the back of Form 940-V, Payment Voucher.   Cat. No. 112340   Form **940** (20--)

Figure 5 (continued)

Part 5: Report your FUTA tax liability by quarter only if line 12 is more than $500. If not, go to Part 6.

16   Report the amount of your FUTA tax liability for each quarter; do NOT enter the amount you deposited. If you had no liability for a quarter, leave the line blank.

16a 1st quarter (January 1 – March 31)	16a	511.95
16b 2nd quarter (April 1 – June 30)	16b	26.91
16c 3rd quarter (July 1 – September 30)	16c	16.90
16d 4th quarter (October 1 – December 31)	16d	6.12

17   Total tax liability for the year (lines 16a + 16b + 16c + 16d = line 17)   17   561.88   Total must equal line 12.

Part 6: May we speak with your third-party designee?

Do you want to allow an employee, a paid tax preparer, or another person to discuss this return with the IRS? See the instructions for details.

☐ **Yes.**   Designee's name and phone number [ ]   ( ) –

Select a 5-digit Personal Identification Number (PIN) to use when talking to IRS   [ ][ ][ ][ ][ ]

☑ **No.**

Part 7: Sign here. You MUST fill out both pages of this form and SIGN it.

Under penalties of perjury, I declare that I have examined this return, including accompanying schedules and statements, and to the best of my knowledge and belief, it is true, correct, and complete, and that no part of any payment made to a state unemployment fund claimed as a credit was, or is to be, deducted from the payments made to employees. Declaration of preparer (other than taxpayer) is based on all information of which preparer has any knowledge.

X **Sign your name here**   *Eileen Green*

Print your name here   **Eileen Green**

Print your title here   **Owner**

Date   1 / 31 / 20--

Best daytime phone   (207) 555 – 7865

Line 14 is the difference between line 12 and line 13 ($561.88 − $421.95 = $139.93). This represents the balance due.

Line 15 is completed if FUTA tax deposited for the year (line 13) is more than the total FUTA tax after adjustments (line 12). This indicates an overpayment.

Part 5:

Lines 16a–d ask for the amount of FUTA tax liability for each quarter.

Line 17 discloses the total tax liability for the calendar year ($561.88). It should equal the amount given on line 12 and the total of lines 16a–d.

The remaining parts of the Form 940 require you to (1) indicate whether you grant permission for third-party inquiries, (2) provide a signature and title of the preparer, and (3) record the date the form is completed.

8-7 WORKERS' COMPENSATION INSURANCE

Most states require employers to provide **workers' compensation insurance** or industrial accident insurance for employees killed or injured on the job. Coverage is available to employers through private insurance companies, authorized by the state, or state-administered plans. The employer usually pays all of the premiums. The premium rate varies with the amount of risk the job entails and the company's claims history. For example, handling molten steel ingots is more dangerous than typing reports. Thus, it is important that employees be identified properly in terms of the insurance premium classifications. The rates are based as a percentage of payroll by job classification. For example, rates may be 0.15 percent on an office work payroll classification and 0.5 percent for sales work, yet industrial labor in heavy manufacturing may be 3.5 percent. These rates are typically expressed as $0.15 per $100 of the salaries or wages for office work, $0.50 per $100 for sales work, and $3.50 per $100 for industrial labor.

Generally, the employer pays a premium in advance based on the estimated payroll for the year. After the year ends, the employer knows the actual amount of the payroll and can calculate the exact premium. At that time, depending on the difference between the estimated and exact premiums, the employer pays an additional premium or gets a credit for having made an overpayment.

At Green Sales Company, there are two work classifications: office work and sales work. At the beginning of the year, the firm's accountant computed the estimated annual premium as follows:

Classification	Estimated Payroll	Rate per Hundred (Percent)	Estimated Premium
Office work	$182,000	0.15	($182,000 ÷ 100) × 0.15 = $ 273.00
Sales work	660,000	0.50	($660,000 ÷ 100) × 0.50 = 3,300.00
			Total estimated premium $3,573.00

The accountant made the following entry, shown in T accounts, when payment was disbursed.

Prepaid Insurance, Workers' Compensation				Cash	
+	−			+	−
Jan. 10 3,573.00					Jan. 10 3,573.00

8-8 END-OF-YEAR PAYROLL RELATED ADJUSTMENTS

8-8a End-of-Year Adjustments for Workers' Compensation

At the end of the year, the accountant calculated the exact premium as follows:

Classification	Actual Payroll	Rate per Hundred (Percent)	Exact Premium
Office work	$188,990	0.15	($188,990 ÷ 100) × 0.15 = $ 283.49
Sales work	672,540	0.50	($672,540 ÷ 100) × 0.50 = 3,362.70
			Total estimated premium $3,646.19

Therefore, the amount of the unpaid premium is

$3,646.19	Total exact premium
3,573.00	Less total estimated premium paid
$ 73.19	Additional premium owed

Now the accountant makes an adjusting entry, similar to the adjusting entry for expired insurance. This entry appears on the work sheet. The accountant also makes an additional adjusting entry for the extra premium owed. By T accounts, the entries are as follows:

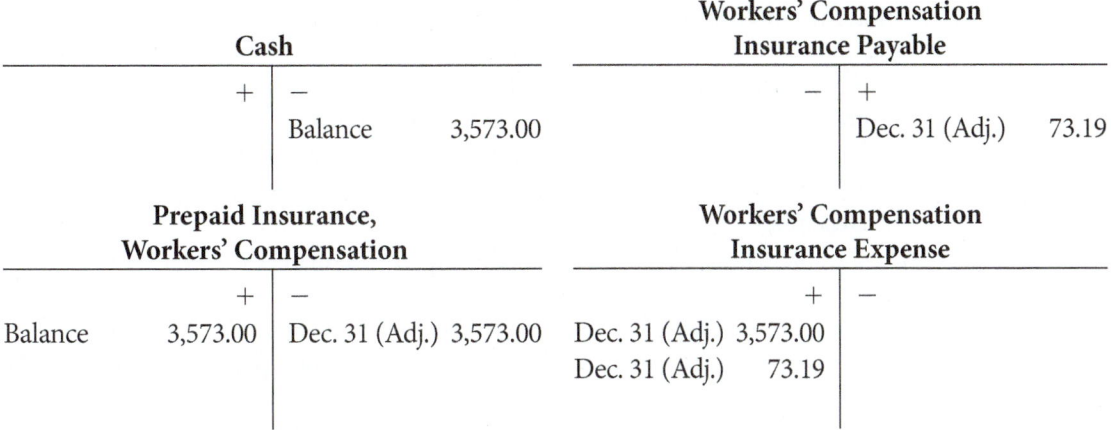

Cash				Workers' Compensation Insurance Payable	
+	−			−	+
	Balance 3,573.00				Dec. 31 (Adj.) 73.19

Prepaid Insurance, Workers' Compensation				Workers' Compensation Insurance Expense	
+	−			+	−
Balance 3,573.00	Dec. 31 (Adj.) 3,573.00		Dec. 31 (Adj.) 3,573.00		
			Dec. 31 (Adj.) 73.19		

Green Sales Company will pay $73.19, the amount of unpaid premium, in January, together with the estimated premium for the next year.

8-8b Adjusting for Accrued Salaries and Wages

Now let's assume that Green Sales Company had $2,400 of wages accrue for the time between the last payday and the end of the year. An adjusting entry is necessary.

Date		Description	Post. Ref.	Debit	Credit
20--		Adjusting Entry			
Dec.	31	Wages Expense		2 4 0 0 00	
		Wages Payable			2 4 0 0 00

8b Determine the amount of the end-of-the year adjustment for accrued salaries and wages and record the adjustment.

Learning Objective

For the accrual adjustment, gross salary and wages are recorded, not the net salary and wages. When the accrued salary and wages are paid, the amounts withheld for federal and state taxes, FICA taxes, and other deductions are recorded.

8-8c Adjusting Entry for Accrual of Payroll Taxes

As you have seen, the following taxes come under the umbrella of the Payroll Tax Expense account: the employer's share of the FICA taxes, the state unemployment tax, and the federal unemployment tax. The employer becomes liable for these taxes only when the employees are actually paid, rather than at the time the liability to the employees is incurred. So there is no adjusting entry for Payroll Tax Expense until the wages are actually paid.

8-8d Tax Calendar

Now let's put it all together. To keep up with the task of paying and reporting the various taxes, the accountant compiles a chronological list of the due dates. We are including only the payroll taxes here, but any kind of taxes, such as sales taxes and property taxes, should also be listed. When you think about the penalties for missing tax deposit or filing due dates, this chronological list seems to be well worth the effort. We assume for this purpose that the employer is a monthly depositor for the federal tax deposit.

Jan.	10	Pay estimated annual premium for workers' compensation insurance. (This is an approximate date, as it varies among the states.)
	15	Make federal tax deposit for employees' income tax withholding, employees' FICA taxes withheld, and employer's FICA taxes for wages paid during December.
	31	Complete Employer's Quarterly Federal Tax Return, Form 941, for the fourth quarter.
	31	Issue Copies B and C of Wage and Tax Statement, Form W-2, to employees.
	31	Pay state unemployment tax liability for the previous quarter and submit state return, employer's tax report.
	31	Pay any remaining federal unemployment tax liability for the previous year and submit Form 940, Employer's Annual Federal Unemployment (FUTA) Tax Return.
	31	Make state deposit for employees' state income tax withholding and submit any required state payroll reports. (Timing and required reports may differ from state to state.)
Feb.	15	Make federal tax deposit for employees' income tax withholding, employees' FICA taxes withholding, and employer's FICA taxes for wages paid during January.
	28	Complete Transmittal of Wage and Tax Statements, Form W-3, and attach Copy A of W-2 forms for employees.
Mar.	15	Make federal tax deposit for employees' income tax withholding, employees' FICA taxes withholding, and employer's FICA taxes for wages paid during February.
Apr.	15	Make federal tax deposit for employees' income tax withholding, employees' FICA taxes withholding, and employer's FICA taxes for wages paid during March.
	30	Pay state unemployment tax liability for the previous quarter and submit state return, employer's tax report.
	30	Complete Employer's Quarterly Federal Tax Return, Form 941, for the first quarter.
	30	Make federal tax deposit for federal unemployment tax liability if it exceeds $500.
	30	Make state deposit for employees' state income tax withholding.

Dan Lee/Shutterstock.com

In the Real World

It is important to report and remit payroll taxes in a timely manner. Failure to do so can result in jail time in addition to financial restitution. A Wisconsin business owner, Jeffrey Grams, learned this the hard way. In 2014, he was sentenced to 15 months in prison, was given three years' supervised release, and was ordered to pay restitution to the IRS in excess of $265,000. According to IRS documents, Mr. Grams failed to deposit and report payroll taxes withheld from employees as well as the required employer's portion for the same time period.

Source: www.irs.gov/compliance/enforcement

8-8e Payroll Fraud

Payroll fraud can be a huge problem for a business in terms of monies lost and time and frustration dealing with the problem. Payroll fraud can be categorized into three general areas:

1. *Ghost employee fraud*—Someone is recorded in the payroll system who does not work for the business.
2. *False wage claim fraud*—Extra hours or other relevant factors are added to wage information to increase the amount of pay.
3. *False expense reimbursement fraud*—Improper claims are made for the reimbursement of business expenses.

Internal controls should be in place to prevent and detect payroll fraud. Some of those controls include the following:

- Require mandatory vacations for those with payroll responsibilities, having other employees perform this function in their absence.
- Use cash payments or checks minimally and increase the use of direct deposit of payroll checks.
- Have employees physically sign and show proper identification to receive their paychecks.
- Conduct periodic unannounced audits to ensure that all employees on the payroll actually work for the company.
- Cross-reference the payroll roster for duplicate addresses or Social Security numbers.
- Conduct a thorough pre-employment reference check for all payroll personnel.
- Compare payroll expense per the payroll register to the actual amounts paid. Also compare amounts to payroll deposits made.
- Outsource payroll administration.

Chapter Review

Study and Practice

Learning Objective   Calculate the amount of payroll tax expense and journalize the entry.

Payroll tax expense consists of the employer's matching portion of FICA taxes plus the **state unemployment tax (SUTA)** and the **federal unemployment tax (FUTA)**. *FICA* taxes consist of Social Security and Medicare taxes. *Employer's* Social Security tax equals total Social Security taxable earnings multiplied by 0.062 (6.2 percent assumed rate) on the taxable earnings. For this text, the maximum taxable earnings is assumed to be $118,500. Total Medicare tax equals Medicare taxable earnings multiplied by 0.0145 (1.45 percent assumed rate). There is no maximum limit for Medicare—all earnings are taxable. *State unemployment tax* equals unemployment taxable earnings multiplied by 0.054 (5.4 percent assumed rate). *Federal unemployment tax* equals unemployment taxable earnings multiplied by 0.006 (0.6 percent assumed rate). Refer to the related journal entry on page 000.

 PRACTICE EXERCISE 1

Quality Roofing has the following payroll information for the week ended May 31:

Total payroll	$56,000
Taxable earnings subject to Social Security	45,000
Taxable earnings subject to unemployment tax	2,000

Using the preceding tax rates, prepare the journal entry to record the employer's payroll tax liability.

PRACTICE EXERCISE 1 • SOLUTION

Date		Description	Post. Ref.	Debit	Credit
20--					
May	31	Payroll Tax Expense		3 7 2 2 00	
		FICA Social Security Tax Payable			2 7 9 0 00
		FICA Medicare Tax Payable			8 1 2 00
		State Unemployment Tax Payable			1 0 8 00
		Federal Unemployment Tax Payable			1 2 00
		To record employer's share of FICA			
		taxes and employer's state and			
		federal unemployment taxes.			

Computations:

FICA taxes payable:	Social Security	$45,000 × 0.062 = $2,790.00
	Medicare	$56,000 × 0.0145 = 812.00
State unemployment tax payable:		$2,000 × 0.054 = $ 108.00
Federal unemployment tax payable:		$2,000 × 0.006 = $ 12.00

2 Journalize the entry for the deposit of employees' federal income taxes withheld and FICA taxes (both employees' withheld and employer's share) and prepare the deposit.

Learning Objective

Refer to the related journal entry at the bottom of page 326.

PRACTICE EXERCISE 2

For the week ended May 31, Quality Roofing withheld the following taxes from its employees:

Federal income taxes withheld	$12,000
FICA Social Security tax withheld	2,790
FICA Medicare tax withheld	812

Prepare the journal entry to record the tax deposit to People's Bank. Include the employees' and the employer's share (computed in Practice Exercise 1) of FICA taxes.

PRACTICE EXERCISE 2 • SOLUTION

Date		Description	Post. Ref.	Debit	Credit
20--					
May	31	Employees' Federal Income Tax Payable		12 0 0 0 00	
		FICA Social Security Tax Payable*		5 5 8 0 00	
		FICA Medicare Tax Payable**		1 6 2 4 00	
		Cash			19 2 0 4 00
		Issued check for federal tax			
		deposit, People's Bank.			

*FICA Social Security Tax Payable includes the employees' share of $2,790 plus the employer's share of $2,790 (see Practice Exercise 1), for a total of $5,580.

**FICA Medicare Tax Payable includes the employee's share of $812, plus the employer's share of $812 (see Practice Exercise 1), for a total of $1,624.

3 Journalize the entries for the payment of employer's state and federal unemployment taxes.

Learning Objective

State unemployment tax is paid on a quarterly basis. Payments are due by the end of the next month following the end of the calendar **quarter**. Refer to the related journal entry on the top of page 328.

If the amount of the accumulated federal unemployment tax liability exceeds $500 at the end of any quarter, the tax is due by the end of the next month following the end of the quarter. If the federal unemployment tax payable is less than $500 at the end of the year, it is due by January 31 of the next year. Refer to the related journal entry on the bottom of page 328.

PRACTICE EXERCISE 3

Assume Best Computers had $90,325 taxable earnings for the first quarter (covering January, February, and March). Assuming that the state unemployment tax rate is 5.4 percent (0.054) and the federal unemployment tax rate is 0.6 percent (0.006) of the first $7,000 paid to each employee during the calendar year, journalize the entries for the payment of Best Computers' state and federal unemployment taxes. Assume that no employee has surpassed the $7,000 limit.

PRACTICE EXERCISE 3 • SOLUTION

Date		Description	Post. Ref.	Debit	Credit
20--					
Apr.	30	State Unemployment Tax Payable		4 8 7 7 55	
		Cash			4 8 7 7 55
		Issued check for payment of			
		state unemployment tax.			
	30	Federal Unemployment Tax Payable		5 4 1 95	
		Cash			5 4 1 95
		Issued check for payment of			
		federal unemployment tax.			

Learning Objective   **4**   Journalize the entry for the deposit of employees' state income taxes withheld.

Employees' state income taxes withheld are paid on a quarterly basis or as required by the state. Payment may be due by the end of the next month following the end of the calendar quarter. Refer to the related journal entry on page 329.

 PRACTICE EXERCISE 4

For the quarter ended June 30, Quality Roofing has a credit balance of $28,000 for Employee's State Income Tax Payable. Assuming the withholdings are deposited on a quarterly basis, prepare the journal entry to record the payment.

PRACTICE EXERCISE 4 • SOLUTION

Date		Description	Post. Ref.	Debit	Credit
20--					
July	31	Employees' State Income Tax Payable		28 0 0 0 00	
		Cash			28 0 0 0 00
		Issued check for state income			
		tax deposit			

Learning Objective   **5**   Complete Employer's Quarterly Federal Tax Return, Form 941.

  PRACTICE EXERCISE 5

Based on the Form 941 shown on pages 332–333, what is the difference between Green Sales Company's taxable Social Security wages and taxable Medicare wages? How are the rates for each determined?

PRACTICE EXERCISE 5 • SOLUTION

For taxable Medicare wages, all wages are taxable; so the amount in Column 1 on line 5c of $197,622 is the same amount as on line 2, Wages, tips and other compensation. For taxable Social Security wages of $177,621, only the first $118,500 of wages is taxable; so in this case, some of the employees of Green Sales Company exceeded this limit. The rates of 0.124 and 0.029 represent both the employer's and employees' share of these taxes:

Social Security   6.2% + 6.2%   =   12.4%, or 0.124
Medicare   1.45% + 1.45% =   2.9%, or 0.029

 6 Prepare W-2 and W-3 forms and Form 940.

Form W-2 (Wage and Tax Statement) is illustrated on page 334. **Form W-3** (Transmittal of Wage and Tax Statements) is illustrated on page 335. **Form 940** (Employer's Annual Federal Unemployment (FUTA) Tax Return) is illustrated on pages 338–339.

 ## PRACTICE EXERCISE 6

What do Form W-2, Form W-3, and Form 940 have in common?

PRACTICE EXERCISE 6 • SOLUTION

Form W-2, Form W-3, and Form 940 all report the name, address, and Employer Identification Number of the company. (See Figures 3, 4, and 5 on pages 334–335, and 338–339, respectively.) The total wages should be the same in Box 1 on Form W-3 and on Line 3 on Form 940. All three forms report state information, in this case for Maine.

 7 Calculate the premium for workers' compensation insurance and prepare the entry for payment in advance.

Rates for **workers' compensation insurance** vary depending on the degree of physical risk involved in different occupations. The amount of the premium equals the predicted annual payroll multiplied by the premium rate. The entry is a debit to Prepaid Insurance, Workers' Compensation and a credit to Cash.

 ## PRACTICE EXERCISE 7

On January 15, Quality Roofing estimated the following payroll for the year:

Classification	Predicted Payroll	Rate (Percent)
Clerical/office work	$150,000	0.11
Project estimators	200,000	0.15
Roofer construction	670,000	2.20

Calculate the estimated premium and prepare the journal entry to record payment.

PRACTICE EXERCISE 7 • SOLUTION

Classification	Predicted Payroll	Rate per Hundred (Percent)	Estimated Premium
Clerical/office work	$150,000	0.11	($150,000 ÷ 100) × 0.11 = $ 165.00
Project estimators	200,000	0.15	($200,000 ÷ 100) × 0.15 = 300.00
Roofer construction	670,000	2.20	($670,000 ÷ 100) × 2.20 = 14,740.00
			Total estimated premium $15,205.00

Date			Description	Post. Ref.	Debit	Credit
20--						
Jan.	15		Prepaid Insurance, Workers'			
			Compensation		15 2 0 5 00	
			Cash			15 2 0 5 00
			To record payment of estimated			
			workers' compensation premium			
			for 20--.			

Learning Objective

8 Determine the amount of the end-of-the-year adjustments for (a) workers' compensation insurance and (b) accrued salaries and wages and record the adjustments.

When the total annual payroll is known, the exact cost of workers' compensation insurance can be determined by multiplying the total payroll by the premium rate. Two adjusting entries are required. The first adjusting entry records the expired insurance as a debit to Workers' Compensation Insurance Expense and a credit to Prepaid Insurance, Workers' Compensation. The second adjusting entry records the difference between the estimated and actual premiums. If the actual premium is greater than the premium that was paid in advance, the entry is a debit to Workers' Compensation Insurance Expense and a credit to Workers' Compensation Insurance Payable. The adjustment for accrued salaries and wages accounts for the additional amount of salaries or wages paid in the next payroll that are incurred in the current fiscal period—a debit to Wages (or Salary) Expense. The credit to Wages (or Salaries) Payable accounts for the additional amount of liability incurred in the current period that will be paid with the next payroll that occurs in the following fiscal period.

 PRACTICE EXERCISE 8

a. At the end of the year, Quality Roofing had the following payroll:

Classification	Actual Payroll	Rate (Percent)
Clerical/office work	$189,000	0.11
Project estimators	195,000	0.15
Roofer construction	695,000	2.20

Determine the amount of the end-of-the-year adjustment for workers' compensation insurance and prepare the journal entries to record the year-end adjustments for the insurance expired and the additional premium.

b. Assume that Quality Roofing had $2,000 of salaries accrue for the time between the last payday and the end of the year. Record the adjusting entry for the accrued salaries.

PRACTICE EXERCISE 8 • SOLUTION

a.

Classification	Actual Payroll	Rate per Hundred (Percent)	Exact Premium
Clerical/office work	$189,000	0.11	($189,000 ÷ 100) × 0.11 = $ 207.90
Project estimators	195,000	0.15	($195,000 ÷ 100) × 0.15 = 292.50
Roofer construction	695,000	2.20	($695,000 ÷ 100) × 2.20 = 15,290.00
			Total exact premium $15,790.40

The amount of the unpaid premium is

$15,790.40	Total exact premium
15,205.00	Less total estimated premium paid (from Practice Exercise 7)
$ 585.40	Additional premium owed

Date		Description	Post. Ref.	Debit	Credit
20--		Adjusting Entries			
Dec.	31	Workers' Compensation Insurance			
		Expense		15 2 0 5 00	
		Prepaid Insurance, Workers'			
		Compensation			15 2 0 5 00
	31	Workers' Compensation Insurance			
		Expense		5 8 5 40	
		Workers' Compensation			
		Insurance Payable			5 8 5 40

b.

Date		Description	Post. Ref.	Debit	Credit
20--		Adjusting Entry			
Dec.	31	Salary Expense		2 0 0 0 00	
		Salaries Payable			2 0 0 0 00

Glossary

Electronic Federal Tax Payment System (EFTPS) Federal tax deposits are made using this system. Payments can be made 24 hours a day, 7 days a week. Businesses can schedule payments up to 120 days in advance of the due date. To be considered on time, tax deposits must be scheduled at least one calendar day prior to the due date. (*p. 325*)

Employer Identification Number (EIN) The number assigned to each employer by the Internal Revenue Service for use in the submission of reports and payments for FICA taxes and federal income tax withheld. (*p. 321*)

Federal unemployment tax (FUTA) A tax levied only on the employer that is equal to 0.6 percent of the first $7,000 of total earnings paid to each employee during the calendar year. This tax is used to help administer unemployment funds. (*p. 323*)

Form 940 An annual report filed by employers showing total wages paid to employees, total wages subject to federal unemployment tax, total federal unemployment tax, and other information. Also called the Employer's Annual Federal Unemployment (FUTA) Tax Return. (*p. 336*)

Form 941 A quarterly report showing the tax liability for withholdings of employees' federal income tax and FICA taxes and the employer's share of FICA taxes. Total tax deposits made in the quarter are also listed on this Employer's Quarterly Federal Tax Return. (*p. 329*)

Form 941-V A payment voucher completed when making payments with the 941 report. (*p. 330*)

Form W-2 A form containing information about employee earnings and tax deductions for the year. Also called Wage and Tax Statement. (*p. 334*)

Form W-3 An annual report sent to the Social Security Administration listing the total wages and tips, total federal income tax withheld, total Social Security and Medicare taxable wages, total Social Security and Medicare tax withheld, and other information for all employees of a firm. Also called the Transmittal of Wage and Tax Statements. (*p. 335*)

Payroll Tax Expense A general expense account used for recording the employer's portion of the FICA taxes, the federal unemployment tax, and the state unemployment tax. (*p. 321*)

Quarter Three consecutive months. (*p. 326*)

State unemployment tax (SUTA) A tax levied against employers by most states based on a portion of employee earnings during the calendar year. Rates and earning limits vary among states. The proceeds are used to pay subsistence benefits to unemployed workers. (*p. 323*)

Workers' compensation insurance This insurance paid for by the employer provides benefits for employees injured or killed on the job. The rates vary according to the degree of risk inherent in the job. The plans may be sponsored by states or by private firms. The employer generally pays the premium in advance at the beginning of the year based on the estimated payroll. The rates are adjusted after the exact payroll is known. (*p. 339*)

Quiz Yourself

_____ 1. Which of the following is *not* considered a payroll tax expense?
   a. FICA Social Security
   b. Federal income tax withholding
   c. FICA Medicare
   d. FUTA
   e. SUTA

_____ 2. When is Form 941 submitted?
   a. Annually
   b. Semiannually
   c. Quarterly

   d. Monthly
   e. Semiweekly

_____ 3. The entry to record the payment of state unemployment tax is _____.
   a. Payroll Tax Expense DR; State Unemployment Tax Payable CR
   b. State Unemployment Tax Payable DR; Payroll Tax CR
   c. State Unemployment Tax Payable DR; Cash CR
   d. Cash DR; State Unemployment Tax Payable CR
   e. None of the above

_____ 4. The payment of employees' state income tax results in which of the following?
   a. DR Cash
   b. CR Employees' State Income Tax Payable
   c. CR Cash
   d. DR Employees' State Income Tax Expense
   e. None of the above

_____ 5. The federal unemployment tax (FUTA) is paid by the _____.
   a. Employee
   b. State government
   c. Local government
   d. Employer
   e. Employee and employer equally

_____ 6. The form also known as the Wage and Tax Statement is _____.
   a. Form 941
   b. Form 940
   c. the State Income Reporting Form
   d. Form W-3
   e. Form W-2

_____ 7. Workers' compensation insurance premiums are based on which of the following?
   a. Job risk
   b. Percentage of payroll
   c. Job classification
   d. Company's claim history
   e. All of the above

_____ 8. The adjusting entry for expired workers' compensation premium is _____.
   a. Workers' Compensation Insurance Payable DR; Cash CR
   b. Cash DR; Workers' Compensation Insurance Expense CR
   c. Workers' Compensation Insurance Expense DR; Prepaid Insurance CR
   d. Prepaid Insurance DR; Workers' Compensation Insurance Expense CR
   e. Workers' Compensation Insurance Expense DR; Cash CR

_____ 9. Which of the following is *not* an internal control for preventing or detecting payroll fraud?
   a. Having only one person responsible for the payroll function, due to confidentiality concerns
   b. Requiring mandatory vacations for payroll personnel
   c. Increasing the use of direct deposits
   d. Outsourcing payroll administration
   e. Conducting periodic unannounced audits

Answers:
1. b 2. c 3. c 4. c 5. d 6. e 7. e 8. c 9. a

Chapter Assignments

Discussion Questions

1. What taxes are employers accounting for that increase the debit to Payroll Tax Expense?
2. Describe the journal entry to:
   a. Record the payroll.
   b. Record the employer's payroll tax contributions.
   c. Pay the payroll.
   d. Pay the state and federal unemployment taxes.
   e. Pay the FICA (Social Security and Medicare) and Federal Income Tax withholding.
   f. Pay the state income tax withholding.
3. Explain the deposit requirement for federal unemployment tax.
4. What is the purpose of Form 941? How often is it prepared, and what are the due dates?

5. How many copies are made of a Form W-2? Who uses the copies of the W-2 form?
6. What is the purpose of Form 940? How often is it prepared, and what is the due date?
7. Generally, what is the time schedule for payment of workers' compensation insurance premiums?
8. Explain the advantage of establishing a tax calendar.
9. Explain how payroll fraud can be prevented.

Exercises

LO 1 ....

Practice Exercise 1

EXERCISE 8-1 Signature Company's partial payroll register for the week ended January 7 is as follows:

	A	C	F	G	H	I	J
1						TAXABLE EARNINGS	
2		BEGINNING		ENDING			
3		CUMULATIVE	TOTAL	CUMULATIVE		SOCIAL	
4	NAME	EARNINGS	EARNINGS	EARNINGS	UNEMPLOYMENT	SECURITY	MEDICARE
5	Barney, R. S.	——	1932.00	1932.00	1932.00	1932.00	1932.00
6	Fisk, M. C.	——	567.00	567.00	567.00	567.00	567.00
7	Hayes, W. O.	——	483.00	483.00	483.00	483.00	483.00
8	Lee, L. B.	——	679.00	679.00	679.00	679.00	679.00
9	Parks, S. J	——	578.00	578.00	578.00	578.00	578.00
10	Tempy, E. B.	——	546.00	546.00	546.00	546.00	546.00
11			4,785.00	4,785.00	4,785.00	4,785.00	4,785.00
12							

Assume that the payroll is subject to an employer's Social Security tax of 6.2 percent on the first $118,500 and a Medicare tax of 1.45 percent on all earnings. Also assume that the federal unemployment tax is 0.6 percent, and that the state unemployment tax is 5.4 percent of the first $7,000. Prepare the entry in general journal form to record the payroll tax expense.

LO 1 ....

Practice Exercise 1

EXERCISE 8-2 On January 14, at the end of the second week of the year, the totals of Castle Company's payroll register showed that its store employees' wages amounted to $33,482 and that its warehouse wages amounted to $13,560. Withholdings consisted of federal income taxes, $5,110, employer's Social Security taxes at the rate of 6.2 percent, and employees' Social Security taxes at a rate of 6.2 percent. Both the employer's and employees' Social Security taxes are based on the first $118,500, and no employee has reached the limit. Additional withholdings were Medicare taxes at the rate of 1.45 percent on all earnings and charitable contributions withheld, $845.

a. Calculate the amount of Social Security and Medicare taxes to be withheld and prepare the general journal entry to record the payroll. Round answers to two decimal places.
b. Prepare the general journal entry to record the employer's payroll taxes, assuming that the federal unemployment tax is 0.6 percent of the first $7,000, that the state unemployment tax is 5.4 percent of the same base, and that no employee has surpassed the $7,000 limit.

EXERCISE 8-3 Go Systems had the following payroll data for wages for the week ended February 5. The state income tax is assumed to be 20% of the federal income tax.

Practice Exercise 1

	F	G	H	I	J	K	L	M	N
1			**TAXABLE EARNINGS**			**DEDUCTIONS**			
2		**ENDING**						**SOCIAL**	
3	**TOTAL**	**CUMULATIVE**		**SOCIAL**		**FEDERAL**	**STATE**	**SECURITY**	**MEDICARE**
4	**EARNINGS**	**EARNINGS**	**UNEMPLOYMENT**	**SECURITY**	**MEDICARE**	**INCOME TAX**	**INCOME TAX**	**TAX**	**TAX**
5									
6	6,770.00	27,850.00	6,770.00	6,770.00	6,770.00	1,015.00	203.00	419.74	98.17
7									

a. Prepare the general journal entry to record the payroll.
b. Prepare the general journal entry to record the employer's payroll taxes. Assume rates of 0.6 percent for federal unemployment tax and 5.4 percent for state unemployment tax based on the first $7,000 for each employee. Also assume that no employee has earned more than $7,000. Round answers to two decimal places.

EXERCISE 8-4 The information on earnings and deductions for the pay period ended December 14 from King Company's payroll records is as follows:

Practice Exercise 1

Name	Gross Pay	Beginning Cumulative Earnings
Burgess, J. L.	$ 410	$ 6,750
Clayton, M. E.	785	40,200
Drugden, T. F.	860	38,500
Lui, L. W.	990	39,700
Sparks, C. R.	4,094	115,700
Stevers, D. H.	850	6,810

For each employee, the Social Security tax is 6.2 percent of the first $118,500, and the employer's Social Security tax is 6.2 percent on the same earnings limit. The Medicare tax is 1.45 percent on all earnings. The federal unemployment tax rate is 0.6 percent of the first $7,000 of earnings of each employee. The state unemployment tax rate is 5.4 percent of the same base. Determine the total taxable earnings for unemployment, Social Security, and Medicare. Prepare a general journal entry to record the employer's payroll taxes. Round answers to the two decimal places.

EXERCISE 8-5 Selected columns of Envirocon Company's payroll register for March are as follows. The employer's Social Security tax amount has already been calculated as $3,124.34. The employees' FICA Medicare tax rate is matched by the employer.

Practice Exercise 2

Payment Date	Employees' Federal Income Tax	Employees' Social Security Tax	Employees' Medicare Tax
March 7	1,125.00	686.43	108.75
14	1,250.00	764.22	121.08
21	1,385.00	845.22	133.91
28	1,357.00	828.47	131.25

(Continued)

Envirocon Company deposits taxes monthly. In general journal form, record the entry for the April 15 payment of FICA and federal income taxes for employees and employer.

LO 2, 3

Practice Exercises 2, 3

EXERCISE 8-6 On September 30, Cody Company's selected account balances are as follows:

Employees' Federal Income Tax Payable	$4,738.00
FICA Social Security Tax Payable (employer, $2,110.80; employee, $2,110.80)	4,221.60
FICA Medicare Tax Payable (employer, $493.66; employee, $493.66)	987.32
State Unemployment Tax Payable	2,200.00
Federal Unemployment Tax Payable	570.00

(Some employees have reached the limit.)

In general journal form, prepare the entries to record the following:

Oct. 15 Payment of liabilities for FICA taxes and the federal income tax.
    31 Payment of liability for state unemployment tax.
    31 Payment of liability for federal unemployment tax.

LO 2, 3

Practice Exercises 2, 3

EXERCISE 8-7 On September 30, Hilltop Company's selected payroll accounts are as follows:

FICA Social Security Tax Payable		FICA Medicare Tax Payable		Employees' Federal Income Tax Payable	
−	+	−	+	−	+
	Sept. 30 1,876.08 (employer)		Sept. 30 438.76 (employer)		Sept. 30 3,210.85
	Sept. 30 1,876.08 (employee)		Sept. 30 438.76 (employee)		
	Bal. 3,752.16		Bal. 877.52		

Federal Unemployment Tax Payable		State Unemployment Tax Payable	
−	+	−	+
	Sept. 30 575.32		Sept. 30 1,183.40

Prepare general journal entries to record the following:

Oct. 15 Payment of federal tax deposit of FICA taxes and the federal income tax.
    31 Payment of state unemployment tax.
    31 Payment of federal unemployment tax.

LO **7, 8**

Practice Exercises 7, 8

EXERCISE 8-8 Great Manufacturing Company received and paid a premium notice on January 2 for workers' compensation insurance stating the rates for the new year. Estimated employees' earnings for the year are as follows:

Classification	Estimated Wages and Salaries	Rate per Hundred (Percent)	Estimated Premium
Office clerical	$ 92,000	0.11	$ 101.20
Warehouse work	29,000	0.92	266.80
Manufacturing	264,000	2.20	5,808.00
			$6,176.00

At the end of the year, the exact figures for the payroll are as follows:

Classification	Actual Wages and Salaries	Rate per Hundred (Percent)	Exact Premium
Office clerical	$ 93,000	0.11	$ 102.30
Warehouse work	30,000	0.92	276.00
Manufacturing	267,000	2.20	5,874.00
			$6,252.30

a. Record the estimated premium entry for the payment on January 2, in general journal form.
b. Record the adjusting entries on December 31 for the insurance expired and for the additional premium.

Problem Set A

LO **1**

PROBLEM 8-1A Mooney Labs had the following payroll for the week ended February 28:

Salaries		Deductions	
Technicians' salaries	$6,955.00	Federal income tax withheld	$1,145.00
Office salaries	2,260.00	Social Security tax withheld	571.33
Total	$9,215.00	Medicare tax withheld	133.62
		Charity withheld	165.00
		Total	$2,014.95

(Continued)

Assumed tax rates are as follows:

a. FICA: Social Security, (employer) 6.2 percent (0.062) and (employee) 6.2 percent (0.062) on the first $118,500 for each employee, and Medicare, 1.45 percent (0.0145) on all earnings for each employee.

b. State unemployment tax, 5.4 percent (0.054) on the first $7,000 for each employee.

c. Federal unemployment tax, 0.6 percent (0.006) on the first $7,000 for each employee.

Check Figure
Payroll Tax Expense,
$1,034.35

Required

Record the following entries in general journal form:

1. The payroll entry as of February 28.
2. The entry to record the employer's payroll taxes as of February 28 assuming that the total payroll is subject to the FICA taxes (combined Social Security and Medicare) and that $5,490 is subject to unemployment taxes.
3. The payment to the employees on March 2. (Assume that the company has transferred cash to Cash—Payroll Bank Account for this payroll.)

LO 1 ••

PROBLEM 8-2A Complete Accounting Services has the following payroll information for the week ended December 7. State income tax is computed as 20 percent of federal income tax.

	A	C	F	K	L
1				DEDUCTIONS	
2		BEGINNING			
3		CUMULATIVE		FEDERAL	STATE
4	NAME	EARNINGS	TOTAL EARNINGS	INCOME TAX	INCOME TAX
5	Denato, T.	6,820.00	480.00	24.00	4.80
6	Herrera, M.	6,840.00	470.00	23.00	4.60
7	Joyner, J.	36,320.00	740.00	58.00	11.60
8	King, L.	26,200.00	540.00	30.00	6.00
9	Wilson, M.	116,060.00	2,720.00	456.78	91.36
10	Yee, N.	28,426.00	605.00	37.00	7.40
11					

Assumed tax rates are as follows:

a. FICA: Social Security, (employer) 6.2 percent (0.062) and (employee) 6.2 percent (0.062) on the first $118,500 for each employee, and Medicare, 1.45 percent (0.0145) on all earnings for each employee.

b. State unemployment tax, 5.4 percent (0.054) on the first $7,000 for each employee.

c. Federal unemployment tax, 0.6 percent (0.006) on the first $7,000 for each employee.

Check Figure
Payroll Tax Expense,
$428.00

Required

1. Complete the payroll register. Payroll checks begin with Ck. No. 5714 in the payroll register.
2. Prepare a general journal entry to record the payroll as of December 7. The company's general ledger contains a Salary Expense account and a Salaries Payable account.
3. Prepare a general journal entry to record the payroll taxes as of December 7.
4. Journalize the entry to pay the payroll on December 9. (Assume that the company has transferred cash to the Cash—Payroll Bank Account for this payroll.)

LO 1

PROBLEM 8-3A For the third quarter of the year, Johnson Company, 415 Circle Avenue, Chicago, Illinois 60652, received Form 941 from the Internal Revenue Service. The identification number of Johnson Company is 91-4213171. Its payroll for the quarter ended September 30 is as follows:

	A	F	I	J	K	M	N
1				TAXABLE EARNINGS		DEDUCTIONS	
2							
3		TOTAL	SOCIAL		FEDERAL	SOCIAL	MEDICARE
4	NAME	EARNINGS	SECURITY	MEDICARE	INCOME TAX	SECURITY TAX	TAX
5	Brown, D. D.	16,629.00	16,629.00	16,629.00	2,494.00	1,031.00	241.12
6	Carey, L. R.	18,528.00	18,528.00	18,528.00	2,780.00	1,148.74	268.66
7	Domzalski, T. P.	14,665.00	14,665.00	14,665.00	2,100.00	909.23	212.64
8	Grisson, R. O.	13,721.00	13,721.00	13,721.00	2,058.00	850.70	198.95
9	Tyler, J. L.	17,406.00	17,406.00	17,406.00	2,510.00	1,079.17	252.39
10	Valdez, K. R.	15,287.00	15,287.00	15,287.00	2,295.00	947.79	221.66
11		96,236.00	96,236.00	96,236.00	14,237.00	5,966.63	1,395.42
12							

The company has had six employees throughout the year. Assume that the FICA Social Security (employer) rate is 6.2 percent, the FICA Social Security (employee) rate is 6.2 percent on the first $118,500, and the Medicare tax is 1.45 percent of all earnings. The employer matches the employees' FICA Medicare taxes. There are no taxable tips, adjustments, backup withholding, or earned income credits. Johnson Company has submitted the following federal tax deposits and written the accompanying checks:

On August 15 for the July Payroll		On September 15 for the August Payroll		On October 15 for the September Payroll	
Employees' income tax withheld	$4,370.00	Employees' income tax withheld	$5,122.00	Employees' income tax withheld	$4,745.00
Employees' Social Security and Medicare tax withheld	2,259.76	Employees' Social Security and Medicare tax withheld	2,326.28	Employees' Social Security and Medicare tax withheld	2,776.01
Employer's Social Security and Medicare tax contributed	2,259.76	Employer's Social Security and Medicare tax contributed	2,326.28	Employer's Social Security and Medicare tax contributed	2,776.01
	$8,889.52		$9,774.56		$10,297.02

Required

Complete Part 1 of Form 941 for the third quarter for Johnson Company.

Check Figure
Total taxes, $28,961.10

LO 1, 2, 3

PROBLEM 8-4A Lynden Company has the following balances in its general ledger as of June 1 of this year:
a. FICA Social Security Tax Payable (employee and employer) is $1,393.50.
   FICA Medicare Tax Payable (employee and employer) is $325.90.
b. Employees' Federal Income Tax Payable (liability for May), $995.00.
c. Federal Unemployment Tax Payable (liability for April and May), $380.00.
d. State Unemployment Tax Payable (liability for April and May), $1,205.75.

(Continued)

The company completed the following transactions involving the payroll during June and July:

June 13 Issued check for $2,714.40, payable to Security Bank, for the monthly deposit of May FICA taxes and employees' federal income tax withheld.

30 Recorded the payroll entry in the general journal from the payroll register for June. The payroll register has the following column totals:

Sales salaries	$11,490.00	
Office salaries	5,147.00	
Total earnings		$16,637.00
Employees' federal income tax deductions	$ 1,725.00	
Employees' Social Security tax deductions	1,031.49	
Employees' Medicare tax deductions	241.24	
Total deductions		2,997.73
Net pay		$13,639.27

30 Recorded payroll taxes. FICA Social Security rates are 6.2 percent (employee) and 6.2 percent (employer). The employer matches the employee's FICA Medicare rate of 1.45 percent. State unemployment tax is 5.4 percent, and federal unemployment tax is 0.6 percent. At this time, all employees' earnings are taxable for FICA and unemployment taxes.

30 Issued check for $13,639.27 from Cash—Payroll Bank Account to pay salaries for the month.

July 14 Issued check for $4,270.46, payable to Security Bank, for the monthly deposit of June FICA taxes (employee and employer) and employees' federal income tax withheld.

31 Issued check for $2,104.15, payable to the State Tax Commission, for state unemployment tax for April, May, and June. The check was accompanied by the quarterly tax return.

31 Issued check for $479.82, payable to Security Bank, for the deposit of federal unemployment tax for April, May, and June.

Check Figure
Payroll Tax Expense,
$2,270.95

*If using Working Papers, record the transactions on pages 77–78 of the general journal.

 LO 6 ·

Problem 8-5A Jack's Lawn Service Company has the following information related to its current year payroll as of December 31:

a. Federal Unemployment Tax Payable as of December 31, $336.00
b. FUTA taxable earnings limit of $7,000, rate 0.6 percent (0.006)
c. First-quarter FUTA taxable liability, $504.00, paid April 30
d. Second-quarter FUTA taxable liability, $168.00 (liability under $500, no payment made)
e. Third-quarter FUTA taxable liability, $112.00 (total liability under $500, no payment made)
f. Fourth-quarter FUTA taxable liability, $56.00 (payment to be made January of the following year)
g. FUTA taxable earnings for the year, $140,000
h. Total Lawn Care Wages, $310,000
i. Jack's Lawn Service Company EIN, 75-1209347
j. No exempt FUTA payments
k. Address: 1515 W. Main Street, Rice, TX 75155

(Continued)

Required

Go to www.irs.gov to locate Form 940. Prepare Form 940 for the year. Then record the appropriate FUTA payment entry in the journal.

Check Figure
Line 14 Balance Due, 336.00

Problem Set B

LO 1

PROBLEM 8-1B Kovarik Company had the following payroll for the week ended March 21:

Salaries		Deductions	
Sales salaries	$7,620.00	Federal income tax withheld	$1,094.00
Office salaries	1,790.00	Social Security tax withheld	583.42
Total	$9,410.00	Medicare tax withheld	136.45
		Charity withheld	153.00
		Total	$1,966.87

Assumed tax rates are as follows:
a. FICA: Social Security, (employer) 6.2 percent (0.062) and (employee) 6.2 percent (0.062) on the first $118,500 for each employee, and Medicare, 1.45 percent (0.0145) on all earnings for each employee.
b. State unemployment tax, 5.4 percent (0.054) on the first $7,000 for each employee.
c. Federal unemployment tax, 0.6 percent (0.006) on the first $7,000 for each employee.

Required

Record the following entries in general journal form:
1. The payroll entry as of March 21.
2. The entry to record the employer's payroll taxes as of March 21, assuming that the total payroll is subject to the FICA taxes (combined Social Security and Medicare) and that $4,965 is subject to unemployment taxes.
3. The payment of the employees on March 23. (Assume that the company has transferred cash to Cash—Payroll Bank Account for this payroll.)

Check Figure
Payroll Tax Expense, $1,017.77

LO 1

PROBLEM 8-2B Kay's Agency has the following payroll information for the week ended December 14. State income tax is computed as 20 percent of federal income tax.

	A	C	F	K	L
1				DEDUCTIONS	
2		BEGINNING			
3		CUMULATIVE		FEDERAL	STATE
4	NAME	EARNINGS	TOTAL EARNINGS	INCOME TAX	INCOME TAX
5	Arivilo, R.	10,650.00	460.00	22.00	4.40
6	Baca, T.	38,820.00	970.00	92.00	18.40
7	Eubanks, E.	115,955.00	2,790.00	474.28	94.86
8	Ling, D.	6,750.00	385.00	14.00	2.80
9	Metcalf, S.	31,670.00	694.00	50.00	10.00
10	Quinn, D.	48,961.00	1040.00	103.00	20.60
11					

(Continued)

Assumed tax rates are as follows:

a.   FICA: Social Security, (employer) 6.2 percent (0.062) and (employee) 6.2 percent (0.062) on the first $118,500 for each employee, and Medicare, 1.45 percent (0.0145) on all earnings for each employee.

b.   State unemployment tax, 5.4 percent (0.054) on the first $7,000 for each employee.

c.   Federal unemployment tax, 0.6 percent (0.006) on the first $7,000 for each employee.

Check Figure
Payroll Tax Expense,
$484.75

Required

1.   Complete the payroll register. Payroll checks begin with Ck. No. 5923 in the payroll register.

2.   Prepare a general journal entry to record the payroll as of December 14. The company's general ledger contains a Salary Expense account and a Salaries Payable account.

3.   Prepare a general journal entry to record the payroll taxes as of December 14.

4.   Journalize the entry to pay the payroll on December 16. (Assume that the company has transferred cash to the Cash—Payroll Bank Account for this payroll.)

 5 ···

PROBLEM 8-3B   For the third quarter of the year, Barney Construction, 715 Red Rock Boulevard, San Francisco, California 94121, received Form 941 from the District Office of the Internal Revenue Service. The identification number for Barney Construction is 91-7382476. Its payroll for the quarter ended September 30 is as follows.

	A	F	I	J	K	M	N
1			**TAXABLE EARNINGS**			**DEDUCTIONS**	
2							
3		**TOTAL**	**SOCIAL**		**FEDERAL**	**SOCIAL**	**MEDICARE**
4	**NAME**	**EARNINGS**	**SECURITY**	**MEDICARE**	**INCOME TAX**	**SECURITY TAX**	**TAX**
5	Britton, D. L.	13,387.00	13,387.00	13,387.00	2,010.00	829.99	194.11
6	Finn, J. A.	16,753.00	16,753.00	16,753.00	2,510.00	1,038.69	242.92
7	Harrell, N. E.	17,780.00	17,780.00	17,780.00	2,767.00	1,102.36	257.81
8	Kelly, T. L.	16,243.00	16,243.00	16,243.00	2,430.00	1,007.07	235.52
9	Morton, S. M.	14,215.00	14,215.00	14,215.00	2,130.00	881.33	206.12
10	Rieck, A. J.	20,264.00	20,264.00	20,264.00	3,040.00	1,256.37	293.83
11		98,642.00	98,642.00	98,642.00	14,887.00	6,115.81	1,430.31
12							

The company has had six employees throughout the year. Assume that the FICA Social Security (employer) is 6.2 percent, the FICA Social Security (employee) is 6.2 percent on the first $118,500, and the Medicare tax is 1.45 percent of all earnings. The employer matches the employees' FICA Medicare taxes. There are no taxable tips, adjustments, backup withholding, or earned income credits. Barney Construction has submitted the following federal tax deposits and written the accompanying checks:

On August 15 for the July Payroll		On September 15 for the August Payroll		On October 15 for the September Payroll	
Employees' income tax withheld	$ 5,226.00	Employees' income tax withheld	$ 5,059.00	Employees' income tax withheld	$4,602.00
Employees' Social Security and Medicare tax withheld	2,597.21	Employees' Social Security and Medicare tax withheld	2,591.58	Employees' Social Security and Medicare tax withheld	2,357.33
Employer's Social Security and Medicare tax contributed	2,597.21	Employer's Social Security and Medicare tax contributed	2,591.58	Employer's Social Security and Medicare tax contributed	2,357.33
	$10,420.42		$10,242.16		$9,316.66

(Continued)

Check Figure
Total taxes, $29,979.23

LO 1, 2, 3

CHAPTER ASSIGNMENTS

Required
Complete Part 1 of Form 941 for the third quarter for Barney Construction.

PROBLEM 8-4B Grande Company has the following balances in its general ledger as of March 1 of this year:

a. FICA Taxes Payable (liability for February), $9,180.00 (total for employee and employer). The FICA Social Security Tax Payable is $7,440.00, and the FICA Medicare Tax Payable is $1,740.00.
b. Employees' Federal Income Tax Payable (liability for February), $9,000.00.
c. State Unemployment Tax Payable (liability for January and February), $3,442.50.
d. Federal Unemployment Tax Payable (liability for January and February), $510.00.

The company completed the following transactions involving the payroll during March and April:

Mar. 12 Issued check for $18,180.00, payable to Coast Bank, for the monthly deposit of February FICA taxes and employees' federal income tax withheld.

31 Recorded the payroll entry in the general journal from the payroll register for March. The payroll register had the following column totals:

Sales salaries	$47,654.00	
Office salaries	11,982.00	
Total earnings		$59,636.00
Employees' federal income tax deductions	$ 8,945.40	
Employees' Social Security tax deductions	3,697.43	
Employees' Medicare tax deductions	864.72	
Total deductions		13,507.55
Net pay		$46,128.45

31 Recorded payroll taxes. FICA Social Security rates are 6.2 percent (employee) and 6.2 percent (employer). The employer matches the employee's FICA Medicare rate of 1.45 percent. State unemployment tax is 5.4 percent. Federal unemployment tax is 0.6 percent. At this time, all employees' earnings are taxable for FICA and $1,000 of the earnings are taxable for unemployment taxes.

31 Issued check for $46,128.45 from Cash—Payroll Bank Account to pay salaries for the month.

Apr. 14 Issued check for $18,069.70, payable to Coast Bank, for the monthly deposit of March FICA taxes (employee and employer) and employees' federal income tax withheld.

30 Issued check for $3,496.50, payable to State Department of Revenue, for state unemployment tax for January, February, and March. The check was accompanied by the quarterly tax return.

30 Issued check for $516.00, payable to Coast Bank, for the deposit of federal unemployment tax for the months of January, February, and March.

Check Figure
Payroll Tax Expense,
$4,622.15

LO 6

*If using Working Papers, record the transactions on pages 77–78 of the general journal.

Problem 8-5B Sharon's Dance Studio has the following information related to its current year payroll as of December 31:

a. Federal Unemployment Tax Payable as of December 31, $110.00
b. FUTA taxable earnings limit of $7,000, rate 0.6 percent (0.006)

(Continued)

c.   First-quarter FUTA taxable liability, $520.00, paid April 30
d.   Second-quarter FUTA taxable liability, $45.00 (liability under $500, no payment made)
e.   Third-quarter FUTA taxable liability, $39.00 (total liability under $500, no payment made)
f.   Fourth-quarter FUTA taxable liability, $26.00 (payment to be made in January of the following year)
g.   FUTA taxable earnings for the year, $105,000
h.   Total Dance Instructor Wages, $195,000
i.   Sharon's Dance Studio EIN, 75-9182736
j.   No exempt FUTA payments
k.   Address: 392 E. Michigan Ave., Smithville, TX 78957

Check Figure
Line 14 Balance Due,
110.00

Required

Go to www.irs.gov to locate Form 940. Prepare Form 940 for the year. Then record the appropriate FUTA payment entry in the journal.

Accounting with ![qb] QuickBooks® Online

Go to the QuickBooks Online Chapter 8 Appendix located on the Cengage Learning companion site at Cengage.com. Review the *Accounting with QuickBooks Online* (step-by-step guide to using QuickBooks Online). *Accounting with QuickBooks Online*, Chapter 8, will introduce you to recording a journal entry to recognize employer taxes and creating payroll reports.

Activities

Why Does It Matter?

TRUGREEN, Memphis, Tennessee

PAWTUCKET RED SOX, Pawtucket, Rhode Island

HOCK IT TO ME, Albuquerque, New Mexico

TruGreen is the world's largest lawn and landscape company, employing over 10,000 employees and serving more than 1.7 million customers.

The Pawtucket Red Sox is a minor league baseball affiliate of the Boston Red Sox. The team's current roster consists of 25 active players, along with the team's manager, coaches, and mascots.

Hock It To Me is a privately owned pawn shop. The company has annual revenue of less than $500,000 and employs a staff of one to four people.

Even though each of these businesses has a unique payroll due to different amounts of salaries or wages, benefits, and withholdings, explain why each business needs to (a) accurately calculate the amount of payroll for each employee, (b) determine the amount of payroll taxes for which the employer is liable, (c) make the payroll tax deposits as required, and (d) file the appropriate payroll tax returns on a timely basis.

What Would You Do?

Between the end of one month and the 15th day of the next month, the balance in the employer's business bank account has been getting smaller and smaller. An employee prepares the next payroll and correctly computes the necessary withholding taxes. The employer is supposed to pay accumulated employment taxes on the 15th of the next month. Payday is the last day of the month. However, the employer has used the funds withheld from employees to pay some of the business's bills. He hopes that enough of the customers who owe him money will pay their outstanding debts. If his assumption is true, the checking account will have enough in it to pay the federal deposit on the 15th of the month. Is the employer acting ethically? After all, he says he intends to have enough money in the account for the deposit. Explain your answer.

Before a Test Check: Chapters 6–8

PART I: Completion

1. Checks issued by the depositor that have been paid or have cleared the bank are called _____ checks.

2. A deposit that is not recorded on the bank statement because it was made after the bank's closing date for preparation of bank statements is called a(n) _____.

3. The process by which the payee transfers ownership of the check to a bank or another party is called a(n) _____.

4. The person to whom a check is payable is called the _____.

5. A cash fund used to make small immediate cash payments is called a(n) _____.

PART II: Application

1. Cheryl Chang's salary is $3,550 per month. If she works more than 40 hours in one week, she is entitled to overtime pay at the rate of 1½ times her regular hourly rate. During the current week, she worked 45 hours. Calculate her gross pay.

2. On June 30, the column totals of Expert Training's payroll register showed that its training employees had earned $18,000 and its office employees had earned $6,000. Social Security taxes were withheld at 6.2 percent, and Medicare taxes were withheld at 1.45 percent. All earnings are taxable. Other deductions consisted of federal income tax, $3,600, and charitable contributions to the United Way, $500. Determine the amount of Social Security and Medicare taxes that should be withheld. Give the general journal entry to record the payroll, crediting Salaries Payable for the net pay.

3. Roxy Company's payroll for the week ended December 31 is as follows:

Gross earnings of employees	$155,000
Social Security taxable earnings	143,000
Medicare taxable earnings	155,000
Federal unemployment taxable earnings	22,000
State unemployment taxable earnings	22,000

Assume that the payroll is subject to employer's Social Security tax of 6.2 percent (0.062), Medicare tax of 1.45 percent (0.0145), federal unemployment tax of 0.6 percent (0.006), and state unemployment tax of 5.4 percent (0.054). Write the entry in general journal form to record the employer's payroll tax expense.

PART III: True/False

T F 1. There is no limit on the amount of taxable earnings for Medicare.

T F 2. When journalizing the entry to reimburse the Petty Cash Fund, include a credit to Petty Cash Fund.

T F 3. When journalizing the entry to account for a customer's NSF check, debit Accounts Payable.

T F 4. An employee's net pay is the result of subtracting his or her deductions from gross pay.

T F 5. The gross pay for an employee who works 45 hours, earns $8.50 per hour, and receives time and a half for hours worked over 40 hours is $402.75.

Answers: Part I

1. canceled   2. deposit in transit or late deposit   3. endorsement   4. payee   5. petty cash fund

Answers: Part II

1.

$3,550 per month × 12 months = $42,600 per year

$42,600 per year ÷ 52 weeks   = $819.23 per week (rounded)

$819.23 per week ÷ 40 hours   = $20.48* per regular hour (rounded)

$20.48 per regular hour × 1.5   = $30.72 per overtime hour

Earnings for 45 hours:

40 hours at straight time (Calculated hourly above)		= $819.20*
5 hours overtime	(5 × $30.72) =	153.60
Total gross earnings		$972.80

2.

		GENERAL JOURNAL				**Page ___**
Date		Description	Post. Ref.	Debit	Credit	
20--						
June	30	Training Salary Expense		18 0 0 0 00		
		Office Salary Expense		6 0 0 0 00		
		Employee's Federal Income Tax				
		Payable			3 6 0 0 00	
		FICA Social Security Tax Payable			1 4 8 8 00	
		FICA Medicare Tax Payable			3 4 8 00	
		Employees' United Way Payable			5 0 0 00	
		Salaries Payable			18 0 6 4 00	
		Payroll register for the week ended,				
		June 30, 20--.				

FICA Social Security Tax Payable: ($24,000 × 0.062) = $1,488.00

FICA Medicare Tax Payable: ($24,000 × 0.0145)   = $348.00

3.

Date		Description	Post. Ref.	Debit					Credit				
20--													
Dec.	31	Payroll Tax Expense		12	4	3	3	50					
		FICA Social Security Tax Payable							8	8	6	6	00
		FICA Medicare Tax Payable							2	2	4	7	50
		State Unemployment Tax Payable							1	1	8	8	00
		($22,000 × 0.054)											
		Federal Unemployment Tax Payable								1	3	2	00
		($22,000 × 0.006)											
		To record employer's share of FICA											
		Taxes and employer's state and											
		federal unemployment taxes.											

FICA Social Security Tax Payable: ($143,000 × 0.062) = $8,866.00

FICA Medicare Tax Payable: ($155,000 × 0.0145) = $2,247.50

Answers: Part III

1. T   2. F   3. F   4. T   5. F

BEFORE A TEST CHECK

Sales and Purchases

Learning Objectives

After you have completed this chapter, you will be able to do the following:

1. Describe the nature of a merchandising business.

2. Using a general journal and the periodic inventory system, record sales and sale-related transactions; then post to the general ledger and the accounts receivable ledger.

3. Prepare a schedule of accounts receivable.

4. Using a general journal and the periodic inventory system, record purchase and purchase-related transactions; then post to the general ledger and the accounts payable ledger.

5. Prepare a schedule of accounts payable.

6. Using a general journal and the perpetual inventory system, record sales and sale-related transactions.

7. Using a general journal and the perpetual inventory system, record purchase and purchase-related transactions.

8. Record transactions in a sales journal and post to the general ledger and accounts receivable ledger.

9. Record transactions in a three-column purchases journal and post to the general ledger and accounts payable ledger.

To: Amy Roberts, CPA
Subject: Sales and Purchases

Hi Amy,
So far things are going well with the business. Thanks for all of your help and advice. I think I'm ready to expand into the next stage of my business plan. Up until now, I have been offering services, but I would like to start selling products as well. When you get some time, can you help me understand the accounting process for recording sales and purchases of merchandise?
Thanks,
Janie

To: Janie Conner
Subject: RE: Sales and Purchases

Hi Janie,
Because you are expanding into a merchandising business, you need to use some new accounts for recording sales and purchases and to understand how to record sales tax, merchandise returns, and freight. Let's plan on meeting next week to discuss the following:

_____ 1. What specific accounts you will use with your new merchandise line.
_____ 2. How to journalize sales transactions, sales tax, and sales returns and allowances in the general journal.
_____ 3. How to post to the accounts receivable ledger and general ledger.
_____ 4. How to journalize purchase-related transactions in the general journal.
_____ 5. How to post to the accounts payable ledger and general ledger.
_____ 6. How to handle freight charges on merchandise.
_____ 7. How to prepare schedules for accounts receivable and accounts payable.

I'll give you a call the first of next week to set up a meeting.

Amy

iStockPhoto.com/Ann Baldwin

In the previous chapters, we discussed companies that specialized in providing a service, such as Conner's Whitewater Adventures. Now we will turn our focus to companies that buy and sell goods. These types of companies are known as **merchandising businesses**. A merchandising business can be a wholesale or retail business. A wholesale business, which is sometimes called a middleman or a distributor, buys goods from manufacturers and sells them to retailers. A retail business sells goods directly to consumers (the public). Before we begin analyzing transactions, let's take a moment to review the specific accounts for merchandising firms.

9-1 NATURE OF MERCHANDISING BUSINESS

Merchandise inventory consists of a stock of goods that a company buys and intends to resell at a profit. Merchandise should be differentiated from other assets, such as furniture and equipment, that are acquired for use in the business and are not for resale.

Merchandise inventory can be recorded using the periodic inventory system or the perpetual inventory system. The **periodic inventory system** requires that companies periodically take a physical count of merchandise on hand and then attach a value to it. Under the **perpetual inventory system**, companies keep continuous records of inventories so that at any given time they know what they should have on hand and the current cost of each item. In the first part of this chapter, we will assume that the company records merchandise inventory using the periodic inventory system. Later in the chapter, we will demonstrate how to record the journal entries for merchandise inventory under the perpetual inventory system.

9-1a Sales Transactions

When merchandising firms record sales of merchandise, they use the **Sales account**. The Sales account is a revenue account, has a normal credit balance, and appears on the Income Statement.

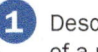 Describe the nature of a merchandising business.

Learning Objective

9-1b Source Documents Related to Sales

In a retail business, a salesperson usually prepares a sales ticket in duplicate or triplicate for a sale on account. One copy goes to the customer, and another copy goes to the accounting department, where it serves as the basis for an entry in the journal. A third copy may be used as a record of sales—to compute sales commissions or control inventory, for example.

In a wholesale business, the company usually receives a written order directly from a customer or through a salesperson who obtained the order from the customer. The credit department approves the order and then sends it to the billing department, where the sales invoice is prepared.

Invoices are prepared in multiple copies and serve as evidence for recording the transaction. Invoice copies should be sent to multiple parties throughout the business, such as the sales department, accounting, and the credit department. In addition, the customer should receive a copy of the invoice. The sales invoice for Whitewater Raft Supply's sale of merchandise to Mesa River Raft Company is shown in Figure 1.

Figure 1
Sales invoice

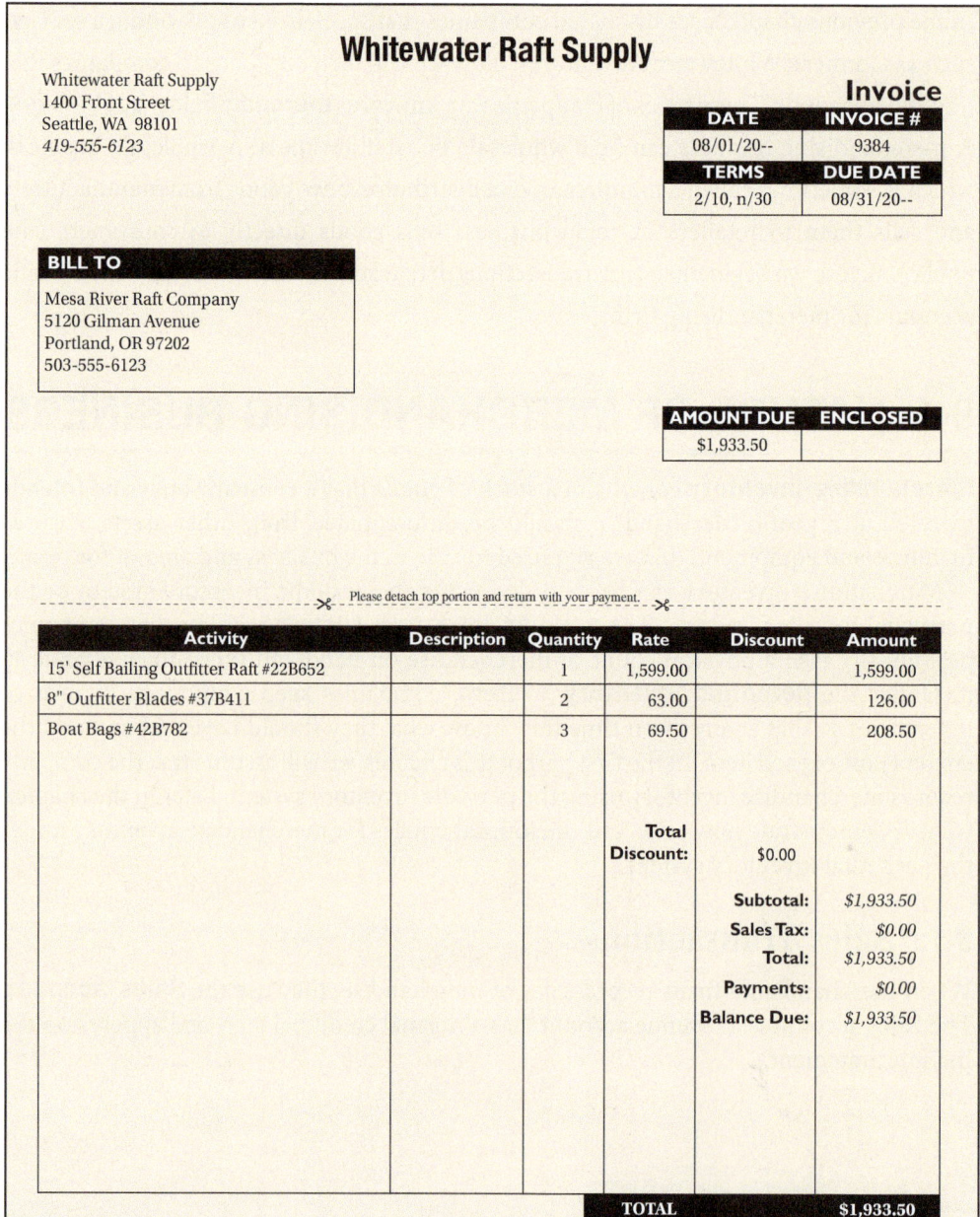

9-2 RECORDING SALES TRANSACTIONS IN A GENERAL JOURNAL

Sales transactions can be recorded two ways—by recording directly into the general journal or by using a special journal called the sales journal. We will introduce sales transactions using the general journal first. Then, because of the importance of understanding accounting systems, we will introduce the use of the sales journal later in this chapter.

In the previous chapters, we examined the transactions for Conner's Whitewater Adventures. Conner purchases the Whitewater rafts she uses on her tours from Whitewater Raft Supply. Whitewater Raft Supply is a wholesaler specializing in selling rafts, kayaks, oars, paddles, and other accessories to businesses across the nation.

We will introduce recording sales by looking at five transactions on the books of Whitewater Raft Supply for August.

2 Using a general journal and the periodic inventory system, record sales and sale-related transactions; then post to the general ledger and the accounts receivable ledger.

Learning Objective

Aug. 1 Sold merchandise on account to Mesa River Raft Company, invoice no. 9384, $1,933.50.

8 Sold merchandise on account to Green River Rafts, invoice no. 9385, $1,116.

14 Sold merchandise on account to Marty's Fly Fishing Adventures, invoice no. 9386, $1,594.

19 Sold merchandise on account to Hi-Flying Adventures, Inc., invoice no. 9387, $552.30.

25 Sold merchandise on account to Hi-Flying Adventures, Inc., invoice no. 9388, $1,674.

Whitewater Raft Supply will record the transactions into the general journal as follows:

Date		Description	Post. Ref.	Debit	Credit
GENERAL JOURNAL					Page 26
20--					
Aug.	1	Accounts Receivable, Mesa River			
		Raft Company		1 9 3 3 50	
		Sales			1 9 3 3 50
		Sold merchandise to Mesa			
		River Raft Company,			
		invoice no. 9384.			
	8	Accounts Receivable, Green			
		River Rafts		1 1 1 6 00	
		Sales			1 1 1 6 00
		Sold merchandise to Green			
		River Rafts, invoice no. 9385.			
	14	Accounts Receivable, Marty's Fly			
		Fishing Adventures		1 5 9 4 00	
		Sales			1 5 9 4 00
		Sold merchandise to Marty's			
		Fly Fishing Adventures,			
		invoice no. 9386.			

(Continued)

GENERAL JOURNAL					Page 26
Date	Description	Post. Ref.	Debit	Credit
20--				
Aug. 19	Accounts Receivable, Hi-Flying			
	Adventures, Inc.		5 5 2 30	
	Sales			5 5 2 30
	Sold merchandise to			
	Hi-Flying Adventures, Inc.,			
	invoice no. 9387.			
25	Accounts Receivable, Hi-Flying			
	Adventures, Inc.		1 6 7 4 00	
	Sales			1 6 7 4 00
	Sold merchandise to			
	Hi-Flying Adventures, Inc.,			
	invoice no. 9388.			

Whitewater Raft Supply's accountant records a debit to Accounts Receivable to record the amount each customer owes the company and a credit to Sales for each transaction. The Sales account is credited because it is a revenue account that is used for recording sales of merchandise.

Here's how the accounts appear in the fundamental accounting equation:

Assets	=	Liabilities	+	Capital	−	Drawing	+	Revenue	−	Expenses
+ −		− +		− +		+ −		− +		+ −
Debit Credit		Debit Credit		Debit Credit		Debit Credit		Debit Credit		Debit Credit

Accounts Receivable

+	−
1,933.50	
1,116.00	
1,594.00	
552.30	
1,674.00	

Sales

−	+
	1,933.50
	1,116.00
	1,594.00
	552.30
	1,674.00

Remember that the transactions are recorded assuming that Whitewater Raft Supply records merchandise inventory using the periodic inventory method. If Whitewater Raft Supply used the perpetual inventory method instead, an additional journal entry would be required. This additional journal entry will be discussed later in this chapter.

9-2a Sales Returns and Allowances

Occasionally customers will need to return inventory or will ask for a reduction in the original price for a specific reason, such as damaged or defective goods. The **Sales Returns and Allowances account** handles these types of transactions. A *return* is a physical return of the goods. An *allowance* is a reduction from the original price for an agreed-upon reason, such as goods that were defective or damaged. To avoid writing a formal business letter each time to inform customers of their account adjustments, businesses use a special form called a **credit memorandum**. A credit memorandum is a written statement indicating a seller's willingness to reduce the amount of a buyer's debt.

The Sales Returns and Allowances account is a contra account that is deducted from Sales. Using an account separate from Sales provides a better record of the total returns and allowances. Accountants deduct Sales Returns and Allowances from Sales on the income statement to determine net sales.

Returning to the Whitewater Raft Supply example, here's an example of a return. The original sale is repeated here for reference, followed by the issuance of a credit memorandum.

TRANSACTION (a). On August 14, Whitewater Raft Supply sold merchandise on account to Marty's Fly Fishing Adventures, $1,594, and recorded the sale in the general journal.

TRANSACTION (b). On September 5, Marty's Fly Fishing Adventures returned $254 worth of the merchandise. Whitewater Raft Supply issued credit memorandum no. 1069.

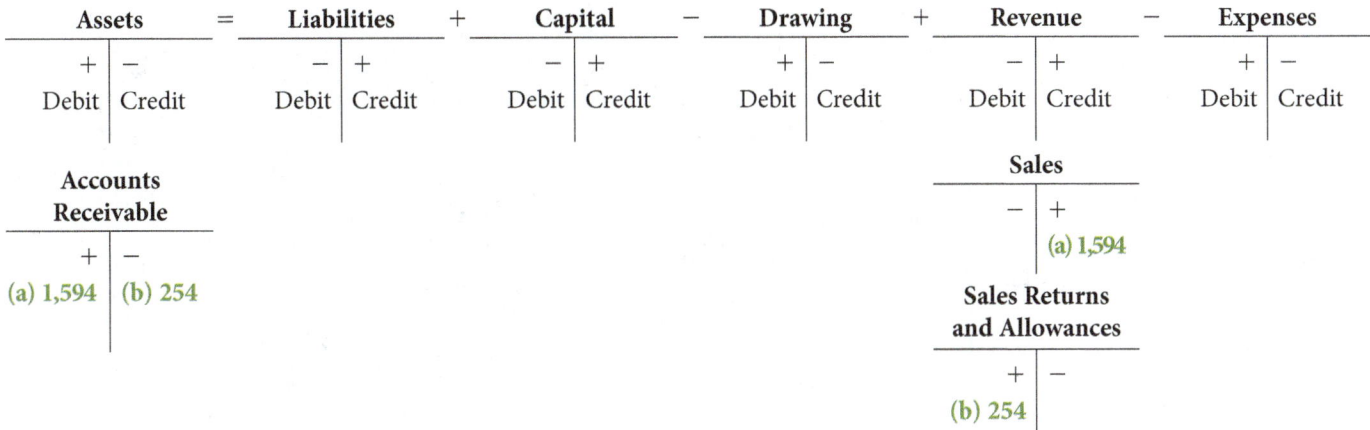

Whitewater Raft Supply's accountant debits Sales Returns and Allowances to increase it. Then, the accountant credits Accounts Receivable to decrease it because the credit customer, Marty's Fly Fishing Adventures, owes less than before.

GENERAL JOURNAL										Page 27			
Date		Description	Post. Ref.		Debit					Credit			
20--													
Sept.	5	Sales Returns and Allowances			2	5	4	00					
		Accounts Receivable, Marty's											
		Fly Fishing Adventures								2	5	4	00
		Issued credit memo no. 1069.											

9-2b Sales Transactions Involving Sales Tax

Most states and some cities levy a sales tax on retail sales of goods and services. The retailer collects the sales tax from customers and later pays it to the tax authorities.

When goods or services are sold, the sales tax is charged to the customer and recorded at the time of the sale. The amount of the sales tax must be computed for each transaction and recorded in the **Sales Tax Payable account**. The customer owes the amount of the sale plus the applicable sales tax.

FYI

As of the writing of this text, nonpublic organizations, like sole proprietorships, will apply the new revenue recognition standards, announced by the Financial Accounting Standards Board (FASB), to annual reporting periods after December 15, 2018. The changes in revenue recognition will affect the reporting of Sales Returns and Allowances.

Revenue from Contracts with Customers, Topic 606, FASB Accounting Standards Update, Financial Accounting standards Board, Norwalk, CT, August 2015.

Assume that David Fly Fishing Outfitters, a retail store, had the following transaction, which includes sales tax computed on the amount of the sale of merchandise:

Jan.   3   Sold merchandise on account to R. Martinez, invoice no. 101, $153.50 plus sales tax of $12.28.

The transaction would be recorded in T accounts and in the general journal as follows:

Assets	=	Liabilities	+	Capital	−	Drawing	+	Revenue	−	Expenses
+ −		− +		− +		+ −		− +		+ −
Debit Credit		Debit Credit		Debit Credit		Debit Credit		Debit Credit		Debit Credit

Accounts Receivable	Sales Tax Payable				Sales
+ −	− +				− +
165.78	12.28				153.50

GENERAL JOURNAL						Page 5
Date	Description	Post. Ref.	Debit		Credit	
20--						
Jan. 3	Accounts Receivable, R. Martinez		1 6 5 78			
	Sales				1 5 3 50	
	Sales Tax Payable				1 2 28	
	Sold merchandise to					
	R. Martinez, invoice no. 101.					

At the end of the first quarter, the accountant for David Fly Fishing Outfitters determines that the total sales tax payable for the quarter is $3,240.50. When the sales tax is paid to the state, the accountant debits Sales Tax Payable and credits Cash for the total amount due.

GENERAL JOURNAL						Page 8
Date	Description	Post. Ref.	Debit		Credit	
20--						
Apr. 20	Sales Tax Payable		3 2 4 0 50			
	Cash				3 2 4 0 50	
	Paid sales tax due for first					
	quarter.					

SALES RETURNS INVOLVING SALES TAX

If a customer who returns merchandise to a retail store was originally charged a sales tax, the amount of the sale and the sales tax must be returned to the customer. Review the following two transactions for David Fly Fishing Outfitters.

TRANSACTION (a). On May 1, David Fly Fishing Outfitters sold merchandise on account to B. Hill, $1,550, plus $124 sales tax.

TRANSACTION (b). On May 5, B. Hill returned the merchandise, and David Fly Fishing Outfitters issued credit memorandum no. 1152.

Following is the general journal entry required for this type of return:

	GENERAL JOURNAL				Page 9	
Date	Description	Post. Ref.	Debit		Credit	
20--						
May 5	Sales Returns and Allowances		1 5 5 0 00			
	Sales Tax Payable		1 2 4 00			
	Accounts Receivable, B. Hill				1 6 7 4 00	
	Issued credit memo no. 1152.					

Notice that David Fly Fishing Outfitters credited B. Hill's account for the amount of the sale ($1,550) and the amount of the sales tax payable ($124).

9-3 ACCOUNTS RECEIVABLE LEDGER AND SCHEDULE OF ACCOUNTS RECEIVABLE

In the sales transactions for Whitewater Raft Supply, we recorded the receivable directly into the Accounts Receivable account. The general journal entry serves as the posting source for crediting the Accounts Receivable account in the general ledger. In addition, to know how much each credit customer owes a business, the firm also maintains an **accounts receivable ledger**. This ledger is a separate record containing a list of the credit customers, in alphabetical order or by account number, with their respective balances. It is important to maintain an accounts receivable ledger so that the company will know at any point in time what amount is owed by the customer, whether the amount is past due, and what payments have been made on the account.

3 Prepare a schedule of accounts receivable.

Learning Objective

Even though an accounts receivable ledger is maintained, the Accounts Receivable account in the general ledger should still be maintained. When all of the postings are up-to-date, the balance of the Accounts Receivable account should equal the total of all of the credit customers' individual account balances. This means in a manual accounting system, the accountant must post to *both* the Accounts Receivable account in the general ledger *and* the accounts receivable ledger. The Accounts Receivable *account* in the general ledger is called a **controlling account**. The accounts receivable *ledger*, containing the accounts of all credit customers, is a special type of ledger called a **subsidiary ledger**.

If the accountant was using a computerized accounting system, the software would automatically post the transaction to the Accounts Receivable controlling account and the customer's account in the accounts receivable ledger. In a manual system, to take care of this double posting for Accounts Receivable, the accountant draws a slanted line in the Post. Ref. column. When the amount has been posted as a debit to the general ledger account, the accountant writes the account number of Accounts Receivable in the left part of the Post. Ref. column. After the debit has been posted to the customer's account in the subsidiary ledger, the accountant puts a check mark in the right portion of the Post. Ref. column. The following entries in the general journal, general ledger, and accounts receivable ledger are shown for Mesa River Raft Company's August 1st transaction after posting is complete.

GENERAL JOURNAL							Page 26	
Date		Description	Post. Ref.	Debit		Credit		
20--								
Aug.	1	Accounts Receivable, Mesa River						
		Raft Company	113 ✓	1 9 3 3 50				
		Sales	411			1 9 3 3	50	
		Sold merchandise to Mesa						
		River Raft Company,						
		invoice no. 9384.						

GENERAL LEDGER

ACCOUNT Accounts Receivable   ACCOUNT NO. 113

Date		Item	Post. Ref.	Debit	Credit	Balance Debit	Balance Credit
20--							
Aug.	1		J26	1 9 3 3 50		1 9 3 3 50	

ACCOUNTS RECEIVABLE LEDGER

NAME   Mesa River Raft Company

ADDRESS 5120 Gilman Avenue

Portland, OR 97202

Date		Item	Post. Ref.	Debit	Credit	Balance
20--						
Aug.	1		J26	1 9 3 3 50		1 9 3 3 50

From the information contained in the accounts receivable subsidiary ledger, the accountant can prepare a schedule of accounts receivable, such as the one shown in Figure 2, listing each credit customer's account balance.

Figure 2
Schedule of accounts receivable

Whitewater Raft Supply Schedule of Accounts Receivable August 31, 20--	
Green River Rafts	$1,116.00
Hi-Flying Adventures, Inc.	2,226.30
Marty's Fly Fishing Adventures	1,594.00
Mesa River Raft Company	1,933.50
Total Accounts Receivable	$6,869.80

Figure 3 diagrams the interrelationships of the subsidiary ledger, general ledger, and schedule of accounts receivable for Whitewater Raft Supply for August. Notice that each entry is posted to Accounts Receivable and Sales in the general ledger. Also, the

Figure 3

Interrelationship of the accounts receivable ledger, general ledger, and schedule of accounts receivable

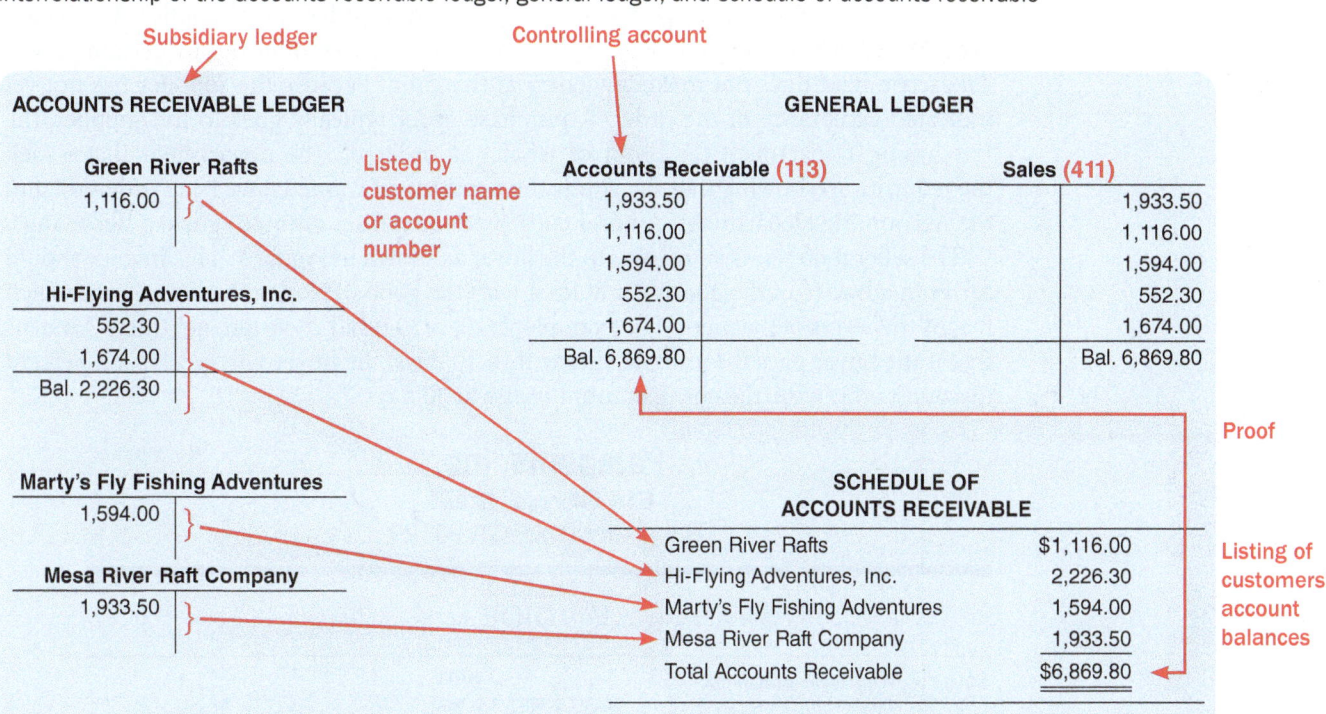

amount owed by the customer is posted to the subsidiary accounts receivable ledger to maintain a running balance of the amount that each customer owes. If performing the posting manually, the accountant should post the individual amounts to the accounts receivable ledger every day, so that this ledger will have up-to-date information. Finally, the Accounts Receivable controlling account in the general ledger will have the same balance, $6,869.80, as the schedule of accounts receivable.

In the simplified illustration in Figure 2, it just so happens that because no payments were received from credit customers, the total of the Sales account equals the balance of Accounts Receivable. However, if $1,200 had been received from credit customers, both the balance of the Accounts Receivable controlling account and the total of the schedule of accounts receivable would be $5,669.80 ($6,869.80 − $1,200.00). The total of the Sales account would still be $6,869.80. Also, if some sales were cash-only transactions, this would cause a difference between total Sales and the balance of Accounts Receivable.

9-4 PURCHASE TRANSACTIONS

The **Purchases account** is used to record the cost of merchandise bought for resale. The Purchases account is considered an expense and has a normal debit balance.

9-4a Source Documents Related to Purchases

In a small retail store, the owner may do the buying. In large retail and wholesale businesses, department heads or division managers do the buying, after which the Purchasing Department goes into action: It places purchase orders, follows up on the orders, and sees that deliveries are made to the correct departments. The Purchasing Department also acts as a source of information on current prices, price trends, quality of goods, prospective suppliers, and reliability of suppliers.

 Using a general journal and the periodic inventory system, record purchase and purchase-related transactions; then post to the general ledger and the accounts payable ledger.

Learning Objective

The Purchasing Department normally requires that any requests to buy merchandise be in writing in the form of a purchase requisition. After the purchase requisition is approved, the Purchasing Department sends a purchase order to the supplier. A purchase order (often referred to as a "PO") is the company's written offer to buy certain goods. The accountant does not make any entry at this point because the supplier has not yet indicated acceptance of the order. A purchase order typically goes to the supplier, the Purchasing Department (as proof of what was ordered), the department that issued the requisition (showing that the goods the department wanted have been ordered), and the Accounting Department. A blind copy (with quantities omitted) goes to Receiving.

The seller then sends an invoice to the buyer as shown in Figure 4. This invoice should arrive in advance of the goods (or at least *with* the goods). Notice the line *Terms,* which means the terms of payment. For example, 2/10, n/30 (read "two-ten, net thirty") means that if the buyer pays the amount due within 10 days, the buyer will receive a 2 percent discount; otherwise, the entire amount is due in 30 days.

Figure 4
Purchase invoice

Pataponia, Inc.
1614 Olivera Street
San Francisco, CA 94129

No. 2706

INVOICE

SOLD TO	Whitewater Raft Supply	DATE:	July 31, 20--
	1400 Front Street	CUSTOMER'S P.O. NO.:	7918
	Seattle, WA 98101	SHIPPED BY:	Western Freight Line
		TERMS:	2/10, n/30

YOUR ORDER NO.	SALESPERSON	TERMS
7918	C. L.	2/10, n/30

DATE SHIPPED	SHIPPED BY	FOB
July 31, 20--	Western Freight Line	San Francisco

QUANTITY	DESCRIPTION	UNIT PRICE	TOTAL
12	Rio Frio Personal Flotation Device (PFD) #772R	142 50	1,710 00
	Freight		85 50
	Total		1,795 50

Pataponia, Inc. (the seller) prepaid the freight cost and added the $85.50 to the bill, listing it separately. This is similar to buying something by mail order or online. Accounting for freight charges is discussed in more detail below and later in the chapter.

9-4b Recording Purchase Transactions in a General Journal

Now that we have reviewed the source documents for purchase transactions, let's move on to recording purchase transactions. Purchase transactions can be recorded in two ways—by recording directly into the general journal or by using a special journal called the purchases journal. We will introduce purchase transactions using the general journal first. Then we will discuss how to record the transactions into the purchases journal later in this chapter.

Let's look at four purchase transactions on the books of Whitewater Raft Supply for August. Some of these transactions include the cost of delivering the merchandise, called Freight In. The Freight In account is used to record the transportation charges on incoming merchandise intended for resale.

Aug.   2   Bought merchandise on account from Pataponia, Inc., invoice no. 2706, $1,710; terms 2/10, n/30; dated July 31; freight prepaid and added to the invoice, $85.50 (total $1,795.50).

10   Bought merchandise on account from Langseth and Son, invoice no. 982, $2,772; terms net 30 days; dated August 8; freight prepaid and added to the invoice, $157 (total $2,929).

17   Bought merchandise on account from Dana Manufacturing Company, invoice no. 10611, $564; terms 2/10, n/30; dated August 15; freight paid by the seller.

26   Bought merchandise on account from Pataponia, Inc., invoice no. 2801, $2,503.70; terms 2/10, n/30; dated August 24; freight prepaid and added to the invoice, $102.30 (total $2,606).

Whitewater Raft Supply will record the transactions into the general journal as follows:

	GENERAL JOURNAL				Page 26	
Date	Description	Post. Ref.	Debit		Credit	
20--						
Aug. 2	Purchases		1 7 1 0 00			
	Freight In		8 5 50			
	Accounts Payable, Pataponia, Inc.				1 7 9 5 50	
	Purchased merchandise from					
	Pataponia, Inc., invoice no.					
	2706, invoice dated 7/31,					
	terms 2/10, n/30.					
10	Purchases		2 7 7 2 00			
	Freight In		1 5 7 00			
	Accounts Payable, Langseth					
	and Son				2 9 2 9 00	
	Purchased merchandise from					
	Langseth and Son, invoice					
	no. 982, invoice dated 8/8,					
	terms n/30.					
17	Purchases		5 6 4 00			
	Accounts Payable, Dana					
	Manufacturing Company				5 6 4 00	
	Purchased merchandise from					
	Dana Manufacturing Company,					
	invoice no. 10611, invoice dated					
	8/15, terms 2/10, n/30.					
26	Purchases		2 5 0 3 70			
	Freight In		1 0 2 30			
	Accounts Payable, Pataponia, Inc.				2 6 0 6 00	
	Purchased merchandise from					
	Pataponia, Inc., invoice no.					
	2801, invoice dated 8/24,					
	terms 2/10, n/30.					

Whitewater Raft Supply's accountant records a debit to the Purchases account to record the cost of merchandise bought for resale. Remember that the Purchases account is similar to an expense account and therefore has a normal debit balance. Freight In (if applied) is also debited to record the increase to the cost of purchases for the transportation charges on incoming merchandise. The corresponding credit is to the Accounts Payable account. Note that the transactions are recorded on the day the merchandise is received.

Here's how the accounts appear in the fundamental accounting equation:

Assets	=	**Liabilities**	+	**Capital**	−	**Drawing**	+	**Revenue**	−	**Expenses**
+ | −		− | +		− | +		+ | −		− | +		+ | −
Debit | Credit		Debit | Credit		Debit | Credit		Debit | Credit		Debit | Credit		Debit | Credit

Accounts Payable		**Purchases**
− | +		+ | −
1,795.50		1,710.00
2,929.00		2,772.00
564.00		564.00
2,606.00		2,503.70

Freight In
+ | −
85.50
157.00
102.30

9-4c Purchases Returns and Allowances

Occasionally a business will need to return merchandise or request an allowance for reasons such as damaged merchandise. The **Purchases Returns and Allowances account** handles these types of transactions. In both cases, there is a reduction in the amount owed to the supplier. The buyer sends a letter or printed form to the supplier, who acknowledges the reduction by sending a credit memorandum. The buyer should wait for notice of the agreed deduction before making an entry.

The Purchases Returns and Allowances account is a contra account to Purchases and is considered to be a deduction from Purchases. Using a separate account provides a better record of the total returns and allowances. Purchases Returns and Allowances is deducted from the Purchases account on the income statement. Let's look at an example consisting of a return on the books of Whitewater Raft Supply. The original transaction is shown here for review and then the credit memorandum is shown.

TRANSACTION (a). On September 2, bought merchandise on account from Dana Manufacturing Company, $830.

TRANSACTION (b). On September 8, Whitewater Raft Supply returned some merchandise and received credit memorandum no. 1629 from Dana Manufacturing Company for $270.

First, here is how the transactions appear in the fundamental accounting equation:

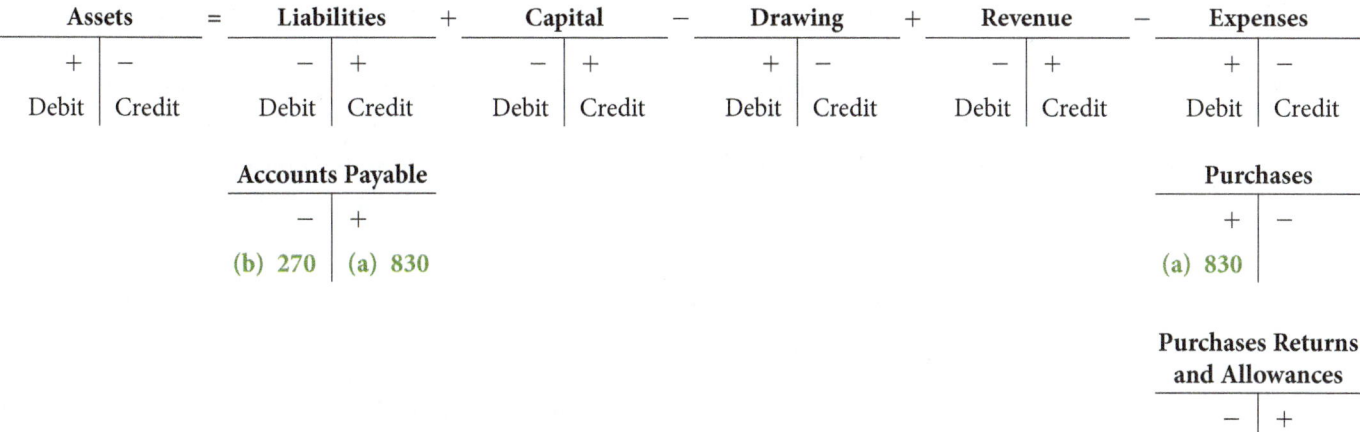

In the general journal, transaction (a) was journalized as a debit to Purchases and a credit to Accounts Payable. Transaction (b) is journalized as follows:

GENERAL JOURNAL				Page 27
Date	**Description**	**Post. Ref.**	**Debit**	**Credit**
20--				
Sept. 8	Accounts Payable, Dana			
	Manufacturing Company		2 7 0 00	
	Purchases Returns and			
	Allowances			2 7 0 00
	Credit memo no. 1629 for			
	return of merchandise.			

Purchases Returns and Allowances is credited because Whitewater Raft Supply's amount of returns and allowances has increased. Accounts Payable is debited because Whitewater Raft Supply owes less than before.

9-4d Freight Charges on Incoming Merchandise

Companies use the Freight In account to keep a record of all separately charged delivery costs on incoming merchandise.

Freight costs are expressed as FOB (free on board) destination or shipping point. **(Destination is the buyer's location; shipping point is the seller's location.)** In both cases, the supplier loads the goods on board the carrier. Beyond that point, there must be an understanding as to who is responsible for paying the freight charges. **If the seller assumes the entire cost of transportation, without any reimbursement from the buyer, the terms are FOB destination**. In this case, title or ownership changes hands when the buyer receives the goods. **If the buyer is responsible for paying the freight cost, the shipping terms are called FOB shipping point**. In this case, title or ownership changes hands when goods are transferred to a common carrier (freight company).

Briefly, when goods are shipped FOB destination, the freight charges are not stated and the seller simply pays the amount of the freight. Suppose Whitewater Raft Supply, which

FYI

Unless the title to the goods is expressly reserved by the seller, whoever pays the freight charges customarily has title to the goods.

is in Seattle, buys merchandise from a supplier in Chicago with shipping terms of FOB Seattle listed on the invoice. The total of the invoice is $1,740, and there is no separate listing of freight charges. In other words, the seller has included the transportation costs in the price.

When goods are shipped FOB shipping point, with the buyer responsible for paying the freight charges, transportation costs may be handled in two ways:

1. The buyer may pay the freight charges directly to the transportation company. For example, an automobile dealer in Houston buys cars FOB Detroit. In this case, the automobile dealer makes one check payable to the manufacturer and another check payable to the carrier for the freight charges. (FOB Detroit is the same as FOB shipping point.)

2. The transportation or shipping costs may be listed separately on the invoice. For example, suppose a person orders a computer from a company online. The company has prepaid (paid in advance) the freight charges as a favor or convenience for the buyer. However, the freight charges are listed on the bill or invoice, and the buyer is responsible for reimbursing the company for the freight charges. Similarly, when a business buys merchandise, the amount of the freight charges may be prepaid by the seller and listed separately on the invoice.

Look again at the invoice from Pataponia, Inc., on page 376. Note that the freight cost is listed separately, and the terms are FOB shipping point (San Francisco). Pataponia paid the transportation cost, and Whitewater Raft Supply must reimburse Pataponia for this cost.

The transaction for the purchase from Pataponia, Inc., was recorded as follows:

			GENERAL JOURNAL										Page 26				
Date			Description	Post. Ref.		Debit						Credit				
20--																
Aug.	2	Purchases			1	7	1	0	00						
		Freight In					8	5	50						
		Accounts Payable, Pataponia, Inc.									1	7	9	5	50
		Purchased merchandise from													
		Pataponia, Inc., invoice no.													
		2706, invoice dated 7/31,													
		terms 2/10, n/30.													

Notice that the transportation cost is recorded separately as a debit to the Freight In account for $85.50. Also notice that because this purchase was FOB shipping point, the buyer (Whitewater Raft Supply) must reimburse the seller for the transportation costs by paying the total invoice cost of $1,795.50.

When the buyer pays for the cost of freight, the buyer records the cost as Freight In, which is included in the cost of purchases and reported on the income statement. If the seller pays for the cost of freight, the seller records the cost as a selling expense in the Delivery Expense or Freight Out account.

9-4e Freight Charges on the Buying of Goods and Services Other Than Merchandise

Any freight charges incurred when buying other assets, such as supplies or equipment, should be debited to the respective asset accounts. The Freight In account is used only to record the incoming transportation charges on merchandise intended for resale. For example, assume that Whitewater Raft Supply bought display cases on account from Carter Cabinet Shop at a cost of $2,700 plus freight charges of $290. The seller of the display cases prepaid the transportation costs for Whitewater Raft Supply and then added the $290 to the invoice price of the cases. Let's visualize this with T accounts.

Store Equipment		Accounts Payable	
+	−	−	+
2,990			2,990

Notice that Whitewater Raft Supply did not use the Freight In account to record the transportation costs. Instead, the company recorded the transportation costs directly into the Store Equipment account.

9-5 ACCOUNTS PAYABLE LEDGER AND SCHEDULE OF ACCOUNTS PAYABLE

Previously, we called the Accounts Receivable account in the general ledger a controlling account, and we saw that the accounts receivable ledger consists of an individual account for each credit customer.

Accounts Payable is a parallel case. It is also a controlling account in the general ledger. The **accounts payable ledger** is a subsidiary ledger. It consists of individual accounts for all of the creditors, listed in either alphabetical or numerical order.

Even though an accounts payable ledger is used, the Accounts Payable account in the general ledger should still be maintained. When all of the postings are up-to-date, the balance of the Accounts Payable account should equal the total of all of the creditors' individual account balances. As with sales transactions, the accountant using a manual accounting system must post purchase transactions daily to both the general ledger and the accounts payable ledger.

In a computerized accounting system, when the purchase is recorded, the software automatically posts to the appropriate accounts payable ledger. When posting manually for Accounts Payable, the accountant draws a slanted line in the Post. Ref. column. The account number of Accounts Payable is shown in the left portion to signify the posting to the general ledger, and a check mark is shown in the right portion to signify posting to the accounts payable ledger.

 5 Prepare a schedule of accounts payable.

Learning Objective

Remember

Creditors are companies or individuals to whom we owe money.

The following entries in the general journal, general ledger, and accounts payable ledger are shown for the August 2 transaction after posting is complete.

				GENERAL JOURNAL						Page 26	
Date		Description	Post. Ref.		Debit			Credit			
20--											
Aug.	2	Purchases	511	1 7 1 0	00						
		Freight In	514	8 5	50						
		Accounts Payable, Pataponia, Inc.	212 ✓				1 7 9 5	50			
		Purchased merchandise from									
		Pataponia, Inc., invoice no.									
		2706, invoice dated 7/31,									
		terms 2/10, n/30.									

GENERAL LEDGER

ACCOUNT **Accounts Payable**   ACCOUNT NO. **212**

Date		Item	Post. Ref.	Debit	Credit	Balance Debit	Balance Credit
20--							
Aug.	2				1 7 9 5 50		1 7 9 5 50

ACCOUNTS PAYABLE LEDGER

NAME   **Pataponia, Inc.**
ADDRESS   **1614 Olivera Street**
          San Francisco, CA 94129

Date		Item	Post. Ref.	Debit	Credit	Balance
20--						
Aug.	2		J26		1 7 9 5 50	1 7 9 5 50

Assuming that there were no previous balances in the creditors' accounts and that no other transactions for Whitewater Raft Supply involved Accounts Payable, the schedule of accounts payable, as of the end of August, would appear as shown in Figure 5. Note that the schedule of accounts payable lists each creditor's account balance, and that it equals the Accounts Payable account shown in the general ledger (Figure 6).

Figure 5
Schedule of accounts payable

Whitewater Raft Supply Schedule of Accounts Payable August 31, 20--	
Assets	
Dana Manufacturing Company	$ 564.00
Langseth and Son	2,929.00
Pataponia, Inc.	4,401.50
Total Accounts Payable	$7,894.50

GENERAL LEDGER

ACCOUNT Accounts Payable   ACCOUNT NO. 212

Date		Item	Post. Ref.	Debit	Credit	Balance	
						Debit	Credit
20--							
Aug.	2		J26		1 7 9 5 50		1 7 9 5 50
	10		J26		2 9 2 9 00		4 7 2 4 50
	17		J26		5 6 4 00		5 2 8 8 50
	26		J26		2 6 0 6 00		7 8 9 4 50

Figure 6
Accounts Payable controlling account

9-5a Internal Control of Purchases

Purchases is one of the areas in which internal control is essential. Efficiency and security require most companies to work out careful procedures for buying and paying for goods. This is understandable, as large sums of money are usually involved. The control aspect generally involves the following measures:

1. Purchases are made only after proper authorization is given. Purchase requisitions and purchase orders are prenumbered so that each form can be accounted for.
2. The receiving department, which received a copy of the purchase order without quantities listed, carefully checks all goods upon receipt for count, damages, and description. Later, the report of the receiving department is verified against the purchase order and the purchase invoice.
3. The person who authorizes the payment is neither the person doing the ordering nor the person writing the check. Payment is authorized only after the purchase invoice data are verified against the receiving report and purchase order.
4. The person who actually writes the check has not been involved in any of the foregoing purchasing procedures.

To: **Amy Roberts, CPA**
Subject: **Sales and Purchases**

Hi Amy
Well, I can see there are some differences between a merchandising business and a service business. I believe I now understand how to record my merchandising sales and purchases transactions. What should we discuss next?
Thanks,
Janie

(Continued)

To: Janie Conner
Subject: RE: Sales and Purchases

Hi Janie,
Now that you understand how to handle various activities for the merchandising side of your business, we should discuss what type of inventory system you should use (periodic or perpetual). It would also be a good time to discuss whether you should record transactions in the general journal or special journals. Are you available later this week for a conference call on the following topics?

_____ 1. Periodic versus perpetual inventory systems.

_____ 2. Special journals versus the general journal for recording transactions.

I will be in the office the rest of the week. Just let me know what time works best for you.
Amy

9-6 THE PERPETUAL INVENTORY SYSTEM

Up until now, we have discussed how to record sales and purchases transactions in the general journal using the periodic inventory system. The periodic inventory system requires that companies periodically take a physical count of inventory at the end of the period to determine the amount of inventory on hand.

On the other hand, the perpetual inventory system keeps continuous records of inventories by recording all transactions so that at any given time, companies know the current amount of inventory on hand, and have a better understanding of their profits. Under the perpetual inventory system, sales and purchases are recorded differently than they are under the periodic inventory system.

9-6a Sales Transactions

Learning Objective 6
Using a general journal and the perpetual inventory system, record sales and sale-related transactions.

Let's review the first two sales transactions on the books of Whitewater Raft Supply for August.

Aug. 1 Sold merchandise on account to Mesa River Raft Company, invoice no. 9384, $1,933.50. *Cost of inventory sold is $1,643.48.*

       8 Sold merchandise on account to Green River Rafts, invoice no. 9385, $1,116. *Cost of inventory sold is $948.60.*

Note that the new information regarding the cost of inventory sold is shown in italics. This information concerning the cost of the inventory sold is needed when sales transactions are recorded using the perpetual inventory system.

Whitewater Raft Supply's accountant would record the transactions in the general journal as follows:

GENERAL JOURNAL				Page 26
Date	Description	Post. Ref.	Debit	Credit
20--				
Aug. 1	Accounts Receivable, Mesa River			
	Raft Company		1 9 3 3 50	
	Sales			1 9 3 3 50
	Sold merchandise to Mesa			
	River Raft Company, invoice			
	no. 9384.			
	Cost of Goods Sold		1 6 4 3 48	
	Merchandise Inventory			1 6 4 3 48
	Cost of merchandise sold to			
	Mesa River Raft Company, invoice			
	no. 9384.			
8	Accounts Receivable, Green			
	River Rafts		1 1 1 6 00	
	Sales			1 1 1 6 00
	Sold merchandise to Green			
	River Rafts, invoice no. 9385.			
	Cost of Goods Sold		9 4 8 60	
	Merchandise Inventory			9 4 8 60
	Cost of merchandise sold to			
	Green River Rafts, invoice			
	no. 9385.			

The sales portion of the transaction is recorded the same under either method. Whitewater Raft Supply's accountant records a debit to Accounts Receivable to record the amount that each customer owes the company and a credit to Sales for each transaction. **However, using the perpetual inventory system, the accountant must also record a debit to Cost of Goods Sold for the cost of the inventory sold and a credit to Merchandise Inventory**. The **Cost of Goods Sold account** represents the cost of the inventory sold and is an expense account that is reported on the income statement. Cost of Goods Sold increases when there is a sale and, therefore, is debited. The Merchandise Inventory account must decrease by the cost of the inventory sold, so the accountant records a credit to Merchandise Inventory.

By recording sales transactions in this manner, the company can easily calculate the profit on the sale of the inventory by subtracting Cost of Goods Sold from Sales. Whitewater Raft Supply's gross profit is $290.02 ($1,933.50 − $1,643.48) on the August 1 sale.

9-6b Sales Returns and Allowances

Sales returns and allowances is also recorded differently under the perpetual inventory system. Let's look at Whitewater Raft Supply's return on September 5, with the original sale described first.

FYI

Only returned merchandise that can be resold is debited to Merchandise Inventory. Damaged goods that are returned but cannot be resold should be expensed.

TRANSACTION (a). On August 14, Whitewater Raft Supply sold merchandise on account to Marty's Fly Fishing Adventures, $1,594, and recorded the sale in the general journal. *Cost of inventory sold is $1,354.90.*

TRANSACTION (b). On September 5, Marty's Fly Fishing Adventures returned $254 worth of the merchandise *having a cost of $215.90.* Whitewater Raft Supply issued credit memorandum no. 1069.

Again, note the additional information provided describing the cost of the inventory sold and returned. This information is necessary to record the transactions using the perpetual inventory system.

Whitewater Raft Supply's accountant would record the return on September 5 as follows:

	GENERAL JOURNAL			Page 27
Date	Description	Post. Ref.	Debit	Credit
20--				
Sept. 5	Sales Returns and Allowances		2 5 4 00	
	Accounts Receivable, Marty's			
	Fly Fishing Adventures			2 5 4 00
	Issued credit memo no. 1069.			
	Merchandise Inventory		2 1 5 90	
	Cost of Goods Sold			2 1 5 90
	Cost of merchandise returned,			
	credit memo no. 1069.			

The first part of the journal entry is the same as when using the periodic inventory system. The accountant debits Sales Returns and Allowances and credits Accounts Receivable to decrease it because the customer owes less than before. However, because Whitewater Raft Supply is using the perpetual inventory system, the company must also record the effect of this return on merchandise inventory by debiting Merchandise Inventory to increase it for the returned items and crediting Cost of Goods Sold to decrease the expense.

9-7 PURCHASE TRANSACTIONS

7 Using a general journal and the perpetual inventory system, record purchase and purchase-related transactions.

As we learned earlier in the chapter, when using the periodic inventory system, the accountant uses the Purchases and Freight In (if applied) accounts to record transactions involving purchases. **Under the perpetual inventory system, all transactions related to the purchase of inventory are recorded in the Merchandise Inventory account.** The accountant never uses the Purchases and Freight In accounts when recording purchase transactions under the perpetual inventory system because *all* costs of merchandise inventory (including freight) are included in the Merchandise Inventory account.

Let's look at two purchase transactions on the books of Whitewater Raft Supply for August.

Aug. 2   Bought merchandise on account from Pataponia, Inc., invoice no. 2706, $1,710; terms 2/10, n/30; dated July 31; FOB San Francisco, freight prepaid and added to the invoice, $85.50 (total $1,795.50).

10   Bought merchandise on account from Langseth and Son, invoice no. 982, $2,772; terms net 30 days; dated August 8; FOB Cleveland, freight prepaid and added to the invoice, $157 (total $2,929).

Whitewater Raft Supply's accountant will record the transactions in the general journal as follows:

Date		Description	Post. Ref.	Debit	Credit
GENERAL JOURNAL					**Page 26**
20--					
Aug.	2	Merchandise Inventory		1 7 9 5 50	
		Accounts Payable, Pataponia, Inc.			1 7 9 5 50
		Purchased merchandise from			
		Pataponia, Inc., invoice no.			
		2706, invoice dated 7/31,			
		terms 2/10, n/30.			
	10	Merchandise Inventory		2 9 2 9 00	
		Accounts Payable, Langseth and Son			2 9 2 9 00
		Purchased merchandise from			
		Langseth and Son, invoice			
		no. 982, invoice dated 8/8,			
		terms n/30.			

Note that Whitewater Raft Supply records a debit to the Merchandise Inventory account (not Purchases and Freight In) to record the cost of merchandise, including freight, bought for resale.

9-7a Purchases Returns and Allowances

Under the perpetual inventory system, purchases returns and allowances transactions are recorded directly into the Merchandise Inventory account, and the Purchases Returns and Allowances account is not used.

Let's look at a return on September 8 for Whitewater Raft Supply, with the original purchase described first.

TRANSACTION (a). On September 2, bought merchandise on account from Dana Manufacturing Company, $830.

TRANSACTION (b). On September 8, Whitewater Raft Supply returned some merchandise and received credit memorandum no. 1629 from Dana Manufacturing Company for $270.

Under the perpetual inventory system, the accountant would record the return on September 8 as follows:

Date		Description	Post. Ref.	Debit	Credit
GENERAL JOURNAL					**Page 27**
20--					
Sept.	8	Accounts Payable, Dana			
		Manufacturing Company		2 7 0 00	
		Merchandise Inventory			2 7 0 00
		Credit memo no. 1629 for			
		return of merchandise.			

Whitewater Raft Supply's accountant debits the creditor's Accounts Payable account to decrease it and credits Merchandise Inventory (not Purchases Returns and Allowances) to decrease it. Recording the credit to the Merchandise Inventory account automatically decreases it for the cost of the inventory returned.

9-7b Periodic Inventory System versus Perpetual Inventory System

Following is an abbreviated version of the chart of accounts for both the periodic and perpetual inventory systems. Note that in the periodic inventory system, the company uses accounts such as Purchases, Purchases Returns and Allowances, and Freight In. These accounts are not used in the perpetual inventory system.

PERIODIC INVENTORY SYSTEM	PERPETUAL INVENTORY SYSTEM
Revenue (400–499)	**Revenue (400–499)**
411 Sales	411 Sales
412 Sales Returns and Allowances	412 Sales Returns and Allowances
Cost of Goods Sold (500–599)	**Cost of Goods Sold (500–599)**
511 Purchases	511 Cost of Goods Sold
512 Purchases Returns and Allowances	
514 Freight In	

Now that we have reviewed the main differences between the periodic and perpetual inventory systems, let's take a moment to reflect on those differences. Figure 7 shows a comparison of the transactions we learned for both inventory systems. Make sure you are familiar with both systems and their differences.

Figure 7

Comparison of journal entries for periodic and perpetual inventory systems

Comparison: Periodic Versus Perpetual Inventory Systems		
Transaction	**Periodic Inventory System**	**Perpetual Inventory System**

Sold merchandise, having a cost of $1,643.48, to customer on account, $1,933.50.	Accounts Receivable, Mesa River Raft Company 1,933.50
	  Sales 1,933.50
		Accounts Receivable, Mesa River Raft Company 1,933.50
		  Sales 1,933.50
		
		Cost of Goods Sold 1,643.48
		  Merchandise Inventory 1,643.48

Customer returned merchandise, $254, having a cost of $215.90.	Sales Returns and Allowances 254.00
	  Accounts Receivable,
	  Marty's Fly Fishing Adventures 254.00
		Sales Returns and Allowances 254.00
		  Accounts Receivable,
		  Marty's Fly Fishing Adventures 254.00
		
		Merchandise Inventory 215.90
		  Cost of Goods Sold 215.90

Purchased merchandise from supplier on account, $1,710, with prepaid freight of $85.50.	Purchases 1,710.00
	Freight In 85.50
	  Accounts Payable,
	  Pataponia, Inc. 1,795.50
		Merchandise Inventory 1,795.50
		  Accounts Payable,
		  Pataponia, Inc. 1,795.50

Returned merchandise to supplier, $270.	Accounts Payable, Dana Manufacturing Company 270.00
	  Purchases Returns and Allowances 270.00
		Accounts Payable, Dana Manufacturing Company 270.00
		  Merchandise Inventory 270.00

In the Real World

In order to be profitable, low margin, discount merchandising companies such as Dollar Tree, need to carefully track their sales, purchases, cost of goods sold, sales discounts, and sales returns and allowances. With over 13,600 store locations across the country, it is also important for companies like Dollar Tree to know what inventory is on hand and where that inventory is located. With a fixed sales price of $1 per item sold, there is little room for purchasing mistakes or inventory discrepancies.

9-8 SPECIAL JOURNALS

We have demonstrated sales and purchases by recording the transactions directly into the general journal. Companies can, however, also record sales and purchases into a special journal. **Special journals** are books of original entry used to simplify the recording process. One or more of these journals may be used in a manual accounting system, or they may be used in certain computerized systems designed to facilitate specialized types of repetitive transactions. The four most commonly used special journals are as follows:

Sales journal (S) Used to record sales of merchandise sold on account *only*. For example, if Whitewater Raft Supply sold a kayak to a customer on account, Whitewater Raft Supply could use this journal to record the sale. However, if the customer paid cash for the kayak, the sale would not be recorded in this journal. Also, if Whitewater Raft Supply sold an old computer on account, this journal would not be used because the equipment was not part of the business's merchandise sales.

Purchases journal (P) Used to record purchases of merchandise purchased on account for resale *only*. For example, Whitewater Raft Supply could use this journal for its purchase, on account, of rafts to resell to customers. However, Whitewater Raft Supply would not use this journal when buying a copy machine or supplies for the office, even though they are purchased on account, because those goods are not intended for resale to customers.

Cash receipts journal (CR) Used to record all transactions that include a debit to Cash, such as cash sales, checks received, or interest earned on a checking account.

Cash payments journal (CP) Used to record all transactions that include a credit to Cash, such as payments by check or bank service charges.

In this chapter, we will demonstrate how Whitewater Raft Supply records sales and purchases transactions using the sales journal and purchases journal. In the next chapter, we will discuss the cash receipts journal and cash payments journal.

Learning Objective

8   Record transactions in a sales journal and post to the general ledger and accounts receivable ledger.

9-8a The Sales Journal

The sales journal is used to record sales of merchandise **on account only.** This specialized type of transaction calls for debits to Accounts Receivable and credits to Sales.

Recall the sales transactions introduced for Whitewater Raft Supply for August:

Aug. 1   Sold merchandise on account to Mesa River Raft Company, invoice no. 9384, $1,933.50.

8   Sold merchandise on account to Green River Rafts, invoice no. 9385, $1,116.

14   Sold merchandise on account to Marty's Fly Fishing Adventures, invoice no. 9386, $1,594.

19   Sold merchandise on account to Hi-Flying Adventures, Inc., invoice no. 9387, $552.30.

25   Sold merchandise on account to Hi-Flying Adventures, Inc., invoice no. 9388, $1,674.

Assume that Whitewater Raft Supply uses the sales journal *instead of* the general journal to record the five transactions. The accountant will record each transaction into the sales journal only.

Remember

The sales journal is a book of original entry. Do not duplicate the transaction in the general journal.

SALES JOURNAL				Page 38	
Date	Inv. No.	Customer's Name	Post. Ref.	Accounts Receivable Dr. Sales Cr.	
20--					
Aug. 1	9384	Mesa River Raft Company		1 9 3 3	50
8	9385	Green River Rafts		1 1 1 6	00
14	9386	Marty's Fly Fishing Adventures		1 5 9 4	00
19	9387	Hi-Flying Adventures, Inc.		5 5 2	30
25	9388	Hi-Flying Adventures, Inc.		1 6 7 4	00

Because *one* column is labeled "Accounts Receivable Dr./Sales Cr.," each transaction requires only a single line. Repetition is avoided, and all entries for sales of merchandise on account are found in one place. Listing the invoice number makes it easier to check the details of a particular sale at a later date. It also ensures that no invoice is missed, since they are clearly listed in number order.

As with the general journal, the amount of each sale should be posted daily to the account of each credit customer in the accounts receivable ledger. After you post an amount from the sales journal to a credit customer's account in the accounts receivable ledger, put a check mark in the Post. Ref. column of the sales journal.

POSTING FROM THE SALES JOURNAL TO THE GENERAL LEDGER

Using the sales journal also saves time and space in posting to the ledger accounts. Because every entry is a debit to Accounts Receivable and a credit to Sales, you can make a single posting to these accounts for the amount of the total as of the last day of the month. This entry is called a summarizing entry because it summarizes one month's transactions. Because Whitewater Raft Supply had no more sales transactions after August 25, the amounts in the Accounts Receivable Dr./Sales Cr. Column from the sales journal are added up and totaled. The total ($6,869.80) is then posted to the Accounts Receivable and Sales accounts in the general ledger. In the Post. Ref. columns of the ledger accounts, the letter *S* designates the sales journal.

GENERAL LEDGER

ACCOUNT Accounts Receivable   ACCOUNT NO. 113

Date	Item	Post. Ref.	Debit	Credit	Balance Debit	Balance Credit
20--						
Aug. 31		S38	6 8 6 9 80		6 8 6 9 80	

GENERAL LEDGER

ACCOUNT Sales   ACCOUNT NO. 411

Date	Item	Post. Ref.	Debit	Credit	Balance Debit	Balance Credit
20--						
Aug. 31		S38		6 8 6 9 80		6 8 6 9 80

After posting the total of the sales journal to the Accounts Receivable account in the general ledger, write the account number of Accounts Receivable at the left below the total of the sales journal. Repeat the process of posting for the total of the sales journal to the Sales account in the general ledger, placing the account number of Sales at the right below the total of the sales journal. **Don't record these account numbers until you have completed the postings.** Figure 8 shows the completed sales journal for Whitewater Raft Supply for August.

SALES JOURNAL   Page 38

Date	Inv. No.	Customer's Name	Post. Ref.	Accounts Receivable Dr. Sales Cr.
20--				
Aug. 1	9384	Mesa River Raft Company	✓	1 9 3 3 50
8	9385	Green River Rafts	✓	1 1 1 6 00
14	9386	Marty's Fly Fishing Adventures	✓	1 5 9 4 00
19	9387	Hi-Flying Adventures, Inc.	✓	5 5 2 30
25	9388	Hi-Flying Adventures, Inc.	✓	1 6 7 4 00
31		Total		6 8 6 9 80
				(113) (411)

Figure 8
Sales journal

SALES JOURNAL WITH SALES TAX PAYABLE

When recording sales transactions that involve sales tax, the sales journal will need to include three columns: Accounts Receivable Debit, Sales Tax Payable Credit, and Sales Credit.

Recall the transaction given for David Fly Fishing Outfitters earlier in the chapter.

Jan.   3   Sold merchandise on account to R. Martinez, invoice no. 101, $153.50 plus sales tax of $12.28.

Remember

The sales journal is used to record only the sales of merchandise (goods) on account.

As shown below, David Fly Fishing Outfitters would record the transaction in the sales journal as follows:

SALES JOURNAL							Page 3
Date	Inv. No.	Customer's Name	Post. Ref.	Accounts Receivable Debit	Sales Tax Payable Credit	Sales Credit	
20--							
Jan. 3	101	R. Martinez		1 6 5 78	1 2 28	1 5 3 50	

At the end of the month, the accountant for David Fly Fishing Outfitters would total the columns and post them as a debit to Accounts Receivable, a credit to Sales Tax Payable, and a credit to Sales. However, with a journal that has more than one column, before posting to the general ledger accounts you should use the column totals to prove that the total debits equal the total credits. After posting, the respective account numbers are recorded in parentheses below the totals.

9-9 PURCHASES JOURNAL (THREE COLUMN)

Learning Objective

9 Record transactions in a three-column purchases journal and post to the general ledger and accounts payable ledger.

Following are the purchase transactions for Whitewater Raft Supply for August. We will use these transactions to demonstrate the purchases journal.

Aug. 2 Bought merchandise on account from Pataponia, Inc., invoice no. 2706, $1,710; terms 2/10, n/30; dated July 31; FOB San Francisco, freight prepaid and added to the invoice, $85.50 (total $1,795.50).

10 Bought merchandise on account from Langseth and Son, invoice no. 982, $2,772; terms net 30 days; dated August 8; FOB Cleveland, freight prepaid and added to the invoice, $157 (total $2,929).

17 Bought merchandise on account from Dana Manufacturing Company, invoice no. 10611, $564; terms 2/10, n/30; dated August 15; FOB Los Angeles.

26 Bought merchandise on account from Pataponia, Inc., invoice no. 2801, $2,503.70; terms 2/10, n/30; dated August 24; FOB San Francisco, freight prepaid and added to the invoice, $102.30 (total $2,606).

As shown below, Whitewater Raft Supply's accountant will record each transaction into the purchases journal. Notice that by including a separate column for each account, Whitewater Raft Supply can record a typical purchase of merchandise on account on one line.

PURCHASES JOURNAL								Page 29
Date	Supplier's Name	Inv. No.	Inv. Date	Terms	Post. Ref.	Accounts Payable Credit	Freight In Debit	Purchases Debit
20--								
Aug. 2	Pataponia, Inc.	2706	7/31	2/10, n/30		1 7 9 5 50	8 5 50	1 7 1 0 00
10	Langseth and Son	982	8/8	n/30		2 9 2 9 00	1 5 7 00	2 7 7 2 00
17	Dana Manufacturing Co.	10611	8/15	2/10, n/30		5 6 4 00		5 6 4 00
26	Pataponia, Inc.	2801	8/24	2/10, n/30		2 6 0 6 00	1 0 2 30	2 5 0 3 70

POSTING FROM THE PURCHASES JOURNAL TO THE GENERAL LEDGER

If using a manual system, each purchase should be posted daily to the accounts payable ledger. After you post an amount from the purchases journal to the accounts payable ledger, put a check mark in the Post. Ref. column of the purchases journal. The accountant also posts the totals of each column into the appropriate general ledger accounts at the end of each month. Figure 9 shows the journal entries in the purchases journal for Whitewater Raft Supply for all transactions involving the purchase of merchandise on account for August and the related ledger accounts for the same time period. In the Post. Ref. column of the ledger accounts, *P* designates the purchases journal. After posting the column totals for the month to the ledger accounts, the accountant goes back to the purchases journal and records the account numbers in parentheses directly below the total.

> **Remember**
>
> Transactions involving the buying of supplies or other assets should not be journalized in the three-column purchases journal. This purchases journal may be used only for purchases of merchandise for resale.

PURCHASES JOURNAL   Page 29

Date		Supplier's Name	Inv. No.	Inv. Date	Terms	Post. Ref.	Accounts Payable Credit	Freight In Debit	Purchases Debit
20--									
Aug.	2	Pataponia, Inc.	2706	7/31	2/10, n/30	✓	1 7 9 5 50	8 5 50	1 7 1 0 00
	10	Langseth and Son	982	8/8	n/30	✓	2 9 2 9 00	1 5 7 00	2 7 7 2 00
	17	Dana Manufacturing Co.	10611	8/15	2/10, n/30	✓	5 6 4 00		5 6 4 00
	26	Pataponia, Inc.	2801	8/24	2/10, n/30	✓	2 6 0 6 00	1 0 2 30	2 5 0 3 70
	31	Totals					7 8 9 4 50	3 4 4 80	7 5 4 9 70
							(2 1 2)	(5 1 4)	(5 1 1)

GENERAL LEDGER

ACCOUNT Accounts Payable   **ACCOUNT NO. 212**

Date		Item	Post. Ref.	Debit	Credit	Balance Debit	Balance Credit
20--							
Aug.	31		P29		7 8 9 4 50		7 8 9 4 50

ACCOUNT Purchases   **ACCOUNT NO. 511**

Date		Item	Post. Ref.	Debit	Credit	Balance Debit	Balance Credit
20--							
Aug.	31		P29	7 5 4 9 70		7 5 4 9 70	

ACCOUNT Freight In   **ACCOUNT NO. 514**

Date		Item	Post. Ref.	Debit	Credit	Balance Debit	Balance Credit
20--							
Aug.	31		P29	3 4 4 80		3 4 4 80	

Figure 9
Purchases journal and general ledger accounts

Chapter Review

Study and Practice

 Learning Objective   **1** Describe the nature of a merchandising business.

A **merchandising business** is a company that buys and sells inventory.
The **Merchandise Inventory** account is an asset account representing the cost of goods bought for resale.
Merchandise inventory can be recorded using the **periodic inventory system** or the **perpetual inventory system**.

 PRACTICE EXERCISE 1

Identify the appropriate inventory system (periodic or perpetual) below.

In the _____ inventory system, companies keep continuous records of inventories.

The _____ inventory system requires companies periodically to take a physical count of merchandise.

PRACTICE EXERCISE 1 • SOLUTION

In the *perpetual* inventory system, companies keep continuous records of inventories. The *periodic* inventory system requires companies periodically to take a physical count of merchandise.

 Learning Objective   **2** Using a general journal and the periodic inventory system, record sales and sale-related transactions; then post to the general ledger and the accounts receivable ledger.

Sales transactions are recorded in the general journal by debiting Accounts Receivable and crediting Sales. The entry is posted to the Accounts Receivable and Sales accounts in the general ledger. The entries are also posted daily to the **accounts receivable ledger**.

When a customer returns merchandise, or when his or her bill is reduced by an allowance for defective or damaged merchandise, the Sales Returns and Allowances account is debited and the Accounts Receivable account is credited. The entry is recorded in the general journal and posted to both the general ledger and the accounts receivable ledger.

Where required, sales tax is collected from customers by the retailer and later paid to the appropriate tax authorities. When goods are sold, the sales tax is charged to the customer and recorded at the time of sale. The entry involves recording a debit to Accounts Receivable or Cash and credits to Sales and Sales Tax Payable.

PRACTICE EXERCISE 2

Record the following transactions for Rodgers Refrigerator Supply in general journal form.

Aug. 23   Sold merchandise on account to Robbins Hardware Store, invoice no. 3209, $1,340.

Sept. 1   Robbins Hardware Store returned $81 of the merchandise. Rodgers Refrigerator Supply issued credit memo no. 114.

     14   Sold merchandise on account to C. Heald, invoice no. 3210, $560 plus $44.80 sales tax.

PRACTICE EXERCISE 2 • SOLUTION

GENERAL JOURNAL						Page ___
Date		Description	Post. Ref.	Debit	Credit	
20--						
Aug.	23	Accounts Receivable, Robbins				
		Hardware Store		1 3 4 0 00		
		Sales			1 3 4 0 00	
		Sold merchandise to Robbins				
		Hardware Store, invoice				
		no. 3209.				
Sept.	1	Sales Returns and Allowances		8 1 00		
		Accounts Receivable, Robbins				
		Hardware Store			8 1 00	
		Issued credit memo no. 114.				
	14	Accounts Receivable, C. Heald		6 0 4 80		
		Sales			5 6 0 00	
		Sales Tax Payable			4 4 80	
		Sold merchandise to C. Heald,				
		invoice no. 3210.				

   Prepare a schedule of accounts receivable.

Learning Objective

The schedule of accounts receivable consists of a listing of the individual account balances of the credit customers taken from the accounts receivable ledger.

 PRACTICE EXERCISE 3

Fill in the missing amounts in the accounts receivable subsidiary ledgers for Willis Spas and Pools. Then, using the information from the ledgers, prepare a schedule of accounts receivable as of May 31.

ACCOUNTS RECEIVABLE LEDGER

NAME J. Hersch
ADDRESS 3540 Key Avenue
Lampasas, TX 76550

Date		Item	Post. Ref.	Debit	Credit	Balance
20--						
May	2		J26	7 8 1 40		7 8 1 40
	8		J26	1 7 8 0 00		(a)
	22		J26		1 2 0 5 00	(b)

NAME M. Hill
ADDRESS 220 Lawrence Avenue
Copperas Cove, TX 76522

Date		Item	Post. Ref.	Debit	Credit	Balance
20--						
May	15		J26	4 8 1 40		4 8 1 40
	18		J26		2 0 4 80	(c)

NAME R. D. Moen
ADDRESS 416 Fifth Avenue
Dallas, TX 75204

Date		Item	Post. Ref.	Debit	Credit	Balance
20--						
May	31		J26	3 1 2 60		3 1 2 60

PRACTICE EXERCISE 3 • SOLUTION

(a) $2,561.40
(b) $1,356.40
(c) $276.60

Willis Spas and Pools
Schedule of Accounts Receivable
May 31, 20--

J. Hersch	$1,356.40
M. Hill	276.60
R. D. Moen	312.60
Total Accounts Receivable	$1,945.60

Learning Objective

 4 Using a general journal and the periodic inventory system, record purchase and purchase-related transactions; then post to the general ledger and the accounts payable ledger.

Purchase transactions are recorded in the general journal by debiting the Purchases account and crediting Accounts Payable. If the company pays for freight, the company will also record a debit to Freight In. The purchase transactions are posted to the general ledger as a debit to Purchases, a debit to Freight In, and a credit to Accounts Payable. Each transaction must also be posted daily to the **accounts payable ledger**.

When a credit memo is received for the return of merchandise or as an allowance for damaged goods, the buyer credits Purchases Returns and Allowances. If the merchandise was bought on account, the buyer debits Accounts Payable. The entry is recorded in the general journal and posted to both the general ledger and the accounts payable ledger.

The Freight In account is debited for the cost of transportation charges on incoming merchandise intended for resale. Freight costs that apply to non-merchandise assets purchased are added to the asset account that applies.

 PRACTICE EXERCISE 4

Record the following transaction for Byrne Corporation in general journal form.

Apr. 14 Bought merchandise on account from Jabari, Inc., invoice no. C3009, $1,125; terms net 30 days; dated April 12; FOB shipping point, freight prepaid and added to the invoice, $72.50 (total $1,197.50).

24 Byrne Corporation received credit memo no. 117 from Jabari, Inc., for merchandise returned, $127.

PRACTICE EXERCISE 4 • SOLUTION

		GENERAL JOURNAL			Page ___	
Date		Description	Post. Ref.	Debit	Credit	
20--						
Apr.	14	Purchases		1 1 2 5 00		
		Freight In		7 2 50		
		Accounts Payable, Jabari, Inc.			1 1 9 7 50	
		Purchased merchandise from				
		Jabari, Inc., invoice no. C3009,				
		invoice dated 4/12, terms n/30.				
	24	Accounts Payable, Jabari, Inc.		1 2 7 00		
		Purchases Returns and Allowances			1 2 7 00	
		Credit memo no. 117 for				
		return of merchandise.				

 Prepare a schedule of accounts payable.

Learning Objective

A schedule of accounts payable, which lists the balance of each creditor's account, is prepared from the accounts payable ledger.

 PRACTICE EXERCISE 5

Fill in the missing amounts in the accounts payable subsidiary ledgers for Updike Train Supply. Then, using the information from the ledgers, prepare a schedule of accounts payable as of June 30.

ACCOUNTS PAYABLE LEDGER

NAME **J. Fletcher and Sons**

ADDRESS **326 Fairway Drive**

Richmond, CA 94805

Date		Item	Post. Ref.	Debit	Credit	Balance
20--						
June	1		J73		1 7 5 1 55	1 7 5 1 55
	14		J73	1 5 7 6 15		(a)

NAME **Rocky and Schlink**

ADDRESS **542 Roselle Blvd.**

Oakland, CA 94601

Date		Item	Post. Ref.	Debit	Credit	Balance
20--						
June	13		J73		2 1 8 00	2 1 8 00

NAME **Tan Supplies**

ADDRESS **120 Fish Road**

Berkeley, CA 94720

Date		Item	Post. Ref.	Debit	Credit	Balance
20--						
June	5		J73		2 7 1 0 00	2 7 1 0 00
	23		J73		1 7 4 0 25	(b)
	29		J73	1 5 0 0 00		(c)

PRACTICE EXERCISE 5 • SOLUTION

(a) $175.40

(b) $4,450.25

(c) $2,950.25

Updike Train Supply Schedule of Accounts Payable June 30, 20--	
J. Fletcher and Sons	$ 175.40
Rocky and Schlink	218.00
Tan Supplies	2,950.25
Total Accounts Payable	$3,343.65

Learning Objective

 Using a general journal and the perpetual inventory system, record sales and sale-related transactions.

The perpetual inventory system keeps continuous records of inventories by recording all transactions. This system allows companies, at any given time, to know the current cost of inventory on hand and provides them with a better understanding of their sales profits. With the perpetual inventory system, sales, sales returns and allowances, and purchases are recorded differently than in the periodic inventory system. While the actual sales portion of the sales transaction is recorded the same under both methods, the perpetual inventory system requires an additional step in the recording process. To track the inventory and costs, accountants using the perpetual inventory system debit Cost of Goods Sold and credit Merchandise Inventory.

 PRACTICE EXERCISE 6

Record the following transactions for North Company in general journal form. North Company uses the perpetual inventory system.

July 1 Sold merchandise on account to Ryder, Inc., invoice no. 5865, $1,450.50. Cost of inventory sold is $1,125.40.

6 Sold merchandise on account to Dean Co., invoice no. 5866, $2,240.25. Cost of inventory sold is $1,950.30.

8 Ryder, Inc., returned $475.00 worth of merchandise purchased on July 1, with a cost of $230.25. North Company issued credit memorandum no. 149.

PRACTICE EXERCISE 6 • SOLUTION

GENERAL JOURNAL				Page __	
Date		Description	Post. Ref.	Debit	Credit
20--					
July	1	Accounts Receivable, Ryder, Inc.		1 4 5 0 50	
		Sales			1 4 5 0 50
		Sold merchandise on account to			
		Ryder, Inc., invoice no. 5865.			
		Cost of Goods Sold		1 1 2 5 40	
		Merchandise Inventory			1 1 2 5 40
		Cost of merchandise sold			
		to Ryder, Inc., invoice no. 5865			
	6	Accounts Receivable, Dean Co.		2 2 4 0 25	
		Sales			2 2 4 0 25
		Sold merchandise to Dean Co.,			
		invoice no. 5866			
		Cost of Goods Sold		1 9 5 0 30	
		Merchandise Inventory			1 9 5 0 30
		Cost of merchandise sold to Dean Co.,			
		invoice no. 5866			
	8	Sales Returns and Allowances		4 7 5 00	
		Accounts Receivable, Ryder, Inc.			4 7 5 00
		Issued credit memo no. 149			
		Merchandise Inventory		2 3 0 25	
		Cost of Goods Sold			2 3 0 25
		Cost of merchandise returned credit			
		memo no. 149			

Learning Objective	7	Using a general journal and the perpetual inventory system, record purchase and purchase-related transactions.

Under the perpetual inventory system, all transactions related to the purchase of inventory (including freight in) are recorded in the Merchandise Inventory account. In addition, the return of merchandise is recorded as a credit to Merchandise Inventory.

 ### PRACTICE EXERCISE 7

Record the following transactions for Mitchell Co., in general journal form. Mitchell Co. uses the perpetual inventory system.

Aug. 1 Bought merchandise on account from Engel Industries, invoice no. 2516, $3,542.15; terms 2/10, n/30; FOB Detroit, freight prepaid and added to the invoice, $115.00 (total $3,657.15).

 10 Received credit memorandum no. 1115 from Engel Industries for $450.00.

PRACTICE EXERCISE 7 • SOLUTION

		GENERAL JOURNAL				Page ___	
Date		Description	Post. Ref.	Debit		Credit	
20--							
Aug.	1	Merchandise Inventory		3 6 5 7 15			
		Accounts Payable, Engel Industries				3 6 5 7 15	
		Purchased merchandise from Engel					
		Industries, invoice no. 2516,					
		invoice dated 8/1, terms 2/10, n/30					
	10	Accounts Payable, Engel Industries		4 5 0 00			
		Merchandise Inventory				4 5 0 00	
		Credit memo no. 1115 for return of					
		merchandise.					

Learning Objective	8	Record transactions in a sales journal and post to the general ledger and accounts receivable ledger.

The **sales journal** is used to record only sales of merchandise on account. The entries are posted daily to the accounts receivable ledger. At the end of the month, the total is posted to the general ledger as a debit to the Accounts Receivable controlling account and a credit to the Sales account.

 ### PRACTICE EXERCISE 8

Record the following sales of merchandise on account on page 25 of the sales journal and then post to the general ledger. (The company uses the same account numbers as Whitewater Raft Supply.)

Apr. 1 Sold merchandise on account to West Company, invoice no. 1054, $1,378.95.

 15 Sold merchandise on account to Ruiz Company, invoice no. 1055, $578.15.

PRACTICE EXERCISE 8 • SOLUTION

			SALES JOURNAL				Page 25				
Date		Inv. No.	Customer's Name		Post. Ref.	Accounts Receivable Dr. Sales Cr.					
20--											
Apr.	1	1054	West Company			1	3	7	8	95	
	15	1055	Ruiz Company				5	7	8	15	
	30		Total			1	9	5	7	10	
							(113)		(411)		

GENERAL LEDGER

ACCOUNT Accounts Receivable   **ACCOUNT NO. 113**

Date	Item	Post. Ref.	Debit					Credit						Balance Debit					Credit				
20--																							
Apr.	30	S25	1	9	5	7	10							1	9	5	7	10					

ACCOUNT Sales   **ACCOUNT NO. 411**

Date	Item	Post. Ref.	Debit					Credit						Balance Debit					Credit				
20--																							
Apr.	30	S25						1	9	5	7	10							1	9	5	7	10

> **9** Record transactions in a three-column purchases journal and post to the general ledger and accounts payable ledger.

Learning Objective

The three-column **purchases journal** handles the purchase of merchandise on account and freight charges that are prepaid by the seller and included in the invoice total. Amounts in the Accounts Payable credit column are posted daily to the accounts payable ledger. At the end of the month, the totals are posted to the general ledger as a debit to Purchases, a debit to Freight In, and a credit to Accounts Payable.

PRACTICE EXERCISE 9

Record the following purchases of merchandise on account on page 52 of the purchases journal and then post to the general ledger. (The company uses the same account numbers as Whitewater Raft Supply.)

Jan. 4   Bought merchandise on account from Switzer Corporation, invoice no. A459, $578; terms net 60 days; dated January 2; FOB destination.

      24   Bought merchandise on account from Stevens Company, invoice no. 48512, $799.80; terms 2/10, n/30; dated January 22; FOB shipping point, freight prepaid and added to the invoice, $50 (total $849.80).

CHAPTER REVIEW

PRACTICE EXERCISE 9 • SOLUTION

								Accounts Payable Credit	Freight In Debit	Purchases Debit
Date		Supplier's Name	Inv. No.	Inv. Date	Terms	Post. Ref.				
20--										
Jan.	4	Switzer Corporation	A459	1/2	n/60			5 7 8 00		5 7 8 00
	24	Stevens Company	48512	1/22	2/10, n/30			8 4 9 80	5 0 00	7 9 9 80
	31	Totals						1 4 2 7 80	5 0 00	1 3 7 7 80
								(2 1 2)	(5 1 4)	(5 1 1)

PURCHASES JOURNAL — Page 52

GENERAL LEDGER

ACCOUNT Accounts Payable   ACCOUNT NO. 212

Date	Item	Post. Ref.	Debit	Credit	Balance Debit	Balance Credit
20--						
Jan. 31		P52		1 4 2 7 80		1 4 2 7 80

ACCOUNT Purchases   ACCOUNT NO. 511

Date	Item	Post. Ref.	Debit	Credit	Balance Debit	Balance Credit
20--						
Jan. 31		P52	1 3 7 7 80		1 3 7 7 80	

ACCOUNT Freight In   ACCOUNT NO. 514

Date	Item	Post. Ref.	Debit	Credit	Balance Debit	Balance Credit
20--						
Jan. 31		P52	5 0 00		5 0 00	

Glossary

Accounts payable ledger A subsidiary ledger that lists the individual accounts of creditors in alphabetical or numerical order with their respective balances. (p. 381)

Accounts receivable ledger A subsidiary ledger that lists the individual accounts of credit customers in alphabetical or numerical order, with their respective transactions and balances. (p. 373)

Controlling account An account in the general ledger that summarizes the balances of a subsidiary ledger. (p. 373)

Cost of Goods Sold account An account, used in the perpetual inventory system, that represents the cost of the inventory sold. (p. 385)

Credit memorandum A written statement indicating a seller's willingness to reduce the amount of a buyer's debt. The seller records the amount of the credit memorandum in the Sales Returns and Allowances account. (p. 371)

FOB destination Shipping terms under which the seller pays the freight charges and includes them in the selling price. Title or ownership changes hands when the buyer receives the goods. (p. 379)

FOB shipping point Shipping terms under which the buyer pays the freight charges between the point of shipment and the destination. Payment may be made directly to the carrier upon receiving the goods or to the supplier if the supplier prepaid the freight charges on behalf of the buyer. Title or ownership changes hands when goods are transferred to the freight company. (*p. 379*)

Invoices Business forms prepared by the seller that list the items shipped, their cost, the terms of the sale, and the mode of shipment. They may also state the freight charges. The buyer considers them purchase invoices; the seller considers them sales invoices. (*p. 368*)

Merchandise inventory Goods (an asset account) that a company buys and intends to resell at a profit. (*p. 367*)

Merchandising businesses Businesses that buy and sell goods. (*p. 367*)

Periodic inventory system A method of recording inventory that requires the company to determine the amount of goods on hand by periodically taking a physical count and then attaching a value to it. (*p. 367*)

Perpetual inventory system A method of recording inventory that provides the firm with a running balance of inventory. (*p. 367*)

Purchases account An account for recording the cost of merchandise acquired for resale. (*p. 375*)

Purchases journal A special journal used to record only the buying of goods on account. It may be used to record the purchase of merchandise only. (*p. 389*)

Purchases Returns and Allowances account An account that records a company's return of merchandise it has purchased or a reduction in the bill for an agreed-upon reason. It is treated as a deduction from Purchases. (*p. 378*)

Sales account A revenue account for recording the sale of merchandise. (*p. 367*)

Sales journal A special journal for recording only the sale of merchandise on account. (*p. 389*)

Sales Returns and Allowances account The account a seller uses to record the physical return of merchandise by customers or a reduction in a bill for an agreed-upon reason. Sales Returns and Allowances is treated as a deduction from Sales. This account is usually evidenced by a credit memorandum issued by the seller. (*p. 370*)

Sales Tax Payable account An account used to record a tax levied by a state or city government on the retail sale of goods and services. The tax is paid by the consumer but collected by the retailer. (*p. 371*)

Special journals Books of original entry in which specialized types of repetitive transactions are recorded. (*p. 389*)

Subsidiary ledger A group of accounts representing individual subdivisions showing the debits and credits of a controlling account. (*p. 373*)

Quiz Yourself

_____ 1. Which of the following is true about the Sales Returns and Allowances account?
   a. It is used to record the sale of merchandise.
   b. It is used to record the reduction of inventory.
   c. It is a contra account, deducted from sales.
   d. It is used to record discounts for prompt payment.
   e. None of the above.

_____ 2. What is the accounts receivable ledger?
   a. A record of credit customers and their balances
   b. A record of vendors and their balances
   c. Part of the sales journal
   d. Part of the general journal
   e. Part of the general ledger

_____ 3. Using the information contained in the accounts receivable ledger, the accountant can prepare _____.
   a. The general ledger balance
   b. The balance sheet
   c. The income statement
   d. A schedule of accounts receivable
   e. None of the above

_____ 4. Which of the following is a written statement indicating a seller's willingness to reduce the amount of a buyer's debt?
   a. Debit memorandum
   b. Credit memorandum
   c. Letter of intent
   d. Sales Returns and Allowances memorandum
   e. None of the above

CHAPTER REVIEW

_____ 5. What does the "2" in 2/10, n/30 mean?
   a. Pay in 2 days to ensure early payment
   b. 2% discount for early payment within 10 days
   c. 2% extra payment due if paid between 10 days and 30 days
   d. $2 discount if paid within 10 days
   e. None of the above

_____ 6. Which of the following is a subsidiary ledger that consists of individual accounts for all creditors?
   a. Accounts receivable ledger
   b. Controlling ledger
   c. Accounts payable ledger
   d. Inventory ledger
   e. Purchase ledger

_____ 7. The schedule of accounts payable lists each creditor's account balance, and the total equals the _____.
   a. Controlling account in the journal
   b. Accounts Payable account in the general ledger
   c. Accounts Receivable account in the general ledger
   d. Purchases account in the general ledger
   e. Sales account in the general ledger

_____ 8. If the seller assumes the entire cost of transportation, without any reimbursement from the buyer, the freight terms are considered _____.
   a. FOB shipping point
   b. FOB destination
   c. Freight in
   d. Freight out
   e. FOB freight

_____ 9. Under the perpetual inventory system, how does the seller record sales made on account?

a. Accounts Payable	DR	
Sales		CR
b. Sales	DR	
Accounts Payable		CR
c. Accounts Receivable	DR	
Sales		CR
d. Accounts Receivable	DR	
Sales		CR
Cost of Goods Sold	DR	
Merchandise Inventory		CR
e. Sales	DR	
Accounts Receivable		CR
Merchandise Inventory	DR	
Cost of Goods Sold		CR

10. Purchases on account of merchandise for resale would be recorded in the _____.
   a. Sales journal
   b. Purchases journal
   c. Cash receipts journal
   d. Cash payments journal
   e. None of the above

Answers:
1. c   2. a   3. d   4. b   5. b   6. c   7. b
8. b   9. d   10. b

Chapter Assignments

Discussion Questions

1. What is the difference between a wholesale business and a retail business?
2. For each of the following accounts, identify whether the normal balance is a debit or a credit. Also specify whether the account is a contra account.
   a. Sales Returns and Allowances
   b. Merchandise Inventory
   c. Sales
   d. Freight In
   e. Purchases Returns and Allowances
   f. Sales Tax Payable
   g. Purchases

3. What is the purpose of each of the following?
   a. Schedule of accounts receivable
   b. Schedule of accounts payable
4. Why is an accounts receivable ledger or an accounts payable ledger necessary for a business with large numbers of credit customers or large numbers of vendors/suppliers?
5. Why is it a good practice to post daily to the accounts receivable or accounts payable ledgers?
6. With regard to goods sold and purchased, explain how sales returns and allowances and purchases returns and allowances are different from each other.
7. Explain the meaning and importance of the shipping terms FOB destination and FOB shipping point. Who has title to the goods once they have been shipped?
8. Describe the four procedures that most companies follow to maintain internal control of purchases of merchandise.
9. Describe the posting procedures to the general ledger and the rules for totaling and ruling the following.
   a. Sales journal
   b. Purchases journal
10. Describe the procedure for posting each of the following:
    a. From the sales journal to the accounts receivable ledger
    b. From the purchases journal to the accounts payable ledger
11. Who issues a credit memorandum and why?
12. What is the difference between a periodic inventory system and a perpetual inventory system?

Exercises

EXERCISE 9-1 Record the following transactions in general journal form.
a. Sold merchandise on account to D. North, invoice no. 4556, $2,515.25.
b. Sold merchandise on account to NexStar Industries, invoice no. 4557, $775.00.
c. NexStar Industries returned $225.50 worth of the merchandise. Issued credit memo no. 101.

LO 2

Practice Exercise 2

EXERCISE 9-2 Post the following entry to the general ledger and subsidiary ledger.

LO 2

Practice Exercises 2, 3

		GENERAL JOURNAL					Page 52	
Date		Description	Post. Ref.	Debit		Credit		
20--								
August	16	Sales Returns and Allowances		2 8 6 42				
		Accounts Receivable, F. E. Dixon				2 8 6 42		
		Issued credit memo no. 131.						

GENERAL LEDGER

ACCOUNT Accounts Receivable   ACCOUNT NO. 113

Date		Item	Post. Ref.	Debit	Credit	Balance Debit	Balance Credit
20--							
August	1	Balance	✓			5 2 1 4 36	

(Continued)

ACCOUNT	Sales Returns and Allowances				ACCOUNT NO. 412	
		Post.			Balance	
Date	Item	Ref.	Debit	Credit	Debit	Credit
20--						
August 1	Balance	✓			2 1 8 40	

ACCOUNTS RECEIVABLE LEDGER

NAME F. E. Dixon

ADDRESS 416 Fifth Avenue

Dallas, TX 75204

Date	Item	Post. Ref.	Debit	Credit	Balance
20--					
July 31		J51	4 6 0 15		4 6 0 15

Practice Exercise 2

LO 2

EXERCISE 9-3 Record the following transactions in general journal form.

a. Sold merchandise on account to A. Bauer, $680 plus $54.40 sales tax (invoice no. D446).

b. Bauer returned $105.50 of the merchandise. Issued credit memo no. 114 for $113.94 ($105.50 for the amount of the sale plus $8.44 for the amount of the sales tax).

LO 4

Practice Exercise 4

EXERCISE 9-4 Journalize the following transactions in general journal form.

a. Bought merchandise on account from Brewer, Inc., invoice no. B2997, $914; terms net 30 days; FOB destination.

b. Received credit memo no. 96 from Brewer, Inc., for merchandise returned, $238.

LO 4

Practice Exercises 4, 5

EXERCISE 9-5 Post the following entry to the general ledger and the subsidiary ledger.

		GENERAL JOURNAL			Page 92	
Date		Description	Post. Ref.	Debit	Credit	
20--						
Sept.	15	Accounts Payable, Jensen and Silva		2 9 1 50		
		Purchases Returns and				
		Allowances			2 9 1 50	
		Credit memo no. 942 for				
		return of merchandise.				

GENERAL LEDGER

ACCOUNT	Accounts Payable				ACCOUNT NO. 212	
		Post.			Balance	
Date	Item	Ref.	Debit	Credit	Debit	Credit
20--						
Sept. 1	Balance	✓				2 8 7 2 45

(Continued)

ACCOUNT	Purchases Returns and Allowances				ACCOUNT NO.	512	
		Post.			Balance		
Date	Item	Ref.	Debit	Credit	Debit	Credit	
20--							
Sept. 1	Balance	✓				1 6 0 30	

ACCOUNTS PAYABLE LEDGER

NAME Jensen and Silva
ADDRESS 542 Roselle Blvd.
Chicago, IL 60141

Date	Item	Post. Ref.	Debit	Credit	Balance
20--					
Sept. 6		J92		3 1 5 00	3 1 5 00

LO 2, 4

Practice Exercises 2, 4

EXERCISE 9-6 Record the following transactions in general journal form for Ford Education Outfitters and Romero Textbooks, Inc.

a. Ford Educational Outfitters bought merchandise on account from Romero Textbooks, Inc., invoice no. 10594, $1,875.34; terms net 30 days; FOB destination. Romero Textbooks, Inc., paid $93.80 for shipping.

b. Ford Education Outfitters received credit memo no. 513A from Romero Textbooks, Inc., for merchandise returned, $135.78.

LO 6, 7

Practice Exercises 6, 7

EXERCISE 9-7 Record the following transactions for a perpetual inventory system in general journal form.

a. Sold merchandise on account to Southridge Manufacturing, Inc., invoice no. 6910, $1,815.24. The cost of merchandise was $1,320.

b. Issued credit memorandum no. 56 to Southridge Manufacturing, Inc., for merchandise returned, $622. The cost of the merchandise was $485.

c. Bought merchandise on account from Michal's Inc., invoice no. 1685, $850; terms 1/10, n/30; dated April 14; FOB Dallas, freight prepaid and added to the invoice, $65.00 (total $915).

d. Received credit memorandum no. 219 from Michal's Inc. for merchandise returned, $210.

LO 8

Practice Exercise 8

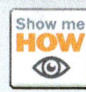

EXERCISE 9-8 Toby Company had the following sales transactions for March:

Mar. 6 Sold merchandise on account to Osbourne, Inc., invoice no. 1128, $563.17.
14 Sold merchandise on account to Ortiz Company, invoice no. 1129, $823.50.
20 Sold merchandise on account to Bailey Corporation, invoice no. 1130, $2,350.98.
24 Sold merchandise on account to Shannon Corporation, invoice no. 1131, $1,547.07.

Assume that Toby Company had beginning balances on March 1 of $3,569.80 (Sales 411) and $2,450.39 (Accounts Receivable 113). Record the sales of merchandise on account in the sales journal (page 24) and then post to the general ledger.

LO 9

Practice Exercise 9

EXERCISE 9-9 Williams Corporation had the following purchases for May:

May   3   Bought ten lawn rakes from Owens Company, invoice no. J34Y9, $250.25; terms net 15 days; dated May 1; FOB shipping point, freight prepaid and added to the invoice, $15 (total $265.25).

11   Bought one weed trimmer from Lionel's Lawn & Landscaping, invoice no. R7740, $219.72; terms 2/10, n/30; dated May 9; FOB shipping point, freight prepaid and added to the invoice, $35 (total $254.72).

15   Bought five bags of fertilizer from Wright's Farm Supplies, invoice no. 478, $210.97; terms net 30 days; dated May 13; FOB destination.

25   Bought one lawn mower from Gutierrez Corporation, invoice no. 2458, $425.39; terms net 30 days; dated May 22; FOB destination.

Assume that Williams Corporation had beginning balances on May 1 of $3,492.29 (Accounts Payable 212), $4,239.49 (Purchases 511), and $234.89 (Freight In 514). Record the purchases of merchandise on account in the purchases journal (page 13) and then post to the general ledger.

LO 8, 9

Practice Exercises 8, 9

EXERCISE 9-10 Kelley Company has completed the following October sales and purchases journals:

a.   Total and post the journals to T accounts for the general ledger and the accounts receivable and accounts payable ledgers.

b.   Complete a schedule of accounts receivable for October 31, 20--.

c.   Complete a schedule of accounts payable for October 31, 20--.

d.   Compare the balances of the schedules with their respective general ledger accounts. If they are not the same, find and correct the error(s).

SALES JOURNAL					Page 18				
Date	Inv. No.	Customer's Name	Post. Ref.	Accounts Receivable Dr. Sales Cr.					
20--									
Oct. 3	414	Anderson Company			4	4	3	24	
4	415	R. T. Holcomb		1	4	2	6	90	
7	416	Gray and Malo		1	6	4	7	00	
11	417	Mercer Mobil		3	1	1	2	16	
16	418	J. L. Anthony		2	1	3	0	00	
22	419	C. A. Goldschmidt		1	9	4	4	05	
31	420	F. A. Baumann		2	7	9	1	00	
31		Total							
				(	)	(	)		

(Continued)

						PURCHASES JOURNAL									Page **10**

Date		Supplier's Name	Inv. No.	Inv. Date	Terms	Post. Ref.	Accounts Payable Credit				Freight In Debit			Purchases Debit		
20--																
Oct.	2	Colter, Inc.	2706	7/31	2/10, n/30		7	5	9	00		4	9	00	7 1 0	00
	3	Thomas and Son	982	8/2	n/30		8	2	9	00		5	7	00	7 7 2	00
	5	Archer Manufacturing Co.	10611	8/3	2/10, n/30		5	6	4	00					5 6 4	00
	9	Spence Products Co.	B643	8/6	1/10, n/30		1	6	5	00		1	0	00	1 5 5	00
	18	L. C. Walter	46812	8/17	n/60		2	2	8	00					2 2 8	00
	25	Delaney and Cox	1024	8/23	2/10, n/30		3	7	6	00		1	4	00	3 6 2	00
	26	Colter, Inc.	2801	8/25	2/10, n/30		4	0	6	00		2	2	00	3 8 4	00
	31	Totals														

Problem Set A

LO **2, 3**

PROBLEM 9-1A Bell Florists sells flowers on a retail basis. Most of the sales are for cash; however, a few steady customers have credit accounts. Bell's sales staff fills out a sales slip for each sale. There is a state retail sales tax of 5 percent, which is collected by the retailer and submitted to the state. The balances of the accounts as of March 1 have been recorded in the general ledger in your Working Papers or in CengageNow. The following represent Bell Florists' charge sales for March:

Mar. 4 Sold potted plant on account to C. Morales, sales slip no. 242, $27, plus sales tax of $1.35, total $28.35.

6 Sold floral arrangement on account to R. Dixon, sales slip no. 267, $54, plus sales tax of $2.70, total $56.70.

12 Sold corsage on account to B. Cox, sales slip no. 279, $16, plus sales tax of $0.80, total $16.80.

16 Sold wreath on account to All-Star Legion, sales slip no. 296, $104, plus sales tax of $5.20, total $109.20.

18 Sold floral arrangements on account to Tucker Funeral Home, sales slip no. 314, $260, plus sales tax of $13, total $273.

21 Tucker Funeral Home complained about a wrinkled ribbon on the floral arrangement. Bell Florists allowed a $30 credit plus sales tax of $1.50, credit memo no. 27.

23 Sold flower arrangements on account to Price Savings and Loan Association for its fifth anniversary, sales slip no. 337, $180, plus sales tax of $9, total $189.

24 Allowed Price Savings and Loan Association credit, $25, plus sales tax of $1.25, because of a few withered blossoms in floral arrangements, credit memo no. 28.

Required

1. Record these transactions in the general journal.*
2. Post the amounts from the general journal to the general ledger and accounts receivable ledger: Accounts Receivable 113, Sales Tax Payable 214, Sales 411, Sales Returns and Allowances 412.
3. Prepare a schedule of accounts receivable and compare its total with the balance of the Accounts Receivable controlling account.

*If using Working Papers, use pages 57 and 58 in the journal.

Check Figure
Schedule of Accounts Receivable total, $726.52

LO **4, 5** ....

PROBLEM 9-2A Berry's Pet Store records purchase transactions in the general journal. The company is located in Boston, Massachusetts. In addition to a general ledger, Berry's Pet Store also uses an accounts payable ledger. Transactions for April related to the purchase of merchandise are as follows:

Apr. 2 Bought ten Carefree Pet Bedding bags from Blackburn Company, $399.90, invoice no. 4R48, dated April 1; terms net 30 days; FOB destination.

  5 Bought seven Marine Betta Kits from Herrera Company, $83.93, invoice no. 4851, dated April 3; terms 2/10, n/30; FOB shipping point, freight prepaid and added to the invoice, $15 (total $98.93).

  6 Bought 15 Two Door Deluxe Kennels from Barrett, Inc., $719.85, invoice no. 1845R, dated April 5; terms 1/10, n/30; FOB destination.

  8 Bought five Dome Top Bird Cages from Faulkner Company, $1,849.95, invoice no. 1485, dated April 7; terms 2/10, n/30; FOB shipping point, freight prepaid and added to the invoice, $76 (total $1,925.95).

  13 Received credit memo no. 415 from Faulkner Company for merchandise returned, $589.13.

  23 Bought three Five Tiered Cat Trees from Rhodes Manufacturing, $1,107, invoice no. 246J, dated April 21; terms net 60 days; FOB destination.

  27 Bought 30 Glitter Collection Leashes from Solomon Products Company, $299.70, invoice no. 2675, dated April 25; terms net 30 days; FOB destination.

  30 Received credit memo no. 861 from Solomon Products Company for merchandise returned, $76.25.

Check Figure
Accounts Payable account balance, $7,048.50 credit

Required

1. If using Working Papers, open the following accounts in the accounts payable ledger and record the April 1 balances, if any, as given: Barrett, Inc., $185.25; Blackburn Company, $254.64; Faulkner Company, $485.12; Herrera Company; Rhodes Manufacturing, $452.31; Solomon Products Company, $1,785.23. For the accounts having balances, write *Balance* in the Item column and place a check mark in the Post. Ref. column. Skip this step if using CengageNow.

2. If using working papers, record the April 1 balances in the general ledger as given: Accounts Payable 212 controlling account, $3,162.55; Purchases 511, $559.06; Purchases Returns and Allowances 512, $123.50; Freight In 514, $15.20. Write *Balance* in the Item column and place a check mark in the Post. Ref. column. Skip this step if using CengageNow.

3. Record the transactions in the general journal. If using Working Papers, begin on page 115.

4. Post to the general ledger and the accounts payable ledger.

5. Prepare a schedule of accounts payable and compare the balance of the Accounts Payable controlling account with the total of the schedule of accounts payable.

LO **2, 3, 4, 5** ....

PROBLEM 9-3A Shirley's Beauty Store records sales and purchase transactions in the general journal. In addition to a general ledger, Shirley's Beauty Store also uses an accounts receivable ledger and an accounts payable ledger. Transactions for January related to the sales and purchase of merchandise are as follows:

Jan. 3 Bought 30 Mango Bath and Shower Gels from Madden, Inc., $660, invoice no. 3487, dated January 1; terms 2/10, n/30; FOB shipping point, freight prepaid and added to the invoice, $125.43 (total $785.43).

  4 Bought ten Beauty Candle Travel Sets from Calhoun Candles, Inc., $420, invoice no. 4513, dated January 1; terms net 45; FOB destination.

(Continued)

12   Sold four Mango Bath and Shower Gels on account to R. Kielman, sales slip no. 1456, $120, plus sales tax of $9.60, total $129.60.

13   Received credit memo no. 8715 from Calhoun Candles, Inc., for merchandise returned, $84.

21   Bought five Winter Skin Essentials Kits from Whitney and Waters, $197.50, invoice no. A875, dated January 18; terms 2/15, n/45; FOB destination.

25   Sold three Winter Skin Essentials on account to A. Benner, sales slip no. 1457, $135.75, plus sales tax of $10.86, total $146.61.

27   Issued credit memo no. 33 to A. Benner for merchandise returned, $45.25 plus $3.62 sales tax, total $48.87.

Required

Check Figure
Schedule of Accounts
Payable total, $2,297.56

1. If using Working Papers, open the following accounts in the accounts receivable ledger and record the balances as of January 1: A. Benner, $45.77; R. Kielman, $175.39. Write *Balance* in the Item column and place a check mark in the Post. Ref. column. Skip this step if using CengageNow.

2. If using Working Papers, open the following accounts in the accounts payable ledger and record the balances as of January 1: Calhoun Candles, Inc., $355.23; Madden, Inc., $573.15; Whitney and Waters, $50.25. Write *Balance* in the Item column and place a check mark in the Post. Ref. column. Skip this step if using CengageNow.

3. If using Working Papers, record the January 1 balances in the general ledger as given: Accounts Receivable 113 controlling account, $221.16; Accounts Payable 212 controlling account, $978.63; Sales Tax Payable 214, $128.45. Write *Balance* in the Item column and place a check mark in the Post. Ref. column. Skip this step if using CengageNow.

4. Record the transactions in the general journal. If using Working Papers, begin on page 25.

5. Post the entries to the general ledger and accounts receivable ledger or accounts payable ledger as appropriate.

6. Prepare a schedule of accounts receivable.

7. Prepare a schedule of accounts payable.

8. Compare the totals of the schedules with the balances of the controlling accounts.

LO 6, 7

PROBLEM 9-4A The following transactions relate to Hawkins, Inc., an office store wholesaler, during June of this year. Terms of sale are 2/10, n/30. The company is located in Los Angeles, California.

June   1   Sold merchandise on account to Hendrix Office Store, invoice no. 1001, $451.20. The cost of the merchandise was $397.06.

3   Bought merchandise on account from Krueger, Inc., invoice no. 845A, $485.15; terms 1/10, n/30; dated June 1; FOB San Diego, freight prepaid and added to the invoice, $15 (total $500.15).

10   Sold merchandise on account to Ballard Stores, invoice no. 1002, $2,483.65. The cost of the merchandise was $2,235.29.

13   Bought merchandise on account from Kennedy, Inc., invoice no. 4833, $2,450.13; terms 2/10, n/30; dated June 11; FOB San Francisco, freight prepaid and added to the invoice, $123 (total $2,573.13).

18   Sold merchandise on account to Lawson Office Store, invoice no. 1003, $754.99. The cost of the merchandise was $671.94.

20   Issued credit memo no. 33 to Lawson Office Store for merchandise returned, $103.25. The cost of the merchandise was $91.89.

(Continued)

25   Bought merchandise on account from Villarreal, Inc., invoice no. 4R32, $1,552.30; terms net 30; dated June 18; FOB Santa Rosa, freight prepaid and added to the invoice, $84 (total $1,636.30).

30   Received credit memo no. 44 for merchandise returned to Villarreal, Inc., for $224.50.

Check Figure
Net Merchandise Inventory,
$1,272.68 debit

Required

Record the transaction in the general journal using the perpetual inventory system. If using Working Papers, use pages 25 and 26.

 2, 3, 8 ....

PROBLEM 9-5A Gomez Company sells electrical supplies on a wholesale basis. The balances of the accounts as of April 1 have been recorded in the general ledger in your Working Papers and CengageNow. The following transactions took place during April of this year:

Apr.   1   Sold merchandise on account to Myers Company, invoice no. 761, $570.40.

5   Sold merchandise on account to L. R. Foster Company, invoice no. 762, $486.10.

6   Issued credit memo no. 50 to Myers Company for merchandise returned, $40.70.

10   Sold merchandise on account to Diaz Hardware, invoice no. 763, $293.35.

14   Sold merchandise on account to Brooks and Bennett, invoice no. 764, $640.16.

17   Sold merchandise on account to Powell and Reyes, invoice no. 765, $582.12.

21   Issued credit memo no. 51 to Brooks and Bennett for merchandise returned, $68.44.

24   Sold merchandise on account to Ortiz Company, invoice no. 766, $652.87.

26   Sold merchandise on account to Diaz Hardware, invoice no. 767, $832.19.

30   Issued credit memo no. 52 to Diaz Hardware for damage to merchandise, $98.50.

Check Figure
Accounts Receivable
account balance,
$5,018.97 debit

Required

1. Record these sales of merchandise on account in the sales journal. If using Working Papers, use page 39. Record the sales returns and allowances in the general journal. If using Working Papers, use page 74.

2. Immediately after recording each transaction, post to the accounts receivable ledger.

3. Post the amounts from the general journal daily. Post the sales journal amount as a total at the end of the month: Accounts Receivable 113, Sales 411, Sales Returns and Allowances 412.

4. Prepare a schedule of accounts receivable. Compare the balance of the Accounts Receivable controlling account with the total of the schedule of accounts receivable.

 5, 9 ....

PROBLEM 9-6A Patterson Appliance uses a three-column purchases journal. The company is located in Fresno, California. In addition to a general ledger, Patterson Appliance also uses an accounts payable ledger. Transactions for January related to the purchase of merchandise are as follows:

Jan.   2   Bought eighty 12-inch, 3-speed Brighton Oscillating Fans from Snyder and Jordan, $1,890, invoice no. 268J, dated January 2; terms net 60 days; FOB Fresno.

(Continued)

4   Bought ten 35-pint-capacity Crystal Humidifiers from Simpson Company, $2,300, invoice no. 39426, dated January 2; terms 2/10, n/30; FOB Durango, freight prepaid and added to the invoice, $90 (total $2,390).

7   Bought ten 16-inch Axel Window Fans from Tran, Inc., $360, invoice no. 452AD, dated January 6; terms 1/10, n/30; FOB Fresno.

10   Bought twenty-four 4-blade Tiempo Ceiling Fans, Model 2760, from Ukele Company, $3,550, invoice no. D7742, dated January 7; terms 2/10, n/30; FOB Sacramento, freight prepaid and added to the invoice, $84 (total $3,634).

14   Bought four Charger Electric Hedge Trimmers from Fernandez Products Company, $186, invoice no. 2542, dated January 13; terms net 30 days; FOB Fresno.

22   Bought 40 Lindon Electric Bug Killers from Snyder and Jordan, $2,265, invoice no. 392J, dated January 22; terms net 60 days; FOB Fresno.

28   Bought ten Charger Electric Blowers from Fernandez Products Company, $830, invoice no. 2691, dated January 27; terms net 30 days; FOB Fresno.

30   Bought ten Kole Powered Attic Ventilators from Porter Company, $446, invoice no. 664CC, dated January 27; terms 2/10, n/30; FOB Seattle, freight prepaid and added to the invoice, $48 (total $494).

Required

Check Figure
Accounts Payable account balance, $12,608.06 credit

1. If using Working Papers, open the following accounts in the accounts payable ledger and record the January 1 balances, if any, as given: Fernandez Products Company; Porter Company, $163.17; Simpson Company, $167.19; Snyder and Jordan; Tran, Inc., $228.70; Ukele Company. For the accounts having balances, write *Balance* in the Item column and place a check mark in the Post. Ref. column. Skip this step if using CengageNow or CLGL.

2. If using Working Papers, record the balance of $559.06 in the Accounts Payable 212 controlling account as of January 1. Write *Balance* in the Item column and place a check mark in the Post. Ref. column. Skip this step if using CengageNow or CLGL.

3. Record the transactions in the purchases journal. If using Working Papers, begin on page 81.

4. Post to the accounts payable ledger daily. Skip this step if using CLGL.

5. Post to the general ledger at the end of the month. Skip this step if using CLGL.

6. Prepare a schedule of accounts payable and compare the balance of the Accounts Payable controlling account with the total of the schedule of accounts payable.

Problem Set B

LO 2, 3

PROBLEM 9-1B Abbott Florists sells flowers on a retail basis. Most of the sales are for cash; however, a few steady customers have credit accounts. Abbott's sales staff fills out a sales slip for each sale. There is a state retail tax of 5 percent, which is collected by the retailer and submitted to the state. The balances of the accounts as of March 1 have been recorded in the general ledger in your Working Papers or in CengageNow. Abbott Florists' charge sales for March are as follows:

Mar. 4   Sold floral arrangement on account to R. Duarte, sales slip no. 236, $45, plus sales tax of $2.25, total $47.25.

(Continued)

7   Sold potted plant on account to C. Meadows, sales slip no. 272, $61, plus sales tax of $3.05, total $64.05.

12   Sold wreath on account to Anthony Realty, sales slip no. 294, $63, plus sales tax of $3.15, total $66.15.

17   Sold floral arrangements on account to Travis Dress Shop, sales slip no. 299, $170, plus sales tax of $8.50, total $178.50.

20   Travis Dress Shop returned a flower spray, complaining that there were dead blooms. Abbott Florists allowed a credit of $36, plus sales tax of $1.80, credit memo no. 27.

21   Sold flower arrangements on account to Porter Computers for its anniversary, sales slip no. 310, $236, plus sales tax of $11.80, total $247.80.

22   Allowed Porter Computers credit, $25, plus sales tax of $1.25, because of withered blossoms in floral arrangements, credit memo no. 28.

27   Sold corsage on account to B. Crosby, sales slip no. 332, $30, plus sales tax of $1.50, total $31.50.

Check Figure
Schedule of Accounts
Receivable total, $682.42

Required

1. Record these transactions in the general journal.*
2. Post the amounts from the general journal to the general ledger and accounts receivable ledger: Accounts Receivable 113, Sales Tax Payable 214, Sales 411, Sales Returns and Allowances 412.
3. Prepare a schedule of accounts receivable and compare its total with the balance of the Accounts Receivable controlling account.

*If using Working Papers, use pages 57 and 58 in the journal.

LO 4, 5 ....

PROBLEM 9-2B Lowery's Pet Depot records purchase transactions in the general journal. The company is located in Cleveland, Ohio. In addition to a general ledger, Lowery's Pet Depot also uses an accounts payable ledger. Transactions for October related to the purchase of merchandise are as follows:

Oct.   3   Bought 12 Automatic Fish Feeders from Barrera Company, $959.88, invoice no. 5493, dated October 2; terms net 30 days; FOB shipping point, freight prepaid and added to the invoice, $79.45 (total $1,039.33).

4   Bought two 18 x 18 Terrarium Stands from Hickman Company, $259.98, invoice no. 2JYX, dated October 2; terms 2/10, n/30; FOB destination.

7   Bought four Chinchilla Bath Houses from Baldwin, Inc., $67.96, invoice no. 4183, dated October 6; terms 1/10, n/30; FOB destination.

10   Received credit memo no. 123 from Baldwin, Inc., for merchandise returned, $13.94.

Oct. 14   Bought 20 Zoo Slider Hoods from Douglas, Inc., $2,599.80, invoice no. X431, dated October 12; terms 2/10, n/30; FOB shipping point, freight prepaid and added to the invoice, $140.50 (total $2,740.30).

15   Bought four Hanging Bird Baths from Krause, Inc., $71.96, invoice no. A499, dated October 11; terms net 60 days; FOB destination.

24   Bought eight Automatic Cat Litter Boxes from Villa Manufacturing, $2,399.92, invoice no. 4429, dated October 21; terms net 30 days; FOB destination.

27   Received credit memo no. 452 from Villa Manufacturing for merchandise returned, $346.78.

(Continued)

Required

Check Figure
Accounts Payable account
balance, $8,372.74 credit

1. If using Working Papers, open the following accounts in the accounts payable ledger and record the October 1 balances, if any, as given: Baldwin, Inc., $46.57; Barrera Company, $743.15; Douglas, Inc., $615.20; Hickman Company; Krause, Inc., $23.45; Villa Manufacturing, $725.64. For the accounts having balances, write *Balance* in the Item column and place a check mark in the Post. Ref. column. Skip this step if using CengageNow.

2. If using Working Papers, record the October 1 balances in the general ledger as given: Accounts Payable 212 controlling account, $2,154.01; Purchases 511, $2,485.12; Purchases Returns and Allowances 512, $287.52; Freight In 514, $48.57. Write *Balance* in the Item column and place a check mark in the Post. Ref. column. Skip this step if using CengageNow.

3. Record the transactions in the general journal. If using Working Papers, begin on page 95.

4. Post to the general ledger and the accounts payable ledger.

5. Prepare a schedule of accounts payable, and compare the balance of the Accounts Payable controlling account with the total of the schedule of accounts payable.

LO **2, 3, 4, 5**

PROBLEM 9-3B May's Beauty Store records sales and purchase transactions in the general journal. In addition to a general ledger, May's Beauty Store also uses an accounts receivable ledger and an accounts payable ledger. Transactions for January related to the sales and purchase of merchandise are as follows:

Jan.　2　Bought nine Matte Nail Color Kits from Mejia, Inc., $450, invoice no. 4521, dated January 1; terms 2/10, n/30; FOB shipping point, freight prepaid and added to the invoice, $87.50 (total $537.50).

　　　5　Bought 30 Perfume Cocktail Rings from Braun, Inc., $1,200, invoice no. 37A, dated January 3; terms 2/10, n/30; FOB destination.

　　　8　Sold two Matte Nail Color Kits on account to J. Herbert, sales slip no. 113, $110, plus sales tax of $8.80, total $118.80.

　　11　Received credit memo no. 455 from Braun, Inc., for merchandise returned, $315.25.

　　18　Bought 15 Eye Palettes from Vargas, Inc., $660, invoice no. 910, dated January 14; terms net 30; FOB destination.

　　23　Sold four Eye Palettes on account to T. Cantrell, sales slip no. 114, $200, plus sales tax of $16, total $216.

　　26　Issued credit memo no. 12 to T. Cantrell for merchandise returned, $50 plus $4 sales tax, total $54.

Required

Check Figure
Schedule of Accounts Payable
balance, $2,776.00

1. If using Working Papers, open the following accounts in the accounts receivable ledger and record the balances as of January 1: T. Cantrell, $86.99; J. Hebert, $63.47. Write *Balance* in the Item column and place a check mark in the Post. Ref. column. Skip this step if using CengageNow.

2. If using Working Papers, open the following accounts in the accounts payable ledger and record the balances as of January 1: Braun, Inc., $513.20; Mejia, Inc., $113.40; Vargas, Inc., $67.15. Write *Balance* in the Item column and place a check mark in the Post. Ref. column. Skip this step if using CengageNow.

3. If using Working Papers, record the January 1 balances in the general ledger as given: Accounts Receivable 113 controlling account, $150.46; Accounts Payable 212 controlling account, $693.75; Sales Tax Payable 214, $237.89. Write *Balance* in the

(Continued)

Item column and place a check mark in the Post. Ref. column. Skip this step if using CengageNow.

4. Record the transactions in the general journal. If using Working Papers, begin on page 17.
5. Post the entries to the general ledger and accounts receivable ledger or accounts payable ledger as appropriate.
6. Prepare a schedule of accounts receivable.
7. Prepare a schedule of accounts payable.
8. Compare the totals of the schedules with the balances of the controlling accounts.

LO 6, 7

PROBLEM 9-4B The following transactions relate to Khan, Inc., a sporting goods wholesaler, during November of this year. Terms of sale are 2/10, n/30. The company is located in Denver, Colorado.

Nov. 3 Sold merchandise on account to Spence Tennis Shop, invoice no. 5420, $2,482.51. The cost of the merchandise was $1,961.18.
     5 Issued credit memo no. 38 to Spence Tennis Shop for merchandise returned, $287.45. The cost of the merchandise was $227.09.
     7 Bought merchandise on account from Maldonado Manufacturing, Inc., invoice no. 1548, $3,854.16; terms n/45; dated November 4; FOB Memphis, freight prepaid and added to the invoice, $135 (total $3,989.16).
     9 Bought merchandise on account from Lozano, Inc., invoice no. 8755, $426.65; terms 1/15, n/30; dated November 5; FOB New York City, freight prepaid and added to the invoice, $67 (total $493.65).
    12 Received credit memo no. 542 to Lozano, Inc., for merchandise returned, $102.20.
    17 Sold merchandise on account to Jack's Golfing Shop, invoice no. 5421, $486.35. The cost of the merchandise was $432.85.
    23 Sold merchandise on account to Yates Sporting Goods, invoice no. 5422, $2,465.99. The cost of the merchandise was $1,972.79.
    28 Bought merchandise on account from Fields, Inc., invoice no. 4599, $441.29; terms 2/10, n/30; dated November 25; FOB Austin, freight prepaid and added to the invoice, $102 (total $543.29).

Check Figure
Total Gross Sales, $5,434.85 credit

Required

Record the transaction in the general journal using the perpetual inventory system. If using Working Papers, use pages 84 and 85.

LO 2, 3, 8

PROBLEM 9-5B R. J. Hinton Company sells electrical supplies on a wholesale basis. The balances of the accounts as of April 1 have been recorded in the general ledger in your Working Papers and CengageNow. The following transactions took place during April of this year:

Apr. 3 Sold merchandise on account to Maxwell Company, invoice no. 822, $652.80.
     7 Sold merchandise on account to B. A. Fitzpatrick Company, invoice no. 823, $462.15.
     8 Sold merchandise on account to Durham Hardware, invoice no. 824, $205.60.
    13 Issued credit memo no. 61 to B. A. Fitzpatrick Company for merchandise returned, $136.50.

(Continued)

15 Sold merchandise on account to Briggs and Campos, invoice no. 825, $831.47.

21 Sold merchandise on account to Pena and Carr, invoice no. 826, $590.34.

24 Issued credit memo no. 62 to Briggs and Campos for merchandise returned, $80.45.

Apr. 26 Sold merchandise on account to O'Neill Company, invoice no. 827, $569.90.

28 Issued credit memo no. 63 to Durham Hardware for damage to merchandise, $52.48.

30 Sold merchandise on account to Durham Hardware, invoice no. 828, $735.50.

Required

1. Record these sales of merchandise on account in the sales journal. If using Working Papers, use page 39. Record the sales returns and allowances in the general journal. If using Working Papers, use page 74.
2. Immediately after recording each transaction, post to the accounts receivable ledger.
3. Post the amounts from the general journal daily. Post the sales journal amount as a total at the end of the month: Accounts Receivable 113, Sales 411, Sales Returns and Allowances 412.
4. Prepare a schedule of accounts receivable. Compare the balance of the Accounts Receivable controlling account with the total of the schedule of accounts receivable.

Check Figure
Accounts Receivable account balance, $4,947.75 debit

LO 5, 9

PROBLEM 9-6B West Bicycle Shop uses a three-column purchases journal. The company is located in Topeka, Kansas. In addition to a general ledger, the company also uses an accounts payable ledger. Transactions for January related to the purchase of merchandise are as follows:

Jan. 4 Bought fifty 10-speed bicycles from Nielsen Company, $4,775, invoice no. 26145, dated January 3; terms net 60 days; FOB Topeka.

7 Bought tires from Barton Tire Company, $792, invoice no. 9763, dated January 5; terms 2/10, n/30; FOB Topeka.

8 Bought bicycle lights and reflectors from Gross Products Company, $384, invoice no. 17317, dated January 6; terms net 30 days; FOB Topeka.

11 Bought hand brakes from Bray, Inc., $470, invoice no. 291GE, dated January 9; terms 1/10, n/30; FOB Kansas City, freight prepaid and added to the invoice, $36 (total $506).

19 Bought handle grips from Gross Products Company, $96.50, invoice no. 17520, dated January 17; terms net 30 days; FOB Topeka.

24 Bought thirty 5-speed bicycles from Nielsen Company, $1,487, invoice no. 26942, dated January 23; terms net 60 days; FOB Topeka.

29 Bought knapsacks from Davila Manufacturing Company, $304.80, invoice no. 762AC, dated January 26; terms 2/10, n/30; FOB Topeka.

31 Bought locks from Lamb Safety Net, $415.47, invoice no. 27712, dated January 26; terms 2/10, n/30; FOB Dodge City, freight prepaid and added to the invoice, $22 (total $437.47).

Required

1. If using Working Papers, open the following accounts in the accounts payable ledger and record the January 1 balances, if any, as given: Barton Tire Company, $156; Bray, Inc.; Davila Manufacturing Company, $82.88; Gross Products Company; Lamb Safety Net, $184.20; Nielsen Company. For the accounts having balances, write *Balance* in the Item column and place a check mark in the Post. Ref. column. Skip this step if using CengageNow or CLGL.

Check Figure
Accounts Payable account balance, $9,205.85 credit

(Continued)

2. If using Working Papers, record the balance of $423.08 in the Accounts Payable 212 controlling account as of January 1. Write *Balance* in the Item column and place a check mark in the Post. Ref. column. Skip this step if using CengageNow or CLGL.

3. Record the transactions in the purchases journal. If using Working Papers, begin on page 81.

4. Post to the accounts payable ledger daily. Skip this step if using CLGL.

5. Post to the general ledger at the end of the month. Skip this step if using CLGL.

6. Prepare a schedule of accounts payable, and compare the balance of the Accounts Payable controlling account with the total of the schedule of accounts payable.

Accounting with qb QuickBooks® Online

Go to the QuickBooks Online Chapters 9 and 10 Appendix located on the Cengage Learning companion site at Cengage.com. Review *Accounting with QuickBooks Online* (step-by-step guide to using QuickBooks Online). *Accounting with QuickBooks Online* Chapters 9 and 10 will introduce you to (1) recording checkbook entries using the Check, Deposit, Pay Bills, Sales Receipt, and Receive Payment functions; (2) recording transactions with vendors on account, using the Bills function; and (3) recording transactions with customers on account, using the Invoice function..

Activities

Why Does It Matter?

Jax Mercantile Co. has been northern Colorado's premier outdoor gear source for over 50 years. Jax sells men's, women's, and children's clothing for any outdoor activity. Customers can also find camping and fishing gear, mountaineering tools, and hunting items. If a customer is not the outdoor type, Jax still offers plenty of other products, such as specialty kitchenware and household decorative items. Jax also carries a full line of optics and photography products, agricultural and automotive accessories, animal care products, and lawn and garden accessories.

Jax has succeeded in stocking a large inventory that meets customers' outdoor and indoor gear needs. When Jax purchases inventory for resale, it must have a way of recording these purchases. Jax also must have a way to record the sales of goods to customers and be able to handle returns and discounts. Considering the size of Jax's inventory (in items and in dollar amount), would Jax use a periodic or perpetual inventory system? Explain your answer.

What Would You Say?

You are the bookkeeper at a small merchandising firm. You are comparing the income statements from the last three years. You notice that the Purchases Returns and Allowances account (as a percentage of net sales) has been increasing at an alarming rate. If you were a manager, to whom would you speak in the organization to help you understand why so much merchandise is being returned? What types of questions would you ask?

What Do You Think?

TO: Accounting Clerk

FROM: Senior Accountant

DATE: April 1, 20--

SUBJECT: Errors in trial balance

Following is a trial balance prepared just before you were hired. Two accounts are missing, and the amount for Sales is off. Here are a few facts to consider. Our business is in a state that collects sales tax. I ran some totals, and we collected $1,800 in sales tax. Customers returned $900 in goods, which would reduce the above sales tax by $70. Our books need to reflect these events. The former accounting clerk said that she recorded everything—somewhere. She said that she may have credited the $1,800 sales tax to Sales and not to Sales Tax Payable. And she looked confused when Sales Returns and Allowances was mentioned. She asked, "Why not just debit Sales?" Determine the two missing accounts and correct the accounts that are off.

Pierce Retail Outlet
Trial Balance
March 31, 20--

Account Name	Debit	Credit
Cash	8,940	
Accounts Receivable	480	
Store Equipment	9,460	
Accounts Payable		958
D. Pierce, Capital		11,959
D. Pierce, Drawing	4,480	
Sales		18,000
Rent Expense	2,400	
Wages Expense	4,864	
Supplies Expense	175	
Miscellaneous Expense	118	
	30,917	30,917

1. Think about where these amounts might have been put, think about what accounts are missing, and use T accounts to solve the problems.
2. Prepare a corrected trial balance.

Sales and Purchases

Ms. Valli of All About You Spa has decided to expand her business by adding two lines of merchandise—a selection of products used in the salon for the body, the feet, and the face, as well as logo mugs, T-shirts, and baseball caps that can provide advertising benefits. She believes she will be able to increase her profits significantly.

July Journal Entries

So that you can complete the journal entries for the month of July, Ms. Valli has also left the information you will need and directions on how to proceed.

Note that with the expansion of the business into merchandising, new accounts have been added to the chart of accounts. For example, an additional revenue account, Merchandise Sales, is needed. Because All About You Spa now needs a Purchases account, the chart of accounts needs to be modified as follows: The 500–599 range is used for the purchase-related accounts (for example, Purchases 511 and Freight In 515). Your new chart of accounts is as follows:

CHART OF ACCOUNTS FOR ALL ABOUT YOU SPA

Assets

111 Cash
113 Accounts Receivable
114 Office Supplies
115 Spa Supplies
116 Merchandise Inventory
117 Prepaid Insurance
124 Office Equipment
125 Accum. Depr., Office Equip.
128 Spa Equipment
129 Accum. Depr., Spa Equip.

Liabilities

211 Accounts Payable
212 Wages Payable
215 Sales Tax Payable

Owner's Equity

311 A. Valli, Capital
312 A. Valli, Drawing
313 Income Summary

Revenue

411 Income from Services
412 Merchandise Sales
413 Sales Discounts
414 Sales Returns & Allow.

Purchases

511 Purchases
512 Purchases Discounts
513 Purch. Returns & Allow.
515 Freight In

Expenses

611 Wages Expense
612 Rent Expense
613 Office Supplies Expense
614 Spa Supplies Expense
615 Laundry Expense
616 Advertising Expense
617 Utilities Expense
618 Insurance Expense
619 Depr. Expense, Office Equip.
620 Depr. Expense, Spa Equip.
630 Promotional Expense

Also note that because you will be making purchases on account and sales on account, subsidiary ledgers will be needed to track what is due from individual customers and owed to individual vendors. A listing of customers and vendors with current balances are as follows:

ACCOUNTS RECEIVABLE LEDGER		ACCOUNTS PAYABLE LEDGER	
About Face Spa	$ 0.00	Adco, Inc.	$ 415.00
Jill Anson	350.00	Giftco	0.00
Chaco's	0.00	Golden Spa Supplies	685.00
Holmes Condos	0.00	Logo Products	0.00
Tory Ligman	345.00	Office Staples	125.00
Los Obrigados Lodge	0.00	Spa Equipment, Inc.	0.00
Mini Spa	0.00	Spa Goods	0.00
Jack Morgan	468.00	Spa Magic	0.00
Pleasant Spa	0.00	Superior Office Equipment	1,345.00
Judy Wilcox	110.00		

All About You
Spa

Checkbook Register

Check No.	Date	Explanation	√	Deposits	Check Amount
	7/1	Owner invested cash in business.		20,000.00	
2027	7/3	Bought additional spa equipment from Spa Equipment, Inc., for $8,150.00, paying $2,000.00 cash down, invoice no. 2731, dated 7/3; terms 2/10, n/60.			2,000.00
2028	7/3	Paid July's rent.			1,500.00
2029	7/5	Paid on account to Golden Spa Supplies, invoice no. 904, dated June 3 (no discount). Paid in full.			685.00
2030	7/5	Paid on account to Office Staples, invoice no. 222, dated June 5 (no discount). Paid in full.			125.00
2031	7/5	Paid Celebrate, Inc., for promotional flowers and balloons for lobby			125.00
2032	7/5	Paid on account to Adco, Inc., invoice no. 215, dated June 5 (no discount). Paid in full.			415.00
2033	7/5	Paid week's wages. (A portion of this payment was recorded as an adjusting entry on June 30.) *Note:* Payroll taxes related to wages will be ignored here for purposes of simplification.			2,075.00
	7/7	Deposited first week's cash sales: merchandise, $1,510.00; services, $3,225.00; sales tax collected, $132.13.		4,867.13	
	7/7	Deposited check from Jill Anson, invoice no. 20, dated June 7 (balance due in August, $200.00).		150.00	
2034	7/12	Paid week's wages.			2,075.00
	7/14	Deposited check from Jack Morgan, invoice no. 21, dated June 14 (balance due in August, $268.00).		200.00	
	7/14	Deposited second week's cash sales: merchandise, $1,525.00; services, $2,510.00; sales tax collected, $122.00.		4,157.00	
1035	7/18	Paid on account to Superior Equipment, invoice no. 4315, dated June 5 (no discount). Paid in full.			520.00
1036	7/19	Paid week's wages.			2,075.00
	7/21	Deposited check from Tory Ligman, invoice no. 22, dated June 21 (balance due in August, $160.00).		185.00	

(Continued)

All About You
Spa

Check No.	Date	Explanation	√	Deposits	Check Amount
	7/21	Deposited third week's cash sales: merchandise, $3,490.00; services, $4,476.55; sales tax collected, $279.20.		8,245.75	
1037	7/25	Bought new nail cart for cash (debit Spa Equipment).			155.00
1038	7/26	Paid week's wages.			2,075.00
1039	7/28	Paid month's laundry bill.			55.00
	7/28	Deposited check from Judy Wilcox, invoice no. 23, dated June 28 (paid in full).		110.00	
	7/31	Deposited end of month's cash sales: merchandise, $4,930.00; services, $3,151.23; sales tax collected, $394.40.		8,475.63	
1040	7/31	Owner withdrew cash for personal use.			2,500.00
1041	7/31	Paid July telephone bill.			125.00
1042	7/31	Paid July power and water bill.			155.00

Purchases Invoices for Merchandise Bought on Account During July

All About You Spa will pay all freight costs associated with purchases of merchandise to the supplier. Use the new accounts Purchases 511 and Freight In 515.

Date of Purchase	Transaction Information	Amount
July 1	Bought aromatherapy products from Spa Goods; invoice no. 512, dated 7/1; terms 2/10, n/60.	$5,300.00 plus $125.00 freight
1	Bought logo merchandise from Logo Products; invoice no. 2579, dated 7/1; terms 2/10, n/60.	$3,692.00 plus $101.00 freight
2	Bought bath and beauty products from Spa Magic; invoice no. 3503, dated 7/2; terms 2/10, n/30.	$2,623.00 plus $95.00 freight
5	Bought logo merchandise from Giftco; invoice no. 613, dated 7/5; terms 2/10, n/60.	$1,253.00 plus $65.00 freight

Sales Invoices for Gift Certificates Sold on Account During July

All About You Spa is responsible for collecting and paying the sales tax on merchandise that it sells. The sales tax rate where All About You Spa does business is 8 percent of each sale (for example, $340.00 × 0.08 = $27.20).

Date of Sale	Transaction Information	Sales Amount (Before Tax)
July 2	Los Obrigados Lodge, invoice no. 24.	$ 340.00
4	Chaco's, invoice no. 25.	475.50
5	Pleasant Spa, invoice no. 26.	1,518.59
10	Holmes Condos, invoice no. 27.	325.50
10	Mini Spa, invoice no. 28.	226.00
12	About Face Spa, invoice no. 29.	465.95

Note: All gift certificates were redeemed for merchandise by the end of the month.

Other July Transactions

There were five other transactions in July. None involved cash.

Date	Transaction Information	Amount
July 1	Bought spa supplies on account from Golden Spa Supplies, invoice no. 1368, dated 7/1; terms n/45.	$ 410.00
5	Bought office equipment on account from Superior Equipment, invoice no. 4608, dated 7/5; terms 2/10, n/60.	395.00
5	Bought self-help books for the waiting room on account (Miscellaneous Expense) from Office Staples, invoice no. 2417, dated 7/5; terms n/30.	179.00
5	Bought office supplies on account from Office Staples, invoice no. 2418, dated 7/5; terms n/30.	109.00
31	Owner invested additional personal spa equipment (treadmill and bicycle) valued at $2,000.00.	2,000.00

Required

1. Journalize the transactions for July (in date order). Ask your instructor whether you should use the special journals or the general journal for this problem.
   - If you are preparing the journal entries using Working Papers, enter your transactions beginning on page 6.
2. Post the entries to the accounts receivable, accounts payable, and general ledgers.
   - Ignore this step if you are using CLGL.
3. Prepare a trial balance as of July 31, 20--.
4. Prepare a schedule of accounts receivable as of July 31, 20--.
5. Prepare a schedule of accounts payable as of July 31, 20--.

Check Figures
3. Trial balance total, July 31, $107,122.18
4. Schedule of accounts receivable total, July 31, $4,247.67
5. Schedule of accounts payable total, July 31, $21,322.00

10

Cash Receipts and Cash Payments

Learning Objectives

After you have completed this chapter, you will be able to do the following:

1 Determine cash discounts according to credit terms.

2 In the general journal, record sales transactions involving cash receipts and cash discounts.

3 In the general journal, record purchase transactions involving cash payments and cash discounts.

4 Record transactions involving trade discounts.

5 In the cash receipts journal, record transactions for a merchandising business and post from a cash receipts journal to a general ledger and an accounts receivable ledger.

6 In the cash payments journal, record transactions for a merchandising business and post from a cash payments journal to a general ledger and an accounts payable ledger.

To: Amy Roberts, CPA
Subject: **Cash Receipts and Cash Payments**

Hi Amy,
Well, the business continues to grow. Thanks again for all of your help. I do have a couple more questions. Is there any way I can speed up the collection of my Accounts Receivable? At certain times during the month, I'm finding that my cash flow is a little tight. Also, some customers have talked to me about trade discounts. What are these? Are they something I should be using in my business?
Thanks,
Janie

To: Janie Conner
Subject: **RE: Cash Receipts and Cash Payments**

Hi Janie,
I'm happy to hear that your business continues to grow. I do have some suggestions for you. First, implementing sales discounts with your charge customers may help encourage early payment. Sales discounts could significantly improve your cash flow situation. As a buyer, you may also want to deal with companies that offer you a purchases discount. Purchases discounts can save you money as well. Regarding trade discounts, these are a reduction from your list prices. The amount of the discount can vary. Trade discounts are not journalized; they are simply a reduction in the published price for certain customers. To be more competitive, you may want to consider offering some type of trade discount to your larger customers. Below is a summary of the agenda we can use when we talk.

_____ 1. Using cash discounts according to credit terms
_____ 2. Journalizing sales transactions and cash receipts from customers entitled to cash discounts
_____ 3. Journalizing purchase transactions and cash payments when you are entitled to cash discounts
_____ 4. Using trade discounts

Janie, let's talk on Friday afternoon. Give me a call anytime after 1 P.M.
Amy

In the previous chapter, we discussed sales and purchases on account. Now we will learn how a company records cash receipts and cash payments for those transactions. We will begin by reviewing discounts and terms available to purchasers and sellers and then discuss recording the cash associated with merchandising transactions.

10-1 CREDIT TERMS

When we discussed sales and purchases of merchandise in Chapter 9, we noted that each sale or purchase was associated with a *term*. The seller stipulates the *terms*—how much credit a customer is allowed and how much time a customer is given to pay in full. The **credit period** is the time the seller allows the buyer before full payment has to be made. Retailers generally allow 25 to 30 days for payment.

1 Determine cash discounts according to credit terms.

Learning Objective

Wholesalers and manufacturers often specify a **cash discount** in their credit terms. A cash discount is an amount that a customer can deduct if a bill is paid within a specified time. The discount is based on the *total amount of the invoice after any returns and allowances and freight charges billed on the invoice have been deducted*. Naturally, this discount acts as an incentive for credit customers to pay their bills promptly.

Let's say that a wholesaler offers customers credit terms of 2/10, n/30. In Chapter 9, we discussed that these terms mean that the customer gets a 2 percent discount if the bill is paid within 10 days after the invoice date. The discount period begins the day after the invoice date. If the bill is not paid within the 10 days, the entire amount is due within 30 days after the invoice date. Other types of cash discounts may be used, such as:

- **1/15, n/60**—The seller offers a 1 percent discount if the bill is paid within 15 days after the invoice date, and the whole bill must be paid within 60 days after the invoice date.

- **2/10, EOM, n/60**—The seller offers a 2 percent discount if the bill is paid within 10 days after the end of the month, and the whole bill must be paid within 60 days after the last day of the month.

A wholesaler or manufacturer that offers a cash discount adopts a single cash discount as a credit policy and makes this available to all of its customers. The seller considers cash discounts as sales discounts under both the periodic and perpetual inventory systems. The buyer, on the other hand, considers cash discounts as purchases discounts under the periodic inventory system and a reduction to Merchandise Inventory under the perpetual inventory system.

10-2 RECORDING TRANSACTIONS INTO THE GENERAL JOURNAL

Occasionally, sales or purchases of merchandise will involve various discounts. In this section, we will discuss discounts and learn how they are recorded in the general journal.

10-2a Sales Discounts

First, we will concentrate on the **sales discount**. *The Sales Discounts account, like Sales Returns and Allowances, is a contra revenue account and is, therefore, deducted from Sales.*

To illustrate, we return to Whitewater Raft Supply. We will record the following transactions in the general journal and T accounts.

TRANSACTION (a). On August 1, Whitewater Raft Supply sold merchandise on account to Mesa River Raft Company, invoice no. 9384, $1,933.50; terms 2/10, n/30. (Take a moment to review the source document on page 368 in Chapter 9 and identify the terms on the invoice.)

TRANSACTION (b). On August 10, received check from Mesa River Raft Company for $1,894.83 in payment of invoice no. 9384, less cash discount ($1,933.50 × 0.02 = $38.67; $1,933.50 − $38.67 = $1,894.83).

FYI

As of the writing of this text, nonpublic organizations, like sole proprietorships, will apply the new revenue recognition standards, announced by the Financial Accounting Standards Board (FASB), to annual reporting periods after December 15, 2018. The changes in revenue recognition will affect the reporting of sales discounts.

Revenue from Contracts with Customers, Topic 606, FASB Accounting Standards Update, Financial Accounting standards Board, Norwalk, CT, August 2015.

		GENERAL JOURNAL				Page 26	
Date		Description	Post. Ref.	Debit		Credit	
20--							
Aug.	1	Accounts Receivable, Mesa River					
		Raft Company		1 9 3 3 50			
		Sales				1 9 3 3 50	
		Sold merchandise to Mesa River					
		Raft Company, invoice no. 9384.					
	10	Cash		1 8 9 4 83			
		Sales Discounts		3 8 67			
		Accounts Receivable, Mesa River					
		Raft Company				1 9 3 3 50	
		Collected cash on account,					
		invoice no. 9384.					

In the Real World

Dun & Bradstreet is a business credit rating organization that looks at a company's collection period ratio as one of its rating measurements. Therefore, businesses should make sure credit periods and terms encourage prompt payment.

To record the receipt of payment from the customer on August 10, the accountant records a debit to Cash for the amount of cash received. The amount of discount granted is recorded as a debit to Sales Discounts. The Accounts Receivable account is credited so that the customer's account will decrease. Notice that the accountant records a credit to Accounts Receivable, Mesa River Raft Company for the total invoice amount, $1,933.50. This is important because if the receivable was credited for only the cash received, the customer's account would still show a balance owed.

Remember

When recording a cash receipt involving a sales discount, be sure to credit Accounts Receivable for the total amount of the sales transaction.

Assets	=	Liabilities	+	Capital	−	Drawing	+	Revenue	−	Expenses
+ | −		− | +		− | +		+ | −		− | +		+ | −
Debit | Credit		Debit | Credit		Debit | Credit		Debit | Credit		Debit | Credit		Debit | Credit

Accounts Receivable
+ | −
(a) 1,933.50 | (b) 1,933.50

Sales
− | +
| (a) 1,933.50

Cash
+ | −
(b) 1,894.83 |

Sales Discounts
+ | −
(b) 38.67 |

When a company receives a return of merchandise sold, the sales discount is calculated by excluding the amount of the returned items. Let's take a look at this example. The journal and T accounts for the following transactions are shown on the next page.

TRANSACTION (a). On September 1, Whitewater Raft Supply sold merchandise on account to Rugged River Company, invoice no. 9391; $3,614, terms 2/10, n/30; and recorded the sale in the general journal.

TRANSACTION (b). On September 5, Rugged River Company returned $254 worth of the merchandise. Whitewater Raft Supply issued credit memorandum no. 1069 and recorded the transaction. *Notice that after the return, there is a balance in Accounts Receivable of $3,360, the amount of the original invoice less the return ($3,614 − $254).*

TRANSACTION (c). On September 8, received check from Rugged River Company for $3,292.80 in payment of invoice no. 9391, less return and cash discount [($3,614 − $254) × 0.02 = $67.20; ($3,614 − $254) − $67.20 = $3,292.80].

		GENERAL JOURNAL			Page 27
Date		Description	Post. Ref.	Debit	Credit
20--					
Sept.	1	Accounts Receivable, Rugged River			
		Company		3 6 1 4 00	
		Sales			3 6 1 4 00
		Sold merchandise to Rugged			
		River Company, invoice no. 9391.			
	5	Sales Returns and Allowances		2 5 4 00	
		Accounts Receivable, Rugged			
		River Company			2 5 4 00
		Issued credit memo no. 1069.			
	8	Cash		3 2 9 2 80	
		Sales Discounts		6 7 20	
		Accounts Receivable, Rugged			
		River Company			3 3 6 0 00
		Collected cash on account,			
		invoice no. 9391.			

Assets	=	Liabilities	+	Capital	−	Drawing	+	Revenue	−	Expenses
+ | −		− | +		− | +		+ | −		− | +		+ | −
Debit | Credit		Debit | Credit		Debit | Credit		Debit | Credit		Debit | Credit		Debit | Credit

Accounts Receivable

+	−
(a) 3,614.00	(b) 254.00
	(c) 3,360.00

Sales

−	+
	(a) 3,614.00

Sales Returns and Allowances

+	−
(b) 254.00	

Cash

+	−
(c) 3,292.80	

Sales Discounts

+	−
(c) 67.20	

Notice that when the accountant records the receipt of cash, the discount is calculated less the sales return. This is because the company would grant a discount only on the remaining amount owed, not for the original sale amount.

10-2b No Sales Discounts Involved

When a transaction does not involve a sales discount or the discount has expired, the seller records the receipt of payment on account by debiting Cash and crediting Accounts Receivable. Assume that Blue Merchandise Company recorded the following transactions:

TRANSACTION (a). On April 1, Blue Merchandise Company sold merchandise on account to Yellow Company, invoice no. 1294, $9,450; terms 2/10, n/30; and recorded the sale in the general journal.

TRANSACTION (b). On April 26, received check from Yellow Company for $9,450 in payment of invoice no. 1294.

Blue Merchandise Company's accountant would record the transactions in the general journal as follows:

	GENERAL JOURNAL				Page 65
Date	**Description**	**Post. Ref.**	**Debit**	**Credit**	
20--					
Apr. 1	Accounts Receivable, Yellow				
	Company		9 4 5 0 00		
	Sales			9 4 5 0 00	
	Sold merchandise to Yellow				
	Company, invoice no. 1294.				
26	Cash		9 4 5 0 00		
	Accounts Receivable, Yellow				
	Company			9 4 5 0 00	
	Collected cash on account,				
	invoice no. 1294.				

Notice that because Yellow Company did not make payment within ten days, the discount was not applied to the invoice amount. Yellow Company paid the invoice in full.

POSTING TO THE GENERAL LEDGER AND SUBSIDIARY LEDGER

To post cash receipts of sales, post each entry to Cash and any other accounts involved in the general ledger. Also, post the amounts paid by customers to the subsidiary accounts receivable ledger to maintain a running balance of the amount each customer owes.

POSTING TO THE GENERAL LEDGER AND SUBSIDIARY LEDGER—A COMPUTERIZED APPROACH

Many computerized accounting software applications allow businesses to post cash receipts for sales and apply discounts. In Figure 1, the cash receipt of $1,894.83 in payment of invoice no. 9384 is being recorded into the accounting software.

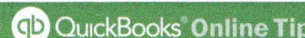
QuickBooks® Online Tip

As of the writing of this text, QuickBooks Online does not have the ability to automatically apply sales discounts to a paid invoice.

Figure 1
Recording a cash receipt using accounting software

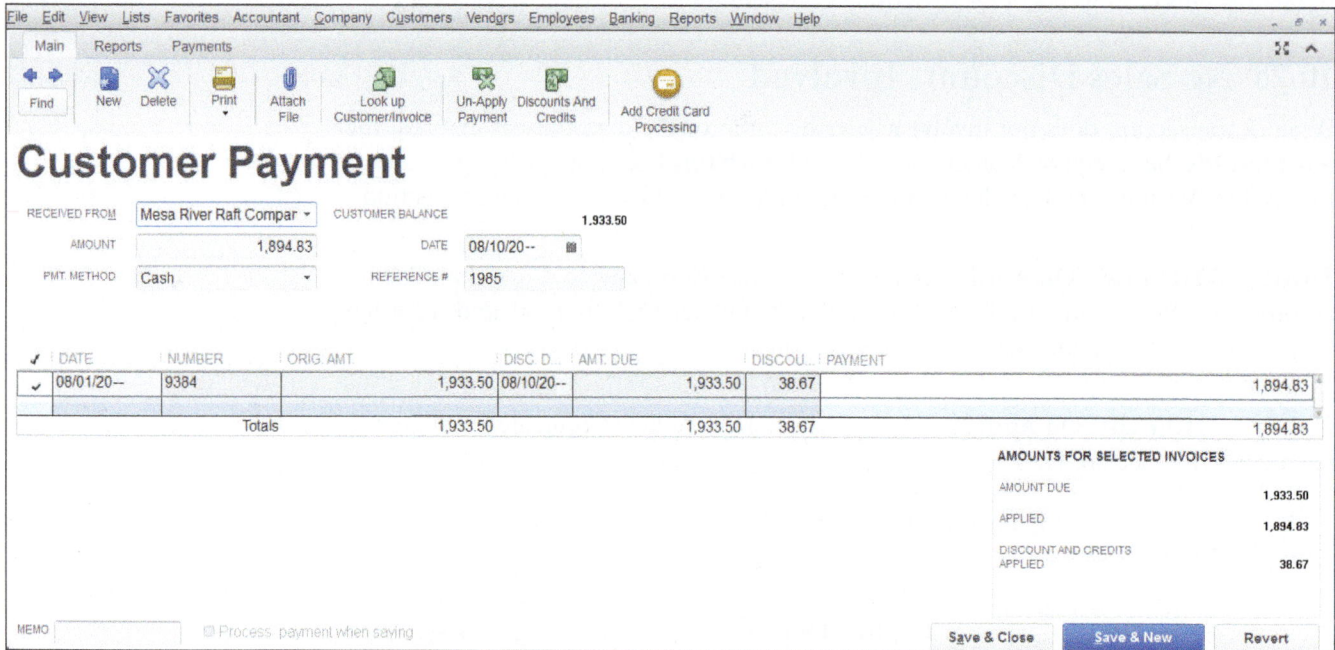

Figure 2
Recording a cash discount using accounting software

Notice that this software system allows the accountant to apply a discount. Look in the lower right corner to see the discount application button. In Figure 2, the accountant is recording the discount into the system.

After the discount has been applied, the invoice is shown as having been paid (Figure 3) and the balance due is $0.00. Using a computerized accounting system is an excellent way for businesses to keep track of cash receipts and discounts. Most computerized accounting software can also handle returns and allowances of merchandise that has been sold.

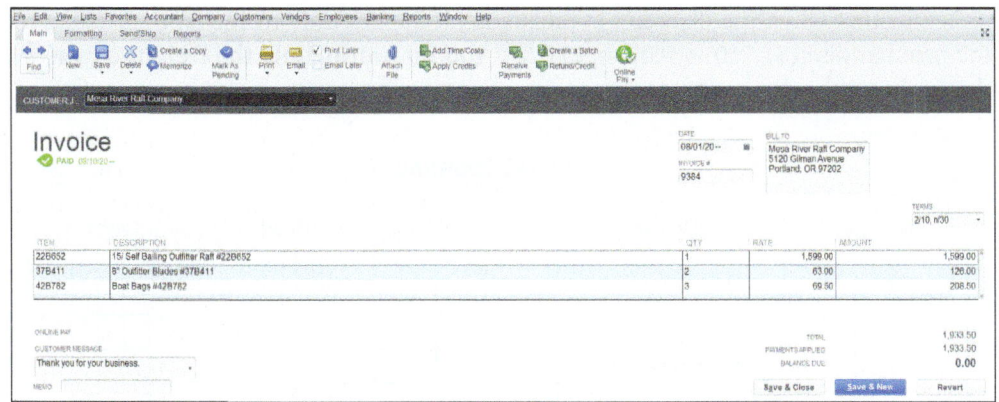

Figure 3
Paid invoice

10-2c Sales Returns and Allowances and Sales Discounts on an Income Statement

On the income statement, the Sales Returns and Allowances and Sales Discounts are placed under Sales. Both accounts are contra accounts, so we subtract their totals from Sales. The Revenue from Sales section of the annual income statement of Whitewater Raft Supply is shown in Figure 4.

Figure 4
Revenue from Sales section of income statement

Whitewater Raft Supply			
Income Statement			
For the Year Ended December 31, 20--			
Revenue from Sales:			
Sales			$257,180
Less: Sales Returns and Allowances		$ 940	
Sales Discounts		1,980	2,920
Net Sales			$254,260

10-3 PURCHASES DISCOUNTS

Recall that a cash discount is the amount the buyer may deduct from the bill. This acts as an incentive to get the buyer to pay the bill promptly. The buyer considers the cash discount to be a **purchases discount** because it relates to the buyer's purchase of merchandise. *Under the periodic inventory system, the Purchases Discounts account, like Purchases Returns and Allowances, is a contra account and is treated as a deduction from Purchases on the buyer's income statement.*

Let's return to Whitewater Raft Supply and assume that the following transactions take place.

3 In the general journal, record purchase transactions involving cash payments and cash discounts.

Learning Objective

Remember

The cash discount does not apply to freight charges billed separately on an invoice.

TRANSACTION (a). On August 2, Whitewater Raft Supply bought merchandise on account from Pataponia, Inc., invoice no. 2706, $1,710; terms 2/10, n/30; dated July 31; FOB San Francisco, freight prepaid and added to the invoice, $85.50 (total $1,795.50).

TRANSACTION (b). On August 8, issued Ck. No. 2076 to Pataponia, Inc., in payment of invoice no. 2706, less cash discount of $34.20, $1,761.30 ($1,795.50 − $34.20).

Notice that when the discount is calculated, it applies only to the amount billed for the merchandise ($1,710 × 0.02 = $34.20). **You do not include the freight cost when determining the discount**.

GENERAL JOURNAL					Page 26
Date	Description	Post. Ref.	Debit	Credit	
20--					
Aug. 2	Purchases		1 7 1 0 00		
	Freight In		8 5 50		
	Accounts Payable, Pataponia, Inc.			1 7 9 5 50	
	Purchased merchandise from				
	Pataponia, Inc., invoice no. 2706,				
	invoice dated 7/31,				
	terms 2/10, n/30.				
8	Accounts Payable, Pataponia, Inc.		1 7 9 5 50		
	Cash			1 7 6 1 30	
	Purchases Discounts			3 4 20	
	Paid Pataponia, Inc., for				
	invoice no. 2706, Ck. No. 2076.				

To record the payment to Pataponia, Inc., the accountant records a debit to Accounts Payable and a credit to Cash for the amount of cash paid. The amount of discount received is recorded as a credit to Purchases Discounts. Notice that the accountant records a debit to Accounts Payable, Pataponia, Inc., for the total invoice amount, $1,795.50. This is important because if the payable was debited for only the cash paid, the account would still show a balance due.

Assets	=	Liabilities	+	Capital	−	Drawing	+	Revenue	−	Expenses
+ | −		− | +		− | +		+ | −		− | +		+ | −
Debit | Credit		Debit | Credit		Debit | Credit		Debit | Credit		Debit | Credit		Debit | Credit

Cash

+	−
(b) 1,761.30	

Accounts Payable

−	+
(b) 1,795.50	(a) 1,795.50

Purchases

+	−
(a) 1,710.00	

Purchases Discounts

−	+
	(b) 34.20

Freight In

+	−
(a) 85.50	

Similar to sales returns, purchase returns and allowances are also not included when calculating the discount. Remember to omit any prepaid freight and returns and allowances when determining the amount of the discount.

10-3a No Purchases Discounts Involved

When a transaction does not involve a purchases discount or the discount has expired, the buyer will record the payment by debiting Accounts Payable and crediting Cash. Assume that Blue Merchandise Company recorded the following transactions:

TRANSACTION (a). On November 1, Blue Merchandise Company bought merchandise on account from Grey, Inc., invoice no. 3901, $4,600; terms 2/10, n/30; dated October 31.

TRANSACTION (b). On November 28, issued Ck. No. 1151 to Grey, Inc., in payment of invoice no. 3901, $4,600.

Blue Merchandise Company's accountant would record the transactions in the general journal as follows:

	GENERAL JOURNAL				Page 81	
Date	Description	Post. Ref.	Debit		Credit	
20--						
Nov. 1	Purchases		4 6 0 0 00			
	Accounts Payable, Grey, Inc.				4 6 0 0 00	
	Purchased merchandise from					
	Grey, Inc., invoice no. 3901,					
	invoice dated 10/31,					
	terms 2/10, n/30.					
28	Accounts Payable, Grey, Inc.		4 6 0 0 00			
	Cash				4 6 0 0 00	
	Paid Grey, Inc., for invoice no. 3901,					
	Ck. No. 1151.					

Notice that because Blue Merchandise Company did not make payment within ten days, the discount was not applied to the invoice amount. Blue Merchandise Company paid the invoice in full.

POSTING TO THE GENERAL LEDGER AND SUBSIDIARY LEDGER

To post cash payments of purchases, post each entry to Cash, Accounts Payable, and any other accounts involved in the general ledger. Also, post the amounts owed to vendors to the subsidiary accounts payable ledger to maintain a running balance of the amount owed to each vendor.

POSTING TO THE GENERAL LEDGER AND SUBSIDIARY LEDGER—A COMPUTERIZED APPROACH

Businesses can use a computerized accounting program to enter cash payments to vendors. Cash payments are applied to vendor invoices that are created by the accountant in the software. In Figure 5, the accountant is beginning to record the payment of the invoice by selecting the correct invoice due.

After the accountant has selected the bill on which to make payment, he or she can apply any discount granted and process the payment. Figure 6 shows the bill payment verification screen showing that payment has been applied to the invoice.

Figure 5
Recording a cash payment
using accounting software

Figure 6
Bill payment

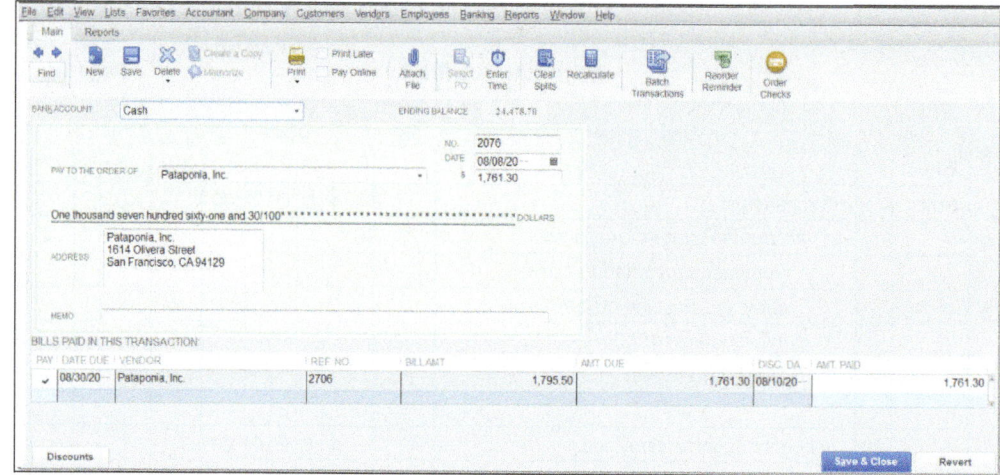

10-3b Purchases Returns and Allowances, Purchases Discounts, and Freight In on an Income Statement

On the income statement, the Purchases Returns and Allowances and Purchases Discounts are placed under Purchases. Both accounts are contra accounts, so we subtract their totals from Purchases. Because Freight In increases the cost of purchases, it must be added. A portion of the Cost of Goods Sold section of the annual income statement of Whitewater Raft Supply, as well as the Revenue from Sales section (taken from Figure 4, on page 431), is shown in Figure 7.

10-4 TRADE DISCOUNTS

 4 Record transactions involving trade discounts.

Manufacturers and wholesalers of many lines of products publish annual catalogs listing their products at retail prices. These organizations offer their customers substantial reductions (often as much as 40 percent) from the list or catalog prices. The reductions from the list prices are called **trade discounts**. Trade discounts are not journalized. Remember, firms grant cash discounts for prompt payment of invoices. Trade discounts are *not related* to cash payments. Manufacturers and wholesalers use trade discounts to avoid the high cost of reprinting catalogs when selling prices change and to encourage customers to purchase goods. To change prices, the manufacturer or wholesaler simply

Whitewater Raft Supply
Income Statement
For the Year Ended December 31, 20--

Revenue from Sales:			
Sales			$ 257,180
Less: Sales Returns and Allowances		$ 940	
Sales Discounts		1,980	2,920
Net Sales			$254,260
Cost of Goods Sold:			
Merchandise Inventory, January 1, 20--			$ 67,000
Purchases		$87,840	
Less: Purchases Returns and Allowances	$ 932		
Purchases Discounts	1,348	2,280	
Net Purchases		$85,560	
Add Freight In		2,360	
Delivered Cost of Purchases			87,920
Cost of Goods Available for Sale			$154,920

Figure 7

Partial income statement for Whitewater Raft Supply

issues a sheet or an online posting that shows a new list of trade discounts to be applied to the catalog prices. Trade discounts can also be used to differentiate between classes of customers. For example, a manufacturer may use one schedule of trade discounts for wholesalers and another schedule for retailers.

Firms may quote trade discounts as a single percentage. *For example, a* distributor of furnaces grants a single discount of 40 percent off the listed catalog price of $8,000. In this case, the selling price is calculated as follows:

List or catalog price	$8,000
Less trade discount of 40% ($8,000 × 0.40)	3,200
Selling price	$4,800

Neither the seller nor the buyer records trade discounts in the accounts. They enter only the selling price. Using T accounts, the furnace distributor records the sale like this:

Accounts Receivable		Sales	
+	−	−	+
4,800			4,800

The buyer records the purchase as follows:

Purchases		Accounts Payable	
+	−	−	+
4,800			4,800

Firms may also quote trade discounts as a chain, or series, of percentages. For example, a distributor of automobile parts grants discounts of 30 percent, 10 percent, and

10 percent off the listed catalog price of $900. In this case, the selling price is calculated as follows:

List or catalog price	$900.00
Less first trade discount of 30% ($900 × 0.30)	270.00
Remainder after first discount	$630.00
Less second trade discount of 10% ($630 × 0.10)	63.00
Remainder after second discount	$567.00
Less third discount of 10% ($567 × 0.10)	56.70
Selling price	$510.30

Using T accounts, the automobile parts distributor records the sale as follows:

Accounts Receivable			Sales	
+	−		−	+
510.30				510.30

The buyer records the purchase as follows:

Purchases			Accounts Payable	
+	−		−	+
510.30				510.30

In the situation involving a chain of discounts, the additional discounts are granted for large-volume transactions, in either dollar amount or size of shipment, such as carload lots.

Cash discounts could also apply in situations involving trade discounts. *Example:* Suppose the credit terms of the preceding sale include a cash discount of 2/10, n/30, and the buyer pays the invoice within ten days. The seller applies the cash discount to the selling price. The seller records the transaction as shown in the following T accounts:

Cash			Sales Discounts			Accounts Receivable	
+	−		+	−		+	−
500.09			10.21				510.30

The buyer records the transaction as follows:

Cash			Purchases Discounts			Accounts Payable	
+	−		−	+		−	+
	500.09			10.21		510.30	

10-4a A Review of Purchases and Sales Transactions

Now that we have covered all of the transactions involving purchases and sales, let's take a moment to review. Remember that each transaction affects a purchaser and a seller. In Figure 8, we show how each transaction would be recorded by a purchaser (Able Company) and a seller (Baker Company). Note that Able Company is using a periodic inventory system. For companies using a perpetual inventory system, Merchandise Inventory would be debited for purchases and credited for purchases returns and allowances and purchases discounts.

Remember

To the seller, a cash discount is a sales discount, and to the purchaser, a cash discount is a purchases discount.

Purchaser's Books—Able Company			Seller's Books—Baker Company		
Bought merchandise from Baker Company, $500; terms 2/10, n/30.			Sold merchandise to Able Company, $500; terms 2/10, n/30.		
Purchases	500		Accounts Receivable	500	
Accounts Payable		500	Sales		500
Received credit memo from			Issued credit memo to Able		
Baker Company for return of			Company for return of		
merchandise, $100.			merchandise, $100.		
Accounts Payable	100		Sales Returns and		
Purchases Returns and			Allowances	100	
Allowances		100	Accounts Receivable		100
Paid Baker Company within			Received cash from Able		
the discount period, $392			Company within the discount		
($500 − $100 = $400; $400 × 0.02 = $8;			period, $392.		
$400 − $8 = $392).					
Accounts Payable	400		Cash	392	
Cash		392	Sales Discounts	8	
Purchases Discounts		8	Accounts Receivable		400

Figure 8

Transactions for two companies' purchases and sales using the periodic inventory system

Remember

For companies using a perpetual inventory system, purchases for Able Company are recorded as:

   Merchandise
   Inventory   500
      Accounts
      Payable   500

Merchandise Inventory is credited for purchases returns and allowances and purchase discounts.

To: Amy Roberts, CPA
Subject: Cash Receipts and Cash Payments

Hi Amy,

I think I understand discounts. Thanks again for your help. I did come up with another question. Is there any way to speed up the journalizing process for cash receipts and cash payments? It seems like I spend a lot of time posting to the same accounts. Can you suggest something that might reduce the time I spend recording transactions?

Thanks,

Janie

To: Janie Conner
Subject: RE: Cash Receipts and Cash Payments

Hi Janie,

I do have a few suggestions regarding your process for recording cash receipts and cash payments. We can discuss the benefits of using the cash receipts and cash payment journals, as well as using the accounts receivable and accounts payable ledgers.

    Below is a summary of the items for us to discuss the next time we talk.

        _____ 1. Journalizing transactions using the cash receipts journal and posting to the accounts receivable ledger

        _____ 2. Journalizing transactions using the cash payments journal and posting to the accounts payable ledger

Just give me a call when you have some time later this week.

Amy

SMALL BUSINESS **SUCCESS**

Credit Cards: Are They Worth It?

Accepting credit cards for sales of merchandise or services has become a natural part of business for most companies. However, some small businesses still don't accept credit cards and rely only on cash sales. The decision to accept credit cards comes at a cost to the business in the form of a fee. The bank that processes your credit card sales will charge your company a fee for any credit card sales. The amount of the fee varies based on the bank you are using and the amount of transactions your company processes. In addition to banks, specific companies, often called merchant service companies, offer credit card processing services.

Why would a company choose to accept credit cards in the form of payment? There are many reasons. One is that it may increase sales by allowing customers more flexibility in payment methods. Also, the bank or processing company assumes all risk associated with non-paying customers. Unlike uncollectible accounts receivables, the company always gets paid when a transaction involves a credit card sale.

How does a company begin accepting credit cards? The first step is to apply for merchant status. Applying for merchant status is similar to applying for a loan. Your company must fill out an application and have its financial records reviewed. Once merchant status is approved for your company, you will be able to accept most common credit cards. The bank or merchant services company that you partner with will transfer the cash proceeds, less the fee, for each credit card sale to your bank account. The transaction fee or service charge usually ranges from 1.5 to 5 percent of the sale. In addition, there may be monthly or other fees associated with credit card transactions.

10-5 **RECORDING TRANSACTIONS IN THE CASH RECEIPTS SPECIAL JOURNAL**

In Chapter 9, we saw that using a sales journal and a purchases journal enables an accountant to carry out the journalizing and posting processes more efficiently. These special journals make it possible to post column totals rather than individual figures. They also make the division of labor more efficient because the journalizing functions can be delegated to different people. The *cash receipts journal* and the *cash payments journal* further extend these advantages.

The **cash receipts journal** contains all transactions in which cash is received, or increased. When a cash receipts journal is used, all transactions in which cash is debited *must* be recorded in it. It may be used for a service as well as a merchandising business. Let's list some typical transactions of a merchandising business, Whitewater Raft Supply, that result in an increase in cash. To get a better picture of the transactions, let's record them in T accounts and then in the general journal.

Oct. 1   **Sold merchandise on account to Green River Rafts, invoice no. 10050, $3,500; terms 2/10, n/30.**

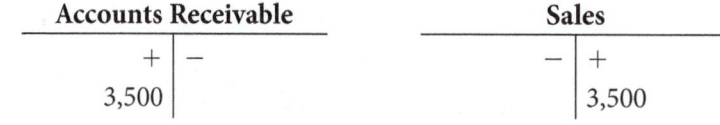

Oct. 4   Sold merchandise, $500, and the customer used a credit card.

The bank issuing the card bills the customer directly each month. The business, on the other hand, deposits the bank credit card receipts every day. The bank *deducts a discount* and credits the firm's account for the cash difference. We will assume that the discount is 4 percent. The firm therefore records the amount of the discount under Credit Card Expense: $500 \times 0.04 = \$20$ credit card expense; $500 - \$20 = \$480$.

Cash			Credit Card Expense			Sales	
+	−		+	−		−	+
480			20				500

As an alternative, many businesses postpone recording the amount of bank credit card expense until they receive notification from their bank on their bank statement. For example, total credit card sales for a restaurant for a time period amount to $10,600 plus 8 percent sales tax. The entry is as follows:

Cash			Sales Tax Payable			Sales	
+	−		−	+		−	+
11,448				848			10,600

The restaurant's next bank statement includes a debit memorandum for credit card charges of $457.92, using an assumed 4 percent discount rate ($11,448 \times 0.04$). The business handles this in a similar manner to a check service charge.

Credit Card Expense			Cash	
+	−		+	−
457.92				457.92

Oct. 5   Collected cash on account from L. R. Ray, a charge customer, $416.

Cash			Accounts Receivable	
+	−		+	−
416				416

Oct. 7   The owner, D. M. Bruce, invested cash in the business, $9,000.

Cash			D. M. Bruce, Capital	
+	−		−	+
9,000				9,000

Oct. 8   Sold equipment at cost for cash, $500.

Cash			Equipment	
+	−		+	−
500				500

Oct. 10   **Received check from Green River Rafts for \$3,430 in payment of invoice no. 10050, less cash discount (\$3,500 × 0.02 = \$70; \$3,500 − \$70 = \$3,430).**

Cash		Sales Discounts		Accounts Receivable	
+	−	+	−	+	−
3,430		70			3,500

Oct. 15   **Cash sales for first half of the month, \$2,460.**

Cash		Sales	
+	−	−	+
2,460			2,460

The same transactions are shown in general journal form as follows:

GENERAL JOURNAL   **Page 29**

Date		Description	Post. Ref.	Debit	Credit
20--					
Oct.	1	Accounts Receivable, Green River Rafts		3 5 0 0 00	
		Sales			3 5 0 0 00
		Sold merchandise to Green			
		River Rafts, invoice no. 10050.			
	4	Cash		4 8 0 00	
		Credit Card Expense		2 0 00	
		Sales			5 0 0 00
		Sold merchandise involving a credit			
		card.			
	5	Cash		4 1 6 00	
		Accounts Receivable, L. R. Ray			4 1 6 00
		Collected cash on account.			
	7	Cash		9 0 0 0 00	
		D. M. Bruce, Capital			9 0 0 0 00
		Owner invested cash.			
	8	Cash		5 0 0 00	
		Equipment			5 0 0 00
		Sold equipment at cost.			
	10	Cash		3 4 3 0 00	
		Sales Discounts		7 0 00	
		Accounts Receivable, Green River Rafts			3 5 0 0 00
		Received a check in payment of			
		invoice no. 10050, less cash			
		discount.			
	15	Cash		2 4 6 0 00	
		Sales			2 4 6 0 00
		Cash sales for the first half			
		of the month.			

Now let's analyze these seven transactions: The transaction on October 1 does not involve cash; therefore, it would not be recorded in the cash receipts journal. Instead, this transaction would be recorded in either the general journal or the sales journal. The transactions occurring on 10/4, 10/5, 10/10, and 10/15 would occur frequently; the transactions on 10/7 and 10/8 would occur less frequently. When designing a cash receipts journal, it is logical to include a Cash Debit column because all of the transactions involve an increase in cash. If a business regularly collects cash from credit customers, there should be an Accounts Receivable Credit column and Sales Discounts Debit column. If a firm often sells merchandise for cash and collects a sales tax, there should be a Sales Credit column and a Sales Tax Payable Credit column. If the business accepts credit cards and wants to record the amount of the discount at the time of each transaction, there should be a Credit Card Expense Debit column for the amount deducted by the bank.

However, the credit to D. M. Bruce, Capital and the credit to Equipment do not occur very often, so it would not be practical to set up special columns for these credits. They can be handled adequately by an Other Accounts Credit column, which can be used for credits to all accounts that have no special column.

The accountant would record these transactions in a cash receipts journal, as shown in Figure 9. Notice that there are columns for each of the most common cash transactions. The accountant would record each transaction directly into the cash receipts journal by placing each amount in the appropriate column.

Figure 9
Cash receipts journal

CASH RECEIPTS JOURNAL — Page 41

Date		Account Credited	Post. Ref.	Cash Debit	Credit Card Expense Debit	Sales Discounts Debit	Accounts Receivable Credit	Sales Credit	Other Accounts Credit
20—									
Oct.	4	_____		4 8 0 00	2 0 00			5 0 0 00	
	5	L. R. Ray		4 1 6 00			4 1 6 00		
	7	D. M. Bruce,							
		Capital		9 0 0 0 00					9 0 0 0 00
	8	Equipment		5 0 0 00					5 0 0 00
	10	Green							
		River Rafts		3 4 3 0 00		7 0 00	3 5 0 0 00		
	15	_____		2 4 6 0 00				2 4 6 0 00	

10-5a Posting from the Cash Receipts Journal

Here are some other transactions that involve increases in cash during the month. These transactions are recorded in the sales journal shown in Figure 10.

Oct. 16   Received check from Floyd Mercantile for $1,366.12 in payment of invoice no. 10052, less cash discount ($1,394.00 − $27.88 = $1,366.12).

   17   Borrowed $9,000 from the bank, receiving cash and giving the bank a promissory note.

   21   Received check from Hartman Guides for $3,696.80 in payment of invoice no. 10055, less cash discount ($3,772.24 − $75.44 = $3,696.80).

   30   Received check from Bowers River Co. for $1,710 in payment of invoice no. 10054. (This is longer than the 10-day period, so the cash discount is not allowed.)

   31   Cash sales for second half of the month, $2,620.

Remember

Special journals include a sales journal (S), a purchases journal (P), a cash receipts journal (CR), and a cash payments journal (CP). Using these special journals saves time in posting totals of the special columns rather than individual amounts to the general ledger.

Figure 10

Posting from the cash receipts journal to the general ledger and accounts receivable ledger

CASH RECEIPTS JOURNAL — Page 41

Date		Account Credited	Post. Ref.	Cash Debit	Credit Card Expense Debit	Sales Discounts Debit	Accounts Receivable Credit	Sales Credit	Other Accounts Credit
20--									
Oct.	4	_____	—	4 80 00	2 0 00			5 0 0 00	
	5	L. R. Ray	✓	4 16 00			4 1 6 00		
	7	D. M. Bruce,							
		Capital	311	9 0 0 0 00					9 0 0 0 00
	8	Equipment	124	5 0 0 00					5 0 0 00
	10	Green River							
		Rafts	✓	3 4 30 00		7 0 00	3 5 0 0 00		
	15	_____	—	2 4 60 00				2 4 6 0 00	
	16	Floyd							
		Mercantile	✓	1 3 66 12		2 7 88	1 3 9 4 00		
	17	Notes Payable	211	9 0 0 0 00					9 0 0 0 00
	21	Hartman							
		Guides	✓	3 6 96 80		7 5 44	3 7 7 2 24		
	30	Bowers River Co.	✓	1 7 10 00			1 7 1 0 00		
	31	_____	—	2 6 20 00				2 6 2 0 00	
	31	Total		34 6 78 92	2 0 00	1 7 3 32	10 7 9 2 24	5 5 8 0 00	18 5 0 0 00
				(1 1 1)	(6 1 5)	(4 1 3)	(1 1 3)	(4 1 1)	(X)

Accounts Receivable Ledger

Bowers River Co.

	+		−	
Beg. Bal.	2,500.00	Oct. 30		1,710.00
End. Bal.	790.00			

Floyd Mercantile

	+		−	
Beg. Bal.	1,394.00	Oct. 16		1,394.00

Green River Rafts

	+		−	
Beg. Bal.	5,000.00	Oct. 10		3,500.00
End. Bal.	1,500.00			

Hartman Guides

	+		−	
Beg. Bal.	3,772.24	Oct. 21		3,772.24

L. R. Ray

	+		−	
Beg. Bal.	416.00	Oct. 5		416.00

General Ledger

Cash   111

	+		−
Oct. 31	34,678.92		

Accounts Receivable   113

	+		−
Oct. 31	10,792.24		

Equipment   124

	+		−
Oct. 8	500.00		

Notes Payable   211

	−		+
		Oct. 17	9,000.00

D. M. Bruce, Capital   311

	−		+
		Oct. 7	9,000.00

Sales   411

	−		+
		Oct. 31	5,580.00

Sales Discounts   413

	+		−
Oct. 31	173.32		

Credit Card Expense   615

	+		−
Oct. 31	20.00		

In the transaction of October 17, in which $9,000 was borrowed from the bank, the bank was given a **promissory note** (a written promise to pay a specified amount at a specified time) as evidence of the debt. The account **Notes Payable**, instead of Accounts Payable, is used to represent the amount owed on the promissory note. The Accounts Payable account is reserved for charge accounts with creditors, which are normally paid on a 30-day basis.

Let's assume that all of the month's transactions involving debits to Cash have been recorded in the cash receipts journal. The cash receipts journal and the T accounts following it in Figure 10, illustrate the postings to the general ledger and the accounts receivable ledger.

Individual amounts in the Accounts Receivable Credit column of the cash receipts journal are usually posted daily to the accounts receivable ledger. Individual amounts in the Other Accounts Credit column are also usually posted daily.

At the end of the month, we can post the special column totals in the cash receipts journal to the general ledger accounts. These columns include Cash Debit, Credit Card Expense Debit, Sales Discounts Debit, Accounts Receivable Credit, and Sales Credit.

In the Post. Ref. column, the check marks (✓) indicate that the amounts in the Accounts Receivable Credit column have been posted to the individual credit customers' accounts as credits. The account numbers show that the amounts in the Other Accounts Credit column have been posted separately to the accounts described in the Account Credited column. An (X) goes under the total of the Other Accounts Credit column. It means "do not post—the figures have already been posted separately." This column is totaled to make it easier to prove that the debits equal the credits.

Debit Totals		Credit Totals	
Cash	$34,678.92	Accounts Receivable	$10,792.24
Credit Card Expense	20.00	Sales	5,580.00
Sales Discounts	173.32	Other Accounts	18,500.00
	$34,872.24		$34,872.24

ADVANTAGES OF A CASH RECEIPTS JOURNAL

The advantages of using a cash receipts journal are as follows:

- Transactions generally can be recorded on one line.

- All transactions involving debits to Cash are recorded in one place.

- It eliminates much repetition in posting to the general ledger when there are numerous transactions involving Cash debits. The Cash Debit side can be posted as one total.

- Special columns can be used for similar transactions and posted as one total.

10-6 RECORDING TRANSACTIONS IN THE CASH PAYMENTS SPECIAL JOURNAL

6 In the cash payments journal, record transactions for a merchandising business and post from a cash payments journal to a general ledger and an accounts payable ledger.

Learning Objective

The **cash payments journal**, as the name implies, is a special journal used to record all transactions in which cash goes out, or decreases. When the cash payments journal is used, all transactions in which cash is credited *must* be recorded in it. This journal may be used for either a service or a merchandising business.

To get acquainted with the cash payments journal, let's list some typical transactions of a merchandising business that result in a decrease in cash. To illustrate, we record the following transactions in T accounts:

Oct. 2 **Bought merchandise on account from Pataponia, Inc., invoice no. 2746, $2,500; terms 2/10, n/30; dated September 30; FOB San Francisco, freight prepaid and added to the invoice, $100.25 (total $2,600.25).**

Accounts Payable		Purchases		Freight In	
−	+	+	−	+	−
	2,600.25	2,500.00		100.25	

Oct. 8 **Issued Ck. No. 2226 to Pataponia, Inc., in payment of invoice no. 2746, less cash discount of $50.00, $2,550.25 ($2,600.25 − $50.00).** [Notice that the discount applies only to the amount billed for the merchandise (2 percent of $2,500).]

Cash		Accounts Payable		Purchases Discounts	
+	−	−	+	−	+
	2,550.25	2,600.25			50.00

Oct. 10 Paid cash for liability insurance, Ck. No. 2227 $4,890.

Prepaid Insurance		Cash	
+	−	+	−
4,890			4,890

Oct. 12 Paid wages for two weeks, Ck. No. 2228, $6,220 (previously recorded in the payroll entry).

Wages Payable		Cash	
−	+	+	−
	6,220		6,220

Oct. 14 Paid rent for the month, Ck. No. 2229, $2,950.

Rent Expense		Cash	
+	−	+	−
2,950			2,950

The same transactions are shown in general journal form as follows:

		GENERAL JOURNAL			Page 29	
Date		Description	Post. Ref.	Debit	Credit	
20--						
Oct.	2	Purchases		2 5 0 0 00		
		Freight In		1 0 0 25		
		Accounts Payable, Pataponia, Inc.			2 6 0 0 25	
		Purchased merchandise from				
		Pataponia, Inc., invoice no. 2746,				
		invoice dated 9/30, terms 2/10, n/30.				
	8	Accounts Payable, Pataponia, Inc.		2 6 0 0 25		
		Cash			2 5 5 0 25	
		Purchases Discounts			5 0 00	
		Paid on account, Ck. No. 2226.				
	10	Prepaid Insurance		4 8 9 0 00		
		Cash			4 8 9 0 00	
		Paid liability insurance,				
		Ck. No. 2227.				
	12	Wages Payable		6 2 2 0 00		
		Cash			6 2 2 0 00	
		Paid wages for two weeks,				
		Ck. No. 2228.				
	14	Rent Expense		2 9 5 0 00		
		Cash			2 9 5 0 00	
		Paid rent for month, Ck. No. 2229.				

Now let's analyze these five transactions. The transaction on October 2 does not involve cash; therefore, it would not be recorded in the cash payments journal. Instead, this transaction would be recorded in either the general journal or the purchases journal. The transaction on October 8 would occur frequently, as payments to creditors are made several times a month. Of the other transactions, the debit to Wages Payable might occur only twice a month, the debit to Rent Expense once a month, and the debit to Prepaid Insurance only occasionally.

It is logical to include a Cash Credit column in a cash payments journal because all transactions recorded in this journal involve a decrease in cash. Because payments to creditors are made often, there should also be an Accounts Payable Debit column and a Purchases Discounts Credit column. You can set up any other column that is used often enough to warrant it. Otherwise, an Other Accounts Debit column takes care of all other transactions.

Now let's record these same transactions in a cash payments journal and include a column titled Ck. No., as illustrated in Figure 11. If you think for a moment, you will see that this is consistent with good management of cash. All expenditures except Petty Cash expenditures should be paid for by check.

Figure 11

Cash payments journal

					Other Accounts Debit	Accounts Payable Debit	Purchases Discounts Credit	Cash Credit
CASH PAYMENTS JOURNAL								**Page 62**
Date	Ck. No.	Account Debited	Post. Ref.		Other Accounts Debit	Accounts Payable Debit	Purchases Discounts Credit	Cash Credit
20--								
Oct. 8	2226	Pataponia, Inc.				2 6 0 0 25	5 0 00	2 5 5 0 25
10	2227	Prepaid Insurance			4 8 9 0 00			4 8 9 0 00
12	2228	Wages Payable			6 2 2 0 00			6 2 2 0 00
14	2229	Rent Expense			2 9 5 0 00			2 9 5 0 00

Here are some other transactions of Whitewater Raft Supply involving decreases in cash during October. Note that credit terms vary among the different creditors.

Oct. 15 Issued Ck. No. 2230 to Gibbs Company in payment of invoice no. 10611 ($564), less return ($270); less cash discount, terms 2/10, n/30; $288.12 [$564 − $270 = $294; $294.00 × 0.02 = $5.88; $294.00 − $5.88 = $288.12].

16 Issued Ck. No. 2231 to Gardner Products Company in payment of invoice no. B643 ($1,245), less return ($315); less cash discount, terms 1/10, n/30; $921.60 [$1,245 − $315 = $930. Freight charges totaled $90 ($930 − $90 = $840); $840.00 × 0.01 = $8.40; $930.00 − $8.40 = $921.60].

17 Bought merchandise for cash, Ck. No. 2232, payable to Jones and Son, $200.

19 Received bill and issued Ck. No. 2233 to Monroe Express for freight charges on merchandise purchased earlier from Gibbs Company, $60.

23 Voided Ck. No. 2234.

25 Paid wages for two-week period, Ck. No. 2235, $1,750 (previously recorded in the payroll entry).

27 Paid F. P. Franz for merchandise returned on a cash sale, Ck. No. 2236, $51.

27 Issued Ck. No. 2237 to Langseth and Son in payment of invoice no. 902, $1,180; terms net 30 days.

The transaction of October 19 paying the freight bill to Monroe Express increases the Freight In account, as the transportation charges are for merchandise purchased.

You should list all checks in consecutive order, even those checks that must be voided. In this way, *every* check is accounted for, which is necessary for internal control.

These transactions are recorded in the cash payments journal illustrated in Figure 12. Notice that an (X) is placed under the Other Accounts column. That means "do not post—the figures have already been posted separately."

The posting process for the cash payments journal is similar to the posting process for the cash receipts journal. Individual amounts in the Accounts Payable Debit column are usually posted daily to the subsidiary ledger. After posting, put a check mark (✔) in the Post. Ref. column. Individual amounts in the Other Accounts Debit column are also usually posted daily to the general ledger. Post these figures individually; then place the account number in the Post. Ref. column. Totals of the Cash Credit column, Purchases Discounts Credit column, and Accounts Payable Debit column are posted to the general

Figure 12
Cash payments journal

					Other Accounts Debit	Accounts Payable Debit	Purchases Discounts Credit	Cash Credit
Date	Ck. No.	Account Debited	Post. Ref.					
20--								
Oct. 8	2226	Pataponia, Inc.	✓			2 6 0 0 25	5 0 00	2 5 5 0 25
10	2227	Prepaid Insurance	116		4 8 9 0 00			4 8 9 0 00
12	2228	Wages Payable	213		6 2 2 0 00			6 2 2 0 00
14	2229	Rent Expense	612		2 9 5 0 00			2 9 5 0 00
15	2230	Gibbs Company	✓			2 9 4 00	5 88	2 8 8 12
16	2231	Gardner Products Company	✓			9 3 0 00	8 40	9 2 1 60
17	2232	Purchases	511		2 0 0 00			2 0 0 00
19	2233	Freight In	514		6 0 00			6 0 00
23	2234	Void	—					
25	2235	Wages Payable	213		1 7 5 0 00			1 7 5 0 00
27	2236	Sales Returns and Allowances	412		5 1 00			5 1 00
27	2237	Langseth and Son	✓			1 1 8 0 00		1 1 8 0 00
31		Totals			16 1 2 1 00	5 0 0 4 25	6 4 28	21 0 6 0 97
					(X)	(2 1 2)	(5 1 3)	(1 1 1)

CASH PAYMENTS JOURNAL — Page 62

ledger accounts at the end of the month. Write the appropriate general ledger account number in parentheses below the column totals. Put an (X) below the total of the Other Accounts Debit column to indicate that the total amount is not posted.

At the end of the month, after totaling the columns, check the accuracy of the footings by proving that the sum of the debit totals equals the sum of the credit totals. Because you have posted the individual amounts in the Other Accounts Debit column to the general ledger, the only posting that remains is the credit to the Cash account for $21,060.97, the credit to the Purchases Discounts account for $64.28, and the debit to the Accounts Payable (controlling) account for $5,004.25.

> **Remember**
>
> The (X) below the total of the Other Accounts Debit column means "do not post total."

Debit Totals		Credit Totals	
Accounts Payable	$ 5,004.25	Cash	$21,060.97
Other Accounts	16,121.00	Purchases Discounts	64.28
	$21,125.25		$21,125.25

ADVANTAGES OF A CASH PAYMENTS JOURNAL

The advantages of the cash payments journal are similar to the advantages of the cash receipts journal.

- Transactions generally can be recorded on one line.
- All transactions involving credits to Cash are recorded in one place.
- For numerous transactions involving Cash credits, the Cash Credit side can be posted in the general ledger as one total.
- Special columns can be used for similar transactions and posted as one total.

10-6a Comparison of the Five Types of Journals

We have now looked at four special journals and the general journal. It is important for a business to select and use the journals that provide the most efficient accounting system possible. Figure 13 summarizes the applications of the journals we have discussed and the correct procedures for using them.

Figure 13
Using special journals

Types of Transactions

Sale of merchandise on account	Purchase of merchandise on account	Receipt of cash	Payment of cash	All other

Evidenced by Source Documents

Sales invoice	Purchase invoice	Credit card receipts Cash Checks Electronic funds transfers	Check stub Electronic funds transfers	Miscellaneous

Types of Journals

Sales journal	Purchases journal	Cash receipts journal	Cash payments journal	General journal

Posting to Ledger Accounts

Individual amounts posted daily to the accounts receivable ledger and the total posted monthly to the general ledger.	Individual amounts posted daily to the accounts payable ledger and the totals of the special columns posted monthly to the general ledger.	Individual amounts in the Accounts Receivable Credit column posted daily to the accounts receivable ledger. Individual amounts in the Other Accounts columns posted daily to the general ledger. Totals of special columns posted monthly to the general ledger.	Individual amounts in the Accounts Payable Debit column posted daily to the accounts payable ledger. Individual amounts in the Other Accounts columns posted daily to the general ledger. Totals of special columns posted monthly to the general ledger.	Entries posted daily to the subsidiary ledgers and the general ledger.

Chapter Review

Study and Practice

 1 Determine cash discounts according to credit terms.

The amount of the discount is determined by multiplying the invoice total (excluding freight charges and any returns and allowances) by the **cash discount** rate.

 1 PRACTICE EXERCISE 1

For the following purchases of merchandise, determine the amount of cash to be paid.

Purchase	Invoice Date	Credit Terms	FOB	Amount of Purchase	Freight Charges	Total Invoice Amount	Returns and Allowances	Date Paid
a.	June 12	1/10, n/30	Destination	$700	—	$ 700	$100	June 21
b.	June 14	2/10, n/30	Shipping point	940	$60	1,000	—	June 20
c.	June 18	n/30	Shipping point	820	40	860	30	July 17

PRACTICE EXERCISE 1 • SOLUTION

a. $594   ($700 − $100) − ($600 × 0.01) = $600 − $6 = $594

b. $981.20   ($940 + $60) − ($940 × 0.02) = $1,000 − $18.80 = $981.20

c. $830   ($820 + $40) − $30 = $830

2 In the general journal, record sales transactions involving cash receipts and cash discounts.

When recording a cash receipt from a customer within the discount period, the business records a debit to Cash for the amount received, a debit to Sales Discounts for the amount of the discount, and a credit to Accounts Receivable for the full amount of the invoice less any returns and allowances.

 2 PRACTICE EXERCISE 2

Record the following sales transactions in general journal form on the books of Fry Company (the seller).

a. Sold merchandise on account to Lee Company, invoice no. 8765, $1,500; terms 2/10, n/30.

b. Issued credit memo no. 967 to Lee Company for damaged merchandise, $100.

c. Lee Company paid the account in full within the discount period.

CHAPTER REVIEW

PRACTICE EXERCISE 2 • SOLUTION

		GENERAL JOURNAL				Page ___
Date		Description	Post. Ref.	Debit	Credit	
	a.	Accounts Receivable, Lee Company		1 5 0 0 00		
		Sales			1 5 0 0 00	
		Sold merchandise to Lee				
		Company, invoice no. 8765.				
	b.	Sales Returns and Allowances		1 0 0 00		
		Accounts Receivable, Lee Company			1 0 0 00	
		Issued credit memo no. 967.				
	c.	Cash		1 3 7 2 00		
		Sales Discounts		2 8 00		
		Accounts Receivable, Lee Company			1 4 0 0 00	
		Received payment in full.				
		[($1,500 − $100) × 0.02]				

Learning Objective   In the general journal, record purchase transactions involving cash payments and cash discounts.

When recording a payment to a vendor within the discount period, the business records a debit to Accounts Payable for the full amount of the invoice less any returns and allowances, a credit to Purchases Discounts for the amount of the discount, and a credit to Cash for the amount paid.

③ PRACTICE EXERCISE 3

Record the following purchase transactions in general journal form on the books of Lee Company (the buyer).

a. Purchased merchandise on account from Fry Company, invoice no. 8765, $1,500; terms 2/10, n/30.
b. Received credit memo no. 967 from Fry Company for damaged merchandise, $100.
c. Paid Fry Company in full within the discount period.

PRACTICE EXERCISE 3 • SOLUTION

		GENERAL JOURNAL			Page ___	
Date		Description	Post. Ref.	Debit	Credit	
	a.	Purchases		1 5 0 0 00		
		Accounts Payable, Fry Company			1 5 0 0 00	
		Purchased merchandise from				
		Fry Company, invoice no. 8765.				
	b.	Accounts Payable, Fry Company		1 0 0 00		
		Purchases Returns and Allowances			1 0 0 00	
		Received credit memo no. 967.				
	c.	Accounts Payable, Fry Company		1 4 0 0 00		
		Purchases Discounts			2 8 00	
		Cash			1 3 7 2 00	
		Paid invoice no. 8765 in full.				
		[($1,500 − $100) × 0.02]				

4 Record transactions involving trade discounts.

Learning Objective

In transactions involving **trade discounts**, the trade discounts are deducted from the list prices to arrive at the selling prices. Both sellers and buyers record the transactions at the selling prices.

PRACTICE EXERCISE 4

Record the following transaction involving a trade discount.

Feb. 2 Bought merchandise on account from Coffee Company, $3,500, received a 40% trade discount, invoice no. 234C, dated Jan. 31; terms 2/10, n/EOM.

PRACTICE EXERCISE 4 • SOLUTION

		GENERAL JOURNAL			Page ___	
Date		Description	Post. Ref.	Debit	Credit	
20--						
Feb.	2	Purchases		2 1 0 0 00		
		Accounts Payable, Coffee Company			2 1 0 0 00	
		Purchased merchandise from				
		Coffee Company, invoice no. 234C.				
		[$3,500 − ($3,500 × 0.40)]				

Learning Objective **5** In the cash receipts journal, record transactions for a merchandising business and post from a cash receipts journal to a general ledger and an accounts receivable ledger.

A transaction for a merchandising business can be recorded on one line in a **cash receipts journal**. The cash receipts journal usually contains the following columns: Date, Account Credited, Post. Ref., Cash Debit, Credit Card Expense Debit, Sales Discounts Debit, Accounts Receivable Credit, Sales Credit, Sales Tax Payable Credit, and Other Accounts Credit.

The accountant posts daily from the Accounts Receivable Credit column to the individual credit customers' accounts in the accounts receivable ledger. After posting, the accountant puts a check mark (✓) in the Post. Ref. column. The accountant also posts the amounts daily in the Other Accounts Credit column and records the account numbers in the Post. Ref. column. The special columns are posted as totals at the end of the month. The accountant then writes the account numbers in parentheses under the totals. An (X) below the total of the Other Accounts Credit column shows that amounts are posted individually and the total is not posted.

 5 **PRACTICE EXERCISE 5**

Indicate the appropriate columns in which each of the following transactions would be recorded in the cash receipts journal.

Transaction	Cash Debit	Credit Card Expense Debit	Sales Discounts Debit	Accounts Receivable Credit	Sales Credit	Other Accounts Credit
a. Collected cash on account from a charge customer.						
b. Received check from a charge customer in payment of an invoice within the discount period.						
c. Borrowed money from the bank, receiving cash and giving the bank a promissory note.						
d. Received check from a charge customer in payment of an invoice past the discount period.						
e. Recorded cash sales for the month.						

PRACTICE EXERCISE 5 • SOLUTION

Transaction	Cash Debit	Credit Card Expense Debit	Sales Discounts Debit	Accounts Receivable Credit	Sales Credit	Other Accounts Credit
a. Collected cash on account from a charge customer.	✓			✓		
b. Received check from a charge customer in payment of an invoice within the discount period.	✓		✓	✓		
c. Borrowed money from the bank, receiving cash and giving the bank a promissory note.	✓					✓
d. Received check from a charge customer in payment of an invoice past the discount period.	✓			✓		
e. Recorded cash sales for the month.	✓				✓	

In the cash payments journal, record transactions for a merchandising business and post from a cash payments journal to a general ledger and an accounts payable ledger.

Learning Objective

A cash payment by a merchandising business that includes a purchases discount can be recorded on one line in a **cash payments journal**. The cash payments journal usually contains the following columns: Date, Ck. No., Account Debited, Post. Ref., Other Accounts Debit, Accounts Payable Debit, Purchases Discounts Credit, and Cash Credit.

The accountant posts daily from the Accounts Payable Debit column to the individual suppliers' accounts in the accounts payable ledger. After posting, the accountant puts a check mark (✓) in the Post. Ref. column. The accountant also posts the amounts daily in the Other Accounts Debit column and records the account numbers in the Post. Ref. column. The special columns are posted as totals at the end of the month. The accountant then writes the account numbers in parentheses under the totals. An (X) below the total of the Other Accounts Debit column shows that amounts are posted individually and the total is not posted.

PRACTICE EXERCISE 6

Indicate the appropriate columns in which each of the following transactions would be recorded in the cash payments journal.

Transaction	Other Accounts Debit	Accounts Payable Debit	Purchases Discounts Credit	Cash Credit
a. Issued check to vendor in payment of an invoice within the discount period.				
b. Paid customer for merchandise returned on a cash sale.				
c. Paid wages for two weeks.				
d. Issued check to vendor in payment of an invoice past the discount period.				
e. Paid rent for the month.				

PRACTICE EXERCISE 6 • SOLUTION

Transaction	Other Accounts Debit	Accounts Payable Debit	Purchases Discounts Credit	Cash Credit
a. Issued check to vendor in payment of an invoice within the discount period.		✓	✓	✓
b. Paid customer for merchandise returned on a cash sale.	✓			✓
c. Paid wages for two weeks.	✓			✓
d. Issued check to vendor in payment of an invoice past the discount period.		✓		✓
e. Paid rent for the month.	✓			✓

Glossary

Cash discount The amount a customer can deduct for paying a bill within a specified period of time; used to encourage prompt payment. Not all sellers offer cash discounts. (*p. 425*)

Cash payments journal A special journal used to record all transactions involving cash payments or decreases to the Cash account. (*p. 443*)

Cash receipts journal A special journal used to record all transactions involving cash receipts or increases to the Cash account. (*p. 438*)

Credit period The time the seller allows the buyer before full payment on a charge sale has to be made. (*p. 425*)

Notes Payable The account containing the balance of promissory notes. (*p. 443*)

Promissory note A written promise to pay a specified amount at a specified time. (*p. 443*)

Purchases discount A cash discount granted by suppliers in return for prompt payment; it is treated as a deduction from Purchases. (*p. 431*)

Sales discount A deduction from the original price granted by the seller to the buyer for the prompt payment of an invoice. (*p. 426*)

Trade discounts Substantial discounts from the list or catalog prices of goods, granted by the seller; not recorded by the buyer or the seller. (*p. 434*)

Quiz Yourself

_____ 1. What do credit terms of 2/10, n/30 mean?
   a. 2–10 days to pay on time or 30 days before going to collection.
   b. 2 percent discount if paid within 10 days, but 30 days to pay on time
   c. 2–10 days to pay with a discount, net 30 days to pay after the discount period
   d. 2–10 percent discount if paid within 30 days
   e. None of the above

_____ 2. What is the entry to record the cash received on a sale of $500, credit terms 1/15, n/30, if the payment is received within the discount period?
   a. Accounts Receivable 500 DR; Cash 500 CR
   b. Cash 500 DR; Accounts Receivable 500 CR
   c. Cash 495 DR, Sales Discount 5 DR; Accounts Receivable 500 CR
   d. Accounts Receivable 500 DR; Cash 495 CR, Sales Discount 5 CR
   e. Cash 500 DR; Sales Discount 5 CR, Accounts Receivable 495 CR

_____ 3. Which of the following statements is true?
   a. Sales discounts are taken on freight charges.
   b. Credit terms are established by the buyer.
   c. Purchases discounts are taken on returns.
   d. Purchases discounts are not taken on freight costs.
   e. None of the above.

_____ 4. Which of the following is *not* an advantage of the cash receipts journal?
   a. Transactions do not have to be posted on a regular basis.
   b. Transactions can be recorded on one line.
   c. Transactions involving debits to Cash are recorded in one place.
   d. Repetition in posting is eliminated.
   e. Special columns can be used for similar transactions.

_____ 5. Which of the following is an advantage of the cash payments journal?
   a. It provides notification of early payment.
   b. Transactions do not have to be posted on a regular basis.
   c. Purchases and payments are recorded in the same place.
   d. Transactions involving credits to Cash are recorded in one place.
   e. None of the above.

Chapter Assignments

Discussion Questions

1. What is the normal balance for each of the following accounts: (a) Purchases? (b) Sales Discounts? (c) Purchases Returns and Allowances? (d) Sales? (e) Purchases Discounts? (f) Sales Returns and Allowances?
2. What does an X under the total of a special journal's Other Accounts column signify?
3. Explain the following credit terms: (a) n/30; (b) 2/10, n/60; (c) 1/15, EOM, n/30.
4. In a cash receipts journal, both the Accounts Receivable Credit column and the Cash Debit column were mistakenly underadded by $700. How will this error be discovered?
5. If a cash payments journal is supposed to save time spent writing, why are there so many entries in the Other Accounts Debit column?
6. Describe the posting procedure for a cash payments journal with an Other Accounts Debit column and several special columns, including an Accounts Payable Debit column.
7. An electronics business purchased speakers for resale. The total of the invoice is $2,580, and it is subject to trade discounts of 15 percent, 10 percent, and 5 percent. Compute the amount the dealer will pay for the speakers.
8. What is the difference between a cash discount and a trade discount?

Exercises

 1, 3

EXERCISE 10-1 For the following purchases of merchandise, determine the amount of cash to be paid:

Practice Exercises 1, 3

Purchase	Invoice Date	Credit Terms	FOB	Amount of Purchase	Freight Charges	Total Invoice Amount	Returns and Allowances	Date Paid
a.	June 1	2/10, n/30	Destination	$550	—	$ 550	—	June 30
b.	June 12	1/10, n/30	Destination	700	—	700	$100	June 21
c.	June 14	2/10, n/30	Shipping point	940	$60	1,000	—	June 23
d.	June 21	n/30	Shipping point	830	70	900	130	July 20
e.	June 24	1/10, n/30	Shipping point	760	50	810	90	July 3

LO 2

Practice Exercise 2

EXERCISE 10-2 Describe the transactions recorded in the following T accounts:

Cash		Accounts Receivable				Sales	
(c) 5,042.10		(a) 5,320	(b) 175			(a)	5,320
			(c) 5,145				

Sales Returns and Allowances		Sales Discounts	
(b) 175		(c) 102.90	

LO 3

Practice Exercise 3

EXERCISE 10-3 Describe the transactions recorded in the following T accounts:

Cash		Accounts Payable				Purchases	
(c) 1,176	(b) 150	(a) 1,350		(a) 1,350			
	(c) 1,200						

Purchases Returns and Allowances		Purchases Discounts	
(b) 150		(c) 24	

LO 2, 3

Practice Exercises 2, 3

EXERCISE 10-4 Record the following transactions in general journal form using the periodic inventory system:

June 5   Sold merchandise on account to Wilson, Inc., $520; terms 1/10, n/30.
  12   Bought merchandise on account from Mastercraft Company, $425; terms 2/10, n/45; FOB shipping point.
  15   Paid Alliance Freight Lines for freight charges on merchandise purchased from Mastercraft Company, $45.
  15   Received full payment from Wilson, Inc.
  20   Received a credit memo from Mastercraft Company for defective merchandise returned, $75.
  25   Paid Mastercraft Company in full within the discount period.
  29   Bought merchandise on account from Boze Industries, $1,090; terms 1/15, n/30; freight prepaid and added to the invoice, $52 (total $1,142).

LO 2, 3

Practice Exercises 2, 3

EXERCISE 10-5 Record the following transactions in general journal form on the books of the seller (Fuentes Company) and then on the books of the buyer (Lowe Company) using the periodic inventory system.

Fuentes Company

a. Sold merchandise on account to Lowe Company, $1,500; terms 2/10, n/30.
b. Issued a credit memo to Lowe Company for damaged merchandise, $100.
c. Lowe Company paid the account in full within the discount period.

(Continued)

Lowe Company

a. Purchased merchandise on account from Fuentes Company, $1,500; terms 2/10, n/30.

b. Received a credit memo from Fuentes Company for damaged merchandise, $100.

c. Paid Fuentes Company in full within the discount period.

LO 2, 3, 4

Practice Exercises 2, 3, 4

EXERCISE 10-6 Record general journal entries to correct the errors described below. Assume that the incorrect entries were posted in the same period in which the errors occurred and were recorded using the periodic inventory system.

a. A freight cost of $85 incurred on equipment purchased for use in the business was debited to Freight In.

b. The issuance of a credit memo to Lang Company for $119 for merchandise returned was recorded as a debit to Purchases Returns and Allowances and a credit to Accounts Receivable, Lang Company.

c. A cash sale of $68 to J. L. LaSalle was recorded as a sale on account.

d. A purchase of merchandise from James Company in the amount of $750 with a 25 percent trade discount was recorded as a debit to Purchases and a credit to Accounts Payable of $750 each.

LO 5

Practice Exercise 5

EXERCISE 10-7 Label the blanks in the column heads as either Debit or Credit.

			CASH RECEIPTS JOURNAL				Page ___
Date	Account Credited	Post. Ref.	Cash ___	Sales Discounts ___	Accounts Receivable ___	Sales ___	Other Accounts ___

LO 5

Practice Exercise 5

EXERCISE 10-8 Describe the transaction recorded.

Cash	Sales Tax Payable	Sales	Credit Card Expense
593.60	44.80	560.00	11.20

LO 6

Practice Exercise 6

EXERCISE 10-9 Label the blanks in the column heads as either Debit or Credit.

				CASH PAYMENTS JOURNAL			Page ___
Date	Ck. No.	Account Debited	Post. Ref.	Other Accounts ___	Accounts Payable ___	Purchases Discounts ___	Cash ___

LO 5, 6

EXERCISE 10-10 Indicate the journal in which each of the following transactions should be recorded. Assume a three-column purchases journal.

		Journal			
Transaction	S	P	CR	CP	J
a. Paid a creditor on account.					
b. Bought merchandise on account.					
c. Sold merchandise for cash.					
d. Adjusted for insurance expired.					
e. Received payment on account from a charge customer.					
f. Received a credit memo for merchandise returned.					
g. Bought equipment on credit.					
h. Sold merchandise on account.					
i. Recorded a customer's NSF check.					
j. Invested personal noncash assets in the business.					
k. Withdrew cash for personal use.					

Problem Set A

LO 1, 2, 3

PROBLEM 10-1A The following transactions were completed by Hammond Auto Supply during January, which is the first month of this fiscal year. Terms of sale are 2/10, n/30. The balances of the accounts as of January 1 have been recorded in the general ledger in your Working Papers or in CengageNow. Hammond Auto Supply does not track cash sales by customer.

Jan. 2 Issued Ck. No. 6981 to JSS Management Company for monthly rent, $775.
  2 J. Hammond, the owner, invested an additional $3,500 in the business.
  4 Bought merchandise on account from Valencia and Company, invoice no. A691, $2,930; terms 2/10, n/30; dated January 2.
  4 Received check from Vega Appliance for $980 in payment of $1,000 invoice less discount.
  4 Sold merchandise on account to L. Paul, invoice no. 6483, $850.
  6 Received check from Petty, Inc., $637, in payment of $650 invoice less discount.
  7 Issued Ck. No. 6982, $588, to Fischer and Son, in payment of invoice no. C1272 for $600 less discount.
  7 Bought supplies on account from Doyle Office Supply, invoice no. 1906B, $108; terms net 30 days.
  7 Sold merchandise on account to Ellison and Clay, invoice no. 6484, $787.
  9 Issued credit memo no. 43 to L. Paul, $54, for merchandise returned.
  11 Cash sales for January 1 through January 10, $4,863.20.
  11 Issued Ck. No. 6983, $2,871.40, to Valencia and Company, in payment of $2,930 invoice less discount.
  14 Sold merchandise on account to Vega Appliance, invoice no. 6485, $2,050.

(Continued)

Jan. 18 Bought merchandise on account from Costa Products, invoice no. 7281D, $4,854; terms 2/10, n/60; dated January 16; FOB shipping point, freight prepaid and added to the invoice, $147 (total $5,001).

21 Issued Ck. No. 6984, $194, to M. Miller for miscellaneous expenses not recorded previously.

21 Cash sales for January 11 through January 20, $4,591.

23 Issued Ck. No. 6985 to Forbes Freight, $96, for freight charges on merchandise purchased on January 4.

23 Received credit memo no. 163, $376, from Costa Products for merchandise returned.

29 Sold merchandise on account to Bruce Supply, invoice no. 6486, $1,835.

31 Cash sales for January 21 through January 31, $4,428.

31 Issued Ck. No. 6986, $53, to M. Miller for miscellaneous expenses not recorded previously.

31 Recorded payroll entry from the payroll register: total salaries, $6,200; employees' federal income tax withheld, $872; FICA Social Security tax withheld, $384.40, FICA Medicare tax withheld, $89.90.

31 Recorded the payroll taxes: Social Security tax, $384.40, FICA Medicare tax, $89.90; state unemployment tax, $334.80; federal unemployment tax, $37.20.

31 Issued Ck. No. 6987, $4,853.70, for salaries for the month.

31 J. Hammond, the owner, withdrew $1,000 for personal use, Ck. No. 6988.

Required

1. Record the transactions in the general journal for January. If you are using Working Papers, start with page 1 in the journal. Assume the periodic inventory method is used.

Check Figure
Trial balance totals, $65,276.40

The chart of accounts is as follows:

111 Cash
113 Accounts Receivable
114 Merchandise Inventory
115 Supplies
116 Prepaid Insurance
121 Equipment

212 Accounts Payable
215 Salaries Payable
216 Employees' Federal Income
    Tax Payable
217 FICA Social Security Tax Payable
218 FICA Medicare Tax Payable
219 State Unemployment Tax Payable
220 Federal Unemployment Tax
    Payable

311 J. Hammond, Capital
312 J. Hammond, Drawing

411 Sales
412 Sales Returns and Allowances
413 Sales Discounts

511 Purchases
512 Purchases Returns and Allowances
513 Purchases Discounts
514 Freight In

621 Salary Expense
622 Payroll Tax Expense
627 Rent Expense
631 Miscellaneous Expense

2. Post daily all entries involving customer accounts to the accounts receivable ledger.
3. Post daily all entries involving creditor accounts to the accounts payable ledger.
4. Post daily the general journal entries to the general ledger. Write the owner's name in the Capital and Drawing accounts.
5. Prepare a trial balance.
6. Prepare a schedule of accounts receivable and a schedule of accounts payable. Do the totals equal the balances of the related controlling accounts?

CHAPTER ASSIGNMENTS

LO 1, 5 ••

PROBLEM 10-2A Preston Company sells candy wholesale, primarily to vending machine operators. Terms of sales on account are 2/10, n/30, FOB shipping point. The following transactions involving cash receipts and sales of merchandise took place in May of this year:

May 1   Received $2,156 cash from L. Reilly in payment of April 22 invoice of $2,200, less cash discount.

4   Received $1,096 cash in payment of $1,000 note receivable and interest of $96.

7   Received $588 cash from K. L. Shannon in payment of April 29 invoice of $600, less cash discount.

8   Sold merchandise on account to D. Padilla, invoice no. 272, $489.

16   Cash sales for first half of May, $2,265.

17   Received cash from D. Padilla in payment of invoice no. 272, less cash discount.

20   Received $325 cash from L. N. Salas in payment of April 16 invoice, no discount.

21   Sold merchandise on account to R. O. Wilcox, invoice no. 273, $935.

24   Received $220 cash refund for return of defective equipment that was originally bought for cash.

27   Sold merchandise on account to R. Jarvis, invoice no. 274, $450.

31   Cash sales for second half of May, $2,845.

Check Figure
Total Cash Debit, $9,974.22

Required

1. Journalize the transactions for May in the cash receipts journal and the sales journal. Assume the periodic inventory method is used.

2. If you are using Working Papers, total and rule the journals and prove the equality of the debit and credit totals.

LO 1, 6 ••

PROBLEM 10-3A MacDonald Bookshop had the following transactions that occurred during February of this year:

Feb. 3   Issued Ck. No. 4312, $892, to Kent Company for invoice no. 68172, recorded previously for $910.20, less 2 percent cash discount.

4   Issued Ck. No. 4313 to Kirby Express Company for freight charges, $35, for books purchased.

6   Issued Ck. No. 4314 to Morse Land Company for monthly rent, $590.

11   Received and paid bill for advertising in the *Ballard News*, $105.79, Ck. No. 4315.

11   Issued Ck. No. 4316, $1,078.11, to Contreras Book Company for invoice no. A3322, recorded previously for $1,089, less 1 percent cash discount.

17   Paid wages recorded previously for first half of February, $487; Ck. No. 4317.

21   R. D. MacDonald, the owner, withdrew $1,200 for personal use; Ck. No. 4318.

26   Issued Ck. No. 4319 to First National Bank for payment on bank loan, $560, consisting of $500 on the principal and $60 interest.

27   Issued Ck. No. 4320, $645, to Graham Publishing Company for invoice no. 7768, recorded previously (no discount).

28   Voided Ck. No. 4321.

28   Paid wages recorded previously for second half of February, $641; Ck. No. 4322.

(Continued)

Required

1. Journalize the transactions for February in the cash payments journal. Assume the periodic inventory method is used.
2. If you are using Working Papers, total and rule the journal. Prove the equality of the debit and credit totals.

Check Figure
Total Cash Credit,
$6,233.90

 LO 1, 2, 3, 5, 6

PROBLEM 10-4A Refer to the information for Problem 10-1A on pages 458–459.

Required

1. Record the transactions for January using a sales journal, page 73; a purchases journal, page 56; a cash receipts journal, page 38; a cash payments journal, page 45; and a general journal, page 100. Assume the periodic inventory method is used.

Check Figure
Schedule of Accounts
Receivable total,
$5,468.00

111 Cash
113 Accounts Receivable
114 Merchandise Inventory
115 Supplies
116 Prepaid Insurance
121 Equipment

212 Accounts Payable
215 Salaries Payable
216 Employees' Federal Income
    Tax Payable
217 FICA Social Security Tax Payable
218 FICA Medicare Tax Payable
219 State Unemployment Tax Payable
220 Federal Unemployment Tax
    Payable

311 J. Hammond, Capital
312 J. Hammond, Drawing

411 Sales
412 Sales Returns and Allowances
413 Sales Discounts

511 Purchases
512 Purchases Returns and Allowances
513 Purchases Discounts
514 Freight In

621 Salary Expense
622 Payroll Tax Expense
627 Rent Expense
631 Miscellaneous Expense

2. Post daily all entries involving customer accounts to the accounts receivable ledger.
3. Post daily all entries involving creditor accounts to the accounts payable ledger.
4. Post daily those entries involving the Other Accounts columns and the general journal to the general ledger. Write the owner's name in the Capital and Drawing accounts.
5. Add the columns of the special journals and prove the equality of the debit and credit totals.
6. Post the appropriate totals of the special journals to the general ledger.
7. Prepare a trial balance.
8. Prepare a schedule of accounts receivable and a schedule of accounts payable. Do the totals equal the balances of the related controlling accounts?

LO 1, 2, 3, 4, 5, 6

Problem 10-5A The following transactions were completed by Nelson's Boutique, a retailer, during July. Terms of sales on account are 2/10, n/30, FOB shipping point.

July 3 Received cash from J. Smith in payment of June 29 invoice of $350, less cash discount.
      6 Issued Ck. No. 1718, $742.50, to Designer, Inc., for invoice. no. 2256, recorded previously for $750, less cash discount of $7.50.

(Continued)

July 9 Sold merchandise in the amount of $250 on a credit card. Sales tax on this sale is 6%. The credit card fee the bank deducted for this transaction is $5.

10 Issued Ck. No. 1719, $764.40, to Smart Style, Inc., for invoice no. 1825, recorded previously on account for $780. A trade discount of 25% was applied at the time of purchase, and Smart Style, Inc.'s credit terms are 2/10, n/30.

12 Received $180 cash in payment of June 20 invoice from R. Matthews. No cash discount applied.

18 Received $1,575 cash in payment of a $1,500 note receivable and interest of $75.

21 Voided Ck. No. 1720 due to error.

25 Received and paid utility bill, $152; Ck. No. 1721, payable to City Utilities Company.

31 Paid wages recorded previously for the month, $2,586, Ck. No. 1722.

Check Figure
Total Cash Credits,
$4,244.90

Required

1. Journalize the transactions for July in the cash receipts journal, the general journal (for the transaction on July 9th), or the cash payments journal as appropriate. Assume the periodic inventory method is used.

2. If you are using Working Papers, total and rule the journals. Prove the equality of debit and credit totals.

Problem Set B

LO 1, 2, 3

PROBLEM 10-1B The following transactions were completed by Yang Restaurant Equipment during January, the first month of this fiscal year. Terms of sale are 2/10, n/30. The balances of the accounts as of January 1 have been recorded in the general ledger in your Working Papers or in CengageNow. Yang Restaurant Equipment does not track cash sales by customer.

Jan. 2 Issued Ck. No. 6981 to Tri-County Management Company for monthly rent, $850.

2 L. Yang, the owner, invested an additional $4,500 in the business.

4 Bought merchandise on account from Valentine and Company, invoice no. A694, $2,830; terms 2/10, n/30; dated January 2.

4 Received check from Velez Appliance for $980 in payment of invoice for $1,000 less discount.

4 Sold merchandise on account to L. Parrish, invoice no. 6483, $755.

6 Received check from Peck, Inc., $637, in payment of $650 invoice less discount.

7 Issued Ck. No. 6982, $588, to Frost and Son, in payment of invoice no. C127 for $600 less discount.

7 Bought supplies on account from Dudley Office Supply, invoice no. 190B, $93.54; terms net 30 days.

7 Sold merchandise on account to Ewing and Charles, invoice no. 6484, $1,115.

9 Issued credit memo no. 43 to L. Parrish, $47, for merchandise returned.

11 Cash sales for January 1 through January 10, $4,454.87.

11 Issued Ck. No. 6983, $2,773.40, to Valentine and Company, in payment of $2,830 invoice less discount.

14 Sold merchandise on account to Velez Appliance, invoice no. 6485, $2,100.

14 Received check from L. Parrish, $693.84, in payment of $755 invoice, less return of $47 and less discount.

(Continued)

Jan. 19   Bought merchandise on account from Crawford Products, invoice no. 7281, $3,700; terms 2/10, n/60; dated January 16; FOB shipping point, freight prepaid and added to invoice, $142 (total $3,842).

    21   Issued Ck. No. 6984, $245, to A. Bautista for miscellaneous expenses not recorded previously.

    21   Cash sales for January 11 through January 20, $3,689.

    23   Received credit memo no. 163, $87, from Crawford Products for merchandise returned.

    29   Sold merchandise on account to Bradford Supply, invoice no. 6486, $1,697.20.

    29   Issued Ck. No. 6985 to Western Freight, $64, for freight charges on merchandise purchased January 4.

    31   Cash sales for January 21 through January 31, $3,862.

    31   Issued Ck. No. 6986, $65, to M. Pineda for miscellaneous expenses not recorded previously.

    31   Recorded payroll entry from the payroll register: total salaries, $5,899.95; employees' federal income tax withheld, $795; FICA Social Security tax withheld, $365.80, FICA Medicare tax withheld, $85.50.

    31   Recorded the payroll taxes: FICA Social Security tax, $365.80; FICA Medicare tax, $85.50; state unemployment tax, $318.60; federal unemployment tax, $35.40.

    31   Issued Ck. No. 6987, $4,653.65, for salaries for the month.

    31   L. Yang, the owner, withdrew $1,000 for personal use, Ck. No. 6988.

Required

1. Record the transactions in the general journal for January. If you are using Working Papers, start with page 1 in the journal. Assume the periodic inventory method is used.

Check Figure
Trial balance totals, $63,228.81

The chart of accounts is as follows:

111 Cash	311 L. Yang, Capital
113 Accounts Receivable	312 L. Yang, Drawing
114 Merchandise Inventory	
115 Supplies	411 Sales
116 Prepaid Insurance	412 Sales Returns and Allowances
121 Equipment	413 Sales Discounts
212 Accounts Payable	511 Purchases
215 Salaries Payable	512 Purchases Returns and Allowances
216 Employees' Federal Income Tax Payable	513 Purchases Discounts
217 FICA Social Security Tax Payable	514 Freight In
218 FICA Medicare Tax Payable	
219 State Unemployment Tax Payable	621 Salary Expense
220 Federal Unemployment Tax Payable	622 Payroll Tax Expense
	627 Rent Expense
	631 Miscellaneous Expense

2. Post daily all entries involving customer accounts to the accounts receivable ledger.
3. Post daily all entries involving creditor accounts to the accounts payable ledger.
4. Post daily the general journal entries to the general ledger. Write the owner's name in the Capital and Drawing accounts.
5. Prepare a trial balance.
6. Prepare a schedule of accounts receivable and a schedule of accounts payable. Do the totals equal the balances of the related controlling accounts?

LO   1, 5

PROBLEM 10-2B C. R. McIntyre Company sells candy wholesale, primarily to vending machine operators. Terms of sales on account are 2/10, n/30, FOB shipping point. The following transactions involving cash receipts and sales of merchandise took place in May of this year:

May   2   Received $411.60 cash from N. Rojas in payment of April 23 invoice of $420, less cash discount.

5   Received $2,085 cash in payment of $2,000 note receivable and interest of $85.

8   Sold merchandise on account to G. Soto, invoice no. 862, $830.

9   Received $11,838.40 cash from D. Maddox in payment of April 30 invoice of $12,080, less cash discount.

15   Received cash from G. Soto in payment of invoice no. 862, less cash discount.

16   Cash sales for first half of May, $3,259.

19   Received $296 cash from R. O. Higgins in payment of April 14 invoice, no discount.

22   Sold merchandise on account to N. T. Jennings, invoice no. 863, $753.

25   Received $239 cash refund for return of defective equipment bought in April for cash.

28   Sold merchandise on account to M. E. Mueller, invoice no. 864, $964.

31   Cash sales for second half of May, $4,728.

Check Figure
Total Cash Debit,
$23,670.40

Required

1. Journalize the transactions for May in the cash receipts journal and the sales journal. Assume the periodic inventory method is used.

2. If you are using Working Papers, total and rule the journals. Prove the equality of the debit and credit totals.

LO   1, 6

PROBLEM 10-3B Jacobs Company had the following transactions that occurred during February of this year:

Feb.   1   Issued Ck. No. 4311, $637, to Barker Company for invoice no. 3113E, recorded previously for $650, less cash discount of $13.

2   Issued Ck. No. 4312 to Bonilla Express Company for freight charges, $48, for merchandise purchased.

4   Issued Ck. No. 4313 to Dillon Realty for monthly rent, $560.

9   Received and paid bill for advertising in *The Nickel News*, $84, Ck. No. 4314.

10   Issued Ck. No. 4315, $990, to Dorsey Company for invoice no. D642, recorded previously for $1,000, less 1 percent cash discount.

15   Paid wages recorded previously for first half of month, $1,678; Ck. No. 4316.

19   R. Jacobs, the owner, withdrew $900 for personal use; Ck. No. 4317.

25   Issued Ck. No. 4318 to First National Bank for payment on bank loan, $896, consisting of $800 on principal and $96 interest.

27   Issued Ck. No. 4319, $430, to Long Company for invoice no. 6317, recorded previously (no discount).

28   Voided Ck. No. 4320.

28   Paid wages recorded previously for second half of month, $1,648; Ck. No. 4321.

28   Received and paid telephone bill, $86; Ck. No. 4322, payable to Southwestern Telephone Company.

Check Figure
Total Cash Credit,
$7,957

Required

1. Journalize the transactions for February in the cash payments journal. Assume the periodic inventory method is used.

(Continued)

2. If you are using Working Papers, total and rule the journal. Prove the equality of the debit and credit totals.

LO **1, 2, 3, 5, 6**

PROBLEM 10-4B Refer to the information for Problem 10-1B on pages 462–463.

Required

Check Figure
Schedule of Accounts
Receivable total,
$4,912.20

1. Record the transactions for January using a sales journal, page 91; a purchases journal, page 74; a cash receipts journal, page 56; a cash payments journal, page 63; and a general journal, page 119. Assume the periodic inventory method is used.

111 Cash	311 L. Yang, Capital
113 Accounts Receivable	312 L. Yang, Drawing
114 Merchandise Inventory	
115 Supplies	411 Sales
116 Prepaid Insurance	412 Sales Returns and Allowances
121 Equipment	413 Sales Discounts
	511 Purchases
212 Accounts Payable	512 Purchases Returns and Allowances
215 Salaries Payable	513 Purchases Discounts
216 Employees' Federal Income	514 Freight In
Tax Payable	
217 FICA Social Security Tax Payable	621 Salary Expense
218 FICA Medicare Tax Payable	622 Payroll Tax Expense
219 State Unemployment Tax Payable	627 Rent Expense
220 Federal Unemployment Tax Payable	631 Miscellaneous Expense

2. Post daily all entries involving customer accounts to the accounts receivable ledger.
3. Post daily all entries involving creditor accounts to the accounts payable ledger.
4. Post daily those entries involving the Other Accounts columns and the general journal to the general ledger. Write the owner's name in the Capital and Drawing accounts.
5. Add the columns of the special journals and prove the equality of the debit and credit totals.
6. Post the appropriate totals of the special journals to the general ledger.
7. Prepare a trial balance.
8. Prepare a schedule of accounts receivable and a schedule of accounts payable. Do the totals equal the balances of the related controlling accounts?

LO **1, 2, 3, 4, 5, 6**

Problem 10-5B The following transactions were completed by Nelson's Hardware, a retailer, during September. Terms on sales on account are 1/10, n/30, FOB shipping point.

Sept. 4   Received cash from M. Alex in payment of August 25 invoice of $275, less cash discount.

    7   Issued Ck. No. 8175, $915.75, to Top Tools, Inc., for invoice. no. 2256, recorded previously for $925, less cash discount of $9.25.

    10   Sold merchandise in the amount of $175 on a credit card. Sales tax on this sale is 8%. The credit card fee the bank deducted for this transaction is $5.

    11   Issued Ck. No. 8176, $653.40, to Snap Tools, Inc. for invoice no. 726, recorded previously on account for $660. A trade discount of 15% was applied at the time of purchase, and Snap Tools, Inc.'s credit terms are 1/10, n/45.

    15   Received $95 cash in payment of August 20 invoice from N. Johnson. No cash discount applied.

(Continued)

19   Received $1,165 cash in payment of a $1,100 note receivable and interest of $65.

22   Voided Ck. No. 8177 due to error.

26   Received and paid telephone bill, $62; Ck. No. 8178, payable to Southern Telephone Company.

30   Paid wages recorded previously for the month, $3,266, Ck. No. 8179.

Check Figure
Total Cash Credit,
$4,897.15

Required

1. Journalize the transactions for September in the cash receipts journal, the general journal (for the transaction on Sept. 10th), or the cash payments journal as appropriate. Assume the periodic inventory method is used.

2. If you are using Working Papers, total and rule the journals. Prove the equality of debit and credit totals.

Accounting with qb QuickBooks® Online

Go to the QuickBooks Online Appendix, Chapters 9 and 10 located on the Cengage Learning companion site at Cengage.com. Review *Accounting with QuickBooks Online* (step-by-step guide to using QuickBooks Online). *Accounting with QuickBooks Online* Chapters 9 and 10 will introduce you to (1) recording checkbook entries using the Check, Deposit, Pay Bills, Sales Receipt, and Receive Payment functions; (2) recording transactions with vendors on account, using the Bills function; and (3) recording transactions with customers on account, using the Invoice function.

Activities

Why Does It Matter?

BOOKSHOP SANTA CRUZ, Santa Cruz, California

If you're ever in Santa Cruz, California, take some time to visit Bookshop Santa Cruz. You'll find books "that entertain, help solve problems, or occasionally, change a life."

Since opening in 1966, Bookshop Santa Cruz has been a vital part of the Bay Area. The bookstore takes immense pride in being an independent bookseller, a rare commodity in today's world of large corporate booksellers such as Barnes & Nobles.

The bookstore has several buyers who are responsible for spotting reading trends, reordering current books, and purchasing the newest and hottest books on the market.

Each time a buyer makes a purchase and every time Bookshop Santa Cruz makes a sale, a transaction must be recorded. Discuss the advantages a store such as Bookshop Santa Cruz would gain by recording the receipt of cash from sales in the cash receipts journal and the payment of cash for purchases in the cash payments journal.

What Would You Say?

You are the manager of the Accounts Receivable Department for a merchandising business. Your billing clerk sent a bill for $2 to a customer who had charged $100 in goods (including sales tax) with terms 2/10, n/30. The customer called and indicated his displeasure. He can't understand an error like this because he paid on time. Explain to your billing clerk why Accounts Receivable is credited for $100 and not $98. How was permission given to send less than the full amount?

What Do You Think?

You work for Gregory Plumbing Supply. You are responsible for training a new accounting clerk. She has the following questions for you to answer about this invoice.

Gregory Plumbing Supply
14 Indiana Avenue
Chicago, Illinois 60612

No. 320

INVOICE

SOLD TO: C. P. Lund Company
5210 Gilman Avenue
San Diego, CA 92102

DATE:	August 1, 20--
CUSTOMER'S P.O. NO.:	5384
SHIPPED BY:	Faster Freight
TERMS:	2/10, n/30
SALESPERSON:	H. T.

QUANTITY	DESCRIPTION	UNIT PRICE		TOTAL	
6	Olin single-control tub shower faucet #44B652	51	50	309	00
6	Olin dual-control washerless lavatory faucet #59B641	22	20	133	20
12	Olin massage shower head, antique brass #37B411	11	56	138	72
	Subtotal			580	92
	Freight			63	80
	Total			644	72

---

1. Who is the buyer?
2. Who is paying the freight?
3. What is the customer's order number?
4. What percentage of the goods bought is the cost of the freight?
5. What are the credit terms? What do they mean?
6. How much will the buyer actually have to pay if the money is received within ten days?
7. What is the dollar amount of the discount?
8. Who receives the discount?
9. What is the due date for payment to get the discount?
10. Why would a seller give a buyer a discount?

What's Wrong with This Picture?

Suppose we collected cash from a charge customer and the debit was to Cash and the credit to Sales. How and when would this error be discovered?

Before a Test Check: Chapters 9–10

PART I: Completion

1. The normal balance of the Purchases Discounts account is on the _____ side.
2. Entries in the Accounts Payable Debit column of a cash payments journal are posted daily to the _____.
3. A(n) _____ is the amount a customer may deduct for paying a bill within a specified period of time.
4. The form sent to the supplier of merchandise is called a(n) _____.
5. The _____ account is used to record the buying of merchandise only.
6. If the freight charges are FOB shipping point, the _____ pays the transportation charges.
7. The time the seller allows the buyer before full payment has to be made is the _____.
8. Increases in Sales Returns and Allowances are recorded on the _____ side.
9. The schedule of accounts receivable lists the balances of all _____ accounts at the end of the month.

PART II: Matching: Special Journals Versus General Journal

_____ 1. Paid freight bill on merchandise purchased.
_____ 2. Bought office equipment on account.
_____ 3. Received a credit memo for merchandise returned.
_____ 4. Bought office equipment for cash.
_____ 5. Sold merchandise on account.
_____ 6. Journalized the closing entries.
_____ 7. Paid state sales tax to the state revenue department.
_____ 8. Bought merchandise on account.
_____ 9. Sold merchandise for cash.
_____ 10. Bought merchandise for cash.

S   Sales journal
P   Purchases journal
CR   Cash receipts journal
CP   Cash payments journal
J   General journal

PART III: True/False

T F 1. The Purchases Discounts account is classified as a revenue account.
T F 2. The normal balance of the Sales Discounts account is on the debit side.
T F 3. On the income statement, Freight In is subtracted from Purchases.

Answers: Part I

1. credit   2. accounts payable ledger   3. cash discount   4. purchase order
5. Purchases   6. buyer   7. credit period   8. debit   9. credit customers'

Answers: Part II

1. CP   2. J   3. J   4. CP   5. S   6. J   7. CP   8. P   9. CR   10. CP

Answers: Part III

1. F   2. T   3. F

All About You Spa

August Journal Entries

Ms. Valli has provided the transactions for the month of August to be entered in the system. All About You Spa does not track cash sales by customer.

CLGL

Checkbook Register

Check No.	Date	Explanation	√	Deposits	Check Amount
2044	8/1	Paid August rent.			1,500.00
	8/1	Deposited Chaco's payment received on account, invoice no. 25.		513.54	
	8/1	Deposited Mini Spa's payment received on account, invoice no. 28. Paid in full.		244.08	
2045	8/1	Paid accumulated sales tax payable to State Revenue Dept.			1,195.86
2046	8/2	Paid advertising bill for August photo ad.			555.00
2047	8/2	Paid week's wages.			2,075.00
2048	8/2	Paid Spa Magic for invoice no. 3503, dated June 2. Paid in full.			2,718.00
2049	8/3	Bought balloons for salon promotional event.			96.80
	8/3	Deposited balance of Tory Ligman's payment on account, invoice no. 22. Paid in full.		160.00	
2050	8/4	Bought spa supplies—5 cases of bottled water for clients.			65.00
	8/4	Deposited Jill Anson's payment received on account.		75.00	
2051	8/5	Bought a digital camera for confidential before-and-after spa pictures.			386.00
2052	8/5	Paid Office Staples for invoice 2417, dated July 5. Paid in full.			179.00
2053	8/5	Paid Giftco for invoice no. 613, dated July 5. Paid in full.			1,318.00
	8/6	Deposited Pleasant Spa's payment received on account, invoice no. 26.		995.00	
2054	8/6	Paid Golden Spa Supplies for invoice no. 1368, dated July 1. Paid in full.			410.00
	8/7	Deposited first week's cash sales: merchandise, $1,860.00; services, $3,350.00; sales tax collected, $148.80.		5,358.80	

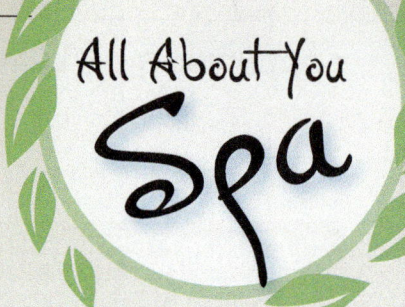
All About You Spa

CONTINUING PROBLEM

Check No.	Date	Explanation	√	Deposits	Check Amount
	8/8	Deposited Los Obrigados Lodge's payment received on account, invoice no. 24.		200.00	
	8/9	Deposited Holmes Condo's payment received on account, invoice no. 27.		150.00	
2055	8/9	Paid week's wages.			2,075.00
2056	8/10	Paid Giftco for invoice no. 616, dated August 1. Paid in full less applicable discount.			4,198.00
	8/14	Deposited second week's cash sales: merchandise, $2,360.00; services, $1,340; sales tax collected, $188.80.		3,888.80	
	8/15	Deposited About Face Spa's payment received on account, invoice no. 29.		300.00	
2057	8/16	Paid week's wages.			2,075.00
2058	8/18	Paid Superior Equipment for invoice no. 4608, dated July 5. Paid in full.			395.00
	8/19	Deposited balance of Jack Morgan's payment on account, invoice no. 21. Paid in full.		268.00	
	8/21	Deposited third week's cash sales: merchandise, $2,440.00; services, $2,520.00; sales tax collected, $195.20.		5,155.20	
2059	8/22	Paid on account to Logo Products, invoice no. 2579, dated July 1.			2,000.00
	8/23	Deposited Mini Spa's payment on account, invoice no. 35. Paid in full less applicable discount.		925.38	
2060	8/23	Paid on account to Spa Goods, invoice no. 512, dated July 1.			2,000.00
2061	8/23	Paid week's wages.			2,075.00
2062	8/28	Paid month's laundry bill.			55.00
2063	8/28	Owner withdrew cash for personal use.			2,000.00
2064	8/30	Paid week's wages.			2,075.00
	8/31	Deposited end of month's cash sales: merchandise, $2,160.00; services, $3,716.00; sales tax, $172.80.		6,048.80	
2065	8/31	Paid August telephone bill.			185.00
2066	8/31	Paid on account to Spa Equipment, Inc., invoice no. 2731, dated July 3.			4,000.00
2067	8/31	Paid August power and water bill.			236.00

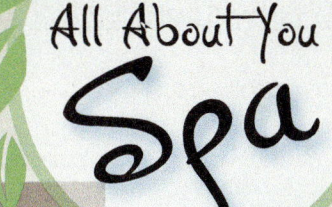

Purchases Invoices for Merchandise Bought on Account During August

All About You Spa will pay all freight costs associated with purchases of merchandise to the supplier. Invoice 616 was paid within the discount period on 8/10. The remaining August purchases were not paid until September.

Date of Purchase	Transaction Information	Amount
Aug. 1	Bought logo merchandise from Giftco; invoice no. 616, dated 8/1; terms 2/10, n/30.	$4,100.00 plus $180.00 freight
1	Bought bath and beauty products from Spa Magic; invoice no. 3525, dated 8/1; terms 2/10, n/30.	$2,625.00 plus $155.00 freight
2	Bought logo merchandise from Logo Products; invoice no. 2680, dated 8/2; terms 2/10, n/30.	$2,541.00 plus $144.00 freight
5	Bought spa accessories from Spa Goods; invoice no. 587, dated 8/5; terms 2/10, n/30.	$1,210.00 plus $110.00 freight

Sales Invoices for Gift Certificates Sold on Account During August

All About You Spa is responsible for collecting and paying the sales tax on merchandise that it sells. The sales tax rate where All About You Spa does business is 8 percent of each sale (for example, $560.00 $\times$ 0.08 = $44.80). Invoice 25 was received within the discount period on 8/23. (Apply the discount to the invoice amount. Disregard the sales tax when calculating the discount.) The remaining August sales were not received until September.

Date of Sale	Transaction Information	Sales Amount (Before Tax)
Aug. 1	About Face Spa, invoice no. 30; terms 2/10, n/45.	$ 560.00
5	Chaco's, invoice no. 31; terms 2/10, n/45.	194.00
8	Holmes Condos, invoice no. 32; terms 2/10, n/45.	993.00
9	Pleasant Spa, invoice no. 33; terms 2/10, n/45.	1,650.00
11	Los Obrigados Lodge, invoice no. 34; terms 2/10, n/45.	365.00
14	Mini Spa, invoice no. 35; terms 2/10, n/45.	873.00

Note: All gift certificates were redeemed for merchandise by the end of the month.

All About You
Spa

Other August Transactions

There were two other transactions in August. Neither involved cash.

Date	Transaction Information	Amount
Aug. 9	Issued credit memorandum no. 1 to About Face Spa for an allowance for damaged goods.	$ 70.00
29	Received a credit memorandum for damaged spa accessories from Spa Magic.	168.00

Required

1. Journalize the transactions for August. Ask your instructor whether you should use the special journals or the general journal.

   * If you are preparing the journal entries manually, enter your transactions beginning on page 11.

2. Post the entries to the accounts receivable, accounts payable, and general ledger.

   * Ignore this step if you are using CLGL.

3. Prepare a trial balance as of August 31, 20--.

4. Prepare a schedule of accounts receivable as of August 31, 20--.

5. Prepare a schedule of accounts payable as of August 31, 20--.

Check Figure
3. Trial balance total, August 31, $125,230.72
4. Schedule of accounts receivable total, August 31, $5,335.01
5. Schedule of accounts payable total, August 31, $14,919.00

The Voucher System of Accounting

1 Prepare vouchers.

2 Record vouchers in a voucher register.

3 Record payment of vouchers in a check register.

4 Record transactions involving canceling or altering an original voucher.

Accounting Language

Voucher (p. 473)
Voucher register (p. 477)

The voucher system is a means of achieving internal control and enabling the owner or manager to maintain contact with day-to-day transactions. This system promotes the delegation of duties and responsibilities.

OBJECTIVE OF THE VOUCHER SYSTEM

The objective of the voucher system is to control the incurrence of all liabilities and the payment of all expenditures—in other words, to control the purchase of (1) merchandise or materials, (2) other assets, and (3) services. The voucher system is suitable for companies of varying sizes that require a clear separation of duties. The voucher system has the following components: vouchers, voucher register, check register, unpaid voucher file, paid voucher file, and general journal.

VOUCHERS

A **voucher** is a document that serves as proof of a transaction and, from a business point of view, also serves as a full description of the transaction. **When a business is using the voucher system, a voucher must be filled out for every invoice or bill received, whether it is to be paid immediately or in the future. The invoice or bill is usually stapled to the voucher.**

Characteristics of Vouchers

Just as the form of invoices varies from one company to another, so too the form of vouchers varies from one company to another. However, the following characteristics are usually present:

- Vouchers are numbered consecutively.
- The name and address of the payee or creditor appear on the voucher.
- The amount and credit terms of the invoice appear on the voucher.
- Vouchers state due dates so that firms can take advantage of any cash discounts.
- For internal control, vouchers require signatures approving payment.
- Vouchers record payment, date paid, and check number.

A completed voucher, with the invoice or bill stapled to it, describes an entire transaction as well as the procedure for processing the voucher. So that you can see the big picture, Figure 1 presents the steps involved in processing a voucher for a purchase of merchandise.

Figure 1
Steps for processing a voucher for a purchase of merchandise

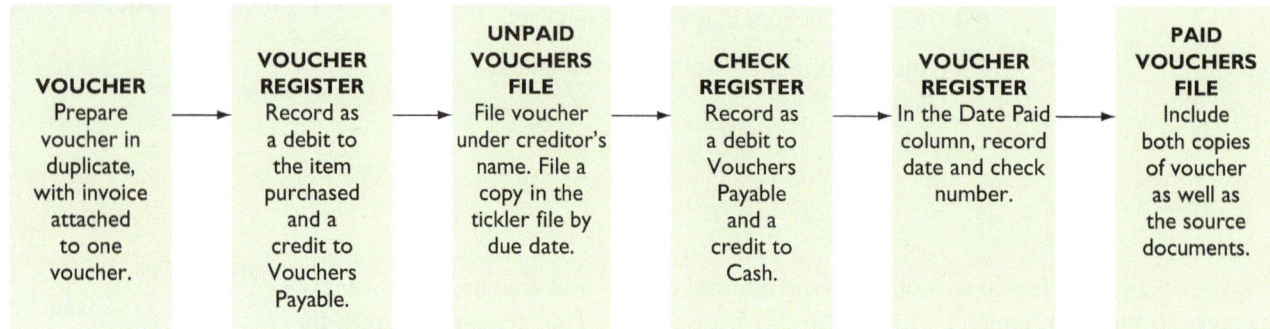

VOUCHER	VOUCHER REGISTER	UNPAID VOUCHERS FILE	CHECK REGISTER	VOUCHER REGISTER	PAID VOUCHERS FILE
Prepare voucher in duplicate, with invoice attached to one voucher.	Record as a debit to the item purchased and a credit to Vouchers Payable.	File voucher under creditor's name. File a copy in the tickler file by due date.	Record as a debit to Vouchers Payable and a credit to Cash.	In the Date Paid column, record date and check number.	Include both copies of voucher as well as the source documents.

10A-1 PREPARATION OF VOUCHERS

Learning Objective

1 Prepare vouchers.

To cite a familiar example, let's assume that Whitewater Raft Supply has now achieved such a volume of business that it is using a voucher system. Let's also assume that Whitewater Raft Supply has received from its supplier, Pataponia, Inc., the invoice shown here.

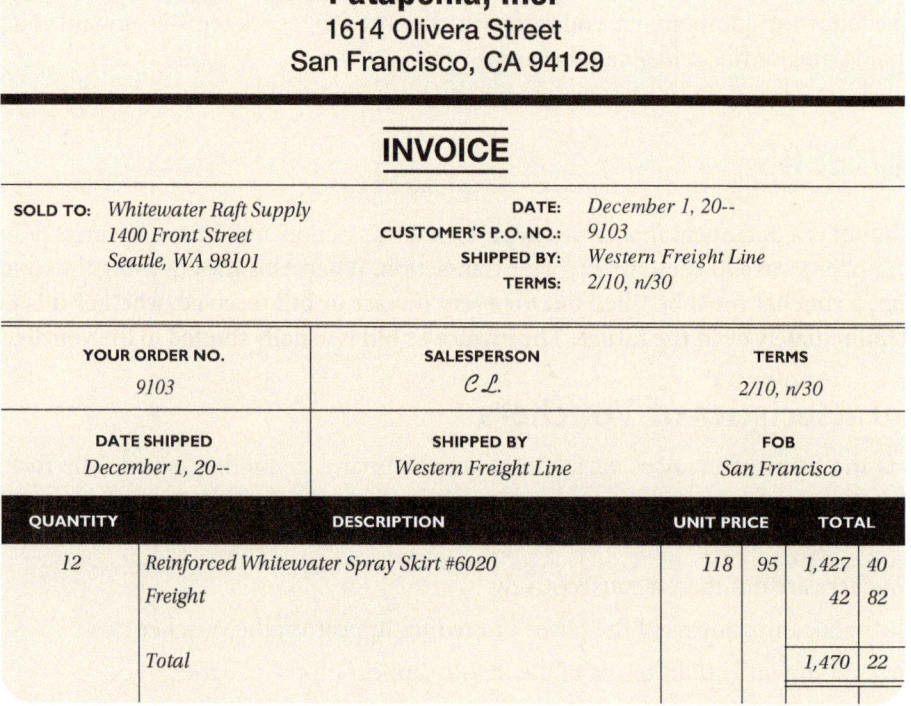

Pataponia, Inc.   No. 3101
1614 Olivera Street
San Francisco, CA 94129

INVOICE

SOLD TO: Whitewater Raft Supply
1400 Front Street
Seattle, WA 98101

DATE: December 1, 20--
CUSTOMER'S P.O. NO.: 9103
SHIPPED BY: Western Freight Line
TERMS: 2/10, n/30

YOUR ORDER NO.	SALESPERSON	TERMS
9103	C.L.	2/10, n/30

DATE SHIPPED	SHIPPED BY	FOB
December 1, 20--	Western Freight Line	San Francisco

QUANTITY	DESCRIPTION	UNIT PRICE	TOTAL
12	Reinforced Whitewater Spray Skirt #6020	118 95	1,427 40
	Freight		42 82
	Total		1,470 22

Whitewater Raft Supply's accountant, using the invoice as the source of information, fills out the following voucher. The face of the voucher lists the details of the transaction.

WHITEWATER RAFT SUPPLY

No. 118

1400 Front Street
Seattle, WA 98101

VOUCHER

PAY TO: Pataponia, Inc.
1614 Olivera St.
San Francisco, CA 94129

DATE _____ 12/1/20-- _____

DATE OF INVOICE	TERMS	DESCRIPTION	AMOUNT	
12/1	2/10, n/30	Invoice No. 3101	1,427	40
		Less discount	28	55
		Freight	42	82
		Net amount payable	1,441	67

APPROVAL	DATES	APPROVED BY
Extensions and footings verified	12/2	M. C. L.
Prices in agreement with purchase order	12/2	S. T.
Credit terms in agreement with purchase order	12/2	S. T.
Quantities in agreement with receiving report	12/2	J. D. S.
Approved for payment	12/7	R. L. R.

ACCOUNT DISTRIBUTION

VOUCHER NO. ___118___

ACCOUNT DEBITED	AMOUNT
Purchases	1,427.40
Freight In	42.82
Wages Payable	
Supplies	
Miscellaneous Expense	
Total Vouchers Payable Cr.	**1,470.22**

DUE DATE: 12/8

PAY TO: Pataponia, Inc.
1614 Olivera Street
San Francisco, CA 94129

SUMMARY OF CHARGES

Amount of invoice	1,470.22
Less cash discount	28.55
Net amount	1,441.67

RECORD OF PAYMENT

Paid by check no.	2815
Date of check	12/8
Amount of check	1,441.67

ACCOUNT DISTRIBUTION by _____ R. R. H. _____

ENTERED IN VOUCHER REG. by _____ M. C. L. _____

> ### Remember
>
> Because the check register replaces the cash payments journal and the voucher register replaces the purchases journal, the special-column totals from the voucher register must be posted before those from the check register.

The *due date* represents the last day on which a company can take advantage of the cash discount. For example, the invoice of Pataponia, Inc., was dated December 1, with terms of 2/10, n/30. The discount period ends on December 11. Therefore, at the latest, the check must be sent on December 8 to receive the discount.

The Account Distribution section is used to record the account titles and amounts to be debited, the total amount to be credited to Vouchers Payable, and the initials of the person authorized to determine the distribution.

When you use a voucher system, you substitute the Vouchers Payable account for Accounts Payable. For example, when a firm buys merchandise on account, the accountant enters it as a debit to Purchases and a credit to Vouchers Payable. Similarly, when a firm buys store equipment on account, the accountant records it as a debit to Store Equipment and a credit to Vouchers Payable. Also, if a company incurs an expense on account, such as Advertising, the entry is a debit to Advertising Expense and a credit to Vouchers Payable.

When a check is issued in payment of a voucher, record the entry in the check register as a debit to Vouchers Payable and a credit to Cash. Remember that *all* liabilities are recorded in the Vouchers Payable account.

Date	Vou. No.	Creditor	Payment Date	Ck. No.	Vouchers Payable Credit	Purchases Debit
20--						
Dec. 1	117	Fast-Way Freight	12 1	2808	63 00	
1	118	Pataponia, Inc.	12 8	2815	1 470 22	1 427 40
3	119	Dell Office Supply	12 3	2809	48 72	
5	120	Stable Ins. Company	12 5	2812	174 00	
9	121	Langseth and Son	12 18	2829	328 00	306 00
10	122	Payroll Bank Account	12 10	2818	1 690 00	
12	123	Southland Journal			176 00	
12	124	Bradley Construction	12 12	2820	116 00	
15	125	D. M. Bruce	12 15	2824	500 00	
15	126	C. A. Waters, Inc.	12 18	Note	421 00	421 00
29	149	Dana Mfg. Company			714 00	714 00
30	150	Safety National Bank	12 30	2837	1 507 50	
31		Totals			11 674 90	5 095 10
					(212)	(511)

	Debits		Credit
Purchases	$ 5,095.10	Vouchers Payable	$11,674.90
Freight In	234.32		
Wages Payable	3,314.00		
Supplies	121.79		
Miscellaneous Expense	83.69		
Other Accounts	2,826.00		
	$11,674.90		

10A-2 THE VOUCHER REGISTER

The **voucher register** has the status of a journal. It is a book of original entry. All vouchers must be recorded in it, in numerical order. Think of it as a multicolumn purchases journal. The voucher register has only one credit column, Vouchers Payable Credit, but a number of debit columns. Headings for the debit columns are selected on the basis of their frequency of use. In addition to the special columns, the voucher register also has space for recording the voucher number, the name of the creditor, the date of payment, and the check number. The voucher register for Whitewater Raft Supply appears below.

When you first record the voucher, leave the Payment Date and Ck. No. columns blank. After you have recorded the payment in the check register, go back to the voucher register and enter the date of payment and the number of the check.

2 Record vouchers in a voucher register.

Learning Objective

10A-2a Posting from the Voucher Register

The entries in the Other Accounts columns are posted *daily* to the general ledger, just as the Other Accounts columns of the other special journals are posted daily.

Remember

A voucher is prepared for every invoice or bill the company receives.

VOUCHER REGISTER   Page 3

Freight In Debit	Wages Payable Debit	Supplies Debit	Miscellaneous Expense Debit	Other Accounts Debit Account	Post. Ref.	Amount
	6 3 00					
	4 2 82					
		4 8 72				
				Prepaid Insurance	116	1 7 4 00
	2 2 00					
	1 6 9 0 00					
				Advertising Expense	618	1 7 6 00
				Sales Returns and Allowances	412	1 1 6 00
				D. M. Bruce, Drawing	312	5 0 0 00
				Notes Payable	211	1 5 0 0 00
				Interest Expense	634	7 50
2 3 4 32	3 3 1 4 00	1 2 1 79	8 3 69			2 8 2 6 00
(5 1 4)	(2 1 3)	(6 2 2)	(6 1 9)			(X)

The (X) under the column total means "do not post." At the end of the month, total all of the columns, and prove the equality of the debit and credit entries by comparing the combined total of the debit columns with the total of the Vouchers Payable Credit column.

10A-3 THE CHECK REGISTER

Learning Objective

3 Record payment of vouchers in a check register.

Any company or organization using a voucher system uses both the voucher register and the check register as books of original entry. Now let's look at the procedure for the check register. Because checks are issued only in payment of approved and recorded vouchers, the entry in the check register is always a debit to Vouchers Payable and a credit to Cash. A Vouchers Payable Debit column in the check register offsets the Vouchers Payable Credit column in the voucher register. Recall that after you record the entry in the check register, you enter the date and check number on the appropriate line in the voucher register and on the outside of the voucher in the Record of Payment section.

	CHECK REGISTER								Page 11	
Date	Ck. No.	Payee	Vou. No.	Vouchers Payable Debit		Purchases Discounts Credit		Cash Credit		
20--										
Dec. 1	2808	Fast-Way Freight	117		63 00				63 00	
3	2809	Dell Office Supply	119		48 72				48 72	
3	2810	Gardner Products Company	114	2 06 00			2 06	2 03 94		
4	2811	Dana Manufacturing Company	115	5 40 00			10 80	5 29 20		
5	2812	Stable Insurance Company	120	1 74 00				1 74 00		
6	2813	Void								
6	2814	Langseth and Son	116	4 64 00			9 28	4 54 72		
8	2815	Pataponia, Inc.	118	1 4 70 22			28 55	1 4 41 67		
30	2837	Safety National Bank	150	1 5 07 50				1 5 07 50		
31		Totals		7 2 81 20			90 09	7 1 91 11		
				(2 1 2)		(5 1 3)		(1 1 1)		

	Debit	Credit
	$7,281.20	$ 90.09
		7,191.11
		$7,281.20

10A-3a Handling of Unpaid Vouchers

Firms usually prepare vouchers in duplicate. In the system used by Whitewater Raft Supply, the invoice is attached to the original copy of the voucher. Then the voucher is circulated within the company for the necessary signatures. After a voucher is recorded in the voucher register, it is filed under the name of the creditor. (Other companies may prepare only one copy of the voucher and file it under the date on which it is supposed to be paid.)

At Whitewater Raft Supply, the Unpaid Vouchers file contains all outstanding vouchers or credit memos. This file, organized by names of creditors, now acts as a subsidiary ledger. In fact, at Whitewater Raft Supply, this file substitutes for the accounts payable ledger.

The *second* copy of the voucher goes to the treasurer, who files it chronologically by due date. This tickler file (a file of unpaid vouchers filed by due date) helps the treasurer forecast the amount of cash that will be needed to pay outstanding bills and take advantage of cash discounts.

Whitewater Raft Supply
Schedule of Vouchers Payable
December 31, 20--

Vou. No.	Name of Creditor	Amount
123	Southland Journal	$176
149	Dana Manufacturing Company	714
	Total Vouchers Payable	$890

At the end of the month, the accountant lists all of the vouchers payable, taking the information directly from the Unpaid Vouchers file.

10A-3b Filing Paid Vouchers

Now let's assume that the firm has paid its bill. The payment is recorded in the check register and in the Payment columns of the voucher register. Then the voucher is stapled to the copy in the tickler file, marked paid, and filed in numerical order in a Paid Vouchers file.

10A-4 SITUATIONS REQUIRING SPECIAL TREATMENT

When a firm is using the voucher system, it inevitably runs into an occasional nonroutine transaction that does not fit in the fixed channels of the voucher system and therefore may require an entry in the general journal. You can consider such treatment as an adjustment to the voucher system.

4 Record transactions involving canceling or altering an original voucher.

Learning Objective

10A-4a Return of a Purchase Before Original Voucher Has Been Recorded

Normally, if a business with an efficient purchasing department is going to return any merchandise, it returns the merchandise before the vouchers are recorded in the voucher register. The accountant records the deduction directly on the invoice and records the invoice in the voucher register for the net amount.

10A-4b Return of a Purchase After Original Voucher Has Been Recorded

Assume that a business purchased merchandise for $566. The transaction was recorded in the voucher register as a debit to Purchases and a credit to Vouchers Payable. Later, the company returns $26 worth of defective merchandise. The return is recorded in the general journal as a debit to Vouchers Payable and a credit to Purchases Returns and Allowances. The notation "Return" is entered in the Payment column of the voucher register.

10A-4c Installment Payments Planned at Time of Original Purchase

In a voucher system, invoices not subject to cash discounts are generally paid in full. Sometimes, however, management prefers to pay for an item in installments. When this happens, the company's accountant prepares a separate voucher for each installment and records each of these vouchers in the voucher register. Each voucher's due date corresponds to the date on which that installment is to be paid.

10A-4d Installment Payments After Original Voucher Has Been Recorded

However, suppose the buyer records the entire amount of the invoice on one voucher and *later* decides to pay the invoice in installments. The accountant must now cancel the original voucher by means of a general journal entry and issue a new voucher for each installment. A notation listing the new voucher numbers is made in the Payment column of the voucher register.

10A-4e Correcting an Amount After Original Voucher Has Been Recorded

If an error in the purchase of merchandise is discovered after the voucher has been recorded in the voucher register, the original voucher must be canceled by means of a general journal entry debiting Vouchers Payable and crediting Purchases. Next, a new entry is made in the voucher register for the correct amount, debiting Purchases and crediting Vouchers Payable. A notation listing the new voucher number is made in the Payment column of the voucher register.

10A-4f Issuing a Note Payable After Original Voucher Has Been Recorded

If a note is issued for the amount of an unpaid invoice after the voucher has been recorded, an entry must be made in the general journal to cancel the original voucher. The entry is a debit to Vouchers Payable and a credit to Notes Payable. The notation "Note" is made in the Date Paid column of the voucher register. When the note is to be paid, a new voucher is issued for the amount of the principal and interest, debiting Notes Payable and Interest Expense and crediting Vouchers Payable.

Glossary

Voucher A document that serves as proof of a transaction and, from a business point of view, also serves as a full description of the transaction. (*p. 473*)

Voucher register A book of original entry in which all vouchers are recorded in numerical order. (*p. 477*)

Problems

LO 2, 3

PROBLEM 10A-1 Saenz Company uses a voucher system in which it records invoices at the gross amount. The following vouchers were issued during February and were unpaid on March 1:

Voucher Number	Company	For	Date of Voucher	Amount
1729	Kipley Company	Merchandise, FOB destination	Feb. 26	$3,436
1732	J. R. Steven	Merchandise, FOB destination	Feb. 28	4,710

The following transactions were completed during March:

Mar. 3 Issued voucher no. 1734 in favor of Larry Company for March rent, $1,220.

 3 Issued Ck. No. 1829 in payment of voucher no. 1734, $1,220.

 5 Bought merchandise on account from Lorenzo, Inc., $3,890; terms 2/10, n/30; FOB shipping point; freight prepaid and added to the invoice, $72 (total, $3,962). Issued voucher no. 1735.

 5 Issued Ck. No. 1830 in payment of voucher no. 1729, $3,401.64 ($3,436 less 1 percent cash discount).

 9 Issued voucher no. 1736 in favor of Mario Electric Company for electric bill, $216.

 9 Issued Ck. No. 1831 in payment of voucher no. 1736, $216.

 9 Issued Ck. No. 1832 in payment of voucher no. 1732, $4,615.80 ($4,710 less 2 percent cash discount).

 13 Issued Ck. No. 1833 in payment of voucher no. 1735, less the cash discount, $3,884.20. Recall that the freight portion is not eligible for discount.

 16 Bought merchandise on account from McGinnis Manufacturing Company, $6,260; terms 2/10 EOM; FOB destination. Issued voucher no. 1737.

 25 Issued voucher no. 1738 for note payable previously recorded in the general journal: principal, $4,000, plus $30 interest. The note is payable to the Keller State Bank.

 25 Issued Ck. No. 1834 in payment of voucher no. 1737, $6,134.80 ($6,260 less 2 percent cash discount).

 31 Issued voucher no. 1739 for wages payable, $4,985, in favor of the payroll bank account. (Assume that the payroll entry was previously recorded in the general journal.)

 31 Paid voucher no. 1739 by issuing Ck. No. 1835, $4,985, payable to Payroll Bank Account.

Required

1. Using the voucher issue date, enter the unpaid invoices in the voucher register (page 65) beginning with voucher no. 1729. Then draw double lines across all columns to separate the vouchers of February from those of March.
2. Record the transactions for March in the voucher register. Also record the appropriate transactions in the check register (page 71).
3. Total and rule the voucher register and the check register.
4. Prove the equality of the debits and credits in the voucher register and the check register.

Check Figure
Voucher Register,
Vouchers Payable
Credit total, $20,673

LO 2, 3, 4

PROBLEM 10A-2 Hartman Company, which uses a voucher system, has the following unpaid vouchers on July 1. The firm follows the practice of recording vouchers at the gross amount.

Voucher Number	Company	For	Date of Voucher	Amount
4789	Garrison and Son	Store equipment	June 15	$ 4,996
4795	Fenner and Company	Merchandise, FOB destination	June 28	8,571
4797	J. R. Paige Company	Merchandise, FOB destination	June 28	10,710

The company completed the following transactions during July:

July 1 Issued voucher no. 4800 in favor of Mortenson Insurance Company for a premium on a 12-month fire insurance policy, $890.
     2 Paid voucher no. 4789 by issuing Ck. No. 8219, $4,996.
     2 Issued Ck. No. 8220 in payment of voucher no. 4800, $890.
     3 Issued voucher no. 4801 in favor of Quinn Quick Freight for transportation charges on merchandise purchases, $223.
     5 Paid voucher no. 4801 by issuing Ck. No. 8221, $223.
     7 Issued Ck. No. 8222 in payment of voucher no. 4795, $8,485.29 ($8,571 less 1 percent cash discount).
     8 Issued Ck. No. 8223 in payment of voucher no. 4797, $10,602.90 ($10,710 less 1 percent cash discount).
   11 Established a petty cash fund of $250. Issued voucher no. 4802.
   11 Paid voucher no. 4802 by issuing Ck. No. 8224, $250.
   13 Issued voucher no. 4803 in favor of Mohammad Company for merchandise, $14,708; terms 2/10, n/30; FOB shipping point; freight prepaid and added to the invoice, $384 (total, $15,092).
   15 Received bill for advertising in the *Weekly Ads*. Issued voucher no. 4804 in the amount of $410.
   17 Received a credit memo for $764 from Mohammad Company for merchandise returned to it, credit memo no. 540 (pertaining to voucher no. 4803).
   20 Issued voucher no. 4805 in favor of Vinson County for six months' property tax (Prepaid Property Taxes), $2,272.
   20 Paid voucher no. 4805 by issuing Ck. No. 8225, $2,272.
   21 Issued Ck. No. 8226 in payment of voucher no. 4803, $14,049.12 ($14,708 less $764 return, less cash discount, plus freight).
   23 Bought merchandise on account from Summers and Company, $6,039; terms 1/10, n/30; FOB destination. Issued voucher no. 4806.
   27 Received a credit memo for $984 from Summers and Company for damaged merchandise, credit memo no. 437 (pertaining to voucher no. 4806).
   31 Issued voucher no. 4807 to reimburse petty cash fund. The charges were:

Supplies Expense	$110.43
H. Hartman, Drawing	75.00
Miscellaneous Expense	39.67

(Continued)

July 31 Issued Ck. No. 8227 in payment of voucher no. 4807, $225.10.

31 Issued voucher no. 4808 for wages payable, $8,448, in favor of the payroll bank account. (Assume that the payroll entry was recorded previously in the general journal.)

31 Paid voucher no. 4808 by issuing Ck. No. 8228, payable to Payroll Bank Account.

Required

Check Figure
Check Register,
Cash Credit total,
$50,441.41

1. Using the voucher issue date, enter the unpaid invoices in the voucher register (page 75) beginning with voucher no. 4789. Then draw double lines across all columns to separate the vouchers of June from those of July.

2. Enter the transactions for July in the voucher register at the gross amount. Also record the appropriate transactions in the check register (page 86) and the general journal (page 41).

3. Total and rule the voucher register and the check register for the transactions recorded during July.

4. Prove the equality of the debits and credits on the voucher register and the check register.

LO **2, 3, 4**

PROBLEM 10A-3 Nathan Systems uses a voucher system in which it records invoices at the gross amount. During October, it completed the following transactions:

Oct. 2 Issued voucher no. 2632 in favor of Myers and Horn for the purchase of merchandise with an invoice price of $5,831; terms n/30; FOB shipping point; freight prepaid and added to the invoice, $192 (total, $6,023). Leave an extra line after this entry.

3 Issued voucher no. 2633 for $1,010, no. 2634 for $1,010, and no. 2635 for $1,010. The debt arose because Nathan Systems bought a laptop and printer from Fitzpatrick, Inc. The terms are $1,010 cash on delivery, $1,010 in 30 days, and $1,010 in 60 days. (Use three lines.)

5 Issued Ck. No. 2725 in payment of voucher no. 2633, $1,010.

9 Issued voucher no. 2636 in favor of Cordero Company for the purchase of supplies, $360.50; terms n/30.

12 Issued voucher no. 2637 in favor of Goode Realty for rent for the month, $1,650.

12 Issued Ck. No. 2726 in payment of voucher no. 2637, $1,650.

16 Issued voucher no. 2638 in favor of French Cargo for freight charges on merchandise purchased, $104.

16 Issued voucher no. 2639 in favor of Holley Company for the purchase of merchandise having a list price of $6,512 with a 25 percent trade discount (record voucher for $4,884); terms 2/10, n/30; FOB shipping point. Leave an extra line after this entry.

16 Issued Ck. No. 2727 in payment of voucher no. 2638, $104.

16 Canceled voucher no. 2632 because the invoice will be paid in two installments as follows: voucher no. 2640, payable November 1, $3,011.50; voucher no. 2641, payable November 15, $3,011.50. Issued voucher no. 2640 and no. 2641.

17 Received a credit memo from Holley Company for merchandise returned, $352, credit memo no. 580, voucher no. 2639.

22 Issued voucher no. 2642 in favor of Pardo Telephone Company for telephone bill, $164.90.

22 Issued Ck. No. 2728 in payment of voucher no. 2642, $164.90.

(Continued)

Oct. 23 Issued Ck. No. 2729 in payment of voucher no. 2639, $4,441.36. ($4,884 less $352 return, less cash discount.)

   31 Issued voucher no. 2643 for wages payable, $4,550, in favor of Payroll Bank Account. (Assume that the payroll entry was recorded previously in the general journal.)

   31 Issued Ck. No. 2730 in payment of voucher no. 2643, $4,550.

   31 Issued voucher no. 2644 in favor of N. S. Nathan, the owner, for personal withdrawal, $1,400.

   31 Issued Ck. No. 2731 in payment of voucher no. 2644, $1,400.

Check Figure
Schedule of Vouchers
Payable total,
$8,403.50

Required

1. Record the transactions for October in the voucher register (page 32), the check register (page 34), and the general journal (page 18).

2. Total and rule the voucher register and the check register.

3. Prove the equality of the debits and credits on the voucher register and the check register.

4. Post the amounts from the registers and the general journal to the Vouchers Payable account, No. 212. Assume no previous balance in the account. (Posting from the voucher register should be marked as VR32. Posting from the check register should be marked as CkR34.)

5. Prepare a schedule of vouchers payable. Compare this total with the balance of the Vouchers Payable account.

Work Sheet and Adjusting Entries

To: Amy Roberts, CPA
Subject: **Work Sheet and Adjusting Entries**

Hi Amy,
A while back you helped me understand adjusting entries for the service side of my business. Are there any differences regarding adjusting entries for the merchandising side of my business that I should know about?
Thanks,
Janie

To: Janie Conner
Subject: **RE: Work Sheet and Adjusting Entries**

Hi Janie,
For the merchandising side of your business, you will still do adjustments for items such as insurance, depreciation, supplies, and accrued wages as we talked about before. However, there are two more adjusting entries that you will need to learn. One involves unearned revenues; the other involves merchandise inventory. The adjustment for unearned revenues can be used with the service side or the merchandising side of your business. The adjusting entry for merchandise inventory applies only to the merchandising side of your business, and the entry you make will depend on the inventory method you use (periodic or perpetual).
Take some time to review the following concepts and let's talk again next week.

_____ 1. Adjusting entries for insurance, depreciation, supplies, and accrued wages

_____ 2. Adjusting entries for unearned revenues

_____ 3. Adjusting entries for merchandise inventory

Amy

We have talked about the journals and accounts that a merchandising business keeps. Now we take another step toward completing the accounting cycle by presenting the related adjustments and the work sheet. First, let's briefly review the adjusting entries you have learned so far. The data and related adjusting entries are below.

Accounting Language

Inventory shrinkage (p. 498)
Physical inventory (p. 489)
Revenue recognition principle (p. 488)
Unearned revenue (p. 488)

Supplies

	+		−
Bal.	1,540	Adj.	1,125
Bal.	415		

Supplies Expense

	+	−
Adj.	1,125	

Supplies used, $1,125. (Used supplies become supplies expense)

Prepaid Insurance

	+		−
Bal.	4,000	Adj.	3,600
Bal.	400		

Insurance Expense

	+	−
Adj.	3,600	

Insurance expired, $3,600. (The amount expired is the amount used.)

Depreciation Expense, Equipment

	+	−
Adj.	1,800	

Accumulated Depreciation Equipment

	−		+
		Bal.	11,000
		Adj.	1,800
		Bal.	12,800

Additional depreciation, $1,800. (Add to both accounts.)

Wages Expense

	+	−
Bal.	25,000	
Adj.	2,900	
Bal.	27,900	

Wages Payable

	−		+
		Adj.	2,900

Accrued wages (owed but not yet paid), $2,900. (Add to both accounts.)

This chapter introduces two more adjusting entries:

1. **Unearned revenue.** This adjustment could apply to a merchandising, manufacturing, or service business.
2. **Merchandise inventory.** This adjustment is used exclusively for a merchandising business. We will show adjusting entries for both the periodic and perpetual inventory methods.

11-1 ADJUSTMENT FOR UNEARNED REVENUE

Learning Objective

1 Prepare an adjustment for unearned revenue.

FYI

As of the writing of this text, nonpublic organizations, like sole proprietorships, will apply the new revenue recognition standards, announced by the Financial Accounting Standards Board (FASB), to annual reporting periods after December 15, 2018.

Revenue from Contracts with Customers, Topic 606, FASB Accounting Standards Update, Financial Accounting Standards Board, Norwalk, CT, August 2015.

Another type of adjusting entry occurs when previously unearned revenues are earned. **Unearned revenue** occurs when cash is received in advanced for goods that will be delivered or services that will be performed later. This entry could pertain to a service business as well as to a merchandising or manufacturing business. Frequently, cash is received in advance for services to be performed in the future. For example, a professional sports team sells tickets in advance, a concert association sells season tickets in advance, a magazine publisher sells subscriptions in advance, and an insurance company receives premiums in advance. According to the **revenue recognition principle**, revenues are recorded when they are earned, which may occur at a time different from when cash is received. Therefore, if the cash amounts received by each of these organizations are earned during the present fiscal period, the amounts should be credited to revenue accounts. On the other hand, if some or all of the amounts received are *not* earned during the current fiscal period, the amounts should be credited to unearned revenue accounts. **An unearned revenue account is classified as a liability** because an organization is liable for (owes) the amount received in advance until it is earned.

To illustrate, assume that on April 1, Ressor Publishing Company receives $73,000 in cash for subscriptions paid in advance and records them originally as debits to Cash and credits to Unearned Subscriptions. At the end of the year, Ressor finds that $32,400 of the subscriptions has been earned. Accordingly, Ressor's accountant makes an adjusting entry, debiting Unearned Subscriptions and crediting Subscriptions Income. In other words, the accountant takes the earned portion out of Unearned Subscriptions and adds it to Subscriptions Income. The T accounts below show how this situation would be recorded.

As another example, suppose Trey's Landscape Supply offers a how-to course in landscape maintenance. On November 1, Trey's Landscape Supply receives $2,400 in fees for a three-month course. Because Trey's Landscape Supply's fiscal period ends on December 31, only two of the three months' worth of fees received in advance will be earned during this fiscal period. Therefore, Trey's Landscape Supply's accountant records the transaction as a debit to Cash of $2,400 and a credit to Unearned Course Fees of $2,400. Unearned Course Fees is a liability account because Trey's Landscape

Supply must complete the how-to course or refund a portion of the money it collected. **Any account beginning with the word *Unearned* is a liability.**

On December 31, because two months' worth of course fees have now been earned, Trey's Landscape Supply's accountant makes an adjusting entry to transfer $1,600 (⅔ of $2,400) from Unearned Course Fees to Course Fees Income. T accounts for the entries look like this:

Cash		
	+	−
Nov. 1	2,400	

Unearned Course Fees		
	−	+
Adj.	**1,600**	Nov. 1 2,400
		Bal. 800

Course Fees Income		
	−	+
		Adj. 1,600

11-2 ADJUSTMENT FOR MERCHANDISE INVENTORY USING THE PERIODIC INVENTORY SYSTEM

Under the periodic inventory system, we do not make an entry in the Merchandise Inventory account until an actual **physical inventory** or count of the stock of goods on hand has been taken. Instead, we record the purchase of merchandise as a debit to Purchases for the cost amount and the sale of the merchandise as a credit to Sales for the amount of the selling price. Finally, after a physical count of merchandise has been taken, one method of adjusting inventory is to make two entries to record the dollar amount of the inventory. The first adjusting entry is to remove the beginning inventory. The second entry is to enter the ending inventory.

Consider this example. A firm has a Merchandise Inventory balance of $183,000, which represents the cost of the inventory at the beginning of the fiscal period. At the end of the fiscal period, the firm takes an actual count of the stock on hand and determines the cost of the ending inventory to be $186,000. Naturally, in any business, goods are constantly being bought, sold, and replaced. The cost of the ending inventory is larger than the cost of the beginning inventory because the firm bought more than it sold. When we adjust the Merchandise Inventory account, we place the new figure of $186,000 in the account. This method requires two steps.

STEP 1. Eliminate the amount of the beginning inventory from the Merchandise Inventory account by transferring the amount into Income Summary. (Remove the beginning inventory.)

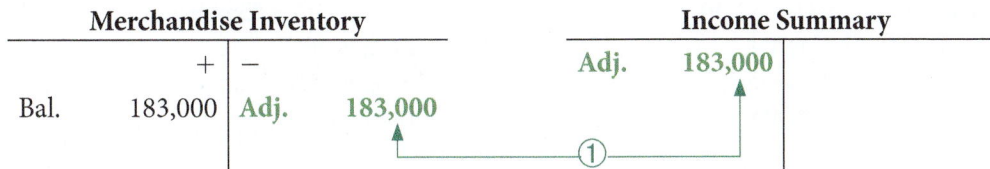

We debit Income Summary and then credit Merchandise Inventory.

STEP 2. Enter the ending or latest physical count of Merchandise Inventory because you must record on the books the cost of the asset remaining on hand. (Enter the ending inventory.)

2 Prepare an adjustment for merchandise inventory under the periodic inventory system.

Learning Objective

Remember

The Income Summary account is the same Income Summary account we used to record closing entries for service businesses. Income Summary now has the extra function of being the balancing or offsetting account in the adjustment of Merchandise Inventory.

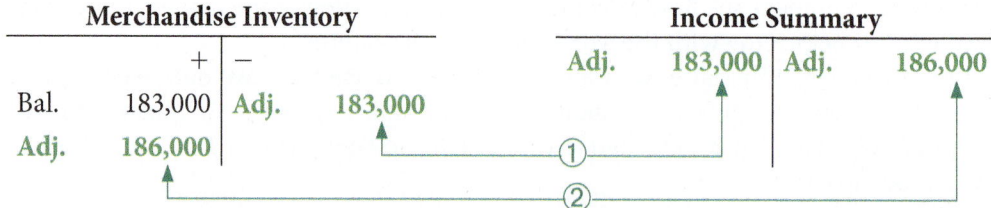

In Step 2, we debit Merchandise Inventory (recording the asset on the plus side of the account) and credit Income Summary.

The reason for adjusting the Merchandise Inventory account in these two steps is that both the beginning and ending amounts appear as distinct figures in the Income Statement columns of a work sheet, and these columns are used as the basis for preparing the income statement.

Whitewater Raft Supply's chart of accounts follows. Notice that Whitewater Raft Supply has an account titled Unearned Course Fees. In addition to selling rafting supplies, Whitewater Raft Supply provides courses to small business owners on how to start and run a successful rafting company. If the small business owner pays in advance for the course before it is offered, the receipt of cash is recorded as Unearned Course Fees. The account number arrangement will be discussed in Chapter 12.

Assets (100–199)
111 Cash
112 Notes Receivable
113 Accounts Receivable
114 Merchandise Inventory
116 Prepaid Insurance
121 Land
122 Building
123 Accumulated Depreciation, Building
124 Equipment
125 Accumulated Depreciation, Equipment

Liabilities (200–299)
211 Notes Payable
212 Accounts Payable
213 Wages Payable
217 Unearned Course Fees
221 Mortgage Payable

Owner's Equity (300–399)
311 J. Conner, Capital
312 J. Conner, Drawing
313 Income Summary

Revenue (400–499)
411 Sales
412 Sales Returns and Allowances
413 Sales Discounts
421 Course Fees Income
422 Interest Income

Cost of Goods Sold (500–599)
511 Purchases
512 Purchases Returns and Allowances
513 Purchases Discounts
514 Freight In

Expenses (600–699)
611 Wages Expense
622 Supplies Expense
623 Insurance Expense
624 Depreciation Expense, Building
625 Depreciation Expense, Equipment
626 Property Tax Expense
634 Interest Expense

© iStockPhoto.com/Anthony Rosenberg

In the Real World

Companies such as Walmart utilize RFID (radio frequency identification) systems to improve inventory accuracy. RFID systems help retailers identify and track their merchandise. By using RFID technology, Walmart has improved inventory accuracy, noting the need for fewer manual inventory adjustments and eliminating some unnecessary inventory. When retailers have better control over their merchandise inventory, they are able to maintain more affordable prices for their customers.

Before we demonstrate how to record adjustments, let's look at the trial balance section of Whitewater Raft Supply's work sheet (Figure 1).

	A	B	C	D	E
1	Whitewater Raft Supply				
2	Work Sheet				
3	For Month Ended December 31, 20--				
4					
5		TRIAL BALANCE		ADJUSTMENTS	
6	ACCOUNT NAME	DEBIT	CREDIT	DEBIT	CREDIT
7	Cash	24,154.00			
8	Notes Receivable	4,000.00			
9	Accounts Receivable	29,546.00			
10	Merchandise Inventory	67,000.00			
11	Supplies	1,540.00			
12	Prepaid Insurance	960.00			
13	Land	122,100.00			
14	Building	129,000.00			
15	Accumulated Depreciation, Building		51,000.00		
16	Equipment	33,100.00			
17	Accumulated Depreciation, Equipment		16,400.00		
18	Notes Payable		36,600.00		
19	Accounts Payable		3,300.00		
20	Unearned Course Fees		1,200.00		
21	Mortgage Payable		7,800.00		
22	J. Conner, Capital		253,774.00		
23	J. Conner, Drawing	77,000.00			
24	Sales		257,180.00		
25	Sales Returns and Allowances	940.00			
26	Sales Discounts	1,980.00			
27	Interest Income		220.00		
28	Purchases	87,840.00			
29	Purchases Returns and Allowances		932.00		
30	Purchases Discounts		1,348.00		
31	Freight In	2,360.00			
32	Wages Expense	45,900.00			
33	Property Tax Expense	1,860.00			
34	Interest Expense	474.00			
35		629,754.00	629,754.00		
36					
37					

◄◄ ◄ ► ►◄   Sheet1 ⟋ Sheet2 ⟋ Sheet3 ⟋   ⟨ ||| ⟩

Figure 1

Trial balance section of Whitewater Raft Supply's work sheet

11-3 DATA FOR THE ADJUSTMENTS

Listing the adjustment data appears to be a relatively minor task. In a business situation, however, someone must take actual physical counts of the inventories and match them up with costs. Someone must check insurance policies to determine the amount of insurance that has expired. In addition, it is important to determine the actual supplies on hand versus those that have been used. Finally, someone must systematically write off, or depreciate, the *used-up* portion of costs on fixed assets, such as buildings and equipment.

Here are the adjustment data for Whitewater Raft Supply. We will show the adjustments recorded in T accounts.

a–b. Ending merchandise inventory, $64,800.

Merchandise Inventory			Income Summary	
	+	−	(a) Adj. 67,000 | (b) Adj. 64,800	
Bal.	67,000	(a) Adj. 67,000		
(b) Adj.	64,800			

c. Course fees earned, $800.

Unearned Course Fees			Course Fees Income	
	−	+	− | +	
(c) Adj.	800	Bal. 1,200	(c) Adj. 800	

d. Supplies used, $1,125.

Supplies			Supplies Expense	
	+	−	+ | −	
Bal.	1,540	(d) Adj. 1,125	(d) Adj. 1,125	

e. Insurance expired, $520.

Prepaid Insurance			Insurance Expense	
	+	−	+ | −	
Bal.	960	(e) Adj. 520	(e) Adj. 520	

f. Additional year's depreciation of building, $3,500.

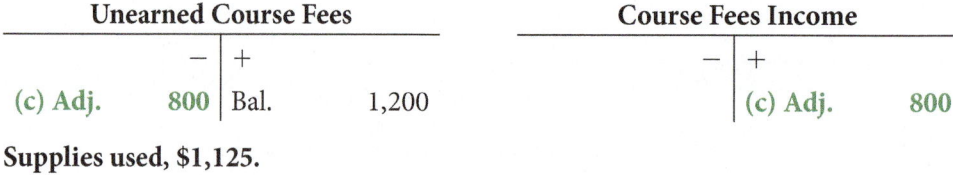

Accumulated Depreciation, Building			Depreciation Expense, Building	
	−	+	+ | −	
		Bal. 51,000	(f) Adj. 3,500	
		(f) Adj. 3,500		

g. Additional year's depreciation of equipment, $4,900.

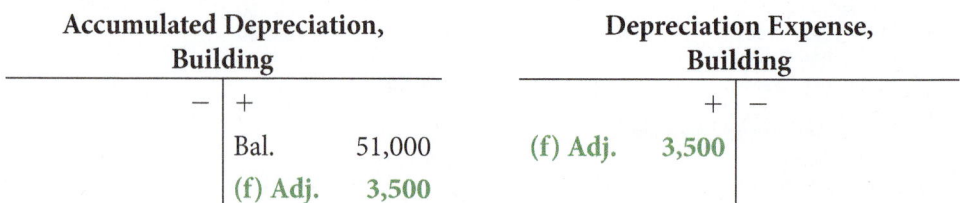

Accumulated Depreciation, Equipment			Depreciation Expense, Equipment	
	−	+	+ | −	
		Bal. 16,400	(g) Adj. 4,900	
		(g) Adj. 4,900		

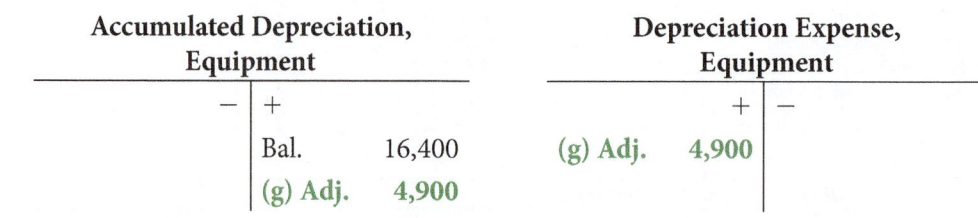

h. Wages owed but not paid to employees at end of year, $1,030

Wages Payable			Wages Expense	
−	+		+	−
	(h) Adj. 1,030		Bal. 45,900	
			(h) Adj. 1,030	

We now record these in the Adjustments columns of the work sheet, using the same letters to identify the adjustments. (See Figure 2.)

Figure 2
Trial balance and adjustments sections of Whitewater Raft Supply's work sheet

	A	B	C	D	E
1			Whitewater Raft Supply		
2			Work Sheet		
3			For Month Ended December 31, 20--		
4					
5			TRIAL BALANCE		ADJUSTMENTS	
6	ACCOUNT NAME	DEBIT	CREDIT	DEBIT	CREDIT
7	Cash	24,154.00			
8	Notes Receivable	4,000.00			
9	Accounts Receivable	29,546.00			
10	Merchandise Inventory	67,000.00		(b) 64,800.00	(a) 67,000.00
11	Supplies	1,540.00			(d) 1,125.00
12	Prepaid Insurance	960.00			(e) 520.00
13	Land	122,100.00			
14	Building	129,000.00			
15	Accumulated Depreciation, Building		51,000.00		(f) 3,500.00
16	Equipment	33,100.00			
17	Accumulated Depreciation, Equipment		16,400.00		(g) 4,900.00
18	Notes Payable		36,600.00		
19	Accounts Payable		3,300.00		
20	Unearned Course Fees		1,200.00	(c) 800.00	
21	Mortage Payable		7,800.00		
22	J. Conner, Capital		253,774.00		
23	J. Conner, Drawing	77,000.00			
24	Sales		257,180.00		
25	Sales Returns and Allowances	940.00			
26	Sales Discounts	1,980.00			
27	Interest Income		220.00		
28	Purchases	87,840.00			
29	Purchases Returns and Allowances		932.00		
30	Purchases Discounts		1,348.00		
31	Freight In	2,360.00			
32	Wages Expense	45,900.00		(h) 1,030.00	
33	Property Tax Expense	1,860.00			
34	Interest Expense	474.00			
35		629,754.00	629,754.00		
36	Income Summary			(a) 67,000.00	(b) 64,800.00
37	Course Fees Income				(c) 800.00
38	Supplies Expense			(d) 1,125.00	
39	Insurance Expense			(e) 520.00	
40	Depreciation Expense, Building			(f) 3,500.00	
41	Depreciation Expense, Equipment			(g) 4,900.00	
42	Wages Payable				(h) 1,030.00
43				143,675.00	143,675.00
44					
45					

Sheet1   Sheet2   Sheet3

11-4 COMPLETION OF THE WORK SHEET

Previously, in introducing work sheets, we included the Adjusted Trial Balance columns as a means of verifying that the accounts were in balance after the adjusting entries were recorded. At this time, to reduce the number of columns in the work sheet, we will eliminate the Adjusted Trial Balance columns. The account balances after the adjusting entries will be carried directly into the Income Statement and Balance Sheet columns.

Figure 3 shows the completed work sheet.

Figure 3

Completed work sheet for Whitewater Raft Supply

	A	B	C	D	E	
1				Whitewater Raft Supply		
2				Work Sheet		
3				For Month Ended December 31, 20--		
4						
5		TRIAL BALANCE		ADJUSTMENTS		
6	ACCOUNT NAME	DEBIT	CREDIT	DEBIT	CREDIT	
7	Cash	24,154.00				
8	Notes receivable	4,000.00				
9	Accounts Receivable	29,546.00				
10	Merchandise Inventory	67,000.00		(b) 64,800.00	(a) 67,000.00	
11	Supplies	1,540.00			(d) 1,125.00	
12	Prepaid Insurance	960.00			(e) 520.00	
13	Land	122,100.00				
14	Building	129,000.00				
15	Accumulated Depreciation, Building		51,000.00		(f) 3,500.00	
16	Equipment	33,100.00				
17	Accumulated Depreciation, Equipment		16,400.00		(g) 4,900.00	
18	Notes Payable		36,600.00			
19	Accounts Payable		3,300.00			
20	Unearned Course Fees		1,200.00	(c) 800.00		
21	Mortgage Payable		7,800.00			
22	J. Conner, Capital		253,774.00			
23	J. Conner, Drawing	77,000.00				
24	Sales		257,180.00			
25	Sales Returns and Allowances	940.00				
26	Sales Discounts	1,980.00				
27	Interest Income		220.00			
28	Purchases	87,840.00				
29	Purchases Returns and Allowances		932.00			
30	Purchases Discounts		1,348.00			
31	Freight In	2,360.00				
32	Wages Expense	45,900.00		(h) 1,030.00		
33	Property Tax Expense	1,860.00				
34	Interest Expense	474.00				
35		629,754.00	629,754.00			
36	Income Summary			(a) 67,000.00	(b) 64,800.00	
37	Course Fees Income				(c) 800.00	
38	Supplies Expense			(d) 1,125.00		
39	Insurance Expense			(e) 520.00		
40	Depreciation Expense, Building			(f) 3,500.00		
41	Depreciation Expense, Equipment			(g) 4,900.00		
42	Wages Payable				(h) 1,030.00	
43				143,675.00	143,675.00	
44	Net Income					
45						
46						

Observe in particular the way we carry forward the figures for Merchandise Inventory and Income Summary. **Income Summary is the only account in which we don't combine the debit and credit figures. Instead, we carry them into the Income Statement columns in Figure 3 as two distinct figures—move the two figures as a pair to the Income Statement columns.** The reason for moving them as a pair is that both figures are needed for completion of the income statement. The debit amount in Income Summary in the Income Statement Debit column is the *beginning* merchandise inventory. The credit amount in Income Summary in the Income Statement Credit column is the *ending* merchandise inventory. We will talk about this topic in greater detail in Chapter 12 when we formulate the income statement for a merchandising entity.

	F	G	H	I
	INCOME STATEMENT		**BALANCE SHEET**	
	DEBIT	**CREDIT**	**DEBIT**	**CREDIT**
			24,154.00	
			4,000.00	
			29,546.00	
			64,800.00	
			415.00	
			440.00	
			122,100.00	
			129,000.00	
				54,500.00
			33,100.00	
				21,300.00
				36,600.00
				3,300.00
				400.00
				7,800.00
				253,774.00
			77,000.00	
		257,180.00		
	940.00			
	1,980.00			
		220.00		
	87,840.00			
		932.00		
		1,348.00		
	2,360.00			
	46,930.00			
	1,860.00			
	474.00			
	67,000.00	64,800.00		
		800.00		
	1,125.00			
	520.00			
	3,500.00			
	4,900.00			
				1,030.00
	219,429.00	325,280.00	484,555.00	378,704.00
	105,851.00			105,851.00
	325,280.00	325,280.00	484,555.00	484,555.00

When completing a work sheet, complete one stage at a time before moving to the next stage:

STEP 1. Record the trial balance and make sure the total of the Debit column equals the total of the Credit column before going to the adjustments.

STEP 2. Record the adjustments in the Adjustments columns, and make sure the totals are equal before extending the new totals into the Income Statement and Balance Sheet columns.

STEP 3. Complete the Income Statement and Balance Sheet columns by recording the adjusted balance of each account. The accounts and classifications pertaining to a merchandising business using the periodic inventory system appear in these columns:

Income Statement		Balance Sheet	
Debit	**Credit**	**Debit**	**Credit**
Expenses	Revenues	Assets	Accumulated
+	+	+	Depreciation
Sales Returns	Purchases Returns	Drawing	+
and Allowances	and Allowances		Liabilities
+	+		+
Sales Discounts	Purchases		Capital
+	Discounts		
Purchases	+		
+	Income Summary		
Freight In			
+			
Income Summary			

Study the following example of a work sheet, noting in particular the way we treat these accounts for a merchandising business using the periodic inventory system.

	Location on Work Sheet			
	Income Statement		Balance Sheet	
Account Name	**Debit**	**Credit**	**Debit**	**Credit**
Merchandise Inventory			64,800.00	
Sales		257,180.00		
Sales Returns and Allowances	940.00			
Sales Discounts	1,980.00			
Purchases	87,840.00			
Purchases Returns and Allowances		932.00		
Purchases Discounts		1,348.00		
Freight In	2,360.00			
Income Summary	67,000.00	64,800.00		

11-5 ADJUSTING ENTRIES USING THE PERIODIC INVENTORY SYSTEM

Figure 4 shows the adjusting entries as taken from the Adjustments columns of the work sheet and recorded in the general journal.

⑤ Journalize the adjusting entries for a merchandising business under the periodic inventory system.

Learning Objective

Figure 4
Adjusting entries for Whitewater Raft Supply

Date		Description	Post. Ref.	Debit	Credit
20--		Adjusting Entries			
Dec.	31	Income Summary		67 0 0 0 00	
(a)		Merchandise Inventory			67 0 0 0 00
(b)	31	Merchandise Inventory		64 8 0 0 00	
		Income Summary			64 8 0 0 00
(c)	31	Unearned Course Fees		8 0 0 00	
		Course Fees Income			8 0 0 00
(d)	31	Supplies Expense		1 1 2 5 00	
		Supplies			1 1 2 5 00
(e)	31	Insurance Expense		5 2 0 00	
		Prepaid Insurance			5 2 0 00
(f)	31	Depreciation Expense, Building		3 5 0 0 00	
		Accumulated Depreciation, Building			3 5 0 0 00
(g)	31	Depreciation Expense, Equipment		4 9 0 0 00	
		Accumulated Depreciation, Equipment			4 9 0 0 00
(h)	31	Wages Expense		1 0 3 0 00	
		Wages Payable			1 0 3 0 00

GENERAL JOURNAL — Page 96

11-6 ADJUSTMENT FOR MERCHANDISE INVENTORY UNDER THE PERPETUAL INVENTORY SYSTEM

Before we demonstrate how to record the adjustment for the perpetual inventory system, let's look at a portion of the trial balance section of Whitewater Raft Supply's work sheet (Figure 5 on the next page), assuming the company used the perpetual inventory system.

Under the perpetual inventory system, a business continually maintains a record of each item in stock. **When merchandise is purchased, the Merchandise Inventory account (not the Purchases account) is debited for the cost of the merchandise and Accounts Payable or Cash is credited. When merchandise is sold, two journal entries**

⑥ Prepare and journalize the adjusting entry for merchandise inventory under the perpetual inventory system.

Learning Objective

Figure 5

A portion of the trial balance section of Whitewater Raft Supply's work sheet (perpetual inventory system)

	A	B	C
23			
24	Sales		257,180.00
25	Sales Returns and Allowances	940.00	
26	Sales Discounts	1,980.00	
27	Interest Income		220.00
28	Cost of Goods Sold	90,120.00	
29	Wages Expense	46,930.00	
30			

Sheet1 Sheet2 Sheet3

are required. First, debit Accounts Receivable or Cash and credit Sales. Second, debit the Cost of Goods Sold account for the cost of merchandise and credit the Merchandise Inventory account for the same amount.

Many firms use electronic devices to keep track of stock items under the perpetual inventory system. For example, when a sale is made at a supermarket checkout counter, as the bar code on each item is scanned, the price and stock number are recorded. The cash register is connected to a computer that updates the inventory record and records the cost of the item. So the business perpetually (always) knows how much inventory it should have on hand.

However, to verify the inventory record, a physical count should be taken from time to time. The amount shown by the physical count may be less than the computer record as a result of errors, shrinkage, or shoplifting. This difference is called **inventory shrinkage**, and an adjusting entry must be made. This entry is a debit to the Cost of Goods Sold account (an expense account) and a credit to the Merchandise Inventory account. The opposite is true if the physical count is more than the computer record. The adjusting entry would be a debit to Merchandise Inventory and a credit to Cost of Goods Sold.

11-6a Adjusting Entry Under the Perpetual Inventory System

Here are examples of entries under the perpetual inventory system when the physical count does not agree with the computer record of merchandise inventory. Assume a beginning inventory of $75,000.

1. Bought merchandise on account, $50,000.

Merchandise Inventory			Accounts Payable		
+	−			−	+
Bal. 75,000				(1)	50,000
(1) 50,000					

2. Sold merchandise for $84,000 having a cost of $60,300.

Accounts Receivable			Sales		
+	−			−	+
(2) 84,000				(2)	84,000

Cost of Goods Sold			Merchandise Inventory		
+	−			+	−
(2) 60,300			Bal. 75,000	(2)	60,300
			(1) 50,000		
			Bal. 64,700		

3a. The adjusting entry for the perpetual inventory system is computed by determining the difference between the computer record and the physical count for ending inventory, $63,200. The recorded balance of the perpetual inventory is $64,700 ($75,000 + $50,000 − $60,300).

The difference of $1,500 ($64,700 − $63,200) is the adjustment amount under the perpetual inventory system. The adjusting entry required to record the $1,500 loss involves a debit to Cost of Goods Sold and a credit to Merchandise Inventory (shown in Figure 6).

Remember

The ending inventory of one period becomes the beginning inventory of the next period.

Cost of Goods Sold			
	+	−	
(2)	60,300		
(3) Adj.	1,500		
Bal.	61,800		

Merchandise Inventory				
		+	−	
Bal.	75,000	(2)	60,300	
(1)	50,000	(3) Adj.	1,500	
Bal.	63,200			

3b. Suppose, on the other hand, that the physical count of the stock of merchandise ($65,200) was more than the recorded amount ($64,700). The adjusting entry would need to increase the Merchandise Inventory account with a debit to Merchandise Inventory and corresponding credit to Cost of Goods Sold (account) for the difference ($65,200 − $64,700 = $500). (Refer to Figure 6.)

		GENERAL JOURNAL						Page 96	
Date		Description	Post. Ref.	Debit			Credit		
20--		Adjusting Entries							
Dec.	31	Cost of Goods Sold		1 5 0 0	00				
3a.		Merchandise Inventory					1 5 0 0	00	
3b.	31	Merchandise Inventory		5 0 0	00				
		Cost of Goods Sold					5 0 0	00	

Figure 6
Adjusting entry for ending inventory under the perpetual inventory system

On the income statement under the perpetual inventory system, the Cost of Goods Sold account is listed on one line rather than there being a Cost of Goods Sold section. The following is a comparison of income statements under the periodic and perpetual inventory systems, assuming scenario 3a from above.

Periodic

Sales (net)		$84,000
Cost of Goods Sold:		
Merchandise Inventory (beginning)	$ 75,000	
Purchases (net)	50,000	
Cost of Goods Available for Sale	$125,000	
Less Merchandise Inventory (ending)	63,200	
Cost of Goods Sold		61,800
Gross Profit		$22,200

Perpetual

Sales (net)	$84,000
Cost of Goods Sold	61,800
Gross Profit	$22,200

YOU Make the Call

You and a college friend have decided to start a merchandising business that markets green products: people- and earth-friendly products for the home and business. You have identified approximately 100 different items, including bath soaps, home cleaning products, plant-friendly foods and pesticides, and a line of organic canned foods. Both of you have taken accounting courses and are trying to decide whether to use the periodic or perpetual inventory system. What are the advantages, disadvantages, and implications of each system?

SOLUTION

For simplicity, using the periodic inventory system would be the way to go. It is less complicated than the perpetual inventory system, requires fewer accounting entries, and is less costly than the perpetual inventory system because you do not have to buy software, hardware, or other electronic inventory tracking devices. However, the perpetual inventory system offers a higher degree of control. It is a better way to manage proper inventory levels because it provides up-to-the-minute data for determining purchasing needs—an advantage that may very well outweigh the disadvantages.

Chapter Review

Study and Practice

Learning Objective   **1**   Prepare an adjustment for unearned revenue.

According to the **revenue recognition principle**, revenues are recorded when they are earned. The receipt of cash and the earning of revenue may occur at different times. For revenue received in advance, an adjustment is required to separate the portion that has been earned from the portion that is unearned. We assume that the amount of cash received in advance was originally recorded as **unearned revenue**, which is a liability. In the adjusting entry for the amount actually earned, debit the unearned revenue account (for example, Unearned Course Fees) and credit the revenue account (such as Course Fees Income).

 PRACTICE EXERCISE 1

On June 1, Thompson Company receives $148,540 in cash for subscriptions covering two years. At the end of the year, December 31, Thompson finds that $94,302 of the subscriptions have been earned. Record in general journal form (a) the original receipt of cash on June 1 and (b) the year-end adjusting entry for Thompson Company.

PRACTICE EXERCISE 1 • SOLUTION

			GENERAL JOURNAL								Page ___			
Date			Description	Post. Ref.		Debit					Credit			
20--														
June	1		Cash		148	5	4	0	00					
(a)			Unearned Subscriptions							148	5	4	0	00
			Adjusting Entries											
Dec.	31		Unearned Subscriptions		94	3	0	2	00					
(b)			Subscriptions Income							94	3	0	2	00

 2 Prepare an adjustment for merchandise inventory under the periodic inventory system. **Learning Objective**

The adjustment for merchandise inventory under the periodic inventory system requires two adjusting entries. In the first adjusting entry (to remove the beginning inventory), debit Income Summary and credit Merchandise Inventory. In the second adjusting entry (to enter the ending inventory), debit Merchandise Inventory and credit Income Summary.

 ### PRACTICE EXERCISE 2

Morkin Company's beginning inventory amounted to $264,072. A physical count at the end of the year reveals that the ending inventory amount is $267,322. Record the necessary adjustments in the T accounts.

PRACTICE EXERCISE 2 • SOLUTION

Merchandise Inventory			**Income Summary**	
+	**–**		(a) Adj. 264,072	(b) Adj. 267,322
Bal. 264,072	(a) Adj. 264,072			
(b) Adj. 267,322				

 3 Record adjustment data in a work sheet, including merchandise inventory, unearned revenue, supplies used, expired insurance, depreciation, and accrued wages or salaries. **Learning Objective**

In the Adjustments columns of the work sheet, record the following adjusting entries:

For merchandise inventory: Debit Income Summary and credit Merchandise Inventory (to remove the beginning inventory); then debit Merchandise Inventory and credit Income Summary (to enter the ending inventory).

For unearned revenue: Debit the unearned revenue account and credit the revenue account (to record revenue earned).

For supplies used: Debit Supplies Expense and credit Supplies.

For expired insurance: Debit Insurance Expense and credit Prepaid Insurance.

For depreciation: Debit Depreciation Expense and credit Accumulated Depreciation.

For accrued wages or salaries: Debit Wages Expense or Salaries Expense and credit Wages Payable or Salaries Payable.

PRACTICE EXERCISE 3

Following are the adjustment data for Majors Company:

a–b. Merchandise inventory (ending), $64,800.
  c. Course fees earned, $1,800.
  d. Supplies inventory (on hand), $2,415.
  e. Insurance expired, $1,520.
  f. Depreciation of building, $13,500.
  g. Depreciation of equipment, $5,900.
  h. Wages accrued, $2,030.

Record these data in the Adjustments column of the following work sheet.

	A	B	C	D	E
1		Majors Company			
2		Work Sheet			
3		For Year Ended December 31, 20--			
4					
5		TRIAL BALANCE		ADJUSTMENTS	
6	ACCOUNT NAME	DEBIT	CREDIT	DEBIT	CREDIT
7	Cash	23,010.00			
8	Notes Receivable	6,000.00			
9	Accounts Receivable	28,540.00			
10	Merchandise Inventory	68,000.00			
11	Supplies	12,440.00			
12	Prepaid Insurance	2,110.00			
13	Land	120,100.00			
14	Building	128,000.00			
15	Accumulated Depreciation, Building		50,000.00		
16	Equipment	34,100.00			
17	Accumulated Depreciation, Equipment		19,600.00		
18	Notes Payable		34,600.00		
19	Accounts Payable		4,300.00		
20	Unearned Course Fees		2,200.00		
21	Mortgage Payable		8,800.00		
22	R. L. Majors, Capital		252,774.00		
23	R. L. Majors, Drawing	65,000.00			
24	Sales		253,980.00		
25	Sales Returns and Allowances	940.00			
26	Sales Discounts	1,880.00			
27	Interest Income		1,220.00		
28	Purchases	88,840.00			
29	Purchases Returns and Allowances		832.00		
30	Purchases Discounts		1,448.00		
31	Freight In	2,460.00			
32	Wages Expense	44,900.00			
33	Property Tax Expense	2,860.00			
34	Interest Expense	574.00			
35		629,754.00	629,754.00		
36	Income Summary				
37	Course Fees Income				
38	Supplies Expense				
39	Insurance Expense				
40	Depreciation Expense, Building				
41	Depreciation Expense, Equipment				
42	Wages Payable				
43					
44					

Sheet1 / Sheet2 / Sheet3

PRACTICE EXERCISE 3 • SOLUTION

	A	B	C	D	E
1		Majors Company			
2		Work Sheet			
3		For Year Ended December 31, 20--			
4					
5		TRIAL BALANCE		ADJUSTMENTS	
6	ACCOUNT NAME	DEBIT	CREDIT	DEBIT	CREDIT
7	Cash	23,010.00			
8	Notes Receivable	6,000.00			
9	Accounts Receivable	28,540.00			
10	Merchandise Inventory	68,000.00		(b) 64,800.00	(a) 68,000.00
11	Supplies	12,440.00			(d) 10,025.00
12	Prepaid Insurance	2,110.00			(e) 1,520.00
13	Land	120,100.00			
14	Building	128,000.00			
15	Accumulated Depreciation, Building		50,000.00		(f) 13,500.00
16	Equipment	34,100.00			
17	Accumulated Depreciation, Equipment		19,600.00		(g) 5,900.00
18	Notes Payable		34,600.00		
19	Accounts Payable		4,300.00		
20	Unearned Course Fees		2,200.00	(c) 1,800.00	
21	Mortgage Payable		8,800.00		
22	R. L. Majors, Capital		252,774.00		
23	R. L. Majors, Drawing	65,000.00			
24	Sales		253,980.00		
25	Sales Returns and Allowances	940.00			
26	Sales Discounts	1,880.00			
27	Interest Income		1,220.00		
28	Purchases	88,840.00			
29	Purchases Returns and Allowances		832.00		
30	Purchases Discounts		1,448.00		
31	Freight In	2,460.00			
32	Wages Expense	44,900.00		(h) 2,030.00	
33	Property Tax Expense	2,860.00			
34	Interest Expense	574.00			
35		629,754.00	629,754.00		
36	Income Summary			(a) 68,000.00	(b) 64,800.00
37	Course Fees Income				(c) 1,800.00
38	Supplies Expense			(d) 10,025.00	
39	Insurance Expense			(e) 1,520.00	
40	Depreciation Expense, Building			(f) 13,500.00	
41	Depreciation Expense, Equipment			(g) 5,900.00	
42	Wages Payable				(h) 2,030.00
43				167,575.00	167,575.00
44					

Sheet1 / Sheet2 / Sheet3

 4 Complete the work sheet.

Carry the Income Summary account from the Adjustments columns into the Income Statement columns as two separate figures. For merchandise inventory, record the amount of the ending inventory in the Balance Sheet Debit column. For unearned revenue, record the unearned revenue account in the Balance Sheet Credit column and the revenue account in the Income Statement Credit column.

 ## PRACTICE EXERCISE 4

Complete the Income Statement and Balance Sheet columns of the work sheet for Majors Company from Practice Exercise 3.

(Continued)

PRACTICE EXERCISE 4 • SOLUTION

	A	B	C	D	E
1			Majors Company		
2			Work Sheet		
3			For Year Ended December 31, 20--		
4					
5		TRIAL BALANCE		ADJUSTMENTS	
6	ACCOUNT NAME	DEBIT	CREDIT	DEBIT	CREDIT
7	Cash	23,010.00			
8	Notes Receivable	6,000.00			
9	Accounts Receivable	28,540.00			
10	Merchandise Inventory	68,000.00		(b) 64,800.00	(a) 68,000.00
11	Supplies	12,440.00			(d) 10,025.00
12	Prepaid Insurance	2,110.00			(e) 1,520.00
13	Land	120,100.00			
14	Building	128,000.00			
15	Accumulated Depreciation, Building		50,000.00		(f) 13,500.00
16	Equipment	34,100.00			
17	Accumulated Depreciation, Equipment		19,600.00		(g) 5,900.00
18	Notes Payable		34,600.00		
19	Accounts Payable		4,300.00		
20	Unearned Course Fees		2,200.00	(c) 1,800.00	
21	Mortgage Payable		8,800.00		
22	R. L. Majors, Capital		252,774.00		
23	R. L. Majors, Drawing	65,000.00			
24	Sales		253,980.00		
25	Sales Returns and Allowances	940.00			
26	Sales Discounts	1,880.00			
27	Interest Income		1,220.00		
28	Purchases	88,840.00			
29	Purchases Returns and Allowances		832.00		
30	Purchases Discounts		1,448.00		
31	Freight In	2,460.00			
32	Wages Expense	44,900.00		(h) 2,030.00	
33	Property Tax Expense	2,860.00			
34	Interest Expense	574.00			
35		629,754.00	629,754.00		
36	Income Summary			(a) 68,000.00	(b) 64,800.00
37	Course Fees Income				(c) 1,800.00
38	Supplies Expense			(d) 10,025.00	
39	Insurance Expense			(e) 1,520.00	
40	Depreciation Expense, Building			(f) 13,500.00	
41	Depreciation Expense, Equipment			(g) 5,900.00	
42	Wages Payable				(h) 2,030.00
43				167,575.00	167,575.00
44	Net Income				
45					
46					

Sheet1 / Sheet2 / Sheet3

	F	G	H	I
	INCOME STATEMENT		**BALANCE SHEET**	
	DEBIT	**CREDIT**	**DEBIT**	**CREDIT**
			23,010.00	
			6,000.00	
			28,540.00	
			64,800.00	
			2,415.00	
			590.00	
			120,100.00	
			128,000.00	
				63,500.00
			34,100.00	
				25,500.00
				34,600.00
				4,300.00
				400.00
				8,800.00
				252,774.00
			65,000.00	
		253,980.00		
	940.00			
	1,880.00			
		1,220.00		
	88,840.00			
		832.00		
		1,448.00		
	2,460.00			
	46,930.00			
	2,860.00			
	574.00			
	68,000.00	64,800.00		
		1,800.00		
	10,025.00			
	1,520.00			
	13,500.00			
	5,900.00			
				2,030.00
	243,429.00	324,080.00	472,555.00	391,904.00
	80,651.00			80,651.00
	324,080.00	324,080.00	472,555.00	472,555.00

CHAPTER REVIEW

Learning Objective   Journalize the adjusting entries for a merchandising business under the periodic inventory system.

  Take the adjusting entries recorded in the journal directly from the Adjustments columns of the work sheet.

 PRACTICE EXERCISE 5

Prepare the year-end adjusting entries from the Adjustments column of Majors Company's work sheet from Practice Exercise 3.

PRACTICE EXERCISE 5 • SOLUTION

	GENERAL JOURNAL				Page ___
Date	Description	Post. Ref.	Debit	Credit
20--	Adjusting Entries			
Dec. 31	Income Summary		68 0 0 0 00	
(a)	Merchandise Inventory			68 0 0 0 00
(b) 31	Merchandise Inventory		64 8 0 0 00	
	Income Summary			64 8 0 0 00
(c) 31	Unearned Course Fees		1 8 0 0 00	
	Course Fees Income			1 8 0 0 00
(d) 31	Supplies Expense		10 0 2 5 00	
	Supplies			10 0 2 5 00
(e) 31	Insurance Expense		1 5 2 0 00	
	Prepaid Insurance			1 5 2 0 00
(f) 31	Depreciation Expense, Building		13 5 0 0 00	
	Accumulated Depreciation, Building			13 5 0 0 00
(g) 31	Depreciation Expense, Equipment		5 9 0 0 00	
	Accumulated Depreciation, Equipment			5 9 0 0 00
(h) 31	Wages Expense		2 0 3 0 00	
	Wages Payable			2 0 3 0 00

Learning Objective   Prepare and journalize the adjusting entry for merchandise inventory under the perpetual inventory system.

Assuming that the amount of the physical count of the stock of merchandise is less than the recorded amount, the adjusting entry is a debit to Cost of Goods Sold and a credit to Merchandise Inventory for the amount of the difference. On the other hand, if the physical count of the stock of merchandise is more than the recorded amount, the adjusting entry is to debit Merchandise Inventory and credit Cost of Goods Sold for the amount of the difference.

PRACTICE EXERCISE 6

Larkin Company employs the perpetual inventory system. Cost of Goods Sold for the year before any adjustment is $553,250. The computer record shows the amount of ending inventory to be $369,583, while the physical count shows ending inventory to be $362,720. Record the adjustment into T accounts and then journalize the adjusting entry.

PRACTICE EXERCISE 6 • SOLUTION

Cost of Goods Sold				Merchandise Inventory		
	+	–			+	–
Bal.	553,250			Bal.	369,583	Adj. 6,863*
Adj.	6,863					

*Adjustment = $362,720 − $369,583 = $(6,863)

		GENERAL JOURNAL				Page ___
Date		Description	Post. Ref.	Debit	Credit	
20--		Adjusting Entries				
Dec.	31	Cost of Goods Sold		6 8 6 3 00		
		Merchandise Inventory			6 8 6 3 00	

Glossary

Inventory shrinkage The amount by which inventory diminishes due to theft, misplacement, loss, or mismarking. (*p. 498*)

Physical inventory An actual count of the stock of goods on hand. (*p. 489*)

Revenue recognition principle An accrual-based accounting principle that requires revenue to be recognized when it is earned, regardless of when payment is received. (*p. 488*)

Unearned revenue Cash received in advance for goods or services to be delivered later; considered to be a liability until the revenue is earned. (*p. 488*)

Quiz Yourself

_____ 1. Which of the following is the adjusting entry for depreciation on Equipment?
   a. Debit Depreciation Expense, Equipment and credit Equipment
   b. Debit Equipment and credit Depreciation Expense, Equipment
   c. Debit Depreciation Expense, Equipment and credit Accumulated Depreciation, Equipment
   d. Debit Accumulated Depreciation, Equipment and credit Depreciation Expense, Equipment
   e. None of the above

_____ 2. The adjusting entry for unearned revenue pertains to which of the following types of businesses?
a. Service
b. Merchandising
c. Manufacturing
d. Service and merchandising
e. All of the above

_____ 3. An account that has *unearned* in its name is classified as what type of account?
a. Asset
b. Liability
c. Revenue
d. Owner's equity
e. Expense

_____ 4. This type of inventory system does not require an entry to Merchandise Inventory until a physical inventory has been taken.
a. Periodic inventory system
b. Perpetual inventory system
c. Merchandise inventory system
d. Beginning inventory system
e. Ending inventory system

_____ 5. The Supplies account has a $1,400 balance. A physical inventory is taken at the end of the fiscal year, and the amount on hand is determined to be $300. What adjusting entry is required to record the supplies used?
a. Supplies 300 DR, Cash 300 CR
b. Supplies Expense 1,400 DR, Supplies 1,400 CR
c. Supplies 1,100 DR, Supplies Expense 1,100 CR
d. Supplies Expense 1,100 DR, Supplies 1,100 CR
e. None of the above

_____ 6. Which of the following accounts would *not* be listed in the Income Statement column(s) of the work sheet?
a. Income Summary
b. Freight In
c. Sales Returns and Allowances
d. Purchases Discounts
e. Merchandise Inventory

_____ 7. The amount of inventory shown on the company books may be different than the physical inventory count. Which of the following is *not* a reason for this difference?
a. Errors in accounting
b. Shrinkage
c. Shoplifting
d. Errors in receiving merchandise
e. A change in supplier

Answers:
1.c 2.e 3.b 4.a 5.d 6.e 7.e

Chapter Assignments

Discussion Questions

1. What is a physical inventory? What does the word *periodic* mean in the term *periodic inventory*?
2. On the Income Summary line of a work sheet, $126,220 appears in the Income Statement Debit column and $123,300 appears in the Income Statement Credit column. Which figure represents the beginning inventory?
3. Using the perpetual inventory system, what account is debited when a business finds that its physical count of inventory is greater than the recorded amount?
4. On a work sheet, where will the amount of the ending merchandise inventory be recorded?
5. Explain what is meant by unearned revenue. Why it is treated as a liability?
6. Why is it necessary to adjust the Merchandise Inventory account under a periodic inventory system?

7. A merchandising company shows $8,842 in the Supplies account on the preadjusted trial balance. After taking inventory of the actual supplies, the company still owns $3,638.
    a.   How much was used or expired?
    b.   Write the adjusting entry.
8. Assume that a college receives $84,000 for one semester's dormitory rent in advance and an entry is made debiting Cash and crediting Unearned Rent. At the end of the year, $68,000 of the rent has been earned. What adjusting entry would be made?

Exercises

EXERCISE 11-1 For the university football program's Unearned Season Tickets account, list the debits and credits for each amount posted to the account and briefly describe each transaction.

LO 1

Practice Exercise 1

ACCOUNT Unearned Season Tickets					ACCOUNT NO. 214		
Date	Item	Post. Ref.	Debit	Credit	Balance Debit	Balance Credit	
20--							
Jan. 1	Balance	✓				19 2 0 0 00	
Oct. 15		J42		28 6 7 0 00		47 8 7 0 00	
Nov. 1		J43		46 2 0 0 00		94 0 7 0 00	
Dec. 31	Adj.	J52	45 3 1 2 00			48 7 5 8 00	

EXERCISE 11-2 On October 31, the Vermillion Igloos Hockey Club received $800,000 in cash in advance for season tickets for eight home games. The transaction was recorded as a debit to Cash and a credit to Unearned Admissions. By December 31, the end of the fiscal year, the team had played three home games and received an additional $450,000 cash admissions income at the gate.
a.   Journalize the adjusting entry as of December 31.
b.   List the title of the account and the related balance that will appear on the income statement.
c.   List the title of the account and the related balance that will appear on the balance sheet.

LO 1

Practice Exercise 1

EXERCISE 11-3 Basga Company uses the periodic inventory system. Beginning inventory amounted to $241,072. A physical count reveals that the latest inventory amount is $256,339. Record the adjusting entries, using T accounts.

LO 2

Practice Exercise 2

EXERCISE 11-4 Indicate the work sheet columns (Income Statement Debit, Income Statement Credit, Balance Sheet Debit, Balance Sheet Credit) in which the balances of the following accounts should appear:
a.   S. Moon, Drawing
b.   Utilities Expense
c.   Merchandise Inventory (ending)

LO 4

Practice Exercise 4

(Continued)

d.   Purchases Discounts
e.   Unearned Rent
f.   Sales Returns and Allowances
g.   Accumulated Depreciation, Equipment
h   Income Summary
i.   Service Income
j.   Prepaid Insurance

LO 5

Practice Exercise 5

EXERCISE 11-5 Journalize the required adjusting entries for the year ended December 31 for Butler Spa and Pool Accessories. Butler Spa and Pool Accessories uses the periodic inventory system.

a–b.   On December 31, a physical count of inventory was taken. The physical count amounted to $22,624. The Merchandise Inventory account shows a balance of $21,696.

  c.   On July 1 of this year, $2,400 was paid for a one-year insurance policy.

  d.   On November 1 of this year, $420 was paid for three months of advertising.

  e.   As of December 31, the balance of the Unearned Membership Fees account is $15,600. Of this amount, $9,200 has been earned.

  f.   Equipment purchased on May 1 of this year for $8,000 is expected to have a useful life of five years with a trade-in value of $500. All other equipment has been fully depreciated. The straight-line method is used.

  g.   As of December 31, three days' wages at $250 per day had accrued.

  h.   As of December 31, the balance of the supplies account is $4,200. A physical inventory of the supplies was taken, with an amount of $1,650 determined to be on hand.

LO 5

Practice Exercise 5

EXERCISE 11-6 On December 31, the end of the year, the accountant for *Fireside Magazine* was called away suddenly because of an emergency. However, before leaving, the accountant jotted down a few notes pertaining to the adjustments. Journalize the necessary adjusting entries. Assume that *Fireside Magazine* uses the periodic inventory system.

a–b.   A physical count of inventory revealed a balance of $199,830. The Merchandise Inventory account shows a balance of $202,839.

  c.   Subscriptions received in advance amounting to $156,200 were recorded as Unearned Subscriptions. At year-end, $103,120 has been earned.

  d.   Depreciation of equipment for the year is $12,300.

  e.   The amount of expired insurance for the year is $1,612.

  f.   The balance of Prepaid Rent is $2,400, representing four months' rent. Three months' rent has expired.

  g.   Three days' salaries will be unpaid at the end of the year; total weekly (five days') salaries are $4,000.

  h.   As of December 31, the balance of the supplies account is $1,800. A physical inventory of the supplies was taken, with an amount of $920 determined to be on hand.

LO 6

Practice Exercise 6

EXERCISE 11-7 On December 31, Marchant Company took a physical count of its merchandise inventory. It operates under the perpetual inventory system. The physical count amounted to $185,294. The Merchandise Inventory account shows a balance of $187,936. Journalize the adjusting entry.

Problem Set A

LO **3, 4**

PROBLEM 11–1A The trial balance of Hadden Company as of December 31, the end of its current fiscal year, is as follows:

Hadden Company		
Trial Balance		
December 31, 20--		
Account Name	**Debit**	**Credit**
Cash	9,246.52	
Merchandise Inventory	63,674.80	
Supplies	1,466.34	
Prepaid Insurance	1,420.00	
Store Equipment	36,230.00	
Accumulated Depreciation, Store Equipment		22,726.00
Accounts Payable		13,196.96
Sales Tax Payable		1,236.98
R. M. Hadden, Capital		56,339.32
R. M. Hadden, Drawing	28,000.00	
Sales		175,864.31
Sales Returns and Allowances	1,573.72	
Purchases	77,300.04	
Purchases Returns and Allowances		1,744.32
Purchases Discounts		1,413.62
Freight In	2,427.00	
Salary Expense	35,458.85	
Rent Expense	14,600.00	
Miscellaneous Expense	1,124.24	
	272,521.51	272,521.51

Here are the data for the adjustments.

a–b. Merchandise Inventory at December 31, $64,742.80.
  c. Store supplies inventory (on hand), $420.20.
  d. Insurance expired, $738.
  e. Salaries accrued, $684.50.
  f. Depreciation of store equipment, $3,620.

Required

Complete the work sheet after entering the account names and balances onto the work sheet.

Check Figure
Net income, $41,517.76

LO   1, 3, 4, 5 ....

PROBLEM 11–2A The balances of the ledger accounts of Beldren Home Center as of December 31, the end of its fiscal year, are as follows:

Cash	$ 10,592
Accounts Receivable	43,962
Merchandise Inventory	120,838
Supplies	1,570
Prepaid Insurance	2,628
Store Equipment	35,924
Accumulated Depreciation, Store Equipment	29,420
Office Equipment	10,436
Accumulated Depreciation, Office Equipment	1,720
Notes Payable	5,000
Accounts Payable	29,822
Unearned Rent	3,200
A. P. Beldren, Capital	120,532
A. P. Beldren, Drawing	29,000
Sales	653,000
Sales Returns and Allowances	9,748
Purchases	519,374
Purchases Returns and Allowances	12,440
Purchases Discounts	8,634
Freight In	24,724
Wages Expense	54,200
Interest Expense	772

Data for the adjustments are as follows:

a–b. Merchandise Inventory at December 31, $102,765.
  c. Wages accrued at December 31, $1,834.
  d. Supplies inventory (on hand) at December 31, $645.
  e. Depreciation of store equipment, $5,782.
  f. Depreciation of office equipment, $1,791.
  g. Insurance expired during the year, $845.
  h. Rent earned, $2,500.

Check Figure
Net income, $38,506

Required

1. Complete the work sheet after entering the account names and balances onto the work sheet. Ignore this step if using CLGL.
2. Journalize the adjusting entries. If using manual working papers, record adjusting entries on journal page 16.

LO 3, 4, 5

PROBLEM 11-3A A portion of the work sheet of Sadie's Flowers for the year ended December 31 is as follows:

	A	F	G	H	I
4					
5		INCOME STATEMENT		BALANCE SHEET	
6	ACCOUNT NAME	DEBIT	CREDIT	DEBIT	CREDIT
7	Cash			9,340.00	
8	Merchandise Inventory			76,940.00	
9	Supplies			256.00	
10	Prepaid Insurance			240.00	
11	Store Equipment			39,280.00	
12	Accumulated Depreciation, Store Equipment				26,220.00
13	Accounts Payable				14,600.00
14	S. R. Rodriguez, Capital				68,940.00
15	S. R. Rodriguez, Drawing			27,600.00	
16	Sales		173,420.00		
17	Sales Returns and Allowances	1,520.00			
18	Purchases	82,312.00			
19	Purchases Returns and Allowances		940.00		
20	Purchases Discounts		1,600.00		
21	Freight In	1,948.00			
22	Salary Expense	37,560.00			
23	Rent Expense	14,800.00			
24					
25	Income Summary	65,680.00	76,940.00		
26	Depreciation Expense, Store Equipment	4,040.00			
27	Insurance Expense	760.00			
28	Supplies Expense	944.00			
29	Salaries Payable				560.00
30		209,564.00	252,900.00	153,656.00	110,320.00
31					

Sheet1 / Sheet2 / Sheet3

Required

1. Determine the entries that appeared in the Adjustments columns and present them in general journal form on page 41.
2. Determine the net income for the year.
3. What is the amount of the ending capital?

Check Figure
Increase in Capital, $15,736

LO 3, 4, 6

PROBLEM 11–4A Here are the accounts in the ledger of Misha's Jewel Box, with the balances as of December 31, the end of its fiscal year.

Cash	$ 13,242
Accounts Receivable	3,984
Merchandise Inventory	126,540
Supplies	2,484
Prepaid Insurance	2,655
Land	18,000
Building	97,000
Accumulated Depreciation, Building	38,240
Store Equipment	46,170
Accumulated Depreciation, Store Equipment	16,250
Accounts Payable	8,270
Sales Tax Payable	2,371
Mortgage Payable	77,871
M. Beloit, Capital	185,000
M. Beloit, Drawing	48,000

(Continued)

Sales	$379,354
Sales Returns and Allowances	3,892
Cost of Goods Sold	279,198
Salary Expense	54,400
Advertising Expense	3,526
Utilities Expense	2,538
Property Tax Expense	1,162
Miscellaneous Expense	1,613
Interest Expense	2,952

Here are the data for the adjustments. Assume that Misha's Jewel Box uses the perpetual inventory system.

a. Merchandise Inventory at December 31, $124,630.
b. Insurance expired during the year, $1,294.
c. Depreciation of building, $3,300.
d. Depreciation of store equipment, $6,470.
e. Salaries accrued at December 31, $2,470.
f. Store supplies inventory (on hand) at December 31, $1,959.

Check Figure
Net income, $14,104

Required

1. Complete the work sheet after entering the account names and balances onto the work sheet. Ignore this step if using CLGL.
2. Journalize the adjusting entries. If using manual working papers, record adjusting entries on journal page 63.

LO 1, 3, 4, 5

PROBLEM 11–5A A portion of Anderson Publishing's work sheet for the year ended December 31 follows:

	A	F	G	H	I
		INCOME STATEMENT		BALANCE SHEET	
	ACCOUNT NAME	DEBIT	CREDIT	DEBIT	CREDIT
7	Cash			100,000.00	
8	Accounts Receivable			114,050.00	
9	Publishing Supplies			1,480.00	
10	Merchandise Inventory			15,000.00	
11	Prepaid Insurance			2,000.00	
12	Publishing Equipment			42,250.00	
13	Accumulated Depreciation, Publishing Equipment				16,900.00
14	Accounts Payable				5,562.00
15	Unearned Subscription Renewals				9,050.00
16	J. Anderson, Capital				218,450.00
17	J. Anderson, Drawing			48,000.00	
18	Magazine Sales		125,000.00		
19	Subscription Renewals		92,000.00		
20	Sales Returns and Allowances	5,425.00			
21	Purchases	65,000.00			
22	Purchases Returns and Allowances		4,500.00		
23	Purchases Discounts		9,000.00		
24	Freight In	7,500.00			
25	Salaries Expense	57,825.00			
26	Rent Expense	9,600.00			
28	Income Summary	16,325.00	15,000.00		
29	Depreciation Expense, Publishing Equipment	8,950.00			
30	Insurance Expense	2,800.00			
31	Salaries Payable				1,113.00
32	Publishing Supplies Expense	370.00			
33		173,795.00	245,500.00	322,780.00	251,075.00

Sheet1 Sheet2 Sheet3

(Continued)

Required

1. Determine the entries that appeared in the Adjustments columns and prepare the general journal entries for the adjustments. If using Working Papers, start on page 120 in the general journal.
2. Determine the net income for the year.
3. What is the amount of ending capital?

Check Figure
Increase in Capital,
$23,705

Problem Set B

LO **3, 4**

PROBLEM 11-1B The trial balance of Jillson Company as of December 31, the end of its current fiscal year, is as follows:

Jillson Company Trial Balance December 31, 20--		
Account Name	**Debit**	**Credit**
Cash	8,463.92	
Merchandise Inventory	47,356.00	
Supplies	1,321.12	
Prepaid Insurance	1,660.00	
Store Equipment	26,580.00	
Accumulated Depreciation, Store Equipment		15,320.00
Accounts Payable		25,578.80
Sales Tax Payable		1,243.36
G. L. Jillson, Capital		75,630.00
G. L. Jillson, Drawing	28,440.00	
Sales		82,026.74
Sales Returns and Allowances	1,542.04	
Purchases	43,348.45	
Purchases Returns and Allowances		1,748.09
Purchases Discounts		1,987.90
Freight In	2,775.00	
Salary Expense	25,758.80	
Rent Expense	15,300.00	
Miscellaneous Expense	989.56	
	203,534.89	203,534.89

Here are the data for the adjustments.

a–b. Merchandise Inventory at December 31, $54,845.00.
  c. Store supplies inventory (on hand), $488.50.
  d. Insurance expired, $680.
  e. Salaries accrued, $692.
  f. Depreciation of store equipment, $3,760.

(Continued)

Check Figure
Net loss, $2,426.74

Required

Complete the work sheet after entering the account names and balances onto the work sheet.

LO   1, 3, 4, 5

PROBLEM 11-2B The balances of the ledger accounts of Pelango Furniture as of December 31, the end of its fiscal year, are as follows:

Cash	$ 12,482
Accounts Receivable	38,962
Merchandise Inventory	118,628
Supplies	1,850
Prepaid Insurance	2,488
Store Equipment	32,824
Accumulated Depreciation, Store Equipment	26,420
Office Equipment	11,236
Accumulated Depreciation, Office Equipment	3,410
Notes Payable	6,000
Accounts Payable	23,420
Unearned Rent	3,150
L. Pelango, Capital	120,532
L. Pelango, Drawing	28,000
Sales	647,090
Sales Returns and Allowances	8,848
Purchases	519,374
Purchases Returns and Allowances	12,440
Purchases Discounts	8,634
Freight In	22,824
Wages Expense	52,800
Interest Expense	780

Data for the adjustments are as follows:

a–b. Merchandise Inventory at December 31, $104,565.
  c. Wages accrued at December 31, $934.
  d. Supplies inventory (on hand) at December 31, $755.
  e. Depreciation of store equipment, $4,982.
  f. Depreciation of office equipment, $1,531.
  g. Insurance expired during the year, $935.
  h. Rent earned, $2,450.

Check Figure
Net income, $42,448

Required

1. Complete the work sheet after entering the account names and balances onto the work sheet. Ignore this step if using CLGL.
2. Journalize the adjusting entries. If using manual working papers, record adjusting entries on journal page 16.

LO   1, 3, 4, 5

PROBLEM 11-3B A portion of the work sheet of Habib Company for the year ended December 31 follows.

(Continued)

	A	F	G	H	I
4					
5		INCOME STATEMENT		BALANCE SHEET	
6	**ACCOUNT NAME**	**DEBIT**	**CREDIT**	**DEBIT**	**CREDIT**
7	Cash			7,736.00	
8	Merchandise Inventory			74,298.00	
9	Supplies			298.00	
10	Prepaid Insurance			250.00	
11	Store Equipment			37,960.00	
12	Accumulated Depreciation, Store Equipment				29,440.00
13	Accounts Payable				13,760.00
14	O. B. Habib, Capital				75,142.00
15	O. B. Habib, Drawing			30,800.00	
16	Sales		171,816.00		
17	Sales Returns and Allowances	1,434.00			
18	Purchases	85,934.00			
19	Purchases Returns and Allowances		964.00		
20	Purchases Discounts		1,636.00		
21	Freight In	2,658.00			
22	Salary Expense	37,852.00			
23	Rent Expense	14,400.00			
24					
25	Income Summary	68,228.00	74,298.00		
26	Depreciation Expense, Store Equipment	4,360.00			
27	Insurance Expense	552.00			
28	Supplies Expense	884.00			
29	Salaries Payable				588.00
30		216,302.00	248,714.00	151,342.00	118,930.00
31					

Sheet1 Sheet2 Sheet3

Required

1. Determine the entries that appeared in the Adjustments columns and present them in general journal form on page 41.
2. Determine the net income for the year.
3. What is the amount of the ending capital?

Check Figure
Increase in capital, $1,612

LO 3, 4, 6

PROBLEM 11-4B The accounts and their balances in the ledger of Markey's Mountain Shop as of December 31, the end of its fiscal year, are as follows:

Cash	$ 12,840
Accounts Receivable	3,242
Merchandise Inventory	137,757
Store Supplies	1,530
Prepaid Insurance	2,845
Land	22,000
Building	86,000
Accumulated Depreciation, Building	36,940
Store Equipment	54,952
Accumulated Depreciation, Store Equipment	13,348
Notes Payable	10,500
Accounts Payable	18,540
Sales Tax Payable	5,706
B. Markey, Capital	171,000
B. Markey, Drawing	52,000
Sales	458,905
Sales Returns and Allowances	7,590
Cost of Goods Sold	265,315
Salary Expense	52,973

(Continued)

Advertising Expense	$ 6,288
Utilities Expense	7,355
Property Tax Expense	800
Miscellaneous Expense	775
Interest Expense	677

Data for the adjustments are as follows. Assume that Markey's Mountain Shop uses the perpetual inventory system.

a. Merchandise Inventory at December 31, $140,357.
b. Store supplies inventory (on hand) at December 31, $540.
c. Depreciation of building, $3,400.
d. Depreciation of store equipment, $3,800.
e. Salaries accrued at December 31, $1,250.
f. Insurance expired during the year, $1,480.

Check Figure
Net income, $108,812

Required

1. Complete the work sheet after entering the account names and balances onto the work sheet. Ignore this step if using CLGL.
2. Journalize the adjusting entries. If using manual working papers, record adjusting entries on journal page 63.

LO   1, 3, 4, 5

PROBLEM 11-5B A portion of Johnson's Farm Supply work sheet for the year ended December 31 follows:

	A	F	G	H	I
4		INCOME STATEMENT		BALANCE SHEET	
5	ACCOUNT NAME	DEBIT	CREDIT	DEBIT	CREDIT
6	Cash			95,000.00	
7	Accounts Receivable			75,250.00	
8	Supplies			750.00	
9	Merchandise Inventory			75,262.00	
10	Prepaid Insurance			400.00	
11	Equipment			96,375.00	
12	Accumulated Depreciation, Equipment				38,550.00
13	Accounts Payable				12,446.00
14	Unearned Revenues				3,600.00
15	V. Johnson, Capital				268,933.75
16	V. Johnson, Drawing			27,250.00	
17	Sales		325,024.00		
18	Sales Returns and Allowances	7,526.20			
19	Purchases	205,576.00			
20	Purchases Returns and Allowances		38,026.00		
21	Purchases Discounts		2,500.00		
22	Freight In	10,836.40			
23	Salaries Expense	62,185.00			
24	Rent Expense	11,400.00			
25					
26	Income Summary	74,852.00	75,262.00		
27	Depreciation Expense, Equipment	19,275.00			
28	Insurance Expense	3,600.00			
29	Salaries Payable				1,195.85
30		395,250.60	440,812.00	370,287.00	324,725.60
31					

Sheet1   Sheet2   Sheet3

Check Figure
Increase in Capital, $18,311.40

Required

1. Determine the entries that appeared in the Adjustments columns and prepare the general journal entries for the adjustments in the general journal, page 19.
2. Determine the net income for the year.
3. What is the amount of the ending capital?

Accounting with qb QuickBooks® Online

Go to the QuickBooks® Online Appendix, Chapter 11, located on the Cengage Learning companion site at Cengage.com. Review *Accounting with QuickBooks® Online* (step-by-step guide to using QuickBooks® Online). *Accounting with QuickBooks® Online* Chapter 11 will introduce you to (1) preparing an adjusting entry for merchandise inventory under the periodic inventory system; (2) preparing adjusting entries for suppliers, insurance, depreciation, and payroll; and (3) preparing an adjusted trial balance.

Activities

Why Does It Matter?

BURT'S BEES, Durham, North Carolina

Burt's Bees describes itself as an "Earth-Friendly, Natural Personal Care Company" that produces products for health, beauty, and personal hygiene. The company manufactures over 197 products distributed in nearly 30,000 retail outlets worldwide. As a merchandising company, Burt's Bees follows its inventory closely. This requires monitoring the receipt, production, purchasing, and planning of inventory. At the end of each time period, Burt's Bees must make adjusting entries to prepare its financial statements accurately. Many of the adjustments are entries you have already learned, such as depreciation, expiration of prepaid expenses, adjustment of supplies used, and recording of accrued expenses. However, merchandising companies also require adjusting entries related to merchandise inventory. Companies such as Burt's Bees monitor inventory, prepare a worksheet, and record adjusting entries using either the perpetual or periodic inventory system. Using your book and/or conducting a brief Internet search to find the differences between perpetual and periodic inventory systems, answer the following questions:

1. What type of inventory system do you think Burt's Bees uses? Why?

2. Using the inventory system you selected in no. 1, what is an example of the type of journal entry Burt's Bees would make when purchasing merchandise on account?

3. Using the inventory system you selected in no. 1, what journal entry would Burt's Bees use to record the sale of merchandise on account?

What Would You Say?

You have a friend who is a seamstress specializing in Renaissance costumes. She receives cash well in advance of the required date, often in the fiscal period prior to the date of delivery of the costume, not only to enable her to purchase material but also to cover her labor. She always debits Cash and credits Costume Income. First, explain to her why this entry violates the revenue recognition principle. Second, identify the classification of Unearned Revenue. Third, explain when the Unearned Revenue account is used.

What Do You Think?

On November 1, an exterior painting company received $5,310 for a paint job that will not be finished for a few months. As of December 31, which is the end of the fiscal period, $2,400 worth of painting will not have been completed. The bookkeeper completed the following entries prior to leaving on vacation:

Cash		Painting Income	
11/1 5,310		12/31 2,400	11/1 5,310

Unearned Painting Income	
	12/31 2,400

The owner wants to get a bank loan by December 1. The bank requires interim financial statements to be submitted as of December 1. How will the bookkeeper's entries affect the accuracy of the interim balance sheet and income statements? What difference will the bookkeeper's methods make in the December 31 balance sheet and income statement?

What Would You Do?

The owner of a motorcycle shop allows his two sons to take motorcycles home to try them out on different types of surfaces because he believes that his sons need to be familiar with the products they sell. Sometimes the motorcycles are not returned to the store by the time the physical count of inventory takes place. Respond to this practice.

What's Wrong with This Picture?

What could happen if a business spent the cash it received in advance for services it promised to perform at a later date?

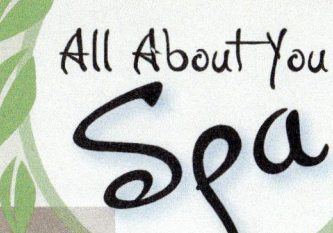

Adjusting Entries

Two months (July and August) have passed since Ms. Valli has seen the financial statements for All About You Spa. It is time to begin their preparation. Several accounts need adjusting. These include the accounts you adjusted in Chapter 4 as well as any accounts involved with merchandising.

CLGL

Adjusting Entry Information

Merchandise Inventory Adjustment (a)

A physical count of inventory was taken, and the inventory was valued at $11,310.

Supplies Adjustments (b) and (c)

A physical count has been taken of the two supplies accounts. The values of the remaining inventories of supplies are as follows:

Office Supplies	$100.00
Spa Supplies	425.00

Prepaid Insurance Adjustment (d)

A review of the insurance records determined that $233.34 in liability insurance coverage had been used during the last two months.

Depreciation Adjustments (e) and (f)

Estimated depreciation amounts for the two equipment accounts are as follows:

Office Equipment	$ 30.00
Spa Equipment	660.54

Wages Expense/Wages Payable Adjustment

There is no need for a Wages Expense/Wages Payable adjustment because the end of the fiscal period did not come in the middle of a pay period.

Required

1. Complete a work sheet (if required by your instructor). Ignore this step if using CLGL.

2. Journalize the adjusting entries in the general journal.
   - If you are preparing the adjusting entries with Working Papers, enter your transactions beginning on page 16.

3. Post the adjusting entries to the general ledger accounts.
   - Ignore this step if you are using CLGL.

4. Prepare an adjusted trial balance as of August 31, 20--.

Check Figures
3. Adjusting entries general journal report total, $12,672.88
4. Adjusted trial balance total, $37,231.226

chapter

12

Financial Statements, Closing Entries, and Reversing Entries

To: **Amy Roberts, CPA**
Subject: **Financial Statements, Working Capital, and Current Ratio**

Hi Amy,
I am talking to my bank about obtaining a line of credit, and the loan officer asked for a classified income statement and balance sheet. Can you explain to me how these are prepared? I was also asked for Whitewater Raft Supply's working capital and current ratio. What are these?
Thanks,
Janie

To: **Janie Conner**
Subject: **RE: Financial Statements, Working Capital, and Current Ratio**
Hi Janie,
A classified income statement and balance sheet is just a more detailed version of the income statement and balance sheet you currently use. The additional breakdown of information will give you and the bank a better idea of your financial position. Here is a list of items that we will need to talk about at our next meeting, so that you will be prepared to meet with the bank. I've also attached a copy of a classified income statement and balance sheet for you to review before our meeting.

_____ 1. Prepare a classified income statement.

_____ 2. Prepare a classified balance sheet.

_____ 3. Compute working capital and current ratio.

Let's get started with these items. Let me know if you have any questions.
Amy

In this chapter, we review how to prepare financial statements directly from a work sheet. We will also look at financial statements in their entirety and explain their various subdivisions. Finally, we will explain the functions of closing entries and reversing entries as means of completing the accounting cycle.

First, here is the chart of accounts for Whitewater Raft Supply.

<table>
<tr><td>

PERIODIC INVENTORY CHART OF ACCOUNTS

Assets (100–199)
111 Cash
112 Notes Receivable
113 Accounts Receivable
114 Merchandise Inventory
115 Supplies
116 Prepaid Insurance
121 Land
122 Building
123 Accumulated Depreciation, Building
124 Equipment
125 Accumulated Depreciation, Equipment

Liabilities (200–299)
211 Notes Payable
212 Accounts Payable
213 Wages Payable
217 Unearned Course Fees
221 Mortgage Payable

Owner's Equity (300–399)
311 J. Conner, Capital
312 J. Conner, Drawing
313 Income Summary

</td><td>

PERPETUAL INVENTORY CHART OF ACCOUNTS

Assets (100–199)
111 Cash
112 Notes Receivable
113 Accounts Receivable
114 Merchandise Inventory
115 Supplies
116 Prepaid Insurance
121 Land
122 Building
123 Accumulated Depreciation, Building
124 Equipment
125 Accumulated Depreciation, Equipment

Liabilities (200–299)
211 Notes Payable
212 Accounts Payable
213 Wages Payable
217 Unearned Course Fees
221 Mortgage Payable

Owner's Equity (300–399)
311 J. Conner, Capital
312 J. Conner, Drawing
313 Income Summary

</td></tr>
</table>

© Digital Vision/Getty Images

PERIODIC INVENTORY CHART OF ACCOUNTS	PERPETUAL INVENTORY CHART OF ACCOUNTS
Revenue (400–499)	**Revenue (400–499)**
411 Sales	411 Sales
412 Sales Returns and Allowances	412 Sales Returns and Allowances
413 Sales Discounts	413 Sales Discounts
421 Course Fees Income	421 Course Fees Income
422 Interest Income	422 Interest Income
Cost of Goods Sold (500–599)	**Cost of Goods Sold (500–599)**
511 Purchases	511 Cost of Goods Sold
512 Purchases Returns and Allowances	
513 Purchases Discounts	**Expenses (600–699)**
514 Freight In	611 Wages Expense
	622 Supplies Expense
Expenses (600–699)	623 Insurance Expense
611 Wages Expense	624 Depreciation Expense, Building
622 Supplies Expense	625 Depreciation Expense, Equipment
623 Insurance Expense	626 Property Tax Expense
624 Depreciation Expense, Building	634 Interest Expense
625 Depreciation Expense, Equipment	
626 Property Tax Expense	
634 Interest Expense	

12-1 THE INCOME STATEMENT

 1 Prepare a classified income statement for a merchandising firm.

Learning Objective

As you know, the work sheet is merely a tool that accountants use to prepare the financial statements. In Figure 1 (on the next page), we present the part of the work sheet for Whitewater Raft Supply that includes the Income Statement columns. Of course, **each of the amounts that appear in the Income Statement columns of the work sheet will be used in the income statement**. Notice that the amounts for the beginning and ending merchandise inventory appear separately on the Income Summary line. Recall that, in Chapter 11, you were asked to pick up the two figures and move them—not to take the difference between the two. Figure 2 (on page 526) shows the entire income statement. Take your time to look it over carefully. Then we will break it down into its components.

The income statement follows a logical pattern that is much the same for any type of merchandising business. The ability to interpret the income statement and extract parts from it is very useful when gathering information for decision making. To realize the full value of an income statement, however, you need to know the basic format of an income statement. Let's look at the statement section by section.

	Net Sales	$254,260
−	Cost of Goods Sold	90,120
	Gross Profit	$164,140
−	Operating Expenses	58,835
	Income from Operations	$105,305

To illustrate the concepts of **gross** and **net**, the following is an example of a simple single-sale transaction.

Figure 1

Partial work sheet for Whitewater Raft Supply

	A	B	C	D	E	H	I
1		Whitewater Raft Supply					
2		Work Sheet					
3		For Month Ended December 31, 20--					
4							
5		TRIAL BALANCE		ADJUSTMENTS		INCOME STATEMENT	
6	ACCOUNT NAME	DEBIT	CREDIT	DEBIT	CREDIT	DEBIT	CREDIT
7	Cash	24,154.00					
8	Notes Receivable	4,000.00					
9	Accounts Receivable	29,546.00					
10	Merchandise Inventory	67,000.00		(b) 64,800.00	(a) 67,000.00		
11	Supplies	1,540.00			(d) 1,125.00		
12	Prepaid Insurance	960.00			(e) 520.00		
13	Land	122,100.00					
14	Building	129,000.00					
15	Accumulated Depreciation, Building		51,000.00		(f) 3,500.00		
16	Equipment	33,100.00					
17	Accumulated Depreciation, Equipment		16,400.00		(g) 4,900.00		
18	Notes Payable		36,600.00				
19	Accounts Payable		3,300.00				
20	Unearned Course Fees		1,200.00	(c) 800.00			
21	Mortgage Payable		7,800.00				
22	J. Conner, Capital		253,774.00				
23	J. Conner, Drawing	77,000.00					
24	Sales		257,180.00				257,180.00
25	Sales Returns and Allowances	940.00				940.00	
26	Sales Discounts	1,980.00				1,980.00	
27	Interest Income		220.00				220.00
28	Purchases	87,840.00				87,840.00	
29	Purchases Returns and Allowances		932.00				932.00
30	Purchases Discounts		1,348.00				1,348.00
31	Freight In	2,360.00				2,360.00	
32	Wages Expense	45,900.00		(h) 1,030.00		46,930.00	
33	Property Tax Expense	1,860.00				1,860.00	
34	Interest Expense	474.00				474.00	
35		629,754.00	629,754.00				
36	Income Summary			(a) 67,000.00	(b) 64,800.00	67,000.00	64,800.00
37	Course Fees Income				(c) 800.00		800.00
38	Supplies Expense			(d) 1,125.00		1,125.00	
39	Insurance Expense			(e) 520.00		520.00	
40	Depreciation Expense, Building			(f) 3,500.00		3,500.00	
41	Depreciation Expense, Equipment			(g) 4,900.00		4,900.00	
42	Wages Payable				(h) 1,030.00		
43				143,675.00	143,675.00	219,429.00	325,280.00
44	Net Income					105,851.00	
45						325,280.00	325,280.00
46							

Sheet1   Sheet2   Sheet3

Several years ago Della Reyes bought an antique table at a secondhand store for $800. She sold the table for $1,850. She advertised it in the daily newspaper at a cost of $73. How much did she make as clear profit?

Sale of Table	$1,850
Less Cost of Table	800
Gross Profit	$1,050
Less Advertising Expense	73
Net Income or Net Profit (gain on the sale)	$ 977

Gross Profit is the profit on the sale of the table before any operating expenses have been deducted; in this case, Gross Profit is $1,050. **Net Income**, or **Net Profit**, is the final or clear profit after all operating expenses have been deducted. In a single-sale situation such as this, we refer to the final outcome as the net profit. But for a business that has many sales and expenses, most accountants prefer the term *net income*. Regardless of which word you use, *net* refers to clear profit—after all expenses have been deducted.

Figure 2

Income statement for
Whitewater Raft Supply

Whitewater Raft Supply
Income Statement
For Year Ended December 31, 20--

Revenue from Sales:			
Sales		$ 257,180	
Less: Sales Returns and Allowances	$ 940		
Sales Discounts	1,980	2,920	
Net Sales			$254,260
Cost of Goods Sold:			
Merchandise Inventory, January 1, 20--		$ 67,000	
Purchases	$87,840		
Less: Purchases Returns and Allowances	$ 932		
Purchases Discounts	1,348	2,280	
Net Purchases		$85,560	
Add Freight In		2,360	
Delivered Cost of Purchases		87,920	
Cost of Goods Available for Sale		$154,920	
Less Merchandise Inventory, December 31, 20--		64,800	
Cost of Goods Sold			90,120
Gross Profit			$164,140
Operating Expenses:			
Wages Expense		$ 46,930	
Supplies Expense		1,125	
Insurance Expense		520	
Depreciation Expense, Building		3,500	
Depreciation Expense, Equipment		4,900	
Property Tax Expense		1,860	
Total Operating Expenses			58,835
Income from Operations			$105,305
Other Income:			
Course Fees Income	$ 800		
Interest Income	220		
Total Other Income	$ 1,020		
Other Expenses:			
Interest Expense	474	546	
Net Income			$105,851

12-1a Revenue from Sales

Now let's look at the Revenue from Sales section of the income statement for Whitewater
Raft Supply:

Revenue from Sales:			
Sales		$ 257,180	
Less: Sales Returns and Allowances	$ 940		
Sales Discounts	1,980	2,920	
Net Sales			$254,260

When we introduced Sales Returns and Allowances and Sales Discounts, we treated them as deductions from Sales. You can see that on the income statement, they are deducted from Sales to give us **Net Sales**. Note that we record these items in the same order in which they appear in the ledger.

> **Remember**
>
> Returns and Allowances (Sales or Purchases) is listed on one line, and Discounts (Sales or Purchases) is listed below.

RATIO ANALYSIS

An important function of accounting is to provide tools for interpreting the financial statements or the results of operations. One ratio that is frequently used to analyze financial statements is *gross profit percentage*.

Southern Office Furniture will serve as our example. (See the comparative income statement below.)

GROSS PROFIT PERCENTAGE

Southern Office Furniture Comparative Income Statement For Years Ended January 31, 2018, and January 31, 2017	2018		2017	
	Amount	Percent	Amount	Percent
Revenue from Sales:				
Sales	$533,600	101 %	$510,000	102%
Less Sales Returns and Allowances	5,600	1	10,000	2
Net Sales	$528,000	100 %	$500,000	100%
Cost of Goods Sold:				
Merchandise Inventory, February 1	$ 46,000	9 %	$ 64,000	13%
Delivered Cost of Purchases	290,000	55	230,000	46
Cost of Goods Available for Sale	$336,000	64 %	$294,000	59%
Less Merchandise Inventory, January 31	58,000	11	46,000	9
Cost of Goods Sold	$278,000	53 %	$248,000	50%
Gross Profit	$250,000	47 %	$252,000	50%
Operating Expenses:				
Sales Salary Expense	$ 63,600	12 %	$ 58,000	12%
Rent Expense	24,000	5	24,000	5
Advertising Expense	21,400	4	16,000	3
Depreciation Expense, Equipment	20,000	4	18,000	4
Insurance Expense	2,000	—	2,000	—
Store Supplies Expense	1,000	—	1,000	—
Miscellaneous Expense	1,000	—	1,000	—
Total Operating Expenses	$133,000	25 %	$120,000	24%
Net Income	$117,000	22 %	$132,000	26%

(Continued)

For each year, net sales is the base (100 percent). All other items on the income statement can be expressed as a percentage of net sales for the particular year involved. For example, let's look at the following percentages:

$$\text{Gross Profit \% (2018)} = \frac{\text{Gross Profit for 2018}}{\text{Net Sales for 2018}} = \frac{\$250,000}{\$528,000} = 0.473 = 47\%$$

$$\text{Gross Profit \% (2017)} = \frac{\text{Gross Profit for 2017}}{\text{Net Sales for 2017}} = \frac{\$252,000}{\$500,000} = 0.504 = 50\%$$

$$\text{Sales Salary Expense \% (2018)} = \frac{\text{Sales Salary Expense for 2018}}{\text{Net Sales for 2018}}$$

$$= \frac{\$63,600}{\$528,000} = 0.120 = 12\%$$

$$\text{Sales Salary Expense \% (2017)} = \frac{\text{Sales Salary Expense for 2017}}{\text{Net Sales for 2017}}$$

$$= \frac{\$58,000}{\$500,000} = 0.116 = 12\%$$

Here's how you might interpret a few of the percentages.

2018
- For every $100 in net sales, gross profit amounted to $47.
- For every $100 in net sales, sales salary expense amounted to $12.
- For every $100 in net sales, net income amounted to $22.

2017
- For every $100 in net sales, gross profit amounted to $50.
- For every $100 in net sales, sales salary expense amounted to $12.
- For every $100 in net sales, net income amounted to $26.

The gross profit percentage declined from 50% in 2017 to 47% in 2018 because the Cost of Goods Sold percentage increased from 50% in 2017 to 53% in 2018.

12-1b Cost of Goods Sold

The section of the income statement that requires the greatest amount of concentration is the Cost of Goods Sold section, where the cost of the goods we sold is computed. We've repeated the section below.

Cost of Goods Sold:			
Merchandise Inventory, January 1, 20--			$ 67,000
Purchases		$87,840	
Less: Purchases Returns and Allowances	$ 932		
Purchases Discounts	1,348	2,280	
Net Purchases		$85,560	
Add Freight In		2,360	
Delivered Cost of Purchases			87,920
Cost of Goods Available for Sale			$154,920
Less Merchandise Inventory, December 31, 20--			64,800
Cost of Goods Sold			90,120

First, let's look closely at the Purchases section.

Purchases		$87,840
Less: Purchases Returns and Allowances	$ 932	
Purchases Discounts	1,348	2,280
Net Purchases		$85,560
Add Freight In		2,360
Delivered Cost of Purchases		87,920

Note the parallel to the Revenue from Sales section. To arrive at **Net Purchases**, we deduct the sum of Purchases Returns and Allowances and Purchases Discounts from Purchases. To complete the Purchases section, we add Freight In to Net Purchases to get **Delivered Cost of Purchases**.

Now let's look at the full Cost of Goods Sold section. You might think of Cost of Goods Sold like this:

Amount we started with (beginning inventory)	$ 67,000
+ Net amount we purchased, including freight charges	87,920
Total amount that could have been sold (available)	$154,920
− Amount left over (ending inventory)	64,800
Cost of the goods that were actually sold	$ 90,120

Here's the Cost of Goods Sold expressed in proper wording.

Merchandise Inventory, January 1, 20--	$ 67,000
+ Delivered Cost of Purchases	87,920
Cost of Goods Available for Sale	$154,920
− Merchandise Inventory, December 31, 20--	64,800
Cost of Goods Sold	$ 90,120

12-1c Operating Expenses

Operating expenses, as the name implies, are the regular expenses of doing business. We list the accounts and their respective balances in the order in which they appear in the ledger.

Many firms use subclassifications of operating expenses, such as the following:

1. **Selling Expenses** Any expenses directly connected with the selling activity:
   - Sales Salary Expense
   - Sales Commissions Expense
   - Advertising Expense
   - Store Supplies Expense
   - Delivery Expense
   - Depreciation Expense, Store Equipment

2. **General Expenses** Any expenses related to the office or administration, or any expense that cannot be directly connected with a selling activity:
   - Office Salary Expense
   - Property Tax Expense
   - Depreciation Expense, Office Equipment
   - Rent Expense
   - Insurance Expense
   - Office Supplies Expense
   - Miscellaneous General Expense

FYI

In preparing the income statement, classifying expense accounts as selling expenses or general expenses is a matter of judgment.

If the Cash Short and Over account has a debit balance (net shortage), the balance is added to and reported as Miscellaneous General Expense. Conversely, if the Cash Short and Over account has a credit balance (net overage), the balance is added to and reported as Miscellaneous Income, which is classified as Other Income.

12-1d Income from Operations

Now let's repeat the skeleton outline:

> Net Sales
> − Cost of Goods Sold
> Gross Profit
> − Operating Expenses
> Income from Operations

If Operating Expenses are the regular, recurring expenses of doing business, Income from Operations should be the regular or recurring income from normal business operations. When you compare the results of operations over a number of years, Income from Operations is the figure to use as a basis for comparison.

12-1e Other Income and Other Expenses

The Other Income classification, as the name implies, includes any revenue account other than Revenue from Sales. We are trying to isolate Sales at the top of the income statement as the major revenue account, so that the Gross Profit figure represents the profit made on the sale of merchandise *only*. Additional accounts that may appear under the heading Other Income are Rent Income (the firm is subletting part of its premises), Interest Income (the firm holds an interest-bearing note or contract), Gain on Disposal of Property and Equipment (the firm makes a profit on the sale of property and equipment), and Miscellaneous Income (the firm has an overage recorded in the Cash Short and Over account).

The classification Other Expenses records various nonoperating expenses, such as Interest Expense or Loss on Disposal of Property and Equipment.

> **Remember**
>
> Net income appears on both the income statement and the statement of owner's equity.

12-1f The Statement of Owner's Equity

Figure 3 is a partial work sheet for Whitewater Raft Supply. Here again we find that **every figure in the Balance Sheet columns of the work sheet is used in the statement of owner's equity or the balance sheet.**

Preparation of the financial statements follows the same order we presented before: first, the income statement; second, the statement of owner's equity; third, the balance sheet. The statement of owner's equity shows why the balance of the Capital account has changed from the beginning of the fiscal period to the end of it. In preparing the statement of owner's equity, always look in the ledger for the owner's Capital account to find any changes, such as additional investments, made during the year.

In Figure 3, we observe the balance of J. Conner, Capital listed on the work sheet as $253,774. We note from the ledger account a credit of $9,000 representing an additional investment. Therefore, the beginning balance of J. Conner, Capital was $244,774 ($253,774 − $9,000).

> **Remember**
>
> The columns on the financial statements *do not* represent debit or credit columns. The columns are for making computations and listing totals.

Figure 3

Partial work sheet for Whitewater Raft Supply

	A	B	C	D	E	J	K
1		Whitewater Raft Supply					
2		Work Sheet					
3		For Month Ended December 31, 20--					
4							
5		TRIAL BALANCE		ADJUSTMENTS		BALANCE SHEET	
6	ACCOUNT NAME	DEBIT	CREDIT	DEBIT	CREDIT	DEBIT	CREDIT
7	Cash	24,154.00				24,154.00	
8	Notes Receivable	4,000.00				4,000.00	
9	Accounts Receivable	29,546.00				29,546.00	
10	Merchandise Inventory	67,000.00		(b) 64,800.00	(a) 67,000.00	64,800.00	
11	Supplies	1,540.00			(d) 1,125.00	415.00	
12	Prepaid Insurance	960.00			(e) 520.00	440.00	
13	Land	122,100.00				122,100.00	
14	Building	129,000.00				129,000.00	
15	Accumulated Depreciation, Building		51,000.00		(f) 3,500.00		54,500.00
16	Equipment	33,100.00				33,100.00	
17	Accumulated Depreciation, Equipment		16,400.00		(g) 4,900.00		21,300.00
18	Notes Payable		36,600.00				36,600.00
19	Accounts Payable		3,300.00				3,300.00
20	Unearned Course Fees		1,200.00	(c) 800.00			400.00
21	Mortgage Payable		7,800.00				7,800.00
22	J. Conner, Capital		253,774.00				253,774.00
23	J. Conner, Drawing	77,000.00				77,000.00	
24	Sales		257,180.00				
25	Sales Returns and Allowances	940.00					
26	Sales Discounts	1,980.00					
27	Interest Income		220.00				
28	Purchases	87,840.00					
29	Purchases Returns and Allowances		932.00				
30	Purchases Discounts		1,348.00				
31	Freight In	2,360.00					
32	Wages Expense	45,900.00		(h) 1,030.00			
33	Property Tax Expense	1,860.00					
34	Interest Expense	474.00					
35		629,754.00	629,754.00				
36	Income Summary			(a) 67,000.00	(b) 64,800.00		
37	Course Fees Income				(c) 800.00		
38	Supplies Expense			(d) 1,125.00			
39	Insurance Expense			(e) 520.00			
40	Depreciation Expense, Building			(f) 3,500.00			
41	Depreciation Expense, Equipment			(g) 4,900.00			
42	Wages Payable				(h) 1,030.00		1,030.00
43				143,675.00	143,675.00	484,555.00	378,704.00
44	Net Income						105,851.00
45						484,555.00	484,555.00
46							

Sheet1 / Sheet2 / Sheet3

Figure 4

Statement of owner's equity for Whitewater Raft Supply

Whitewater Raft Supply
Statement of Owner's Equity
For Year Ended December 31, 20--

J. Conner, Capital, January 1, 20--		$244,774
Investment during the Year	$ 9,000	
Net Income for the Year	105,851	
Subtotal	$114,851	
Less Withdrawals for the Year	77,000	
Increase in Capital		37,851
J. Conner, Capital, December 31, 20--		$282,625

12-2 BALANCE SHEET

Learning Objective

2 Prepare a classified balance sheet for any type of business.

Balance sheet classifications are generally uniform for all types of business enterprises. You are strongly urged to take the time to learn the following definitions of the classifications and the order of accounts within them. As you read, refer to Figure 5.

12-2a Current Assets

Current Assets consist of cash and any other assets or resources that are expected to be realized in cash or to be sold or consumed during the normal operating cycle of the business (or one year if the normal operating cycle is less than 12 months).

Figure 5
Balance sheet for Whitewater Raft Supply

Whitewater Raft Supply
Balance Sheet
December 31, 20--

Assets

Current Assets:			
Cash		$ 24,154	
Notes Receivable		4,000	
Accounts Receivable		29,546	
Merchandise Inventory		64,800	
Supplies		415	
Prepaid Insurance		440	
Total Current Assets			$123,355
Property and Equipment:			
Land		$122,100	
Building	$129,000		
Less Accumulated Depreciation	54,500	74,500	
Equipment	$ 33,100		
Less Accumulated Depreciation	21,300	11,800	
Total Property and Equipment			208,400
Total Assets			$331,755

Liabilities

Current Liabilities:		
Notes Payable	$ 36,600	
Mortgage Payable (current portion)	2,000	
Accounts Payable	3,300	
Wages Payable	1,030	
Unearned Course Fees	400	
Total Current Liabilities		$ 43,330
Long-Term Liabilities:		
Mortgage Payable		5,800
Total Liabilities		$ 49,130

Owner's Equity

J. Conner, Capital	282,625
Total Liabilities and Owner's Equity	$331,755

Accountants list current assets in the order of their convertibility into cash—in other words, their **liquidity**. (If you have an asset, such as a car or a stereo, and you sell it quickly and turn it into cash, you are said to be turning it into a *liquid* state.) If a company has the first four accounts shown under Current Assets in Figure 5, they are presented in the following order: (1) Cash, (2) Notes Receivable, (3) Accounts Receivable, and (4) Merchandise Inventory.

Notes Receivable (current) are short-term (one year or less) promissory notes (promise-to-pay notes) held by the firm. A note is generally received from a customer as a substitute for a charge account.

Prepaid Insurance and Supplies are considered prepaid items that will be used up or will expire within the following operating cycle or year. Generally, these prepaid items are not converted into cash, which is why they appear at the bottom of the Current Assets section.

12-2b Property and Equipment

Property and Equipment are relatively long-lived assets that are held for use in the production or sale of other assets or services. Some accountants refer to them as *fixed assets*. The three types of accounts that usually appear in this category are Land, Building, and Equipment. (Refer to Figure 5.) Note that the Building and Equipment accounts are followed by their respective Accumulated Depreciation accounts. We list these assets in order of their length of life, with the longest-lived asset placed first.

12-2c Current Liabilities

Current Liabilities are debts that will become due within the normal operating cycle of the business, usually within one year. They normally will be paid, when due, from current assets. List current liabilities in the order of their expected payment. Notes Payable represents the amount owed on promissory notes. Mortgage Payable is the payment made to reduce the principal of the mortgage in a given year. Accounts Payable are debts owed to creditors. Wages Payable and any other accrued liabilities, such as Commissions Payable and the current portion of unearned revenue accounts, usually fall at the bottom of the list of current liabilities.

12-2d Long-Term Liabilities

Long-Term Liabilities are debts that are payable over a comparatively long period, usually longer than one year. The current portion of notes, contracts, and loans (the amount of principal due within the next year) is shown as a current liability. The remaining amount is shown as a long-term liability. Note that for Whitewater Raft Supply, $2,000 of the Mortgage Payable represents the current portion and is shown as a current liability. The remaining $5,800 is shown as a long-term liability. (Refer to Figure 5.)

12-3 WORKING CAPITAL AND CURRENT RATIO

Both the management and the short-term creditors of a firm are vitally interested in two questions:

1. Does the firm have a sufficient amount of capital to operate?
2. Does the firm have the ability to pay its debts?

 Compute working capital and current ratio.

Learning Objective

Two measures used to answer these questions are a firm's working capital and its current ratio. The necessary data are taken from a classified balance sheet.

Working capital is determined by subtracting current liabilities from current assets; thus,

$$\text{Working capital} = \text{Current assets} - \text{Current liabilities}$$

The normal operating cycle for most firms is less than one year. Because current assets equal cash—or items that can be converted into cash or used up within one year—and current liabilities equal the total amount the company must pay out within one year, working capital is appropriately named. It is the amount of capital the company has available to use or to work with. The working capital for Whitewater Raft Supply is as follows:

$$\text{Working capital} = \$123,355 - \$43,330 = \$80,025$$

The **current ratio** is useful in revealing a firm's ability to pay its bills. It is determined by dividing current assets by current liabilities.

$$\text{Current ratio} = \frac{\text{Current assets (amount of cash coming in within one year)}}{\text{Current liabilities (amount of cash going out within one year)}}$$

The current ratio for Whitewater Raft Supply is calculated like this:

$$\text{Current ratio} = \frac{\$123,355}{\$43,330} = 2.85$$

In the case of Whitewater Raft Supply, $2.85 in current assets is available to pay every dollar currently due on December 31.

Remember

The current ratio has a weakness. It favors companies with many current assets. However, the current ratio does not attempt to measure the overall strength of a company.

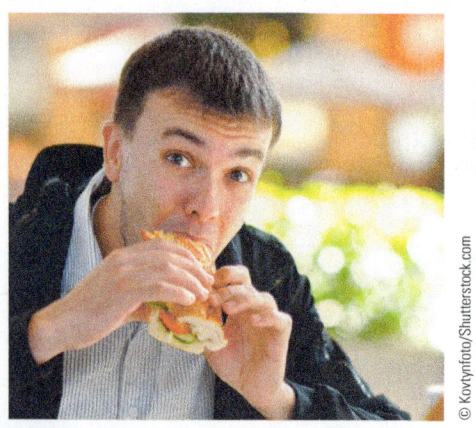

© Koviynfoto/Shutterstock.com

In the Real World

In franchises such as Subway, minimum working capital standards are used to make sure franchisees have adequate financial resources to run their businesses successfully. Each franchise-granting organization has its own financial requirements regarding minimum working capital standards. These standards are typically based on the location of the business and on minimum performance standards.

YOU Make the Call

J. J. Marston owns Woodland Toys, a small business selling handmade wooden toys. Sales have been a bit slow, so he has come up with some strategies to increase sales as well as to begin exporting his specialty toys. The problem is that he needs cash to hire assistants and to purchase several woodworking tools to increase production. He has tried to figure out how he can manage the investment. He has no idea how to analyze his financial statements to provide valuable decision-making information. How would you recommend that he use his most recent balance sheet (shown below) and the two formulas discussed in the chapter to help him decide whether to expand his operation?

Woodland Toys
Balance Sheet
December 31, 20--

Assets		
Current Assets:		
Cash	$22,751	
Accounts Receivable	7,692	
Merchandise Inventory	45,018	
Prepaid Insurance	1,265	
Total Current Assets		$76,726
Property and Equipment:		
Shop Equipment	$18,357	
Less Accumulated Depreciation	6,020	
Total Property and Equipment		12,337
Total Assets		$89,063
Liabilities		
Current Liabilities:		
Accounts Payable	$10,340	
Total Current Liabilities		$10,340
Long-Term Liabilities:		
Mortgage Payable		3,500
Total Liabilities		$13,840
Owner's Equity		
J. J. Marston, Capital		75,223
Total Liabilities and Owner's Equity		$89,063

(Continued)

YOU Make the Call

SOLUTION

While many more tools are available for analyzing financial statements than have been introduced, you have learned two formulas in this chapter that can assist Mr. Marston in determining his ability to expand his business—working capital and current ratio.

Working capital is the amount of capital the company has available to use or to work with. To compute Woodland Toys' working capital, subtract its current liabilities from its current assets:

$$\text{Working capital} = \$76,726 - \$10,340$$
$$= \$66,386$$

While J. J. Marston does not want to liquidate all of his assets, he can see that there is adequate capital to begin planning his business expansion.

A second formula that can help in making the decision to expand is the current ratio. It is useful in revealing a firm's ability to pay its bills. To compute Woodland Toys' current ratio, divide its current assets by its current liabilities.

$$\text{Current ratio} = \frac{\$76,726}{\$10,340} = 7.42$$

This means that $7.42 in current assets is available to pay every dollar of debt currently due on December 31. The higher the current ratio, the better position the company is in to pay short-term debt. A current ratio of 7.42 shows that Woodland Toys is in a very favorable position.

12-3a Chart of Accounts

When we introduced the chart of accounts and the account number arrangement, we said that the first digit represents the classification of an account. Because we are now acquainted with classified income statements and balance sheets, we can introduce the second digit. The second digit stands for the subclassification.

Assets	1--	Revenue	4--
Current Assets	11-	Revenue from Sales	41-
Property and Equipment	12-	Other Income	42-
Liabilities	2--	Cost of Goods Sold	5--
Current Liabilities	21-	Purchases	51-
Long-Term Liabilities	22-	Expenses	6--
Owner's Equity	3--	Selling Expenses	61-
Capital	31-	General Expenses	62-
		Other Expenses	63-

The third digit indicates the placement of the account within the subclassification. For example, account number 411 represents Sales, which is the first account listed under Revenue. Account number 512 represents Purchases Returns and Allowances, which is the second account listed under Cost of Goods Sold. Account number 312 represents Drawing, which is the second account listed under Owner's Equity.

To: **Amy Roberts, CPA**
Subject: **End of the Year**

Hi Amy,

Thanks for sending the examples of a classified income statement and balance sheet. These were very helpful. Now that we are approaching the end of the year, do you have time to discuss the closing entries that I need to do for Whitewater Raft Supply? Are these entries different for a merchandising business?

Janie

To: **Janie Conner**
Subject: **RE: End of the Year**

Hi Janie,

Closing entries for your merchandising business are handled in the same way as the entries you completed for your service business. The closing process involves the same four steps, which include resetting your temporary accounts to a zero balance.

In addition to closing entries, you may also need to do reversing entries. Reversing entries let routine transactions continue to be posted in their usual manner without worrying about how the adjusting entry may interfere. Here's what we'll talk about at our next meeting.

_____ 1. Review closing entries.

_____ 2. Record reversing entries and understand why your company might use them.

Congratulations on wrapping up your first year. Let me know if I can help you with anything else.

Amy

12-4 CLOSING ENTRIES

Now let's look at closing entries for a merchandising business. You follow the same four steps to close, or zero out, the revenue, expense, and Drawing accounts as you do for a service business.

At the end of a fiscal period, you close the revenue and expense accounts so that you can start the next fiscal period with zero balances. You close the Drawing account because it, too, applies to one fiscal period. Recall in Chapter 5 we discussed that these accounts are called **temporary-equity accounts**, or *nominal accounts*.

Figure 6 shows the isolated Income Statement columns. After you have looked them over, we'll discuss at the four steps of the closing procedure.

Figure 6

Partial work sheet for Whitewater Raft Supply

	A	B	C	H	I
1		Whitewater Raft Supply			
2		Work Sheet			
3		For Month Ended December 31, 20--			
4					
5		TRIAL BALANCE		INCOME STATEMENT	
6	ACCOUNT NAME	DEBIT	CREDIT	DEBIT	CREDIT
7	Cash	24,154.00			
8	Notes Receivable	4,000.00			
9	Accounts Receivable	29,546.00			
10	Merchandise Inventory	67,000.00			
11	Supplies	1,540.00			
12	Prepaid Insurance	960.00			
13	Land	122,100.00			
14	Building	129,000.00			
15	Accumulated Depreciation, Building		51,000.00		
16	Equipment	33,100.00			
17	Accumulated Depreciation, Equipment		16,400.00		
18	Notes Payable		36,600.00		
19	Accounts Payable		3,300.00		
20	Unearned Course Fees		1,200.00		
21	Mortgage Payable		7,800.00		
22	J. Conner, Capital		253,774.00		
23	J. Conner, Drawing	77,000.00			
24	Sales		257,180.00		257,180.00
25	Sales Returns and Allowances	940.00		940.00	
26	Sales Discounts	1,980.00		1,980.00	
27	Interest Income		220.00		220.00
28	Purchases	87,840.00		87,840.00	
29	Purchases Returns and Allowances		932.00		932.00
30	Purchases Discounts		1,348.00		1,348.00
31	Freight In	2,360.00		2,360.00	
32	Wages Expense	45,900.00		46,930.00	
33	Property Tax Expense	1,860.00		1,860.00	
34	Interest Expense	474.00		474.00	
35		629,754.00	629,754.00		
36	Income Summary			67,000.00	64,800.00
37	Course Fees Income				800.00
38	Supplies Expense			1,125.00	
39	Insurance Expense			520.00	
40	Depreciation Expense, Building			3,500.00	
41	Depreciation Expense, Equipment			4,900.00	
42	Wages Payable				
43				219,429.00	325,280.00
44	Net Income			105,851.00	
45				325,280.00	325,280.00
46					

12-4a Four Steps in the Closing Procedure

These four steps should be followed when closing:

STEP 1. Close the revenue accounts and the other accounts that appear on the income statement and that have credit balances (all temporary or nominal accounts with credit balances) into Income Summary. **(Debit the figures that are credited in the Income Statement columns of the work sheet, except the figure on the Income Summary line.)** This entry is illustrated for Whitewater Raft Supply as follows:

Date		Description	Post. Ref.	Debit					Credit				
GENERAL JOURNAL									**Page 97**				
20--		Closing Entries											
Dec.	31	Sales		257	1	8	0	00					
		Interest Income			2	2	0	00					
		Purchases Returns and Allowances			9	3	2	00					
		Purchases Discounts		1	3	4	8	00					
		Course Fees Income			8	0	0	00					
		Income Summary							260	4	8	0	00

STEP 2. Close the expense accounts and the other accounts appearing on the income statement that have debit balances (all temporary or nominal accounts with debit balances) into Income Summary. **(Credit the figures that are debited in the Income Statement columns of the work sheet, except the figure on the Income Summary line.)**

Note that you close Purchases Discounts and Purchases Returns and Allowances in Step 1 along with the revenue accounts. Note also that in Step 2, you close Sales Discounts and Sales Returns and Allowances along with the expense accounts.

Date		Description	Post. Ref.	Debit					Credit				
GENERAL JOURNAL									**Page 97**				
Dec.	31	Income Summary		152	4	2	9	00					
		Sales Returns and Allowances								9	4	0	00
		Sales Discounts							1	9	8	0	00
		Purchases							87	8	4	0	00
		Freight In							2	3	6	0	00
		Wages Expense							46	9	3	0	00
		Supplies Expense							1	1	2	5	00
		Property Tax Expense							1	8	6	0	00
		Interest Expense								4	7	4	00
		Insurance Expense								5	2	0	00
		Depreciation Expense, Building							3	5	0	0	00
		Depreciation Expense, Equipment							4	9	0	0	00

STEP 3. Close the Income Summary account into the Capital account, transferring the net income or loss to the Capital account.

GENERAL JOURNAL					Page 97
Date	Description	Post. Ref.	Debit	Credit	
Dec. 31	Income Summary		105 8 5 1 00		
	J. Conner, Capital			105 8 5 1 00	

Here is what the T accounts look like. Note that the Income Summary account already contains adjusting entries for merchandise inventory.

Income Summary

Adj. (Beginning Merchandise Inventory)	67,000	Adj. (Ending Merchandise Inventory)	64,800
Closing (Expenses and other debit balance accounts)	152,429	Closing (Revenue and other credit balance accounts)	260,480
Closing (Net Income)	105,851		

J. Conner, Capital

−	+	
	Bal.	253,774
	Closing (Net Income)	105,851

STEP 4. Close the Drawing account into the Capital account.

GENERAL JOURNAL					Page 97
Date	Description	Post. Ref.	Debit	Credit	
Dec. 31	J. Conner, Capital		77 0 0 0 00		
	J. Conner, Drawing			77 0 0 0 00	

Here is what the T accounts would look like.

J. Conner, Drawing

+		−	
Bal.	77,000	Closing	77,000

J. Conner, Capital

−		+	
Closing (Drawing)	77,000	Bal.	253,774
		Closing (Net Income)	105,851
		Bal.	282,625

12-5 **REVERSING ENTRIES**

Reversing entries are general journal entries that are the exact reverse of certain adjusting entries. A reversing entry enables the accountant to record routine transactions in the usual manner, *even though* an adjusting entry affecting one of the accounts involved in the transaction has intervened. We can understand this concept best by looking at an example.

> **5** Determine which adjusting entries can be reversed and record the reversing entries.
>
> **Learning Objective**

Suppose there is an adjusting entry for accrued wages owed to employees at the end of the fiscal year. Assume that, altogether, the employees of Mason Company earn $400 per day for a five-day week and that payday occurs every Friday throughout the year. When the employees get their checks at 5 p.m. on Friday, the checks include their wages for that day and for the preceding four days. And assume that December 31, the last day of the fiscal year, falls on a Wednesday. A diagram of this situation would look like this:

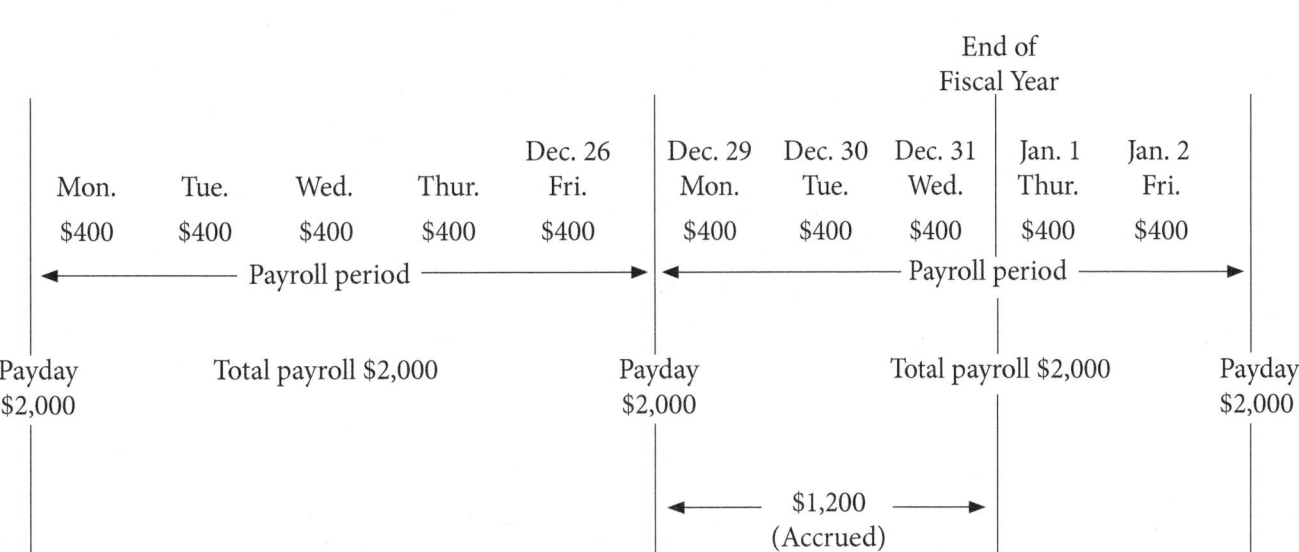

Each Friday during the year, the payroll has been debited to the Wages Expense account and credited to the Cash account. As a result, Wages Expense has a debit balance of $102,000 as of December 26. The year-end adjusting entry, in T account form, would be:

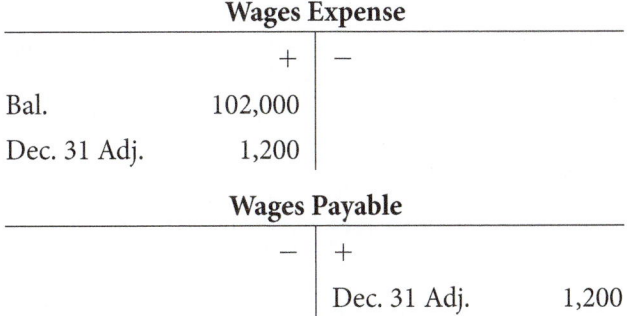

Next, when all of the expense accounts are closed, Wages Expense is closed by crediting it for $103,200. However, Wages Payable continues to have a credit balance of $1,200. The $2,000 payroll on January 2 must be allocated by debiting Wages Payable $1,200, debiting Wages Expense $800, and crediting Cash $2,000.

The employee who records the payroll not only has to record this particular payroll differently from all other weekly payrolls for the year, but also has to refer back to the adjusting entry to determine what portion of the $2,000 is debited to Wages Payable and what portion is debited to Wages Expense. In many companies, however, the employee who records the payroll does not have access to the adjusting entries.

There is a solution to this problem. The need to refer to the earlier entry and allocate the debit total between the two accounts is eliminated *if a reversing entry is made on the first day of the following fiscal period.* You make an entry that is the reverse of the adjusting entry as follows:

		GENERAL JOURNAL			Page 118
Date		Description	Post. Ref.	Debit	Credit
20--		Reversing Entries			
Jan.	1	Wages Payable		1 2 0 0 00	
		Wages Expense			1 2 0 0 00

Now let's bring the T accounts up to date.

Wages Expense

	+	−	
Bal.	102,000		
Dec. 31 Adj.	1,200	Dec. 31 Closing	103,200
Bal.	———	Jan. 1 Reversing	1,200

Wages Payable

	−	+	
Jan. 1 Reversing	1,200	Dec. 31 Adj.	1,200

The reversing entry has the effect of transferring the $1,200 liability from Wages Payable to the credit side of Wages Expense. Wages Expense will temporarily have a credit balance until the next payroll is recorded in the routine manner. In our example, this occurs on January 2 as follows:

Wages Expense

	+	−	
Bal.	102,000		
Dec. 31 Adj.	1,200	Dec. 31 Closing	103,200
Bal.	———		
Jan. 2	2,000	Jan. 1 Reversing	1,200
Bal.	800		

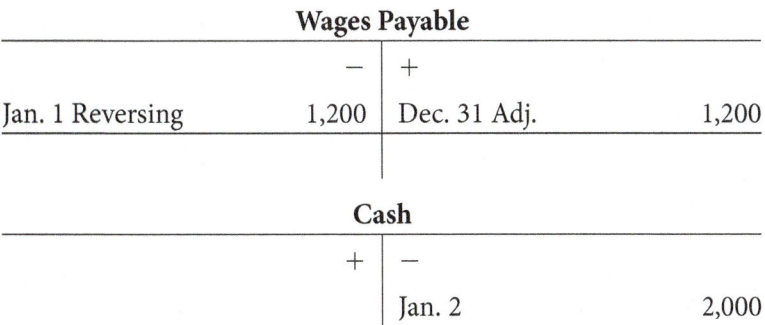

Wages Payable

	–	+	
Jan. 1 Reversing	1,200	Dec. 31 Adj.	1,200

Cash

	+	–	
		Jan. 2	2,000

There is now a *net debit balance* of $800 in Wages Expense, which is the correct amount ($400 for January 1 and $400 for January 2). To see this, look at the following ledger accounts. December 26 was the last payday of one year, and January 2 is the first payday of the next year.

GENERAL LEDGER

ACCOUNT Wages Expense   **ACCOUNT NO.** 611

Date		Item	Post. Ref.	Debit	Credit	Balance Debit	Balance Credit
20--							
Dec.	26		CP16	2 0 0 0 00		102 0 0 0 00	
	31	Adjusting	J116	1 2 0 0 00		103 2 0 0 00	
	31	Closing	J117		103 2 0 0 00	———	———
20--							
Jan.	1	Reversing	J118		1 2 0 0 00		1 2 0 0 00
	2		CP17	2 0 0 0 00		8 0 0 00	

ACCOUNT Wages Payable   **ACCOUNT NO.** 213

Date		Item	Post. Ref.	Debit	Credit	Balance Debit	Balance Credit
20--							
Dec.	31	Adjusting	J116		1 2 0 0 00		1 2 0 0 00
20--							
Jan.	1	Reversing	J118	1 2 0 0 00		———	———

The reversing entry for accrued salaries or wages applies to service as well as merchandising companies. You can see that a reversing entry simply switches an adjusting entry. The question is, Which adjusting entries should be reversed? Here are two handy rules for reversing. **If an adjusting entry is to be reversed, it must meet both of the following qualifications:**

1. **The adjusting entry increases an asset or liability account.**

2. **The asset or liability account did not have a previous balance.**

With the exception of the first year of operations, Merchandise Inventory and contra accounts—such as Accumulated Depreciation—always have previous balances. Consequently, adjusting entries involving these accounts should never be reversed.

Let's apply these rules to the adjusting entries for Whitewater Raft Supply.

Do not reverse: Merchandise Inventory is an asset, but it was decreased and has a previous balance.

Merchandise Inventory				Income Summary			
	+	−		Adj.	67,000		
Bal.	67,000	Adj.	67,000				

Do not reverse: Merchandise Inventory is an asset, but it has a previous balance.

Merchandise Inventory				Income Summary			
	+	−		Adj.	67,000	Adj.	64,800
Bal.	67,000	Adj.	67,000				
Adj.	64,800						

Do not reverse: Unearned Course Fees is a liability, but it was decreased and has a previous balance.

Course Fees Income				Unearned Course Fees			
	−	+			−	+	
		Adj.	800	Adj.	800	Bal.	1,200

Do not reverse: Supplies is an asset account, but it was decreased and has a previous balance.

Supplies				Supplies Expense			
	+	−			+	−	
Bal.	1,540	Adj.	1,125	Adj.	1,125		

Do not reverse: Prepaid Insurance is an asset account, but it was decreased and has a previous balance.

Insurance Expense				Prepaid Insurance			
	+	−			+	−	
Adj.	520			Bal.	960	Adj.	520

Do not reverse: Accumulated Depreciation is a contra asset, and it always has a previous balance after the first year.

Depreciation Expense, Building				Accumulated Depreciation, Building			
	+	−			−	+	
Adj.	3,500					Bal.	51,000
						Adj.	3,500

Do not reverse: Accumulated Depreciation is a contra asset, and it always has a previous balance after the first year.

Depreciation Expense, Equipment				Accumulated Depreciation, Equipment			
	+	−			−	+	
Adj.	4,900					Bal.	16,400
						Adj.	4,900

Reverse: Wages Payable is a liability account. It was increased, and it had no previous balance.

Wages Expense				Wages Payable			
	+	−			−	+	
Bal.	45,900					Adj.	1,030
Adj.	1,030						

Remember

Reversing entries are optional.

Whenever additional adjusting entries are introduced, we make it a point to state whether they can be reversed.

Chapter Review

Study and Practice

 1 Prepare a classified income statement for a merchandising firm.

Learning Objective

The outline of the income statement looks like this:

Revenue from Sales {
Gross Sales
− Sales Returns and Allowances
− Sales Discounts
= **Net Sales**
}

− Cost of Goods Sold {
Beginning Merchandise Inventory
+ Delivered Cost of Purchases {
Gross Purchases
− Purchases Returns and Allowances
− Purchases Discounts
+ Freight In
= Delivered Cost of Purchases
}
= Cost of Goods Available for Sale
− Ending Merchandise Inventory
= Cost of Goods Sold
}

= Gross Profit
− Operating Expenses { **Selling Expenses** / **General Expenses** }

= Income from Operations

+ Other Income {
Interest Income
Rent Income
Gain on Disposal of Property and Equipment
}

− Other Expenses {
Interest Expense
Loss on Disposal of Property and Equipment
}

= Net Income

 PRACTICE EXERCISE 1

Using the following information, prepare the Cost of Goods Sold section of an income statement.

Purchases Discounts	$ 9,000
Merchandise Inventory, December 31	192,000
Purchases	480,000
Merchandise Inventory, January 1	188,000
Purchases Returns and Allowances	16,000
Freight In	27,000

PRACTICE EXERCISE 1 • SOLUTION

Cost of Goods Sold:			
Merchandise Inventory, January 1, 20--			$188,000
Purchases		$480,000	
Less: Purchases Returns and Allowances	$16,000		
Purchases Discounts	9,000	25,000	
Net Purchases		$455,000	
Add Freight In		27,000	
Delivered Cost of Purchases			482,000
Cost of Goods Available for Sale			$670,000
Less Merchandise Inventory, December 31, 20--			192,000
Cost of Goods Sold			478,000

Learning Objective **2** Prepare a classified balance sheet for any type of business.

The outline of the balance sheet looks like this:

Assets

Current Assets (listed in the order of their convertibility into cash; the most liquid asset is listed first)

1. Cash
2. Notes Receivable
3. Accounts Receivable
4. Merchandise Inventory
5. Prepaid items (Supplies; Prepaid Insurance)

Property and Equipment (listed in the order of their length of life; the asset with the longest life is placed first)

1. Land
2. Buildings
3. Equipment

Liabilities

Current Liabilities (listed in the order of their urgency of payment; the most pressing obligation is placed first)

1. Notes Payable
2. Mortgage Payable or Contracts Payable (current portion)
3. Accounts Payable
4. Accrued liabilities (Wages Payable; Commissions Payable)
5. Unearned Revenue

Long-Term Liabilities (Contracts Payable; Mortgage Payable)

Owner's Equity Capital balance at end of the fiscal year

 PRACTICE EXERCISE 2

Identify each of the following items relating to sections of a balance sheet as Current Assets (CA), Property and Equipment (PE), Current Liabilities (CL), Long-Term Liabilities (LTL), or Owner's Equity (OE).

a. Land
b. Unearned Course Fees
c. Merchandise Inventory
d. Cash
e. Salaries Payable

f. Accumulated Depreciation, Building
g. Note Payable (current)
h. Note Payable (due in ten years)
i. F. R. Fred, Capital

PRACTICE EXERCISE 2 • SOLUTION

a. Land, PE
b. Unearned Course Fees, CL
c. Merchandise Inventory, CA
d. Cash, CA
e. Salaries Payable, CL

f. Accumulated Depreciation, Building, PE
g. Note Payable (current), CL
h. Note Payable (due in ten years), LTL
i. F. R. Fred, Capital, OE

 3 Compute working capital and current ratio.

Learning Objective

These two measures help analysts determine whether a firm has enough capital to operate and whether it can pay its debts.

$$\text{Working capital} = \text{Current assets} - \text{Current liabilities}$$

$$\text{Current ratio} = \frac{\text{Current assets}}{\text{Current liabilities}}$$

 ## PRACTICE EXERCISE 3

On December 31, 20--, Laredo Company's balance sheet shows that total current assets equal $450,784 and that total current liabilities equal $435,209. Determine the amount of Laredo Company's working capital and current ratio and explain what these measures mean.

PRACTICE EXERCISE 3 • SOLUTION

$$\text{Working capital} = \$450{,}784 - \$435{,}209 = \$15{,}575$$

$$\text{Current ratio} = \frac{\$450{,}784}{\$435{,}209} = 1.04$$

Laredo Company's working capital shows that it has $15,575 to use or to work with (for example, for expansion or other improvements). Its current ratio shows that the company has $1.04 available to pay for every dollar currently due.

 4 Record the closing entries for a merchandising firm.

Learning Objective

There are four steps in making closing entries for a merchandising business:

STEP 1. Close the revenue accounts and the other accounts that appear on the income statement and that have credit balances (all temporary or nominal accounts with credit balances) into Income Summary.

STEP 2. Close the expense accounts and the other accounts appearing on the income statement that have debit balances (all temporary or nominal accounts with debit balances) into Income Summary.

STEP 3. Close the Income Summary account into the Capital account, transferring the net income or loss to the Capital account.

STEP 4. Close the Drawing account into the Capital account.

 PRACTICE EXERCISE 4

From the following partial work sheet for Glasco Company, journalize the closing entries dated December 31.

	A	B	C	H	I
4					
5		TRIAL BALANCE		INCOME STATEMENT	
6	ACCOUNT NAME	DEBIT	CREDIT	DEBIT	CREDIT
7					
22	O. E. Glasco, Capital		250,800.00		
23	O. E. Glasco, Drawing	77,000.00			
24	Sales		256,150.00		256,150.00
25	Sales Returns and Allowances	960.00		960.00	
26	Sales Discounts	1,860.00		1,860.00	
27	Interest Income		1,230.00		1,230.00
28	Purchases	87,840.00		87,840.00	
29	Purchases Returns and Allowances		922.00		922.00
30	Purchases Discounts		1,348.00		1,348.00
31	Freight In	2,460.00		2,460.00	
32	Wages Expense	45,900.00		46,930.00	
33	Supplies Expense	1,540.00		1,125.00	
34	Property Tax Expense	1,960.00		1,960.00	
35	Interest Expense	344.00		344.00	
36		630,631.00	630,631.00		
37	Income Summary			65,740.00	62,700.00
38	Course Fees Income				730.00
39	Supplies				
40	Insurance Expense			550.00	
41	Depreciation Expense, Building			5,000.00	
42	Depreciation Expense, Equipment			3,400.00	
43	Wages Payable				
44				218,169.00	323,080.00
45	Net Income			104,911.00	
46				323,080.00	323,080.00
47					

Sheet1 / Sheet2 / Sheet3

PRACTICE EXERCISE 4 • SOLUTION

GENERAL JOURNAL Page ___

Date		Description	Post. Ref.	Debit	Credit
20--		Closing Entries			
Dec.	31	Sales		256 1 5 0 00	
		Interest Income		1 2 3 0 00	
		Purchases Returns and Allowances		9 2 2 00	
		Purchases Discounts		1 3 4 8 00	
		Course Fees Income		7 3 0 00	
		Income Summary			260 3 8 0 00
	31	Income Summary		152 4 2 9 00	
		Sales Returns and Allowances			9 6 0 00
		Sales Discounts			1 8 6 0 00
		Purchases			87 8 4 0 00
		Freight In			2 4 6 0 00
		Wages Expense			46 9 3 0 00
		Supplies Expense			1 1 2 5 00
		Property Tax Expense			1 9 6 0 00

	Interest Expense					3 4 4 00		
	Insurance Expense					5 5 0 00		
	Depreciation Expense, Building					5 0 0 0 00		
	Depreciation Expense, Equipment					3 4 0 0 00		
31	Income Summary*		104 9 1 1 00					
	O. E. Glasco, Capital					104 9 1 1 00		
	*($62,700 + $260,380) −							
	($65,740 + $152,429)							
31	O. E. Glasco, Capital		77 0 0 0 00					
	O. E. Glasco, Drawing					77 0 0 0 00		

5 Determine which adjusting entries can be reversed and record the reversing entries.   **Learning Objective**

The use of **reversing entries** is optional. Reverse the adjusting entries that increase asset or liability accounts that do not have previous balances. A contra account, such as Accumulated Depreciation, should not be reversed. Reversing entries are dated as of the first day of the next fiscal period.

PRACTICE EXERCISE 5

From the following T accounts, determine which adjusting entries can be reversed and journalize the reversing entries.

Merchandise Inventory			Income Summary		
+	−		Adj.	68,500	
Bal. 68,500	Adj. 68,500				

Merchandise Inventory			Income Summary		
+	−		Adj.	68,500	Adj. 70,320
Bal. 68,500	Adj. 68,500				
Adj. 70,320					

Course Fees Income			Unearned Course Fees		
−	+		−	+	
	Adj. 800		Adj. 800	Bal. 850	

Supplies			Supplies Expense		
+	−		+	−	
Bal. 1,620	Adj. 735		Adj. 735		

Insurance Expense			Prepaid Insurance		
+	−		+	−	
Adj. 1,620			Bal. 2,110	Adj. 1,620	

(Continued)

Depreciation Expense, Building		
	+	−
Adj.	3,200	

Accumulated Depreciation, Building		
	−	+
		Bal.	46,000
		Adj.	3,200

Depreciation Expense, Equipment		
	+	−
Adj.	4,300	

Accumulated Depreciation, Equipment		
	−	+
		Bal.	21,400
		Adj.	4,300

Wages Expense		
	+	−
Bal.	32,560	
Adj.	2,230	

Wages Payable		
	−	+
		Adj.	2,230

PRACTICE EXERCISE 5 • SOLUTION

GENERAL JOURNAL   Page ___

Date		Description	Post. Ref.	Debit	Credit
20--		Reversing Entries			
Jan.	1	Wages Payable		2 2 3 0 00	
		Wages Expense			2 2 3 0 00

Glossary

Current Assets Cash and any other assets or resources that are expected to be realized in cash or to be sold or consumed during the normal operating cycle of the business (or one year if the normal operating cycle is less than 12 months). (*p. 532*)

Current Liabilities Debts that will become due within the normal operating cycle of a business, usually within one year, and that are normally paid from current assets. (*p. 533*)

Current ratio A firm's current assets divided by its current liabilities. Portrays a firm's short-term debt-paying ability. (*p. 534*)

Delivered Cost of Purchases Net Purchases plus Freight In:

Net Purchases
+ Freight In
Delivered Cost of Purchases (*p. 529*)

General Expenses Expenses incurred in the administration of a business, including office expenses and any expenses that are not completely classified as Selling Expenses or Other Expenses. (*p. 529*)

Gross Profit Net Sales minus Cost of Goods Sold, or profit before deducting operating expenses:

Net Sales
− Cost of Goods Sold
Gross Profit (*p. 525*)

Liquidity The ability of an asset to be quickly turned into cash by selling it or by putting it up as security for a loan. (*p. 533*)

Long-Term Liabilities Debts payable over a comparatively long period, usually more than one year. (*p. 533*)

CHAPTER REVIEW

Net Income or **Net Profit** The final figure on an income statement after all expenses have been deducted from revenues. (*p. 525*)

Net Purchases Purchases minus Purchases Returns and Allowances, minus Purchases Discounts:

Purchases
— Purchases Returns and Allowances
— Purchases Discounts
_____
Net Purchases   (*p. 529*)

Net Sales Sales minus Sales Returns and Allowances, minus Sales Discounts:

Sales
— Sales Returns and Allowances
— Sales Discounts
_____
Net Sales   (*p. 527*)

Notes Receivable (current) Written promises to pay the seller/lender the amount due in a period of less than one year. (*p. 533*)

Property and Equipment Long-lived assets that are held for use in the production or sale of other assets or services; also called *fixed assets*. (*p. 533*)

Reversing entries The reverse of certain adjusting entries, reversing entries are recorded as of the first day of the following fiscal period. The use of reversing entries is optional. (*p. 541*)

Selling Expenses Expenses directly connected with the selling activity, such as salaries of sales staff, advertising expenses, and delivery expenses. (*p. 529*)

Temporary-equity accounts Accounts whose balances apply to one fiscal period only, such as revenues, expenses, and the Drawing account. Temporary-equity accounts are also called *nominal accounts*. (*p. 538*)

Working capital A firm's current assets less its current liabilities. The amount of capital a firm has available to use or to work with during a normal operating cycle. (*p. 534*)

Quiz Yourself

_____ 1. What is the term used for the profit on a sale before any operating expenses have been deducted?
a. Net Income
b. Net Profit
c. Gross Profit
d. Gain on Sale
e. All of the above

_____ 2. Which of the following is *not* an example of a current asset?
a. Cash
b. Merchandising Inventory
c. Prepaid Expenses
d. Equipment
e. Supplies

_____ 3. The data needed to calculate working capital and its current ratio can be found on which of the following?
a. Classified balance sheet
b. Statement of owner's equity
c. Classified income statement
d. Chart of accounts
e. All of the above

_____ 4. What is the third entry of the closing procedure for a merchandising business?
a. Sales to Income Summary
b. Income Summary to Capital
c. Expenses to Income Summary
d. Drawing to Capital
e. Capital to Income Summary

_____ 5. What general journal entry is used to undo a previously made adjusting entry?
a. Adjusting entry
b. Closing entry
c. Special journal entry
d. Correcting entry
e. Reversing entry

Answers: 1.c 2.d 3.a 4.b 5.e

Chapter Assignments

Discussion Questions

1. What is the order for listing accounts in the Current Assets section of the balance sheet?
2. What is the difference between the cost of goods available for sale and the cost of goods sold?
3. What are the basic classifications found on an income statement for a merchandising business as compared to a service business?
4. On a balance sheet, what is the difference between Current Liabilities and Long-Term Liabilities? Give an example of an account in each classification.
5. On an income statement, what is the difference between income from operations and net income? Which is more useful in comparing the results of operations over a number of years?
6. Explain the calculation of net sales and net purchases.
7. In the closing procedure, what happens to (a) Purchases Discounts, (b) Sales Returns and Allowances, (c) Freight In, and (d) Gain on Disposal of Property and Equipment?
8. What are the rules for recognizing whether an adjusting entry should be reversed?
9. What two measures are used to determine whether a firm has sufficient capital to operate and whether the firm has the ability to pay its debts?

Exercises

 1

EXERCISE 12-1 Calculate the missing items in the following:

Practice Exercises 1

	Sales	Sales Returns and Allowances	Net Sales	Beginning Merchandise Inventory	Net Purchases	Cost of Goods Available for Sale	Ending Merchandise Inventory	Cost of Goods Sold	Gross Profit
a.	$242,000	$ 6,000	_____	$152,000	$170,000	_____	$136,000	$186,000	_____
b.	304,000	_____	$297,000	134,000	_____	$404,000	176,000	228,000	_____
c.	_____	10,000	628,000	_____	416,000	486,000	89,000	_____	_____

LO 1

Practice Exercise 1

EXERCISE 12-2 Using the following information, prepare the Cost of Goods Sold section of an income statement.

Purchases Discounts	$ 8,500
Merchandise Inventory, December 31	189,000
Purchases	476,000
Merchandise Inventory, January 1	185,000
Purchases Returns and Allowances	9,000
Freight In	12,000

LO 1

Practice Exercise 1

EXERCISE 12-3 Identify each of the following items relating to sections of an income statement as Revenue from Sales (S), Cost of Goods Sold (CGS), Selling Expenses (SE), General Expenses (GE), Other Income (OI), or Other Expenses (OE).

a. Utilities Expense
b. Advertising Expense
c. Purchases Discounts
d. Sales Returns and Allowances
e. Interest Income
f. Freight In
g. Depreciation Expense, Equipment
h. Interest Expense
i. Rent Expense
j. Sales

LO 1

Practice Exercise 1

EXERCISE 12-4 The Income Statement columns of the August 31 (year-end) work sheet for Ralley Company are shown here. From the information given, prepare an income statement for the company. To save time and space, the expenses have been grouped together into two categories.

	A	H	I
		INCOME STATEMENT	
4			
5		INCOME STATEMENT	
6	ACCOUNT NAME	DEBIT	CREDIT
7			
23	Income Summary	32,000.00	31,000.00
24	Sales		324,000.00
25	Sales Returns and Allowances	13,310.00	
26	Sales Discounts	7,700.00	
27	Purchases	126,360.00	
28	Purchases Returns and Allowances		1,200.00
29	Purchases Discounts		1,300.00
30	Freight In	7,500.00	
31	Selling Expenses	61,560.00	
32	General Expenses	50,884.00	
33		299,314.00	357,500.00
34	Net Income	58,186.00	
35		357,500.00	357,500.00
36			

Sheet1   Sheet2   Sheet3

LO 2

Practice Exercise 2

EXERCISE 12-5 Identify each of the following items relating to sections of a balance sheet as Current Assets (CA), Property and Equipment (PE), Current Liabilities (CL), Long-Term Liabilities (LTL), or Owner's Equity (OE).

a. Accounts Payable
b. Equipment
c. Accounts Receivable
d. Prepaid Insurance
e. Mortgage Payable (current)
f. Office Supplies
g. Mortgage Payable (due in 3 years)
h. Unearned Rent
i B. Marley, Capital
j. Notes Payable (due in 3 months)

LO 3

Practice Exercise 3

EXERCISE 12-6 On December 31, 20--, the following selected accounts and amounts appeared on the balance sheet for Duncan Company. Determine the amount of the working capital and the current ratio. (Round to two decimal places.)

Building	$180,000
Prepaid Insurance	1,800
Merchandise Inventory	85,000
Store Equipment	11,000
Unearned Fees	1,200
Notes Payable (due in six months)	6,000
Accumulated Depreciation, Building	62,000
Accounts Payable	25,000
Land	50,000
Cash	50,000
Store Supplies	1,400
Accumulated Depreciation, Store Equipment	8,000
Notes Receivable (due in four months)	1,500
Mortgage Payable (current portion)	4,400
Salaries Payable	1,600
M. Duncan, Capital	161,500
Mortgage Payable (due in four years)	86,000

EXERCISE 12-7 From the following T accounts, journalize the closing entries dated December 31 for Baylor Company.

Practice Exercise 4

Salary Expense		H. Baylor, Drawing		Purchases Returns and Allowances	
+	−	+	−	−	+
65,000		55,000			8,600

Purchases		Miscellaneous Expense		Rent Expense	
+	−	+	−	+	−
235,600		12,200		22,000	

Sales Returns and Allowances		Freight In		Sales	
+	−	+	−	−	+
7,400		11,200			502,000

Income Summary		H. Baylor, Capital		Purchases Discounts	
87,000	103,000	−	+	−	+
			335,000		4,300

EXERCISE 12-8 From the following information, journalize the last two closing entries and present a statement of owner's equity for Nishimoto Company.

Practice Exercise 4

H. Nishimoto, Capital		
−	+	
	Jan. 1 Bal.	450,000
	Apr. 7	18,000

Income Summary			
Dec. 31 Adj.	190,000	Dec. 31 Adj.	206,000
Dec. 31 Closing	415,000	Dec. 31 Closing	492,000

H. Nishimoto, Drawing		
	+	−
Mar. 1	35,000	
Dec. 9	40,000	

Problem Set A

 LO **1, 4**

PROBLEM 12-1A A partial work sheet for The Fan Shop is presented here. The merchandise inventory at the beginning of the year was $52,300. P. G. Ochoa, the owner, withdrew $30,500 during the year.

	A	H	I
1	The Fan Shop		
2	Work Sheet		
3	For Year Ended December 31, 20--		
4			
5		INCOME STATEMENT	
6	ACCOUNT NAME	DEBIT	CREDIT
7			
24	Sales		324,000.00
25	Sales Returns and Allowances	3,400.00	
26	Sales Discounts	2,707.00	
27	Interest Income		1,830.00
28	Purchases	201,490.00	
29	Purchase Returns and Allowances		2,880.00
30	Freight In	9,790.00	
31	Wages Expense	46,240.00	
32	Rent Expense	12,610.00	
33	Commissions Expense	8,310.00	
34	Supplies Expense	1,842.00	
35	Interest Expense	854.00	
36	Income Summary	52,300.00	54,580.00
37	Insurance Expense	1,240.00	
38	Depreciation Expense, Building	4,600.00	
39	Depreciation Expense, Equipment	2,600.00	
40			
41		347,983.00	383,290.00
42	Net Income	35,307.00	
43		383,290.00	383,290.00
44			

Sheet1   Sheet2   Sheet3

Check Figure
Cost of Goods Sold,
$206,120

Required

1. Prepare an income statement.
2. Journalize the closing entries.

PROBLEM 12-2A Here is the partial work sheet for Eckland Stereo.

	A	J	K
1	Eckland Stereo		
2	Work Sheet		
3	For Year Ended December 31, 20--		
4			
5		BALANCE SHEET	
6	ACCOUNT NAME	DEBIT	CREDIT
7	Cash	14,815.00	
8	Notes Receivable	7,500.00	
9	Accounts Receivable	30,170.00	
10	Merchandise Inventory	50,244.00	
11	Prepaid Property Taxes	2,115.00	
12	Prepaid Insurance	1,640.00	
13	Land	16,700.00	
14	Building	50,000.00	
15	Accumulated Depreciation, Building		15,900.00
16	Computer Equipment	6,892.00	
17	Accumulated Depreciation, Computer Equipment		5,674.00
18	Store Equipment	7,230.00	
19	Accumulated Depreciation, Store Equipment		4,424.00
20	Delivery Equipment	4,300.00	
21	Accumulated Depreciation, Delivery Equipment		3,470.00
22	Notes Payable		5,215.00
23	Accounts Payable		27,140.00
24	Mortgage Payable (current portion)		2,800.00
25	Mortgage Payable		65,200.00
26	M. J. Eckland, Capital		57,314.00
27	M. J. Eckland, Drawing	23,000.00	
28			
41	Wages Payable		1,984.00
42		214,606.00	189,121.00
43	Net Income		25,485.00
44		214,606.00	214,606.00
45			

Sheet1 / Sheet2 / Sheet3

Required
1. Prepare a statement of owner's equity (no additional investment).
2. Prepare a balance sheet.
3. Determine the amount of the working capital.
4. Determine the current ratio (carry to two decimal places).

Check Figure
Working capital, $69,345

PROBLEM 12-3A The following partial work sheet covers the affairs of Masanto and Company for the year ended June 30.

ACCOUNT NAME	INCOME STATEMENT DEBIT	CREDIT	BALANCE SHEET DEBIT	CREDIT
		Masanto and Company		
		Work Sheet		
		For Year Ended June 30, 20--		
Cash			21,034.00	
Accounts Receivable			89,016.00	
Merchandise Inventory			116,400.00	
Prepaid Insurance			3,210.00	
Delivery Equipment			12,400.00	
Accumulated Depreciation, Delivery Equipment				4,600.00
Store Equipment			30,400.00	
Accumulated Depreciation, Store Equipment				8,700.00
Accounts Payable				55,300.00
P. R. Masanto, Capital				172,720.00
P. R. Masanto, Drawing			26,000.00	
Sales		516,000.00		
Purchases	399,101.00			
Purchases Returns and Allowances		9,600.00		
Purchases Discounts		6,800.00		
Freight In	14,000.00			
Salary Expense	46,000.00			
Delivery Equipment Expense	10,600.00			
Supplies Expense	2,700.00			
Miscellaneous Expense	1,459.00			
Income Summary	112,200.00	116,400.00		
Salaries Payable				1,240.00
Insurance Expense	2,840.00			
Depreciation Expense, Delivery Equipment	1,400.00			
Depreciation Expense, Store Equipment	2,600.00			
	592,900.00	648,800.00	298,460.00	242,560.00
Net Income	55,900.00			55,900.00
	648,800.00	648,800.00	298,460.00	298,460.00

Sheet1 / Sheet2 / Sheet3

Check Figure
Reversing entry amount, $1,240

Required
1. Journalize the six adjusting entries.
2. Journalize the closing entries.
3. Journalize the reversing entry as of July 1, for the salaries that were accrued in the June adjusting entry.

PROBLEM 12-4A The following accounts appear in the ledger of Celso and Company as of June 30, the end of this fiscal year.

Cash	$ 15,349
Accounts Receivable	13,810
Merchandise Inventory	50,280
Store Supplies	1,935
Prepaid Insurance	1,385
Store Equipment	18,640
Accumulated Depreciation, Store Equipment	6,882
Accounts Payable	10,065
B. E. Celso, Capital	96,524
B. E. Celso, Drawing	30,000
Sales	208,030
Sales Returns and Allowances	1,740
Purchases	133,050
Purchases Returns and Allowances	4,295

(Continued)

Purchases Discounts	$ 3,853
Freight In	8,350
Wages Expense	35,400
Advertising Expense	7,710
Rent Expense	12,000

The data needed for the adjustments on June 30 are as follows:

a–b. Merchandise inventory, June 30, $54,600.
 c. Insurance expired for the year, $475.
 d. Depreciation for the year, $4,380.
 e. Accrued wages on June 30, $1,492.
 f. Supplies on hand at the end of the year, $100.

Required

1. Prepare a work sheet for the fiscal year ended June 30. Ignore this step if using CLGL.
2. Prepare an income statement.
3. Prepare a statement of owner's equity. No additional investments were made during the year.
4. Prepare a balance sheet.
5. Journalize the adjusting entries.
6. Journalize the closing entries.
7. Journalize the reversing entry as of July 1, for the wages that were accrued in the June adjusting entry.

Check Figure
Net income, $14,066

Problem Set B

PROBLEM 12-1B A partial work sheet for McKnight Music Store is presented here. The merchandise inventory at the beginning of the fiscal period was $48,473. W. J. McKnight, the owner, withdrew $40,000 during the year.

LO 1, 4

	A	H	I
1	McKnight Music Store		
2	Work Sheet		
3	For Year Ended December 31, 20--		
4			
5		INCOME STATEMENT	
6	ACCOUNT NAME	DEBIT	CREDIT
7			
24	Sales		315,483.00
25	Sales Returns and Allowances	4,348.00	
26	Sales Discounts	1,817.00	
27	Interest Income		925.00
28	Purchases	185,272.00	
29	Purchases Returns and Allowances		1,547.00
30	Freight In	9,173.00	
31	Wages Expense	40,615.00	
32	Rent Expense	10,840.00	
33	Commissions Expense	8,220.00	
34	Supplies Expense	1,826.00	
35	Interest Expense	1,258.00	
36	Income Summary	48,473.00	48,850.00
37	Insurance Expense	2,624.00	
38	Depreciation Expense, Building	4,220.00	
39	Depreciation Expense, Equipment	4,500.00	
40			
41		323,186.00	366,805.00
42	Net Income	43,619.00	
43		366,805.00	366,805.00
44			

Sheet1 Sheet2 Sheet3

(Continued)

Check Figure
Cost of Goods Sold,
$192,521

Required

1. Prepare an income statement.
2. Journalize the closing entries.

 2, 3 ....

PROBLEM 12-2B Here is the partial work sheet for Meyer Mountain Shop.

	A	J	K	
1	Meyer Mountain Shop			
2	Work Sheet			
3	For Year Ended December 31, 20--			
4				
5		**BALANCE SHEET**		
6	ACCOUNT NAME	DEBIT	CREDIT	
7	Cash	18,525.00		
8	Notes Receivable	4,500.00		
9	Accounts Receivable	22,680.00		
10	Merchandise Inventory	53,542.00		
11	Prepaid Property Taxes	1,820.00		
12	Prepaid Insurance	2,450.00		
13	Land	18,600.00		
14	Building	42,000.00		
15	Accumulated Depreciation, Building		22,500.00	
16	Computer Equipment	4,424.00		
17	Accumulated Depreciation, Computer Equipment		2,250.00	
18	Store Equipment	7,480.00		
19	Accumulated Depreciation, Store Equipment		5,085.00	
20	Delivery Equipment	5,740.00		
21	Accumulated Depreciation, Delivery Equipment		3,225.00	
22	Notes Payable		6,500.00	
23	Accounts Payable		19,455.00	
24	Mortgage Payable (current portion)		2,500.00	
25	Mortgage Payable		54,600.00	
26	M. E. Meyer, Capital		75,085.00	
27	M. E. Meyer, Drawing	35,250.00		
28				
41	Wages Payable		1,460.00	
42		217,011.00	192,660.00	
43	Net Income		24,351.00	
44		217,011.00	217,011.00	
45				

Sheet1 / Sheet2 / Sheet3

Check Figure
Working capital, $73,602

Required

1. Prepare a statement of owner's equity (no additional investment).
2. Prepare a balance sheet.
3. Determine the amount of the working capital.
4. Determine the current ratio (carry to two decimal places).

LO **4, 5**

PROBLEM 12-3B The following partial work sheet covers the affairs of Ketcher and Company for the year ended June 30.

	A	H	I	J	K	
1		Ketcher and Company				
2		Work Sheet				
3		For Year Ended June 30, 20--				
4						
5		INCOME STATEMENT		BALANCE SHEET		
6	ACCOUNT NAME	DEBIT	CREDIT	DEBIT	CREDIT	
7	Cash			37,302.00		
8	Accounts Receivable			97,557.00		
9	Merchandise Inventory			117,274.00		
10	Prepaid Insurance			2,410.00		
11	Delivery Equipment			12,700.00		
12	Accumulated Depreciation, Delivery Equipment				6,240.00	
13	Store Equipment			35,900.00		
14	Accumulated Depreciation, Store Equipment				10,480.00	
15	Accounts Payable				77,328.00	
16	J. Ketcher, Capital				193,810.00	
17	J. Ketcher, Drawing			40,350.00		
18	Sales		532,262.00			
19	Purchases	397,830.00				
20	Purchases Returns and Allowances		8,817.00			
21	Purchases Discounts		6,935.00			
22	Freight In	23,400.00				
23	Salary Expense	54,700.00				
24	Delivery Equipment Expense	9,492.00				
25	Supplies Expense	2,416.00				
26	Miscellaneous Expense	1,800.00				
27						
28	Income Summary	113,202.00	117,274.00			
29	Salaries Payable				1,645.00	
30	Insurance Expense	2,940.00				
31	Depreciation Expense, Delivery Equipment	2,800.00				
32	Depreciation Expense, Store Equipment	2,718.00				
33		611,298.00	665,288.00	343,493.00	289,503.00	
34	Net Income	53,990.00			53,990.00	
35		665,288.00	665,288.00	343,493.00	343,493.00	
36						

Sheet1 / Sheet2 / Sheet3

Required

1. Journalize the six adjusting entries.
2. Journalize the closing entries.
3. Journalize the reversing entry as of July 1, for the salaries that were accrued in the June adjusting entry.

Check Figure
Reversing entry amount, $1,645

LO **1, 2, 4, 5**

CLGL

PROBLEM 12-4B The following accounts appear in the ledger of Sheldon Company on January 31, the end of this fiscal year.

Cash	$ 16,400
Accounts Receivable	15,100
Merchandise Inventory	55,500
Store Supplies	1,603
Prepaid Insurance	3,080
Store Equipment	24,900
Accumulated Depreciation, Store Equipment	3,860
Accounts Payable	14,400
M. E. Sheldon, Capital	126,484
M. E. Sheldon, Drawing	36,000

(Continued)

Sales	227,000
Sales Returns and Allowances	2,000
Purchases	172,000
Purchases Returns and Allowances	2,375
Purchases Discounts	$ 3,567
Freight In	7,491
Wages Expense	24,800
Advertising Expense	5,912
Rent Expense	12,900

The data needed for adjustments on January 31 are as follows:

a–b. Merchandise inventory, January 31, $55,750.

   c. Insurance expired for the year, $1,285.

   d. Depreciation for the year, $5,482.

   e. Accrued wages on January 31, $1,556.

   f. Supplies used during the year $1,503.

Check Figure
Net loss, $1,737

Required

1. Prepare a work sheet for the fiscal year ended January 31. Ignore this step if using QuickBooks or general ledger.
2. Prepare an income statement.
3. Prepare a statement of owner's equity. No additional investments were made during the year. Ignore this step if using CLGL.
4. Prepare a balance sheet.
5. Journalize the adjusting entries.
6. Journalize the closing entries.

Accounting with ⓺ QuickBooks® Online

Go to the QuickBooks Online Appendix, Chapter 12, located on the Cengage Learning companion site at Cengage.com. Review *Accounting with QuickBooks Online* (step-by-step guide to using QuickBooks Online). *Accounting with QuickBooks Online* Chapter 12 will introduce you to (1) preparing reversing entries for specific adjusting journal entries; (2) preparing, customizing, and saving a comparative income statement for a merchandising firm; (3) preparing, customizing, and saving an income statement for a merchandising firm; (4) preparing, customizing, and saving a comparative balance sheet for a merchandising firm; (5) preparing, customizing, and saving a balance sheet for a merchandising firm; (6) preparing, customizing, and saving a statement of cash flows for a merchandising firm; (7) preparing, customizing, and saving summary aging reports for accounts receivable and accounts payable; and (8) performing an analysis of financial statements and reports.

Activities

Why Does It Matter?

COSTCO WHOLESALE CORPORATION, Issaquah, Washington

Costco is the largest chain of membership warehouse clubs in the world, based on sales volume, and it is the fifth largest general retailer in the United States. Costco focuses on selling products at low prices, often at a very high volume. These goods are usually bulk-packaged and marketed primarily to large families and businesses. Costco became the first company to grow from zero to $3 billion in sales in less than six years. In a recent fiscal year, Costco's sales totaled $116 billion, a 2 percent increase from 2015, and its net income reached $2.35 billion, an 1 percent decrease from 2015. This information, and much more, can be derived from the financial statements that merchandising firms such as Costco prepare on a regular basis to provide shareholders and other interested parties information about the company's activities and financial performance.

1. What type of information would a classified income statement provide to shareholders and other interested parties?

2. What type of information would a classified balance sheet provide to shareholders and other interested parties? Why would this information be important for calculating the working capital and the current ratio, for example?

What Would You Say?

A music store sells new instruments. The store also sells used instruments for people who are willing to give the store part of the sales price. The sales of used instruments, called commissions, amount to about one-fourth of total sales. On the firm's classified income statement under the Revenue heading are both New Instrument Sales and Sales Commissions. Comment on this practice.

What Do You Think?

You are an owner/bookkeeper in a country whose economy has been nearly destroyed. Goods are scarce. In fact, you have no goods to sell at the start of each day. You go out early each morning to purchase goods and haul them back to sell. At the end of the day, you have sold everything. Prepare a Cost of Goods Sold section for a day when you purchased $400 in goods. What conclusion can you draw?

What Would You Do?

Marty is an accountant. Sometimes printouts of financial statements contain errors, making the financial statements unusable. Marty doesn't like to waste anything, so he takes the unusable financial statements to his son's day care center to use for drawing paper. Explain why you think this is or is not unethical behavior.

What's Wrong with This Picture?

What if the freight charges on a new desk for the owner were journalized and posted to the Freight In account? Would this affect the Cost of Goods Sold section? If so, how?

Before a Test Check: Chapters 11–12

PART I: Completion

1. An actual count of a stock of goods is called a(n) _____.

2. Under the _____ system, entries to record the purchase of merchandise are recorded in the Merchandise Inventory account.

3. Unearned revenue is classified as a(n) _____.

4. Under the periodic inventory system, the first adjustment is to debit _____ for the amount of the beginning inventory.

5. Under the perpetual inventory system, after recording the sale of the goods, the accountant debits _____ and credits _____.

6. An increase in Rent Expense results in a(n) _____ to net income.

7. Gross Profit is calculated by subtracting _____ from Net Sales.

8. Current Assets minus Current Liabilities equals _____.

9. Gross Profit minus Total Operating Expenses equals _____.

10. Net Purchases plus _____ equals Delivered Cost of Purchases.

PART II: True/False

T F 1. The second adjustment for Merchandise Inventory under the periodic inventory system is to debit Cost of Goods Sold and credit Merchandise Inventory.

T F 2. Unearned Rent Income is classified as a revenue.

T F 3. The perpetual inventory system requires that each sale of goods has two entries: one to reduce inventory and affix the cost of the goods sold and one to record the sale.

T F 4. The periodic inventory system requires two adjusting entries: one to remove the old inventory amount and one to enter the latest inventory amount.

T F 5. The adjustment to unearned revenue allows the correct amount of liability and revenue to be applied to each fiscal period involved.

T F 6. Freight In is classified in the Operating Expenses section of an income statement.

T F 7. Under the perpetual inventory system, the cost of goods sold is calculated by subtracting ending inventory from the cost of goods available for sale.

T F 8. Reversing entries are optional, and only some adjusting entries are reversed.

T F 9. Delivery Expense is added to Net Purchases to arrive at Delivered Cost of Purchases.

T F 10. Purchases Returns and Allowances increases Income from Operations.

PART III: Application

1. Alphonse Company uses the periodic inventory system. Employees have just taken a physical count of its inventory. This ending inventory has been valued at $136,000. The company's accounting records show the Merchandise Inventory account with a debit balance of $132,000. Journalize the entries on December 31 to adjust the records for this situation.

2. Regletto Company uses the perpetual inventory system. Employees have just taken a physical count of its inventory. This ending inventory has been valued at $146,000. The company's accounting records show the Merchandise Inventory account with a debit balance of $148,000. Journalize the entry on December 31 to adjust the records for this situation.

3. On December 1, Wesley Company collected $20,000 for a remodeling job that will be completed on March 31 of the following year. The revenue will be earned evenly over four months. Wesley Company's fiscal period ends December 31. Journalize the entries to record the collection of the cash and the year-end adjustment to reflect the amount of revenue earned in December.

4. Yorkland Company has total assets of $250,000, of which noncurrent assets amount to $140,000. The company also has total liabilities of $130,000, of which $80,000 are long-term liabilities. Calculate (a) working capital and (b) current ratio.

Answers: Part I

1. physical inventory   2. perpetual inventory   3. current liability   4. Income Summary   5. Cost of Goods Sold; Merchandise Inventory   6. decrease   7. Cost of Goods Sold   8. Working Capital   9. Income from Operations   10. Freight In

Answers: Part II

1. F   2. F   3. T   4. T   5. T   6. F   7. F   8. T   9. F   10. T

Answers: Part III

1.

GENERAL JOURNAL				Page ___	
Date		Description	Post. Ref.	Debit	Credit
20--		Adjusting Entries			
Dec.	31	Income Summary		132 0 0 0 00	
		Merchandise Inventory			132 0 0 0 00
	31	Merchandise Inventory		136 0 0 0 00	
		Income Summary			136 0 0 0 00

2.

GENERAL JOURNAL				Page ___	
Date		Description	Post. Ref.	Debit	Credit
20--		Adjusting Entries			
Dec.	31	Cost of Goods Sold		2 0 0 0 00	
		Merchandise Inventory			2 0 0 0 00

3.

						GENERAL JOURNAL												Page ___	
Date			Description		Post. Ref.		Debit						Credit					
20--																		
Dec.	1	Cash				20	0	0	0	00							
		Unearned Revenue									20	0	0	0	00		
		To record collection of cash for a															
		four-month job.															
		Adjusting Entry															
	31	Unearned Revenue				5	0	0	0	00							
		Remodeling Revenue									5	0	0	0	00		
		To record one month's revenue															
		earned.															

4. a. $250,000 total assets – $140,000 noncurrent assets = $110,000 current assets

$130,000 total liabilities – $80,000 long-term liabilities = $50,000 current liabilities

$110,000 current assets – $50,000 current liabilities = $60,000 working capital

b. $\dfrac{\$110,000 \text{ current assets}}{\$50,000 \text{ current liabilities}} = 2.20$ current ratio

Comprehensive Review Problem

You are to record transactions completed by Fabulous Furnishings during February of this year. Beginning balances for the accounts listed below have been provided in your Working Papers. This company is located in Dallas, TX. To gain practice in completing the steps in the accounting cycle, assume that the fiscal period consists of one month.

CHART OF ACCOUNTS

Assets (100–199)
111 Cash
112 Petty Cash Fund
113 Accounts Receivable
114 Merchandise Inventory
116 Supplies

118 Prepaid Insurance
122 Equipment
123 Accumulated Depreciation, Equipment

Liabilities (200–231)

221 Accounts Payable
226 Employees' Income Tax Payable
227 FICA Social Security Tax Payable
228 FICA Medicare Tax Payable
229 State Unemployment Tax Payable
230 Federal Unemployment Tax Payable
231 Salaries Payable

Owner's Equity (300–399)

311 M. L. Langdon, Capital
312 M. L. Langdon, Drawing
313 Income Summary

Revenue (400–499)

411 Sales
412 Sales Returns and Allowances

Cost of Goods Sold (500–599)

511 Purchases
512 Purchases Returns and Allowances
513 Purchases Discounts
514 Freight In

Expenses (600–699)

611 Salaries Expense
612 Payroll Tax Expense
613 Rent Expense
614 Utilities Expense
616 Supplies Expense
617 Insurance Expense
618 Depreciation Expense, Equipment
619 Miscellaneous Expense

JOURNALS

Sales Journal, page 65
Purchases Journal, page 65
Cash Receipts Journal, page 66
Cash Payments Journal, page 67
General Journal, pages 68–71

*If using Working Papers, reference the journal page numbers listed above.

ACCOUNTS RECEIVABLE

Fashion Decor
Hotel Beritz
Jason and Waldon

ACCOUNTS PAYABLE

Brandon, Inc.
Kingston Fabrics
Magnuson Textiles
Tyson Manufacturing Company

TRANSACTIONS

The following transactions were completed during February of this year.

Fabulous Furnishings does not track cash sales by customer. If you are using CLGL, select "Cash Sales" as the customer for all cash sales transactions.

Feb. 1 Reversed the adjusting entry for accrued salaries, $620.
1 Sold merchandise on account to Hotel Beritz, $12,520.86, invoice no. 5221.
2 Issued Ck. No. 7216, $16,593.46, to Kingston Fabrics, in payment of its invoice no. D1739 for $16,932.10 less 2 percent discount.
5 Bought merchandise on account from Magnuson Textiles, $4,874.80, invoice no. RE275, dated February 2; terms 1/10, n/30; FOB Louisville; freight prepaid and added to the invoice, $158.

(Continued)

Feb. 5   Received an electric bill and paid Countywide Power, Ck. No. 7217, $358.

6   Received check from Jason and Waldon, $10,780.51, in payment of account.

7   Issued Ck. No. 7218, $9,684.18, to Magnuson Textiles, in payment of its invoice no. RE64 for $9,782 less 1 percent discount.

9   Cash sales for February 1 through February 9, $9,745.40.

12   Recorded the payroll in the payroll register for regular biweekly salaries for period ended February 12. Salaries: R. W. Harris, $2,840; T. L. Newkirk, $2,374. Income tax withholdings are $287 for Harris and $216 for Newkirk. Assume the following tax rates and taxable earnings limits (see the payroll register for beginning cumulative earnings in your Working Papers. This information is also provided in CengageNow, or CLGL.):
- Social Security taxable earnings, $118,500, with a rate of 6.2 percent for employees and 6.2 percent for employers.
- Medicare taxable earnings, all earnings, with a rate of 1.45 percent (for both employees and employers).

12   Recorded the payroll entry, crediting Salaries Payable.

12   Issued Ck. No. 7219, $2,335.74, to R. W. Harris. Issued Ck. No. 7220, $1,976.39, to T. L. Newkirk.

12   Recorded payroll taxes. Assume the following tax rates and taxable earnings:
- Federal unemployment taxable earnings, $7,000, with a rate of 0.6 percent.
- State unemployment taxable earnings, $7,000, with a rate of 5.4 percent.

12   Received a credit memo from Magnuson Textiles for defective merchandise, $692, credit memo no. 916.

14   Issued Ck. No. 7221, $2,900.80, to Mid-State Bank for monthly deposit of January employees' federal income tax withheld, $1,285, FICA Social Security tax, $1,309.54 and FICA Medicare tax, $306.26.

14   Sold merchandise on account to Jason and Waldon, $15,781.30, invoice no. 5222.

14   Issued Ck. No. 7222, $4,298.97, to Magnuson Textiles, in payment of its invoice no. RE275 less the credit memo for defective merchandise and less the discount.

18   Bought merchandise on account from Brandon, Inc., $21,375.20, invoice no. 164M, dated February 14; terms 2/10, n/30; FOB Miami; freight prepaid and added to the invoice, $1,242.

18   Cash sales for February 10 through February 18, $7,889.24.

19   Issued Ck. No. 7223 payable to Quicker Printing for invoice forms, $336 (not previously recorded).

19   Received check from Fashion Decor, $4,830.65, in payment of account.

22   Issued Ck. No. 7224, $12,540, to Tyson Manufacturing Company, in payment of its invoice no. 9264D.

22   Sold merchandise on account to Fashion Decor, $17,435.32, invoice no. 5223.

24   Issued credit memo no. 214 to Fashion Decor, $185, for merchandise returned.

24   Bought merchandise on account from Kingston Fabrics, $16,536.90, invoice no. D1797, dated February 22; terms 2/10, n/30; FOB Dallas.

26   Recorded the payroll in the payroll register for regular biweekly salaries for period ended February 26. Salaries: R. W. Harris, $2,840; T. L. Newkirk, $2,374. Income tax withholdings are $287 for Harris and $216 for Newkirk. Note: See the entry of February 12 for taxable earnings limits and tax rates. See the payroll register for this payroll's beginning cumulative earnings.

(Continued)

Feb. 26 Recorded the payroll entry, crediting Salaries Payable.

26 Issued Ck. No. 7225, $2,335.74, to R. W. Harris. Issued Ck. No. 7226, $1,976.39, to T. L. Newkirk. Use two lines and debit Salaries Payable.

26 Ck. No. 7227 voided.

26 Recorded payroll taxes. Assume the following tax rates and taxable earnings:
- Federal unemployment taxable earnings, $7,000, with a rate of 0.6 percent.
- State unemployment taxable earnings, $7,000, with a rate of 5.4 percent.

27 Issued Ck. No. 7228, $1,035, to JIT Freight Line for transportation charge on merchandise purchased from Kingston Fabrics.

28 Issued Ck. No. 7229, $155.60, payable to Cash to reimburse the petty cash fund. Petty cash payments consist of Supplies, $130.24, and Miscellaneous Expense, $25.36.

28 Cash sales for February 19 through February 28, $8,986.60.

28 Issued Ck. No. 7230, $2,290, to Global Rental Agency for monthly rent.

28 M. L. Langdon (owner) withdrew $5,000 for personal use, Ck. No. 7231.

Required

1. Journalize and post the transactions completed during February, using either a general journal or special journals or both. (Your instructor will assign you which one(s) to use.)

   General Journal. Ignore this section if using CLGL.
   a. Post daily all entries involving customer accounts to the accounts receivable ledger.
   b. Post daily all entries involving creditor accounts to the accounts payable ledger.
   c. Post daily the general journal entries to the general ledger.

   Special Journals. Ignore this section if using CLGL.
   a. Post daily the amounts in the Other Accounts columns of the special journals.
   b. Post daily the general journal.
   c. Post the totals of the special columns of the special journals at the end of the month.

2. Prepare a schedule of accounts receivable and a schedule of accounts payable.

3. Complete the work sheet for February. Ignore this step if using CLGL.
   Data for the month-end adjustments are as follows:
   a–b. Merchandise inventory at February 28, $45,484.
   c. Salaries accrued at February 28, $2,084.
   d. Insurance expired during February, $210.
   e. Depreciation of equipment during February, $1,885.
   f. Supplies on hand, $100.

4. Journalize the adjusting entries. If using manual Working Papers, post the adjusting entries to the general ledger.

5. Prepare an income statement.

6. Prepare a statement of owner's equity. (No additional investment was made during the month.)

7. Prepare a balance sheet.

8. Journalize the closing entries. If using manual Working Papers, post to the general ledger.

9. Prepare a post-closing trial balance.

All About You Spa

Closing Entries and Financial Statements

CLGL

It is now August 31. You have journalized and posted the adjustments in the All About You Spa accounting records, and Ms. Valli wants to see financial statements for the last two months (July and August). Then she would like you to prepare the closing entries.

Required

1. Prepare an income statement for the two months ended August 31, 20--.

2. Prepare a statement of owner's equity for the two months ended August 31, 20--. Ignore this step if using QuickBooks.

3. Prepare a balance sheet as of August 31, 20--.

4. Journalize the closing entries in the general journal.
   - If you are preparing the closing entries using Working Papers, enter your transactions beginning on page 5.

5. Post the closing entries to the general ledger accounts.
   - Ignore this step if you are using QuickBooks or CLGL.

6. Prepare a post-closing trial balance as of August 31, 20--.

Congratulations! You have completed your work with All About You Spa.

Check Figures
1. Net income, $15,314.18
2. A. Valli, Capital (end of period), $67,085.93
3. Balance Sheet report total assets, $83,081.33
5. Post-closing trial balance total, $83,935.12

Try it with QuickBooks® Online

Go to the QuickBooks Online Chapter 12 Appendix located on the Cengage Learning companion site at Cengage.com. Review the *Accounting with QuickBooks Online* (step-by-step guide to using QuickBooks Online). *Accounting with QuickBooks Online,* Chapter 12 will cover Reversing Entries, Financial Statements and Report. At the end of this chapter, you can complete the *Review It with QuickBooks* activity, and the *Try It with QuickBooks* problem.

TRY IT WITH QUICKBOOKS ONLINE

The Statement of Cash Flows

Learning Objectives   After you have completed this appendix, you will be able to do the following:

 Classify cash flows as Operating Activities, Investing Activities, and Financing Activities.

 Prepare a statement of cash flows using the indirect method.

The fourth major financial statement is the **statement of cash flows**. The main purpose of the statement of cash flows is to provide a summary of information concerning a company's cash receipts and payments during a fiscal period. A secondary purpose is to provide information about a firm's operating, investing, and financial activities during a fiscal period. Finally, the statement of cash flows also serves to reconcile the beginning and ending cash balance for the period. A profitable company can still go out of business if it runs out of cash. Therefore, the statement of cash flows is an important to a company as an income statement.

Accounting Language

Cash equivalents (p. 572)
Financing activities (p. 571)
Indirect method (p. 572)
Investing activities (p. 571)
Operating activities (p. 571)
Statement of cash flows (p. 571)

12A-1 SECTIONS OF THE STATEMENT OF CASH FLOWS

The statement has three main sections: **Operating Activities**, **Investing Activities**, and **Financing Activities**. Cash flows are subdivided into cash inflows and cash outflows.

Learning Objective 1   Classify cash flows as Operating Activities, Investing Activities, and Financing Activities.

Operating Activities	
Cash Inflows (Receipts):	*Cash Outflows (Payments):*
• From customers for the sale of merchandise and services	• For merchandise purchases • For operating expenses • For interest paid
Investing Activities	
Cash Inflows (Receipts):	*Cash Outflows (Payments):*
• From the sale of property and equipment • From the sale of investments or bonds in a corporation • From the collection of loan principal from borrowers	• To purchase property and equipment • To purchase investments or bonds in a corporation • For loans made to borrowers
Financing Activities	
Cash Inflows (Receipts):	*Cash Outflows (Payments):*
• From short- or long-term borrowings • From investment of cash by owner	• For repayments of loans • For payments to owner (drawings)

Cash, for purposes of the cash flow statement, includes checking and savings accounts as well as **cash equivalents**. A company that has idle cash temporarily during the year may prefer to invest in short-term interest-bearing notes or money market funds. These short-term funds are considered to be cash equivalents.

12A-2 DEVELOPING THE STATEMENT OF CASH FLOWS

<table>
<tr><td>**Learning Objective**</td><td>**2** Prepare a statement of cash flows.</td></tr>
</table>

To prepare the statement of cash flows, we need the company's income statement and statement of owner's equity for the present fiscal period and its balance sheets at the beginning and end of the fiscal period. Preparing a statement of cash flows is easy with QuickBooks Online. QuickBooks Online uses the **indirect method**, which involves adjusting net income to determine cash flows from operating activities, as shown on the statement of cash flows in Step 2 below.

Preparing the statement of cash flows involves four steps:

STEP 1. Determine the change in cash.

STEP 2. Determine the net cash flows from operating activities.

STEP 3. Determine the net cash flows from investing activities.

STEP 4. Determine the net cash flows from financing activities.

The financial statements for Jenny's Paintings are presented here.

Remember

The three categories of cash flows relate to the three sections of the statement of cash flows: operating, investing, and financing activities.

Jenny's Paintings
Income Statement
For Year Ended December 31, 2018

Net Sales		$800,000
Cost of Goods Sold:		
Merchandise Inventory, January 1, 2018	$126,000	
Delivered Cost of Purchases	514,000	
Cost of Goods Available for Sale	$640,000	
Less Merchandise Inventory, December 31, 2018	130,000	
Cost of Goods Sold		510,000
Gross Profit		$290,000
Operating Expenses:		
Salary Expense	$100,000	
Rent Expense	20,000	
Depreciation Expense, Equipment	22,000	
Supplies Expense	1,600	
Insurance Expense	400	
Total Operating Expenses		144,000
Net Income		$146,000

Jenny's Paintings
Statement of Owner's Equity
For Year Ended December 31, 2018

J. K. Kim, Capital, January 1, 2018		$233,200
Investments During the Year	$ 0	
Net Income	146,000	
Subtotal	$146,000	
Less Withdrawals	150,000	
Decrease in Capital		(4,000)
J. K. Kim, Capital, December 31, 2018		$229,200

Jenny's Paintings
Comparative Balance Sheet
December 31, 2018 and December 31, 2017

	2018	2017	Increase (Decrease)
Assets			
Cash	$ 29,400	$ 35,000	$ (5,600)
Accounts Receivable	45,600	33,000	12,600
Merchandise Inventory	130,000	126,000	4,000
Prepaid Insurance	2,300	1,400	900
Equipment	138,600	136,600	2,000
Less Accumulated Depreciation	(62,000)	(40,000)	(22,000)
Total Assets	$283,900	$292,000	$ (8,100)
Liabilities			
Accounts Payable	$ 51,500	$ 56,000	$ (4,500)
Salaries Payable	3,200	2,800	400
Total Liabilities	$ 54,700	$ 58,800	$ (4,100)
Owner's Equity			
J. K. Kim, Capital	229,200	233,200	(4,000)
Total Liabilities and Owner's Equity	$283,900	$292,000	$ (8,100)

STEP 1: DETERMINE THE CHANGE IN CASH

Jenny's Paintings had a $5,600 ($29,400 − $35,000) decrease in cash for the year. This information is found on the comparative balance sheet. This change in cash will be verified on the statement of cash flows at the bottom of the statement, as shown here.

Jenny's Paintings
Statement of Cash Flows
For Year Ended December 31, 2018

Net Increase (Decrease) in Cash	$ (5,600)
Cash, January 1, 20--	35,000
Cash, December 31, 20--	$29,400

STEP 2: DETERMINE THE NET CASH FLOWS FROM OPERATING ACTIVITIES

Convert Net Income to Cash Flows from Operations. The purpose of the statement of cash flows is to show how an increase or a decrease in cash came about. In essence, the company's income statement must be converted to a cash basis. In the Operating Activities section of the statement of cash flows, list only the adjustments necessary to convert net income to cash flows from operations as determined by changes in balance sheet accounts (assets, liabilities, and capital). This is required because under the accrual system, income is counted when it is earned, not when cash is received. The same holds true for expenses. Expenses are deducted when incurred, not when cash is paid. To convert from the accrual to the cash basis, we must add to or deduct from net income to get to the correct amount for cash.

A discussion on how to convert an income statement from the accrual basis to the amount of cash actually received or paid out follows.

STEP 2a: IDENTIFY NET INCOME (LOSS)

The net income for Jenny's Paintings is $146,000, as found on the income statement. This amount is listed first in the Operating Activities section of the statement of cash flows.

Jenny's Paintings
Statement of Cash Flows
For Year Ended December 31, 2018

Cash Flows from (Used by) Operating Activities:	
Net Income	$146,000

STEP 2b: ADD (DEDUCT) NONCASH OPERATING INCOME AND EXPENSE ITEMS

Next, we will add or subtract noncash operating income and expense items. Remember, when preparing the Operating Activities section, we want to convert net income (which includes cash and noncash items) to a cash-only basis. A common noncash operating income and expense item is Depreciation Expense.

Depreciation Expense. Jenny's Paintings had $22,000 recorded as Depreciation Expense, Equipment on the income statement for the current year. Depreciation Expense decreases net income but represents a noncash expense. Because this non-cash amount was deducted from net income, we need to add it back to convert net income to a cash-only basis.

Jenny's Paintings
Statement of Cash Flows
For Year Ended December 31, 2018

Cash Flows from (Used by) Operating Activities:		
Net Income		$146,000
Add (Deduct) Items to Convert Net Income		
from Accrual Basis to Cash Basis:		
Depreciation Expense, Equipment	$22,000	

Next, we will add or deduct changes in current assets (other than cash) and current liabilities.

STEP 2c: ADD (DEDUCT) CHANGES IN CURRENT ASSETS (OTHER THAN CASH) AND CURRENT LIABILITIES

To convert net income from an accrual basis to a cash basis, we will adjust net income for the changes in current assets (other than Cash) and current liabilities that are found on the balance sheet. Let's look at the first current asset—Accounts Receivable.

Increase in Accounts Receivable. The Accounts Receivable account increased by $12,600 ($45,600 − $33,000). An increase in accounts receivable corresponds to an increase in sales. The following summary journal entry explains the effect of accounts receivable and sales:

	GENERAL JOURNAL			Page ___	
Date	Description	Post. Ref.	Debit	Credit	
	Cash		787 4 0 0 00		
	Accounts Receivable		12 6 0 0 00		
	Sales			800 0 0 0 00	

The sales of $800,000 (found on the income statement) is recorded as a credit, and the change in accounts receivable is recorded as a debit. The difference of $787,400 represents the cash received from sales. Notice that not all of the sales recorded on the income statement were received in cash. The $12,600 relates to sales from customers on account.

The $12,600 increase in accounts receivable, representing noncash sales, must be subtracted from net income to determine operating cash flows.

Jenny's Paintings		
Statement of Cash Flows		
For Year Ended December 31, 2018		
Cash Flows from (Used by) Operating Activities:		
Net Income		$146,000
Add (Deduct) Items to Convert Net Income		
from Accrual Basis to Cash Basis:		
Depreciation Expense, Equipment	$ 22,000	
Increase in Accounts Receivable (net)	(12,600)	

If Accounts Receivable *increases* between the beginning and the end of the fiscal period, cash receipts from customers would be *less* than the revenue listed on the income statement and would need to be subtracted from net income. If Accounts Receivable *decreases* between the beginning and the end of the fiscal period, cash receipts from customers would be *more* than the revenue listed on the income statement and would need to be added to net income.

Increase in Merchandise Inventory. Before analyzing the Merchandise Inventory account, we will review all of the T accounts related to cost of goods—Cash, Merchandise Inventory, Accounts Payable, and Cost of Goods Sold.

Cash				Merchandise Inventory			
+	−				+	−	
	(c)	518,500	Jan. 1 (a)	126,000 514,000	(b)		510,000
			Dec. 31	130,000			

Accounts Payable				Cost of Goods Sold			
−	+				+	−	
	Jan. 1	56,000					
(c) 518,500	(a)	514,000	(b)	510,000			
	Dec. 31	51,500					

Transaction (a) represents the purchases of inventory for the year, $514,000. Transaction (b) represents the cost of goods sold that is reported on the income statement, $510,000. Notice that this represents both cash and noncash purchases, while transaction (c) represents the cash payments for inventory for the year, $518,500.

GENERAL JOURNAL					Page ___
Date	Description	Post. Ref.	Debit	Credit	
(a)	Merchandise Inventory		514 0 0 0 00		
	Accounts Payable			514 0 0 0 00	
	To record purchase of inventory.				
(b)	Cost of Goods Sold		510 0 0 0 00		
	Merchandise Inventory			510 0 0 0 00	
	To record cost of goods sold				
	as shown on the income statement.				
(c)	Accounts Payable		518 5 0 0 00		
	Cash			518 5 0 0 00	
	To record payment of cash for				
	inventory.				

The cash payments for inventory sold during the year are $8,500 ($518,500 − $510,000) higher than what is represented as Cost of Goods Sold on the income statement. This difference is comprised of two parts: the change in inventory, $4,000 ($130,000 − $126,000), and the change in accounts payable, $(4,500) ($51,500 − $56,000).

The increase in inventory of $4,000 must be subtracted from net income to eliminate the noncash portion of cost of goods sold.

Jenny's Paintings Statement of Cash Flows For Year Ended December 31, 2018		
Cash Flows from (Used by) Operating Activities:		
Net Income		$146,000
Add (Deduct) Items to Convert Net Income		
from Accrual Basis to Cash Basis:		
Depreciation Expense, Equipment	$ 22,000	
Increase in Accounts Receivable (net)	(12,600)	
Increase in Merchandise Inventory	**(4,000)**	

Increase in Prepaid Insurance. The Prepaid Insurance account for Jenny's Paintings increased by $900 during the year. This means that $900 more in cash than the $400 listed as Insurance Expense on the income statement was paid out. A summary journal entry would look like this:

	GENERAL JOURNAL			Page ___
Date	Description	Post. Ref.	Debit	Credit
	Prepaid Insurance		9 0 0 00	
	Cash			9 0 0 00

Notice that the Cash account decreased but there was no impact on the Insurance Expense account included in net income. Therefore, the $900 increase must be subtracted from net income to reflect the additional decrease in the Cash account.

Jenny's Paintings Statement of Cash Flows For Year Ended December 31, 2018		
Cash Flows from (Used by) Operating Activities:		
Net Income		$146,000
Add (Deduct) Items to Convert Net Income		
from Accrual Basis to Cash Basis:		
Depreciation Expense, Equipment	$ 22,000	
Increase in Accounts Receivable (net)	(12,600)	
Increase in Merchandise Inventory	(4,000)	
Increase in Prepaid Insurance	**(900)**	

If a prepaid expense (for example, Prepaid Rent or Prepaid Insurance) *increases* between the beginning and the end of the fiscal period, cash payments for the item(s) would be *more* than the amount listed as expense (Rent Expense or Insurance Expense) and would need to be subtracted from net income. If a prepaid expense (for example, Prepaid Rent or Prepaid Insurance) *decreases* between the beginning and the end of the fiscal period, cash payments for the item(s) would be *less* than the amount listed as expense (Rent Expense or Insurance Expense) and would need to be added to net income.

Decrease in Accounts Payable. Jenny's Paintings' Accounts Payable account decreased by $4,500. This decrease was reviewed in the T accounts and journal entries shown when we discussed the Merchandise Inventory account on page 576. The reduction in the Accounts Payable account means that the company paid cash of $4,500 to suppliers that was not reflected in the cost of goods sold shown on the income statement. This additional cash outflow of $4,500 needs to be subtracted from net income to reflect operating activities on a cash basis.

Jenny's Paintings Statement of Cash Flows For Year Ended December 31, 2018		
Cash Flows from (Used by) Operating Activities:		
Net Income		$146,000
Add (Deduct) Items to Convert Net Income		
from Accrual Basis to Cash Basis:		
Depreciation Expense, Equipment	$ 22,000	
Increase in Accounts Receivable (net)	(12,600)	
Increase in Merchandise Inventory	(4,000)	
Increase in Prepaid Insurance	(900)	
Decrease in Accounts Payable	**(4,500)**	

Increase in Salaries Payable. The Salaries Payable account increased by $400 during the year. As depicted in the following summary journal entry, Jenny's Paintings' Salary Expense account included $400 of noncash expense.

	GENERAL JOURNAL			Page ___	
Date	Description	Post. Ref.	Debit	Credit	
	Salaries Expense		4 0 0 00		
	Salaries Payable			4 0 0 00	

The company would add the increase in Salary Expense of $400 to net income to adjust for the noncash expense.

Jenny's Paintings Statement of Cash Flows For Year Ended December 31, 2018		
Cash Flows from (Used by) Operating Activities:		
Net Income		$146,000
Add (Deduct) Items to Convert Net Income		
from Accrual Basis to Cash Basis:		
Depreciation Expense, Equipment	$ 22,000	
Increase in Accounts Receivable (net)	(12,600)	
Increase in Merchandise Inventory	(4,000)	
Increase in Prepaid Insurance	(900)	
Decrease in Accounts Payable	(4,500)	
Increase in Salaries Payable	**400**	**400**

Now that we have made adjustments for all noncash operating income and expense items and changes in current assets (other than Cash) and current liabilities, we can compute the net cash flows from operating activities. The net cash flows from operating activities is calculated by adding or subtracting the changes to net income. Therefore, net cash flows from operating activities for Jenny's Paintings is $146,400.

Jenny's Paintings Statement of Cash Flows For Year Ended December 31, 2018		
Cash Flows from (Used by) Operating Activities:		
Net Income		$146,000
Add (Deduct) Items to Convert Net Income		
from Accrual Basis to Cash Basis:		
Depreciation Expense, Equipment	$ 22,000	
Increase in Accounts Receivable (net)	(12,600)	
Increase in Merchandise Inventory	(4,000)	
Increase in Prepaid Insurance	(900)	
Decrease in Accounts Payable	(4,500)	
Increase in Salaries Payable	400	400
Net Cash Flows from Operating Activities		**$146,400**

There is an easy way to remember how to prepare the Operating Activities section. Figure 1 illustrates the adjustments we just made. Take some time to review this figure. It will help when you prepare the Operating Activities section of the statement of cash flows.

Noncash Operating Income and Expense Items	
Depreciation Expense	+
Changes in Current Assets (Other Than Cash) and Current Liabilities	
Increase in Current Assets	−
Decrease in Current Assets	+
Increase in Current Liabilities	+
Decrease in Current Liabilities	−

Figure 1
Items to convert net income from accrual basis to cash basis

STEP 3: DETERMINE THE NET CASH FLOWS FROM INVESTING ACTIVITIES

Investing activities are concerned with changes in property and equipment (long-term assets). During 2018, Equipment increased from 136,600 to 138,600. This represents a purchase of equipment with cash.

The following entry is found in the general journal:

	GENERAL JOURNAL			Page ___	
Date	Description	Post. Ref.	Debit	Credit	
	Equipment		2 0 0 0 00		
	Cash			2 0 0 0 00	

Notice that a purchase of equipment with cash involves a credit to Cash of $2,000. We list the purchase of equipment, $2,000, as a negative cash flow under Investing Activities.

Notice that the Accumulated Depreciation account balance increased from $40,000 to $62,000. This $22,000 change is accounted for by recording $22,000 as Depreciation Expense, Equipment on the income statement. This amount is not paid to anyone and thus represents a noncash item.

The change in depreciation expense is added to net income in the operating activities section, as demonstrated previously.

Notice that the only item included in the Investing Activities section is the purchase of equipment. The adjustment for Depreciation Expense was already made in the Operating Activities section.

Jenny's Paintings
Statement of Cash Flows
For Year Ended December 31, 2018

Cash Flows from (Used by) Operating Activities:		
Purchase of Equipment	$(2,000)	
Net Cash Flows Used by Investing Activities		$(2,000)

STEP 4: DETERMINE THE NET CASH FLOWS FROM FINANCING ACTIVITIES

Record Cash Payments of Drawings. Financing activities include additions to or reductions in owner's equity. On the statement of owner's equity, we note $150,000 personal withdrawals, which we assume are in the form of cash. The withdrawals result in a decrease in cash. We can easily check our assumption that the withdrawals involved cash by reviewing the transactions affecting the J. K. Kim, Drawing account. We record $150,000 as an outflow of cash in the Financing Activities section.

Jenny's Paintings
Statement of Cash Flows
For Year Ended December 31, 2018

Cash Flows from (Used by) Operating Activities:		
Payment of Personal Withdrawals	$(150,000)	
Net Cash Flows Used by Financing Activities		$(150,000)

Putting these cash conversions together, we have the complete statement of cash flows for Jenny's Paintings.

Jenny's Paintings
Statement of Cash Flows
For Year Ended December 31, 2018

Cash Flows from (Used by) Operating Activities:		
Net Income		$ 146,000
Add (Deduct) Items to Convert Net Income		
from Accrual Basis to Cash Basis:		
Depreciation Expense, Equipment	$ 22,000	
Increase in Accounts Receivable (net)	(12,600)	
Increase in Merchandise Inventory	(4,000)	
Increase in Prepaid Insurance	(900)	
Decrease in Accounts Payable	(4,500)	
Increase in Salaries Payable	400	400
Net Cash Flows from Operating Activities		$ 146,400
Cash Flows from (Used by) Investing Activities:		
Purchase of Equipment	$ (2,000)	
Net Cash Flows Used by Investing Activities		(2,000)
Cash Flows from (Used by) Financing Activities:		
Payment of Personal Withdrawals	$(150,000)	
Net Cash Flows Used by Financing Activities		(150,000)
Net Increase (Decrease) in Cash		$ (5,600)
Cash, January 1, 2018		35,000
Cash, December 31, 2018		$ 29,400

Glossary

Cash equivalents Items included in the broad definition of cash. Included are short-term, highly liquid investments (for example, money market accounts, U.S. Treasury bills, and commercial paper) having maturities with a maximum of 90 days from the date acquired. (*p. 572*)

Financing Activities A category on the statement of cash flows (*involving inflows and outflows*) that includes borrowing money or repaying loans and additional cash investments or reducing owner's investments through personal withdrawals. (*p. 571*)

Indirect method A method used to prepare the Operating Activities section of the statement of cash flows that involves adjustments made to net income for noncash operating income and expense items and changes in current assets (other than Cash) and current liabilities. (*p. 572*)

Investing Activities A category on the statement of cash Flows (*involving inflows and outflows*) that includes the buying and selling of property and equipment and the making and collecting of loans. (*p. 571*)

Operating Activities A category on the statement of cash flows (*involving inflows and outflows*) that includes cash receipts from customers for the sale of merchandise and services, cash payments for merchandise purchases, cash payments for operating expenses, and cash payments for interest. (*p. 571*)

Statement of cash flows A financial statement that explains in detail how the balance of cash and cash equivalents has changed between the beginning and the end of a fiscal period. (*p. 571*)

Problems

LO   1, 2

PROBLEM 12A-1 Mahoney Company has the following financial statements for 2017 and 2018. Assume that the purchase of equipment and the withdrawals were in the form of cash.

Mahoney Company
Income Statement
For Year Ended December 31, 2018

Revenue:		
Income from Services		$154,000
Expenses:		
Wages Expense	$67,000	
Rent Expense	8,000	
Depreciation Expense, Equipment	5,000	
Supplies Expense	2,000	
Total Expenses		82,000
Net Income		$ 72,000

Mahoney Company
Statement of Owner's Equity
For Year Ended December 31, 2018

A. M. Mahoney, Capital, January 1, 2018		$85,000
Net Income for the Year	$72,000	
Less Withdrawals for the Year	60,000	
Increase in Capital		12,000
A. M. Mahoney, Capital, December 31, 2018		$ 97,000

(Continued)

Mahoney Company
Comparative Balance Sheet
December 31, 2018 and December 31, 2017

	2018		2017		Increase (Decrease)
Assets					
Cash		$ 18,800		$ 9,000	$ 9,800
Supplies		10,000		4,500	5,500
Equipment	$105,000		$ 98,000		7,000
Less Accumulated Depreciation	(18,000)	87,000	(13,000)	85,000	(5,000)
Total Assets		$115,800		$98,500	$17,300
Liabilities					
Accounts Payable	$ 13,000		$ 7,000		$ 6,000
Rent Payable	5,800		6,500		(700)
Total Liabilities		$ 18,800		$13,500	$ 5,300
Owner's Equity					
A. M. Mahoney, Capital		97,000		85,000	12,000
Total Liabilities and Owner's Equity		$115,800		$98,500	$17,300

Required

Prepare a statement of cash flows for the year ended December 31, 2018.

Check Figure

Net cash flows from operating activities, $76,800

LO 1, 2

PROBLEM 12A-2 The financial statements for Romeo and Company follow. Assume that the additional investment and the withdrawals were in the form of cash.

Romeo and Company
Income Statement
For Year Ended December 31, 2018

Revenue:		
Income from Services		$370,000
Expenses:		
Wages Expense	$161,000	
Rent Expense	18,000	
Depreciation Expense, Equipment	12,000	
Supplies Expense	4,000	
Insurance Expense	1,000	
Total Expenses		196,000
Net Income		$174,000

(Continued)

Romeo and Company
Statement of Owner's Equity
For Year Ended December 31, 2018

R. U. Romeo, Capital, January 1, 2018		$150,000
Investment During the Year	$ 2,000	
Net Income for the Year	174,000	
Subtotal	$176,000	
Less Withdrawals for the Year	150,000	
Increase in Capital		26,000
R. U. Romeo, Capital, December 31, 2018		$176,000

Romeo and Company
Comparative Balance Sheet
December 31, 2018 and December 31, 2017

	2018		2017		Increase (Decrease)
Assets					
Cash		$ 16,800		$ 2,800	$ 14,000
Accounts Receivable		37,000		26,000	11,000
Supplies		10,000		9,400	600
Prepaid Insurance		3,200		600	2,600
Equipment	$155,400		$145,400		10,000
Less Accumulated Depreciation	(36,000)	119,400	(24,000)	121,400	(12,000)
Total Assets		$186,400		$160,200	$ 26,200
Liabilities					
Accounts Payable		$ 10,400		$ 10,200	$ 200
Owner's Equity					
R. U. Romeo, Capital		176,000		150,000	26,000
Total Liabilities and Owner's Equity		$186,400		$160,200	$ 26,200

Check Figure
Net cash flows from operating activities, $172,000

Required

Prepare a statement of cash flows for the year ended December 31, 2018.

PROBLEM 12A-3 The financial statements for Zhang Company follow. Assume that the withdrawals were in the form of cash.

Zhang Company
Income Statement
For Year Ended December 31, 2018

Revenue from Sales:		
Net Sales	$1,042,000	
Less Cost of Goods Sold	853,600	
Gross Profit		$188,400
Operating Expenses:		
Salary Expense	$ 66,900	
Rent Expense	18,000	
Depreciation Expense, Equipment	10,000	
Supplies Expense	4,700	
Insurance Expense	2,800	
Total Operating Expenses		102,400
Net Income		$ 86,000

Zhang Company
Statement of Owner's Equity
For Year Ended December 31, 2018

C. L. Zhang, Capital, January 1, 2018		$196,000
Net Income for the Year	$86,000	
Less Withdrawals for the Year	90,000	
Decrease in Capital		(4,000)
C. L. Zhang, Capital, December 31, 2018		$192,000

(Continued)

Zhang Company
Comparative Balance Sheet
December 31, 2018 and December 31, 2017

	2018		2017		Increase (Decrease)
Assets					
Cash		$ 9,400		$ 10,900	$ (1,500)
Accounts Receivable		56,000		48,600	7,400
Merchandise Inventory		104,600		104,400	200
Supplies		8,200		6,000	2,200
Prepaid Insurance		1,600		1,800	(200)
Equipment	$156,000		$156,000		—
Less Accumulated Depreciation	(76,400)	79,600	(66,400)	89,600	(10,000)
Total Assets		$259,400		$261,300	$ (1,900)
Liabilities					
Accounts Payable	$ 62,700		$ 60,400		$ 2,300
Salaries Payable	4,700		4,900		(200)
Total Liabilities		$ 67,400		$ 65,300	$ 2,100
Owner's Equity					
C. L. Zhang, Capital		192,000		196,000	(4,000)
Total Liabilities and Owner's Equity		$259,400		$261,300	$ (1,900)

Check Figure
Net cash flows used by financing activities, $(90,000)

Required

Prepare a statement of cash flows for the year ended December 31, 2018.

LO 1

PROBLEM 12A-4 The financial statements for Cole Company follow.

Cole Company
Income Statement
For Year Ended December 31, 2018

Net Sales		$540,000
Cost of Goods Sold:		
Merchandise Inventory, January 1, 2018	$103,000	
Delivered Cost of Purchases	390,790	
Cost of Goods Available for Sale	$493,790	
Less Merchandise Inventory, December 31, 2018	137,000	
Cost of Goods Sold		356,790
Gross Profit		$183,210
Operating Expenses:		
Salary Expense	$ 84,000	
Rent Expense	18,000	
Advertising Expense	12,000	
Supplies Expense	845	
Depreciation Expense, Equipment	12,000	
Utilities Expense	1,790	
Insurance Expense	2,400	
Miscellaneous Expense	360	
Total Operating Expenses		131,395
Net Income		$ 51,815

Cole Company
Statement of Owner's Equity
For Year Ended December 31, 2018

A. E. Cole, Capital, January 1, 2018		$120,300
Investments During the Year	$ 0	
Net Income	51,815	
Subtotal	$51,815	
Less Withdrawals	30,000	
Increase in Capital		21,815
A. E. Cole, Capital, December 31, 2018		$142,115

(Continued)

Cole Company
Comparative Balance Sheet
December 31, 2018 and December 31, 2017

	2018	2017	Increase (Decrease)
Assets			
Cash	$ 61,435	$ 27,500	$ 33,935
Accounts Receivable	21,000	30,000	(9,000)
Merchandise Inventory	60,000	58,000	2,000
Prepaid Insurance	2,780	2,560	220
Equipment:	40,000	40,000	0
Less Accumulated Depreciation	(24,000)	(12,000)	(12,000)
Total Assets	$161,215	$146,060	$ 15,155
Liabilities			
Accounts Payable	$ 16,000	$ 22,860	$ (6,860)
Salaries Payable	3,100	2,900	200
Total Liabilities	$ 19,100	$ 25,760	$ (6,660)
Owner's Equity			
A. E. Cole, Capital	142,115	120,300	21,815
Total Liabilities and Owner's Equity	$161,215	$146,060	$ 15,155

Check Figure

Net Cash Flows from Operating Activities, $63,435

Required

Using the statements of Cole Company, prepare a statement of cash flows for the year ended December 31, 2018.

Methods of Depreciation

1 Prepare a schedule of depreciation using the straight-line method.

2 Prepare a schedule of depreciation using the units-of-production method.

3 Prepare a schedule of depreciation using the double-declining-balance method.

4 Prepare a schedule of depreciation for five-year property under the Modified Accelerated Cost Recovery System.

Accounting Language

As you have learned, depreciation is the the process of allocating the cost of an asset to an expense over its useful life. In this appendix, we will illustrate four methods of depreciation (straight-line, units-of-production, double-declining-balance, and Modified Accelerated Cost Recovery System), using the example of a delivery truck. Assume that the truck was bought at the beginning of Year 1 at a cost of $24,000. The truck is estimated to have a useful life of five years and a trade-in value of $6,000 at the end of the five-year period.

Double-declining-balance method (p. A-2)

Modified Accelerated Cost Recovery System (MACRS) (p. A-3)

Straight-line method (p. A-1)

Units-of-production method (p. A-2)

STRAIGHT-LINE METHOD

The **straight-line method** was demonstrated in Chapter 4. This method is popular because it is easy to use and allows a business to calculate an equal amount of depreciation expense for each year of service anticipated. The accountant computes the annual depreciation by dividing the depreciation base (cost minus salvage value, if any) by the number of years of useful life predicted for the asset. See the illustration of the straight-line method below.

1 Prepare a schedule of depreciation using the straight-line method.

Learning Objective

$$\text{Yearly Depreciation} = \frac{\text{Cost of Asset} - \text{Trade-in Value}}{\text{Years of Life}} = \frac{\$24,000 - \$6,000}{5 \text{ years}}$$

$$= \frac{\$18,000}{5 \text{ years}} = \$3,600 \text{ per year}$$

Year	Depreciation for the Year	Accumulated Depreciation	Book Value (Cost Less Accumulated Depreciation)
1	$18,000 ÷ 5 years = $ 3,600	$ 3,600	$24,000 − $ 3,600 = $20,400
2	18,000 ÷ 5 years = 3,600	$ 3,600 + $3,600 = 7,200	24,000 − 7,200 = 16,800
3	18,000 ÷ 5 years = 3,600	7,200 + 3,600 = 10,800	24,000 − 10,800 = 13,200
4	18,000 ÷ 5 years = 3,600	10,800 + 3,600 = 14,400	24,000 − 14,400 = 9,600
5	18,000 ÷ 5 years = 3,600	14,400 + 3,600 = 18,000	24,000 − 18,000 = 6,000
	$18,000*		

*Depreciation expense for straight-line method is constant.

UNITS-OF-PRODUCTION METHOD

The **units-of-production method** calculates depreciation based on usage (miles, hours) instead of the years of service anticipated. This method is useful when the utilization of an asset varies. Assume that the truck used in the straight-line method illustration is now estimated to have a useful life of 100,000 miles. (This is also known as units-of-production or units-of-output.) The truck is anticipated to be driven 30,000 miles during Year 1; 25,000 miles during Year 2; 20,000 miles during Year 3; 15,000 miles during Year 4; and 10,000 miles during Year 5. The accountant determines that the units-of-production method would more accurately reflect the annual depreciation for the truck. The units-of-production method is computed with a two-step process. See the illustration of the units-of-production method below.

STEP 1. Compute the depreciation per unit.

$$\text{Depreciation per unit} = \frac{\text{Cost of Asset} - \text{Trade-in Value}}{\text{Total Units-of-Production}} = \frac{\$24,000 - \$6,000}{100,000 \text{ Miles}}$$

$$= \frac{\$18,000}{100,000} = \$0.18 \text{ per mile}$$

STEP 2. Compute the depreciation expense for Year 1.

Depreciation Expense Year 1 = Depreciation per Mile × Total Units-of-Production for Year 1 (Total Miles Driven)

Depreciation Expense Year 1 = $0.18 × 30,000 miles = $5,400

Year	Depreciation for the Year	Accumulated Depreciation	Book Value (Cost Less Accumulated Depreciation)
1	30,000 miles × $ 0.18 = $ 5,400	$ 5,400	$24,000 − $ 5,400 = $18,600
2	25,000 miles × 0.18 = 4,500	$ 5,400 + 4,500 = 9,900	24,000 − 9,900 = 14,100
3	20,000 miles × 0.18 = 3,600	9,900 + 3,600 = 13,500	24,000 − 13,500 = 10,500
4	15,000 miles × 0.18 = 2,700	13,500 + 2,700 = 16,200	24,000 − 16,200 = 7,800
5	10,000 miles × 0.18 = 1,800	16,200 + 1,800 = 18,000	24,000 − 18,000 = 6,000
	$18,000*		

*Depreciation expense for the units-of-production method varies.

DOUBLE-DECLINING-BALANCE METHOD

The **double-declining-balance method** is an accelerated method of depreciation that allows larger amounts of depreciation to be taken in the early years of an asset's life. In accelerated depreciation, larger amounts of depreciation are taken during the early life of an asset, and smaller amounts are taken during the later years of an asset's life. Some accountants reason that the amount charged to depreciation should be higher during an asset's early years, when it is more productive and efficient, to offset the higher repair and maintenance expenses of the asset's later years. This way the total annual expense tends to be equalized over the entire life of the asset.

The double-declining-balance method calculates depreciation at double the straight-line rate. In the illustration below, with an estimated useful life of five years, the straight-line rate is 1/5, or 0.20. Twice, or double, the straight-line rate is 2/5 (1/5 × 2), or 0.40. Note that the trade-in value is not taken into account until the end of the schedule. To calculate depreciation using the double-declining-balance method, multiply the *book value* at the beginning of each year by twice the straight-line rate.

Year	Depreciation for the Year	Accumulated Depreciation	Book Value (Cost Less Accumulated Depreciation)
1	$24,000 × 0.40 = $ 9,600	$ 9,600	$24,000 − $ 9,600 = $14,400
2	$14,400 × 0.40 = 5,760	$ 9,600 + $5,760 = 15,360	24,000 − 15,360 = 8,640
3	$8,640 − $6,000 = 2,640	15,360 + 2,640 = 18,000	24,000 − 18,000 = 6,000
4	0	18,000	24,000 − 18,000 = 6,000
5	0	18,000	24,000 − 18,000 = 6,000
	$18,000		

If the 40% depreciation rate is applied to Year 3, depreciation expense would be $3,456 ($8,640 × 0.40), accumulated depreciation would be $18,816 ($15,360 + $3,456), and book value would be $5,184 ($24,000 − $18,816). However, the book value cannot drop below the established salvage, or trade-in, value of $6,000. So for Year 3, an adjustment must be made limiting the depreciation for the year to $2,640, which will bring the accumulated depreciation up to $18,000. Consequently, the book value at the end of the year will be $6,000 ($24,000 cost − $18,000 accumulated depreciation) and no further depreciation will be taken.

TAX REQUIREMENT—MACRS

Business firms are entitled to deduct depreciation on their income tax returns. However, the amount recorded on a company's income statement (based on the depreciation method: straight-line method, double-declining-balance, or another method) may differ from the amount recorded on the company's income tax return.

For property acquired after 1986, a schedule of depreciation called the **Modified Accelerated Cost Recovery System (MACRS)** has been established. The term *recovery* is used because MACRS is a means of recovering or deducting the cost of an asset. Most small businesses use MACRS for financial statement reporting and tax reporting. MACRS is a combination of the declining-balance and straight-line depreciation methods. For more information, see IRS Publication 946, available at www.irs.gov.

According to MACRS, property is divided into eight classes, as follows:

4 Prepare a schedule of depreciation for five-year property under the Modified Accelerated Cost Recovery System.

Learning Objective

Property Class	Description
3-year property	Certain horses and tractor units for use over the road
5-year property	Autos, light- and heavy-duty general-purpose trucks, computers, and office equipment (copiers, etc.); also, furniture, appliances, window treatments, and carpeting used in residential rental buildings

(Continued)

7-year property	Office furniture and fixtures and any property that does not have a class life and that is not, by law, in any other class
10-year property	Vessels, barges, tugs, and similar water transportation equipment
15-year property	Wharves, roads, fences, and any municipal wastewater treatment plant
20-year property	Certain farm buildings and municipal sewers
27.5-year residential rental property	Rental houses and apartments
39-year real property	Office buildings, store buildings, and warehouses

Under MACRS, trade-in value is ignored. The following table lists the depreciation rates that a business may use for tax purposes.

Depreciation for Recovery Period				
Year	3-Year	5-Year	7-Year	10-Year
1	33.33%	20.00%	14.29%	10.00%
2	44.45	32.00	24.49	18.00
3	14.81	19.20	17.49	14.40
4	7.41	11.52	12.49	11.52
5		11.52	8.93	9.22
6		5.76	8.92	7.37
7			8.93	6.55
8			4.46	6.55
9				6.56
10				6.55
11				3.28

Our delivery truck qualifies as five-year property.

Year	Depreciation for the Year	Accumulated Depreciation	Book Value (Cost Less Accumulated Depreciation)
1	$24,000 × 0.20 = $ 4,800.00	$ 4,800.00	$24,000.00 − $ 4,800.00 = $19,200.00
2	24,000 × 0.32 = 7,680.00	$ 4,800.00 + $7,680.00 = 12,480.00	24,000.00 − 12,480.00 = 11,520.00
3	24,000 × 0.192 = 4,608.00	12,480.00 + 4,608.00 = 17,088.00	24,000.00 − 17,088.00 = 6,912.00
4	24,000 × 0.1152 = 2,764.80	17,088.00 + 2,764.80 = 19,852.80	24,000.00 − 19,852.80 = 4,147.20
5	24,000 × 0.1152 = 2,764.80	19,852.80 + 2,764.80 = 22,617.60	24,000.00 − 22,617.60 = 1,382.40
6	24,000 × 0.0576 = 1,382.40	22,617.60 + 1,382.40 = 24,000.00	24,000.00 − 24,000.00 = 0
	$24,000.00		

Glossary

Double-declining-balance method An accelerated depreciation method that calculates depreciation at double the straight-line rate. (*p. A-2*)

Modified Accelerated Cost Recovery System (MACRS) A variety of tax rate schedules established by the Internal Revenue Service. MACRS is a combination of declining-balance and straight-line methods. (*p. A-3*)

Straight-line method A popular method of depreciation because it is easy to use and allows a business to calculate an equal amount of depreciation expense for each year of service anticipated. Annual depreciation is calculated by dividing the depreciation base (cost minus salvage value, if any) by the number of years of useful life predicted for the asset. (*p. A-1*)

Units-of-production method A depreciation method that calculates depreciation based on usage (miles, hours) instead of the years of service anticipated. (*p. A-2*)

Problems

LO 1

PROBLEM A-1 A delivery van was bought for $18,000. The estimated life of the van is four years. The trade-in value at the end of four years is estimated to be $2,000.

Required
Prepare a depreciation schedule for the four-year period using the straight-line method.

Check Figure
Year 1 depreciation, $4,000

LO 2

PROBLEM A-2 Use the information in Problem A-1 to solve this problem. Assume the delivery van is expected to have a useful life of 100,000 miles (Year 1, 40,000 miles; Year 2, 30,000 miles; Year 3, 20,000 miles; Year 4, 10,000 miles).

Required
Prepare a schedule of depreciation using the units-of-production method.

Check Figure
Year 3 depreciation, $3,200

LO 3

PROBLEM A-3 Use the information in Problem A-1 to solve this problem.

Required
Prepare a schedule of depreciation using the double-declining-balance method.

Check Figure
Year 2 depreciation, $4,500

LO 4

PROBLEM A-4 Use the information in Problem A-1 to solve this problem. Assume that the van is five-year property for tax purposes.

Required
Prepare a schedule of depreciation under MACRS. Round figures to the nearest whole dollar.

Check Figure
Year 3 depreciation, $3,456

Bad Debts

Accounting Language

Allowance method of accounting for bad debts expense (p. B-1)

Direct write-off method of accounting for bad debts expense (p. B-3)

As you know, not all credit customers pay their bills. In this appendix, we turn our attention to the accounts receivable that will not be collected. There are two basic methods of providing for writing or charging off credit customers' accounts that are considered uncollectible. They are the allowance method and the direct write-off method.

ALLOWANCE METHOD

The **allowance method of accounting for bad debts expense** provides for bad debts expense in advance by estimating them. Although there are a number of ways to estimate the amount of future expenses from open accounts, we will base our estimate on a percentage of credit sales.

For example, based on its experience with bad debts expense, Miami Printing estimates that 1 percent of its revenue from services on account for the year will be uncollectible. Obviously, Miami Printing does not know which credit customers will not pay their bills. If the company were certain that a particular customer would not pay his or her bill, it would not perform services without requiring cash in advance.

Adjusting Entry for Bad Debts

Miami Printing's total income from services on account for last year was $500,000. One percent of $500,000 is $5,000 ($500,000 × 0.01 = $5,000). On its work sheet, Miami Printing makes an adjusting entry. We also show this in T account form, assuming a credit balance of $170 in the Allowance for Doubtful Accounts account.

1 Prepare the adjusting entry for bad debts, using the allowance method based on a percentage of credit sales.

Learning Objective

Bad Debts Expense			Allowance for Doubtful Accounts		
+	−		−	+	
Dec. 31 Adj. 5,000				Bal. 170	
				Dec. 31 Adj. 5,000	

The general journal entry is shown below.

Date		Description	Post. Ref.	Debit	Credit
20—		Adjusting Entry			
Dec.	31	Bad Debts Expense		5 0 0 0 00	
		Allowance for Doubtful Accounts			5 0 0 0 00

Allowance for Doubtful Accounts is treated as a deduction from Accounts Receivable. Consequently, Allowance for Doubtful Accounts is a contra account. The adjusting entry is similar to the entry for depreciation, in that there is a debit to an expense account and a credit to a contra-asset account.

Assume that Miami Printing's Accounts Receivable balance is $90,000. Let's show the accounts and the adjusting entries in T account form.

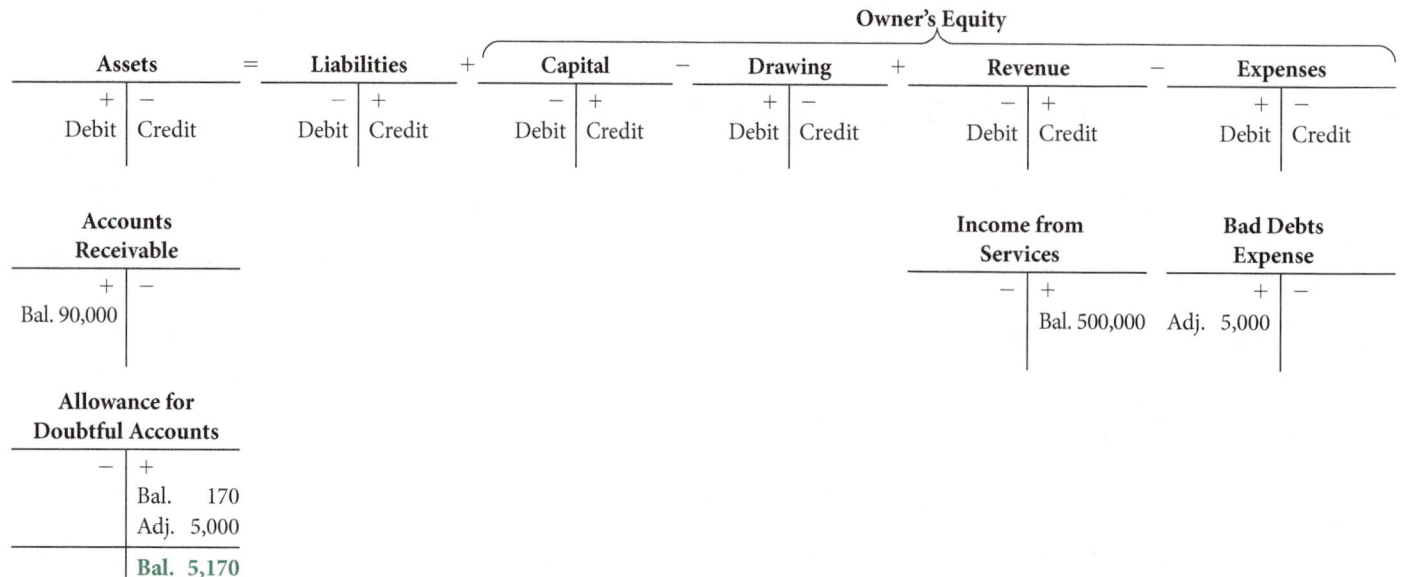

The Bad Debts Expense account comes into existence as an adjusting entry, and it is immediately closed during the closing process.

As certain credit customers' accounts are determined to be uncollectible and are written off, the losses are taken out of Allowance for Doubtful Accounts. Think of the Allowance for Doubtful Accounts as a reservoir. By means of the adjusting entry, the account is filled up at the end of the year and is gradually drained off (reduced) during the next year by write-offs of credit customer accounts. The $170 balance in Allowance for Doubtful Accounts at the end of the year (prior to the adjusting entry of $5,000) indicates that less accounts receivable were actually written off as uncollectible during the year than previously estimated. As a result, Bad Debts Expense in the period was overstated and net income thus understated.

FYI

Companies generally have a credit balance left in the Allowance account.

Learning Objective

2 Prepare the entry to write off an account as uncollectible when the allowance method is used.

Writing Off an Account

Let's go on to the next year. On January 2, Miami Printing finally gives up on its attempts to collect $720 from its credit customer, Ace Computer, which is included in Accounts Receivable. Miami Printing now writes off the account in the amount of $720, shown in T account form.

Accounts Receivable				Allowance for Doubtful Accounts			
	+	−			−	+	
Bal.	90,000	Jan. 2 (write-off)	720	Jan. 2 (write-off)	720	Bal.	5,170
Bal.	**89,280**					**Bal.**	**4,450**

As you can see, the write-off has reduced both the balance of Accounts Receivable and the balance of Allowance for Doubtful Accounts, but has not changed the net realizable value of accounts receivable. The general journal entry is shown below.

		GENERAL JOURNAL					Page ___	
Date		Description	Post. Ref.	Debit		Credit		
20—								
Jan.	2	Allowance for Doubtful Accounts		7 2 0 00				
		Accounts Receivable				7 2 0 00		
		Wrote off the account of Ace						
		Computer as uncollectible.						

An Advantage and a Disadvantage of the Allowance Method

The allowance method is consistent with the accrual basis of accounting in that it matches revenues of one year with expenses of the same year. The bad debts expense potential is provided in the same year in which the revenue is earned. The conformity with the matching principle places the allowance method in compliance with generally accepted accounting principles as recognized by the FASB.

SPECIFIC CHARGE-OFF METHOD

Under the **direct write-off method of accounting for bad debts expense**, when a credit customer's account is determined to be uncollectible, the account is simply written off. The terms *write-off* and *charge-off* mean the same thing. No allowance account is used with the direct write-off method because no estimate of uncollectible accounts receivable is calculated. As an illustration, Walter Company uses the direct write-off method. On May 5, Walter Company writes off the account of Garber Construction, $1,220. For the purpose of this example, we will use a separate Accounts Receivable account for Garber Construction. T accounts pertaining to Garber's account look like this:

 3 Prepare the entry to write off an account as uncollectible when the direct write-off method is used.

Learning Objective

Accounts Receivable, Garber Construction				Bad Debts Expense			
	+	−			+	−	
Bal.	1,220	May 5 (write-off)	1,220	May 5 (write-off)	1,220		

The general journal entry is shown below.

GENERAL JOURNAL					Page ___
Date	Description	Post. Ref.	Debit	Credit	
20—					
May 5	Bad Debts Expense		1 2 2 0 00		
	Accounts Receivable			1 2 2 0 00	
	Wrote off the account of				
	Garber Construction as				
	uncollectible.				

Under this method, entries will be made directly into the Bad Debts Expense account during the year. No adjusting entry is needed, and Allowance for Doubtful Accounts is not used.

Advantages of the Direct Write-off Method

The main advantage is that the method is simple to use. It is not necessary to make an adjusting entry. Also, one less account (Allowance for Doubtful Accounts) is required.

A Disadvantage of the Direct Write-off Method

This method is not consistent with the accrual basis of accounting (recognizing revenue when it is earned and expenses when they are incurred). The method does not match up the revenues of one year with the expenses of the same year. This lack of conformity with the matching principle places the direct write-off method in violation of generally accepted accounting principles. For example, the sale of services on account to Garber Construction could have been made two years ago. Because the account receivable will never be collected, the revenue for that year was too high (overstated). Consequently, net income is also overstated during that year. Now, two years later, $1,220 is written off as an expense. So net income for this year is too low (understated) because of the added expense.

Glossary

Allowance method of accounting for bad debts expense A method that requires an adjusting entry to debit Bad Debts Expense and to credit Allowance for Doubtful Accounts to match expenses from uncollectible accounts with sales of the same period. Write-offs of uncollectible accounts are debited to Allowance for Doubtful Accounts and credited to Accounts Receivable. (*p. B-1*)

Direct write-off method of accounting for bad debts expense A simple method of recognizing bad debts that requires no adjusting entry. The accountant debits Bad Debts Expense and credits Accounts Receivable, when an uncollectible account is written off. This method is not allowed under GAAP. (*p. B-3*)

Problems

LO **1, 2**

PROBLEM B-1 Rogan Company's total sales on account for the year amounted to $327,000. The company, which uses the allowance method, estimated bad debts at 1 percent of its credit sales.

Required
Journalize the following selected entries:

Check Figure
Adjusting entry amount, $3,270

2017
Dec. 31   Record the adjusting entry.

2018
Mar. 2   Write off the account of A. M. Billson as uncollectible, $584.
June 6   Write off the account of W. H. Gilders as uncollectible, $492.

LO **1, 2**

PROBLEM B-2 Hardy's Landscape Service's total revenue on account for 2018 amounted to $273,205. The company, which uses the allowance method, estimates bad debts at ½ percent of total revenue on account.

Required
Journalize the following selected entries:

Check Figure
Adjusting entry amount, $1,366.03

2012
Dec. 12   Record services performed on account for E. E. Morton, $245.
     31   Record the adjusting entry for Bad Debts Expense.
     31   Record the closing entry for Bad Debts Expense.

2013
Feb. 18   Write off the account of E. E. Morton as uncollectible, $245.

LO **3**

PROBLEM B-3 Nillson's Nursery uses the direct write-off method for recording bad debts.

Required
Journalize the following selected entries:

Check Figure
Total amount debited to Bad Debts Expense $726

2012
Apr. 10   Write off the account of P. A. Seldon as uncollectible, $458.
July 27   Write off the account of J. M. Weller as uncollectible, $268.

Inventory Methods

1 Determine the amount of the ending merchandise inventory by the weighted-average-cost method.

2 Determine the amount of the ending merchandise inventory by the first-in, first-out (FIFO) method.

3 Determine the amount of the ending merchandise inventory by the last-in, first-out (LIFO) method.

Accounting Language

First-in, first-out (FIFO) method (p. C-2)

Last-in, first-out (LIFO) method (p. C-2)

Weighted-average-cost method (p. C-2)

To determine the dollar amount of the ending merchandise inventory under the periodic inventory system, it is necessary to take a physical count of the various items in stock and match them up with their costs. In other words, the ending inventory consists of the number of units of each type of item on hand, multiplied by the cost of each unit.

If each unit were purchased at the same price, the job of determining the total cost of the inventory would be simple. For example, if there are 100 units of Product A on hand and all 100 units were bought at \$15, the total cost of the ending inventory is \$1,500 (100 × \$15). However, over a period of time, costs of individual purchases of units may differ. Changes in costs of individual units make the different methods of inventory valuation necessary.

We will use Bruce Medical Supply, a distributor of medical supplies, to illustrate the three methods of inventory valuation. Bruce uses a periodic inventory system to record inventory. Bruce's ending inventory consists of 176 Standard 2.5v diagnostic sets acquired through various purchases, as follows:

Specific Purchase	Number of Units	Cost per Unit	Total Cost
Beginning inventory	34	$145	$ 4,930
First purchase	60	152	9,120
Second purchase	256	156	39,936
Third purchase	164	162	26,568
Total units available	514		$80,554

Of the 514 units available for sale, 176 units are still on hand and 338 have been sold (514 − 176 = 338 units sold).

Bruce Medical Supply may choose any one of the following three methods of recording the total cost of the 176 units in the ending inventory of medical supplies.

WEIGHTED-AVERAGE-COST METHOD

1 Determine the amount of the ending merchandise inventory by the weighted-average-cost method.

An alternative to keeping track of the cost of each item purchased is to use the **weighted-average-cost method**. This method averages the cost per unit of all like articles available for sale during the period. The first step is to find the total cost of the merchandise on hand during the year by multiplying the number of units by their respective purchase costs. (See page C-1.) From this information, you can find the average cost per unit, which will be used to determine the ending inventory value, as shown below:

$$\text{Average Cost per Unit} = \frac{\text{Total Cost}}{\text{Total Units Available}} = \frac{\$80,554}{514} = \$156.72 \text{ (rounded)}$$

Cost of Ending Inventory (176 units) = $156.72 × 176 units = $27,582.72

FIRST-IN, FIRST-OUT METHOD

2 Determine the amount of the ending merchandise inventory by the first-in, first-out (FIFO) method.

The **first-in, first-out (FIFO) method** is based on the assumption that the first units of diagnostic sets purchased will be sold first. The costs of the units left will be those of the most recently purchased units. You may think of this as the way a grocery store sells milk. Because milk will sour, the oldest milk is moved to the front of the display shelf and is sold first. Consequently, the cartons of milk remaining on the shelf are the freshest milk.

Relating to our illustration of diagnostic sets:

Specific Purchase	Number of Units	Cost per Unit	Total Cost
Beginning inventory	34	$145	$ 4,930
First purchase	60	152	9,120
Second purchase	256	156	39,936
Third purchase	164	162	26,568
Total units available	514		$80,554

The cost of the ending merchandise inventory, or the 176 diagnostic sets on hand (most recently purchased), is as follows:

164	units (third purchase)	@ $162 each =	$26,568
12	units (second purchase)	@ $156 each =	1,872
176	units		$28,440

LAST-IN, FIRST-OUT METHOD

3 Determine the amount of the ending merchandise inventory by the last-in, first-out (LIFO) method.

The **last-in, first-out (LIFO) method** is based on the assumption that the last units of diagnostic sets purchased will be sold first. The costs of the units left over will be those of the earliest purchased units. You may think of this as the way a coal yard sells coal. When the coal yard sells coal to its customers, it takes coal off the top of the pile. Consequently, the tons of coal in the ending inventory consist of those first few tons at the bottom of the pile.

Relating to our illustration of diagnostic sets, the cost of the ending merchandise inventory, or the 176 diagnostic sets on hand (earliest purchased), is as follows:

34	units (beginning inventory)	@ $145 each =	$	4,930
60	units (first purchase)	@ $152 each =		9,120
82	units (second purchase)	@ $156 each =		12,792
176	units			$26,842

COMPARISON OF METHODS

If prices don't change very much, all inventory methods give about the same results. However, in a dynamic market where prices are constantly rising and falling, each method may yield different amounts. Here is a comparison of the results of the sale of diagnostic sets, using the three methods we described.

Comparison of Three Methods		
Method	Ending Inventory (176 units)	Cost of Goods Sold (Goods Available for Sale − Ending Inventory) (338 units = 514 − 176)
Weighted-average-cost	$27,582.72	$52,971.28 ($80,554.00 − $27,582.72)
First-in, first-out	28,440.00	52,114.00 ($80,554.00 − $28,440.00)
Last-in, first-out	26,842.00	53,712.00 ($80,554.00 − $26,842.00)

A summary of the effects of the methods is as follows:

1. Weighted-average-cost is a compromise between LIFO and FIFO for both the amount of the ending inventory and the Cost of Goods Sold.
2. FIFO provides the most realistic amount for the ending merchandise inventory in the Current Assets section of the balance sheet. The ending inventory is valued at the most recent costs, referred to as replacement cost.
3. LIFO provides the most realistic amount for the Cost of Goods Sold section of the income statement because the items that have been sold must be replaced at the most recent costs.

Now assume that the diagnostic sets were sold for $245 each.

	Weighted-Average-Cost	First-in, First-out	Last-in, First-out
Sales (338 units × $245 each)	$82,810.00	$82,810.00	$82,810.00
Less: Cost of Goods Sold	52,971.28	52,114.00	53,712.00
Gross Profit	$29,838.72	$30,696.00	$29,098.00

As you can see, the inventory method used can have an effect on the gross profit of a business. Once an inventory method is adopted by a business, the method must be used consistently. If a company wants to change its inventory method for tax purposes, the company must request permission from the Internal Revenue Service.

Glossary

First-in, first-out (FIFO) method An inventory costing method that assumes the first units purchased will be sold first and the costs of the units left in inventory will be from the most recently purchased items. (*p. C-2*)

Last-in, first-out (LIFO) method An inventory costing method that assumes the last units purchased will be sold first and the costs of the units left in inventory will be from the earliest purchased items. (*p. C-2*)

Weighted-average-cost method An inventory costing method that averages the costs of items purchased. The average unit price is then used to determine the total cost of goods sold and the total cost of the remaining inventory. (*p. C-2*)

Problems

LO 1

PROBLEM C-1 Bean Nursery sells bark to its customers at retail. Bean buys bark from a plywood mill in bulk and transports the bark in its own trucks. Information relating to the beginning inventory and purchases of bark is as follows:

Beginning inventory	1,500 cubic yards @ $0.40 per cubic yard
First purchase	2,100 cubic yards @ $0.42 per cubic yard
Second purchase	1,400 cubic yards @ $0.46 per cubic yard
Third purchase	1,000 cubic yards @ $0.47 per cubic yard

Check Figure
Cost of ending inventory,
$519.24

Required

Find the cost of 1,200 cubic yards in the ending inventory by the weighted-average-cost method. Carry average cost per cubic yard to four decimals.

LO 2

PROBLEM C-2 Use the information presented in Problem C-1 to solve this problem.

Check Figure
Cost of ending inventory, $562

Required

Find the cost of the ending inventory by the first-in, first-out method.

LO 3

PROBLEM C-3 Use the information presented in Problem C-1 to solve this problem.

Check Figure
Cost of ending inventory, $480

Required

Find the cost of the ending inventory by the last-in, first-out method.

Notes Payable and Notes Receivable

Learning Objectives

After you have completed this appendix, you will be able to do the following:

1 Calculate the interest on promissory notes.

2 Determine the due dates of promissory notes.

3a Record journal entries for notes given to secure an extension of time on an open account.

3b Record journal entries for payment of an interest-bearing note at maturity.

3c Record journal entries for notes given to secure a cash loan when the bank discounts the note.

3d Record journal entries for payment of a discounted note at maturity.

4a Record the journal entry for receipt of a note from a charge customer.

4b Record the journal entry for receipt of payment of an interest-bearing note at maturity.

4c Record the journal entry for discounting an interest-bearing note receivable.

4d Record the journal entry for a dishonored note receivable.

Accounting Language

Discount (p. D-5)

Discount period (p. D-7)

Discounting a notes payable (p. D-5)

Discounting notes receivable (p. D-7)

Dishonored note receivable (p. D-8)

Duration (p. D-2)

Interest (p. D-2)

Maker (p. D-1)

Maturity date (p. D-2)

Maturity value (p. D-4)

Payee (p. D-1)

Principal (p. D-2)

Proceeds (p. D-5)

Promissory note (p. D-1)

Credit plays an extremely important role in the operation of most business enterprises. Credit may be extended on a charge-account basis, with payment generally due in 25 to 30 days. This type of credit involves the Accounts Payable and Accounts Receivable accounts. Credit may also be granted by giving or receiving notes for specific transactions. This sort of credit involves the Notes Payable and Notes Receivable accounts. The notes which represent formal instruments of credit are known as a **promissory note**. A promissory note—usually referred to simply as a *note*—is a written promise to pay a certain sum at a fixed or determinable future time. They are customarily used as evidence of credit transactions for periods longer than 30 days. For example, promissory notes may be used in sales of equipment on the installment plan and for transactions involving large amounts of money. Promissory notes are also used to grant extensions of credit beyond the original credit terms. Like a check, notes must be payable to the order of a particular person or firm, known as the **payee**. It must also be signed by the person or firm making the promise, known as the **maker**.

Most companies become involved with notes at one time or another by issuing notes to creditors, by receiving notes from customers, or by issuing notes to banks in order to borrow money. Consequently, an accountant must be acquainted with the procedures for handling promissory notes.

CALCULATING INTEREST

Interest is a charge made for the use of money. To the maker of the note, interest is an expense. The amount of interest a maker pays is expressed as a certain percentage of the principal of the note for a period of one year (or less). The following formula is used to calculate interest:

Interest (in dollars)	=	**Principal** of Note (in dollars)	×	**Rate** of Interest (as a percentage of the principal)	×	**Time** of Note (expressed as a year or fraction of a year)

The **principal** is the face amount of the note. The *rate of interest* is a percentage of the principal. *Time,* or the length of life of the note, is usually expressed in days or months. It is the period between the note's date of issue (starting date) and its **maturity date** (the due date or interest payment date). It is stated in terms of a year or fraction of a year. The usual commercial practice is to use a 360-day year, making the denominator of the fraction 360.

Example: $80,000, 6 percent, 60 days

Interest = Principal × Rate × Time

$$\text{Interest} = \$80{,}000 \times 0.06 \times \frac{60}{360} = \underline{\$800}$$

DETERMINING DUE DATES

The period of time between a promissory note's issue date and its maturity date is called the **duration** of the note. The duration of a note may be expressed in days or months. If the time of the note is expressed in months, the maturity date is the corresponding day in the month after the specified number of months has elapsed. When counting the number of days, begin with the day *after* the date the note was issued and end with the last day of the note.

Example

Let's say that the due date of a promissory note is specified as 60 days after April 8. The due date is June 7.

   The due date is determined by the following steps:

STEP 1. Determine the number of days remaining in the month of issue by subtracting the date of the note from the number of days in the month in which it is dated.

STEP 2. Add as many full months as possible without exceeding the number of days in the note, counting the full number of days in these months.

STEP 3. Determine the number of days remaining in the month in which the note matures by subtracting the total days counted so far from the number of days in the note, as shown on the following page.

April							May							June						
S	M	T	W	T	F	S	S	M	T	W	T	F	S	S	M	T	W	T	F	S
		1	2	3	4	5					1	2	3	1	2	3	4	5	6	7
6	7	8	9	10	11	12	4	5	6	7	8	9	10	8	9	10	11	12	13	14
13	14	15	16	17	18	19	11	12	13	14	15	16	17	15	16	17	18	19	20	21
20	21	22	23	24	25	26	18	19	20	21	22	23	24	22	23	24	25	26	27	28
27	28	29	30				25	26	27	28	29	30	31	29	30					

22 days
8th through the 30th
30 − 8 = 22 days left

+ 31 days

= 53 days have passed
60 − 53 = 7 days re-
maining after May 31
June 7 due date

STEP 1. April (30 − 8)   = 22 days left in April

STEP 2. May   = 31 days

Total days so far   = 53 days

STEP 3. June (60 − 53)   = 7th day of June (due date)

In addition to determining the due date using the method above, you can find a loan calculator on the Internet that will automatically find the due date. These calculators require you to input the starting date and time period of the loan. The software then determines the due date.

TRANSACTIONS FOR NOTES PAYABLE

We assume that all notes are due within one year; thus, they are classified on the balance sheet as Current Liabilities. However, if notes are not due within one year, the portion of the note that is due within one year is a Current Liability and the remainder is classified as a Long-Term Liability. Interest expense is classified on the income statement as Interest Expense (if significant) or Other Expense.

Note Given to Secure an Extension of Time on an Open Account

When a company wants to obtain an extension of time for the payment of an account, the company may ask a supplier to accept a note for all or part of the amount due. For example, assume that Whitewater Raft Supply prefers not to pay its open account with Dana Manufacturing Company when the account becomes due. Dana Manufacturing Company agrees to accept a 60-day, 6 percent, $900 note from Whitewater Raft Supply in settlement of the account. The entry that caused the account to be put on Dana Manufacturing Company's books came about when Whitewater Raft Supply bought merchandise on account on April 12, with terms n/30.

3a Record journal entries for notes given to secure an extension of time on an open account.

Learning Objective

ORIGINAL PURCHASE

In general journal form, the entry looks like this:

	GENERAL JOURNAL			Page ___
Date	Description	Post. Ref.	Debit	Credit
20—				
Apr. 12	Purchase		9 0 0 00	
	Accounts Payable, Dana			
	Manufacturing Company			9 0 0 00
	Terms n/30.			

PAYMENT BY NOTE

On May 12, Whitewater Raft Supply records the issuance of the note in its general journal.

	GENERAL JOURNAL			Page ___
Date	Description	Post. Ref.	Debit	Credit
20—				
May 12	Accounts Payable, Dana			
	Manufacturing Company		9 0 0 00	
	Notes Payable			9 0 0 00
	Gave a 60-day, 6 percent			
	note in settlement of our			
	open account.			

Observe that the previous entry cancels the Accounts Payable, Dana Manufacturing Company account and substitutes Notes Payable. The note does not *pay* the debt. It merely changes the liability status from an account payable to a note payable.

Payment of an Interest-Bearing Note at Maturity

When a note payable falls due, payment must be made to the holder. The maker must make payment for the principal of the note plus the interest, or **maturity value**.

> **Learning Objective 3b** Record journal entries for payment of an interest-bearing note at maturity.

Whitewater Raft Supply pays the note on July 11. In general journal form, the entry is as follows:

	GENERAL JOURNAL			Page ___
Date	Description	Post. Ref.	Debit	Credit
20—				
July 11	Notes Payable		9 0 0 00	
	Interest Expense		9 00	
	Cash			9 0 9 00
	Paid note to Dana			
	Manufacturing Company.			

Because Interest = Principal × Rate × Time, we perform this calculation:

$$\text{Interest} = \$900 \times 0.06 \times \frac{60}{360} = \$9$$

Borrowing from a Bank When Bank Discounts Note (Deducts Interest in Advance)

In another type of bank loan, called **discounting a note payable**, the bank deducts the interest in advance. For example, also on June 7, Whitewater Raft Supply borrows $10,000 for 120 days from Westmore National Bank, and the bank requires Whitewater Raft Supply to sign a note. From the face value of the note, the bank deducts 6 percent interest for 120 days, so Whitewater Raft Supply actually gets only $9,800 (($10,000 − $200). This interest deducted in advance by a bank is called the **discount**. The principal of the loan left after the discount has been subtracted is called the **proceeds**, which is the amount the borrower has available to use. Because all of the interest is deducted at the time the loan is made, the note must state that only the face amount is to be paid at maturity. The calculation for the discount is as follows:

3c Record journal entries for notes given to secure a cash loan when the bank discounts the note.

Learning Objective

Interest = Principal × Rate × Time

$$\text{Interest} = \$10,000 \times 0.06 \times \frac{120}{360} = \$200$$

The bank deducts the discount from the face amount of the note before making the money available to the borrower.

Principal	$10,000
− Discount	200
Proceeds	$ 9,800

GENERAL JOURNAL   Page ___

Date		Description	Post. Ref.	Debit	Credit
20—					
June	7	Cash		9 8 0 0 00	
		Interest Expense		2 0 0 00	
		Notes Payable			10 0 0 0 00
		Discounted our 120-day, non-			
		interest-bearing note at Westmore			
		National Bank, discount rate			
		6 percent.			

Note Paid to the Bank at Maturity

When the note becomes due, Whitewater Raft Supply pays the bank only the *face value of the note* and records the transaction as follows:

 3d Record journal entries for payment of a discounted note at maturity.

Learning Objective

GENERAL JOURNAL   Page ___

Date		Description	Post. Ref.	Debit	Credit
20—					
Oct.	5	Notes Payable		10 0 0 0 00	
		Cash			10 0 0 0 00
		Paid Westmore National			
		Bank on our note payable			
		discounted June 7.			

TRANSACTIONS FOR NOTES RECEIVABLE

Now let's see how to journalize transactions involving notes receivable for Whitewater Raft Supply. The accounts involved are Notes Receivable (classified as a current asset on the balance sheet in our examples, although it could be classified as a long-term asset if the repayment period is longer than a year) and Interest Income (classified as other income on the income statement).

Note from a Charge Customer to Extend Time on Account

Learning Objective

4a Record the journal entry for receipt of a note from a charge customer.

On March 7, Whitewater Raft Supply sold $930 worth of merchandise to Green River Rafts, with the customary terms of 2/10, n/30, and made the original entry in its sales journal. On April 6, Green River Rafts sent Whitewater Raft Supply a note for $930, payable within 30 days, at 6 percent interest. The note, dated April 6, was in settlement of the transaction of March 7. Whitewater Raft Supply recorded this new development in its general journal as follows:

Date		Description	Post. Ref.	Debit	Credit
GENERAL JOURNAL					**Page___**
20—					
Apr.	6	Notes Receivable		9 3 0 00	
		Accounts Receivable, Green			9 3 0 00
		River Rafts			
		Received a 30-day, 6 percent			
		note, dated April 6, in			
		settlement of open account.			

Receipt of Payment of an Interest-Bearing Note at Maturity

Learning Objective

4b Record the journal entry for receipt of payment of an interest-bearing note at maturity.

On May 6, Green River Rafts paid Whitewater Raft Supply in full: principal plus interest. Whitewater Raft Supply recorded the transaction in the general journal as follows:

Date		Description	Post. Ref.	Debit	Credit
GENERAL JOURNAL					**Page___**
20—					
May	6	Cash		9 3 4 65	
		Notes Receivable			9 3 0 00
		Interest Income			4 65
		Received full payment of			
		Green River Rafts' note.			
		($930 × 0.06 × 30/360)			

As a reminder, if special journals were used, this transaction would be recorded directly in the cash receipts journal rather than in the general journal. But for the sake of simplicity and clarity, we will use the general journal format to illustrate entries throughout this chapter.

DISCOUNTING NOTE RECEIVABLE

Instead of keeping notes receivable until they come due, a firm can raise cash by selling its notes receivable to a bank or finance company. This type of financing is called **discounting notes receivable** because the bank deducts the interest or discount from the maturity value of the note to determine the proceeds (that is, the amount of money received by the payee). In the process of discounting a note receivable, the payee endorses the note (as it would a check) and delivers it to the financial institution. The financial institution gives out cash now in exchange for the right to collect the principal and interest when the note comes due. The discount rate is the annual rate (percentage of maturity value) charged by the financial institution for buying the note. The financial institution generally discounts at a higher interest rate than stated in the note because the financial institution assumes increased risk of the maker's possible default.

4c Record the journal entry for discounting an interest-bearing note receivable.

Learning Objective

Whitewater Raft Supply granted an extension on an open account by accepting a 60-day, 5 percent note for $1,800, dated April 20, from Bowers River Co. To raise cash to buy additional merchandise, Whitewater Raft Supply sold the note to New National Bank on May 5. The bank charged a discount rate of 6 percent. In handling discounted notes receivable, you should follow a definite step-by-step procedure.

STEP 1. Diagram the Situation. A diagram of the Situation looks like this:

STEP 2. Determine the discount period. The **discount period** of the note consists of the interval between the date the note is given to the bank and the maturity date of the note. (In other words, the discount period is the time the note has left to run.)

Days held by endorser:		Discount period (bank holds note):
April 30 − 20	= 10 days left in April	(Total days − Days held by endorser)
May	= 5 days in May	60 days − 15 days = 45 days
Days held by endorser	= 15 days	

STEP 3. Record the formula. Next, we determine the value of the note at maturity and deduct the amount of the bank's discount from it, using the following formula:

Principal ($1,800)
+ Interest to maturity date (5%, 60 days)
―――――――――――――――――――――――
   Value at maturity
− Discount (6%, 45 days)
―――――――――――――――――――――――
   Proceeds
―――――――――――――――――――――――

STEP 4. **Complete the formula.** After we set up the problem, we can complete the calculation.

Principal	$1,800.00	Interest = Principal × Rate × Time
+ Interest (5%, 60 days)	15.00	
Value at maturity	$1,815.00	Interest = $1,800.00 × 0.05 × $\frac{60}{360}$ = $15.00
− Discount (6%, 45 days)	13.61	
Proceeds	$1,801.39	Discount = $1,815.00 × 0.06 × $\frac{45}{360}$ = $13.61

Note that in our calculations, we figure the discount on the value of the note at maturity ($1,815). The proceeds are the amount that Whitewater Raft Supply receives from the bank. This amount is therefore debited to Cash. *If the amount of the proceeds is greater than the amount of the principal, the difference represents Interest Income because Whitewater Raft Supply made money on the deal. If the amount of the proceeds is less than the principal, on the other hand, the deficiency represents Interest Expense because Whitewater Raft Supply lost money in the deal.*

STEP 5. **Record the entry.** Look at the entry in Whitewater Raft Supply's general journal.

GENERAL JOURNAL					Page ___
Date	Description	Post. Ref.	Debit	Credit	
20—					
May 5	Cash		1 8 0 1 39		
	Notes Receivable			1 8 0 0 00	
	Interest Income			1 39	
	Discounted at the bank Bowers River				
	Co.'s note, dated April 20. The bank				
	discount rate is 6 percent.				

DISHONORED NOTES RECEIVABLE

4d Record the journal entry for a dishonored note receivable.

When the maker of a note fails to pay the principal amount or to renew the note at maturity, the note is said to be a **dishonored note receivable**. The maker of the note is still obligated to pay the principal plus interest, and the creditor should take legal steps to collect the debt. However, the balance of the Notes Receivable account shows only the principal of notes that have not yet matured. A note that is past due, or dishonored, should be removed from the Notes Receivable account and added to the Accounts Receivable account. The amount listed should be the principal plus interest. In other words, once a note receivable comes due and is not collected, it is "in default." But the maker still owes the payee, so the amount owed (principal plus interest) is put back into Accounts Receivable.

For example, Whitewater Raft Supply holds a 60-day, 5 percent note for $950, dated April 20, from Hartman Guides, which fails to pay by the due date. Thus, the note is dishonored at maturity. Whitewater Raft Supply then makes the following entry in its general journal to remove the dishonored note from the Notes Receivable account.

GENERAL JOURNAL											Page ___			
Date		Description	Post. Ref.		Debit					Credit				
20—														
June	19	Accounts Receivable, Hartman												
		Guides			9	5	7	92						
		Notes Receivable								9	5	0	00	
		Interest Income										7	92	
		Hartman Guides dishonored												
		its 60-day, 5 percent note for												
		$950, dated April 20.												
		($950 × 0.05 × 60/360)												

Glossary

Discount Interest deducted in advance by a bank that makes a loan. (*p. D-5*)

Discount period The time between the date a note receivable is discounted and the date it matures. (*p. D-7*)

Discounting a notes payable The procedure by which a bank deducts interest in advance when it loans money with a note. (*p. D-5*)

Discounting notes receivable The process by which a firm may raise cash by selling a note receivable to a bank or finance company. The bank deducts the discount from the maturity value of the note to determine the proceeds (*amount of money*) the firm receives. (*p. D-7*)

Dishonored note receivable A note whose maker fails to pay the principal amount or to renew the note at maturity. (*p. D-8*)

Duration The period of time a note is outstanding; the length of time in days or months from a note's issue date to its maturity date. (*p. D-2*)

Interest A charge made for the use of money. (*p. D-2*)

Maker An individual or a firm that signs a promissory note. (*p. D-1*)

Maturity date The due date of a promissory note. (*p. D-2*)

Maturity value The principal (*face value*) of note plus interest from the date of the note until the due date. (*p. D-4*)

Payee The party receiving payment, such as on a note receivable or an account receivable. (*p. D-1*)

Principal The face amount of a note. (*p. D-2*)

Proceeds The principal of a loan less the discount. (*p. D-5*)

Promissory note A written promise to pay a certain sum at a fixed or determinable future time. (*p. D-1*)

Problems

PROBLEM D-1 **Part A:** Calculate the interest on the following notes:

Principal	Interest Rate (percent)	Number of Days
1. $14,600	5.5%	30 days
2. 11,200	6.5	60 days
3. 6,400	5	90 days
4. 9,500	6	120 days
5. 3,500	7	3 months

Check Figure
1. Interest, $66.92

Part B: Determine the maturity dates on the following notes:

Date of Issue	Life of Note
1. January 18	90 days
2. February 12	6 months
3. June 21	60 days
4. September 10	4 months
5. November 17	30 days

LO 1, 2, 3a, 3b

PROBLEM D-2 Andy Cooke gave a 60-day, 5.5 percent note, dated February 14, to Key Company, a creditor, in the amount of $10,500.

Check Figure
(c) 4/15 Cash,
$10,596.25

a. What is the due date of the note?
b. How much interest is to be paid on the note at maturity?
c. Write the entries in general journal form to record issuance of the note by the maker and payment of the note at maturity as they would appear on Cooke's books.

LO 3c, 3d

PROBLEM D-3 As a result of a loan from Plateau State Bank, Trent Company signed a 90-day note, dated March 12, for $12,700 that the bank discounted at 7 percent. Journalize the entries for the maker in general journal form to record the following, assuming that the note is paid in the same fiscal period.

Check Figure
3/12 Interest Expense,
$222.25

a. Issuance of the note on March 12.
b. Payment of the note at maturity.

LO 3c, 3d

PROBLEM D-4 On August 5, M. Valenty borrowed $8,500 from Costner State Bank for 45 days, with a discount rate of 7 percent. Accordingly, M. Valenty signed a note for $8,500, dated August 5. Write entries in general journal form to record the following transactions:

Check Figure
8/5 Notes Payable, $8,500

a. Issuance of the note on August 5.
b. Payment of the note at maturity on September 19.

LO 4a, 4b

PROBLEM D-5 On March 11, Rainz Company received a 90-day, 6 percent note for $1,500, dated March 11, from J. Rose, a charge customer, to satisfy his open account receivable.

Check Figure
(d) Interest Income, $22.50

a. What is the due date of the note?
b. How much interest is due at maturity?
Given the preceding data, write entries in general journal form on the books of Rainz Company to record the following:
c. Receipt of the note from J. Rose in settlement of his account.
d. Receipt of the principal and interest at maturity.
Given the same data, write entries in general journal form on Rose's books to record the following:
e. Issuance of the note by Rose in settlement of his account.
f. Payment of the note at maturity.

LO **4a, 4c**

PROBLEM D-6 Prepare entries in general journal form to record the following:

June 12 Sold merchandise on account to K. Perrot; terms n/30; $1,740.
July 12 Received $740 in cash from K. Perrot and a 60-day, 7 percent note for
          $1,000, dated July 12.
Aug. 17 Discounted the note at the bank at 7.5 percent.

Check Figure
8/17 Cash, $1006.61

LO **4a, 4b**

PROBLEM D-7 The following T accounts show a series of four transactions concerning a sale of merchandise on account and subsequent payment of the amount owed. Describe what happened in each transaction.

Cash		Accounts Receivable		Sales	
+	−	+	−	−	+
(d) 2,175		(a) 1,500	(b) 130		(a) 1,500
			(c) 2,150		

Interest Income		Notes Receivable		Sales Returns and Allowances	
−	+	+	−	+	−
	(d) 25	(c) 2,150	(d) 2,150	(b) 130	

LO **4d**

PROBLEM D-8 Prepare entries in general journal form to record the following:

Aug. 6 Woodard Company failed to pay its 30-day, 10 percent note for $600, dated
          July 9. The note is thus dishonored at maturity.

Check Figure
Accounts Receivable,
$485.00

Index

Steps in the Accounting Process

STEP 1. Analyze source documents and record business transactions in a journal.

STEP 2. Post journal entries to the accounts in the ledger.

STEP 3. Prepare a trial balance.

STEP 4. Gather adjustment data and record the adjusting entries on a work sheet.

STEP 5. Complete the work sheet.

STEP 6. Journalize and post the adjusting entries from the data on the work sheet.

STEP 7. Prepare financial statements from the data on the work sheet.

STEP 8. Journalize and post the closing entries.

STEP 9. Prepare a post-closing trial balance.

Working with T Accounts

The left side of a T account is called the **debit** side; the right side is called the **credit** side.

					Owner's Equity					
Assets	=	**Liabilities**	+	**Capital**	−	**Drawing**	+	**Revenue**	−	**Expenses**
+ | −		− | +		− | +		+ | −		− | +		+ | −
Debit | Credit		Debit | Credit		Debit | Credit		Debit | Credit		Debit | Credit		Debit | Credit

The following table summarizes debits and credits and the way they are affected by increases and decreases. **The critical rule to remember is that the amount placed on the debit side of one or more accounts *must* equal the amount placed on the credit side of another account or other accounts.**

To summarize debits and credits, increases and decreases:

Debits Signify		**Credits Signify**	
Increases in {	Assets Drawing Expenses	Decreases in {	Assets Drawing Expenses
Decreases in {	Liabilities Capital Revenue	Increases in {	Liabilities Capital Revenue

Assets	The *left* side is the *increase* side.
Liabilities	The *right* side is the *increase* side.
Capital	The *right* side is the *increase* side.
Drawing	The *left* side is the *increase* side.
Revenue	The *right* side is the *increase* side.
Expenses	The *left* side is the *increase* side.

Steps in Analyzing a Transaction

STEP 1. What accounts are involved?

STEP 2. What are the classifications of the accounting involved (asset, liability, capital, drawing, revenue, expenses)?

STEP 3. Are the accounts increased or decreased?

STEP 4. Write the transaction as a debit to one account (or accounts) and a credit to another account (or accounts).

STEP 5. Is the equation in balance after the transaction has been recorded?

Journalizing and Posting

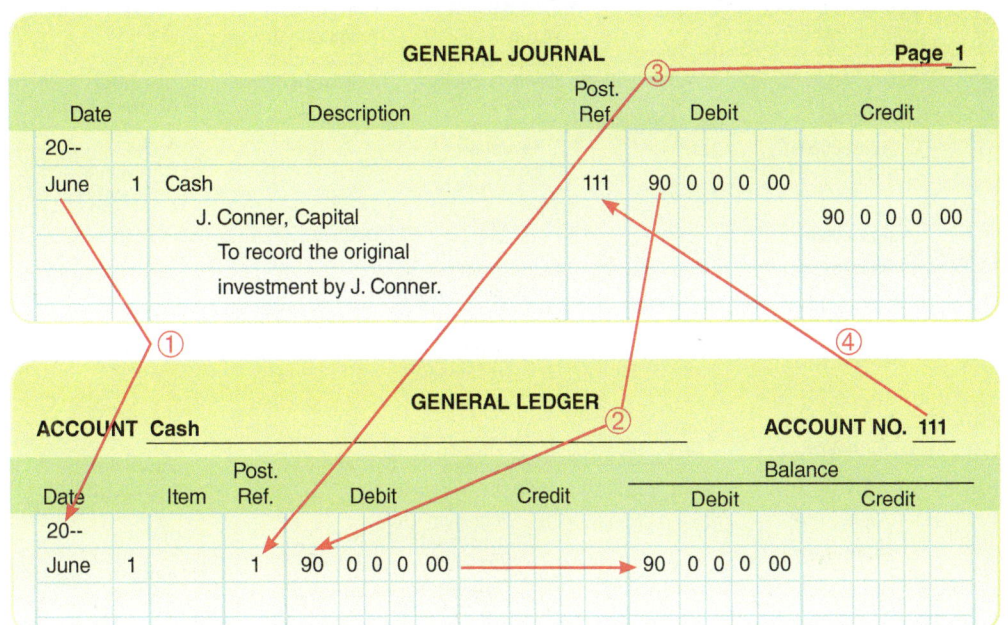

① Date of transaction
② Amount of transaction
③ Page number of the journal
④ Ledger account number

The Work Sheet

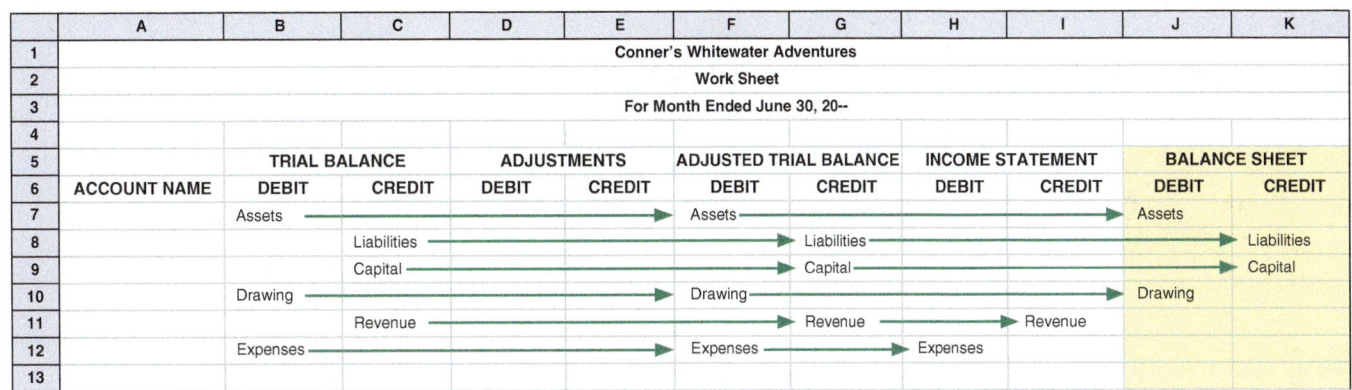

Steps in the Closing Process

STEP 1. Close the revenue account(s) into Income Summary.

STEP 2. Close the expense account(s) into Income Summary.

STEP 3. Close the Income Summary account into the Capital account, transferring the net income or net loss to the Capital account.

STEP 4. Close the Drawing account into the Capital account.

The Accounting Cycle

Using Special Journals

Types of Transactions

Sale of merchandise on account	Purchase of merchandise on account	Receipt of cash	Payment of cash	All other

Evidenced by Source Documents

Sales invoice	Purchase invoice	Credit card receipts Cash Checks Electronic funds transfers	Check stub Electronic funds transfers	Miscellaneous

Types of Journals

Sales journal	Purchases journal	Cash receipts journal	Cash payments journal	General journal

Posting to Ledger Accounts

Individual amounts posted daily to the accounts receivable ledger and the total posted monthly to the general ledger.	*Individual amounts posted daily to the accounts payable ledger and the totals of the special columns posted monthly to the general ledger.*	*Individual amounts in the Accounts Receivable Credit column posted daily to the accounts receivable ledger.* *Individual amounts in the Other Accounts columns posted daily to the general ledger.* *Totals of special columns posted monthly to the general ledger.*	*Individual amounts in the Accounts Payable Debit column posted daily to the accounts payable ledger.* *Individual amounts in the Other Accounts columns posted daily to the general ledger.* *Totals of special columns posted monthly to the general ledger.*	*Entries posted daily to the subsidiary ledgers and the general ledger.*

Steps in the Closing Process

STEP 1. Close the revenue account(s) into Income Summary.

STEP 2. Close the expense account(s) into Income Summary.

STEP 3. Close the Income Summary account into the Capital account, transferring the net income or net loss to the Capital account.

STEP 4. Close the Drawing account into the Capital account.

The Accounting Cycle